IDAHO PLACE NAMES

Idaho counties, 1988.

IDAHO PLACE NAMES
A Geographical Dictionary

Lalia Boone

THE UNIVERSITY OF IDAHO PRESS
MOSCOW, IDAHO

University of Idaho Press
Moscow, Idaho

Photographs throughout are reproduced with the kind permission of the Special Collections Archives of the University of Idaho Library.

Idaho counties map courtesy of Cartographics, Geography Department, University of Idaho. © by Cartographics.

"There Are No Names But Stories" first appeared in *Poetry Northwest* 26(1985): 47, and is reprinted here with kind permission of Kim R. Stafford.

Designed by Caroline Hagen
Printed in the United States of America

Library of Congress Cataloging-in-Publication Data

Boone, Lalia Phipps, 1907–
    Idaho place names : a geographical dictionary / Lalia Boone.
        p. cm.
    Bibliography: p.
    ISBN 0–89301–119–3 (pbk.)
    1. Names, Geographical–Idaho–Dictionaries. 2. Idaho
–History, Local. I. Title.
F744.B66 1987
917.96'003'21–dc19   87–30211
                                                            CIP

There Are No Names But Stories

When the anthropologist asked the Kwakiutl
for a map of their coast, they told him
stories: Here? *Salmon gather.* Here?
Sea otter camps. Here *seal sleep.*
Here we say *body covered with mouths.*

How can a place have a name? A man,
a woman may have a name, but they die.
We are a story until we die.
Then our names are dangerous.
A place is a story happening many times.

Over there? We say *blind women
steaming clover roots become ducks.*
We will tell that story for you at
place of meeting one another in winter.

But now is our time for travel. We will
name those stories as we pass them by:

> *place like smoke*
> *loon on roof*
> *small noise of clapping*
> *hollow of stopping*
> *having many canoe-cedars*
> *place of hiding repeatedly*
> *cedarbark bedding of cradles*
> *mink's grave*
> *insufficient canoe*
> *sound of swans*
> *one turned over covering another*
> *going with tide*
> *hollow thing at rest*
> *hollow of the northwest wind*
> *having everything right*

KIM R. STAFFORD

Contents

Foreword

TO THE PERSON wondering "How did my town happen to get its name?" *Idaho Place Names* provides a ready answer and much more. It notes the county, accurately locates the site geographically, describes the topography, and tells, often in a good deal of detail, what is presently known of its history, traditions, and features of note. Those with a casual interest who take the time to browse beyond a particular entry will find a wealth of information that invites them further to explore Idaho's historical heritage. In addition to early written histories and the publications of county and state historical societies, research for this volume has drawn upon maps, gazetteers, county records, files of old newspapers, and records of federal agencies, including the U.S. Forest Service, the Post Office Department, the U.S. Geological Survey, and the Board on Geographic Names. The information from postal records is of great historic interest, listing as it does some 1300 post offices, only about of fourth of which survive. The ones that have disappeared represent once-active communities which might be forgotten if they were not recorded here.

Although these sources are in principle generally available to researchers, this volume brings them together in convenient and accessible form. In addition, it assembles information from diaries, letters, questionnaires, and hundreds of personal interviews with older residents, some of whose information is nowhere else available. In short, this is an outstanding reference work that will answer the questions and pique the curiosity of the general reader. To the researcher it will be an invaluable source of information.

For Idaho this book fills a real need. Any historian or researcher moving to a new state is likely to look first for a reference work on place names. Other states have long had such comprehensive compilations. Previous studies for Idaho have been too expensive and too cumbersome for private use and are in any event now out of date. The great value of the place name research accomplished here lies in the light it can shed on the history of the state. The names selected reflect the influence not only of Idaho's Indians, explorers, trappers, missionaries, miners, and emigrants during the preterritorial period, but also of such later factors as changes in transportation, the establishment of post offices, Mormon colonization, and the development of irrigation, to name only a few.

Also valuable to note are the patterns of naming that emerge and how names indicate what interested or impressed the people who bestowed them. It is not surprising that 42 percent of the entries, the largest group, involve names of persons. As Simeon Strunsky has said, "The years by themselves do not make a place historic. It is those who give the color of history to a place by their deeds there or by merely having lived there." Most often settlements were named for homesteaders or early settlers. Later town names sometimes honored railroad or church officials, financiers, or community leaders.

The second most important group of names is descriptive. These suggest that colors, artifacts, size, location, and resemblance to familiar forms were good features for identifying places, valuable reminders of what early settlers found. Some of these, of course, have suffered change with the passing of years. One example is American Falls, which endures as the name of a town even though its forty-two foot waterfall, a famous landmark on the Oregon Trail, has been obliterated by a dam since 1927.

A closely related group of names pertains to flora and fauna once plentiful throughout the state but since diminished or gone. Among less frequent types are names transferred to Idaho from other places, which may be seen as expressions either of ambition or of nostalgia. Either type of name tells something valuable about the persons who chose it. Other, less frequent types of place names involve minerals, mining, or historic events. Viewed as a whole, the patterns of naming indicate how people reacted to their new environment and to each other in it.

Valuable as *Idaho Place Names* is, it should not mark the end of place name research in the state. In only a few counties has intensive research been carried out: Boise, Bonneville, Clearwater, Fremont, Latah, Lemhi, Nez Perce, and Owyhee. Most of this has not yet been fully published in reference works specifically on county place names. For example, the coverage of Latah County in the present volume when compared to that in Dr. Boone's recently published *From A to Z in Latah County, Idaho: A Place Name Dictionary* reveals how much more detailed information county compilations can include. Schools, cemeteries, lode mines, churches, mills, parks, and registered farm names are all of interest and value but far too many in number to figure in a realistically sized statewide compendium. Definitive studies of other counties are still very much needed.

Idaho, unlike states which were settled earlier, has the advantage of closeness to its frontier days. Thus, many of its elderly residents are available as sources of valuable, unrecorded information. They should be interviewed and their recollections systematically recorded. County records need to be examined thoroughly for clues regarding place names, particularly records concerning homesteads and water rights. Those willing to undertake such study can expect to be rewarded with a real appreciation for the many persons who have lent their time and their talent to building what Idahoans enjoy today.

Place name research in Idaho demands as well that a place name center be established for use in future work. Such a facility ought to be connected with the state historical society or a university library. It should house all the data used for this book, as well as much that is as yet unpublished, and it should promote research on names for which only location and topography are presently known. It would build on what has been done, provide continual updating, and share data with other states. In short, it would supply a permanent, organized system of public access to information already collected on the various topographical features of Idaho. Such a center would be useful not only to the general public, but to historians, government workers, folklorists, geographers, genealogists, and as a data base for scholarly, popular, and educational publications.

With the publication of the present volume, an excellent start has been made on the study of the place names of Idaho. It points up the directions for further development of the project Dr. Boone has so ably begun, one that will make a unique contribution to the understanding of Idaho's history.

LILLIAN OTNESS
1983 recipient of the
Certificate of Commendation by the
American Association for State and Local History

Acknowledgments

THE COMPILATION OF this dictionary would have been impossible without the help of far too many people to list, help that began with inspiration from Thomas Pyles, my graduate professor from 1946 to 1952, who introduced me to the world of linguistics, and continues to this day. In *American Language*, Supplement II, Mencken's treatment of place names drew my interest and led me to a lifetime venture. Later, George Stewart's *Names on the Land* pointed out the nature of needed research and described some methods of approach. My thanks to these scholars and their followers who compiled place name dictionaries of various areas: Bertha Bloodworth, Florida; Frederick C. Cassidy, Dane County, Wisconsin; Byrd H. Granger, Arizona; Kelsey Harder, the United States and Canada; Lewis A. McArthur, Oregon; Donald Orth, Alaska; and Fritz L. Kramer, *Idaho Town Names*.

Thanks go as well to my students at the University of Idaho, who completed questionnaires by the hundreds for their respective communities and interviewed old-timers, parents, grandparents, and friends. Some worked in forests during their vacations and jogged the memories of their superiors and co-workers for more information. Eight graduate students chose the study of place names for their Master of Arts theses, and I gratefully acknowledge their help in searching out the sources and locations of place names. These paved the way for this statewide study: James Carl Dahl, Mary Jo Geidl, Elizabeth Ann Gordon, Gail Keller Scott, Selway Lysle Mulkey, Marion Jill Thurston, and Mary Walsh Taylor.

A special debt is due Lillian Otness, Keith Peterson, Mary Reed, Stanley A. Shepard, Cort Conley, Kathy Probasco, and Warren Owens for their continued interest and encouragement, and to Dr. Merle Wells for reading and criticizing the manuscript. To Donald Orth for supplying data from the U.S. Board on Geographic Names. And to Professors Harry H. Caldwell, Richard L. Day, Robert Coonrod, William R. Swagerty, and Siegfried B. Rolland for their moral support and advice.

ACKNOWLEDGMENTS

To my staff for assistance in putting collected data into manuscript form. Especially to Brad Sargent, my assistant for nearly two years, who has kept my office and files in respectable order, submitted to unforeseen changes and exigencies, written grant proposals, fed the computer, and made corrections beyond the call of duty; to Eleanor Mahaffy, typist; and to David Kohl, proofreader. Without these three there would be no manuscript. My gratitude to Dave Whelchel for his patient and continued help with manipulating the home computer. To Sharl K. Keskinin for developing a program for sorting and alphabetizing data on the University of Idaho mainframe computer. And to Lane Alexander for her significant help in arriving at a usable computer format for this volume, as also to Judy Austin for her meticulous editing and to the staff of the University of Idaho Press for bringing all the loose ends together and seeing the book through publication.

For financial assistance I am deeply grateful to the American Philosophical Society and the University of Idaho Seed Grants, 1966-68, supporting initial research on Idaho place names; to the Humanities in Idaho and the John Calhoun Smith Scholarship Fund, Department of History, 1983-84, for support in preparing the manuscript; and to the Kaypro Corporation for their donation to the Idaho Place Name Project of a KAYPRO 4 computer.

Publications and holdings of county and state historical societies have been invaluable, as have early newspaper files. The Special Collections department of the University of Idaho Library has been most generous over a long period of time in making available pertinent papers, maps, personal records, and rare books. Forest Service employees and officials have graciously given hours in interviews and have shared the publications of their various National Forests. Histories, gazetteers, county courthouse records, and personal diaries have been of vital importance, as have the official records of the U.S. Post Office Department, the U.S. Geological Survey, and the Board on Geographic Names. A limited bibliography of published sources appears after the dictionary proper. Many other shorter works and hundreds of informants have been omitted, but they are nonetheless important to this study.

My grandchildren Jacque, Phillip, and Shirley have most graciously put up with my preoccupation with work during their infrequent visits and have even helped sort and alphabetize research cards. My friend Irene has generously helped by keeping my house in order, running errands, and just being available for whatever emergency, without a single grumble. It is inevitable that there will be errors in this book. My hope is that they are few. I shall be happy to receive corrections and questions.

Introduction

IDAHO PLACE NAMES: 1800–1863

INDIAN INFLUENCE

Like names in all other parts of the civilized world, those of Idaho reflect the history of the area. Before the first European settlers came to the state, Indians lived here who called themselves by specific names and described the places they frequented, the food they harvested, and their environment. Some of these come down to us today as place names. *Bannock, Shoshone,* and *Kootenai,* the names of tribes, closely approximate their original pronunciation. They serve as names of counties, streams, and other topographical features. In the early 1800s, Canadian French fur trappers bestowed on tribes in northern Idaho names that have survived: *Coeur d'Alene, Pend Oreille,* and *Nez Perce,* all located in the specific areas frequented by these tribes.

Names of Indian tribal leaders are likewise preserved in *Targhee, Benewah, Tygee, Tyee, Pocatello, Wabango,* and *Athol.* Cultural words give us *Wickiup, Tepee, Napias, Potlatch, Picabo,* and *Kinnikinnic,* names of streams, areas, and villages. Descriptive names of specific places result in *Latah, Palouse, Chatcolet, Kuna, Pahsimeroi, Weippe, Ahsahka, Tosioba, Lapwai,* and *Hatwai. Palouse, Chatcolet,* and *Pahsimeroi* bear the stamp of French namers, for French Canadians recorded them using the French orthography of the period. Animal names remaining from earliest times include *Wickahoney, Moolack,* and *Mora. Aggipah* Mountain, *Egin, Menan,* and *Minidoka,* all descriptive words, are appropriately applied to Idaho places. And *Camas* comes to us from the camas root, which all tribes of Indians in the Northwest harvested, preserved, and fed on throughout the winter. Today it names a county and two major prairies, as well as several streams and meadows and early communities. All these are explained individually in the text that follows.

PATHFINDERS AND TRAPPERS

Explorers, trappers, traders, and mappers made Idaho a busy place from 1805 to 1843. As they worked their way along the streams and rivers of the state, many recorded their experiences and impressions by leaving names on the land. Between 1804 and 1806, Lewis and Clark regularly named streams. On 21 August 1805, Captain Clark named the present-day Salmon River the *Lewis River* for Meriwether Lewis. Also recorded by the same expedition are *Fish Creek* for today's North Fork of the Salmon River, 1 September 1805; *Collins* and *Cotton* creeks honoring other expedition members; *Coltkilled Creek,* for the present-day White Sand Creek, 14 September 1805; *Hungry Creek,* 18 September 1805, renamed *Obia Creek* in the early 1900s and finally restored as *Hungery [sic] Creek* after 1960; *Commearp,* 10 May 1806, for Lawyers Canyon; and *Drewyer River* for Palouse River. *Coltkilled Creek,* where the expedition killed a colt for food, should be restored because it illustrates so pointedly the very real difficulties the first pathfinders encountered. Though the names Lewis and Clark bestowed did not for the most part remain in use, their own names did. There are, for instance, *Lewis County, Lewiston, Lewisville, Clark River, Clark Point,* and *Clarkia.*

After the explorers came trappers, to seek out the streams rich in mink, beaver, and other furbearing animals. They flooded into the state over the Rocky Mountains, trapping and trading along the Teton, Snake, Portneuf, and Salmon rivers and their tributaries. In 1810 Andrew Henry of the Missouri Fur Company established Fort Henry, after which *Henrys Fork* and *Henrys Lake* are named. He had been preceded in northern Idaho by David Thompson and Finan McDonald, British fur traders of the Northwest Fur Company. Thompson erected the first building and founded the first commercial firm in the state, Kullyspell House, a trading post on Lake Pend Oreille. In 1811 Wilson Price Hunt, with the forty-six-member Hunt-Astoria Expedition, blazed the trail across Idaho to Astoria, laying the foundation upon which the Oregon Trail developed half a century later. The tragedy the expedition suffered on 28 October 1811 served as a warning to others making their way down the Snake River and led to the name *Caldron Linn,* bestowed, perhaps, by the Scotsman Donald Mackenzie. This expedition won for Hunt the title of World's Greatest Trailblazer. Later he was honored in the naming of *Hunt,* Jerome County, and the important Hunt Project for irrigation after World War II.

Additional names honoring adventurers of this period include *Payette,* 1818; *Pierres Hole,* 1819; *Godin Valley* and *Godin River,* 1820 and 1830; *Ross Fork,* 1824; *Portneuf,* 1825; *Cassia,* ca.1830; *Bonneville,* 1832; *Sublett,* 1832; *Fremont,* 1843; and *Landers Cut-off,* ca. 1850. Among the pathfinders were the missionaries Henry Harmon Spalding, 1835, whose name remains in *Spalding,* Nez Perce County, and Father Jean de Smet, 1842, for whom *Desmet* and *Tensed* are named. Colonel William Craig, veteran fur trapper, settled a few miles from the Spaldings in 1846, leaving his name on *Craig Mountain* and, ultimately, on *Craigmont Development,* 1860-63.

The discovery of gold in Lemhi, Boise, Clearwater, Latah, Owyhee, and Idaho counties between 1861 and 1863 drew thousands of prospectors, miners, and investors. Mining camps quickly gave way to mining towns, some of which last to this day. Streams where gold was found took the names of gold discoverers or of some characteristic of the discovery. Names originating in mining activities during this period include *Centerville, Bogus Basin, Eldorado Gulch, Idaho City, Mores Creek, Pioneerville,* and *Placerville* in Boise County; *Orofino Creek, Pierce,* and *Orogrande;* in Clearwater County; *Warren, Buffalo Hump, Florence, Elk City,* and *Burgdorf* in Idaho County; *Silver City* and *Ruby City* in Owyhee County. Almost every mining camp had its *Slaughterhouse* and *Garden* creeks, for miners had to be fed. Supply bases sprung into being. Lewiston was the earliest and the most important, since it could be reached by steamboat from the Pacific coast, with supplies then trail-packed to the Clearwater and Idaho gold fields. Mount Idaho and Emmett also served as supply bases. Protection for emigrants and settlers was provided by Lapwai Post in the Clearwater area and Boise Barracks in the South.

The problem of transportation was partially solved by opening the *Boise Basin* and the *Lewiston to Elk City Trails.* The *Oregon Trail* was acclaimed the best-known wagon road in the world, with such stopovers as *Beer Springs* (later *Soda Springs*), *Fort Hall, Three Island Crossing,* and *Boise Barracks.* All comers, whether en route to California or Oregon or to the gold fields, rested here. By 1855 Mormons had established Fort Lemhi and by 1860 the first permanent settlement of Franklin; hence new routes opened up between Utah and these points. Emigrants relied upon established landmarks to guide them: *Emigrant, Massacre,* and *Register* rocks; *Big, Twin, Menan,* and *China Hat* buttes.

By 1863 the Snake, Blackfoot, Portneuf, Bear, Malad, Big Wood, Salmon, Boise, Payette, Weiser, and Clearwater rivers had already been named. The Mullan Road in northern Idaho had been completed and named for its builder. Maps of trails bearing the names already given to landmarks, way stations, and streams were in the hands of wagonmasters and emigrants alike. Lewiston and Idaho City were destined to become county seats, and Nez Perce, Idaho, Shoshone, and Owyhee counties had first been established as part of Washington Territory. In short, by 1863 not only was the foundation for building the State of Idaho already laid, but the patterns for place naming had been set.

TERRITORIAL IDAHO: 1863-1890

CREATION OF NEW COUNTIES

Population increased greatly after the creation of Idaho Territory in 1863. Miners, veterans and victims of the Civil War, and disappointed Oregon-bound emigrants poured into the territory from the East, the West, and the South. A brief look at the development of additional counties and towns that would become county seats reflects what was happening throughout the territory.

Thirteen new counties were created from the original four. Ada, Bingham, Cassia, Fremont, and Washington were named directly for people; Custer was named for the General Custer Mine, which in turn was named for the American general who lost his life at the Battle of the Little Bighorn. *Bear Lake, Boise, Kootenai,* and *Latah* were transfer names from already named features in the territory, like *Oneida,* from Oneida in New York state. *Elmore* was named for the super-producer Ida Elmore Mine, and *Lemhi* for *Fort Lemhi,* honoring a figure in the *Book of Mormon.*

Twenty-eight towns later to become county seats were added to Lewiston and Idaho City of the earlier period. Thirteen of the names pay tribute to people important to the specific vicinity: *Pocatello, Paris, Hailey, Bonners Ferry, Caldwell, Challis, Preston, Emmett, Rigby, Coeur d'Alene, Shoshone, Rexburg,* and *Wallace.* Boise, Council, Blackfoot, Payette, Soda Springs, Mountain Home, Grangeville, Salmon, American Falls, Orofino, and *Weiser* are transfer names from existing features within the territory; *Moscow* and *St. Anthony* from features outside the territory. *Sandpoint,* on Lake Pend Oreille, is a descriptive name, and *St. Maries* is biblical.

NEW INFLUENCES

Four new developments affected the choice of names important to the community: the building of railroads, the establishment of post offices, Mormon colonization, and Indian difficulties.

Railroads. Railroads and railroad stations replaced stage coaches, wagon trains, pack wagons, and way stations. And where a trickle of goods, supplies, and people had formerly seeped in to the state during preterritorial days, a flood poured in by railway. Railroad lines established stations, sometimes at sites already named and sometimes at new sites, which called for new names on the land. *Drummond, Kendrick, Burley, Laclede,* and *McCammon,* for example, honor railroad officials. The great number of names honor locals important to the specific site, just as those of the earlier period. There is one notable exception: the Oregon Short Line (OSL), in order not to duplicate any existing names, chose a group of Indian and pseudo-Indian names, including *Bisuka, Kuna, Mora, Owinza, Picabo, Ticeska, Tikura,* and *Wapi.*

Post Offices. The place of postal records in place name research cannot be overlooked. They give a clue to the actual date when a settlement becomes, and ceases to be, a recognized community. Two post offices had been granted in 1862, when this was Washington Territory: *Elk City* and *Well Gate.* By 1890 there were more than four hundred post offices, some closing after very short lives and some continuing to the present. Approximately 1300 post offices would be created by the 1920s, most of which were eliminated as communities died and Rural Free Delivery became a reality. Today there are three hundred and fifty post offices, fourteen percent of which bear the names of first postmasters or members of their families. Among these are *Archer, Bovill, Burns, Driggs, Carey, Conant, Marysville, Sarilda,* and *Starrhs Ferry.* The United States Postal Service directly affected some names, especially those which they could not decipher from handwritten applications: *Fernwood* for Fennwood, *Tensed* for Temsed, *Heglar* for Heglaer, *Osburn* for Osborne, and *Erncliff* for Ern Cliff. Sometimes the Postal Service substituted a name for the one submitted, as *Howe* for Hawley. Near the end of the territorial period guidelines were set for naming: no more two-word, long, or duplicating names. Thus Boise City, Florence City, and Pierce City were simplified to *Boise*, *Florence*, and *Pierce*. *Elk City* and *Idaho City*, however, remained as they were. Paradise Valley, at the request of the Postal Department, was changed to *Moscow*. Names like Beecherville were rejected on the basis of their length, and shorter names were selected.

Mormon Colonization. Mormon settlements followed the naming patterns already established, but often honored church leaders and officials, hence *Burton, Chesterfield, Hammond, Hinckley, Lyman, Rexburg, St. Charles,* and *Thomas.* Evidence that many Mormon settlers came from western Europe can be seen in the names transferred from their former homes, such as *Albion* (Great Britain), *Amsterdam, Bern, Danish Flat, Copenhagen, Dublin, French Creek, Geneva, Irish Canyon, Italian Gulch, Lanark* (Scotland), and *Little Sweden.* During the Mormon disfranchisement period, Mormon communities were often denied the name of their choice, the Postal Department instead assigning a name. Such is the case of *Chester* for Cleveland and *Rudy* for Clark. Railroad stations kept such of these names as fell along the right-of-way.

Indian Difficulties. Indians who had roamed freely over Idaho for generations did not take kindly to the invasion of their hunting and camping grounds and sought ways to halt the intrusion. They preyed first on emigrant trains, killing, robbing, and destroying. Disastrous encounters resulted in names like *Battle Creek, Massacre Rock,* and *Almo Battleground.* Open warfare between whites and Indians and among the Indians themselves, the Nez Perce and the Sheepeaters, left *Soldier Bar, Hospital Bar, Soldiers Grave,* and *Vinegar Hill,* where surrounded soldiers drank vinegar to quench their thirst. The names of military personnel remained where they camped or fought, as on *Bernard Creek, Putnam Mountain, Camp Lyon,* and *Farrow Mountain.* Memory of the fierce skirmishes fought on Pistol and Indian Creeks in 1873 is preserved in names given later: *Artillery, Luger, Mortar, Forty-five, Shrapnel, Colt, Trigger,* and *Winchester* creeks, and *Tommyhawk, Wickiup, Big Chief, Papoose,* and *Wampum* creeks. These names mark a distinct departure from the names of individual Indians and tribes that had been common in the preterritorial period.

Mining Interests. New gold, silver, and lead fields opened up. Each led to new names drawn from those of miners and mines and given to the streams and gulches where claims were located. *Allan, Basinger, Carver, Cary, Chamberlain,* and *Chaney* creeks honor miners. *Ajax Peak, Baby Grand Mountain, Blackhawk Bar, Bluejacket Creek, Champion Creek,* and *Big I Gulch* are named for mines. Prospectors in the 1860s and later dubbed streams and nearby features for the minerals found there. Thus, there is a proliferation of gold, silver, iron, lead, and copper features, but only occasionally stibnite, coal, cobalt, cyanide, or salt. Gold, for example, occurs where only a small amount of the precious substance was found or where it was sought, as well as where it might have produced great wealth. Though one can hardly tell by the number of gold features alone where the richest gold fields were, there is no difficulty in locating the areas where gold was actively sought and often found.

The number of place names increased during this period in proportion to the increase in population. Many earlier names of way stations and trail sites disappeared; others remained but took on new characteristics.

STATEHOOD: AFTER 1890

FEDERAL INFLUENCES

Before Idaho was even a territory, the United States Department of the Interior had sent surveyors to lay out roads and to set boundaries. John Mullan came in 1850 to survey a military road in North Idaho. Others came later to survey roads for emigrant trails, including the Oregon Trail. In 1872 Dr. F.V. Hayden, United States Geological Survey (USGS), came to map the southeastern part of the state. Among the names he bestowed are *Fox, Game,* and *Moose* creeks for the game he found; *Goodfellow* and *Leigh* creeks for members of his party; and *Horseshoe* and *Packsaddle* features for artifacts. He continued his surveying and naming throughout the area now in Teton, Fremont, and Madison counties. In 1905 a small community in Owyhee County honored him by choosing the name *Haden* (sic). Surveys such as Hayden's have been in progress ever since, and many of the surveyors have been honored in prominent features like *Lake Walcott* and *Pinchot Peak,* as well as small features like *Adams* and *Collins* creeks. Recently the USGS has prepared a finding list of all the topographical features in Idaho. Whenever there is a dispute about the name of a feature, it is brought before the US Board on Geographic Names, which researches the data and hands down decisions concerning the name and its spelling.

The United States Forest Service (USFS) has also been active throughout the twentieth century naming streams, promonotories, and other features, pinpointing each for use in firefighting and rescue activities. This naming includes research on who came to the area, when, and what was done there. Thus, many features, even small streams, canyons, and gulches, received the names of the early settlers, squatters, miners, and ranchers that researchers discovered. Most of these pioneers would otherwise have been totally forgotten. When such names could not be found, the namers used descriptive names. Some in North Idaho are as distinctive as the OSL names in South Idaho. The forester W. H. Daugs, for example, during the 1920s and 1930s gave many features descriptive names derived from Chinook jargon, such as *Hyaak, Ipsoot, Kiwa, Sypah,* and *Yakala* creeks. Major Frank Fenn, first Superintendent of Forestry in the West, not only named features, but was later himself honored by having *Fenn Mountain* and other features named for him. Forester C.K. "Andy" Hjort named Fenn Mountain, then later had *Hjort Lake* named for himself. Other features honoring Forest Service officials include *Sevy, Grandjean, Shepherd,* and *Horton* peaks and *Benedict* creek and lakes. All these features, as well as those honoring USGS officials, reflect the history of the Service in preserving the early history of Idaho through the names they placed on the land.

Office Names. Analogical names have been created by office staff members of both the USGS and the USFS. For example, take a name like *Bear Creek* as a major feature. The task is to name the tributaries suitably, and the staff may develop the names *Cub, Kodiak,* and *Polar* as a group of names compatible with the original. *Pistol* and *Indian* creeks have already been mentioned in connection with Indian difficulties. *Pie, Bacon,* and *Coffee* creeks (as well as *Jap Creek, Siam Creek,* and *Siam Lakes*) fall into the same category.

Another characteristic of office names can be seen in duplication. *Dry Creek,* for example, occurs in many areas of the state for the reason that the streams so named all go dry in the summer months. In office naming, the nearby ridges and gulches are also given the same name, creating a cluster.

IRRIGATION

Once the land was fairly well settled, residents looked to ways of improving their surroundings. Irrigation would turn deserts into gardens and enable settlers to produce more and better crops and livestock. In the late 1800s, people like I.B. Perrine had a vision of making the Snake River Plains productive, green and beautiful where formerly it had been dreaded as a desert of sagebrush, sand, rattlesnakes, and intense heat. By 1910, irrigation projects on a large scale were underway. These called for new towns to be laid out and, consequently, new names. Where did a portion of these come from? Naturally, from developers, investors, irrigation engineers, and hundreds of the new settlers attracted to the area by the promise of success in a new land. Dams built to impound river waters were named for their builders, investors, cooperating farmers, and visionaries: *Perrine, Milner, Hansen.* Financiers like Jerome, Buhl, Hollister, Kimberly, Murtaugh, and Burley became namesakes of six towns and one county.

DESCRIPTIVE NAMES

So far, most of the names discussed have related to the names of people, but there are in the state almost as many descriptive names. When settlers reached their new homes, they saw topographical features reminiscent of specific objects, hence the names *Beehive, Castle, Buffalo Hump, Tower, Cathedral, Monument, Catrock, Chimney, Cliff, Clear,* and the like. *Red, black, blue,* and *white* were attached to features of those colors and *sand, clay,* and *lava* to features thus composed. Other features were named for artifacts found in the vicinity, for example, *Acequia, Arrastra, Butcherknife, Chute, Bunkhouse,* and *Bridge. Broad, long, round,* and *central* indicate sizes and location. Places of special beauty received names like *Fairview, Bellevue, Fairylawn, Bridal Falls, Blossom, Bellgrove,* and *Bayview.*

Closely related to descriptive names are those derived from the flora and fauna of the area. The number of *cottonwood* features makes one wonder why half the counties, indeed the entire state, are not named *cottonwood.* The same could be said for *alder, aspen, cedar, cherry, mahogany, pine,* and *willow,* which at one time grew profusely along streams, ridges, and mountain slopes. Names of animals are also repetitive. *Bear* and *beaver* appear so frequently that it is easy to picture the primitive condition of Idaho as being overrun by them. Latah County has *Big Bear, Little Bear,* and *Three Bear* creeks, along with at least two ridges of the same name. Current maps of Idaho County alone list twenty features named *bear,* while Valley County has seventeen, Shoshone County nine, and twenty-one of the remaining counties one or more. *Antelope, cougar, deer, elk, fish, goat,* and *moose* run *bear* and *beaver* close races. Birds that summered and nested along streams and lakes left their names in areas from the southeast to the northwest: *eagle, goose, grouse, loon, mallard,* and *swan.* These names remain, even though the flora, fauna, and minerals for which they are named may be scarce or nonexistent today.

SUMMARY OF NAME SOURCES

The following list indicates the percentages of the various kinds of names discussed above. It illustrates especially the point that new names are almost always related to new developments in transportation, communications, and occupations, as well as to the recognition of local and national leaders:

Persons	42%
Descriptive features	30%
Flora and fauna	14%
Transfer	4%
Minerals and mines	4%
Incidents	2%
Biblical, legendary, mythological characters	2%
Other	2%

A NOTE ON FORMAT

The data for this book have been organized through the use of three basic formats for entries:

Main entries describe a single location or major name.

Cluster entries are used when a group of closely related features derive their names from the same source.

Common-name entries, e.g., *bear, cottonwood, big, dry,* summarize background information on names that are widespread in the state. Because of the large volume of places falling in common-name entries, only those are included for which other than geographical information is available.

In general, only those features for which more than geographical data are available are included here. For example, many of the 150 peaks over 10,000 feet have been omitted for lack of information about the sources for their names.

Main entries have the place name (also called the *entry name*) in boldface and flush with the left-hand margin. In the body of the entry, the place name is given first. The county name and elevation follow. Next, the technical location by township, range, and section is given. Streams are located at the confluence with a larger stream. Next is provided a descriptive location that tells where the place is situated relative to nearby, usually well-known, features. Distances to other features are given in air miles rather than miles by roadways. Finally, the pertinent topographical, historical, and linguistic data available are given. These may include such items as founding, settlement, postal information, industry, and the source of the name.

For example:

Hamer (Jefferson). 4802'. T7N R16E sec 15/22. Lies in the NE quadrant of the county 15 mi N of Roberts, on the UP RR and US 91. Founded by easterners and the first building. . . .

Hamer Post Office opened 20 Apr 1909 with Frank E. Wessler as postmaster. He was followed by. . . .

Named for Colonel Thomas R. Hamer, who was born in Fulton County, Illinois, 4 May 1864. . . .

This entry locates Hamer in Jefferson County at an altitude of 4802 feet in township 7 North, range 16 East, section 15 and 22. It is 15 miles north of Roberts, as the crow flies, and on both the Union Pacific Railroad and US Highway 91. The historical and other data are self-explanatory, and a table of abbreviations is given below.

Cluster entries are used for situations where the name of a place transfers to a group of social features like communities or to a group of topographical features. The cluster contains two or more features, usually found in the same vicinity and always deriving their name from the same source. For example:

Nez Perce County. County seat, Lewiston. Established by the Territorial Legislature of Idaho in 1861 and named for the Nez Perce Indians who occupied the territory. . . .

Nezperce (Lewis) 3200'. T33N R2E sec 5. County seat located in the center of the county 12 mi E of Craigmont and 40 mi SE of Lewiston. . . .

Nez Perce Creek (Lemhi). . . .

Nez Perce Lake (Lemhi). . . .

Nez Perce National Forest. . . .

Nez Perce National Historic Park. . . .

Nez Perce Pass (Lemhi) 6587'. T27N R 16E. At the summit of Bitterroot Mountains on the Nez Perce Trail. . . .

In this cluster entry, Nez Perce County is the entry name, and there are six run-ins under it. All the names stem from the Nez Perce Indians. Nez Perce County is listed and treated as a main entry, and the remaining Nez Perce features are given in alphabetical order as run-in entries under the main heading. The run-in place names are, like the body of each run-in within a cluster entry, in normal paragraph style. The order of information within each run-in is the same as those of the main entries.

Abbreviations

CCC	Civilian Conservation Corps
E	East
Fk	Fork
FS	Forest Service
LDS	Latter-Day Saints
mi	mile(s)
N	North
PFI	Potlatch Forest, Inc.
RR	Railroad
S	South
W	West
USFS	United States Forest Service
USGS	United States Geological Survey

Names of Railroads

BVT	Boise Valley Traction
CAP	Camas Prairie
GN	Great Northern
NP	Northern Pacific
OSL	Oregon Short Line
PIN	Pacific and Idaho Northern
SCP	Spokane, Coeur d'Alene, and Palouse
SI	Spokane and International
UP	Union Pacific
WIM	Washington, Idaho, and Montana

Alturas Lake (Blaine County) in the Sawtooth Mountains.

A

Abandon Creek (Boundary). T63N R3W sec 27. Flows into Caribou Creek in sec 7 of the same township and range. Abandon Mountain is 1 mi SW of the mouth of the creek, in Kaniksu National Forest.

Name descriptive of the remote and deserted aspect of this fire-stricken area.

Abbey (Twin Falls). T9S R14E sec 23/24. In the N part of the county, 4 mi N of Buhl. Originally an agricultural area and a post office; now an abandoned town.

Post office, 1902-1911.

Abbot Gulch (Elmore). T3N R10/11E sec 13, 14, 11/17, 18. In E Elmore County 3 mi E of Featherville and S of S Fk Boise River.

Named for the Abbot family, who pioneered here.

Aberdeen (Bingham). 4404′. T5S R31E sec 33. In the SW part of the county, 13.6 mi N of American Falls and 2 mi W of American Falls Reservoir.

Post office, 1907-.

Named in 1906 by F. A. Sweet, manager of American Falls Canal and Power Company, for Aberdeen, Scotland, because some of the stockholders were Scots emigrants.

Abes Knob (Latah). 4220′. T42N R1W sec 27. A promontory in the NW part of the county, between Feather Creek

and W Fk Potlatch River in the St. Joe National Forest. Named for Abel "Abe" Thompson, who settled here.

Acequia (Minidoka). 4200′. T9S R24E sec 1. Town in the SE part of the county, 5 mi W of Lake Walcott. Laid out by the U.S. Reclamation Service (later the Bureau of Reclamation) at the beginning of the Minidoka Project in 1906. Pronounced ah-SEEK-we-uh.

Post office, formerly Scherrer, 1907-.

The name is Spanish for "canal"; the town is at a division of several canals.

Ada County. County seat, Boise. County established in 1864.

Named for Ada Riggs, the first white child born in the area and the daughter of H. C. Riggs, one of the founders of Boise and a member of the Idaho Territorial Legislature.

Adair Creek (Shoshone). T43N R5E sec 15. In the SE part of the county 11 mi S of Avery. Rises on the SW slope of Round Mountain and flows 5 mi SE to N Fk Clearwater River.

A post office was established at this point in 1910 and discontinued a year later. It was reestablished in 1917 as Delage, with a change back to Adair in 1924-1926.

Named for Ione Adair, a young cook for some firefighters in 1910, who climbed a nearby mountain and left her name in a tobacco can. Her name is also on the Milwaukee RR station on the loop 11 mi NE of Avery.

Adams County. County seat, Council. Established in 1911 from the W part of Washington County. Named for John Adams, the second president of the United States.

Adams Creek (Clearwater). T38N R9E sec 4. Rises on Junction Mountain and flows 3 mi SW into Fourth of July Creek, Clearwater River drainage.

Named for Walter Adams, chief engineer of the party surveying for a road. He accidentally killed himself in 1919 while getting a drink from the creek, as his gun fell out of his holster and discharged. The shot entered his stomach, but he lived long enough to write a letter to his mother explaining what happened.

Adams Creek (Idaho). T27N R3E sec 24. A 2-mi tributary of Mill Creek from the SW; S Fk Clearwater River drainage.

Post office, 1900-1918.

Believed to have been named for an early prospector or trapper.

Adams Creek (Lemhi). T15N R25E sec 10. Originates near Gunsight Peak and flows NE 3 mi, where it goes underground.

Mr. Steeples says the creek was named for George Adams, an early rancher in the area. Leslie W. Adams patented land in the area on 10 June 1913. George Adams was possibly his father, who first settled here.

Adams Gulch (Blaine). T4N R17E sec 1. In the NW part of the county, 1 1/2 mi N of Ketchum; trends 6 mi from NW to SE and empties into Big Wood River.

In the 1860s a man named Adams had a sawmill up this gulch.

Addie (Boundary). 2600'. T65N R2E sec 26/27/34/35. Village in the extreme NE of Boundary County on US 95 and the SIRR.

Post office was established 1908 with Addie Greenway, wife of an early settler, as postmaster.

Adelaide (Minidoka). 4350'. T7S R23E sec 24. A UPRR siding in the SW part of the county, 4 mi SW of Rupert. Founded in 1882 and named for Adelaide Dampier, the first county superintendent of schools.

Post office, 1915-1916.

Advent Hollow (Latah). T40N R5W sec 5/8. A community of 270 people established in 1908, when the Upper Columbia Mission Society of the Seventh-Day Adventists purchased 180 acres 2 mi E of Viola.

The purpose was to provide their people with a place to grow their own food and to educate their children away from the influence of the cities. The school and the church that served as the center of community activities were closed in 1959.

Agatha (Nez Perce). 900'. T37N R2W sec 34. Town 15 mi N of Joseph, 1 mi W of Lenore. Camas Prairie RR station established to ship grain; once a small town. Pronounced uh-GATH-uh.

Post office, 1896-1933.

Informants have given two sources for the name: for an Indian woman who first owned the land; for a little girl.

Agency Creek (Lemhi). T19N R24E sec 20. Forms near Lemhi Pass and flows W 10 mi to enter Lemhi River at Tendoy. In 1872, Indian agent A. J. Smith erected some buildings near the mouth of this stream for the Lemhi Indian Agency.

Aggipah Mountain (Lemhi). 9920'. T21N R16E sec 18. Located 1/2 mi SW of Ship Island Lake, and about 37 mi

W of Salmon, Idaho. Pronounced AG-i-pah.

Chinook jargon meaning "salmon." (Father Paul Tracy, who has had contact with Shoshoni Indians at Fort Hall, says the name means "salmon water.")

Ahrs Creek/Gulch (Benewah). T46N R1E sec 19. Rises at Crystal Lake in the NE corner of the county and flows generally S to St. Joe River.

Named for Thomas Ahr, who homesteaded here.

Ahsahka (Clearwater). T37N R1E sec 33/34. Town 3 mi SW of Orofino. Pronounced Ah-SAH-kah. A post office was established in 1898.

Named for an Indian village across from its site, Ahsahka means "forks of a river," as it is situated at the confluence of the N Fk Clearwater River with the main stream. However, according to Sam Watters, a Nez Perce Indian, the term means "box canyon." Ralph Space (USFS) maintains Ahsahka, originally named by the Salish Indians, means "brushy country."

Airplane Lake (Lemhi). T21N R16E sec 9. Located 1/2 mi NE of Shoban Lake in Bighorn Crags.

From the air, this lake looks like the fuselage and wings of an airplane.

Aishnima (Lewis). See Slickpoo.

Ajax Peak (Lemhi). 10,028′. T23N R23E sec 16. On Idaho-Montana border in the Beaverhead Mountains; Salmon National Forest.

Named for its closeness to the Ajax mine in Montana.

Akers Gulch (Latah). T42N R3W sec 25. A gulch extending SW from Flynn Butte to Meadow Creek, a N tributary of Palouse River.

Named for early settler Thomas R. Aker, through whose land the gulch runs.

Alameda (Bannock). 4460′. T6S R34E sec 23. In the NW part of the county; now annexed to Pocatello. Primarily a residential suburb of Pocatello.

Formerly named Fairview; consolidated with north Pocatello in 1924, when its name was changed to Alameda, for the poplars along the streets.

Albeni Falls (Bonner). T56N R5W sec 29. On Pend Oreille River 4 1/2 mi W of the town of Priest Lake. Albeni Falls Dam is located here. Albeni Falls Creek heads 1 1/2 mi SE of Newport Hill and flows 2 1/2 mi SSW into Pend Oreille River.

Post office, 1907-1965.

Features received their names from Albeni Poirier, a homesteader who first came to the area in 1886. Since he was the only settler in the vicinity of the falls, his first name was applied to it for purposes of identification. Also Albany Falls.

Alberta (Lincoln). 4280′. T4S R19E sec 25/26. Early name for Richfield.

Albertson Spring (Lemhi). T21N R24E sec 18. About midway between Salmon River and Idaho-Montana line on W Fk Wimpey Creek.

Named for Horace Albertson, who had a ranch in this vicinity.

Albion (Cassia). 4750′. T12S R25E sec 6. In the center of the county, 14 mi SE of Burley.

First called Marsh Basin, for the creek on which it was located; then changed to Albion in 1877 on the suggestion of early settler and storekeeper Miles G. Robinson.

Albion became the county seat by election in 1879 and remained the seat until 1919.

Post office, 1879-.

The name means "white," or "white land," or "mountain land." It was the first name by which Great Britain was known and is still a poetic name for Great Britain. Whether Albion was one of several names to be selected by random drawing from a hat has been disputed.

Albion Mountains (Cassia/Box Elder Co., Utah). Mountains 12 mi wide and 32 mi long, extending from a point about 10 mi SE of Burley into Box Elder Co., Utah; elevation of 9200' at Mount Harrison in the N and 10,340' at Cache Peak in the S.

Alder Creek (Custer). T6N R25E sec 6. Stream about 10 mi long, heading at the junction of the Mammoth and Stewart canyons and flowing generally ENE to the Big Lost River about 5.5 mi SE of Mackay and 19 mi NW of Arco.

Alder City. T6N R25E sec 6. Ghost town at the mouth of Alder Creek. The town was established in 1884 and developed around the Big Copper mine.

Post office, 1884-1885.

Named for the stand of alders in the area.

Aldermand Ridge (Clearwater). T39N R1/2E. In the NW extremity of the county, 13 mi N of Orofino. Trends E-W; 4 mi long.

Named for homesteader John Aldermand.

Alexander (Caribou). 5733'. T9S R41E sec 7/18. Community in the W central part of the county, 5 mi N of Grace and 5 mi W of Soda Springs. First called Crater, then renamed for Charles Alexander, said to be an early settler; according to F. W. Lander, the name existed in 1858.

Post office, 1903-1983.

Algoma (Bonner). T56N R2W sec 16. Town 5 1/2 mi S of Sandpoint, 3 mi NNE of Dufort. Algoma Lake is located 7 mi SSW of Sandpoint, 3/4 mi SW of Algoma.

NPRR established in 1881. Its name is of Indian derivation, formed by combining Algonquin and Goma, meaning "lakewaters." It also designates a large district in Canada bordering on Lakes Huron and Superior, and is the name of a town in Ontario.

Alidade Creek (Elmore). T7N R11E sec 3. Rises in Alidade Lake and flows NW 1 mi to Johnson Creek; N Fk Boise system.

Named for an instrument used in surveying.

Allan Creek (Lemhi). T25N R21E sec 6. Headwaters 5 mi W of Gibbonsville, flows 2 mi SW to Hughes Creek; N Fk Salmon River.

Allan Mountain (9137'). T26N R20E sec 11/12. 1 1/4 mi E of Idaho-Montana border; Allan Lake lies .5 mi SE of the mountain.

Named for John F. Allan, an early mining operator in this area.

Allen Creek (Shoshone). T45N R6E sec 24. In the SE part of the county, 8 mi E of Avery. Rises on Little Sister Peak and flows N 3 mi to St. Joe River. Allen Ridge, 4 mi long, lies to the W of the stream; the highest elevation is Allen Point. Another stream by the same name lies 7 mi NW.

Named for trapper John Allen, who built a cabin at the mouth of this stream across the river from Bird Creek.

Allen Creek (Lemhi). T22N R20E sec 3. Two mi long, heads E to enter Moose Creek near the mouth of Beartrap Creek; Salmon River drainage.

Frank Allen leased and operated a ranch on this creek.

Allhands Spring (Lemhi). T13N R27E sec 15. About 2 mi E of Gilmore.

Named for Bernard Allhands, a rancher who patented his land in this vicinity on 1 Mar 1918.

Allison Creek (Lemhi). T17N R21E sec 29. Heads W of Lem Peak and flows W 3 mi, then SW 3 mi to enter Salmon River.

Named in honor of John F. Allison, a pioneer packer and horseman.

Almeda (Latah). T42N R5W sec 4. An early settlement, formerly called Stringtown. In the NW part of the county in the Cedar Creek area; 5 mi SW of Cora and 8 mi NW of Potlatch.

Post office, 1892-1895.

Named for Almeda Comer, who applied for the post office. The name was not popular and was changed locally to Yellow Dog (which see).

Almo (Cassia). T15S R24E sec 22/27. In the S part of the county, 23 mi S of Albion and 8 mi E of the City of Rocks.

Named by Myron B. Durfee in 1881 when he applied for a post office; an early stage station on the Boise-Kelton stage route.

Post office, 1882-.

The source of the name is disputed. One common belief is that it derived from a mythical 1862 massacre, because Almo was the watch word of all emigrants at that time, from "Remember the Alamo," slogan from the Texas War for Independence. Another logical explanation is that it is Spanish for the cottonwood tree, which grew profusely along Almo Creek, on which the town is located. Still another comes from an Indian word said to mean "plenty of water" or "battlefield." The name appears to have already been on the creek and on Almo Hot Springs well before the post office was applied for. A logical explanation is that the name is a transfer from the creek and the hot springs.

Almo Creek. T15S R25E sec 30. Rises in the Albion Mountains in the Sawtooth National Forest in the W part of Cassia County; flows 13 mi SE to empty into Edwards Creek, 2.5 mi E of the town of Almo; Raft River drainage.

Alpha (Valley). 5754'. T12N R4E sec 8. In the upper part of Round Valley, 9 mi SE of Cascade in the SW part of the county. Once a farming community with a post office, 1890-1912.

Named Alpha—first letter of the Greek alphabet—in expectation of a later settlement to have been named Omega—the last letter.

Alpheus Creek (Jerome). T9S R17E sec 19. This outlet of the third of the Blue Lakes NW of Twin Falls is 4' deep and about 40' wide, one of the shortest large streams in existence. Flows W 3 mi to empty into Snake River 4 mi W of Shoshone Falls. Also called Warm Creek. Named for a mythological river god who fell in love with the nymph Arethusa and, when she became a fountain to escape him, changed into a river and mingled with her.

Alpine (Adams). T15N R1W sec 31. Village 3 mi E of the Washington-Adams county boundary and 4 1/2 mi NW of Indian Valley.

Post office, 1891-1907.

Named because of the mountainous area.

Alpine (Bonneville). 5600'. T3S R46E sec 3. Village in extreme E part of Bonneville County on the Idaho-Wyoming line, up the gorge of S Fk Snake River. Alpine Springs is near S Fk Snake River on the S of State Highway 26 a few mi W of Alpine on the Idaho-Wyoming line.

Name suggested by the mountainous surroundings of the spring and the town.

Alpine Creek (Bonner). T57N R3E sec 5. Heads 1 1/4 mi NW of Lightning Mountain and flows 1 1/2 mi W of Rattle Mountain into Rattle Creek; Clark Fork River drainage.

Named because of the alpine character of the terrain.

Alpine Creek (Lemhi). T20N R14E sec 25. Heads at Alpine Lake and runs SW 3 1/2 mi to enter Wilson Creek; Middle Fk Salmon River drainage. Alpine Lake lies near Bighorn Crags 3/4 mi S of Ramshorn Lake.

Named by USFS and U.S. Coast and Geodetic Survey because the area of both the creek and the lake is in the high crags, surrounded by alpine trees.

Alridge (Bingham). 4977'. T2S R38E sec 28/33. In the SE part of the county, 8 mi SE of Goshen; about .5 mi upstream from the mouth of Cedar Creek.

Formerly called Cedar Creek. When a post office was applied for in 1915, the US Post Office Department would not accept the name, and Dewalde Durfee, the applicant, submitted a list of alternate names, from which Alridge was chosen. The entire area is characterized by ridges, hence the name.

Post office, 1915-1950.

Alta (Teton). T5N R46E sec 17. A Mormon settlement near the mouth of Teton Canyon.

The first settlers arrived between 1888 and 1890. They named the place Alta (Spanish for "high") because of the elevation.

Alta Creek (Custer). T8N R16E sec 28. Tributary of Germania Creek; E Fk Salmon River drainage.

Named for the daughter of Wm. H. Horton, forest ranger on Pole Creek District, 1908-1929.

Alta County. Created in 1891 with Hailey as the county seat, from the northern part of Alturas County. Dissolved later the same year by judicial interpretation.

Alton (Bear Lake). 6000'. T14S R45E sec 1. In the SE part of the county, S of Sheep Creek Reservoir, on US 30 16 mi SE of Montpelier. Once a school district and center of a few scattered farms.

Post office, 1902-1908.

May have been named for Alton, Vermont, by analogy with nearby Montpelier.

Alturas (Custer). Post office established 1904. The action was rescinded the same year.

Alturas County. The seventh county created in Idaho (1864), with Esmeralda as the county seat. Included all lands N of the Snake River from the mouth of Bruneau River to Lost River as far N as the Sawtooth Mountains.

County was eliminated in 1895.

Alturas City (Elmore). T5N R11E sec 4. Tiny mining town established in 1864 in Alturas County at the mouth of Yuba River; now gone.

Alturas Lake (Blaine). T7N R14E sec 19/20/29/30. One of the largest of the lakes in Stanley Basin, 2560 acres, the only remnant of the name of the seventh county created in Idaho.

The name derives from a Spanish word meaning "mountainous heights," probably imported by California miners.

Amalga (Minidoka). T10S R23E sec 2. A UPRR siding in an agricultural area in the S part of the county, 4 mi SW of Rupert.

The name is derived from Amalgamated Sugar Factory, 2.7 mi NW of the siding.

Amelia Bay (Bonner). On Lake Pend Oreille, near the mouth of the Clark Fork River.

Named for the wife of General Thomas F. Meagher, the first governor of Montana.

American Falls (Power). 4404'. T7S R31E sec 29. County seat. At the American Falls on Snake River, a famous landmark on the Oregon Trail, in SE Idaho and the N part of Power County.

The name dates from the early 1800s. Some have confused the incident that brought it into being with the Wilson Price Hunt Expedition of 1811, when Antoine Clappine drowned; but Rees, Walgamott, and Steel say it derived from an American Fur Company expedition in 1829, when the company traveling in canoes down Snake River came upon the falls unexpectedly and went over them, and all but one man were drowned. Subsequent maps carried the name as a warning to prevent a recurrence of the tragedy.

The town grew up on the W side of the river at an important campsite on the Oregon Trail until the OSL chose the site for its first RR station. Upon the completion of the first unit of American Falls Dam, the town was moved 1/2 mi E to its present site and the original site was inundated by the waters of Snake River. A concrete elevator tower is all that is visible of the original townsite.

Post office, 1882-.

American Girl Gulch (Boise). T6N R6E sec 9. A 2-mi gulch trending SE into Mores Creek 5 mi NE of Idaho City; Boise River drainage.

The name is derived from a mine of the same name on the banks of the gulch, given it by Winthrop H. Estabrook of Boston, its owner, in 1888.

American Hill Lake (Idaho). T29N R8E sec 35. In the central part of the county, 1 mi S of Elk City, 2 mi from the mouth of American River; 500' in diameter.

The current name was approved 13 Feb 1908. Formerly called Charlie Brown Lake, for Charles Brown, placer miner near the lake; then Poison Lake, because a nearby dredge hole contaminated the lake with arsenic; but eventually named for the nearby stream,. American River. Probably a transfer name given by miners from California.

Ames Creek (Shoshone). T47N R3E sec 28. In the W part of the county. Rises on Cemetery Ridge and flows 3 mi W to Middle Fk Big Creek, 7 mi SW of Wallace; St. Joe River drainage.

A man named Ames, who homesteaded near this stream, lost his life in the great 1910 forest fire.

Ammon (Bonneville). 4714'. T2N R38E sec 27/35. On Sand Creek, 4 mi SE of Idaho Falls. Settled in the 1890s by Mormons, who engaged in agriculture. It was at first an extension of Iona and was called South Iona, but residents applied for a separate post office.

Post office, 1898-.

Named for a Mormon apostle, son of Moscah, chief of missionaries.

Amsterdam (Twin Falls). 4725'. T13S R16E sec 16. In the central part of the county, 4.5 mi N of Rogerson,.5 mi W of US 93. Established in 1909 and named by Dutch settlers for the capital of the Netherlands. Insufficient water for irrigation caused an exodus before 1930; however, Deep Creek Reservoir has since opened up areas once abandoned.

Post office, 1909-1919.

Anderson (Latah). Early settlement in the eastern part of the county in the Bear Creek area about 25 mi E of Moscow.

August, Henry, and Lunue Anderson homesteaded in the area in the 1880s. Post office, 1893-1907.

Andersons Crossing. T39N R2W sec 5. A bridge was built across Big Bear Creek at the bottom of Big Bear Canyon in 1887-88 by August Anderson to shorten the distance between the SE section of the county and Moscow, and later Troy. Eventually a more permanent bridge was built, but none exists today.

Named for Henry and August Anderson, first postmaster and bridge builder respectively.

Anderson Creek (Boise). T9N R4E sec 15. Rises in the N central part of the county and flows 14 mi W into S Fk Payette River at Crouch.

Named by Barent Anderson, of Norway, who settled in the area in 1875.

Anderson Creek (Idaho). T30N R10E sec 29. In the central part of the county; rises on the E slope of Anderson Butte (6847') and flows 3.5 mi NE to Meadow Creek; Selway River drainage.

Both features were named for an early settler.

Anderson Creek (Lemhi). T26N R21E sec 25. Originates near Anderson Mountain and flows S 4 mi to enter Dahlonega Creek at Gibbonsville; N Fk Salmon River drainage.

Named for George D. Anderson, who built the first stamp quartz mill in Montana at Bannock. He made the first mineral location in the Gibbonsville mining district in 1877 and operated mines in this region until his death in 1899. He was also the first mayor of Gibbonsville.

He arrived at Leesburg in 1866 to locate placer ground and built toll bridges in Salmon City and Nevada before he went Gibbonsville.

Anderson Gulch (Lemhi). T19N R17E sec 29. About 1 1/2 mi long, runs into Yellowjacket Creek drainage; Middle Fk Salmon River drainage.

There are two versions of how this feature was named. One says it was named for William Anderson, who mined in the Yellowjacket and later had the old Silver Spur Bar next to McPhersons Dry Goods in Salmon. The other informant says it was named for Charles and Joe Anderson, who owned mining property in this gulch.

Anderson Lake (Kootenai). T48N R3W sec 28/29/32. One of a group of 9 lakes along the lower Coeur d'Alene River, formed partly by overflow of the river during flood stages.

In the late 1800s there was a shipping point named Anderson at the N end of the lake; the name was changed to Springston (which see) in 1901.

Anderson Point (Bonner). T57N R1E sec 31. On Lake Pend Oreille, ESE of Sandpoint 2 1/2 mi SE of Sunnyside.

Named for the Anderson family, who own land here.

Andrews Spring (Lemhi). T18N R22E sec 1. The head of Sawmill Canyon on McDevitt Creek.

Named for the Ernest Andrews family, who owned land in this area.

Angel Butte (Clearwater). 3783'. T37N R3E sec 2. Five mi N of Grangemont.

Al Hansen (USFS) believed the butte was named for a lookout here named Angel. Ralph Space (USFS). Said the name was in existence in 1919, before a lookout was established.

Anna Lukes Meadows (Lewis). See Lapwai Lake.

Named for an Indian woman who had her land allotment on the meadow.

Annis (Jefferson). T5N R38E sec 25/36. In the SE section of the county 4 mi E of Menan on the island between the main channel of Snake River and Great Feeder Canal; the name of an area rather than a town.

James and Annie Browning Kearney were early settlers here and carried the mail for the area. In 1896 Annis Post Office was established and the Kearneys moved it to their store, rather than their home; James Kearney was named post-master.

Name said by Adams (*100 Years of Jefferson County*) to be derived from a respelling of Annie's, as in the local expression, "Let's go to Annie's to get the mail and chat for a while." Others say it is a blend of Annie and island.

Ant Butte (Adams). 7945'. T21N R1W sec 22. Located between Rapid River on the W and Boulder Creek on the E, about 3 mi NW of Brush Mountain and 1 mi SE of North Star Butte. Ant Basin lies E of Ant Butte and is drained by Ant Basin Creek, 3 mi long, flowing W and SW to Boulder Creek; Little Salmon River drainage.

Named for the shape of the butte, which resembles a giant anthill.

Antelope (Butte). T4N R24E sec 19. Ghost town in SW quadrant just E of the Butte-Custer county line. An early mining and ranching center.

Post office, 1882-1904.

Named for the herds of antelope in the area.

Antelope Mountain (Bonner). 4392'. T55N R3E sec 6. Located 3 3/4 mi W of Idaho-Montana border; 2 1/2 mi E of Clark Fork. Antelope Lake lies 2 mi SW of the mountain and 4 3/4 mi W of Idaho-Montana border; 1 1/2 mi ESE of Clark Fork.

The names of these features are derived from the animal, although it was probably never found in the area.

Antelope Valley (Clark). T12N R39/40E. An area extending W from Sheridan Reservoir to N of Kilgore, in the NE extremity of the county.

Named for the herds of antelope that frequent the area.

Anthony Creek (Shoshone). T42N R2E sec 9. In the SE extremity of the county in the Clearwater National Forest. Rises on Anthony Peak and flows about 5 mi NW to Middle Fk St. Maries River, .5 mi N of Clarkia.

A man named Anthony home-steaded near this stream.

Anvil Creek (Lemhi). T18N R16E sec 22. Heads about 2 mi SE of Forge Creek Hot Springs and flows SW 2 1/2 mi to enter Camas Creek; Middle Fk Salmon River drainage.

Named by Irvin Robertson of Salmon when he was a forest ranger. See Forge Creek and Hammer Creek.

Aparejo Creek (Lemhi). T18N R14E sec 3. Heads near source of Soda Creek and runs W 3 mi to enter Middle Fk Salmon River. Aparejo Point lies 1/2 mi NW of the mouth of Aparejo Creek.

Named for an *aparejo*, a Spanish pack saddle made of cowhide, willows, and straw, found at the mouth of this stream.

Apgar Creek (Idaho). T33N R7E sec 11. A 3-mi stream rising on Cedar Knob and flowing SE to Lochsa River, 5 mi NNE of Lowell; in Clearwater National Forest.

Named for Bill Apgar, an early fireman on the Lochsa Ranger District.

Apple Valley (Canyon). T6N R6W sec 24. An agricultural community.

Named c.1913 for the fine quality of apples grown here.

Applejack Creek (Boise). T8N R5E sec 34. Rises 2 mi SW of Grimes Pass and flows 2 mi SW into Muddy Creek 1 mi N of Placerville; Boise River drainage.

The Applejack mine, recorded 16 Dec 1865, was located on its banks.

Arange Creek (Fremont). T14N R42E sec 11. Flows 3 mi S to Hotel Creek, 4 mi N of Island Park Reservoir; Henrys Fork drainage. Arange Peak (8984') is 3 mi N of Island Park Reservoir.

Named for a Swiss business combine, the Arangee Company, which established a hotel, mill, and dairy on the stage line from Kilgore to West Yellowstone c.1881.

Arbon (Power). 5246'. T11S R33E sec 23. In the SE part of the county, 51 mi SE of American Falls. Settled in the late 1890s and early 1900s by farmers along the creeks.

Post office, 1898-.

Arbon Valley (Power/Oneida). T7-12S R33/34E. Lies between Blue Springs Hills on the E and Deep Creek Mountains on the W, separated by a low divide from Holbrook Valley on the S; a very long narrow valley that follows and is drained by Bannock Creek, running S to N in Power County, S of American Falls.

Named in 1897 for Joseph N. Arbon, the oldest among the early settlers.

Archer (Madison). 4915'. T5/4N R40E sec 31/5. Center of an agricultural and dairying area in the SW part of the county, 12 mi S of Rexburg. First settled by Mormons in 1885; in 1903 the townsite was designated as Lyman for Theodore Lyman, first settler in the area. It was later changed to Archer.

Post office, 1902-1910.

Named for John Archer, leading citizen given credit for having established the post office.

Archer Mountain (Idaho). 7492'. T30N R12E sec 23. In the central part of E Idaho County at the W edge of Bitterroot National Forest. Archer Point (5061') lies 3 mi ENE of Archer Mountain, also on the border of Selway- Bitterroot Wilderness Area.

Named for a trapper who lost his life because of a fall from a cliff on Archer Mountain and was buried here.

Arco (Butte). 5318'. T4N R26/27E sec 25/36. County seat. In the S central part of the county at the base of the S extremity of Lost River Mountains in Big Lost River Valley, near the Snake River Plain. Arco Hills (7352') trend 7 1/2 mi NE from a point 3 mi E of Arco, and Arco Peak (7517') is 1 1/2 mi N of Arco.

Began as a stage station named Root Hog at Kennedy Crossing, some 5 mi S of its present site. Old Isaac Smith became the station operator when the Blackfoot-Wood River and Blackfoot-Salmon River stage roads formed a junction at the site and the name became Junction. A little settlement grew up around the stage station.

A post office application for Junction was refused, on the grounds that there were too many Junctions; the US Post Office Department suggested the name Arco to honor a European count visiting the US. It was accepted, partly because the bend or arc in Lost River with the town at the end made it appropriate. Some informants insist that it was named for Arco Isaac Smith, but Smith acquired that name from the town.

In 1880 Arco Stage Station accommodated two 6-horse stages. Then Arco moved to a second site, 4 mi SE of present Arco, and remained there until the RR came through—when it moved again to its permanent site on the RR.

Post office, 1880-.

Argora (Clark) 7500'. T12N R33E sec 8. A grazing area for cattle and sheep in the NW quadrant of the county on Medicine Lodge Creek between May and Edie ranches.

Post office, 1916.

Named for an early settler.

Arimo (Bannock). 4735'. T10S R37E sec 7/17. In the central part of the county, 5 mi S of McCammon. Settled by Latter-day Saints in the 1870s and named Oneida, for the Oneida mine in the area. Arimo is on the RR and US 91.

Post office, 1878-1926.

10

Named by a RR official, supposedly for a red-haired Indian chief.

Arkansas Creek (Bannock). T10S R37E sec 19. Rises in springs 1 mi E of Downey and flows N 9 mi to its confluence with N Fk Arkansas Creek, 5 mi long, then W 1 mi to join Marsh Creek; Portneuf River drainage.

Named because of a settler who came from Arkansas.

Arling (Valley). 4848'. T15N R3E sec 15. In the W part of the county, a RR siding on the NE extremity of Cascade Reservoir.

Post office, 1915-1920.

Originally named Arlington, it became Arling at the request of the US Post Office to avoid duplication of names.

Armstrong Gulch (Clearwater). T36N R6E sec 17. A 2-mi gulch trending N to S; flows S into Orofino Creek 4 mi SE of Pierce; Clearwater River drainage.

Named for John Armstrong, a miner.

Armstrong Lookout (Clearwater). T40N R4E sec 13. Five mi NW of Bertha Hill.

Abe Armstrong settled near here in 1908.

Arnett Creek (Lemhi). T22N R19E sec 22. Heads about 3 mi SW of Haystack Mountain and flows S then SE 7 1/2 mi to enter Napias Creek about 2 mi SW of Leesburg; Salmon River drainage.

Named for a pioneer placer miner.

Arrastra Creek (Lemhi). T18N R17E sec 26. Forms in Black Mountain and flows NW 4 mi to enter Silver Creek; Salmon River drainage.

Arrastra Gulch. T23N R19E sec 16. SE of Smith Gulch, 1 1/2 mi long, runs NE to Pine Creek drainage; Salmon River drainage.

Named for the arrastras located in the area. An arrastra is a construction used to grind gold-bearing rock. It consists of a pit lined with smooth stones and a suspended rock tied to a log, which is pulled around in circles by horses or mules. Once the ore was ground down, it was much easier to separate the gold.

Arrow (Nez Perce). 822'. T36N R3W sec 7. Town 3 mi NE of Spalding.

The NPRR, while excavating for the Clearwater branch line on the E bank of Potlatch Creek, established a telegraph station on the W side of the creek and named it Arrow Junction for the great number of arrowheads found at this site. Now known as Arrow.

Arrow Rock Junction (Elmore). T3N R4E sec 15. On Boise-Elmore county line. Now inundated by waters behind Lucky Peak Dam. Established when Arrowrock Dam was being built. Arrow Rock itself has a cleft at which, according to local tradition, passing Indians fired arrows to test their marksmanship.

Post office, 1911-1917.

Arrowhead, The (Custer). T8N R13E sec 17. Promontory in the Sawtooth Range, .4 mi N of Profile Lake and .8 mi NNE of Mount Cramer.

Named because of its shape.

Arson Creek (Latah). T42N R4W sec 21. Rises in NW part of county near Gold Hill (3800'); flows 2 mi SW to Gold Creek. Palouse River drainage.

Named in 1930 by W. H. Daugs (USFS) because of the number of man-caused fires in this drainage in the summer of 1924.

Artesian City (Twin Falls). T11S R20E sec 31. On the Cassia-Twin Falls county line, 2 mi S of Murtaugh Lake. Formerly Farmington; changed when residents applied for a post office.

Post office, 1909-1911.

Named for its artesian wells.

Ashton (Fremont). 5256'. T9N R42E sec 25/36. Town on US 20 and UPRR 14 mi NE of St. Anthony.

Post office, 1906-.

Named for Walter Ashton, construction engineer on the railroad; incorporated 1906.

Aspendale (Latah). 2589'. T39N R1W sec 32. 1 mi S of Tomer Butte on the Tomer-Lenville Road. Pioneer community named Tin Bell until 1896, when the name was changed for the aspen trees in the area.

Astor Gulch (Owyhee). T6S R4W sec 21. Flows SW into Flint Creek, 1/2 mi E of Flint. The ravine was named for John Jacob Astor.

Athol (Kootenai). 2391'. T53N R3W sec 9/16. In the NW part of the county on US 95, Highway 52, and the NPRR; 20 mi N of Coeur d'Alene. Incorporated in 1909.

Post office, 1895-.

Said to have been named for an Indian chief.

Atlanta (Elmore). 5500'. T5N R11E sec 3. Early mining town, settled by Southern sympathizers, in the NE quadrant of the county on the Middle Fk Boise River, in Boise National Forest.

Gold was discovered here in 1864, opening the gold rush to S Fk Boise River. The discovery ledge was named after the Battle of Atlanta, because both the news of Sherman's victory at Atlanta and the discovery of gold were big events at the time. The town was named for the ledge. Mining continued through the 1930s.

Post office, 1867-.

Atlanta Springs. 2 mi above the mouth of Roaring River; Middle Fk Boise River drainage.

Atomic City (Bingham). T1N R31E sec 3. In the NW extremity of the county, halfway between Arco and Blackfoot; formerly called Midway.

In 1949 when the city was incorporated, the citizens decided to change the name from Midway to Atomic City, as it was more appropriate to the new development near the nuclear engineering site.

Post office, 1949-.

Atwater Lake (Latah). 2400'. A lake between Big Bear Creek and Big Bear Ridge about 5 mi N of Kendrick.

Thomas E. Atwater homesteaded the 160 acres containing this lake.

Auger Falls (Twin Falls). T9S R17E sec 19. On the Snake River, 5 mi NE of Filer.

Named because of the peculiar auger-like formation of the rock in the river channel that causes the water to spiral as it pours through the partly obstructed channel and over a series of ledges.

Auglebright Gulch (Boise). T10N R4E sec 13. In the NW extremity of the county; runs 2 mi W into the Middle Fk Payette River drainage. Pronounced ARE-ge-brite.

Named for the Auglebright family, who settled here in the 1880s.

Aunt Mollys Spring (Valley). T16N R6E sec 23. On S Fk Salmon River in the W part of the county, 2 mi from Knox.

Early settlers used this spring for many years, but it has now fallen into disuse. Named for Molly Smead, Sheepeater Indian wife of Pony Smead.

Austin (Madison). T6N R38E sec 24. A RR station in the NW extremity of the county, 5 mi W of Rexburg.

Established and named by the UPRR for Mark Austin, president of the Fremont Stake of the Mormon church and of the board of education in Rexburg, and the assistant manager of the sugar company in Sugar City.

Austin (Twin Falls). T9S R14E sec 8. In the NW part of the county, SW across Snake River from Banbury Springs; an early settlement.

Post office, 1898-1910. Named for Alice Austin, first postmaster.

Austin Creek (Idaho). T35N R6E sec 36. In the N central part of the county; rises on E slope of Austin Ridge and flows 2 mi SE to Eldorado Creek, tributary of Lolo Creek; Clearwater River drainage. The ridge is 5 mi long, trending NE to SW, with the S extremity the highest elevation, 4731'.

Named for John Austin, who trapped the Musselshell country in the early 1900s. He also served as a lookout and fireman for the USFS.

Auxor Basin (Bonner). T57N R2E sec 20. Located 3 1/2 mi NE of Hope; 5 mi NW of Bee Top Mountain.

Named for a miner who lived in the Hope area and had a mine in the basin.

Avalanche Ridge (Clearwater). T41N R8E sec 5-31. A 5-mi ridge in the NE part of the county, trending SW from the Shoshone-Clearwater county line.

This is steep country with heavy snowfall; thus avalanches are common.

Avelene Creek (Boise). T5N R4E sec 34. In the SW extremity of the county. Flows NE into Mores Creek; Boise River drainage. Pronounced AV-e-lin.

Named after Jane Avelene, whose father once had a claim on this creek.

Avery (Shoshone). 2484'. T45N R5E sec 10/14. Avery Creek rises on Avery Hill and flows SE to St. Joe River at Avery. Once a mining and logging town in the central part of the county, at the junction of the St. Joe River and N Fk St. Joe.

In 1886, Sam "49" Williams homesteaded the site on which Avery is now located. Known as North Fork until the USFS started using the name Pinchot (for Chief Forester Gifford Pinchot) about 1906-07. When the RR was completed in 1908, the station was named Avery by the RR officials for Avery Rockefeller, son of William Rockefeller, who at one time was director of the Chicago, Milwaukee and St. Paul RR.

Post office, 1910-.

Avondale (Owyhee). T4S R3W sec 27. Ranch and landmark 2 1/2 mi N of Silver City.

Mr. and Mrs. Milton Presby had a milk ranch here. Mrs. Presby named it for Avondale, Scotland, as early as 1866. The earlier name of this location was allegedly Crosby Gulch, for a Mr. Crosby who once had a dairy here.

Avondale Lake (Kootenai). T51N R3W sec 7/18. Just N of Bervan Bay at the NW end of Hayden Lake; about .8 mi long. Originally Avondale Lake, then Wrights Lake, renamed after the owner; in 1962, by a decision of the US Board on Geographic Names, was given its original name.

Ax Park (Lemhi). T26N R20E sec 22. Park E of headwaters of Hughes Creek and 2 mi SW of Allan Mountain, on Idaho-Montana line.

A man reportedly lost an axe in this park-like area, and it was never found. Through local usage the place became known as Ax Park.

Ayer (Latah). T40N R6W sec 24. A RR stop on the Spokane and Inland Empire RR. Named for Mary Ayer, whose property the track crossed.

Boise (Ada County), the old Overland Hotel, 1889.

B

Babel, Tower of (Idaho). 9268'. T23N R2W sec 13. One of the promontories in the Seven Devils Mountains. It lies in the Nezperce National Forest just E of Sheep Lake and 1 mi ENE of He Devil.

Named by A. H. Marshall because of a ledge that spirals from the bottom to the top of this peak, resembling the ramp often pictured as ascending the biblical Tower of Babel.

Baboon Creek (Idaho). T29N R8E sec 24. In the N central part of the county, a 1-mi tributary of American River from the E; just E of Elk City.

Named for a French miner, Peter Baboin (or Bablaine), whose nickname was Baboon. Early records carry the name Babboon.

Baby Grand Mountain (Latah). 4744'. T42N R1W sec 7. In the NE quarter of the county, in the St. Joe National Forest, between the headwaters of Mizpah Creek and N Fk Palouse River.

Named for the Baby Grand mine, the first mining claim (1905) on this mountain.

Baby Joe Gulch (Lemhi). T16N R26E sec 23. Heads 1/2 mi S of Grizzly Mountain and runs S 2 mi to enter Canyon Creek drainage just 1 mi W of Leadville; Lemhi River drainage.

Joe Fannin and his wife, Nellie, came to the town of Junction from Kentucky in the 1880s. They had one child, a boy, and named him Baby Joe. When the father discovered an ore deposit in this gulch, he called the claim the Baby Joe mine.

Bacon Creek (Adams). T15N R2W sec 16. Rises in the SW part of the county near Mesa and flows generally W about 7 mi to Weiser River.

Bacon (4534'). T15N R2W sec 14. Community located on Bacon Creek. Both the stream and the community took the name of the original homesteaders.

Bacon Creek (Clearwater). T39N R9E sec 22. Rises in the NE part of the county on Junction Mountain and flows 2 mi NW into N Fk Clearwater River.

Bacon Creek is located less than 4 mi from Pie Creek and Coffee Creek; its name may have been part of a group of names supplied by the USFS.

Bad Bear Creek (Boise). T7N R6E sec 35. Rises in the SW part of the county on Freeman Peak (8111') and Thompson Peak (10,766') and flows 3 mi S into Mores Creek; Boise River drainage.

Legend has it that an early miner was severely mauled by a bear at the head of this creek.

Badger Creek (Teton). T7N R44E sec 20. Rises in Wyoming in North and South creeks, which converge in Idaho 10 mi N of Driggs, and flows SW, NW, and SW to empty into Teton River; about 15 mi from the convergence to the mouth.

Badger. T6N R45E sec 5/6. Post office established on Badger Creek, 1904; the name was changed to Felt in 1913.

Named in 1872 by Dr. F. V. Hayden, USGS, for the badgers in the area.

Bailey Creek (Idaho). T26N R10E sec 22. On Salmon River.

Named for Robert G. Bailey, politician; printing-press operator; author of *The River of No Return*, the first book about the Salmon River.

Bairds Gulch (Boise). T6N R5E sec 35. Rises 2 mi S of Idaho City and flows 2 1/2 mi N into Mores Creek; Boise River drainage.

Named for Calvin Baird, who settled in the area in 1863.

Baker (Lemhi). 4359′. T20N R23E sec 4. Town on Highway 28 near the mouth of Baker Creek, about 9 mi SE of Salmon. Baker Bridge crosses Lemhi River near the mouth of Wimpey Creek.

Post office, 1889-.

Named for William R. Baker, a pioneer rancher in this area, who patented his land 24 Mar 1884. Baker was reportedly a buffalo hunter for the RR in his earlier years.

Baker Draw (Fremont). T12N R44E sec 25. In E central Fremont County; runs SW 2 mi W of Eccles Butte.

Named for the sons of Joseph Baker, early Marysville settler, who ran trap lines in the area.

Baker Peak (Camas). 10,174′. T4N R15E sec 21. On NE boundary of Camas County, in the Smoky Mountains, Sawtooth National Forest. Baker Creek rises 3 mi SW of Baker Peak and flows 15 mi NE to Big Wood River. Baker Lake lies 2 mi NE of the peak.

Named for an early settler who started a shingle mill on Baker Creek.

Balaam (Blaine). T1N R19E sec 20. In the center of the county, 4 mi S of Bellevue. A UPRR siding named for a nearby resident.

Bald Mountain (Blaine). 9230′. T4N R17E sec 27. In the NW part of the county, 2.5 mi SW of Ketchum.

The name is descriptive; there is little vegetation on the summit.

Bald Mountain (Clearwater). 5036′. T37N R4E sec 1.

The mountain was named after a forest fire burned off the timber on it. Believed to be named by the Pierce party (1860).

Bald Mountain (Custer). 10,313′. T12N R18E sec 16. South of Bayhorse Lake in the Challis National Forest. Named because it lacks trees.

Bald Mountain (Latah). 5334′. T43N R2W sec 34. Just S of the Benewah-Latah county line at the N extremity of Cleveland Gulch, in the Hoodoo Mountains, St. Joe National Forest.

Named because the top is bare of trees. Little Bald Mountain (4400′) is about 1 mi S of Bald Mountain.

Bald Peak (Fremont). 10,145′. T16N R43E sec 11. On the border between Idaho and Montana 1 mi W of Lionhead. Also: Targhee Peak.

Named for its appearance: summit is above the timberline.

Baldy Creek (Kootenai). T48N R1W sec 27. Rises on the N slope between Twin Crags and Mt. Wiessner and flows 5 mi N and NW to Latour Creek; Coeur d'Alene River drainage.

The original name of Mt. Wiessner, Mt. Baldy, is preserved in the name of this stream.

Baldy Creek (Lemhi). T19N R24E sec 17. Originates 1 mi S of Tule Lake and flows E 6 mi to enter Lemhi River across the mouth of Pattee Creek; Lemhi River drainage. Baldy Basin lies N of Baldy Creek.

Named for George A. "Balley" Martin, a rancher in this area who patented his land 1 Feb 1906.

Baldy Mountain (Lemhi). 10,773'. T15N R28E sec 26. Three mi SE of Mountain Peak, on the Continental Divide; in the Salmon National Forest.

USFS map calls the feature Mount Baldy, but local usage is usually Baldy Mountain.

Ball Butte (Latah). 3308'. T41N R5 sec 19. In the NW quarter of the county just W of the homestead of Richard and Cora Ball (1891).

Ballard (Owyhee). T6S R4W sec 13. Townsite 8 mi S of Silver City. Post office, 1886-1887.

Named for Bill Ballard, an early miner.

Banbury Springs (Twin Falls). 2910'. T8S R14E sec 32/33. On the S bank of Snake River, 8 mi NW of Buhl.

Named for early rancher Roy W. Banbury, who developed the site.

Bancroft (Caribou). 5423'. T8S R39E sec 14. In the W part of the county, 16 mi NW of Soda Springs. Settled in 1885 by homesteading farmers who came from Arkansas, and first named Squaw. Renamed Bancroft for William H. Bancroft, vice president of Oregon Short Line RR.

Post office, 1892-.

Band Mill (Clearwater). T37N R3E sec 26. Settlement 1 mi W of Grangemont.

The White Pine Lumber Company had a sawmill here that used one of the first band saws in the area.

Banida (Franklin). 4721'. T14S R39E sec 6/7. In the W part of the county about 6 mi SE of Oxford. Formerly Richfield, for the fertility of the soil.

Post office, 1912-.

Named Banida in 1908 from Bannock and Oneida, for its nearness to those counties.

Banks (Boise). T9N R3E sec 29/32.

Village named for the Banks family; W. B. Banks was a local rancher and Emma Banks the first postmaster (1914).

Banks Gulch (Latah). T42N R2W sec 14. One of ten named gulches running parallel to each other and emptying into N Fk Palouse River from the N. Like the others, Banks Gulch was once famous for gold prospecting.

Named for early claim-holder Ida E. Banks.

Bannock County. County seat, Pocatello. Created in 1893 from part of Bingham County and named for the Bannack Indians, the first inhabitants of the area, whose name was spelled Bannock by early settlers.

Bannock Range (Bannock, Oneida, Franklin). Lies N and E of Malad Range and S of Pocatello Range; about 20 mi long and 6 mi wide. Highest peaks: Oxford (9281') and Elkhorn (9001').

Bannock Creek (Power). T6S R32E sec 2. Rises in the mountains 3 mi S of Arbon and flows N and NE into American Falls Reservoir; about 38 mi long. Its waters are used to irrigate tracts of land along the valley.

Named for the Bannock Indians, who frequented the area.

Bannock Pass (Clark). 7670'. T13N R31E sec 1. On the Continental Divide at the Idaho-Montana line in the NW extremity of the county.

Named for the Bannock Indians, who used this pass to go to and from buffalo grounds.

Bannock Pass (Lemhi). 7672'. T17N R27E sec 7. On the Continental Divide, between Idaho and Montana.

It was through this pass that the Nez Perce Indians recrossed from Montana into Idaho during the war of 1877. The Gilmore and Pittsburg RR crossed the Continental Divide by tunneling under this pass.

Named by Leesburg miners in 1868 because this was the main route from Old Junction to Bannock, Montana.

Bar Creek (Clearwater). T40N R8E sec 32. Rises on Bar Point (6418') and flows 3 mi NW into N Fk Clearwater River, just S of Moscow Bar.

The bar at the mouth of the creek was mined for gold.

Barber (Ada). T3N R3E sec 29. Early 20th-century mill town on a spur of the UPRR.

The Barber Lumber Company built the town about 1903 and named it after J. T. Barber, president of the company. The mill operated intermittently until 1935, when the nearby commercial lumber supply was exhausted.

Post office, 1909-.

Bargamin Creek (Idaho). T26N R10E sec 26. Salmon River tributary from the N.

Named for Vic Bargamin, who in 1903 trapped between the Salmon and Clearwater rivers.

Barking Fox Lake (Lemhi). T21N R16E sec 20. In Bighorn Crags about 1/2 mi S of Terrace Lakes.

Named by the USFS and Coast and Geodetic Survey in 1963. Gilbert L. (Tommy) Farr, who was ranger on the Cobalt Ranger District, heard a fox bark one night near this lake.

Barn Creek (Clearwater). T39N R10E sec 26. In the NE part of the county. Flows 3 mi NE into Barnard Creek; Clearwater River drainage.

Barn is a shortened form of Barnard; it is part of a group name, probably supplied by the USFS.

Barnard Creek (Clearwater). T39N R10E sec 23. Rises in the E part of the county on Switchback Hill (6472') and Star Point (5310') and flows 4 mi N into Kelly Creek; Clearwater River drainage.

Named for a USGS topographer.

Baron Creek (Boise). T9N R11E sec 11. Rises on the Boise-Custer county line on Braxon Peak (10,353') and Thompson Peak (10,766') and flows NW into the S Fk Payette River. Upper Baron, Little Baron, and Baron lakes are the sources of the stream. Baron Peak (10,297') lies 4 mi NW of the source of the creek.

It is believed that the original name was Barren, because that is descriptive of the area.

Barth Hot Springs (Idaho). T25N R11E sec 13. Situated on Salmon River. Formerly Guleke Springs, for Salmon River boatman Captain Harry Guleke.

The current name is for Jim Barth, who lived here in the 1920s.

Bartlett Creek (Custer). T8N R21E sec 11. Heads N of Porphyry Peak and flows N to Big Lost River. Bartlett Point is a promontory just SE of the mouth of the creek.

Named for an early settler.

Bartlett Point (Clearwater). T38N R3E sec 14. Peak 14 mi NE of Orofino.

Named for Bill Bartlett, a miner, who settled in the area with his Indian wife.

Barton (Washington). 2475'. T12N R4W sec 10. Station on the PINRR midway between Crane and Midvale, on the Weiser River.

Named for E. M. Barton and the Barton family, who came to Weiser from Missouri in 1882.

Barton Hump (Bonner). T54N R1W sec 11. Hill 2 1/2 mi NE of the town of Cedar Creek; 2 1/4 WNW of Pack Saddle Mountain.

Named for a local resident.

Bartoo Island (Bonner). T60N R4W sec 17/20. On Priest Lake, 1 1/2 mi NW of Fourmile Island; 2 mi SE of Kalispell Island.

Named for George Bartoo, a settler. The name was once written Baritoe on maps.

Basalt (Bingham). 4588′. T1S R37E sec 19. In the N part of the county, 4 mi S of Shelley.

Settled by Mormons in 1885. The entire area had been called Cedar Point, but when the RR came through in 1879, RR officials assigned a new name— first Monroe, and shortly thereafter Basalt. In 1903 Basalt was moved up onto the flat E of the canals and RR.

Named for the basaltic formation along the Snake River.

Basalt Hill (Latah). 3300′. T40N R4W sec 1. This hill lies between the headwaters of Flat and Hatter creeks, 6 mi SE of Princeton.

The name is descriptive of the rock in the area.

Basin (Cassia). T13S R23E sec 32/33. Former townsite in the central part of the county, 4 mi E of Oakley. A Mormon settlement dating from 1878.

Post office, 1883-1909.

Formerly Spring Basin, named for the shape of the valley in which the community is situated.

Basin Creek (Custer). T11N R14E sec 29. N tributary of Salmon River. Heads in the small lakes between Hindman and Valley Creek lakes, flows generally S and SE into Salmon River.

Basin Butte is W of the source of Basin Creek, and East Basin Lake is at the head of East Basin Creek.

The name is derived from Mormon Basin, through which the creek flows.

Basinger Canyon (Lemhi). T11N R27E sec 33/34. Just SE of Bell Mountain in the Lemhi Range. Runs parallel to Bell Mountain Creek, mainly from NE to SW.

Named for Perry Basinger, who had patented mining claims in this area.

Basque Spring (Boise). T9N R5E sec 23.

Named for Basque sheepherders, who used the spring.

Basque Spring (Owyhee). T16S R12E sec 8. Five mi SE of the town of Three Creek.

Many Basque sheepherders in Owyhee County used this spring.

Bates Canyon/Creek (Bonneville). T1N R42E sec 32-33. Lies at about the center of the county. The creek empties into June Creek; Snake River drainage.

Named for Dan Bates, a trapper, hired by the Fall Creek cattlemen to trap wolves in 1898.

Bathtub Mountain (Shoshone). 6225′. T43N R7E sec 10. In the S part of the county, 16 mi SE of Avery. Bathtub Creek rises on the S slopes of the mountain and flows 3 mi SE to Buck Creek; N Fk Clearwater River drainage. Bathtub Meadows lies at the source of Bathtub Creek.

According to a local story, a young man homesteaded on the slopes of the mountain and set about building a cabin and making ready for his bride to join him. She had made one stipulation about coming to this wilderness; she would not come if she could not have a bathtub. He assured her that the tub would be ready. Some say he bought a bathtub, others that he made a wooden bathtub, and in either case he set it in the open yard.

Battle Creek (Franklin). T15S R39E sec 5. Rises on the W slopes of Treasureton Hill and wanders 16 mi SE to Bear River, 3 mi NW of Preston.

Named for the Battle of Bear River, which occurred at the mouth of this creek 29 Jan 1863. On this date Colonel Patrick E. Connor and his Third California Infantry had been sent to avenge Shoshoni Chief Pocatello's purported massacre of a California emigrant train near the City of Rocks, Cassia County. Connor attacked an Indian winter camp on this stream and almost annihilated the band. Two hundred sixty-seven Indians, of which 90 were women and children, were slaughtered.

Post office, 1882-1908.

Battle Creek (Owyhee). T14S R2W sec 1. Flows SW 32 mi into the E Fk Owyhee River. Battle Creek Stage Station was located on this creek.

Named because Michael Jordan, the leader of the original discoverers of gold in the county, was killed here 11 July 1864 by Bannock Indians, who mutilated his body. The settlers were having great difficulty with the Indians, and when they attacked a man and stole 50 horses, Jordan led a group of volunteers to punish the culprits and to regain the horses. They followed the thieves for almost two days and came upon them in a rocky canyon near the Owyhee River, where Jordan was killed.

Battleground (Custer). T7N R23E sec 2. Site of a battle between whites and Indians; also a stage station.

In 1878 a battle occurred at this site between the Bannock Indians and members of Joe Skelton's freighting train. Skelton was hauling goods to Challis for George L. Shoup's store. The place is now under the waters of Mackay Reservoir.

Named for the 1878 battle.

Battles (Clearwater). T36N R4E sec 24/25. Settlement 5 mi N of Weippe.

Charles Battles homesteaded about 4 mi from the location and ran a shingle mill here.

Baugh Creek (Blaine). T2N R20E sec 10. Rises in the NE quadrant and flows 10.5 mi SE to Little Wood River.

Named for a druggist from Shoshone, Idaho, who ran sheep in this area in the early 1900s.

Bayhorse Creek (Custer). T12N R19E sec 7. W tributary of Salmon River.

This creek was prospected as early as 1864 and a claim was staked in 1872. In 1877 a mining district including Bayhorse and Clayton was formed, and smelters were built in both locations.

Bayhorse 6140'. T12N R18E sec 5. Ghost town on Bayhorse Creek. Formerly Aetna and Bay Horse. Bayhorse Lake lies 1 1/4 mi W of the town and Little Bayhorse Lake 1/2 mi E. The post office was first established as Aetna, a name assigned by the US Post Office because Bay Horse, as two words, was considered unacceptable. By 1884 Bay Horse was listed as a post office name and Aetna dropped. Now the name is written Bayhorse. The post office was discontinued in 1927.

Said to have been named for an incident in 1864. A prospector lost his bay horse and in his search discovered an outcropping of ore at the site.

Bayview (Kootenai). 2134'. T54N R2W sec 34. In the northernmost part of the county on Pend Oreille Lake; 8 mi E of Athol and 3 mi N of Farragut State Park. Established in 1894 and first known as a fishing village and winter quarters for trappers, it is now a summer resort.

Post office, 1906-.

Bayview Creek (Bonner/Kootenai). T54N R2W sec 33. A 3-mi long stream; rises 2 mi NW of Cape Horn and flows SW to disappear .3 mi NW of the town of Bayview.

Named for the view from its location on Pend Oreille Lake.

Beachs Corner (Bonneville). 4783'. T3N R38E sec 34. Intersection about 8 mi NE of Idaho Falls.

Named for Aaron W. Beach, who with his wife and eight children settled on 80 acres of land here before 1910.

Beacon Butte (Jefferson). T7N R36E sec 1. In the NE quadrant of the county, 4 mi E of the NE corner of Camas Wildlife Refuge and 3 mi NE of Hamer.

Locally known because an FAA beacon is located at its summit.

Beagle Creek (Lemhi). T19N R17E sec 9. Heads in area S of Red Rock Peak and flows NW for 2 1/2 mi to enter Yellowjacket Creek near the Yellowjacket Ranger Station; Middle Fk Salmon River drainage.

Named for Al and Bill Beagle, early settlers in this region.

Beagle Gulch (Latah). One of ten named gulches emptying into N Fk Palouse River from the N.

Named for homesteader and prospector Oliver H. P. Beagle. See Banks Gulch.

Beals Butte (Latah). 4932'. T41/42N R1W sec 6/31. A promontory central to the headwaters of Torpid and Graves creeks; 6 mi due E of Laird Park, in NE quadrant of county.

W. J. Gamble says this butte commemorates a lumberjack; John B. Miller, in *The Trees Grew Tall*, suggests it may be named for Tom Beall, who went with Captain E. D. Pierce to Orofino in 1861. Also called Beals Mountain and Beals Lookout.

Bean Hill (Latah). T39N R2W sec 29. An area on Big Bear Ridge settled by the D. J. Ingle family in 1884.

Named because the principal crop was beans in the early years.

Bear Canyon Creek (Fremont). T12N R41E sec 11. NW section of county. Flows 3 mi to Island Park Reservoir at W end; Henrys Fork drainage. Bear Creek runs NW 2 mi to Robinson Creek; Warm River drainage. Bear Spring is located in this gulch 1 mi N of Warm River Butte at the head of Twisted Draw. One-half-acre Bear Lake lies 5 mi W of the SW corner of Yellowstone National Park.

Named for the black bear that frequent the area.

Bear Creek (Adams). T19N R3W sec 29. Rises on the SW slopes of Bear Saddle and flows generally SW and S 16 1/2 mi to Crooked River; Snake River drainage.

Bear (4365'). T20N R3W sec 35. Community on Bear Creek about 28 mi NW of Council; a gateway to the Seven Devils area.

Post office, 1892-1966.

The first settlers found black bear plentiful. The earliest record of the name was on Bear Creek: it was given also to the community and other features in the NW part of the county. Apparently the various other bear names in the area sprang up independently.

Bear Creek (Clearwater). T39N R12E sec 21. Rises in the extreme NE part of the county on Bruin Hill and flows 4 1/2 mi SW into Kelly Creek; Clearwater River drainage.

This creek was named first; its tributaries were subsequently named Polar, Kodiak, and Cub creeks. It may have been an office name applied by the USFS since it rises by Bruin Hill.

Bear Gulch (Lemhi). T23N R18E sec 19. Heads approximately 1 mi NE of Sagebrush Lookout and runs NE 2 mi to enter Panther Creek drainage about 1 mi up from the mouth of Panther Creek.

Local reports have it that someone killed a bear in this gulch. Bears were frequently seen eating chokecherries in this drainage.

Bear Lake (Bear Lake). 5923'. T15/16S R43/44E. Lake that lies half in Utah and half in extreme SE Idaho. It is about 20 mi long and 5-7 mi wide, covering 125 square miles.

In the winter of 1811-12 the Hunt-Astoria fur-trapping party (Hoback, Rezner, Robinson, Cass, and Miller) were the first white men to see this lake and Bear River. In 1818 Donald McKenzie made the same trip and named the lake Black Bear Lake for the black bear in the vicinity. In 1826 William Henry Ashley's men called it Little Lake to distinguish it from the Great Salt Lake farther south and west.

All the following entries derive their names from Bear Lake.

Bear Lake Hot Springs. T15S R44E sec 13. At the NE end of Bear Lake.

Bear Lake Valley. A broad depression extending northward beyond Bennington to the vicinity of Nounan, where Bear River escapes through the narrows. The S end is in the vicinity of Laketown, Utah. It extends almost due N for about 45 mi, with a maximum width of 7 mi. It is bounded on the NE by the Aspen Range and on the SW by the Bear River Range.

Bear Lake County. County seat, Paris. Established in 1875 and named for Bear Lake. Settlement of the county began with Mormon colonization in 1863. Paris was the first colony, with forty families who came in wagons, in oxcarts, and on foot over very difficult terrain

from Cache Valley, Utah. Then in rapid succession Bloomington, Georgetown, St. Charles, Liberty, and Montpelier were settled.

Bear Mountain (Custer). 10,744'. T12N R25E sec 23. In NE extremity of the county in Challis National Forest, Lost River Division.

Bear River. Rises in the Uinta Mountains in Utah, flows through Wyoming into the SE corner of Bear Lake County and NW to Soda Springs, where it turns S and flows through Franklin County into Utah, to empty into Salt Lake; about 450 mi long.

The first white visitors to this area came looking for furs in 1811-12 and named the river Miller River for one of their members. Shoshoni Indians called the stream Que-yaw-pah from Que-yaw "tobacco root" and Pah "water," or stream along which tobacco trees grow. Renamed Black Bear River in 1818 by Donald McKenzie; later reduced to Bear River.

Bear River Range. Located in the SE corner of Bear Lake County, it is part of the Wasatch Range of Utah, extending 73 mi into Utah and 22 mi into Idaho. It grows narrower toward the N, terminating in a single broad, rounded summit known as Sheep Rock near Soda Springs. The highest peaks on the Idaho side are Paris (9572') and Sherman (9669').

Bear Run Gulch (Boise). T6N R5E sec 26. Flows SW 3 1/2 mi into Elk Creek 1 mi W of Idaho City; Boise River drainage.

The discoverers of Placerville attempted to keep their find a secret. To explain their absence while exploring the area, they claimed a bear chased them. When their disgruntled comrades at Idaho City discovered the truth, they named a gulch after the event.

Bear Valley (Valley). T12/13N R8/9E. Trends NE to SW in the SE part of the county, in the Boise National Forest, drained by Bear Valley Creek, NW of Cape Horn. About 2 mi wide and 20 mi long, the only valley on the upper waters of the Middle Fk Salmon River.

Bear Valley Creek rises in the mountains N of Lowman and flows 20 mi generally NE to empty into Middle Fk Salmon River. Its drainage is 189 square miles; Salmon River drainage. Bear Valley Mountain is a promontory overlooking Bear Valley on the S and SE, Mountain Meadow on the N, Elk Meadow on the NW, and Corduroy Meadow on the SW.

Like other "bear" features, named for the presence of bears in the area.

Bear Wallow Spring (Lemhi). T26N R20E sec 33. SW of Butcherknife Ridge and about 2 mi NE of Grizzly Spring.

Named by prospectors and USFS personnel to help identify the area and because of the numerous bear wallows here.

Beartrap Ridge (Lemhi). T24N R17E sec 13 through T24N R18E sec 7. Trends SW to NE 2 1/2 mi between Owl and E Fk Owl creeks. Beartrap Lookout (8078') lies at the SW end of the ridge, about 6 mi NE of Long Tom Lookout, Beartrap Spring is just N of Beartrap Lookout.

Named because of log beartraps made by early trappers which could be seen along the ridge.

Beatty (Ada). 2640'. T3N R1E sec 9. A UPRR siding with mail service from Meridian.

Named in 1889 for Idaho Supreme Court Justice James H. Beatty.

Beauty Creek (Kootenai). T49N R3W sec 11. Rises on the W slopes of Red Horse Mountain and flows 5 mi NW to Beauty Bay on the NE arm of Coeur d'Alene Lake.

A descriptive name.

Beaver. The name "Beaver" abounds in Idaho, because it was fur- trapping country in the early 19th century, and beaver fur was commercially valuable as well as being a means of exchange for supplies. The animal left its name on the land that it frequented. Such names indicate the presence of beaver at one time.

Beaver (Clark). T13N R36E sec 35. In the N part of the county. Said to be the earliest settlement in Clark County, located near the present town of Spencer. The Beaver Stage Station was operated by the Edward Kaufman family when the name was shortened to Beaver in the early 1870s.

Post office, 1881-1889.

Named for Beaver Creek.

Beaver Creek (Shoshone). There are three Beaver Creeks in this county, two with a Beaver Peak at their sources. Noah Kellogg, prospecting about two days out of Murray with a Scotsman named Dr. Cooper, named the stream he was working. That particular stream had already been named S Fk Coeur d'Alene River; so a nearby creek received the name, for the many beaver dams present. This 11-mi stream rises in the mountains N of Silverton and flows NNW to Coeur d'Alene River at Prichard.

Beaverdam Pass (Cassia). T15S R20E sec 27. In the SW part of the county, 20 mi SW of Oakley.

In 1880 Johnnie Freisch and a Mr. Worthington located outcroppings of coal-bearing shale here; they mined it and used it as fuel for Albion Normal School for two years.

Beaverhead Mountains (Lemhi). Range of mountains dividing Idaho and Montana, forming the E border of Lemhi County.

23

Bechtel Creek (Shoshone). T42N R1E sec 13. In the SW extremity of the county. Rises between Bechtel Mountain and Cedar Butte and flows 3 mi SE to W Fk St. Maries River.

Named for the Bechtel family, who homesteaded near the base of the mountain.

Beck Canyon (Butte). T4N R25E sec 19-22. In SW quadrant of the county 8 mi WNW of Arco; trends 4 mi W to E.

Named for an early homesteader.

Bedbug Creek (Latah). T38N R1W sec 14. This stream flows SW 3 mi to Kauder Creek; Clearwater River drainage.

From 1914 to 1925 bedbugs infested the entire area: woods, logging camps, rooming houses, hotels, and homes. The church built at Crescent along this creek was called Bedbug Church, because it was full of bedbugs from the blankets used to bed down youngsters during all-night revival meetings.

Bedrock Gulch (Benewah). T43N R3W sec 29. Canyon and stream on Meadow Creek; Palouse River drainage.

Named by W. H. Daugs, USFS ranger. Prospectors were said to have found bedrock close to the surface while prospecting for placers in this area.

Bee Top Mountain (Bonner). 6212'. T56N R2E sec 1. Located 4 1/2 mi W of Idaho-Montana border; 6 mi N of Clark Fork.

Named because it looks like a beehive: the top is cone-shaped and there are slides surrounding it.

Beecherville (Cassia). 5000'. T13S R25E sec 32.

Early name for Elba, which see. Named for the Ranson A. Beecher family, who settled here in 1873. The Post Office Department refused this name for a post office because it was too long.

Beehive Mountain (Lemhi). 9610'. T22N R16E sec 26. SW of Goat Lake and N of Roaring Creek lakes.

Named for its resemblance to a beehive.

Beeman (Nez Perce). T35N R2W sec 1. Early community about 3 mi W of Melrose in the E part of the county.

The town was founded in 1896 by a Mr. Beeman, who applied for and was granted a post office (1896-1901) that was housed on his property.

Beer Springs (Caribou). Early name for Soda Springs, which see.

Named by Capt. Benjamin L. E. Bonneville, 9 May 1834, when he was on his way to rendezvous with his party; named because the natural fountains were somewhat foamy. Later a stage station name for Soda Springs; a favorite stopping place for emigrants on the Oregon Trail because of the effervescing and acid taste of the waters.

Beetville (Cassia). 4225'. T11S R22E sec 1. A freight station on the Oakley branch of the UPRR in the NW part of the county, 2 mi SW of Burley.

Named for the large quantities of sugar beets loaded here.

Belcher Bar (Lemhi). T25N R21E sec 8. On Hughes Creek, near the mouth of Ditch Creek.

Named for an old placer miner called either Byron or Houston Belcher.

Bell Bay (Kootenai). T48N R4W sec 27. In the SW part of the county, on the E side of Coeur d'Alene Lake 4 mi NW of Harrison.

George and Milly Bell homesteaded in this area.

Bell Mountain (Lemhi). 11,612'. T11N R27E sec 36. Near Lemhi-Butte county line, about 5 mi S of Coal Kiln Spring. Bell Mountain Canyon heads N of Bell Mountain and runs 4 1/2 mi N to enter Mammoth Canyon. Bell Mountain Creek heads near Bell Mountain on the Lemhi-Butte county line and flows NE 2 mi, then SW 7 mi to Little Lost River.

Named to honor Robert N. Bell, State Mine Inspector (ca. 1911), who also located and produced gold and silver ore from the Speculation Lode of the Mineral Hill Mining District near Shoup.

Bellevue (Blaine). 5175'. T2N R18E sec 36. In the center of the county, 4 mi S of Hailey. In the 1880s, locally called the Gate City, because it affords access to the Wood River Valley.

Founded in 1880 after the discovery of the Minnie Moore mine. Bellevue was first named Biddyville, but after its opportunity to become the county seat of Logan County in 1890 the legislature was prevailed upon to change the name to one considered more suitable. Bellevue served as the county seat from 1890 to 1895 (when the county was merged in the new Blaine County) and became an important smelter and shipping point. The territorial government granted Bellevue a charter, and it is now the only chartered city in Idaho.

Post office, 1880-.

The name means "beautiful view."

Bellgrove Creek (Kootenai). T48N R5W sec 1. In the SW part of the county, a 4-mi tributary of Rockford Creek trending NW to SE. A small village named Bellgrove serving a farm community here in the late 1800s and early 1900s was situated on the stream.

Post office, 1894-1908; the name was changed from Morris to Bellgrove in 1895.

Said to have been an old Indian encampment. Named for the beautiful grove of trees in the area.

Belmont (Kootenai). 2462'. T53N R2/3W sec 19/24. A district in the N part of the county on Lewellan Creek, on the old Bayview Branch of the SIRR, 5 mi E of Athol. Settled in 1902 as a logging and mill town.

Post office, 1913-1928.

Apparently named by the RR. Name means "beautiful mountain."

Bench (Caribou). 5735'. T10/11S R41E sec 32/4. In the SW part of the county, 4 mi SE of Grace. A stage station on the line between Grace and Lago. Settled in 1879 and named for its location on benchland.

Post office, 1902-1923.

Bench Creek (Boundary). T64N R5W sec 29. Heads in Washington and flows SE, crossing the Idaho boundary between posts 169 and 170 of Washington-Idaho border; empties into Hughes Fork. Formerly Big Creek.

Present name suggested by nearly level area of 50 acres at the mouth of creek; eliminates one of a number of Big Creeks in this vicinity.

Bench Lakes (Custer). T9N R13E sec 7/8/19. Near the head of a western feeder of Redfish Lake. These are approximately 3 mi from the road and the Redfish Lodge. Surrounded by timber, they nestle on a bench against the N side of Mt. Heyburn.

Benedict Creek/Lake (Boise). T8N R12E sec 27/T7N R12E sec 9 Situated on the upper drainage of the S Fk Payette River near Grandjean Peak.

Named for M. S. Benedict, Supervisor of Western Division, USFS, until 1962.

Benewah County. County seat, St. Maries. Created in 1915 by an act of the state legislature from the southern part of Kootenai County. Its early history is included in Kootenai County history. Some settlers came to the area on

25

the completion of the Mullan Road in 1860, but most settlement occurred after 1880, when gold had been discovered near St. Maries.

Benewah. T45N R4W sec 24. On Benewah Creek, a tributary to Benewah Lake. The town was settled in 1910.

Benewah Lake. T46N R3W sec 10,11,13. A lake in Heyburn State Park that becomes three in low water. The other lakes are Chatcolet and Hidden.

All Benewah features derive from the name of a famous and historic Coeur d'Alene chief.

Bennett Creek (Clearwater). T36N R4E sec 5. Flows NW into Orofino Creek at sec 5; Clearwater River drainage.

Named for homesteaders. Records indicate that Charles G. Bennett, Jr., and Milton Bennett located along the creek in the early 1900s. They may have been brothers.

Bennett Creek (Clearwater). T37N R8E sec 26. In the NW part of the county. Flows SW into Weitas Creek; Clearwater River drainage.

Named for a settler, whose first name may have been Lee.

Bennington (Bear Lake). 5708'. T12S R44E sec 9. In the N central part of the county, 5 mi N of Montpelier. Settled in 1864 by Mormon colonizers.

Post office, 1877-.

Named by Evan M. Greene, first presiding elder, for Bennington, Vermont, the community where Brigham Young grew up.

Benson Hill (Latah). T40N R2W sec 13. A promontory E of Deary, so steep it was once used as a testing place for automobiles; it was a very good car that could reach the top of this hill without needing to shift gears.

Named for homesteader John Benson, who also was an engineer for Potlatch Lumber Co. on the WIMRR.

Benton (Nez Perce). Early community. Post office, 1908-1910; named for Henry S. Benton, first postmaster.

Berenice (Butte). T6N R29E sec 22/26. About 4 mi N of Howe.

Settled in 1907 when Martin Woods brought a colony from Kansas and Oklahoma, and named for Berenice Dietrich, one of the settlers.

Post office, 1913-1930.

Berg Creek (Idaho). T24N R2E sec 18. Salmon River tributary from the N.

Named for August Berg, who was born in Germany, came to America with his parents in 1851, and sought a fortune in the California gold rush. He then joined the Florence boom and finally settled on the Salmon River in 1864.

Berg Green Gulch (Lemhi). T16N R24E sec 25. Runs parallel to Swanson Gulch in an E direction for 3 mi; Lemhi River drainage.

Named for Martin Bergreen, who patented the land for his ranch on Little Eightmile Creek in 1921.

Berger (Twin Falls). 4200'. T11S R16E sec 16. An agricultural center in the central part of the county on Desert Creek, about .5 mi W of US 93 and 11 mi SW of Twin Falls.

Settled in 1908 by farmers from the Midwest who came to file under a Carey Act Project. Post office, 1911-1927.

Named for Fred Berger, a pioneer landowner in the area.

Bern (Bear Lake). 6000'. T12S R43E sec 36. In the central part of the county, 4 mi N of Ovid.

Settled by Swiss Mormons in 1880 under the leadership of John Kuntz, with his family of eight sons and two daughters, and George Allemann and his children and grandchildren.

Post office, 1901-1927.

Named for the city of Bern, Switzerland.

Bernard Creek (Valley). T19N R14E sec 22. Rises at 7651' and flows 2 1/2 mi E to Middle Fk Salmon River.

Named for Capt. Reuben F. Bernard, who had command of US Army troops in the Sheepeater War of 1879. At about this point he lost the Sheepeaters he was chasing and with his 56 men turned back to Boise Barracks.

Bernard Creek (Valley). T13N R7E sec 14. Rises on Pilgrim Mountain (8196'), and flows SW 2 mi to Deadwood River. Capt. Reuben F. Bernard and his men camped at the mouth of this stream 20 July 1879.

Bernard Ferry (Canyon/Owyhee). T1N R3W sec 17. Ferry on the Snake River 15 mi S of Caldwell.

Well known to early-day SW Idaho settlers; established in 1882 and named for James C. Bernard. It was run in competition with nearby Walters Ferry.

Post office (named Central), 1888.

Berry Creek (Bonner). T59N R1W sec 31. Heads 1/4 mi N of Keokee Mountain; flows 6 1/2 mi E into a marsh near Pack River 1 mi NE of Colburn.

Named for the wild berries growing in the area.

Bertha Rock. T4N R41E sec 31. A rock formation in Kelley Canyon.

Named for Bertha Gavin; one of three named rocks in that area. See Blanche Rock and Kelley Rock.

Bertha Hill (Clearwater). 5520'. T40N R5E sec 35. Mountain in the N central part of the county.

Some college boys from Moscow working for the Clearwater Timber Protective Association named the two-humped mountain for Bertha, a girl from the railroad district in Moscow. The mountain was formerly called Thun-

der Mountain because of the many storms here.

Bickel (Twin Falls). T10S R19E sec 27. In the NE part of the county on the Snake River, 2 mi NW of Murtaugh and 7 mi E of Kimberly.

An agricultural area, settled about 1908 under the Twin Falls South Side irrigation project.

Named for Paul S. A. Bickel, chief engineer on the Milner Dam project.

Biddyville (Blaine). Early name for Bellevue, which see.

Big Baldy Ridge (Valley). T17N R9E sec 21 to R11E sec 30. Trends 11 mi NW to SE on the breaks of Middle Fk Salmon River about 6 mi W of the river between Pistol and Indian creeks. The ends of the ridge are marked by Baldy Mountain (9070') on the W and Big Baldy (9722') on the E. In early days Big Baldy was a mecca for sheepmen.

Named for the highest point on the ridge, Big Baldy.

Big Bar (Adams). 1340'. T21N R3W sec 30. A point of land on the Snake River at the N end of Hells Canyon.

A survey of this bar by Idaho State University Museum in 1963 yielded hundreds of artifacts, indicating that this had once been an Indian village and a hunting area beginning about 1600.

A generic name; big probably indicates that it is larger and longer than the bar to the S or N.

Big Bear Creek (Latah). T38N R2W sec 24. Rises in East Fork, 4400', just S of Mica Mountain and flows S and SW 7 mi; in Middle Fork, 2920', and flows 6 mi generally SE; and in West Fork, and flows 6 mi SE. All converge 2 mi W of Deary as Big Bear Creek, which flows 13 mi S and empties into the Potlatch River at Kendrick; Clearwater River drainage.

Gerald Ingle believes the name came from an early incident: a very early pioneer named Prather was near a creek crossing and saw a bear on each side of the creek, a little bear on the west side and a big bear on the east side. After that the creek was called Bear Creek; the east ridge, Big Bear Ridge, and the west ridge, Little Bear Ridge.

Big Bear Ridge (Latah). TRS 2000' to 2860'. A ridge running slightly SW from about 2 mi SW of Deary to Potlatch River, between Big Bear Creek on the W and Pine Creek on the E.

Big Bend Ridge (Fremont). T10/11N R41/42E. A range of hills to 7400'. Twelve mi long, running NW/SE from High Point to Snake River Butte.

Named for its shape, bending like a sickle blade from High Point S and then curving E.

Big Black Dome (Custer). 11,359'. T6N R21E sec 28. In the White Knob Mountains. Situated on the divide between Wild Horse Creek drainage and E Fk Big Lost River drainage, about 2 mi NE of Pyramid Peak; Challis National Forest.

Probably named for its dome-shaped summit, in contrast to neighboring Pyramid Peak.

Big Buck Mountain (Elmore). 9867'. T8N R10E sec 36. In the Sawtooth Wilderness Area on the Boise-Elmore county line in the NE extremity of the county. In Boise National Forest.

Named for a large buck deer killed on this mountain.

Big Butte (Butte). 7576'. T1N R29E sec 26. In the SE corner of the county, about 20 mi SE of Arco.

A famous landmark for emigrants and in the 1880s the site of a stage station at the spring here.

Big Butte is a composite volcanic cone that terminates in two ridges about 1 mi apart, with a deep depression between that is apparently the remnant of a crater. Also known as Big Southern Butte.

Named for its size.

Big Canyon Creek (Lewis/Nez Perce). T33N R2W sec 15. Rises in the W part of the county and flows NE and E approximately 15 mi to the Clearwater River in T36N R1W sec 3 at Peck, Nez Perce County; Clearwater River drainage. Flows through Big Canyon.

Named for the size of the canyon in comparison to that of Little Canyon to the E.

Big Cedar Canyon (Cassia). T13S R21E sec 9. Heads in Sawtooth National Forest and trends E and NE; 6.5 mi long; mouth on Cottonwood Creek.

Named for the stand of cedar in the canyon, a wood-gathering spot for early settlers in the area.

Big Cedar Swamp (Shoshone). Early name for Fourth of July Canyon.

Big Cinder Butte (Butte). 6516'. T1N R24E sec 13. In Craters of the Moon National Monument, .6 mi S of of the loop drive. This butte opened up along its E base and lavas poured out toward the NE.

Named for its size.

Big Clear Lake (Lemhi). T21N R16E sec 10. In Bighorn Crags E of Pothole Lake and NE of Crater Lake.

Named by Lester Gutzman and a crew from Copper Creek Ranger Station (now Cobalt R.S.) ca.1940 when they planted fish here, because of the size of the lake and the clarity of the water.

Big Crater (Butte). T1N R24E sec 2. Volcanic crater just E of Silent Cone in the Craters of the Moon National Monument, 1.5 mi S of the entrance. Stands on the Rift; great lava flows oozed out of this butte to the SW.

Named for its size; it covers almost 1/4 square mile, and its flow covers more than 1.5 square miles.

Big Creek (Lemhi). T13N R23E sec 5. Originates where S Fk Big Creek meets N Fk Big Creek and flows NW 11 mi, forming the Lemhi-Custer county border, to enter Pahsimeroi River. Big Creek Peak (11,358′) is about 3 mi NE of the head of Big Creek in the Lemhi Range at the head of Falls Creek, about 4 mi SW of Junction Peak; Salmon National Forest.

The creek is named because it is the biggest stream in the valley, and the name was also given to the nearby peak.

Big Creek (Shoshone). T45N R3E sec 5. In the SW part of the county. Rises in the St. Joe Mountains and flows about 13 mi S to the St. Joe River between Calder and Marble Creek.

Ed Piles homesteaded at the mouth of this stream about 1900. The Piles family ran Piles Eating House at the mouth of Big Creek for many years; the site was known as Piles, Big Creek, and Piles Creek.

Named Big Creek by True and Dennis Blake, because it was a rather large stream spilling into the canyon. Common usage by lumbermen and the USFS led to the permanent name.

Big Creek (Valley). T20N R14E sec 10. E tributary of Middle Fk Salmon River, at Waterfall Creek Rapids. Heads in the mountains 6 mi N of Yellow Pine between Big Creek Point (8810′) and Vern Peak; flows 40 mi generally NE and E to Middle Fk Salmon River, altitude 3390′; the drainage is 594 square miles. One of the largest of Idaho's minor streams.

Big Creek 6000′. T21N R9E sec 26. Old Edwardsburg, a way station and post office that served a large mining area.

Big Creek Point 8990′. T20N R8E sec 22.

Big Creek Summit 6614′. T15N R5E sec 24. A mountain pass in Boise National Forest on Warm Lake Road between Cascade and Warm Lake.

The creek was named for its size and the name then applied to other features.

Big Deer Creek (Lemhi). T21N R18E sec 2. Heads in vicinity of Golden Trout Lake; flows NE for 6 mi, then flows E 5 mi to enter Panther Creek; Salmon River drainage.

This drainage had many deer in it at one time and was part of a state game preserve for many years.

Big Dick Creek (Shoshone). T46N R6E sec 18. In the E part of the county. Rises on Big Dick Point and flows 3 mi NW to the St. Joe River 6 mi N of Avery.

Allegedly named for river poleman Big Dick, who homesteaded near this creek in 1909 but was burned out in the 1910 Idaho fire. A more popular version of the naming of Big Dick and nearby Long Liz creeks is that they were named for Long Liz, a Wallace prostitute, and Big Dick, her pimp.

Big Eightmile Creek (Lemhi). T16N R25E sec 3. Forms in Lemhi Range, just over the divide from the head of Big Creek in the Pahsimeroi; flows N 4 mi, then NE 9 mi to enter the Lemhi River, across from the mouth of Little Eightmile Creek.

Named for its approximate distance from Leadore.

Big Falls (Fremont). T10N R43E sec 13. Five mi upstream on Henrys Fork from its convergence with Warm River. Also called Upper Mesa Falls, which see.

A vertical drop of 114′ with the full flow of Henrys Fork. Biggest waterfall on Henrys Fork.

Big Foot Butte (Ada). 3535′. T2S R2E sec 33. Big Foot Bar lies about 5 mi SW of the butte at T3S R1E sec 35/36.

Named for the renegade Shoshoni, "Bigfoot" or possibly Nam Puh.

Much placer gold was found here and across the Snake River in Owyhee County.

Big Foot Canyon (Owyhee). On Reynolds Creek near the Snake River. Named for the Shoshoni-Bannock Indian "Bigfoot," who roamed through southern Idaho with a small band of Indians, committing depredations. While his followers generally rode on Indian ponies, Bigfoot was always on foot and was said to travel from place to place with great rapidity.

His name was appropriate for he weighed 300 pounds, measured 59 inches around the chest, and stood six feet, eight-and-a-half inches tall. His foot was reputedly 17 1/2 inches long. He is supposedly buried along Reynolds Creek.

Big Grassy (Fremont). T11N R45E sec 9/16/21. Ridge 3 mi long in SE section of Fremont County running NE/SW at the head of Fish Creek.

Said to be named for the long, open, grassy sides of the ridge in an area that is mostly timbered.

Big Hole Mountains (Teton/Fremont). Also called the Snake River Mountains, they are called the Big Hole Mountains by the USFS. They extend some 40 mi in a NW direction from Wyoming into Idaho and vary in width from 12 to 24 mi. The chief peaks are Palisade (9780′), Thompson (9485′), and Baldy (9830′).

Named for the adjacent valley floor, a caldera. Palisade Lakes lie in these mountains not far from Swan Valley. The S Fk of the Snake River parallels them on the S; Rexburg is not far W of

their W extremity; Teton Basin is on the NE; Teton River on the N.

Big I Gulch (Owyhee). T5/6S R4W. Ravine S of Silver City.

Named after the Big I mine.

Big Island (Clearwater). T38N R4E sec 6/7. On the N Fk Big Creek 10 mi W of Headquarters.

This was the largest island on the N Fk. Once surrounded by water at all times, later only during high water. Waters of Dworshak Reservoir now cover it.

Big Jureano Creek (Lemhi). T21N R19E sec 8. Heads about 1 mi SE of Jureano Mountain; flows about 3 1/2 mi SW to enter Panther Creek; Salmon River drainage.

Named for Jules Renaud, a French prospector in this area as early as 1866.

Big Lake Creek (Custer). T10N R18E sec 30/31. Flows E 7 1/2 mi to Jimmy Smith Lake, SE 1 1/2 mi to E Fk Salmon River.

Name originates from the fact that a moderately large lake (Jimmy Smith Lake) is filled and drained by the stream.

Big Lost River (Custer/Butte). T15N R30E sec 1/2. The general contour of this stream, with its tributaries N and E Fks, is like an S. It rises in the Pioneer Mountains in Custer County and flows NE to 15 mi NW of Mackay, SE through Mackay Reservoir, and into Butte County. It then flows S to Arco and circles around the S end of the Lost River and Lemhi ranges, then NE to Big Lost Sinks, where it disappears underground.

Big Lost River Valley. A valley ranging from 8 to 16 mi wide and approximately 30 mi long, drained by Big Lost River and lying E of Lost River Range. Its trend is from NW to SE, approximately from Chilly to Arco. See also Godin Valley.

Big Mallard Creek (Idaho). T25N R10E sec 6. Salmon River tributary .2 mi from Mallard Rapids. Little Mallard Creek is about 1 mi W of the Big Mallard features.

Peter Mallard was an early miner on this stream.

Big Meadow Creek (Latah). T39N R3W sec 7. Rises E of East Moscow Mountain and flows generally SE to Troy, where it empties into W Fk Little Bear Creek; Potlatch River drainage.

Named by E. F. Helmers, USFS ranger, in 1938; there are several large meadows below the former site of a Civilian Conservation Corps camp and above the town of Troy.

Big Meadow. T40N R4W sec 13/14/23/24. A recreational area at the head of Big Meadow Creek 3 mi N of Troy.

A descriptive name.

Big Pine Creek (Boise). T9N R6E sec 33. Rises at the confluence of 5-mi long Middle Fk and 5-mi long E Fk Big Creek and flows 2 mi S into S Fk Payette River at Birch Flat; Payette River drainage.

Named by the USFS for the yellow pine that line the banks of the main creek.

Big Sand Creek (Latah). T42N R2W sec 28. Southern tributary of Palouse River; rises E of Mica Mt., flows 8 1/2 mi N and W to a point 3 mi NE of Camp Grizzly.

Probably named for sandy creek bed in clay country.

Big Sheepeater Creek (Lemhi). T23N R18E sec 10. Heads near source of Horsefly Gulch and Sheepeater Point and flows SE into Salmon River just SW of Cohen Gulch; Salmon River drainage.

Named after Sheepeater or Tukuarika Indians (from *tuku* which meant "mountain sheep" and *arikas* for "to eat").

Named because these Indians lived mainly on bighorn sheep.

Big Silver Creek (Boise). T8N R10E sec 34. Rises on Shepherd Peak (8833') and flows 3 1/2 mi E into N Fk Boise River on the E border of the county.

This creek is at the center of Boise County's silver-producing area. Probably named by developer Matt Graham.

Big Silverlead Creek (Lemhi). T24N R21E sec 16. Forms 2 mi W of Stein Mountain and flows 4 mi SW to enter the Salmon River drainage at N Fk.

Named for the silver claims located on this drainage. Name was once written Big Silver Lead Creek; appears as Silver Creek on USFS 1913 map.

Big Smoky Creek (Camas). T3N R13E sec 9. Source is E of Marshall Peak (9766') in Smoky Mountains, Sawtooth National Forest. Altitude at mouth is 5357'. Flows through timbered mountains and a broad valley. This small stream, only 20 mi long, is a tributary of the S Fk Boise River.

Named for the mountains.

Big Southern Butte (Butte). See Big Butte.

Big Springs (Fremont). 6540'. T14N R44E sec 34. Town 5 mi E of Macks Inn; a resort built and operated by Jack Kooch, the first postmaster, a Swiss. Post office since 1914.

Named for the springs that are one of the sources of Henrys Fork of the Snake River.

Big Springs (Owyhee). T10S R1W sec 10. At the head of Big Springs Creek, tributary of Owyhee River. The water gushes; hence the name.

Big Squaw Creek (Idaho). T25N R12E sec 27. Stream 6.5 mi long flowing SSW to the Salmon River 8.7 mi WSW of Waugh Mountain.

Originally named Squaw Creek during the Sheepeater Indian War in 1879 when some Indian women were captured in this area. The name was later changed to Big Squaw Creek to differentiate it from Little Squaw Creek.6 mi upstream.

Big Tinker Creek (Idaho). T32N R5E sec 13. A 2.7-mi stream flowing NNW to Middle Fk Clearwater River 10 mi E of Kooskia.

Both Big Tinker and Little Tinker creeks were named for a man named Tinker, who homesteaded between the two streams on the bank of Middle Fk Clearwater River.

Big Willow (Canyon). Site of an early community in the NW part of the county. Post office, 1907-1916.

Named for a large willow tree that grew here.

Big Witch Creek (Blaine). T3N R19E sec 10. Rises in the NE part of the county on the W slope of Pioneer Mountains and flows 4.5 mi SW to Cove Creek; E Fk Wood River drainage.

Named by a superstitious miner whose name has been lost.

Big Wood River (Blaine). T1S R14E sec 23. Rises on the S slopes of Boulder Mountains in the NW extremity of Blaine County, flows SE and S, through Magic Reservoir, across the NW corner of Lincoln County, and into Gooding County to empty into the Malad River just above Tuttle; about 85 mi long.

Forks: E Fk Wood River, 17 mi long, converges with Big Wood River 6 mi NNW of Hailey; E Fk of N Fk Big Wood River, 5.5 mi long, converges with N Fk 11 mi NNW of Ketchum; W Fk of N Fk Big Wood River, 5 mi long, converges with N Fk 12 mi NNW of Ketchum; N Fk Big Wood River, 10 mi long, converges with Big Wood River 7.5 mi NNW of Ketchum.

The first hydro plant in Idaho to serve the public was established in 1885 at Hailey, harnessing this river. Before that the river had already seen gold prospectors; some were successful and mining towns sprang up along the main stream.

Named by early pathfinders, explorers, and emigrants for the heavy growth of trees along its banks.

Bighorn Crags (Lemhi). A mountain range E of Middle Fk Salmon River, W of Clear Creek, and N and W of Wilson Creek, beginning in T20N R16E and extending NE for approximately 20 mi to near the mouth of Panther Creek.

Named because it is the habitat of Rocky Mountain bighorn sheep.

Bighorn Point (Clearwater). 4659'. T38N R8E sec 21. Peak 5 mi N of Weitas Ranger Station. Bighorn Creek lies S of the point and flows 2 mi SE into Weitas Creek; Clearwater River drainage.

Horns from bighorn sheep were found here.

Bill Creek (Clearwater). T38N R9E sec 13. In the E part of the county. Rises between Star Point and Windy Bill Camp; flows 4 mi W into Fourth of July Creek; Clearwater River drainage.

Named for Bill Johnson, a cook for USFS crews.

Bill Williams Canyon (Oneida). T12S R36E sec 35. Heads in the Caribou National Forest and trends SE 3.5 mi to Devil Creek; Malad River drainage.

Named for a settler.

Billingsley Creek (Gooding). T7/8S R13/14E. A 7-mi stream in Hagerman Valley that trends erratically N-S along the line between ranges 13 and 14.

Named for a settler. Earlier named La Pree Creek for a man who led a snowbound emigrant train from Little Wood River S and camped on this stream.

Bills Canyon (Lemhi). T25N R21E sec 28. Runs 2 mi W to enter N Fk Salmon River drainage across from mouth of Hull Creek.

Named for Bill Buster, who had a cabin here at one time.

Billy Creek (Idaho). T31N R3W sec 25. A S tributary of Salmon River.

Salmon River Billy and his son Luke Billy, Nez Perce Indians, lived on this creek and planted apple trees beside it before the Nez Perce War.

Billy Creek (Lemhi). T21N R21E sec 14/23. A stream 2 mi long, running SE.

Named for Billy Ostrander, who had a ranch here.

Bimerick Creek (Idaho). T33N R8E sec 3. In the N part of the county, rising on McClendon Butte (5562') and flowing 5.5 mi S to Lochsa River. It drains Bimerick Meadows.

Named for a trapper/prospector from Chicago who worked in the area about 1906.

Bimetallic Ridge (Bonner). T55N R2W sec 11. Heads at Butler Mountain, extends 1 mi E to a point 1 mi SW of Talache. In the Kaniksu National Forest.

Named for a bimetallic mineral claim in the vicinity.

Bingham County. County seat, Blackfoot. Established in 1885 from the E and N parts of Oneida County, and named by Territorial Governor William M. Bunn for his friend Congressman Henry Harrison Bingham, of Pennsylvania. Fremont County was carved out of Bingham in 1893, Bonneville in 1911, Power in 1913, and Butte in 1917.

Bingham County is bordered by Bonneville and Jefferson on the N; Butte, Minidoka, and Power on the W; Caribou and Bannock on the S; and Bonneville on the E. The Snake River cuts across the county from E to W to American Falls Reservoir. Lava beds are in the W and mountains in the E.

Bingo Creek (Boise). T10N R5E sec 4-6. Flows W into the Middle Fk Payette River in the NW corner of the county.

Named by the USFS because a hunting party shot five deer near the creek; five consecutive successful shots comprise a "bingo."

Bingo Saddle (Clearwater). T40N R6E sec 30. Two mi NE of Bertha Hill. Bingo Creek flows S from this saddle to Beaver Creek.

Named by Homer David and Hec Edmondson while they were college students prospecting in this area.

Birch Creek (Clark/Lemhi/Butte). Heads on Gilmore Summit in Lemhi County and flows 35 mi SE through Clark County and into the NE quadrant of Butte County, where it sinks. Named for the birch trees along its banks.

In the early 1880s this was called John Days Defile, named for John Day, member of the Donald McKenzie party on a trapping expedition, who died in February of 1820 and was buried somewhere in what is now Birch Creek Valley.

Birch Creek Valley (Lemhi/Clark). A 35-mi long, 6-mi wide valley lying along Birch Creek; 7000' at the N extremity and 5900' where it joins the Snake River Plain.

The upper Birch Creek Valley is rife with springs and the ground marshy, ending in a basaltic ridge across the valley called The Narrows. The middle valley is less moist, the stream swift and lined with trees. And the lower 5 mi is much like the Snake River plain: dry, sage-covered, with little grass and only occasional clumps of trees.

Bird Creek (Shoshone). T45N R6E sec 24. Rises in the divide between Bluebird Point and Mirror Peak and flows about 7 mi SSE to the St. Joe River 8 mi E of Avery.

Named by Ralph Debbit of the USFS, who was interested in the Ideal mine at the mouth of this creek, in 1906. No reason for the name is known.

Bird Creek (Lemhi). T23N R21E sec 12. Heads 1 mi NE of Diamond Gulch and flows generally E 3 mi to enter the Salmon River just across the Salmon River drainage from Tower Creek.

Named for Henry Bird, an early rancher in this area.

Birdbill Lake (Lemhi). T21N R16E sec 21. In Bighorn Crags S of Shoban Lake.

Named in 1962 by Paul Dalke of the University of Idaho. Birdbill is a name for a high-altitude flower (dodecatheon) that is very common on the shores of this lake in the early spring.

Birdseye Creek (Lemhi). T19N R18E sec 31. Heads 1 1/2 mi NE of Duck Peak and flows generally E 4 mi to enter Silver Creek; Middle Fk Salmon River drainage.

Named for James W. Birdseye, mining engineer and one-time county surveyor.

Bishop Creek (Clearwater). T38N R4E sec 6. In the NW part of the county, N of Dworshak Reservoir; flows 3 mi SE into the reservoir.

Named for homesteader, Lon E. Bishop, who settled about 1 mi from the head of the creek in 1904. Called Deadhorse Creek at one time.

Bishop Mountain (Fremont). 7810'. T12N R42E sec 30. In the central section of the county, 26 mi N of Ashton. Named for John and Thomas Bishop, who homesteaded land nearby in 1889.

Bismark Meadows (Bonner). T61N R5W sec 22/27. Three mi E of Idaho-Washington border; 1 1/2 mi SW of Nordman. Bismark Mountain (4048') overlooks the meadows from the SW.

Name derived from an early trapper, who lived in a cabin in the area.

Bissell Canyon (Oneida). T13S R35E sec 2,3. Canyon.5 mi long in the NE part of the county 10 mi N of Malad City; S of and almost parallel to Bill Williams Canyon.

Named by Dale A. Evans in 1969 for the old Bissell place, near Bissell Creek.

Bisuka (Ada). 3100'. T1S R3E sec 9. Oregon Short Line RR siding. Now Hickey. Believed to be an Indian word meaning "not a large place," pronounced be-SOO-ka.

John Hailey, then librarian of the Idaho State Historical Society, wrote on 6 July 1915 that a Mr. Blinkingdoffer, chief engineer of the railroad, said he deliberately chose Indian names for the sidings and stations to avoid conflict with names on other railroads.

Many of the names have been lost, especially where settlements did not develop. Others have been changed.

Bitch Creek (Fremont). Rises in Wyoming; forms SE border between Fremont and Teton counties until its convergence with Badger Creek; Teton River drainage. Also N Fk Teton River.

The original name, Anse de Biche (Doe) Creek, was reportedly bestowed by French trappers and later corrupted by their American counterparts. The name is a corruption of the French biche "doe" and was changed to N Fk of the Teton by the Hayden expedition of 1872. Also said to be named because its rugged canyon and fast flow make it a "real bitch."

Bitterroot Mountains (Lemhi). The general range of mountains that border

Lemhi County on the N and E, dividing Idaho from Montana.

Bitterroot Springs (Shoshone). T47N R6E sec 5. In the E part of the county, 4 mi E of Mullan; in the Bitterroot Range.

Ultimately named for the Montana state flower, *Lewisia rediviva*, which abounds in and near the springs and whose root Indian tribes used for food. It is reportedly bitter except in the spring.

Bitters Peak (Bonneville). 7190'. T3S R46E sec 18. In the SE part of the county on the Idaho-Wyoming line. Bitters Creek rises on Bitters Peak and flows 3.4 mi NW into McCoy Creek; Snake River drainage.

Named for the quality of water contained therein, which probably reminded pioneers of the tonic of the same name.

Black Bear (Shoshone). T48N R5E sec 8. In the E part of the county on Canyon Creek, 2 mi W of Burke. An early mining camp in the Leland Mining District. Post office, 1903-1919.

Named for the Black Bear mine.

Black Bear Creek (Boise). T9N R5E sec 36. Flows 3 mi NW into the S Fk Payette River. Payette River drainage.

Named for the Black Bear mine, which was located on the banks of this creek.

Black Butte (Lincoln). T3S R18E sec 5/8. In the NW part of the county, in the lava bed where Shoshone Ice Caves are located.

This is a broad low rise in the land, identified as an old volcano by its shallow summit crater; composed of basaltic materials, from which it takes its name.

Black Buttes (Clearwater). T41N R7E sec 21-24. A heavily wooded area NE of Canyon Ranger Station. Black Creek rises on Black Mountain (7210') and flows NW 2 1/2 mi to Isabella Creek; Clearwater River drainage. Black Lake is immediately E of Black Mountain. East Sister and West Sister (buttes) also lie in the area.

Named for the dark appearance created by heavy timber of spruce and hemlock on the slopes of the buttes.

Black Canyon (Clearwater). T40N R10E sec 29/32. Four mi N of Kelly Forks Ranger Station.

Named because the canyon is shaded; little sunlight penetrates the forest.

Black Canyon/Creek (Bonneville). T4S R45E sec 22-26. Extends NW to SE in the SE corner of the county in the Caribou Range. Creek empties into Jackknife Creek; Salt River (Wyoming) drainage.

A descriptive name referring to the color of the terrain.

Black Imp (Adams). 8379'. T22N R2W sec 22. Located in the Seven Devils Mountains in the Payette National Forest, N of the Black Lake area.

An analogical name with the other smaller mountains in the Seven Devils.

Black Jack (Owyhee). T4S R4W. Townsite on Florida Mountain near Dewey.

This town, which once had a post office, was probably named after the Black Jack mine, located on Nigger Gulch in the Carson Mining District on Florida Mountain.

Black Lake (Adams). T21N R2W sec 3. A crater lake, one of many in the Seven Devils Mountains. In the Payette National Forest 1 mi NE of Cuprum and 4 1/4 mi E of Helena.

Black Lake. A mining townsite. The mine tunnel is located high above the lake and ore was transported by cable tramway across the lake and to the mill.

Post office, 1903-1907.

Black Point. 6284′. T21N R3W sec 3/10. Promontory in the Seven Devils Mountains.

Black Lake was named because it is surrounded by high mountains that cast shadows on the water, making it appear black. The name also was applied to the other features in the area.

Black Lake (Kootenai). T47N R3W sec 1/12. One of the nine lakes formed by overflows of Coeur d'Alene River at flood stages; 2 mi long and .5 mi wide at the middle, with 2 distinctive arms on the W.

Post office (at N end of lake), 1911-1927.

Black Mountain (Clark). 8860′. T11N R32E sec 11. In the NW quadrant of the county about 1 mi NW of Antelope Lakes, in the Targhee National Forest.

Named for the black stone of which the mountain is composed.

Black Mountain (Owyhee). 6600′. T3S R3W sec 32. Four mi SE of Share. Named for the black rocks on the mountain.

Black Peak (Adams). 6278′. T21N R3W sec 3. In the Seven Devils Mountains. Located in the Payette National Forest between Grassy Ridge and Snake River, about 1 1/2 mi NW of Kinney Point.

The name black suggests evil in this case, in keeping with the names of other features of the area.

Black Peak (Fremont). 10,239′. T16N R43E sec 11. On the Idaho-Montana line N of Henry's Lake. Also Black Mountain.

Black Pine (Oneida). T15S R30E sec 31. In SW Oneida County, 5 mi from the Utah line. Regarded in 1876 as site of the richest mining strike in the area; a grazing area in 1888 with a few set-tlers, a school, and a Latter-day Saints ward. The name is preserved in Black Pine Canyon, Black Pine Road, and Black Pine Stone Road (T16S R30/31E).

Post office, 1895; reestablished 1910 and discontinued before 1965.

Named for the heavy stand of pine.

Black Pine Cone (Cassia). 8008′. T15S R29E sec 33. Promontory in the SE corner of the county, in the Black Pine Mountains; in Sawtooth National Forest.

Named for the heavy stand of pine in the area.

Black Pine Mountains (Cassia). T14/15/16S R28/29E. In the SE part of the county. Trends NW to SE; about 14 mi long, 2-6 mi wide; highest elevations about the center, War Eagle and Black Pine peaks and Black Pine Cone.

Named for the stand of pine, a woodcutting area for early settlers, that was so heavy on the N side that the whole range was cast in a black shadow.

Black Prince Creek (Shoshone). T45N R3E sec 10. Rises on Mastodon Mountain in the St. Joe National Forest and flows 8 mi SW to the St. Joe River, 5 mi W of Avery.

Named by Dan Davis of the Copper Prince mine in 1890. He originally named it Prince Creek.

Black Rock (Kootenai). 2300′. T48N R4W sec 9/10. A point of land and a bay in the SW part of the county on the W side of Coeur d'Alene Lake, about 11 mi S of Coeur d'Alene.

A post office opened in 1905 under the name of Monitor, for a nearby mine; the name was changed to Blackrock, 1909-1913.

Named for a black rock used as a landmark in early days.

Blackbird Creek (Lemhi). T20N R19E sec 8. Heads E of Blackbird Mountain and flows SE 6 mi to enter Panther

Creek; Salmon River drainage. Blackbird Mountain (9096′) lies at the head of Blackbird Creek, about 5 mi E of Golden Trout Lake.

Blackbird. Town, now Cobalt, which see. Post office, 1892-1907.

Named for the Blackbird mine, which in turn was reportedly named because only one blackbird was ever seen in the area. First applied to the creek and then to the other features.

Blackeagle Creek (Lemhi). T19N R16E sec 10. Heads near McEleny Mountain and runs 2 mi S and then 1 mi W to enter Hoodoo Creek; Salmon River drainage.

Named because the Blackeagle mine is located in the vicinity of the headwaters of the creek.

Blackfoot (Bingham). 4485′. T3S R35E sec 3. County seat. In the central part of the county on Blackfoot River.

Donald McKenzie named the river Blackfoot in 1819, for the Indians he encountered there who called themselves Siksika "black" and Kah "foot." The name of the river was applied to the town and to other topographical features nearby.

Blackfoot was long a stage station for lines to Arco, Mackay, Challis, and other points NW until the UPRR built a branch line in 1901. Then Blackfoot became an important RR station. The town was founded in 1879 on the homesteads of Shilling and Lewis, and when Bingham County was organized it was named as the county seat.

Post office, 1879-.

Blackfoot Lava Field (Caribou). N of Soda Springs.

Three old volcanoes here—China Hat Cone, Middle Cone, and North Cone—are thought to be of the plug type, in which viscous lava clots readily and the core is extruded.

Blackfoot Mountains (Bingham). In the E part of the county, extending NW nearly 30 mi from Wilson Creek and Blackfoot River; about 15 mi at their widest, rising 600′ above Willow Creek in the NE and 1400′ above Blackfoot Valley in the SW. The highest point in the range is Mt. Taylor, 4 mi S of the Bingham-Bonneville county line. Rich phosphate deposits are located in the S part of this range.

Blackfoot River (Bingham/Caribou). T3S R34E sec 28, 1 mi N of Ferry Butte. Rises in the Caribou National Forest at the confluence of Bacon, Lanes, and Sheep creeks in the E part of Caribou County and flows approximately 100 mi generally WNW to empty into the Snake River.

Blackfoot Valley (Bingham). Trends NE to SW between the Blackfoot Mountains on the NE and the Portneuf Mountains on the SW. It varies from 1 to 6 mi wide and its elevation is about 6100′.

Blackhawk Bar, Rapid (Idaho). T26N R1E sec 2. On the Salmon River.

Both features were named for the Blackhawk mine.

Blacklead Mountain (Clearwater). 7525′. T38N R13E sec 17.

Named by Lafe Williams for the silver ore found here; the rock is black with the silver mixed into it.

Blackman Peak (Custer). 10,307′. T7N R15E sec 1,2. In White Cloud Peaks; on divide between E Fk Salmon River and main river.

Named for George Washington Blackman, a black who mined in the area for many years. He began prospecting in Blackman Basin in 1879 and also worked many claims along Fourth of July Creek. His cabin was in Blackman Basin. All who knew him respected him and knew his cabin as a welcome stopping place.

Blackrock Canyon (Bannock). T7S R35E sec 23. Heads 3.5 mi E of Pocatello and trends about 5 mi S, emptying into the Portneuf River. A UNRR station here, named Blackrock, was later renamed Portneuf.

Named for the black rock formation through which the canyon passes.

Blacks Creek (Boise). T10N R8E sec 19. Rises in the N central part of the county and flows 2 mi SE into Clear Creek; Boise River drainage.

Elmer Black lived near this creek and had a claim on it.

Blackstock Spring (Owyhee). T1S R5W sec 28. Two mi W of Piute Butte.

A Blackstock family lived in this area.

Blacktail Canyon (Bonneville). From T1N R42E sec 22-35. Extends NW to SE in mid-county in the Caribou Range. Blacktail Canyon Creek flows 4 mi SE into Fall Creek; Snake River drainage.

Named by John E. Jones for the many blacktail deer in the area.

Blacktail Creek (Bonner). T62N R5W sec 34. Tributary of Granite Creek; 3/4 mi NE of Reeder Mountain; heads on Blacktail Mountain.

The prevalence of blacktail deer in the northern part of the county led to this name, as well as to the name of Blacktail, a community on Lake Pend Oreille, 1 1/4 mi S of Talache; Blacktail Mountain (5521'), on the Idaho-Washington border; Blacktail Mountain (4975'), ENE of Cocolalla; Blacktail Mountain Lookout; and Blacktail Lake, 5 1/2 mi SSE of Mt. Pend Oreille and 3 1/2 mi W of the Idaho-Montana state border.

Blacktail Pass (Teton). 8279'. T4N R43E sec 22. A promontory in the Big Hole Mountains in SW Teton County. Blacktail Creek, a tributary of Canyon Creek, rises on the slopes of Blacktail Pass.

Named for the abundance of blacktail deer in the area.

Blackwell Hump (Shoshone). 4800'. T45N R1E sec 34. A promontory in the extreme E part of the county, 8 mi SE of Calder.

Named for the Blackwell Lumber Company.

Blaine (Camas). 5027'. T1S R16E sec 7. In the E part of Camas County on Elk Creek; a RR siding, established in 1911 when it was still in Blaine County. Post office, 1908-1922. May have been named for the county, which in turn was named for James G. Blaine, Secretary of State (1889-1892) under President Benjamin Harrison.

Blaine (Latah). 2818'. T38N R5W sec 3/10. A thriving village in the 1880s in what was then Nez Perce County.

Post office, 1882-1887.

Said to have been named for James G. Blaine.

Blaine County. County seat, Hailey. Created 5 Mar 1895 (eliminating Alturas and Logan counties) with Hailey as the county seat; includes headwaters of Salmon, Big Wood, and Little Wood rivers and Boulder Mountains, with Sawtooth and Pioneer ranges. It has been reduced by Lincoln County when it was created 18 Mar 1895; Power County, 30 Jan 1913; and Butte and Camas counties, 6 Feb 1917.

Topographically, Blaine County has a most unusual shape, partly because of the continuous chipping away to make other counties and partly because of the long, narrow extension down to Lake Walcott to give it a better tax base, since the RR runs through that section. It is bounded on the N by Custer County; on the E by Butte, Bingham, and Power; on the S by Cassia, Minidoka, and Lincoln; and on the W by Camas. It is drained primarily by Big and Little Wood rivers.

Blake (Clearwater). T36N R2E sec 11. Town 4 mi E of Orofino.

US postal records indicate Edwin W. Blake, for whom the site is named, established a post office here in 1900; the office closed in 1928.

Blakes Fork (Latah). T42N R3W sec 3. Flows 3 mi S to Meadow Creek, Palouse River drainage; in N central part of the county.

Named for Benjamin N. Blake, who homesteaded in 1901 at the mouth of the creek.

Blanchard Creek (Bonner). Tributary of the Spokane River (Washington). Rises in Fish Lake 1/2 mi SE of Blanchard and flows generally NW 4 mi to the Idaho-Washington border 2 mi SSW of Blanchard. Blanchard Lake, a man-made lake fed by Blanchard Creek, is just E of the town of Blanchard.

Blanchard. T54N R5W sec 20. A resort town 2 3/4 mi E of the Idaho-Washington border. The community was once named White, and a post office was established here in 1900. In 1908, the name was changed to Blanchard.

All these names honor a pioneer of the same name who homesteaded on Blanchard Creek.

Blanchard Ridge (Teton). T3N R45E sec 20/28. In the Targhee National Forest in SE Teton County, about 4 mi SW of Chapin.

Ira Blanchard, who homesteaded S of Blanchard, was dragged to death by a horse in this district in 1891.

Blanche (Gooding). 2888'. T5S R13E sec 28/29. A community in the NW part of the county on Clover Creek.

Post office, 1896-1917; Pleasant Blanche Butter, first postmaster, gave her name to the site.

Blanche Rock (Jefferson). T4N R41E sec 32. A rock formation in Kelley Canyon named for Blanche Heise, daughter of Richard C. Heise, founder of Heise Hot Springs Resort.

Similar formations were named for Blanche's sister Bertha and for Peter Kelley, who settled in the canyon.

Blaser (Bannock). 5148'. T9S R38E sec 10. An old UPRR station 2.2 mi N of Lava Hot Springs, on the Portneuf River.

Formerly Lava, for the lava flows nearby; renamed Blaser for a RR official in 1910.

Bliss (Gooding). 3265'. T6S R13E sec 6/8. In the W part of the county, 11 mi W of Gooding; on I-84 and Snake River. The OSLRR built stock pens and loading chutes here; sheep and cattle were driven S from Camas Prairie and N from the Three Forks country to corrals and shearing sheds.

Post office, 1883-.

Named for David B. Bliss, who settled here in 1878 and raised livestock and horses; his place was headquarters for placer miners and cowboys. His wife, Lydia H. Bliss, was instrumental in having the first school district created and taught in Bliss, Clover Creek, and Toponis. The OSLRR came through in 1883 and officially named the place.

Blizzard Mountain (Butte). T2N R24E sec 14. On the divide between Butte and Blaine counties in the Lost River Range.

Locally the mountain has always been known as Blizzard Mountain. When iron was found in the area, people not in the immediate vicinity called it Iron Mountain. When limited amounts of tungsten were found later, the name was changed to Tungsten Mountain. The official name remains Blizzard Mountain and is in strong local use; it presumably commemorates an early blizzard in the area.

Blizzard Mountain (Elmore). T6N R12E sec 9. In the NE part of the county in Boise National Forest, Sawtooth Wilderness Area.

A surveying party was caught in a blizzard on the summit of this mountain.

Blonde Creek (Clearwater). T35N R5E sec 34. Flows NE into Musselshell Creek at sec 36; Clearwater River drainage.

This is possibly part of a group name given by the USFS, since it rises by Brown Creek Lookout.

Bloom Creek (Bonner). T59N R1W sec 12. Tributary of Sand Creek. Rises in Bloom Lake and flows 1 3/4 mi S to 7 mi W of Grouse Mountain and 2 3/4 mi NE of Elmira.

The name Bloom is derived from the lush vegetation surrounding the lake.

Bloom Creek (Clearwater). T41N R1E sec 35. In the NW corner of the county. Rises on Jackson Mountain (4685') and flows 3 mi N into the E Fk Potlatch River. Bloom Meadows lie W of the mouth of this creek.

Named for Henry Bloom, who homesteaded along the creek in 1904. Bloom was the manager of the Elk River Mill for Potlatch Lumber Company.

Bloomington (Bear Lake). 5985'. T14S R43E sec 22/23. In the SW part of the county, 3 mi S of Paris, on Bloomington Creek.

Settled by Mormons in 1864. Charles Rich and his sons laid the area out into 10-acre parcels and subdivided each into 10 lots; they completed 40 cabins by that fall.

Post office, 1872-.

Named by Charles G. Rich as a compliment to the settlers who by their cooperative industry and hard labor soon had the new colony blooming.

Bloomington Creek. T15S R44E sec 8. Rises in S, Middle, and N Fks at T14S R42E sec 28; flows ESE to empty into Bear Lake; about 16 mi long; an important feeder to the Bear River-Bear Lake irrigation system. This stream flows through Bloomington Canyon.

Bloomington Lakes. T15S R42E sec 5. Three deep lakes situated at the head of S Fk Bloomington Creek. Bloomington Peak lies between the head of S and Middle fks. Bloomington Horse Flat lies 1 mi SE of S Fk Bloomington Creek. All the Bloomington names are from the town.

Blossom City (Payette). Nickname for Payette, which see.

Blossom Mountain (Kootenai). 4385'. T50N R5W sec 21. In the NW part of the county, 8.5 mi SW of Coeur d'Alene.

Named for the Glen Blossom family, who homesteaded in this area.

Blowout Canyon (Bonneville). T1S R46E sec 21. Extends NW to SE into Wyoming. Blowout Canyon Creek flows 3 1/2 mi in this canyon.

Blowout 5537'. T1/2S R45E sec 36/1. Community on Bear Creek.

Named for a blowout, a geological term for an outcropping of a mother lode; a rich surface vein was found on the side of Blowout Canyon.

Blowup Creek (Clearwater). T37N R11E sec 7. Just W of the Idaho County line. Rises at Horseshoe Lookout (6985') and flows 2 mi W into Gravey Creek; Clearwater River drainage.

Named for the 1961 fire that got away from fire fighters and "blew up," burning the hillside toward Horseshoe Lake Lookout.

Blue Creek (Bonner). Rises 1 1/2 mi W of Johnny Long Mountain: flows 5 mi W into Priest River 6 3/4 mi N of the town of Priest River.

Named for the color visible in the waters of this stream. The name was applied to other nearby features: Blue Lake, located 4 1/4 mi W of Johnny Long Mountain, 7 1/2 mi NNE of the town of Priest Lake; and Blue Mountain (6700'), 5 1/2 mi W of Colburn and 9 1/2 mi NNW of Sandpoint.

Blue Creek (Fremont). T10N R43E sec 22. Flows 5.5 mi S to Henrys Fork system; easternmost of six parallel canyons NE of Ashton. A second Blue Creek flows 5 mi S to Sheep Creek; Henrys Fork system. Blue Creek Reservoir covers 1/2 acre; its outlet becomes Sand Creek. Another Blue Creek empties into this reservoir.

Named for the color and clarity of the water.

Blue Dome (Clark). T10N R30E sec 32. In the SW quadrant of the county on Birch Creek at the mouth of Skull Canyon.

Maier Kaufman settled on a ranch at the mouth of Skull Canyon in the late 1890s and applied for a post office at that time with the name of Kaufman. The office and name were granted. Later Maier sold his ranch to his sons Edward and Henry Kaufman and the post office closed. The Blue Dome Cafe, then the Blue Dome Inn (now defunct) then opened, so the area was called Blue Dome.

Blue Gulch (Boise). T7N R5E sec 21. A 2-mi gulch 4 mi N of New Centerville. Flows W into Grimes Creek; Boise River drainage.

Named for the blue clay in the gulch.

Blue Jay Canyon (Custer). T7N R25E sec 9-7. Extends from the base of Invisible Mountain 2 mi E to Pass Creek on the Butte-Custer county line, 6 mi N of Leslie.

A gorge in the Lost River Range, very narrow and with almost sheer walls rising 2000'. The lower walls are blue limestone, which grades upward into shale.

Blue Lake (Custer). T15N R13E sec 20. At the head of Little Loon Creek in the Challis National Forest.

Formed when the stream was dammed by a large landslide that filled the canyon to a depth of several hundred feet.

Name derives from the color of the water.

Blue Lake (Kootenai). T48N R3W sec 23/14. One of the nine lakes formed by overflows of Coeur d'Alene River, in the S part of the county, .5 mi N of the Coeur d'Alene River and 2 mi N of Black Lake; 1.25 mi long and .3 mi wide; surrounded by rushes.

Blue Lake Creek heads on the SW slope of Red Horse Mountain and flows 4 mi SW into Blue Lake; to avoid confusion with the Blue Creek that empties into Blue Creek Bay, the name of this stream was changed in 1959 by the US Board of Geographic Names to Cottonwood Creek, for cottonwood trees common to the area.

Blue Lakes (Jerome). T9S R17S sec 28/29. Three small beautiful lakes surrounded by deep canyon walls in the SW part of the county, on the N side of the Snake River about 4 mi N of Twin Falls.

Blue Lakes received its name from the sapphire-colored water, probably as early as the 1860s when gold miners were in the area.

Blue Nose (Lemhi). 8677'. T25N R18E sec 28. On the Idaho-Montana border about 2 mi NW of Valliet Spring.

Two reasons for the name are given: there are blue outcroppings of rock here and in winter it is so cold here one's nose is always blue.

Blue Spring Hills (Oneida). These hills extend from the Pocatello Range on the N through the center of Oneida County to the state line on the S; parallel to Deep Creek Mountains on the W and Malad and Bannock ranges on the E; highest elevation, Samaria Mountain, about 9000'.

Named for Blue Spring in the range, presumably named for the color of its water.

Bluejacket Creek (Latah). T42N R2W sec 28. A 3-mi stream that flows S to Palouse River, 2 1/2 mi NE of Laird Park.

Numerous mining claims were filed as early as 1899 on locations along this creek.

The name Bluejacket was brought by miners from California gold mines and applied both to the stream and to mines in the area.

Bluett Creek (Custer). T9N R17E sec 11. Heads on the E side of Railroad Ridge and flows E and SE to E Fk Salmon River.

Named for a homesteader.

Bluff Station Ferry (Payette). T8N R4W sec 34. Established in 1866 1 1/2 mi from present-day New Plymouth at the site of Black Bridge. On the trail from Boise to Umatilla. Also called Bluff Station.

Named for the bluff overlooking the Payette River at this site.

Boathouse Creek (Clearwater). T39N R4E sec 8. A small stream that flows SE into the upper part of Dworshak Reservoir.

Named for the boat once kept here by the Clearwater Timber Protective Association for use in crossing the river. The boat may have been kept in a small house.

Bob Moore Creek (Lemhi). T22N R22E sec 30. Forms near UP Lake and flows SE 2 mi, then E 3 mi to Salmon River drainage.

Local story has it that Bob Long deserted from the army and changed his name to Moore. He ran a sawmill in this drainage.

Bob Smith Creek (Bannock). T9S R37E sec 23. West Bob Smith Creek rises is Crystal Spring 3 mi NE of McCammon; East Bob Smith rises 6 mi NE of McCammon; and Bob Smith between the two. The three streams converge and empty into the Portneuf River 3 mi W of Lava Hot Springs; drainage, about 8 sections of land.

East and West Bob Smith creeks mark the E and W boundaries of land once owned by an Indian named Bob Smith.

Bobcat Gulch (Lemhi). T24N R21E sec 34. Heads on Napoleon Hill and runs NE 2 mi to the Salmon River.

Named in 1944 by Al Wheeler, USFS ranger, for the bobcats common in the gulch at that time.

Boehls Butte (Clearwater). 3610'. T41N R5E sec 30. Eight mi NW of Bertha Hill.

Named for homesteader Lou Boehls. His cabin, located along Homestead Creek, was later sold to the Clearwater Timber Company.

Bog, The (Boise). 7277'. T10N R6E sec 35/36.

A high spruce bog with excellent drinking water, named by the USFS.

Bogus Creek (Boise). T5N R3E sec 6. Rises on Shafer Butte (7582') and flows 3 1/2 mi NW into Shafer Creek; Payette River drainage. Bogus Basin is drained by the upper reaches of the creek; it is the site of Bogus Basin Ski Area.

Prospectors headed by K. P. Plowman found some fool's gold in this creek in the 1860s.

Bohannon Creek (Lemhi). T21N R23E sec 33. Forms near Center Mountain and flows SW about 9 mi to enter the Lemhi River, about 1 mi NW of Baker. Bohannon Spring is situated near the head of this stream, 1 mi NW of Magpie Spring No. 2.

Named for Isaiah "Tick" Bohannon, who settled on the stream early in the 1870s, maintained a large dairy herd, and raised large gardens to meet the great demand for vegetables.

Boiling Springs (Valley). T12N R5E sec 21/22. On the Middle Fk Payette River about 25 mi N of Garden Valley, in the Boise National Forest. Named for the near-boiling water from the springs here, issuing from rocks at a temperature of 190 degrees.

Boise (Ada). 2739′. T4/3N R2E sec 10. County seat and state capital. Founded and platted in July 1863; chartered by the territorial legislature in 1867. Recognized as a standard metropolitan community by the US Bureau of Census, 1963. Boise is the business, financial, professional, and transportation center of the state.

Post office, 1863-.

Named for the Boise River. Nickname: "City of Trees," from the great variety of trees in the city.

Boise County. County seat, Idaho City. Fourth county to be created in Idaho; created by the Legislature in 1864. It encompasses parts of both the Boise and the Payette river drainage system.

Named for Boise River, which see.

Boise River. Snake River drainage. Rises in the mountains NE of Boise at an altitude of about 8000′; bisects the Boise Valley and empties into the Snake River in Canyon County just W of Parma. Upper portion characterized by rugged mountains and lava canyons, lower portion by a wide valley. Formerly called

Wihinast, "boiling rapidly," by Shoshoni; Reed River, for John Reed of the American Fur Co., who was murdered by Indians while trapping this stream, 1813; and Skamnaugh by Donald McKenzie in 1819, for a local tribe.

Middle Fk Boise River. Rises in the Boise National Forest at 8000′, joins S Fk 7 mi above Arrowrock Dam; 90 mi long.

N Fk Boise River. About 42 mi long, flows generally SW to form the boundary between Boise and Elmore counties.

S Fk Boise River. Rises in the Sawtooth National Forest at 7500′, flows generally S and SW for 75 mi, then NW 35 mi to join the Middle Fk.

Boise Basin. An 18-mile-square area in the middle of Boise County. At the time of the first gold discoveries here in 1862, this was regarded as the most extensive gold district in the Northwest, and the great influx of prospectors and miners led to the establishment of Idaho Territory. See Boise River.

Boise Mountains (Boise/Camas/Elmore/Valley). A long slender range visible on the east of Highway 55 from Boise to McCall and again on the southeast from McCall to Burgdorf; bounded by N Fk Payette River on the W; S Fk Salmon River and the Sawtooth and Soldier mountains on the E; and by the Snake River Plain on the S.

Boise Peak. 6825′. T4N R3E sec 10. Located in Boise National Forest.

All Boise names are transferred from the name given the river by French-Canadian explorers and trappers for the great variety of trees growing along its banks. After traveling over many miles of arid land, they are said to have exclaimed, "Les bois, les bois! Voyes les bois!" (The woods, the woods! See the woods!) The river has been called by other forms of the name: Rivière Boisée,

Boisias River, and Boise; in 1892 the US Board of Geographic Names decided on the current spelling, Boise.

Boles (Idaho). 4500'. T30N R1W sec 30. In the NW part of the county, about 30 mi W of Grangeville.

Named for D. H. Boles, who settled in Lewiston with his family in 1890 and moved to this site as a permanent home. In 1910 he applied for a post office, which was granted with him as the first postmaster.

Bonami Creek (Latah). T41N R2W sec 9. A 2.7-mi stream that flows W to Little Sand Creek, 2 mi SE of Laird Park; Palouse River drainage.

Named by USFS ranger W. H. Daugs, because there was a spring at the head of this creek within a short walking distance of the one-time Sand Mtn. Lookout. The spring furnished a never-ending supply of water for the lookout and was therefore a "good friend" (French *bon ami*).

Bonanza (Custer). 6378'. T12N R14E sec 17. Ghost town located on Yankee Fork, just S of Franklin Creek, in 1878.

Reportedly named by California miners who came to the area. The name Bonanza is Spanish, meaning "prosperity."

Bonanza Bar (Power). T9S R29E sec 16. In the SW quadrant of the county on the N side of the Snake River. Post office, 1916-1921. Named for the Bonanza placer mine located on this bar.

Bonanza Lake. T8S R29E sec 16. In the W part of the county, 17 mi SE of Crystal Ice Caves and 5 mi N of Bonanza Bar, for which it is named. This lake results from the overflow of the Snake River through the old channel partially filled with lava when Cedar Buttes lava flow ponded the river.

Bond Creek (Benewah). T46N R1E sec 20. In the NE corner of the county.

Rises in Shoshone County and flows NW about 4 mi into St. Maries River 8 mi E of St. Maries.

Named for Walter and Lewis Bond, brothers, who lived at the mouth of this stream.

Bone (Bonneville). 6076'. T1S R40E sec 20/29. Village in the E part of the county on Canyon Creek, 23 mi SE of Idaho Falls. First settled in 1905. Post office, 1917-1950.

Named for the Orion G. Bone family, early settlers in the area.

Bonner County. County seat, Sandpoint. Bonner County was created from part of Kootenai County by a legislative act signed by Governor Frank Gooding in 1907. It was named in honor of Edwin L. Bonner, who had established and operated a ferry on the Kootenai River where the town of Bonners Ferry is located.

Bonner Creek (Clearwater). T40N R6E sec 35. In the N central part of the county. Flows W into Beaver Creek; Clearwater River drainage.

Luther Bonner, a good woodsman, got lost coming out of the area during a fire.

Bonner Lake (Boundary). T62N R3E sec 17. Not far from the Kootenai River and about 10 mi NE of Bonners Ferry.

Named for Edwin L. Bonner.

Bonners Ferry (Boundary). 1779'. T62N R1E sec 26/27/28. County seat. Situated on the Kootenai River, about 30 mi from the Canadian line.

In the early 1870s Edwin L. Bonner built a ferry at a point on the river that Indians had used as a crossing, and it became an important site in emigrant travel over the route from Walla Walla to the placer and quartz mines in British Columbia. He operated the ferry for several years and then sold it to Richard Fry in 1866. The first post office was

44

established under the name of Fry, but later the name of the settlement was changed to Bonners Ferry.

Bonners Ferry was incorporated in 1894; and in 1915, when Boundary County was created, it was made the county seat. The city began to grow in importance when the Great Northern RR was built through the area.

Bonneville County. County seat, Idaho Falls. Created in 1911 by the State Legislature from the N and E parts of Bingham County.

A settlement grew up at the site of the Eagle Rock Ferry in 1864. When the Utah and Northern Railway was completed in 1881, Eagle Rock, later Idaho Falls, became a division point and it remained one until 1897. By 1880 permanent settlement had begun. Mormons filed claims, put in irrigation ditches, and established agricultural communities. Today Bonneville County is a rich agricultural area.

The Snake River bisects the county, and its tributaries drain the entire area. The county is bounded by Caribou County on the S; Bingham County on the W; Teton, Madison, and Jefferson counties on the N; and Wyoming on the E.

The following features were also named for Capt. B. L. E. Bonneville, who explored throughout the Snake River area (1834-1836).

Bonneville Hot Springs (Boise). T9N R10E sec 5/6.

Bonneville Peak (Bannock/Caribou). 9260'. T7S R37E sec 33. On the Bannock-Caribou county line 6 mi SE of Inkom; in the Caribou National Forest.

Bonneville Point (Ada). T2N R3E sec 24. Promontory located in the center of the county.

Boom Creek (Boise). T10N R5E sec 6. In the N extremity of the county. Rises in Valley County and flows 3 mi SE into Middle Fk Payette River.

A logging site; boom is a term for a connected line of floating logs across a stream or enclosing an area.

Boomer Canyon (Lemhi). T22N R23E sec 16. Canyon 1/2 mi long, located just SW of the confluence of N Fk and E Fk Kirtley Creek.

Named for Harry Boomer, whose camp was located here during the construction of a canal.

Boomerang (Payette). Early name for Payette, which see.

Named for the log boom in the river, used for holding RR ties.

Boone Creek (Fremont). T9N R45E sec 34. In SE Fremont County. Rises in Wyoming, enters Idaho, flows SW to convergence with Falls River 17 mi E of Ashton.

Named for the young Boone brothers, who in the 1830s accompanied fur trapper William Sublette to the area now in Idaho. The boys, 17 and 18, became homesick and decided to return to Missouri. Over Sublette's protests, they started out, but they were beset by Indians at Jackson Hole. With difficulty they rejoined Sublette.

Booneville (Owyhee). 5850'. T4S R4W sec 36. Early name for Dewey, which see, located on Jordan Creek. The first mining camp established in the future Owyhee County, 1863.

Named for J. C. Boone, one of the original prospecting party.

Boone Peak is 5 mi E of Flint.

Bootjack Creek (Fremont). T14N R44E sec 18. Heads in Bootjack Pass, flows 7 mi SE to Henrys Fork. Bootjack Pass (6791'), T15N R43E sec 21, is directly S of Henrys Lake.

Named for the appearance of the pass, a narrow declivity resembling the

U-shaped end of a bootjack when viewed from Henrys Lake Flats.

Borah (Power). 4400′. T8/7S R30E sec 35/2. A UPRR station.

Named by RR officials to honor William E. Borah, US Senator from Idaho 1907-1940.

Borah, Mount (Custer). 12,655′. T9N R23E sec 6. The tallest peak in Idaho, located in Lost River Range; Challis National Forest.

Named for US Senator William E. Borah in 1933.

Border (Bear Lake). 6100′. T14S R46E sec 11. In the E part of the county on the Idaho-Wyoming border, for which it is named; on US 30 and Bear River.

Post office, 1892-1900.

Bostetter (Cassia). T14S R20E sec 31. In the SW part of the county on Big Cottonwood Creek, S and W of Oakley; Sawtooth National Forest. Once a settlement, then a CCC camp, and now a recreation area S and W of Oakley.

Said to have been named for Jim Bostetter, an early settler.

Boston Gulch (Boise). T7N R5E sec 30-31. A 2-mi gulch that flows S into Grimes Creek 1 mi NE of New Centerville; Boise River drainage.

This gulch is directly N of New Centerville (formerly Old Boston); its name was transferred from Old Boston.

Bottle Bay (Bonner). T62N R4W sec 28. On Priest Lake 3 1/2 mi E of Granite Mountain and 6 mi NE of Nordman. Bottle Creek rises in Bottle Lake and empties into Priest Lake near Bottle Bay.

Named because Harry Bare, Walt Ritaker, and a man named Meyer camped at the bay. Instead of throwing away their beer bottles, they stacked them behind their cabin.

Bottle Bay (Bonner). T57N R1W sec 33. On Lake Pend Oreille, 2 1/4 mi SW of Sunnyside; 5 1/4 mi SE of Sandpoint.

Named because the bay is bottle-shaped.

Bottleneck, Lake (Minidoka). T4S R24E sec 8/9. In the NW part of the county, surrounded on three sides by lava beds, hence the name.

Boulder Creek (Boise). T6N R6E sec 17. Rises in the S central part of the county and flows 3 1/2 mi SW into Mores Creek; Boise River drainage.

This name was transferred from the Boulder mine, which operated on the banks of the creek.

Boulder Creek (Bonner). T63N R5W sec 2. Stream heading 1/2 mi SE of Boulder Mountain and flowing 5 1/2 mi N into Hughes Fork 3 1/2 mi NW of Upper Priest Lake. Boulder Meadows lies 2 1/2 mi E of Idaho-Washington border and 4 1/2 mi SW of Upper Priest Lake. Drained by Boulder Creek. Boulder Mountain (5672′) overlooks the creek and meadows from the S 5 1/2 mi SW of Upper Priest Lake.

Name derived from the rock formation in the area.

Boulder Creek (Latah). T43N R3W sec 20. Rises NE of East Gold Hill, flows 7.7 mi SE to Jerome Creek; Palouse River drainage.

Locally said to be a misnomer because mapmakers confused it with Gold Creek, a creek characterized by large rocks.

Boulder Creek (Latah). T39N R1W sec 30. Heads about 2 mi N of Chambers Mill Lookout, flows SW for about 6 mi, and empties into Potlatch River 2.5 mi N of Linden; Clearwater River drainage.

Named for the large rocks in the creek bed in clay country.

Boulder Lake (Shoshone). T47N R5E sec 10. In the St. Joe National Forest, in the extreme E part of the county, 4 mi SE of Mullan. This lake lies at the head of 3.5-mi-long Boulder Creek.

Boulder Mountains (Custer/Blaine). The crest forming part of the line between the counties and also the divide between drainages of Big Wood River and E Fk Salmon River, extending from Bryan Peak on the E to the point near Galena where the Hailey-Stanley road crosses the divide. Boulder is within Blaine County.

Named for the rocky terrain.

Boulder Peak (Blaine). 10,966′. T6N R16E sec 32. In the N part of the county, 12 mi NW of Ketchum. This is one of the highest peaks on the divide between the Salmon and Big Lost rivers on the N and Wood River on the S.

Named for its boulder-like summit. The name was also given to Boulder Basin, which lies between the headwaters of E and N Fks of Big Wood River; to Boulder Creek, which rises on the S slopes of the peak and flows 4.5 mi S to empty into Big Wood River; and to the mining town of Boulder, located on the creek, later renamed Briggs.

Boulder Basin. T6N R17E sec 19. Just N of Boulder Peak and of Big Wood River. The narrow canyon of Boulder Creek opens out into a meadow with several small lakes, surrounded on three sides by cliffs rising from 1000′ to 1600′.

Boundary County. County seat, Bonners Ferry. Named because it borders Canada on the N, Washington on the W, and Montana on the E as well as Bonner Co. on the S. Created out of Kootenai and then Bonner counties in 1907. The county is entirely mountainous except along the Kootenai River and in the southern area.

Boundary Point (Latah). T41N R2W sec 18. A promontory just E of the St. Joe Forest boundary at the head of E Fk Queener and Little Bear creeks.

Named because it marks the E boundary of the forest.

Boundary Ridge (Bear Lake). T15/16S R46E. A ridge running N-S about 8 mi directly W of the Idaho-Wyoming line; at the headwaters of Bear River.

Named because of its location near the state line.

Bovill (Latah). 2874′. T41N R1W sec 36. An incorporated town in the E part of the county, 9 mi ENE of Deary.

Named for Hugh Bovill, its founder and first postmaster. Originally Warren Meadows, homestead of R. Francis Warren, cattleman; bought by Hugh Bovill, an Englishman, in 1899. He opened the Bovill Hotel and a general store to accommodate sportsmen, homesteaders, and timber cruisers. The WIM and Milwaukee railroads joined E of Bovill in 1910.

Bower Springs (Cassia). T13S R20E sec 17. In the extreme W part of the county, just E of Ramshorn Ridge and Stump Hollow, at the headwaters of E Fk Dry Creek.

Named for J. E. Bower, who first worked for California cattleman A. J. Harrell in 1872 when his herd was in the Goose Creek Mountains, then later became a well-known cattleman with his own herd in this area.

Bowers (Ada). T3N R1E sec 2/1. An old BVTRR station. Today there are two Boise additions in the same township named for the station.

The railroad construction crew met B. N. Bowers, a likeable Shoshoni Indian, and named the station for him.

Bowmont (Canyon). 2655′. T2N R2W sec 2. Village founded in 1911, located in the E part of the county just E of

Highway 45 and 9 mi S of Nampa; noted for its potatoes, lettuce, onions, and clover seed.

Named by its founder, J. F. Bow. Formerly Newell.

Bowns Creek (Camas). T3N R13E sec 11. Stream 5 mi long, flows N to Big Smoky Creek 18 mi NNW of Fairfield.

Named for Charles Bowns, an early settler in the area.

Box Canyon (Boise). T9N R6E sec 4. In the N central part of the county. Trends 3 mi SW into Little Camp Creek, Payette River drainage.

Barent Anderson named this canyon after he lost a herd of cattle in it one winter, when they became boxed in by snow.

Box Canyon (Idaho). T23-27N R1-3W. Snake River Box Canyon begins about 18 mi N of Oxbow Dam and extends N about 30 mi. This is perhaps the most famous of the box canyons in Idaho.

Box Canyon (Idaho). T24-26N R1E. On the Salmon River S of Slate Creek and N of Riggins. A descriptive name; the walls of the canyon form what is known as a box canyon.

Box Creek (Clearwater). T39N R12E sec 19. In the extreme E part of the county. Flows S from Kelly Lake into Kelly Creek; Clearwater River drainage.

Named for the narrow, boxed-in gorge through which it runs, making it difficult to walk along the creek.

Box Spring (Lemhi). T25N R21E sec 19. NW of the head of Monument Gulch and S of Little Hull Creek.

Named because an old watering box was built around this spring to water cattle.

Boyer (Bonner). T57N R1W sec 4. Town 4 mi NE of Sandpoint and 9 1/4 mi WNW of Hope. Boyer Slough lies 2 mi E of the town; it heads 1/4 mi W of

Selle and flows 3 3/4 mi S into Lake Pend Oreille 3 1/2 mi NE of Sandpoint.

Name derived from an early settler, Alfred Boyer, who came to Sandpoint in 1889; first applied to the town, then to the nearby slough.

Boyles Gulch (Boise). T7N R4E sec 14. Trends SW 3 mi into Woof Creek at Placerville; Boise River drainage.

Named for Charles Boyle, who came to Placerville in 1863.

Brady (Lincoln). T6S R18E sec 8. A UPRR station 3 mi SE of Shoshone.

Named for James H. Brady, who moved to Idaho from Pennsylvania in 1895; made a fortune in irrigation and the electric business; governor of Idaho, 1909-1911; US senator, 1913-1918.

Brady Creek (Idaho). T34N R6E sec 7. A short stream that flows W to Lolo Creek, 14 mi S of Pierce; Clearwater River drainage.

Two conflicting explanations are given for this name, the first perhaps more reliable: named for a homesteader named Brady, who settled in Crane Meadow, or for Idaho Governor James H. Brady.

Brady Gulch (Latah). T38N R3W sec 25. A northern tributary of Potlatch River, 4 mi long, mouth just W of Kendrick.

Named for Philip Brady, who homesteaded 160 acres above the mouth of the stream in the 1880s.

Brainard Creek (Boise). T8N R3E sec 27. Rises in the W part of the county on Hawley Mountain (7301') and flows SW 3 mi into Hill Creek; Payette River drainage.

Named for Timothy Brainard, the first cattle rancher in the Jerusalem Valley area.

Bramwell (Gem). T6N R2W sec 21. Station on the UPRR 8 mi SW of Emmett.

This 1902 Latter-day Saints settlement was named for Franklin S. Bramwell, a local LDS leader.

Braxon Peak (Boise/Custer). 10,353′. T9N R12/13E sec 36/30. In the Sawtooth Range W of Redfish Lake on E boundary of Boise National Forest.

Braxon Lake (Boise). Lake .1 mi across, located in the Sawtooth Range 9.3 mi SW of Stanley and 1 mi SW of Braxon Peak.

Named for a family that settled in Stanley.

Bray Creek (Lemhi). T16N R23E sec 19. Originates near Hi Peak and flows NE 3 mi to enter W Fk Hayden Creek; Lemhi River drainage.

Mark Bray was a pioneer settler on this stream, which was named to honor him.

Breakfast Creek (Clearwater). T37N R6E sec 5. In the S part of the county. Rises on Shanghai Mountain (5198′) NE of Jaype and flows 5 mi E into Orogrande Creek; Clearwater River drainage.

Named by the miners during the early days of Pierce.

Breaks, The (Jefferson). 5017′. T7N R35E sec 19/20/21. A topographical feature characterized by a group of promontories, the largest having an elevation of 5017′. Mud and North lakes, surrounded by a border of lowlands, lie immediately S of The Breaks.

A descriptive name.

Breazeale Spring (Lemhi). T12N R28E sec 12. On N Jump Creek, 6 1/2 mi NE of Hahn charcoal kilns. Pronounced bruh-ZILL.

Walt and Bert Breazeale were stockmen in this area.

Breitenback, Mount (Custer). 12,130′. T9N R24E sec 31. In the Lost River Range about 3.1 mi SSE of Leatherman Peak and 9 mi E of Chilly.

Named for John E. (Jake) Breitenback, who was killed on the American expedition to Mount Everest, 1963. Name changed from Hawley Peak.

Brickaville (Latah). A post office serving upper American and Driscoll ridges between 1887 and 1894.

Named for George Bricka, homesteader in whose home the post office was located.

Bridal Wreath Springs (Gooding). T8S R14E sec 8. In the SE part of the county, on the Snake River; local name for a section of Thousand Springs.

Named because the spray looks like a bridal wreath as the water falls over the basalt formation.

Bridge (Cassia). 4750′. T15S R27E sec 7/8. In the SE part of the county near Raft River; 12 mi S of Malta; long a favorite campsite for Indians and later for pioneers.

Named for a bridge built across Raft River about 1878-1879.

Bridgeport (Idaho). T31N R4E sec 28/33. Early name for Harpster, which see.

Named for a station established by William Jackson, who also built a toll bridge across the Clearwater River at this point.

Briggs (Blaine). A mining community, formerly Boulder. Located about 6 mi SE of Boulder Peak and 6.5 mi NW of Ketchum. Named for the first postmaster, Samuel T. Briggs, in 1888.

The Postal Guide lists the name as Boulder in 1883 and 1885, but as Briggs in 1888 and 1890. Neither appears on maps after 1895.

Broad Valley (Teton).

Early descriptive name given Teton Valley by Indians in 1808 when John Colter accompanied a band of Crow Indians over Teton Pass.

Brockman Creek (Bonneville). T2S R42E sec 29. Rises in the E part of the county and flows 4 mi NE into Grays Lake Outlet.

Named for Dan Brockman, who settled here in 1885. He was a former slave of Charles Martin, an early Idaho Falls cattleman.

Broken Crater (Caribou). 6824′. T7S R41E sec 9. In the NW part of the county near the Bonneville County line, 3 mi W of the S end of Blackfoot River Reservoir and 10 mi N of Soda Springs. Little Crater (6540′) lies 2 mi NE of Broken Crater.

The name describes the crater.

Broken Leg Creek (Shoshone). T42N R9E sec 10. In the SE extremity of the county between Needle Peak (6643′) and Elbow Ridge; a 2-mi tributary of the St. Joe River from the N.

Named for an episode in which John H. Siders, a forest ranger, broke his leg in a fall from the rafters of a cabin being built as a district headquarters in 1913. E. A. Hanson recorded this account from M. C. Evendon while Hanson was a lookout in the Pole Mountain District in 1934.

Bromaghin Peak (Blaine). 10,225′. T6N R15E sec 29. Located in the Smoky Mountains 29 mi NW of Hailey. Named for Ralph Bromaghin, US Army captain who lost his life in Italy during World War II.

Bronson Meadow (Latah). 3199′. T41N R1W sec 34. A meadow 2.5 mi W of Bovill.

Named for a homesteader, William E. Branson (sic).

Broom Creek (Clearwater). T40N R7E sec 4. In the N central part of the county. Flows N into N Fk Clearwater River.

Named for Charlie "Broom-face" Brooks, an early-day logger. His nick-name came from the fact that his whiskers stuck out like a broom.

Brown Creek (Benewah). T43N R2W sec 10. Rises in the SE quadrant of the county, 6 mi W of Tyson Peak, and flows SW to E Fk Charlie Creek; St. Maries River drainage.

Henry Brown homesteaded near the creek in 1905.

Brown Creek Ridge (Clearwater). T34N R5E sec 1-5. In the extreme S part of the county, 6 mi SE of Weippe; 3 mi long, trending E-W, 1 mi S of Brown Creek Lookout (4068′).

Named for Jim Brown, a prospector in the early days of Pierce. Jim Brown Creek is also named for him.

Brown Gulch (Shoshone). T46N R1E sec 23. A 1.5-mi gulch trending N to S to the St. Joe River, 4 mi W of Calder.

Named for pioneer physician Dr. Charles G. Brown, who homesteaded nearby.

Brown Gulch (Lemhi). T25N R21E sec 11. One mi long, running W to enter N Fk Salmon River 1 mi N of Sheep Creek.

Racehorse Brown, who ran a hotel in Gibbonsville at one time, had a ranch here.

Brownlee Creek (Boise). T7N R2E sec 3. Rises in the SW extremity of the county and flows generally SE 10 mi into the Payette River at Gardena.

Named for J. Brownlee, an Idaho City miner.

Brownlee Creek (Washington). T17N R5W sec 22. Stream about 3 1/2 mi long, heading at the junction of W and E Brownlee creeks and flowing generally NNW to the Snake River in Brownlee Reservoir, about 12 mi E of Richland and 37 1/2 mi N of Weiser.

Brownlee community lies about 2 mi N of Brownlee Creek; post office, 1878-190?.

The Brownlee family settled here before 1862 and John Brownlee operated a ferry across the Snake River.

All the Brownlee features were named for Brownlee.

Browns Camp Creek (Latah/Clearwater). T38N R1E sec 11. A tributary of Dicks Creek, in the SE corner of Latah County; N Fk Clearwater River drainage.

Thought to be a campsite of C. O. Brown, lumber cruiser for the Weyerhaeuser Company, who recognized the commercial value of the white pine forests in Latah County and thus opened up the area from Bovill throughout the NW and north central part of the county.

Browns Creek (Elmore). T5N R8E sec 10. Rises between the N and Middle fks of the Boise River and flows 5 mi generally SW to Middle Fk Boise River.

On the S side are Browns Springs; these gush out of a granite cliff, and the 100′ flow of hot water cascades down the rock wall and into the river.

A U.S. Board of Geographic Names note of 19 January 1962 says this feature was named for a Mr. Bowns (sic), who in earlier days hunted and trapped here.

Browns Creek (Owyhee). Flows NE into Catherine Creek; Snake River drainage. Browns Gulch, lying 2 mi E of the Bruneau Sand Dunes, flows N into the Snake River.

James L. Brown had property in this area.

Browns Meadow (Latah). T40N R3W sec 6. A meadow E of Basalt Hill at headwaters of Hatter, Little Bear, and Big Bear creeks.

Named for Benjamin Brown, who homesteaded 120 acres here in the 1890s.

Browns Rock (Clearwater). T39N R6E sec 21. Peak 6 mi NE of Headquarters.

A large rock at the location was named for C. O. Brown, a scout for the Weyerhaeuser Timber Company.

Bruce Canyon (Lemhi). T12N R27E sec 10. Heads 3/4 mi S of Sheep Mountain; runs E 3 mi, 1 mi N of Hahn.

Named for A. T. Bruce, a pioneer mining inspector and teacher in the Birch Creek area from 1885 to 1897.

Bruces Eddy (Clearwater). T37N R1E sec 26-28. Two mi NE of Ahsahka on N Fk Clearwater River; now under waters of Dworshak Reservoir.

A. B. Curtis (USFS) says it was named for Bruce Lipscomb, who brought supplies up the river; he drowned at that location. Al Hansen (USFS) thinks it was named for C. R. Bruce, who homesteaded near here.

Bruin Creek (Clearwater). T39N R13E sec 6. In the E extremity of the county. Rises on Bruin Hill (6564′) and flows 3 mi SE into the N Fk Kelly Creek; Clearwater River drainage. Bruin Ridge trends NW-SE for 5 mi between Bruin and Kelly creeks.

Named for bear found in the area.

Brundage Mountain (Adams/Valley). 7803′. T19N R3E sec 7. About 10 mi W of McCall, on the Adams-Valley county line.

Named for Scott Brundage, early rancher in the area.

Bruneau River (Owyhee). Flows the entire length of the E part of the county, NW into the Snake River; drains an area of about 1200 sq mi.

There are many theories concerning the origin of the name Bruneau. Some say the name is of French origin, *brun*, "dark" and *eau*, "water," descriptive of the color of the river at certain times of the year. This name was first believed to have been applied by the French

Canadians of Donald McKenzie's trapping party from the Hudson's Bay Company in 1818. Another theory is that it was named for Baptiste Bruneau or Pruneau, a trapper for the Hudson's Bay Company, who supposedly came to this area in 1815 and discovered the river.

Robert Stuart, leader of the eastbound Astorians in 1812, called the river Rocky Bluff Creek. The name Bruneau was probably given by Ramsey Crooks' detachment of the Astorians; it was first used in 1831 in the journals of John Work. On B.L.E. Bonneville's 1837 map the river is called Powder River.

Bruneau (2559'). T6S R5E sec 24/25. Town 22 mi S of Mountain Home in the NE part of the county. Post office, 1875-.

Bruneau was named for the Bruneau River. Some people say that the town was named for Bruneau John, an old Indian who warned the white people in Mountain Home of the Bannock Indian uprising and saved their lives (1878). In fact, the Indian was named after the village.

Bruneau Canyon. Depth is approximately 1200' to 2000'. It is 67 mi long and runs the length of the Bruneau River.

Bruneau Sand Dunes. T6S R6E. In the NE corner of the county, 4 1/2 mi NE of Bruneau. Covering an area of 4 square miles, rising 452'.

Bruneau Springs. T7S R6E sec 27. S of Bruneau on the E side of the Bruneau River.

Bruneau Valley. T6/7S R5/6E. Near the mouth of the Bruneau River. The town of Bruneau is in the valley. Often called the "valley of tall grass."

Brunning (Clearwater). T36N R3E sec 6. Town 3 mi NE of Grangemont.

Named for Ed Brunning, who had a farm here in 1905.

Brush Creek (Bonner). T54N R1W sec 10. Heads 1 mi NE of Barton Hump; flows 3/4 mi SW, then 1 1/2 mi W into Cedar Creek 1 mi SE of Whiskey Rock.

Named for the density of flora found here.

Brush Creek (Latah). T40N R2W sec 31. A 4-mi stream heading E of Potato Hill and flowing S to the Potlatch River; Clearwater River drainage.

Named from the heavy brush growing along its banks.

Brushy Gulch (Lemhi). T24N R20E sec 6. Heads near Bald Mountain and runs SE about 3 mi to the Indian Creek drainage.

Named because of the extraordinary amount of brush at the mouth of this gulch.

Buck Butte (Clearwater). 4334'. T38N R4E sec 32. Six mi NE of Grangemont.

Named by a homesteader for the deer here.

Buck Mountain (Boundary). 6177'. T60N R2E sec 12. Formerly Buckhorn Mountain; the Buckhorn lode was located here in 1895.

Buckhorn Creek (Cassia). T12S R20E sec 24. Rises near the N boundary of the Sawtooth National Forest in the W part of the county; flows 4 mi NE and sinks into the terrain. It flows through Buckhorn Canyon and is fed by Buckhorn Spring. Buckhorn Ranch, named for the stream, is situated at the mouth of the creek.

Apparently this was a favorite deer-hunting area in the 1870s; the creek and canyon already bore the name Buckhorn at that time.

Buckingham Point (Clearwater). 6772'. T39N R8E sec 27. Peak 5 mi NE of the Bungalow Ranger Station, in the N central part of the county.

Named after USFS ranger W. E. Buckingham, who was in the area in the 1920s.

Buckles Mountain (Kootenai). 4733'. T52N R2W sec 16. In the Chilco Mountains in the N part of the county, 4 mi NE of Hayden Lake.

Named for John Buckles, who mined here in 1885.

Buffalo Creek (Elmore). T2N R6E sec 13. Rises in the mountains between Willow Creek and S Fk Boise River and flows 4 mi NE to empty into S Fk Boise River. Named for the Buffalo mine (1882).

Buffalo Hump (Idaho). 8926'. T26N R6E sec 3. The most prominent of the peaks of the Clearwater Mountains. It rises in the center of a triangle formed by the mining towns of Warren, Florence, and Elk City. Mining commenced at Buffalo Hump in the late 1890s.

Named by miners in 1862, because of its resemblance to the hump of a buffalo.

Buffalo (Idaho) was a townsite adjoining the Big Buffalo mine on the W slope of the mountain.

Buffalo River (Fremont). T13N R43E sec 28. Empties into Island Park Reservoir; Henrys Fork drainage.

Named by George Rea, 1890s trapper and settler, who shot one of the last buffalo in the area while hunting along the river.

Buffalo Skull Lake (Lemhi). T15N R23E. A lake 657' long located 1.9 mi SW of Mill Mountain.

Named for a buffalo skull found nearby, a unique discovery at this elevation.

Bug Creek (Bonner). T57N R3E sec 6. Heads 1/2 mi NNE of Rattle Mountain; flows 1 1/2 mi WSW into Tattle Creek 10 mi NE of Hope.

Named for the bugs that infest the area.

Buggy Spring (Fremont). T8N R46E sec 24. In the SE of the county, between Conant and Elk creeks, 2 mi E of the Wyoming border.

Said to be named for the discovery of a buggy abandoned after an attempt to take it over the Tetons; the spring is located along an old road.

Bugle Creek (Bonner). T63N R4W sec 23. Rises 1 mi NW of Bugle Ridge and flows 4 mi S to E Fk Caribou Creek, which empties into Upper Priest Lake. Bugle Ridge is at the head of Bugle Creek.

Bugle Mountain (Boise). 9209'. T8N R11E sec 11.

Bugle Point (Clearwater). T38N R8E sec 14/23. Peak 4 mi E of Bungalow Ranger Station, in the E central part of the county.

Named for the bugling elk in the area.

Bugtown (Canyon). T4N R3W sec 27. Camp of the OSLRR in the 1880s, located 1/2 mi S of present Caldwell.

A derogatory name, probably from the bugs that troubled many such camps. Also designated Caldwell at times.

Buhl (Twin Falls). 3793'. T9S R14E sec 36. In the N part of the county, 15 mi W of Twin Falls.

Established as part of the then-proposed Twin Falls South Side irrigation project in 1905; post office, 1906-.

Named for Frank H. Buhl, one of the founders of the Twin Falls South Side irrigation project.

Buist (Oneida). T13S R33E sec 4. A ranching community on Deep Creek.

Named for an early settler.

Bull Creek (Idaho). T24N R6E sec 4. Tributary of Salmon River. Bull Creek Ridge parallels Bull Creek on its W side.

Named for Alexander Bull, an early miner.

Bull Creek (Lemhi). T15N R27E sec 14. Forms near Mountain Peak and flows W 3 mi.

E. R. Hawley, who had a ranch on Hawley Creek, herded bulls across this creek to winter them.

Bull Elk Creek (Teton). T7N R44E sec 36. Rises on the W slopes of Teton Range and flows erratically W some 13 mi to Badger Creek.

Named for the herds of elk once found in the area.

Bull Run Creek (Kootenai). T48N R1W sec 16. Rises on Black Rock Ridge and flows NW 3.5 mi through Rose Lake to empty into the Coeur d'Alene River. Bull Run Peak (3969') lies about 1 mi E of the stream.

Named in the late 1860s for the river where the two Civil War Battles of Bull Run were fought in 1861 and 1862; as Union forces were defeated, doubtless named by Confederate-sympathizer settlers.

Bull Spring (Lemhi). T19N R19E sec 31. About 2 1/2 mi E of Rooker Basin.

This spring and pond are used by cattle that graze in Prairie Basin.

Bullion (Blaine). T2N R17E sec 25. About 7 mi W of Hailey at the mouth of Bullion Gulch. Established in 1880, with an estimated 500 miners and a total population of 700.

Named for the gold and silver bullion produced in this area.

Bullion Creek (Shoshone). T47N R5E sec 36. In the E part of the county. Rises in the Bitterroot Mountains on the W slopes of Bullion Pass (5445'), and flows 5 mi SW to N Fk St. Joe River.

Named for the Bullion mine, located 1 mi downstream from its source.

Bulltown (Latah). Early name for Onaway, which see.

Bunch Creek (Boise). T8N R5E sec 8. Rises in the west central part of the county and flows 2 mi N into the S Fk Payette River, 1 1/2 mi W of Grimes Pass.

Lee Bunch located a placer mine on this creek in the 1860s.

Bunchs Creek (Boise). T8N R4E sec 15. Rises on Hawley Mountain (7301') and flows 3 mi NE into Alder Creek, 5 mi S of Garden Valley; Payette River drainage. Davis Bunch had a mine on this creek and later located his ranch near it.

Bundy (Nez Perce). 1253'. T35N R3W sec 19. Town 2 mi SW of Sweetwater on Lapwai Creek.

Named after William Henry Bundy, who was elected state senator from Nez Perce County in 1914. He came to Idaho in 1872 and lived in the Tom Beall section near Culdesac. He was very active in community affairs and initiated a program of planting trees along the highways. Bundy died in 1958.

Bunghole (Idaho). T22N R5E. A tent-town located on the ridge above Bear Creek and below Marshall Lake mines. Established in 1902, this short-lived settlement served as a refuge for miners from Florence, who waited for the heavy snow to melt so they could continue prospecting or go to Thunder Mountain.

A bunghole is a hole in a keg through which liquid is poured in or drained.

Bunker Hill (Jefferson). T7N R35E sec 25. A promontory 3 mi ENE of Mud Lake.

Presumably named for the American Revolutionary War battle.

Bunkhouse Creek (Fremont). T13N R42E sec 14. Flows SW to converge with Sheep Creek; Island Park Reservoir/Henrys Fork drainage.

Named because it flowed W of the living quarters of the Grubb Ranch.

Burch Creek (Cassia). T14S R22E sec 3. Rises in Middle Creek, Southern Mountains, and flows 13 mi N to dissipate near Oakley Airport.

Named for G. D. Burch, who in 1881 filed water rights on Goose Creek, which lies about 1 mi W of Burch Creek.

Appears as Birch Creek on some maps.

Burcham Creek (Clearwater). T35N R5E sec 2. In the extreme S part of the county. Rises in Lew Hard Meadow and flows 4 mi SE into Brown Creek; Clearwater River drainage.

Named for homesteader Billy Burcham.

Burgdorf (Idaho). 5160'. T22N R4E sec 1. In the SW part of the county, 30 mi NE of McCall; from its founding, a resort and a mining town. Established about 1863 as Warm Springs, changed to Resort before 1894, and to Burgdorf in 1914. Its chief attraction was the hot springs. Burgdorf Creek, a 3-mi stream, joins Lake Creek just S of the town, and Burgdorf Summit (8110') lies 15 mi NE.

Named for its founder and first postmaster, Fred C. Burgdorf, a native German who discovered the springs here and secured a deed to them while he was gold mining in the Warrens area.

Burke (Shoshone). 3736'. T48N R5E sec 10. In the E part of the county, 6 mi NE of Wallace, on Canyon Creek. Silver was discovered in 1883 in the canyon where Burke is located; post office 1887.

Named in 1885 to honor J. M. Burke, a local miner and politician. Thirty-five miners had met for the pur-

pose of selecting a name and two were proposed, Burke and Onealville, from the motto "One for all"; the vote was 29 for Burke and 1 for Onealville.

Burley (Cassia). 4157'. T10S R23E sec 19/20. County seat. In the NW part of the county, on the Snake River.

In 1905 J. E. Miller, I. B. Perrine, and David E. Burley platted the town on the S side of Snake River and named it Commerce, in which name the first post office was granted. Then they changed their minds and renamed it to honor Burley, a general passenger agent for the OSLRR. Burley was influential in the growth of the potato industry in Idaho, offering prizes for production. He also discovered a way to ship potatoes that would protect them from bruising, and he adapted techniques used for cleaning and wrapping oranges to the potato industry.

Burn Creek (Lemhi). T16N R14E sec 20. Flows SW 1 1/2 mi to enter Loon Creek; Middle Fk Salmon River drainage.

Reportedly this area was burned off by Indians before Captain Reuben F. Bernard captured them in 1879 during the Sheepeater Campaign.

Burns (Lincoln). T3S R19E sec 17. Early post office in the N part of the county just E of the central lava beds and 3 mi NE of Burmah. Named for the first postmaster, John F. Byrns (sic).

Burns Canyon (Bonneville). T3N R42E sec 1. Rises in Teton County and flows 5 mi from NE to SW across the corner of Madison County into Bonneville County to empty into the Snake River.

Named for trapper Jim Burns, who worked along the Snake River in 1864.

Burns Canyon/Creek (Bonneville). T3N R42E sec 11. Extends 6.7 mi SW in NE part of the county. The creek empties into Snake River, about 25 mi NE of Idaho Falls. Little Burns Canyon/Creek extends NE into Teton County.

Named for William Burns, who lived here with his Indian wife and family (ca.1910) trapping beaver, marten, mink, and otter.

Burns Gulch (Lemhi). T24N R21E sec 21. Three mi long, runs SE between Big Silverlead Creek and Wagonhammer Creek to enter Salmon River drainage.

In the early 1900s Tom "Old Man" Burns fell from the cliff into the river and drowned while he and some other men were bringing a pack string past the mouth of this gulch.

Burnt Creek (Clearwater). T40N R8E sec 32. In the N central part of the county. Flows just S of Moscow Bar SE into N Fk Clearwater River.

Named for the fires here, especially the great 1910 fire, which burned this area.

Burro Creek (Clearwater). T39N R7E sec 15. Rises in the central part of the county on Shin Point and flows E into N Fk Clearwater River.

May be an office name given by the USFS, since the creek is located near Dead Mule Creek.

Burton (Madison). 4839′. T6N R39E sec 34. An agricultural area in the center of the county; 4 mi SW of Rexburg. Site occupied by a trapper in 1876 and settled by Mormons in 1884. Richard "Beaver Dick" Leigh and his first family made their home here and died here.

Named for Robert T. Burton, first counselor and presiding bishop of the Church of Jesus Christ of Latter-day Saints, who designated the area as a townsite.

Bush Creek (Clearwater). T38N R6E sec 4. In the center of the county. A 2-mi stream that flows S into Scofield Creek; Clearwater River drainage.

Named for Ben Bush, head of the Idaho State Land Board, who was responsible for selection of state land.

Bussell Creek (Shoshone). T44N R2E sec 25. In the SW part of the county. Rises on the N slope of Davis Pass and flows 5 mi NE to Toles Creek; St. Joe River drainage.

Named for the head cruiser of the NPRR, Bussell, who had been in a wreck on the NP shortly before coming west. The injuries sustained required that he wear a silver plate in his head. While carrying a packsack up Marble Creek with the use of a head strap, he suddenly lost his mind, probably from the pressure on the head plate. He died before reaching medical help.

Buster Gulch (Lemhi). T24N R20E sec 26. About 2 mi long, heads in vicinity of Whiskey Spring and enters Salmon River drainage.

Named after C. F. "Free" Buster, who ran a saloon on Indian Creek when the mines were active in the 1860s.

Buster Gulch (Lemhi). T26N R21E sec 23. One mi long, runs SW to enter N Fk Salmon River drainage.

Named for John Buster, early rancher and stage driver. He ranched at the mouth of the gulch and drove the stage from Salmon to Gibbonsville in the 1880s.

Buswell (Latah). T40N R6W sec 1. An early community about 3 mi E and 1 mi S of Viola.

Named for L. A. Buswell, who lived here and grew vegetables and small fruits, partly for Advent Hollow.

Butcherknife Ridge (Lemhi). T26N R20E sec 38/29/34. Trends SE to NW about 2 mi.

Named because at a distance this sharp, pointed ridge looks like a butcherknife blade.

Butler Creek (Bonner). T55N R2W sec 18. Heads 3/4 mi SW of Butler Mountain; flows 5 mi WSW into Cocolalla Lake at Cocolalla.

Butler Mountain (4911'), 2 mi NE of the mouth of the stream, is 2 mi SW of Talache and 10 mi SSE of Sandpoint.

Named for a USFS employee, who was killed nearby by lightning.

Butte City (Butte). T3N R27E sec 9. An incorporated city 4 mi SE of Arco.

Named for the county.

Butte County. County seat, Arco. Established in 1917 from parts of Blaine, Jefferson, and Binham counties; and named for the buttes characteristic of the area.

Butte County, located in the SE portion of Idaho, is bordered by Bingham, Jefferson, and Clark counties on the E; Lemhi County on the N; Custer on the W; and Blaine on the SW and S. It is drained by the Big and Little Lost rivers and Birch Creek, all of which dissipate into the terrain. The Challis National Forest extends throughout most of the W and N part of the county and Targhee National Forest into the NE corner. The S extremities of the Lemhi and Lost River ranges stretch into the county from the N. The Craters of the Moon lie in the SW and the Snake River Plain in the S.

Butte Creek (Clearwater). T41N R6E sec 31. Rises on Butte Creek Saddle in the N central part of the county and flows 4 mi N into N Fk Clearwater River, about midway between Telephone and Beaver creeks.

Named for the nearby butte or buttes. Thompson Butte and Beaver Butte are on the E; Micky Point is on the W.

Butter Creek (Clearwater). T37N R11E sec 1. Rises on the S border of the county on Horseshoe Lookout and flows 3 mi NE into Howard Creek; Clearwater River drainage.

Named for the mountain buttercup, a little yellow flower found along the creek.

Buttercup Mountain (Blaine/Camas). 9081'. T2N R16E sec 8. In the SW part of the county on the Camas-Blaine county line. Buttercup Creek (Camas) rises on the W slope of this peak and flows 4 mi SW to Willow Creek.

Both features are named for the Buttercup mine, which lies in the upper reaches of Buttercup Creek.

Butterfield Creek (Clearwater). T39N R1E sec 1. Rises in the NW corner of the county on Neva Hill and flows 5 mi SE into Oviatt Creek; Clearwater River drainage.

Named for A. S. Butterfield, who located along the creek in 1912.

Byram (Canyon).

Named for the only postmaster, Jessie P. Byram.

BM Hill (Clearwater). 6485'. T38N R14E sec 9/10. Mountain 7 mi E of Blacklead Mountain.

Named for the benchmark telling the elevation here.

57

Clarkia (Shoshone County) at the turn of the century.

C

Cabarton (Valley). 2173′. T13N R3E sec 25. An early-20th-century Boise Payette Lumber Company town, on the UPRR, 1 mi W of the N Fk Payette River, 5 mi S of Cascade. The town was established in 1921, but in 1935 all the buildings were removed to McGregor, where the company had acquired new holdings.

Named for C. A. Barton, an official of the Boise Payette Lumber Company.

Cabin Creek (Boise). T8N R9E sec 9. Rises in the E part of the county between Little Silver Creek and Crooked River and flows SW into the Crooked River at Trapper Flat; Boise River drainage.

John Welch had a cabin at the head of this creek.

Cabin Creek (Lemhi). T42N R19E sec 12. Heads near Ulysses Mountain and runs W to Indian Creek; Salmon River drainage.

There used to be an old cabin near the mouth of this creek. At one time people tried to change the name to Marsing Creek after Nels O. Marsing, a pioneer of this district.

Cabin Gulch (Latah). T43N R3W sec 34. Extends 2 mi E from Prospect Peak to Meadow Creek. In St. Joe National Forest; once the scene of much gold prospecting.

Named for a tumbled-down cabin in the gulch, believed to have belonged to a miner.

Cabin Point (Clearwater). T38N R8E sec 32. Peak 3 mi SE of Bungalow Ranger Station.

Named for the Hunch Cabin here, once owned by George Englehorn.

Cabin Spring (Idaho). T25N R12E sec 14. On S slope of Harrington Mountain 7.5 mi NW of Waugh Mountain.

Named for a cabin adjacent to the spring, burned in 1929, leaving only its rock foundation and fireplace.

Cabinet (Bonner). T55N R3E sec 28. Town 1 1/2 mi W of Idaho-Montana border; 6 1/4 mi SE of Clark Fork. Appears as a town as early as 1868.

Cabinet Gorge lies 1 mi E of the town; it is a Z-shaped gorge with 350′ walls through which the Clark Fork River flows.

Cabinet Mountains. A 120-mi range of mountains separating the Kootenai River from Clark Fork, in western Montana and northern Idaho, delimited on the N by that part of Kootenai River between Jennings and Bonners Ferry; on the W by Purcell Trench; on SW by Clark Fork and up that stream to its head, over Haskell Pass, and along an abandoned line of the GNRR down to

Jennings. Peaks to 9000' occupy the middle of the range.

French trappers applied the name Cabinet to the recesses in the walls of the gorge; the name was transferred to the town, the mountains, and a dam.

Cable Creek (Kootenai). T49N R5W sec 17. Rises on the N slope of Cable Peak (4956') and flows 7 mi N into Washington state to empty into the Spokane River.

Both the peak and the creek were named for the logging cables left lying along the stream by early-day loggers.

Cache (Teton). T5N R45E sec 4/5/8/9. An early Latter-day Saint settlement midway between Tetonia and Driggs. The townsite was established in 1907.

Named for Cache Valley, Utah, original home of most of the settlers. The word cache was widely used in fur-trapping days for a place to store pelts and trapping gear. The UPRR name for this place is Dwight.

Cache Bar (Lemhi). 3000'. T23N R16E sec 18. On Salmon River between Cramer Creek on the SE and Fountain Creek on the NW.

One informant says Captain Harry Guleke, a noted river boatman, kept a cache here. Another says a river rat and prospector named Cache lived here. And still another says it was named because placer mining here brought in much cash.

Cache Creek (Clearwater). T38N R7E sec 32. Rises on Elk Mountain in the central part of the county and flows 4 mi S into French Creek, 13 mi NE of Pierce; Clearwater River drainage.

Named in 1919 for Earl Cash (sic), who was a member of a road-surveying crew, by Walter Adams, the chief engineer of the party.

Cache Creek (Lemhi). T17N R14E sec 19. Heads N of Sleeping Deer Mountain and flows 6 mi generally NW to enter Loon Creek; Middle Fk Salmon River drainage.

Captain Reuben F. Bernard reportedly cached some supplies here during the Sheepeater Campaign of 1879 but could never recover them.

Outfitters packing from Challis to Thunder Mountain cached mule shoes and horseshoes and other supplies here to be used on the return trip to Challis.

Cache Peak (Cassia). 10,339'. T14S R24E sec 21. In Albion Range SE of Oakley. This peak has been sculptured by glaciers, and on its N slope is a large cirque in which lie the 5 small Independence Lakes. Descent on the SW is nearly vertical for 3000'. The high, broad dome is 10-12 mi wide.

Calamity Point (Bonneville). 6520'. T1S R45E sec 17. An igneous intrusion through the Swan Valley Fault; in the E part of the county.

Source of name is in dispute: Named because of the dangerous bend in the river where several men lost their lives while floating large rafts of logs to the sawmills; named because large log rafts holding from 10 to 20 thousand board feet of rough lumber were upset in the swift water.

Calder (Shoshone). 2190'. T45N R2E sec 3. In the SW part of the county, 18 mi S of Kellogg; on the St. Joe River and the Milwaukee RR.

Originally settled as a RR construction camp and named for a member of the construction crew. John Rice, an early settler in the area, named it Elk Prairie, but the name did not stick; later names include Gordon (1891) and Remington (1906).

Calderwood Creek (Boise). T8N R5E sec 10. Rises in the W central part of the county on Grimes Pass and flows 2 mi N into the S Fk Payette River.

The Calderwood family lived near this creek.

Caldron Linn (Jerome/Twin Falls). T10S R21E sec 28. Site of a canoe disaster 28 Oct 1811, when Wilson Price Hunt and his party were on their way to Astoria by way of Snake River.

One of the canoes struck a rock at this site and broke into pieces, and the steersman, Antoine Clappine, was drowned. The party cached the supplies that were not ruined, abandoned the remaining canoes, and went on laboriously by foot. The pour-over at this spot, which they designated as Caldron Linn, has also been called the Devil's Scuttle Hole.

Caldron Linn means a "boiling, seething caldron," which exactly describe the site.

Caldwell (Canyon). 2370′. T4N R3W sec 21/22. County seat. Situated in the center of the county on the S shore of the Boise River.

The Idaho and Oregon Land Improvement Company, of which Kansas U.S. Senator C. A. Caldwell was president, owned and platted the townsite of Caldwell in 1883.

Nicknames: Bugtown and Hamburg, which see.

Named for C. A. Caldwell.

Caldwell Creek (Clearwater). T38N R4E sec 7. Rises in the NW quadrant and flows 3 mi NW into Dworshak Reservoir.

Named after a settler.

Caleb (Custer). T14N R19E. A short-lived post office, 1882-1883.

The origin of the name is unknown. It may be biblical from the Israelite Caleb, who spied out Canaan. Certainly whoever settled here in 1882 was spying out the land.

Calendar (Idaho). 6200′. T26N R6E sec 2. Once a thriving mining town, 2 mi E of Buffalo Hump, now a ghost town.

As a result of production at Big Buffalo mine, a town started at this site in 1900. Named by superintendent W. H. Hill for a New Yorker, Thomas O. Callender. It was partially destroyed by fire. Post office 1900-1904.

Calhoun Creek (Clearwater). T38N R5E sec 28. Heads 1 mi S of Headquarters; flows N into Reeds Creek; Clearwater River drainage.

Named after a miner.

California Bar (Lemhi). T21N R20E sec 6. Just NE of Missouri Gulch, on Napias Creek; Salmon River drainage.

It probably reminded early placer miners of the California gold rush, so they named it accordingly.

California Gulch (Boise). T7N R4E sec 3-14. A 4-mi gulch trending 4 mi SE into Woof Creek at Placerville; Boise River drainage.

California Gulch was named by the original settlers of Placerville, many of whom were from California.

California Gulch (Latah). T42N R2W sec 11. Flows SE 2 mi; sixth of the 10 named gulches emptying into N Fk Palouse River.

Believed to be named by prospectors who moved to this district from California gold mines. See Banks Gulch.

Calipeen (Shoshone). T42N R6E sec 27. A 2-mi tributary of Little N Fk Clearwater River in the Clearwater National Forest near the Clearwater county line.

Named by W. H. Daugs, USFS ranger. A pistol thought to have been lost by Indians was found on this stream. Calipeen is a Chinook Indian word for "pistol."

Callahan Creek (Shoshone). T47N R5E sec 28. Rises in the Coeur d'Alene Mountains and flows 2 mi NE to the St. Joe River, in the Mullan-Wallace area.

An Irish man named James Francis (Jim) Callahan, shake-splitter turned prospector, in 1885 located several mines in the area. They became the core of the Callahan Mining Company.

Callopy (Canyon). T2N R1W sec 5. UPRR siding near Nampa.

Named for T. C. Callopy, a train dispatcher.

Camas. Camas as a place name occurs throughout Idaho, as does the lily-like plant with an edible bulb used as a staple food by Indians and as hog fodder by settlers. Features so named lie in areas where the plant once flourished. Pronounced KAM-us.

Camas Creek (Camas/Elmore). T1S R17E sec 22. Rises in Elmore County, in the Boise National Forest on the NE slope of Bennett Mountain (7465'), and flows E 50 mi to the Big Wood River at Magic Reservoir, Camas County. Little Camas Creek rises in the mountains W of Hill City and flows 12 mi N to Little Camas Reservoir and from there to S Fk Boise River; drainage, 47 square miles.

Camas County. County seat, Fairfield. Established in 1917 when Blaine, Butte, and Camas counties were created.

Topographically, the county is divided into three parts. The N is mountainous, the central part is prairie and agricultural, and the S is hilly. The mountainous N is occupied by the Sawtooth National Forest.

Camas Prairie (Camas/Elmore). T1/2S R11E. Plain of Camas Creek extending W for over 40 mi from a point about 5 mi above the confluence of that stream with the Big Wood River. It is bounded on the N by the Smoky and Soldier mountains, on the S and W by Mount Bennett Hills.

Once "food locker of wandering Indian tribes," now an area that produces high-protein hay.

Camas Prairie, Little (Elmore). T1S R9E. At the E end of Camas County, SE of S Fk Boise River and NW of Mount Bennett Hills.

Camas Prairie (Idaho/Lewis/Nez Perce T30-34 R2E-3W). This N prairie rolls N and W from Grangeville, about 30 mi from N to S and 20 mi from E to W. It is still referred to as Camas Prairie, for the camas that once covered the area, or as "The Prairie" by locals.

Camas Creek (Jefferson/Clark). T7N R36E sec 30. Rises on the Continental Divide in the Targhee National Forest N of Kilgore and flows 50 mi across eastern Clark County SSW into Jefferson County to empty into Rays Lake, then into Mud Lake.

Camas (Jefferson). 4816'. T8N R36E sec 21/22. A station on the UPRR in the NE quadrant of the county, on Camas Creek 5 mi N of Hamer.

In the 1880s this was a thriving town with a population of 3000, the largest shipping point between Ogden, Utah, and Butte, Montana, and the principal depot for lead bullion from the Birch Creek mines in Lemhi County.

Post office, 1880-1961.

Named for Camas Meadow. Formerly Lava, for the composition of the soil.

Camas Butte (Jefferson). 4816'. T8N R36E sec 22. Lies 1 mi S of the town of Camas and 1 mi NE of the Camas Wildlife Refuge.

Camas Meadow (Clark). T12N R39E sec 31. About 4.5 mi S and E of Idmon between Camas and Spring creeks.

Site of a battle with the Nez Perce led by Looking Glass, Toohoolhoolzote, and Ollokot with 28 Nez Perce warriors, who came to General Oliver Howard's camp 19 August 1877 to steal horses. A fierce battle ensued. Captain Randolph Norwood and L Company fought a 4-hour battle August 20 with the retreating Indians.

Camas Creek (Latah). T41N R4W sec 12. Flows 4.1 mi S and SE to the Palouse River, 3 mi W of Harvard.

Gold was discovered here in 1870; site of Camas Creek Massacre, 1880, when Chinese placer miners were shot and then robbed of their gold and their boots.

Camas Creek. An early mining community at the mouth of Camas Creek. Post office, 1878-1898. It is believed locally that Chinese miners accounted for most of the settlement; evidence includes the distinctive dams, ditches, flumes, creek channeling, and ground sluices, which moved tremendous quantities of water and earth.

Cambridge (Bannock). T11S R37E sec 22. An early Mormon settlement named for Cambridge, England, original home of some of the settlers; name said to have been suggested by Bishop William B. Preston (1870s).

Cambridge (Washington). 2651'. T14N R3W sec 3/11. Eight mi N of Midvale on the W side of the Weiser River, at the intersection of Highway 71 and US 95.

John Cuddy, an Irish immigrant, came to the area in 1870 and homesteaded 320 acres 5 mi N of present-day Cambridge. He built a grist mill on Rush Creek that had the capacity to produce 3 tons of flour a day and enough bran and other residue for his herd of hogs; he also milled lumber. The nearest settlement was Salubria, forerunner of Cambridge; and as it grew, Cuddy moved his mill to the town.

When the Pacific and Idaho Northern made plans to run their RR through Salubria, there was difficulty getting a right-of-way, because one landowner demanded too much money. A landowner across the river offered to donate every other lot of his holdings if the RR would come by that route. Salubria was by-passed and Cambridge was born. Many of the Salubria businesses moved to the new site.

Named for the location of Harvard University, alma mater of the president of the PINRR.

Camel Gulch (Lemhi). T24N R21E sec 19. About 1 mi long, running NW to the Salmon River drainage about 2 mi SW of N Fk.

A family by the name of Camel lived at the mouth of the gulch.

Camelback Mountain (Bannock). 6582'. T6S R35E sec 22. A distinctive promontory 4.5 mi NE of Pocatello between the N and S forks of Pocatello Creek.

Named for its configuration.

Cameron Creek (Shoshone). T46N R3E sec 7. Rises on Cameron Hill (5082') and flows 2 mi SW to Big Creek; St. Joe River drainage.

A man named Cameron homesteaded this creek.

Cameron Creek (Valley). T16N R12E sec 12. Flows 2 mi SSE into Middle Fk Salmon River from the W.

Named for Kinney Cameron, a Scotsman who ranched here and raised potatoes and apples for miners up Big Creek.

Camp Bay (Bonner). T56N R1E sec 18. On Lake Pend Oreille, 8 mi E of Sagle and 4 3/4 mi SW of Hope.

Named because the spot has been used as a campsite.

Camp Creek (Bonneville). T1S R42E sec 2. Flows 4-5 mi NE into Fall Creek in Caribou Range; Snake River drainage.

Named because it was a suitable campsite during the westward migration, 1860-1890.

Camp Creek (Lemhi). T19N R16E sec 32. Heads just N of Middle Fork Peak; flows SE 2 mi to enter Yellowjacket Creek; Middle Fork Salmon River drainage.

The Thunder Mountain trail crossed the head of this creek, and since there was good grass and water, travelers in the area frequently made their camp here. There was an attempt to change the name to Nate Creek in honor of Nate Smith, the pioneer miner who discovered placer gold on Yellowjacket and Loon creeks, 1866.

Camp Creek (Lemhi). T17N R14E sec 34. Flows W for 2 mi to enter Loon Creek, near Lemhi-Custer county line; Middle Fk Salmon River drainage.

Outfitters going from Salmon to Middle Fk camped at the head of this creek.

Camp Creek (Lemhi). T22N R20E sec 21. Forms SW of Haystack Mountain and flows SE 3 1/2 mi to enter Napias Creek near Leesburg; Salmon River drainage.

Named for Chris Camp, an early miner on this stream.

Camp Dynamo (Lemhi). T22N R18E sec 28. A community located on Panther Creek at the mouth of Clear Creek.

In 1886 a hydro-generator was installed here that lit up the area all the way to the Beaver Creek sawmill, about 1 mi.

Camp George Creek (Clearwater). T38N R9E sec 10. Rises in the SE part of the county on Bee Butte (5393') and in Camp George; flows 3 mi NE into Fourth of July Creek; Clearwater River drainage.

Named after George Englehorn, who trapped around Cook Mountain and camped on this stream. He started trapping in 1906, working for the USFS in the summers.

Camp Lyon (Owyhee). 4664'. T3S R6W sec 26. Military post 5 mi SW of Captain Butte on the Idaho-Oregon line, on Cow Creek. Established on May 6, 1865, to maintain peace on the routes of emigration across Idaho; not actually located until 27 June 1865. The post consisted of several buildings of hand-hewn logs. In March, 1866, there were three companies of troops stationed here.

Named after a slain military officer, Brigadier General Nathaniel Lyon, who was killed at the Civil War Battle of Wilsons Creek, Missouri, on 10 Aug 1861.

Camp Three Forks (Owyhee). T8S R6W sec 22. Military post on the SW slope of South Mountain on Soldier Creek near the Idaho-Oregon line. Camp Three Forks was established in 1866 to guard the road to California. In the early 1870s the United States government sold the entire installation for nine cents an acre.

It was named because of its proximity to the three forks of the Owyhee River.

Campbell's Ferry (Idaho). T25N R9E sec 22. In the S central part of the county; River of No Return Wilderness.

Named for William Campbell, who ran the ferry across the Salmon River on the trail to Thunder Mountain in 1902, when the mining camp was booming.

Campbell Flat (Idaho). T27N R1E sec 10/11. Situated on the E bank of Salmon River 5 mi S of White Bird.

Bill Campbell owned a ranch on this site and raised hay for his cattle until his death in the early 1920s.

Campbells Hot Springs (Washington). T11N R6W sec 16. Six mi W of Weiser, in the foothills. These two springs supply a pool for swimming; one is hot and the other cold.

Leno Campbell was born near here in 1882, his family having settled earlier.

Canal Gulch Creek (Clearwater). T36N R5E sec 2. Just N of Pierce. Flows S into Orofino Creek; Clearwater River drainage.

First known use was by E. D. Pierce, on his discovery of gold in the gulch in 1860. Canals, or ditches, brought water for use in placer mining; a canal from this creek later led around and above the town of Pierce.

Canary Canyon Creek (Bonneville). T1N R44E sec 25. Rises in E Bonneville County and flows 4 mi W into Palisades Creek; Snake River drainage.

Named for the American goldfinch, of the canary family, common to the area.

Canfield (Idaho). 3800'. T29N R1E sec 17. In the NW part of the county, 12 mi NW of White Bird.

Founded in 1890 by Oscar F. Canfield to serve stockmen.

Named for the Oscar F. Canfield family—perhaps officially for Mrs. Canfield, since she was the first postmaster.

Canfield Buttes (Kootenai). 4162'/3967'. T51N R3W sec 28/29. In the central part of the county, 2 mi S of Hayden Lake and 3.5 mi NE of Coeur d'Alene. These buttes, about 1 mi apart, serve as good viewpoints of the area.

Named for a local family.

Canyon County. County seat, Caldwell. Created from a portion of Ada County by an act of the State Legislature 7 March 1891. Located in SW Idaho, with the Snake River as its western and southern boundary. The Boise River furnishes irrigation water throughout the central and southern portions. Owyhee County lies to the S; Ada County to the E; Payette and Gem counties to the N; Oregon to the W.

Current sources attribute the name to the canyon of the Boise River near Caldwell. However, both John Rees and Vardis Fisher believed it was named for the Snake River Canyon, which forms a natural boundary for the county.

Canyon Creek (Madison/Teton). T7N R42E sec 23. Rises in the Black Hole Mountains in Teton County and flows about 26 mi generally NW and N to empty into the Teton River at the Fremont-Madison county line. Canyon Creek Butte (6121') is an isolated promontory 3 mi E of Canyon Creek, for which it is named.

Named in 1872 by Dr. F. V. Hayden of the US Geological Survey for its major feature, a deep gorge that intersects the Teton River Canyon.

Canyon Creek (Madison). T6N R42E sec 6. Community in the E part of the county on Canyon Creek, 3 mi E of Newdale; an agricultural area. The settlement began in 1900 and became a half-way station for freighters, 1901-1920. Post office, 1909-1926.

Canyon Creek (Elmore). T5S R4E. Rises W of Long Tom Reservoir at the confluence of Syrup and Long Tom creeks at an altitude of 4000'. It flows 35 mi SE to empty into the Snake River at an altitude of 2368'; drainage, 265 square miles, deeply entrenched, with a drop of as much as 164' a mile.

Cape Horn (Bonner). T54N R1W sec 30. Cape on Lake Pend Oreille, 3 mi SW of the town of Cedar Creek; 2 1/2 mi NW of Lakeview. Cape Horn Creek heads on the NW side of Cape Horn Peak and flows 3/4 mi SW into Old Maid Creek, 4 3/4 mi ESE of Careywood. Cape Horn Peak (4519'), 4 mi SW of the town of Cedar Creek and 3 3/4 mi NW of Lakeview.

The name Cape Horn derives from the Cape Horn at the southern tip of South America, applied to the cape on Lake Pend Oreille and transferred to the nearby creek and peak, as well as to the Custer County formation independently.

Cape Horn (Custer). 9500'. T12N R10E sec 2. Mountain situated NW of Stanley near the W boundary between Custer and Valley counties. Cape Horn Summit lies 2 mi SW of Cape Horn Mountain.

Capitan, El (Blaine). 9901'. T7N R13E sec 16. Peak located 11 mi SSW of Obsidian, near Lake Alice. Named for El Capitan in Yosemite National Park, which it resembles.

Captain Butte (Owyhee). T3S R5W sec 16. Three mi NE of Camp Lyon. Sergeant Denoile, who was attached to Camp Lyon, was taking his pregnant wife to Fort Boise, accompanied by another soldier and the driver of the ambulance wagon. Near this site the party was ambushed and Denoile was killed. Mrs. Denoile was taken alive. Later the body of a white woman, who had been scalped and disemboweled, and a mutilated body of an unborn baby were found in an Indian camp.

Some people attribute the name to this incident, others to its proximity to Camp Lyon.

Captain John Creek (Nez Perce). T32N R5W sec 35. Flows W into the Snake River.

This creek was named after a Nez Perce Indian who was a follower of Chief

Lawyer and a headman of a small village on the E side of the Snake River S of Lewiston. In 1861 individual Indians began to sell reservation land. Captain John was called Jokais (worthless) by the other Indians because he sold so much land. He acted as a scout for General O. O. Howard during the Nez Perce War of 1877.

Captain Pauls Hot Springs (Owyhee). T6S R2W. On Upper Castle Creek.

Named after Joseph Paul, known as "Captain Paul," who had a ranch and maintained a toll road in this area. Many of the miners from Silver City came to the springs to bathe in hope of curing their rheumatism.

Carbon Creek (Shoshone). T48N R5E sec 7. In the E part of the county 4 mi NE of Wallace. Post office, 1889-1890.

Named for the coal deposits in its drainage.

Carbonate (Shoshone). 2900'. T47N R5E sec 1. In the E part of the county, 7 mi E of Wallace. A mining camp; post office, 1917-1920.

Named for the Carbonate Hill mine at the campsite.

Carbonate (Custer). An early mining community and post office that was later consolidated with Houston to become Mackay. Post office, 1884-1885.

Named for the Carbonate mine.

Cardiff (Clearwater). T37N R5E sec 3. Town 5 mi N of Pierce.

Named for Leonard Cardiff, a sawmill operator.

Carey (Blaine). 4750'. T1S R21E sec 27. In the central part of the county, on the Little Wood River, 35 mi W of Craters of the Moon; an agricultural area. Town established in 1884.

Named for the first postmaster, James Carey.

Careywood (Bonner). T54N R3W sec 12. Town 4 1/4 mi NE of Kelso; 5 mi S of Cocolalla. Careywood Creek rises 2 1/4 mi NW of Cape Horn Peak and flows W and slightly NE to Lake Cocolalla.

This town was first known as King's Spur. In 1907 a post office was built here, and the name was changed to Severance. Shortly afterward, a man named Carey bought a great deal of land in the area, and the name was changed to Careywood.

Caribel (Idaho). T34N R4E sec 34. In the NW part of the county on Tomtaha Creek, 17 mi NE of Kamiah.

Settled by the Huffman family and named for Mrs. Claribelle Huffman. The Rawson Lumber Company built a sawmill town on this site when lumber in the Gregg area became scarce. This town thrived for a while, with a post office and a school. Later it was acquired by the Western States Lumber Company, with a plan to build a large flume to carry lumber from Caribel to the old point of operations on the Clearwater River. The town died when the mill was moved to the river.

Caribou City (Bonneville). 6900'. T4S R44E sec 2. Ghost town in SE Bonneville County in the Caribou Range. Caribou Basin trends 6.3 mi NW to SE just S of Caribou City. Caribou Mountain (9805'), 2 mi W of the city and 3 mi E of Grays Lake, marks the culmination of the Caribou Range. Formerly Mount Pisgah.

Formerly known as Iowa Bar (1889), later as Cariboo City, and after 1920 as Caribou City. It may also have been called Keenan at one time.

Caribou Range. T2S R42E to T4S R44E. Extends across the SE part of the county, NW to SE. One of the larger ranges of the Idaho-Wyoming chain, exceeds 50 mi in length, 15 mi in width;

lies S of and parallels the Big Hole Mountains; bounded by S Fk Snake River on the N, by the Snake River Plain on the W, by the outlet of Grays Lake on the S, and by Star Valley in Wyoming on the E.

Named for Cariboo Fairchild, who had taken part in the gold rush in the Cariboo region of British Columbia in 1860. He discovered gold in this region two years later.

Caribou County. County seat, Soda Springs. Created from the E side of Bannock County in 1919, the last county in Idaho to be created; named for the Caribou Mountains, which in turn are named for Cariboo Fairchild.

The county is rich in phosphate and sulphur deposits, and the mountains in the E half are timbered. Mountainous terrain, slopes lined with creeks with valleys and canyons between, characterizes all the county except the extreme N portion. The Blackfoot, Portneuf, and Bear rivers drain most of the county.

Bounded on the N by Bingham and Bonneville counties, on the E by Wyoming, on the S by Bear Lake and Franklin counties, on the W by Bannock County.

Caribou Creek (Bonner). T63N R4W sec 4. Rises in the hills and ridges of NE Bonner Co. and flows SW approximately 9 mi into Thorofare 1 mi N of Tule Bay. Caribou Hill lies about 1 mi NW of the headwaters of Caribou Creek.

Named for the mountain caribou. The name Caribou appears on several creeks and other topographical features in this county, evidence of the presence of caribou at one time throughout the county.

Caribou Creek (Kootenai). T49N R3W sec 12. Rises W of Beauty Creek Campground and flows NE to Beauty Creek; Coeur d'Alene River drainage.

Named for the Caribou mine, at its mouth.

Carl Gulch (Lemhi). T25N R21E sec 22. Heads N of Bills Canyon and runs NW 1 mi to enter N Fk Salmon River drainage near North Fork Ranger Station.

H. F. Carl, A. Carl, and Charles Carl had a bonanza placer claim in this area that they located in 1888. They also had a ranch here.

Carlin Bay (Kootenai). T48/49N R3W sec 6/31. In the S part of the county on the E side of Coeur d'Alene Lake.

Carlin Creek, a 4.5-mi stream rising on Carrill Peak (4098') and flowing about 5 mi NW, empties into Carlin Bay. A small village grew up at this point and once had a grange and a post office (1903-1965).

Named for General Carlin, US Army.

Carlin Creek (Benewah). T45N R2W sec 20. Rises 6 1/2 mi SW of St. Maries and flows 3 1/4 mi SE to St. Maries River.

Named for the Carlin family, who homesteaded on this stream.

Carlin Creek (Lemhi). T24N R22E sec 17. Flows SW 2 1/2 mi to enter Cottonwood Creek; 14 mi N of Salmon; N Fk Salmon River drainage.

A man named Carlin, an early stockman in this area, brought in 200-300 head of Texas longhorns in the 1870s to start a herd; they were all winter-killed.

Carmen Creek (Lemhi). T22N R22E sec 8. Heads on the Idaho-Montana border and flows SW 11 mi to enter the Salmon River 1/8 mi N of Carmen.

Carmen. 3290'. T22N R22E sec 17. Town established in the 1890s; Post office, 1902-1965.

Named for Benjamin Carmen, who built a sawmill on the stream in the 1870s, or for his wife, Martha.

Lewis and Clark named the stream Salmon Creek on 31 August 1805 because of the number of salmon they found here. In 1832 Captain B. L. E. Bonneville erected a temporary fortification on the stream. Also Carman Creek.

Carpenter Creek (Boise). T8N R5E sec 8. Flows 3 mi SW into the S Fk Payette River 1 1/4 mi W of Grimes Pass.

Nazaire Carpentier, a French immigrant, homesteaded land around the creek in 1867 and left in 1900. Mapmakers changed the name to Carpenter.

Carpenter/Little Carpenter Creek (Benewah). T43N R1E sec 5. Rises on Carpenter Mountain (4400') in SE Benewah County and flows about 8 1/2 mi generally NE to the St. Maries River; Little Carpenter Creek, about 5 1/2 mi long, is the main tributary.

Marshal and Erastus Carpenter settled near this creek by 1891.

Carr Creek (Bonner). T57N R3W sec 26. Heads 3 1/2 mi ENE of Johnny Long Mountain; flows 3 mi S into the Pend Oreille River 5 1/2 mi WSW of Sandpoint.

Named for Carey Carr, who lived near the area in 1888.

Carrie Creek (Camas). T3N R14E sec 35. Stream 7 mi long, flows SW to Little Smokey Creek 14 mi N of Fairfield.

Carrietown (Camas). 6950'. T3N R15E sec 8. Ghost town in SE Camas County, on the Camas-Blaine county line on Carrie Creek; S Fk Boise River drainage.

Named for the Carrie Leonard mine.

Carrol Creek (Lemhi). T16N R23E sec 21. Heads 1 1/2 mi NW of Mogg Mountain and flows N 2 mi to W Fk Hayden Creek; 12 mi SW of Lemhi; Lemhi River drainage.

Carrol Pyeatt lived in this vicinity; John Carroll was an early rancher and miner (ca. 1898) in this same area. Also Carol Creek.

Carter Creek (Bonner). T56N R2E sec 6. Heads 3 1/4 mi E of Hope; flows 2 mi SW to a point 2 3/4 mi NNE of Sheepherder Point.

Named for a man who lived near the creek.

Cartwright Creek (Boise). T6N R2E sec 24. Rises in the extreme SW part of the county near Castle Rock and flows 4 1/2 mi SW into Shafer Creek; Payette River drainage.

Named for homesteader George Cartwright.

Carver Creek (Idaho). T25N R1E sec 14. Salmon River tributary.

Named for Warren miner Amos Carver.

Cary Creek (Lemhi). T22N R23E sec 34. Flows 2 mi SW to Geertson Creek, 6 1/2 mi NE of Carmen; Salmon River drainage.

Named for Cary Wright, a native of Virginia, who placer mined on this stream in the 1870s.

Cascade (Valley). 4790'. T14N R3E sec 25. County seat. Located 1/2 mi from the dam and reservoir in the SW part of the county on the N Fk Payette River, in the S end of Long Valley. Founded in 1912 by the consolidation of Van Wyck, Thunder City, and Crawford.

Named for the Cascade Falls on N Fk Payette River. What was a spectacular cascade at the time of naming is now mostly obscured by Cascade Reservoir.

Cascade Creek (Bonner). T56N R2E sec 25. Heads 1 3/4 mi SSW of Scotchman Peak; flows 1 1/4 mi WNW, 3/4 mi SW, then 3/4 mi NW into Lightning Creek 2 1/2 mi NNE of Clark Fork.

Named for the way the stream tumbles down from the mountain.

Casner Creek (Boise). T9N R9E sec 14. Rises on Eightmile Mountain (7871') in the NE part of the county and flows 4 mi S into the S Fk Payette River. Pronounced KES-ner.

Named for Joseph Casner, an 1870 settler.

Cassel Gulch (Lemhi). T24N R22E sec 29. Runs 1 mi W to Fourth of July Creek drainage; Salmon River drainage.

Named for a rancher, Field Cassel, who had a small place at the mouth of the gulch. Was once known locally as Thrasher Gulch, after Danial B. Thrasher, who planted an orchard here and patented the land in 1914.

Cassia County. County seat, Burley. Established by the Idaho Territorial Legislature in Feb 1879; created from parts of Oneida and Owyhee counties; later reduced in 1913 by the creation of Twin Falls Power counties.

It was named for Cassia Creek, which in turn was named for one of two words: *cajeaux*, peasant French for raft; or for James John Cazier, member of the LDS Church and of the Mormon Battalion (discharged in July 1847), later a colorful captain of an emigrant train. Addison Pratt, a member of an emigrant train, recorded on 15 Sept 1848, "encamped on Cazier, a stream abounding in trout," identified as the company passed City of Rocks. Another diary described it as emptying into one of the large tributaries of the Columbia River. The only large stream in that area is Cassia Creek, spelled Cassier in 1879. Albion, the first permanent settlement, was chosen as county seat.

Bounded on the N by Jerome, Minidoka, and Blaine counties; on the N and E by Power County, on the E by Oneida County, on the S by Utah and Nevada, on the W by Twin Falls County.

Cassia Creek (Cassia). T12S R26E sec 25. Rises on Albion Mountain and flows 19 mi NE to Raft River 4 mi N of Malta.

It is the compiler's belief that it was named for the colorful Frenchman, James John Cazier, whose name was corrupted to Cassia. Locally there is a belief that it derived from the name of a plant.

Castle Butte (Idaho). 6660'. T36N R10E sec 28. In the N central part of the county, between Lochsa River and the Lolo Trail.

Named because of the castle-like shape of the summit of the butte.

Castle Creek (Lemhi). T17N R17E sec 16. Originates in the vicinity of Woods Peak and flows generally W 8 mi to enter Camas Creek; Middle Fk Salmon River drainage.

Named because of a nearby rock formation that looks somewhat like an old castle.

Castle Peak (Custer). 11,815'. T8N R16E sec 9. One of the White Cloud Peaks, at the S end of the range; at the head of Little Boulder Creek in the Challis National Forest and Chamberlain Creek in the Sawtooth National Forest.

Named for immense projections of granite above the timberline, which suggest the towers of a castle.

Castleford (Twin Falls). 3866'. T10S R13/14E sec 25/36. In the NW part of the county, 9 mi SW of Buhl.

Town named for an early crossing on Salmon Falls Creek, because of the obelisks of rhyolite at that point. Used by pioneers as a ford in 1849, it became a famous crossing on the Kelton-Dalles stage route.

Castro Creek (Boise). T10N R9E sec 10. Rises in the NE extremity of the county and flows 4 mi SW into Eightmile Creek, 3 mi S of Red Mountain Lakes; Payette River drainage.

Named for Juan Castro, a Basque sheepherder who worked in this area.

Cat Creek (Lemhi). T21N R20E sec 6. One mi long, flows W to Napias Creek, near California Bar; Salmon River drainage.

Named for the numerous bobcats found in this area.

Cataldo (Kootenai). 2142'. T49N R1E sec 34. In the N part of eastern Kootenai County, on I-90 and the Coeur d'Alene River. Famous for the Coeur d'Alene Mission of the Sacred Heart, or Old Mission, which was built nearby (1848) and is the oldest building in Idaho.

Cataldo Mountain (4124') lies 3 mi N of Old Mission; and Cataldo Flats extend 4 mi along Coeur d'Alene River S of the mountain.

Named for Father Joseph Cataldo, who came to work among the Coeur d'Alenes in 1865 and founded missions at Lapwai and Lewiston, 1867.

Caterpillar Hill (Latah). T41N R1E sec 29. A high, massive hill NE of Bovill, where most of the logging was done by a combination of steam donkeys and Caterpillar tractors. The rough slopes of this hill during the logging days of 1916-18 and for many years thereafter were called Caterpillar Hill.

Cathedral Peak (Shoshone). 4925'. T53N R3E sec 7/18. In the NW part of the county, 14 mi E of Lakeview. East Cathedral Peak lies 1.5 mi E and Cathedral Creek rises on the peak and flows 6 mi S to Coeur d'Alene River.

Named for Cathedral Rocks, 1.3 mi S of the peaks.

Name derived from the configuration of the promontory.

Cathedral Rock (Lemhi). 9411'. T21N R16E sec 24. Rock formation about 1/2 mi NW of Cathedral Lake, in Bighorn Crags, Salmon National Forest. A second Cathedral Rock (7786') is located on the Idaho-Montana border 8 mi NE of Squaw Creek. Cathedral Lake lies 1/2 mi SE of Cathedral Rock and 1 mi NW of Golden Trout Lake. A second Cathedral Lake is located 2 1/2 mi SW of Deer Lake.

Named for the appearance of the rock spires, weathered and eroded to resemble a cathedral.

Catherine Creek (Owyhee). T4S R2E sec 18. Flows 8 mi NE into Castle Creek; Snake River. Named after a girl from Silver City. See Hurry Back Creek. There is a theory that it was named well before Silver City was in existence, but no documentation of this has been found. In the middle 1860s it was called Middle River by some people; it was crossed by the south alternate of the Oregon trail.

Catrock (Washington). T11N R4W sec 9/10. A very early community just S of the Weiser River, 4 mi E of Weiser.

Named for a large rock at this site that looks like a cat.

Cattle Creek (Bonneville). T1S R40E sec 11. Rises in S central Bonneville County and flows 3 1/2 mi SW into Grays Lake Outlet; Grays Lake drainage.

Cattle graze along this stream.

Cattle Creek (Owyhee). Flows NW into Oregon into the Owyhee River.

Many cattle were brought into the area in 1860 and cattle raising is still a major industry.

Cavanaugh Bay (Bonner). T60N R4W sec 23. On Priest Lake, 9 mi SE of Nordman, 4 mi NNE of Coolin.

Named for the Cavanaughs, who settled here prior to 1904.

Cave Creek (Clearwater). T39N R7E sec 26. Rises on Cave Point (4588') in the central part of the county and flows 4 mi SW into N Fk Clearwater River.

Named for holes in the rock ledges about 1 1/4 mi from the river.

Cave Creek (Lemhi). T18N R15E sec 14. Heads near origin of Soda Creek and runs S 2 1/2 mi to enter Camas Creek; Salmon River drainage.

There is a large cave at the mouth of the creek, used as shelter by travelers in stormy weather; Salmon River drainage.

Cavendish (Clearwater). 2400'. T37N R1W sec 11. Town 4 mi N of Ahsahka.

The town was established in the early 1860s on the old trail to a settlement in the Pierce area known as Snell's Mill. In 1886 E. A. Snell established a post office and named it Cavendish for Cavendish, Vermont.

Cayuse Creek (Clearwater). T39N R11E sec 24. Rises in the extreme SE part of the county in Lost Lakes and flows 21 mi W, then 7 mi NE into Kelly Creek; Clearwater River drainage. Cayuse Lake and Cayuse Junction lie 3 mi S of Blacklead Mountain.

Frank Altmiller, USFS in Clearwater NF before 1960, found an Indian pony on the stream and named the creek Cayuse—a term for a western range horse.

Cearley Creek (Custer). Stream 1.5 mi long, flows WSW to Yankee Fork 5.2 mi N of Sunbeam; Salmon River drainage.

Named for James Cearley, Sr. (d. 1902), pioneer and miner who moved to this area in 1880.

Cedar. Cedar as a place name occurs in many areas, always where there is now or has been a grove of cedar trees.

Cedar Butte (Jefferson). Early name for Menan, which see.

Cedar Buttes (Power). T9S R29E sec 1. In the SE part of the county on the N side of Snake River; 9 mi W and 5 mi S of American Falls. These inconspicuous buttes are of the lava-dome type. From their vents lava flowed W, N, and S, filling the old channel of Snake River for 20 mi from below Bonanza Bar N to Aberdeen. The old channel lies 7-8 mi NW of the present channel at American Falls.

Cedar Creek (Clearwater). T36N R3E sec 9. Flows SW into Orofino Creek at T36N R3E sec 9; Clearwater River drainage.

There are three other Cedar Creeks in Clearwater County, tributaries of Elk Creek, Little N Fk Clearwater, and Clearwater River; Old Cedars settlement is 10 mi N of Kelly Creek Work Center, Clearwater NF.

Cedar Creek (Latah). T38N R2W sec 11. SE tributary of Potlatch River in SE part of Latah County; flows 3 mi NW and empties into the river; the southern boundary of Cedar Ridge.

Cedar Ridge. T38N R1/2W. A once heavily populated ridge about 4 mi long and 2 mi wide lying between Boulder Creek, Cedar Creek, and the Potlatch River in the SE part of Latah County; called Cedar Creek Ridge by local residents.

Cedar Creek (Latah). T42N R6W sec 6. Rises on the SW slope of Mission Mountain and flows 6 mi SW into Washington State to empty into the Palouse River.

Cedar Creek. T42N R5W sec 5/6. A pioneer community in the NW corner of Latah County along the banks of Cedar Creek, in existence before 1900.

Cedar Creek (Twin Falls). T11S R14E sec 30. In the SW part of the county. Rises in the mountains close to Nevada at an altitude of 6500′ and flows NW through Cedar Creek Reservoir to empty into Salmon Falls Creek S of Castleford. It is 30 mi long and drains 220 square miles.

Cedar Point (Bingham). 4977′. T2S R38E sec 28/33. An early 1880s settlement on or near Cedar Creek in the SE part of the county.

Most of the settlers were Mormons from Utah, previously from England, Scotland, Wales, and the Scandinavian countries. They were farmers who upon their coming immediately set about diverting water from the Snake and Blackfoot rivers for irrigation.

Cedarhill (Oneida). T13S R32E sec 29/28. In the SW part of the county, in the Sawtooth National Forest; 7 mi NW of Holbrook. Settled about 1880. Post office, 1880-1965.

Appeared as Cedar Mountain on Rand, McNally Pocket Map of Idaho, 1898.

Variant names: Cedar Butte, Cedar Mountain.

Cedars (Twin Falls). 3760′. T10S R21E sec 29. In the NE part of the county; .5 mi E of Milner Dam. Wilson Price Hunt's party of Astorians camped here in 1811 on their way west from Pierre's Hole. Named by this party for the cedar trees growing here at the time, the only trees for miles around, and now gone.

Later emigrants and travelers crossed the river at this point to the north-side alternate of the Oregon Trail. This is also the point at which Twin Falls-area pioneer farmer I. B. Perrine forded the Snake River to deliver his produce to Albion.

Also called The Cedars and later Milner.

Cedarville (Butte). T7N R27E sec 8. Ghost town about 10 mi N of Howe on the E side of Spring Creek. Residents of this settlement worked the Daisy Black mines. Cedarville Canyon extends 5 mi SE and NE to 4 mi from the mining ghost town.

Cedron (Teton). T4N R45E sec 31. Farming community about 3 mi NW of Victor on Trail Creek.

This is a Mormon settlement, begun in 1888 W of the first Trail Creek locators, but the name did not appear until 1911, in the Teton Valley News (Driggs).

Named for the brook that flows through the Garden of Gethsemane.

Cemetery Ridge (Shoshone). T46/47N R3E sec 2,3/34-36. In the W part of the county, 6 mi SW of Wallace in the Coeur d'Alene Mountains; near Big Creek.

Eighteen fire fighters were killed in the 1910 fire a short distance to the N of this point. The bodies were removed to the ridge and temporarily buried, thus the name.

Center Camp Corrals (Boise). T10N R6E sec 28/29.

Probably named by a Mr. McCloud, who had sheep corrals here.

Center Mountain (Lemhi). T22N R24E sec 17/18/19/20. On the corner of four sections near the head of Bohannon Creek on the Idaho-Montana border.

Named for its position in the corners of four sections.

Center Star Mountain (Idaho). T29N R7E sec 34. A prominent three-peak mountain S of S Fk Clearwater River and 7 mi N of Orogrande; in a mining district.

Center Star mine was opened in 1909 on the slopes of this mountain, but it has not been determined whether the name of the mine or that of the mountain came first.

Centerville (Boise). T7N R5E sec 29. A ghost town in the SE part of the county on Grimes Creek. New Centerville lies 2 mi SE.

Centerville was a mining camp founded November, 1862, and a post office (1864-1931). Named by Muford, Standifer, Calloway, and Thatcher because it was halfway between Idaho City and Placerville. When the mines at Centerville seemed to play out, many of its residents relocated at Old Boston, which they renamed New Centerville.

Central (Caribou). 5564'. T9S R40E sec 17/20. In the SW part of the county, 11 mi W of Soda Springs.

Settled in 1895 and named for its central location in Gentile Valley.

Cerro Grande (Bingham). 4650'. T1N R30E sec 3. A grazing area in the NW extremity of the county on the UPRR, just W of the lava beds. Settled in 1910; post office, 1918-1924.

Cerro Grande means "big hill."

Chadville (Franklin). T15S R38E sec 23. Early name for Dayton, which see.

Chair Creek (Idaho). T25N R1E sec 26. Salmon River tributary from the E.

The old-timer who lived on this creek in the 1880s built himself a chair in which to await the mail stage; hence the name.

Challis (Custer). 5283'. T14N R19E sec 28/32. County seat. Situated in the center of the county and surrounded by the Salmon River Range on the W and N; Pahsimeroi Mountains on the E; Sawtooth Mountains on the S; and canyons of the Salmon River on both S and N.

Founded in 1878 and connected to Custer by a toll road, Challis became a trading center for the mining interest in Stanley Basin, Yankee Fork, Loon Creek, and Bayhorse.

Named for Alvan P. Challis, surveyor when Challis townsite was laid out. The name was transferred to several nearby features.

Challis Hot Springs is 2 1/2 mi E of Challis on the Salmon River; formerly Beardsley Springs.

Chamberlain Creek (Clearwater). T41N R10E sec 1. Rises on Chamberlain Mountain (6614') in the NE part of the county and flows 3 mi NE into Vanderbilt Gulch; Clearwater River drainage. Chamberlain Meadows lie 1 1/2 mi N of the mountain and 14 mi N of Kelly Forks Ranger Station.

Named for an early-day prospector and trapper.

Chamberlain Creek (Idaho). T24N R12E sec 1. Stream 30 mi long, heads at the junction of Rim and S Fk Chamberlain creeks, flows NE to Salmon River 18 mi SSE of Dixie.

Named for John Chamberlain, reported to be the first settler in the area in the late 1880s, a beaver trapper along the stream as late as 1895. Chamberlain Basin, once populated by moose, is now an elk calving ground.

Chamberlain Creek (Lemhi). T14N R28E sec 35. Forms on the Idaho- Montana border; flows 52 mi, then W 2 mi just NE of Walters Spring, in Beaverhead Mountains; Salmon National Forest.

Named for George Chamberlain, one of the original discoverers of the Copper Queen mine.

Chambers (Latah). T41N R4W sec 1. An early community and post office in Chambers Flat area, near present-day Princeton.

Named for the first postmaster, Matthew T. Chambers, an early homesteader.

Chambers Mill Lookout (Latah). T39N R1W sec 24. In St. Joe Forest midway between Boulder and Three Bears creeks in SE Latah County. Chambers Creek rises on the E slope of this promontory and flows 3.1 mi SE to

Three Bear Creek; Clearwater River drainage.

Named after John I. and C. C. Chambers, early settlers on the creek.

Champagne Creek (Butte). T3N R25E sec 5. Rises just S of the ghost town of Era and flows S and SE for about 9 mi, then terminates in a lava bed.

The original homesteader at the mouth of the creek called the water champagne. This creek was known as Era Creek during the mining period, 1880s and early 1890s, but has been called Champagne Creek since about 1895.

Champagne Spring (Caribou). T9S R41E sec 12. One of the favorite tourist spots at Soda Springs.

Named because of the effervescence of the water.

Chaney Gulch (Boise). T7N R4E sec 11. A 1-mi gulch trending SW into Woof Creek at Placerville; Boise River drainage.

S. M. Chaney and his family located a claim on this gulch, 1860s.

Chaparral Hollow/Creek (Bonneville). T1S R43E sec 26 to T2S R44E sec 5. Extends 5 1/2 mi NW to SE in the Caribou Range just W of Palisades Reservoir. The creek empties into Bear Creek; Snake River drainage.

The name is descriptive of thick brush common to the area; a Spanish word.

Chapin (Teton). 6151'. T4N R45E sec 26. Early settlement situated 2 mi N of Victor on Fox Creek; dates from 1880s and 1890s; called Fox, 1892-96.

B. W. Driggs says the name came from a man in the US Post Office who wanted to honor himself. It is more likely named for a Mr. Chapin, early trapper and mountaineer in the area.

Charcoal Creek (Boise). T7N R5E sec 10. Flows generally NW to Clear Creek

1 mi S of Placerville; Boise River drainage.

A charcoal kiln on this creek supplied the residents of Placerville.

Charcoal Gulch (Boise). T6N R5E sec 34. A 2-mi gulch trending 2 mi S into Mores Creek 1 mi SW of Idaho City; Boise River drainage.

Site of the Kelly store, whose owner also made charcoal for local blacksmiths.

Charley Creek (Clearwater). T40N R6E sec 13. In the N central part of the county. Flows 2 mi NW into Beaver Creek; Clearwater River drainage.

Charlie Brooks lived on this stream.

Charters Mountain (Boise). T8N R4E sec 17.

Named for William (Scotty) Charters and his family, 1875 settlers near the mountain. He had previously been a miner near Idaho City.

Chas. Johnson Mill (Clearwater). T37N R4E sec 13. Settlement 6 mi NE of Pierce. Named for Charlie Johnson, the mill operator. He was sometimes called "Gin Pole" Johnson, since he used a gin pole operated by horse power to load logs.

Chase Lake (Bonner). T59N R4W sec 14/23. Located 9 3/4 mi E of Idaho-Washington border; 1 3/4 mi SSE of Coolin.

The lake was named for Pete Chase, an early squatter, miner, and moonshiner.

Chatcolet (Benewah). T46/47N R4W sec 36. Town at the S end of Coeur d'Alene Lake in the Coeur d'Alene National Forest in N part of the county. On the site of an old Indian campground, later appropriated by French trappers; an outlaw hideout, 1863-70.

Lake Chatcolet. A body of water on the S end of Coeur d'Alene Lake. At low water its average depth is 14' and it covers about 1200 acres. One of the three lakes that become one in high water; the other two are Benewah and Hidden.

The name is reportedly Coeur d'Alene for "place where animals are trapped."

Chateau Rock (Clearwater). 5670'. T39N R8E sec 31. Mountain 3 mi N of the Bungalow Ranger Station, in the central part of E Clearwater County. Chateau Creek rises on this mountain and flows 2 1/2 mi NW into Cave Creek; Clearwater River drainage.

The rock atop the mountain resembles a house or castle.

Cheney Creek (Lemhi). T20N R23E sec 16. E of Joe Moore Creek; originates 1 mi NW of K Mountain and flows N 2 mi, then NW 1 mi to enter Withington Creek, 11 mi SE of Salmon; Salmon River drainage.

Named for John Cheney, who settled here around 1890.

Chenoweth, Mount (Shoshone). T45N R6E sec 25. In the S central part of the county, 8 mi SE of Avery in St. Joe National Forest; between Allen Creek and Prospector Creek about 1.5 mi S of St. Joe River.

Named in 1944 for Professor C. W. Chenoweth, University of Idaho, who was active in various civic projects.

Cherry Butte (Latah). 3763'. T40N R2W sec 13. Two mi E of Potato Hill and NE of Deary.

Named for the chokecherries that once grew on the slopes of this butte.

Cherry Creek (Camas). T2N R15E sec 36. Rises near the Camas-Blaine county line in the Smoky Mountains and flows 4 1/2 mi SW to Willow Creek, tributary of Camas Creek; Big Wood River drainage.

Wild cherries or chokecherries grew in the foothills of the area.

Cherry Creek (Custer). T4N R24E sec 2. NW tributary of Antelope Creek; heads in Challis National Forest, Lost River Division, and flows SE; Lost River drainage.

Named for Zephaniah V. T. Cherry, who in 1916 packed mail once a week to Hailey, Vienna, and Galena.

Cherry Creek (Lemhi). T19N R24E sec 12. Forms 1 1/4 mi N of First Basin Spring and flows E parallel to Haynes Creek for 3 mi, to enter Lemhi River, about 2 mi S of the mouth of Haynes Creek and 2 1/2 mi N of Tendoy; Lemhi River drainage. Cherry Spring is 2 mi SW of the mouth of the creek and 2 mi W of Tendoy.

Named for the chokecherries found along the creek and around the spring.

Chesley (Nez Perce). 3465'. T35N R2W sec 26. Early community located 3 1/2 mi S of Lookout, 8 mi N of Reubens in the W part of the county.

Oscar B. Chesley founded this community in 1899. He established a general store and ran a way station. The town developed into a sawmill town with a population of more than 200 and with considerable trade until the Camas Prairie RR was built.

Chesley Creek (Latah). T42N R3W sec 9. Rises between headwaters of Big and E Fk Big creeks and flows 2 mi SW to Big Creek, Palouse River drainage.

Named by W. H. Daugs, USFS ranger, after Edward J. Chesley, a homesteader and surveyor for Potlatch Lumber Company before 1890. Appears on 1966 and 1977 St. Joe National Forest Maps as Chelsey Creek; on USGS quadrangle maps and in the Idaho Geographic Names, 1983, as Chesley Creek.

Chester (Fremont). 5068'. T8N R41E sec 24/25. Town 6 mi NE of St. Anthony; settled by pioneers from Utah in the late 1880s, with a post office in 1894.

Formerly Fall River, for its proximity to that river, the name of this settlement was changed to Chester by the Post Office Department.

Chesterfield (Caribou). 5454'. T6S R39E sec 28. In the NW part of the county, 9 mi N of Bancroft. In the early 1870s Chester Call and Christian Nelson, his nephew, from Bountiful, Utah, found this place while searching for grazing land for their horses. Call persuaded 12 families to return with him to make a new settlement. Post office, 1893-1965.

Named by William B. Preston for the birthplace of Chester Call, Chesterfield, England.

Chet Rowe Spring (Lemhi). T21N R23E sec 14. Located 3/4 mi SW of Sawmill Gulch Spring, on Bohannon Creek; Salmon River drainage.

Chet Rowe was a rancher near the mouth of the creek.

Chicago (Lewis). T34N R1W sec 31. Former name of Craigmont. One mi W of present site of Craigmont.

The first settlement in the area (1898), Chicago was platted and dedicated in August, 1901, by Frank Vincent.

Named for Chicago, Illinois. See Ilo.

Chicken Creek (Bonneville). T2N R41E sec 27. Flows 1 1/2 mi SW to Meadow Creek, 18 mi E of Idaho Falls; Snake River drainage. Chicken Peak (8409') lies about 18 mi NE of the mouth of Chicken Creek.

Named for the abundance of "chickens," sage hens, once in the area.

Chicken Creek (Camas). T1N R15E sec 9. A stream 2 1/2 mi long, rising SE of Cannonball Mountain and flowing SE to Deer Creek, a tributary of Camas Creek; Big Wood River drainage.

This stream got its name from the flocks of willow grouse, blue grouse, and sage hens here.

Chicken Creek (Clark). T14N R36E sec 33. Rises 1 mi S of the Continental Divide and flows 3 mi SW to Beaver Creek at Humphrey.

Named for the abundant sage hens here until the 1900s. Early settlers reported them to be so prolific that they never had to worry about chicken on the table when unexpected company stopped by.

Chief Joseph Pass (Lemhi). 7241'. T27N R21E sec 13. In the Bitterroot Range, about 1 mi SE of Lost Trail Pass, 25 mi WNW of Wisdom, Montana, and 36 mi N of Salmon, Idaho.

Named for the famous chief of a band of Nez Perce, who in 1877 travelled through this pass on their flight toward Canada.

Chilly (Custer). 6880'. T9N R22E sec 29. Town in the southern part of the county on Highway 93, 17 mi NW of Mackay.

Settled in 1899 by pioneers from Utah; post office, 1903-1934.

Named for the temperatures that reached 30 to 40 degrees below zero.

Chimney Butte (Idaho). 5642'. T36N R9E sec 32. In the N central part of the county, 28 mi E of Weippe. Someone saw a fissure on the butte that resembled a chimney.

Chimney Peak, Chimney Rock, and Chimney Lake are in The Crags, a rugged group of peaks between the Selway and Lochsa rivers.

The lake is named for the Chimney peaks, which is in turn a descriptive name.

Chimney Creek (Camas). T1S R13E sec 32. Rises in a string of lakes in the SW quadrant of the county N of Sheep Point; flows generally SE to Camas Creek; Magic Reservoir, Big Wood River drainage.

Named for a tumbled-down chimney along this stream, evidence of attempts at settlement before the area was opened in 1877.

Chimney/Chimney Rock (Boundary). 7136'. T61N R3W sec 26. Located E of Priest Lake.

This pinnacle divides three glacial cirques. Chimney itself rises some 200' above its base.

China Butte (Owyhee). T5S R4/3W sec 24. In the Silver City area.

Chinese wood choppers worked here during the gold rush, hence the name.

China Creek (Idaho). T26N R1E sec 34. Flows SE into Salmon River.

Many Chinese were among the early settlers of Lewiston, attracted by the rich placer diggings of the adjacent gold fields. In the 1870s there were 1500 Chinese living in Lewiston, but by 1885 many of them had gone to other mining areas and only 400 remained. The creek was probably named for the large groups of Chinese who carried on their mining operations along this creek.

China Creek (Boise). T7N R7E sec 3. Flows SE into Beaver Creek; Boise River drainage.

Named for the Chinese, who mined the area after the white men abandoned it.

China Fork (Boise). T7N R4E sec 11. Flows 3 1/2 mi SE into Woof Creek; Boise River drainage.

Chinese worked this creek heavily after the white men left it; there was a small Chinese settlement here.

China Garden Creek (Nez Perce). T31N R5W sec 25. Flows SW to Snake River. Variant name: Garden Creek.

The name is derived from the Chinese placer mining along the creek. Chinese also had gardens at the mouth of the creek and raised vegetables to sell to other placer miners.

China Gulch (Lemhi). T24N R19E sec 30. Heads 1 mi N of Stormy Peak, runs W to enter the Salmon River, 1/4 mi NE of Shoup.

Named for a Chinese who reportedly built a hut here.

China Gulch (Owyhee). T4S R4W sec 34. Located 1/2 mi W of Discovery Bar. Flows S into Jordan Creek.

At one time about 700 Chinese were present in this mining area.

China Hat (Caribou). 7164′. T7S R41E sec 24. On the Blackfoot Lava Field; one of three old volcanoes probably of the dome type, the others being Middle Cone and North Cone; near the S shore of Blackfoot River Reservoir. China Hat is a conspicuous landmark, standing nearly 1000′ above the lava plain surrounding it and having a basal circumference of 5 mi. Its profile is that of a smaller dome surmounting a broader mass.

Named for its profile, which bears some resemblance to the shape of a Chinese hat.

China Springs (Lemhi). T20N R20E sec 34. About 3/4 mi W of Lake Mountain; 11 mi SW of Salmon.

Three Chinese were killed and robbed of their gold near here in the 1870s.

Chink Gulch (Lemhi). T26N R22E sec 29. Heads near source of Cyanide Gulch and runs NE 1 mi to enter Dahlonega Creek; Salmon River drainage.

Two reasons for the name. Placer mining was done by Chinese in this area. Also there were many grouse here — sometimes called "chickens" or "chinks" by local people.

Originally China Gulch, but changed by forest ranger Al Wheeler in 1944 because there were too many China Gulches.

Chipmunk Crossing (Owyhee). T4S R4W sec 4. NW of Silver City near the headwaters of Sucker Creek.

May have been named after a ranch that was in this area known as Chipmunk Ranch. One of the first to live at the ranch was a man with the nickname of "Chipmunk," also sometimes referred to as "Hair-Oil Johnny."

Chips Creek (Lemhi). T21N R21E sec 2. Forms N of Baldy Mountain and flows generally E 3 mi to enter Pollard Canyon; 5 mi W of Salmon; Salmon River drainage.

Named for Charles "Chips" Evans, a road agent and gunman who killed a man named Magee in 1886 because Magee wounded Caleb Davis, a saloon owner at the town of Dynamo. Evans was later captured in Butte, Montana. Also Chipps Creek.

Chittam Creek (Idaho). T25N R5E sec 31. A N tributary of Salmon River.

Named for the cascara tree, the bark of which is called chittam and is used as a laxative.

Chloride Gulch (Bonner). T53N R1W sec 15. Heads 1 mi NE of Prospect Peak; extends 2 mi NE to Gold Creek, 2 mi S of Lakeview (originally named Chloride).

Named because of the mining industry in the area.

Chokecherry (Bonneville). 5105′. T3N R42E sec 5. Village in the N part of the county on the S bank of the Snake River, 7 mi E of Poplar. Organized in 1915 as a school district.

Named for the chokecherry trees in the area.

Christmans (Lewis). T33N R1E sec 8. RR siding in the center of the county, 6 mi W of Nezperce.

Named for landowner Robert E. Christman, who filed a claim nearby in 1904.

Christie Creek (Idaho). T26N R1E sec 12. Salmon River tributary from the W. Named for Charles Christie, a miner and storekeeper at Slate Creek.

Churchill (Cassia). T12S R21E sec 24/25. In the NW part of the county 13 mi NW of Oakley.

An early Mormon settlement 1880-1882, originally Golden Valley, but as many of the families were named Church and Hill, the name was changed to Churchill. Post office, 1915-1930.

Chute Creek (Bonner). T59N R2E sec 8. Heads 1 1/4 mi NW of Calder Mountain and flows 1 1/2 mi S into Grouse Creek; Pack River drainage.

Logs were chuted down the mountain here; hence the name.

Cinch Creek (Lemhi). T18N R14E sec 24. Heads about 1 1/2 mi N of Martin Mountain and runs N 2 1/2 mi to enter Camas Creek; Middle Fk Salmon River drainage.

Named for a packsaddle cinch found by Frank Bradley and a construction crew when they built this section of the Camas Trail in the 1920s.

Cinder Butte (Jerome). 4224'. T9S R20E sec 11. In the E part of the county about 2 mi N of Wilson Lake Reservoir.

A generic name: the butte is the remnant of a volcano, a cinder cone. See Wilson Butte Cave.

Cinder Cone Butte (Ada). 3436'. T2S R4E sec 28. Near the Ada- Elmore county line.

Named because its summit is a cinder cone, formed of fragmented volcanic ejecta in the form of cinders, bombs, and ash.

Cinnabar Mountain (Owyhee). 8115'. T5S R3W sec 14/23. Three mi SE of Silver City.

Cinnabar mines were located on the mountain. Cinnabar is a heavy, bright-red mineral that is the principal ore of mercury. This is the highest mountain in Owyhee County, part of the Owyhee Mountain Range. It is sometimes called Cinnabar Ridge. Originally called War Eagle Mountain, which see.

Circular Butte (Jefferson). T6N R33E sec 19. A promontory near the W border of the county, 2.5 mi SW of Antelope Butte.

A descriptive name: the butte is round.

Cirque Lake (Custer). T9N R16E sec 18. A 20-acre lake in the glacial deposits of the White Cloud Peaks at 10,080' elevation.

Glacial erosion has formed the lake by gouging out the lake bed and depositing a large dike at the E end of the lake. "Cirque" is a geological term describing this type of glacial depression.

City of Rocks (Cassia). T15S R23/24E sec 24, 25, 26, 36/19, 29-32. A 25-square-mile area in the S central part of the county; a natural landmark on the California Trail, and site of a later stage station.

The huge bizarre rock formations are named individually for their suggestive shapes. Also called Silent City of Rocks.

City of Rocks (Gooding). T3S R14E sec 27. Rock formation in the NE part of the county, about 13 mi NW of Gooding.

Rock formations of shale and stone, their shapes suggestive of a city in ruins: fallen pillars, columns, and monuments. It is approximately 4 mi long and 1.5 mi wide, with several large gorges. Also called Gooding City of Rocks.

Clagstone (Bonner). 2240'. T54N R4W sec 22. Town on the SIRR and W bank of Hoodoo Lake, about 25 mi SW of Sandpoint. Surveyed in 1906 and started in 1907, this village is now a small summer resort area.

Named for Paul Clagstone, early settler and a Speaker of the House, Idaho State Legislature.

Clark Canyon (Butte). T7N R26E sec 29. Two mi long, trends SW to open out in Big Lost River Valley 5 mi NE of Leslie.

Named for an early resident of the area.

Clark County. County seat, Dubois. Created in 1919 from part of Fremont County and named for Sam K. Clark, early settler on Medicine Lodge Creek who became the first state senator from Clark County.

The county is bounded on the N by the Centennial and Beaverhead mountains of Montana, on the E by Fremont County, on the S by Jefferson County, and on the W by Lemhi and Butte counties.

Clark Fork River (Bonner/Montana). Source is the Silverbow Mountains SW of Butte in Montana. Its length, exclusive of windings, is 420 mi; its drainage 25,800 square miles in Montana, Idaho, Washington, and British Columbia. The river falls nearly 500' in the last 40 mi of its course. It enters Idaho at Cabinet and flows into Lake Pend Oreille in T56N R2E sec 20, 31 and T55N R2E sec 5. It is the chief tributary of the lake.

Clark Fork. T55N R2E sec 2. Town 6 mi W of Idaho-Montana border; 9 1/4 mi SE of Hope. Clark Fork Ranger Station is 1 mi ENE of Clark Fork; 6 mi S of Bee Top Mountain.

The stream was named for William Clark of the Lewis and Clark Expedi-

tion in 1805. (Also known as Bitterroot River, Clarke Fork, Clarks Fork, Deer Lodge River, Hell Gate River, Missoula River, Silverbow River.) The town was named after the river. Its site seems to have been used by fur trappers as early as 1809. The Northern Pacific Railway siding was constructed prior to 1888.

Clarke Mountain (Clearwater). 5285'. T38N R7E sec 14. Two mi W of the Bungalow Ranger Station.

Named for Jimmy Clarke, a lookout at this location during the 1920s.

Clarkia (Shoshone). 2828'. T42N R1E sec 6. In the SW corner of the county, 18 mi S of Calder and 33 mi SE of St. Maries. On State Highway 7 and the Milwaukee RR. Originally a lumber camp. Pronounced KLARK-ee.

Named for William Clark of the Lewis and Clark Expedition.

Clatter Creek (Bonner). T57N R3E sec 5. Heads at Bear Mountain; flows 1 1/2 mi WNW into Rattle Creek 1 mi SW of Rattle Mountain.

Named by the USFS for its sound.

Clawson (Teton). T6N R45E sec 34/35. Town 4 mi N of Driggs on S Leigh Creek. Formerly Leigh. An agricultural center of a rich valley, drained by several streams, and with springs, groves, and forests. The area was settled between 1882-1903 and known as Leigh (for Leigh Creek, named for frontiersman Richard "Beaver Dick" Leigh). The townsite was platted 5 Dec 1915 and renamed Clawson. Post office, 1896-.

Named for Spencer Clawson, who in 1905 offered lots for the townsite if the town were renamed for him.

Clay Creek (Boise). T7N R5E sec 21. Flows 2 mi S into Grimes Creek 1 mi N of Centreville; Boise River drainage.

Named because blue clay is visible on the banks of this stream.

Clayton (Custer). 5471′. T11N R17E sec 25. Town at the mouth of Kinnikinnic Creek, a N tributary of the Salmon River.

This town sprang up in the late 1870s when the Livingston, Kinnikinnic, and Red Bird mines were developing. A smelter was built here in 1902 and processed ore from the Ramshorn, Skylark, and Poverty Flat mines, as well as others.

Named for Clayton Smith, who operated a house of ill-repute in the heyday of the mining rush.

Clayton Creek (Clearwater). T39N R11E sec 21. In the central part of E Clearwater County. Rises on Scurvy Mountain and flows 3 mi E, then N into Kelly Creek; Clearwater River drainage.

Named for Clayton Shoecraft, one of two men who died here of scurvy in 1907.

Claytonia (Owyhee). T3N R4W sec 29. Town. In 1915 a Mr. Fleming built a store in this location and named it Claytonia in honor of Benjamin Clay, who owned the land on which the store was built.

Clear Creek (Bonneville). T3S R44E sec 14. Flows 6.2 mi into McCoy Creek SE in the S part of the county; Snake River drainage.

Named because the water is exceptionally clear.

Clear Creek (Lemhi). T14N R27E sec 3. Forms in Beaverhead Mountains on the Continental Divide; flows W 8 1/2 mi to enter Lemhi Valley; Lemhi River drainage.

The clear stream was once called Stephenson Creek after Elijah M. Stephenson, an early settler on the stream.

Clear Creek (Lemhi). T23N R18E sec 28. Headwaters in Bighorn Crags, flows

NE 13 mi to enter Panther Creek, 5 mi SW of Shoup; Salmon River drainage.

This creek has crystal-clear water. Named by miners in the vicinity of the mouth of the creek in the 1880s.

Clear Lakes (Gooding). T9S R14E sec 2. In the SE part of the county in the Snake River Canyon. Small lakes, deep and clear, fed by numerous springs.

Named for the clear water.

Clearlake. T9S R14E sec 2. In the SE part of the county, 2 mi S of Thousand Springs.

Clear Lakes (Twin Falls). T9S R14E sec 10. In the Snake River Canyon N of Buhl.

Lakes 40′ deep are so clear that the springs which feed them can be seen on the white sands on the bottom.

Clear Creek, a 5-mi stream flowing N from Buhl, empties into the Snake River; it takes its name from the lakes. The early town of Abbey sprang up in this area in 1900.

Clearwater County. County seat, Orofino.

Established 1911, by an act of the State Legislature from the eastern half of Nez Perce County, as the 25th county in Idaho; 2,508 square miles. Bounded on the E by the Bitterroot Mountains, on the S and SE by Idaho County, on the SW by Lewis County, on the NW by Latah County, and on the N by Shoshone County. Drained primarily by N Fk Clearwater River.

Named for the Clearwater River, which see.

Clearwater River. Tributary of the Snake River.

The Clearwater River drainage, including its major tributaries, drains the area between the Salmon and St. Joe drainages. All or part of five counties lie in this area: Clearwater, Latah, Nez Perce, Lewis, and Idaho. The river rises in the mountainous plateaus bordered on the E by the Bitterroot Range; drainage, 10,000 square miles; main stream formed by the junction of Middle and S fks at Kooskia; additional significant tributaries, N Fk, Little N Fk, Selway, Lochsa, and Potlatch rivers.

The name was translated from the Nez Perce term Koos-Koos-Kai-Kai, describing clear water. Clearwater was applied first to the river, then the county and the other features that follow.

Clearwater (Idaho). T31N R4E sec 36. Town in the NW portion of the county at the headwaters of Clear Creek about 6 mi E of S Fk Clearwater. Post office, 1872.

Clearwater Gulch (Clearwater). T36N R6E sec 5. Runs W into Rhodes Creek at T36N R5E sec 1; Clearwater River drainage. A descriptive name given by miners in the 1860s because of its connection with the Clearwater River.

Clearwater Mountains. The largest single block of mountains in Idaho. They are bounded on the N by the St. Joe Mountains; on the E by the Bitterroot Mountains; on the S by the Salmon River; and on the W by the Clearwater and St. Maries rivers. They extend 125 mi in length and 40 to 70 mi in width and rarely exceed 8000′ in elevation.

Middle Fk Clearwater River. T32N R5W sec 4. Formed by the junction of the Lochsa and Selway rivers near Lowell, converging with S Fk at Ahsahka. It is 75 mi long; its drainage area 3250 square miles; and its terrain, chiefly canyons and narrow valleys.

N Fk Clearwater River (Clearwater). T38N R1E sec 34. Rises on the W slopes of the Bitterroot Range and flows erratically SW to empty into the Clearwater River at Ahsahka. It is 90 mi long and drains almost all of Clearwater County, 2450 square miles. Principal tributaries: Little N Fk River; Weitas Creek; and

Elk Creek. Near Orofino, Dworshak Dam is located on this stream.

S Fk Clearwater River. T38N R1E sec 34. Rises in the watershed E and S of Elk City in the Nezperce National Forest; flows W and N to Ahsahka. It is 55 mi long and drains 865 square miles; the terrain, rough with narrow canyons and valleys.

Cleft (Elmore). 3220′. T2S R5E sec 22. A UPRR station.

Cleft Crater Rings. Explosion pits about 2 mi S of Cleft. There are two immense pits with only a narrow ridge of older bedded lavas between them. The pits are about 250′ deep, with windblown soil covering their level floors. Their diameter at the top is about 1/2 mi. The presence nearby of deposits of lapilli indicate they are of volcanic, eruptive origin.

Cleft Fissure. Located in Cleft just S of the water tank and across the RR tracks. The sides of the fissure are columnar, gaping 1′-2′ apart. In some places it is possible to descend 20′-30′. The fissure extends 1/2 mi E, and one wall stands 10′-15′ above the others.

The name Cleft is descriptive of the main feature of the area.

Clementsville (Teton). 5163′. T6N R43E sec 3. Town in the NW part of the county between the rim of Teton Basin and Canyon Creek.

This area was organized (as a branch of the Teton Stake of the Church of Jesus Christ of Latter-day Saints) 30 May, 1915. At the time, the community had a church, a school, and a general store.

Named for Cecil Clements, the first presiding elder of the branch.

Cleveland (Franklin). 4930′. T12S R40E sec 26. In the NE part of the county, 24 mi NE of Preston.

First known as Cottonwood; settled about 1880 and named for President Grover Cleveland; an agricultural and stock-raising community. Post office, 1893-1960.

Cleveland (Jefferson). 4880'. T4N R39E sec 3. Early name for Labelle; changed before 1884 to Cleveland for President Grover Cleveland.

Cleveland Gulch (Latah). T42N R2W sec 14. Fourth of the 10 named gulches emptying into N Fk Palouse River from the N; in the Hoodoo Mining District.

Probably named for C. L. Cleveland, who according to Jake J. Johnson prospected in this gulch in 1903. See Banks Gulch. This gulch was extensively mined by Chinese during the late 1880s.

Cleveland, Lake (Cassia). T13S R24E sec 4. In the central part of the county, 6 mi S of Albion; Sawtooth National Forest; 1 mi NE of Mt. Harrison.

Named for President Grover Cleveland, who was defeated for re-election by Bnejamin Harrison in the 1888 election. See Mt. Harrison.

Clicks (Lewis). 3675'. T34N R2W sec 24. RR siding and spur situated in the NW section of the county, 4 mi NE of Winchester.

Named for Quincy R. Click, owner of a local lumber mill.

Cliff (Custer). 8475'. T6N R23E sec 1.

This town was brought into being by the White Knob mining boom in 1884. Its main claim to fame was the only two-stack smelter in Idaho. Post office, 1884-1891. Ghost town.

Named for terrain in which it is located.

Cliff Canyon (Lemhi). T11N R29E sec 35. Heads 1/4 mi S of Mahogany Mountain and runs SW 6 mi, 1 1/2 mi SW of Reno.

Large rocks and cliffs are found at the mouth of the canyon.

Cliff Creek (Clearwater). T41N R8E sec 22. In the central part of N Clearwater County. Rises in Cliff Lake and flows 4 1/2 mi E into Collins Creek; Clearwater River drainage.

Named for the rough country, with many cliffs.

Cliffs (Owyhee). 5200'. T9S R6W sec 11. Town in W part of the county, 40 mi SW of Silver City close to the Oregon line.

Named for the cliffs on N Fk Owyhee River.

Clifton (Franklin). 4893'. T14S R38E sec 22. In the NW part of the county, immediately W of Twin Lakes.

Settled by Mormons from Franklin in 1864-65; surveyed in 1869 and named by John Saut for a high cleft in rocks nearby.

Clover (Twin Falls). 4106'. T10S R15E sec 34. In the W part of the county between Buhl and Filer; a community settled in 1914.

The town never developed, as it lay between the developing towns of Buhl and Filer.

Named for the clover fields that surrounded the area.

Clover (Valley). T21N R12E sec 28. On Big Creek, at its junction with Garden Creek. The E terminal on the road to Warrens, Idaho County, by way of Elk Summit. Post office, 1914-1929.

Named for the native clover in the area.

Clover Creek (Gooding). T5S R12E sec 18. Rises in the NW corner of Gooding County and flows about 32 mi SE and then SW through Pioneer Reservoir to the Snake River SE of King Hill, Elmore County.

The Clover Creek system, including its tributaries, drains the NW quadrant of the county.

Wilson Price Hunt camped at the mouth of this stream in 1811 after his expedition separated, with 19 members on the S side of the river and 19 on the N.

Named for the clover in the area.

Cloverdale (Ada). T3N R1E sec 4/10. Once a farming community lying SW of Ustick.

Named for the natural grazing land in the area.

Coal Banks Creek (Cassia). T16S R21E sec 13. Rises in the SW part of the county in the Sawtooth National Forest; flows 4.5 mi to empty into Goose Creek, 4 mi N of the Nevada border.

Named for the outcrops of lignite along the upper drainages.

Coal Camp Fork (Custer). T10N R16E sec 12. Stream 2.5 mi long, flows NE to French Creek.

In the early 1900s there was a large charcoal-producing camp in the area.

Coal Kiln Canyon (Lemhi). T12N R28E sec 19. Heads in the Lemhi Range N of Mammoth Canyon and runs NE 5 mi to Birch Creek Valley, 8 mi SW of Nicholia. Coal Kiln Spring is SE of Coal kiln Canyon and very near the charcoal kilns.

Charcoal was made in kilns here for use in the mines at Nicholia.

Coal Pit Butte (Cassia). 7291'. T13S R19E sec 35. Near the center of the W border of the county; the site of a coal outcropping that was once worked. Coal Pit Creek rises on the SE slope of Coal Pit Butte in Coal Pit Spring. In the Sawtooth National Forest.

Coalmine Canyon (Madison). T4N R43E sec 30. One mi long; trends SE along the course of Coalmine Creek to Burns Canyon.

Named for a coal mine at the head of the ravine.

Coalpit Mountain (Owyhee). T15 R3W sec 28. Near Reynolds Creek.

Named because at one time there was a coal mine here. Previously known as Tennessee Mountain.

Coates (Latah). T42N R4W sec 3. Named for Crawford Coates, a homesteader between the sources of Gold and Water Hole creeks.

Cobalt (Lemhi). 5050'. T20N R19E sec 4. Town on Panther Creek near the mouth of Spring Creek, 3 1/2 mi S of the confluence of Napias and Panther creeks.

Named for the mineral deposit found here.

Cochran Draw (Bonner). T57N R1E sec 15. Heads 1 mi NE of Mount Eagen; extends 2 mi NW to Trestle Creek 3 1/2 mi NNW of Hope.

Named for Frank Cochrane's (sic) father, who homesteaded here.

Cocolalla (Bonner). T55N R2W sec 19. Town at the S end of Cocolalla Lake. Post office established 1903.

Cocolalla Creek heads 1/2 mi E of Little Black Mountain and empties into Careywood Creek, which empties into Cocolalla Lake. A second Cocolalla Creek heads on Black Pine Mountain and winds E almost to Cocolalla Lake, then NE and NW through Round Lake and into the Pend Oreille River from the SE.

Cocolalla is said to be derived from a Coeur d'Alene word describing water as "very cold." It was first given the lake and then transferred to the nearby topographical features.

Coddington Gulch (Shoshone). T45N R5E sec 13. A 1.5-mi stream and gulch emptying into the St. Joe River from the NE 1 mi E of Avery.

Named for a Mr. Coddington, who had a claim near the mouth of the gulch. He was trained as a lawyer and also worked for the USFS a few years, beginning in 1926.

Coeur d'Alene (Kootenai). T50N R4W sec 7/18. County seat. This is the largest city N of Lewiston, headquarters for Coeur d'Alene National Forest, located on the N shore of Lake Coeur d'Alene and near the Chilco Mountains.

The US Government established a military post here in 1879 on the recommendation of General William Tecumseh Sherman, of Civil War fame, setting aside 999 acres now occupied by North City Park and North Idaho College. Sherman named the fort Coeur d'Alene, but on his death it was renamed Ft. Sherman to honor him. The town remained Coeur d'Alene.

The name Coeur d'Alene was first given the Indians of the area by French fur trappers and traders. It has been interpreted in a variety of ways: "awl," "pointed," or "needle-hearted," for the shrewd trading ability of the Indians. The name was transferred to the land and waters of the area. Sherman transferred it to the fort, and it was then applied to the city. The following features stem from the same source.

Coeur d'Alene Lake (Kootenai/ Benewah). The lake extends southward from the city about 30 mi, its tip in Benewah county; it receives most of its water from the Coeur d'Alene, St. Joe, and St. Maries rivers, which rise along the Pend Oreille Divide and the Bitterroot Range. The outlet river for Coeur d'Alene Lake is the Spokane River, a tributary of the Columbia, and the S end is a bay-like area named Lake Chatcolet (which see). This is the center of a large resort area.

Coeur d'Alene Mountain (Kootenai). 4439'. T49N R3W sec 23. In the Coeur d'Alene National Forest. Formerly Sticker Mountain (which see), but citizens of Coeur d'Alene asked for a change, as the mountain is in full view of the city.

Coeur d'Alene Mountains (Kootenai and Shoshone counties; Idaho, Mineral and Sanders counties, Montana). NW-SE trending mountain group about 95 mi long and 35 mi wide, comprising, along with the St. Joe Mountains, the NW part of the Bitterroot Range just NW of the Bitterroot Mountains; they are bounded on the N, NE, and E by Pend Oreille Lake and the Clark Fork; on the S by the Coeur d'Alene River and its S Fk, Lookout Pass, the Saint Regis River, and the Clark Fork; and on the W by Coeur d'Alene Lake and Rathdrum Prairie.

Coeur d'Alene River (Shoshone/ Kootenai). T47N R4W sec 1. Rises on the Pend d'Oreille Divide and flows in a S direction through Beaver, McPherson, Rock City, and Big Creek to Prichard; and thence SW through Enaville, Rose Lake, and Medimont. It empties into Lake Coeur d'Alene at Harrison. Length is about 100 mi. The terrain in the upper reach is the timbered slopes of the Coeur d'Alene National Forest; in the lower reach rolling valley. Its S Fk passes Mullan, Wallace, and Kellogg to its junction at Enaville. Its N Fk heads near Lakeview and joins the main stream at Linfor. It drains the NW corner of Kootenai County and the N third of Shoshone County. Its streams have been profitably prospected for gold and silver and its drainage is an important source of lumber.

Coeur d'Alene Valley (Kootenai/ Shoshone). Drained by the Coeur d'Alene River and its S Fk, a remarkably even depression. The valley of the N Fk is of canyon-like dimensions in most of its length, but below the junction at Kingston, it becomes broader down to its mouth at Lake Coeur d'Alene. Its floor in the lower portion is a large expanse of meadowland. The valley of the S Fk is for the most part fairly broad, although it passes through a gorge between Mullan and Wallace.

Coffee Creek (Clearwater). T38N R9E sec 3. Rises in the NE part of the county in Junction Lake and flows SW into Fourth of July Creek; Clearwater River drainage.

Possibly a group name given by the USFS, since Pie Creek and Bacon Creek are nearby.

Coffee Gulch (Lemhi). T23N R20E sec 35/25. Just W of Racetrack Meadows; trends NE and SW; 2 mi N of Leesburg.

This gulch was originally called Sierra Gulch by the Sharkey party, who first discovered gold at Leesburg when they were on their way back to Montana, because it reminded them so much of Sierra Gulch in Montana.

There was an earlier Coffey Gulch in the W portion of T22N R20E sec 11, about 1 mi SE of the present Coffee Gulch. It was named for William Coffey, who was elected president of the Summit Mining District in 1866.

A local belief has it that the place was named because early miners found gold there that looked like coffee beans.

Coffee Gulch (Owyhee). One mi SW of Silver City. Flows E into Long Gulch and eventually into Jordan Creek. A coffee can was found in the gulch by the miners in the 1860s.

Coffee Pot Creek (Fremont). T13N R43E sec 32. Flows 6 mi SE into Henrys Fork 1/2 mi downstream from Coffee Pot Rapids, 3 mi downstream from Macks Inn.

Named by George Rea, early trapper and settler, after his canoe overturned in the rapids, and he lost everything but the coffee pot.

Cohen Gulch (Lemhi). T23N R18E sec 3. About 2 mi long, runs SE to enter the Salmon River drainage between Little Sheepeater Creek on the NE and Big Sheepeater Creek on the SW; Salmon River drainage.

Named for Michael Cohen, a hardrock miner who made a strike in the late 1860s and alone drove almost 2000' of tunnel behind his cabin, but never processed or carried his ore out.

Colburn (Bonner). T58N R2W sec 12. Town 9 mi N of Sandpoint; 2 1/4 mi W of Samuels. Colburn Creek lies W of town.

Named for an early settler named Coburn, but the GNRR changed the name to Colburn. H. E. Brown established a timber company and sawmill here in 1908.

Cold Creek (Custer). T11N R16E sec 29/31/32. A small creek flowing into Salmon River in sec 29. Located in the Challis National Forest. Variant name: Cold Springs Creek.

There is no spring on the creek but the water is very cold.

Cold Lake (Clearwater). T40N R9E sec 22/23. In the NE part of the county. Cool Creek rises on Cold Springs Peak (6731') and empties into Cold Springs Creek, a tributary of N Fk Clearwater River.

Named for the nearby cold springs and for its cold water.

Cold Springs Creek (Elmore). T6S R9E sec 6. Formed by the junction of its E and W fks; flows generally S 16 mi to the Snake River at a point opposite Schoffs Island about 1.8 mi SE of Hammett. Formerly Cold Spring Creek.

Named for the cold springs at the source of the creek.

Cole Creek (Clearwater). T36N R6E sec 27. Rises on Lost Hat Saddle in the SE part of the county and flows S into Musselshell Creek; Clearwater River drainage.

Named for Frank "Daddy" Cole, who had claims on nearby Gold and Musselshell creeks in the 1860s.

Cole Creek (Clearwater). T38N R2E sec 18. In the NW part of the county. Rises on Alderman Ridge and flows 5 mi SE into Dworshak Reservoir.

Named for a homesteader, Alvin Cole.

Coleman (Bonner). T54N R5W sec 25. Town 10 1/2 mi W of Granite; 3 1/2 mi E of Blanchard.

Named for Harry Coleman, a local settler, homesteader, and businessman in the 1890s.

Coleman Canyon (Fremont). T9N R43E sec 5-20. In S central Fremont County. Trends NE to SW to Henrys Fork; one of the parallel canyons NE of Ashton. Coleman Ridge parallels Coleman Canyon. Local name; unmarked on maps.

Named for Joe Coleman, an early homesteader at the mouth of the canyon.

Coles Flat (Latah). T40N R4W sec 31. Owned in 1903 by Annie R. Cole, for whom the area is named. The Cole sawmill was located here. Later became known as Rowlands Park.

Colgate Warm Springs (Idaho). T36N R12E sec 15. In the NE part of the county on the Lochsa River; Clearwater National Forest.

Named for the cook of a hunting party who went into Lochsa Valley in the winter of 1893. The party abandoned him when he became ill and his body was found the following spring 8 mi from the place where he was abandoned. His grave is near Colgate Springs.

Also Colgate Hot Springs.

Collins (Latah). T41N R1E sec 18. An early lumbering community 2 mi N of Slabtown and 4 mi N of Bovill. Settled in 1890s; post office 1908-1915. A railroad station on the Chicago, Milwaukee, and St. Paul RR appears on the 1883 and 1907 GLO Maps of Idaho.

Named for John H. Collins, a timber cruiser and homesteader in the area before 1895.

Collins Creek (Clearwater). T41N R8E sec 27. Rises on Surveyors Peak in Shoshone County and flows 11 mi S into Skull Creek; Clearwater River drainage. The settlement of Collins Creek is situated at the mouth of this stream.

Named for John Collins, packer and guide for the US Geological Survey. This may be the same John Collins who lived in the area and had mining claims here as early as 1903.

Collister (Ada). T4N R2E sec 29. Originally a community NW of Boise, but now a part of the city.

Named for Dr. George Collister, prominent physician and resident of the area, 1890s-1900s.

Color Creek (Shoshone). T43N R9E sec 32. Rises in the Clearwater National Forest and flows 2 mi NW to the St. Joe River just E of Copper Point, in the extreme SE part of the county.

Named by W. H. Daugs, USFS ranger, in 1929 because the water has a rust or brick color, especially in the fall.

Colson Creek (Lemhi). T23N R16E sec 25. Heads near Long Tom Ridge and runs 6 mi S to enter the Salmon River.

The Colson brothers were packers and placer miners on this creek in the 1960s.

Colt Creek (Clearwater). T38N R11E sec 36. Rises on Horseshoe Lookout (6985') on the S border of the county and flows NW into Cayuse Creek; Clearwater River drainage.

This developed as a group name. The creek is a tributary of Cayuse Creek.

Coltkilled Creek (Idaho). T37N R14E sec 34. E tributary of the Lochsa River.

On 14 September 1805, William Clark recorded that the Lewis and Clark Expedition was compelled to kill a colt for want of meat, and named the S Fk of the main stream Coltkilled Creek and the main stream Koos Koos Ke. Now White Sand Creek, which see.

Coltman (Bonneville). 4778'. T3N R38E sec 5/8. Village just N of Idaho Falls.

Residents chose Coltman as the name for their school district, honoring the postmaster of Idaho Falls, 1894.

Columbia Gulch (Lemhi). T19N R16E sec 13,14. Settlement near Blackeagle Creek, which runs NW to enter Hoodoo Creek drainage; Middle Fk Salmon River drainage.

Named for the Columbia Mining Company, which had holdings in this gulch.

Combe Canyon (Butte). T4N R28E sec 6. Canyon 3/5 mi long, trends NW to open 9 mi NE of Arco.

Named for a homesteader.

Combination Creek (Owyhee). T7S R4W sec 10. Flows NE into Boulder Creek; Owyhee River drainage.

Named for the wild horses found in this area. They were of many different colors and therefore called combination herds.

Comet Creek (Lemhi). T23N R21E sec 12. Forms 1 1/2 mi N of Diamond Gulch and flows NE 3 1/2 mi to enter the Salmon River, 6 mi N of Carmen.

Named for the Comet Mines, which are located in this drainage; possibly discovered around 1910, when Halley's Comet was seen.

Commearp (Lewis). Early name for Lawyer Canyon Creek, which forms a part of the S boundary of Lewis County. See Lawyers Canyon.

Named by Lewis and Clark 14 September 1806; a Nez Perce word supposedly meaning "pretty valley."

Commerce (Cassia). Early name for Burley, which see.

Commissary Ridge (Bonneville). 7400'. T1/2S R43E sec 29/11. About the center of E Bonneville County in the Caribou Range, 12 mi W of Palisades Reservoir.

Named because a sheep wagon carrying food and supplies owned by Henry L. Finch was abandoned here in 1905.

Con Shea Basin (Owyhee). T2S R1W. Near Murphy.

Named for Con Shea, one of the early cattle kings of the Owyhee country.

Conant (Cassia). T13S R26E sec 20. In the E part of the county, once a thriving trade center on Cassia Creek on the road from Boise to Kelton, Utah; a stage station on the California Trail's Hudspeth cutoff; 11 mi SE of Albion in a valley surrounded by low hills, with Mt. Harrison and Mt. Independence on the W.

The Conant brothers opened a general store here in 1880, established a mill, and opened a post office 1890-1917.

Conant Creek (Fremont). T8N R43E sec 18. In SE Fremont County; rises in Wyoming, enters Fremont County, flows 21 mi W to Fall River.

Named by Richard "Beaver Dick" Leigh in 1870 for Al Conant, who came to the mountains in 1865 and who very nearly lost his life on the stream.

Conant Valley (Bonneville). T2N R43E sec 19-32. Extends NW to SE in NE

Bonneville County, upriver from Burns Creek.

Named for Charles Conant, a trapper in the area in the 1870s. During a smallpox outbreak in 1876-1877 he took vaccine to the trappers in Swan Valley.

Concord (Idaho). T26N R6E sec 14. Located by John Leffler in 1898 in the Buffalo Hump area near the Atlas mine; a small mining town that vied for importance with ghost towns Calendar and Humptown.

Named for the Concord mine.

Conda (Caribou). 6100'. T8S R42E sec 15. In the central part of the county, 6 mi NE of Soda Springs. A model industrial town built in 1920 by the Anaconda Copper Company to serve its employees in the phosphate mines. Now the J. R. Simplot Company owns and operates a phosphate mine at the site. The phosphate outcrop is 13 mi long; open-pit mining.

Named for the Anaconda Mining Company.

Confederate Gulch (Boise). T7N R4E sec 9. Runs 4 mi SW to Granite Creek at Quartzburg; Boise River drainage.

Confederate sympathizers made the first big strike in this gulch and are said to have contributed 50 pounds of gold to the Confederate treasury.

Conkling Park (Kootenai). T47N R3W sec 19. A resort in the S part of the county on the W shore of the S extremity of Coeur d'Alene Lake.

Developed as a resort in 1916 by the original homesteader, A. B. Conkling, whose name it bears.

Connor Creek (Cassia). T13S R25E sec 23. Rises on Connor Ridge about 7 mi S of Albion and flows 10 mi SE to Cassia Creek. The settlement of Connor is situated at the mouth of this stream. Connor Flat lies near the head of the stream.

Named for Colonel Patrick Connor, stationed at Camp Douglas, Utah, who ordered the punishment of Indians for depredations on emigrant trains in Cassia County. In 1864 Captain Samuel P. Smith was ordered to Raft River, Idaho Territory, to take steps to capture or kill the male adults of five lodges of Snake Indians who for years had been stealing from and attacking emigrants to Idaho. In 1864, soldiers led by Smith, under orders from Connor, virtually annihilated a band of Indians at Connor Creek.

Variant: Conner Creek.

Contest Point (Bonner). T57N R1E sec 19. On Lake Pend Oreille, 2 1/2 mi E of Sandpoint; 2 1/2 mi SSE of Kootenai.

Named because boat races were held near here in the 1910s.

Continental Mountain (Boundary). 6725'. T65N R5W sec 36. On the border of Kaniksu National Forest. Continental Creek rises in the NW corner of the county and flows into Priest River.

The name is applied to the summit and not to the entire ridge surrounding the head of Blue Joe Creek, as shown on some maps. The name of the creek derives from the mountain on which it rises.

Named for the Idaho Continental Company, owned by A. K. Klockmann.

Cony Peak (Boise). 9638'. T8N R12E sec 5. In the extreme E part of the county 2 mi W of the Custer-Boise county line. Cony Lake lies immediately E.

Named by Will C. Barnes of the USFS in 1928; rock rabbits or conies are numerous on this mountain.

Cook Creek (Clearwater). T36N R3E sec 18. Rises in SW Clearwater County and flows 5 1/2 mi W into Orofino Creek 4 mi E of Orofino; Clearwater River drainage.

Named for Robert Cook, who operated a sawmill along the creek.

Cook Mountain (Clearwater). 6534'. T37/38N R9E sec 2,3/35. In the lower E part of the county. Cook Creek rises on this mountain and flows 5 mi N into Fourth of July Creek; Clearwater River drainage.

A man named Hughes, who was cooking for a camp in the vicinity of Junction Mountain, became ill and died. Although he was buried on Junction Mountain, George Engelhorn, an employee of the Clearwater National Forest, thought he was buried on the mountain later named Cook Mountain; thus the name was mistakenly applied.

Cooks Canyon (Latah). T38N R3W. A small canyon in the Fix Ridge area.

Named for Asa Cook, an early settler on the ridge, who came with his parents James W. and Hattie Cook in 1892.

Cool Gulch (Lemhi). T27N R21E sec 27. Runs E and W for approximately 1 mi; enters N Fk Salmon River drainage.

Named ca. 1940 by Al Wheeler, forest ranger at North Fork, because it is usually shady in this canyon and the water is always cool.

Cooley Creek (Boise). T9N R7E sec 31. Rises in the Charters Mountain region and flows 4 mi SE into the S Fk Payette River.

A large number of Chinese (coolies) worked on this creek.

Coolin (Bonner). T59N R4W sec 10. Town on Priest Lake, 8 3/4 mi E of the Idaho-Washington state border; 4 3/4 mi SSE of Bartoo Island. Coolin Mountain is 1 1/2 mi SW of Coolin.

This resort town was named by Andrew Coolin, an early resident of the area. It was renamed Williams while Walt Williams was postmaster, but the name eventually reverted to Coolin. Post office, 1893-.

Coolwater Creek (Idaho). T33N R8E sec 4. In the N central part of the county; a 5.5-mi tributary of the Lochsa River from the S. Coolwater Lake lies 1.5 mi E of the source of this stream and Coolwater Ridge SE of the lake. The lake is 4 acres, cool and deep and clear. Coolwater Mountain (6929'), near the lake, offers a magnificent view.

Named for the water in the stream and lake.

Coon Creek (Benewah). T43N R3W sec 29. Rises on Holaki Knob near the Benewah-Latah county line in the SW quadrant and flows 1 mi SE to Meadow Creek; Palouse River drainage.

Named by W. H. Daugs, USFS ranger. The name was selected because a USFS employee reported finding a dead raccoon on this creek, the first report of a raccoon in the area.

Cooney Canyon (Fremont). T12N R41E sec 11. In NW Fremont County. Runs 5 mi N to the extreme western end of Island Park Reservoir.

Relatively recent (1930s) name said to commemorate a local lumberman.

Coons Canyon (Lemhi). T12N R29E sec 2. N of head of Cedar Gulch; runs 1 mi N to Willow Creek drainage; Lemhi River drainage.

John Coons, who mined at Nicholia in its early days, had a cabin in this canyon.

Cooper (Clearwater). T36N R3E sec 23. Settlement 9 mi W of Orofino on Cooper Creek, which flows W into Orofino Creek; Clearwater River drainage.

Named for Frank Cooper, a homesteader in the area.

Cooper Bar (Idaho). T28N R1E sec 36. A bench on the Salmon River.

Ben and Frances Cooper settled here in 1908, raised alfalfa, and ran a ferry.

Cooper Creek (Lemhi). T16N R23E sec 9. Originates near Mogg Mountain and flows N 4 mi to enter Hayden Creek, across from the mouth of Squaw Creek; Lemhi River drainage.

Newt Cooper was a pioneer stockman in this area.

Copeland (Boundary). T64N R1E sec 7/18. Town on the Kootenai River in the northern part of the county. Named for an employee of the Great Northern RR. Post office, 1900-.

Copenhagen Canyon (Bear Lake). T12S R43E sec 30. Heads in Copenhagen Basin, along the Bear Lake-Franklin county border; trends ENE 5 mi to North Creek; Bear River drainage.

Many Danish Mormons settled in this area between Liberty and Mill Canyon, most of them from Liberty, Bennington, Bloomington, Ovid, St. Charles, and Paris, between 1863 and 1888. Many of these people retained their Danish ways and dress and lived very much as they might have in their old country.

Named for the capital of the native country of the settlers.

Copenhagen Point (Nez Perce). Near Melrose.

Said to be named because all the Swedish settlers in the area chewed tobacco; evidently their brand was Copenhagen.

Copper Bar Devils Garden (Idaho). T30N R1W sec 36. On a S bend in the Salmon River about 10 mi SE of Cottonwood.

Named for the rocky terrain and for a nearby bar in the river on which there was some prospecting for copper.

Copper Basin (Custer). T5/6N R22E. A depression in the southern part of the county near the head of E Fk Big Lost River, Lemhi National Forest. Copper Basin Knob (10,784'). T5N R22E

sec 16. Peak on the edge of Copper Basin.

Much copper prospecting and mining went on here in the 1880s, hence the name. Tungsten was found here in 1957.

Copper Creek (Boundary). T65N R2/3E. Tributary to Moyie River from the E between Addie and Eastport. Copper Falls are near the mouth of the creek. Copper Lake, Copper Mountain, and Copper Ridge lie E of the creek.

There was much prospecting in this area, 1864-1874. Both copper and zinc were found.

Copper Mountain (Lemhi). T23N R19E sec 19. Copper Canyon heads about 1/2 mi SW of Copper Mountain; runs SW 1 1/2 mi to enter Beaver Creek drainage; Salmon River drainage.

Named for the Copper King mine and other copper mines in the area.

Copperville (Idaho). T28N R1E sec 14. At the mouth of White Bird Creek on the Salmon River. A small settlement founded in 1904, 1 mi from the town of White Bird. No sign of the settlement remains.

Presumably named for the copper deposits nearby.

Cora (Latah). T42N R5W sec 3. An early community with a store and post office serving an estimated 600 people, 1896-1907; located 7 mi NW of Potlatch.

Named for the first postmaster, Cora Caruthers.

Corbin (Kootenai). 2336'. T55N R3W sec 33. In the N part of the county, 17 mi N of Coeur d'Alene. A RR station and shipping point built on the 30-mile-long Coeur d'Alene RR and Navigation Company branch from St. Maries Mission to Kingston, Murray, Wallace, Burke, and Ryan; built by D. C. Corbin in 1886.

Corbin supplemented his RR line with three riverboats: the *Coeur d'Alene* and the *General Sherman*, which he bought, and the *Kootenai*, which he built. He also built a branch line from Hauser Junction to Coeur d'Alene and down to the steamboat docks. In 1888 Corbin sold out to the NPRR. Though the community of Corbin began as a construction camp, it became a shipping point for timber and farm products.

Named for D. C. Corbin.

Corder (Elmore). T1N R5E sec 18. Early settlement and post office later replaced by Mayfield, which see.

Corder Creek (Elmore/Ada). T4S R3E sec 31. Rises in the SE corner of Ada County and trends SW to the Snake River.

Named for the founding family and the first postmaster, James O. Corder.

Corinth (Bear Lake). 6300'. T13S R46E sec 22. Formerly Raymond, which see.

Corn Creek (Lemhi). T24N R14E sec 35. Heads on Long Ridge Camp; flows 6 mi to enter the Salmon River at 2000'. Corn Lake is at the head of Corn Creek, 3 1/2 mi NW of Long Tom Ridge Camp.

Some informants say the creek was named because early prospectors found gold nuggets here the size of kernels of corn. Another informant says packers spilled some corn when passing through here and it started to grow.

Cornell (Latah). T40N R1W sec 15. Between Deary and Bovill, one of eight WIM railroad stations (1907) bearing the names of colleges, and one of six said to be named by college students working on the railroad.

Named for Cornell University.

Cornice Lake (Custer). T8N R16E sec 5. Lake .15 mi long, .6 mi NE of

Patterson Peak. Seasonally, there is a snow cornice above the lake.

Cornwall (Latah). 2611'. T39N R4W sec 19. An early community (1887) between Moscow and Troy on the head of Little Potlatch Creek, on the NPRR.

Named for Mason Cornwall, homesteader and developer in the area. Formerly Otto, which see; first known as Bronta Cabin. Post office, 1887-1901.

Corral. Wherever corral appears in a place name, there is a strong indication that the place once served as a corral, in many instances for stage lines. Later cattlemen and loggers designated places to pasture their horses while they were not needed.

Corral (Camas). 5092'. T1S R13E sec 7. In the SW quadrant of the county on Corral Creek, 8 mi W of Fairfield. This town has been in six different counties: Boise, Alturas, Alta, Logan, Blaine, and Camas.

Named for the numerous natural corrals found by early white settlers and along Corral Creek, a 15-mi tributary from the N to Camas Creek; Big Wood River drainage.

Corral Creek (Bonneville). T2N R46E sec 30. Rises in the E part of the county and flows 4.1 mi NW into Palisades Creek; Snake River drainage.

Named because the creek banks were excellent areas for grazing stock, with food and water available. Other Corral Creeks occur in Boise, Clark, and Latah counties.

Corral Flat (Lemhi). T23N R17E sec 27. Situated midway between the mouth of Panther Creek and Middle Fk Salmon River and 2 mi S of the Salmon River.

Many wild horses were in this area at one time, and cowboys who were after them built corrals for them on this flat.

Corto Creek (Benewah). T43N R1W sec 19. Flows NE 1 mi to E Fk Charlie Creek; St. Maries River drainage.

Named by USFS ranger W. H. Daugs, 24 November 1923. The name means "short" in Spanish.

Coski Creek (Boise). T9N R4E sec 35. Flows NE into the S Fk Payette River 1 1/2 mi W of Garden Valley Airport.

Named after David Coski, an early settler in the Garden Valley region, ca. 1870.

Cottage Island (Bonner). T56N R1E sec 3. On Lake Pend Oreille, 2 mi S of Hope; 2 1/2 mi E of Glengary.

Named for a building erected on the island. Once known as Twin Island.

Cotterel Mountains (Cassia). A N-S range of mountains 16 mi long extending S from T10S R25E sec 25 to T13S R26E sec 18. The ridge follows closely the range line between R25E and R26E, between Marsh Creek and Raft River.

Cotterel. T12S R26E sec 30. Small village on the mountain.

Town is named for the first postmaster, Samuel Cotteral, who was no doubt a descendant of the early homesteader for whom Cotterel Mountains are named. Post office, 1912-1917.

Cottonwood. As a place name, "cottonwood" signifies the presence of a great number of cottonwood trees along a stream or in an area. Such streams appear in nearly every section of Idaho, and the name is often transferred to other features.

Cottonwood (Idaho). 3550'. T31N R1E sec 6. In the NW part of the county, 12 mi N of Grangeville.

Settled in the 1860s during the gold rush and named for the creek on which it is situated. Incorporated in 1901. Post office, 1862-.

Cottonwood Creek (Adams). T16N R1W sec 28. Rises on the S slope of Council Mountain and flows about 13 mi to the Weiser River, 2 mi below Council Valley. The community of Cottonwood (2935') is located 2 1/2 mi S of Council on Cottonwood Creek. Also called Vista.

Cottonwood Basin lies at the head of Cottonwood Creek, 1 mi W of Council Mountain. A second Cottonwood Creek rises in the W part of the county and flows S and SE to N Hornet Creek; Weiser River drainage.

Cottonwood Creek (Bannock/Caribou). T12S R41E sec 31. Rises in Bannock County near its E boundary in the SE section of the county; flows 7 mi SSE into Caribou County, then 10 mi ESE to Bear River, 2 mi N of Maple Grove Springs; about 17 mi long. Cottonwood Peak (7924') is 2 mi W of the upper reaches of this stream and 9 mi E of Downey.

In 1876 Jefferson Hunt built a sawmill in Cottonwood Valley, which is drained by this stream. There was a plentiful supply of trees in the valley for the lumber business; many pioneer homes were built entirely of cottonwood logs.

Cottonwood Creek (Kootenai). T48N R3W sec 12. A 2-mi stream in the Coeur d'Alene National Forest, heading on the NE slope of Cottonwood Peak (3925') and flowing generally S and then W to Blue Lake Creek, about 2.5 mi above Blue Lake.

Named for the cottonwood trees in the area, though it was originally Blue Creek or Blue Lake Creek; the name was changed to avoid confusion with another stream by the same name.

Cottonwood Creek (Twin Falls). T11S R20E sec 21. In the NE extremity of the county, rising in the Sawtooth National Forest and flowing 5.5 mi W and N to empty into Murtaugh Lake.

Old water rights along this stream date to the early settlement of this valley.

Cottonwood Peak (Lemhi/Montana). 11,024′. T13N R29E sec 5. On the Continental Divide in Beaverhead Mountains; 13 mi E of Gilmore.

Couch Summit (Camas). 7008′. T2N R14E sec 9. In the center of the county in the Soldier Mountains, Sawtooth National Forest; 12 mi N of Fairfield. A mountain pass and a winter-sports area.

Cougar Creek (Bonner). T60N R4W sec 23. Heads in Boundary County and flows 5 mi W into Priest Lake at Cavanaugh Bay.

Named for a cougar that used to come into the area and, from the top of a large rock, prey on deer.

Cougar Creek (Kootenai). T50N R4W sec 22. Rises on the E side of Mica Peak (5241′) and flows 8.5 mi NE to Cougar Bay, on Coeur d'Alene Lake. The stream flows through Cougar Gulch.

The entire area is known locally as Cougar Gulch, as residents hunted cougar here for bounty.

Cougar Creek (Latah). T41N R1W sec 10. Rises 6 mi E of Laird Park and flows 3.9 mi E to W Fk Potlatch River, 2 mi W of Collins and 5 mi NW of Bovill; Clearwater River drainage.

Cougar Meadow. Just W of Collins, bounded on the N by Cougar Creek and W Fk Potlatch River.

Named because hunters often came here to shoot wildcats.

Cougar Creek (Lemhi). T22N R18E sec 6. Headwaters near Indian Point; flows N 3 mi to enter Clear Creek; Salmon River drainage.

This feature was unnamed prior to 1930. While working as a fire guard and lookout on the Sagebrush Lookout in 1930, Willard Rood frequently referred to this drainage as Cougar Creek because

he had killed cougar here in previous years. The USFS then added the name to the Clear Creek drainage system.

Coulter Summit (Boise). T8N R6E sec 27.

Tim Coulter froze to death while attempting to snowshoe from Pioneerville to the Mammoth mines with the mail and was buried on this summit.

Council (Adams). 2911′. T16N R1W sec 10. County seat. Situated in the Council Valley of the Weiser River in the center of the county; S of the Seven Devils. Council Mountain (8124′) is on the divide between Council and Long valleys in the Payette National Forest.

Homesteading began here in 1876. By 1899 there were several permanent settlers and the PINRR had been built this far. The town incorporated in 1903 and became the county seat when Adams County was created in 1911.

The town, valley, and mountain are named for the councils held here, especially on the butte, for a great many years. Reportedly, Nez Perce, Coeur d'Alenes, Shoshonis, Umatillas, Sheepeaters, Lemhi, Bannocks, and Sioux met regularly for trade, games, and salmon fishing. Post office, 1878-.

Courier Gulch (Blaine). T4N R18E sec 25. Extends 2 mi NW to SE to E Fk Wood River at Triumph.

Named for the Courier mine in this gulch.

Cove (Latah). 2670′. T40N R6W sec 25. A RR stop 2 mi N of Viola on the Spokane and Inland Empire Railroad.

The name was in official use by 1910. Also referred to as Mountain Cove.

Named for its location on a strip of open land extending into the woods.

Cove Creek (Lemhi). T23N R17E sec 14. Salmon River tributary from the N, 4 mi long.

So called for the small inlet above the mouth. There is a bridge on the Salmon River at this point. There is also a Cove Creek on Middle Fk Salmon River, named for the same reason (T18N R14E sec 22).

Cow Creek (Clearwater). T36N R4E sec 5. In the SW extremity of the county. Flows S into Orofino Creek 12 mi E of Orofino; Clearwater River drainage.

Named by the miners for the domestic animal in the 1860s. A few cattle escaped when they were driven from their summer range to their winter range along the creek and were found alive the next spring.

Cow Creek (Latah). T37N R6W sec 13. Rises above Blaine and flows 14.2 mi S through Genesee and Nez Perce County into Washington State.

In 1883 there was an old fort on this creek surrounded by an 8' stockade enclosing .5 acre of land; used as both a schoolhouse and a church.

Named because cows grazed here.

Cow Creek (Latah). T42N R3W sec 25. Rises on Flynn Butte in St. Joe National Forest, north central Latah County and flows SW about 2 mi to Meadow Creek, between and parallel to Pup Creek on the N and Akers Gulch on the S; Palouse River drainage.

Named because cows were allowed to graze here.

Cow Creek (Lemhi). T19N R24E sec 25. Heads on the Idaho-Montana border 9 mi E of Tendoy and flows W 2 mi, then NW 2 1/2 mi to enter Agency Creek; Lemhi River drainage.

Named by the Pattee family because of the numerous cow skeletons found here after the cows had died from eating larkspur or other poisonous plants.

Cow Creek (Lemhi). T17N R14E sec 18. S of Heifer Creek, flows 1 1/2 mi

generally W to enter Middle Fk Salmon River.

Charles Matley took 200 cows into the Middle Fork country in 1886. He lost most of them on what is now Cow Creek because the mountainsides were so steep that they fell to their deaths.

Cow Creek (Owyhee). Flows NW into Soda Creek; Owyhee River drainage. The town of Cowcreek is 11 mi NE of Jordan Valley, Oregon, on Cow Creek.

Cow Creek (Owyhee). Flows SE into Peach Creek; Owyhee River drainage.

The ranges of both Owyhee County Cow Creeks were speedily covered with immense herds after the first cattle were brought into the county in the 1860s.

Cox (Bingham). 4643'. T1N R37E sec 36. An agricultural community in the NE part of the county, 4 mi E of Shelley.

Named for Edward E. Cox, businessman and homesteader in the county, who was one of the first to use the area's irrigation system (1886).

Coyote Creek (Owyhee). Flows NE into Mountain Creek; Owyhee River drainage.

Named for the prevalence of coyotes along the stream.

Coyote Gulch (Nez Perce). T36N R4W sec 21. Ravine 1/2 mi N of North Lapwai. Flows S into the Clearwater River.

An old Nez Perce Indian known as "Coyote" or "Poor Coyote" lived on the N side of the Clearwater River, 1 mi W of Spalding. The ravine bears his name. His Indian name was Its-I-ah Yow-its, which means "coyote poor." He was so named because when he was born, his mother saw a scruffy coyote through the opening of the tepee.

Crabb Butte (Owyhee). T6S R6E sec 20. Near Bruneau.

Named for Charlie Crabb, a cowboy on the ranch of Barney Horn, one of Owyhee County's most successful cattlemen and owner of the T Ranch.

Cradle Creek (Idaho). T22N R14E sec 25. Empties into the Middle Fk Salmon River about 88 mi S of Dagger Falls. Cradle Creek Rapids lie just below the mouth of the creek.

Named for Earl Parrott's sluice box, used on this stream.

Crag Canyon/Creek (Bonneville). T3N R44E sec 4-3. Extends 1 1/2 mi NW to SE in the NE part of the county; Snake River Range, Targhee National Forest. The creek empties into Red Creek; Snake River drainage.

Name derives from the steep, rugged character of the canyon.

Crags, The (Idaho). T33N R10E. In the Selway-Bitterroot Wilderness Area at its NW border; the most rugged section of Nezperce National Forest.

It is a spectacular jumble of mountains that look like gigantic towers and walls; between the Selway and Lochsa rivers.

Craig Creek (Clearwater). T40N R11E sec 31. Rises in the E central part of the county on Moose Creek Buttes and flows NE to Deadwood Creek; Clearwater River drainage.

George W. Craig settled near the creek in 1905.

Craig Mountain Plateau. An extensive area between the Snake, Salmon, and Clearwater rivers, south of Culdesac. Craig Junction, a RR junction, is 3 mi S of Reubens.

Named for Colonel William Craig, the first permanent white settler in Idaho. He was born in Greenbrier County, Virginia, in 1807 and joined the Rocky Mountain trappers in 1829. He met the Nez Perce Indians at a trappers' gathering and settled on Lapwai Creek shortly after the Reverend Henry Spalding's arrival at Lapwai in 1836.

He established permanent residence in Idaho in 1846 and, in accordance with the Oregon Donation Act of 1850, he and his Nez Perce wife, Isabel, claimed and patented 640 acres at Lapwai. He also aided Gov. I. I. Stevens in treaty negotiations in 1855 and 1856; because he was trusted by the Indians, he was placed on Stevens' staff as lieutenant colonel. He later served as Indian agent at Lapwai. He was buried near Lapwai in 1869.

Craig Mountains (Nez Perce). Rise at the Clearwater River at Lewiston and extend into the NW part of Idaho County. Also known as Craig Mountain and Craigs Mountain, but they were recorded as Craig Mountains as early as 1877.

Craigmont (Lewis). 3688'. T34N R1W sec 32. Town in the center of the county.

The town of Craigmont officially received its name in 1920 after the former towns of Ilo and Vollmer consolidated. Ilo, formerly Chicago, was founded in 1898, and Vollmer in 1906. A bitter rivalry existed between the two towns situated across the RR tracks from each other, and many believed that if this friction had not existed when Lewis County was formed, the county seat would have been located here instead of at Nezperce.

Post office 1920-. Named directly for Craig Mountain, ultimately for William Craig.

Cramer Creek (Lemhi). T23N R16E sec 20. Heads about 2 mi SW of Long Tom Lookout and runs 2 mi SW to enter Salmon River.

Named for Jack Cramer, who took a herd of horses into this county in the

1860s and wintered them while he did some prospecting.

Cranberry Creek (Clearwater). T38N R2E sec 24. In the SW part of the county. Rises above Five Corners and flows SW into Dworshak Reservoir.

Wild vine cranberries (*Oxycoccus intermedius*) grew along a section of the creek.

Crandall Spring (Teton). T4N R46E sec 20. About 5 mi SE of Driggs near the head of Sorensen Creek.

In 1896 H. L. Crandall homesteaded land near the mouth of the stream that flows from the spring, about 3 mi S of Driggs.

Crane Creek (Ada). T3N R2E sec 5. Rises in Boise County and flows SW 7 mi to the Boise River. Crane Creek Gulch, a tributary of Crane Creek, extends NE to T4N R3E sec 24/26.

Named for C. W. Crane, who had a berry and grape farm in the gulch.

Crane Creek (Clearwater). T34N R5E sec 24. Rises on Brown Creek Ridge and flows SE into Lolo Creek at the S border of the county; Clearwater River drainage.

Ralph Space (USFS) thought the creek was named for the birds seen here; Al Hansen (USFS) believes it was named for a homesteader by the name of Crane.

Crane Creek (Latah). T42N R4W sec 32. Rises NW of Prospect Peak at the Benewah County line, flows SW and SE for about 9 mi to Gold Creek 2 mi NE of Onaway; Palouse River drainage.

Named for a family who lived here in the 1890s. Also Craine Creek.

Crane Creek (Washington). T11N R4W sec 14. Rises on the divide between Weiser and Payette rivers and flows through Crane Creek Reservoir W and SW to the Weiser River; 28 mi long, drains 300 square miles.

Crane was an early settlement on Crane Creek 3 1/2 mi E of Weiser. Post office, 1884-1919.

The name derives from the great numbers of sandhill cranes that once frequented the stream and meadows.

Crater Meadows (Clearwater). T37N R9E sec 11/12.

The glaciated meadows have the appearance of craters.

Crater Mountain (Caribou). 8697'. T5S R41E sec 14. In the NE part of the county at the S end of Webster Range. The remnant of a volcano E of the N arm of Blackfoot River Reservoir and W of Pelican Ridge.

Crater Rings (Elmore). T3S R5E sec 3/4. Three mi S of Cleft.

On a featureless plain are two circular depressions with vertical walls and elevated rims; level floor of fine yellow soil; both 250' deep, one 800' diameter, the other 1100' diameter. They originated from volcanic eruption.

Craters of the Moon (Butte). T1/2N R24/25E. National Monument 18 mi W of Arco, and almost entirely within this county. An 83-square-mile area set aside in 1924 by President Calvin Coolidge because of its outstanding geological values. Named for its resemblance to the surface of the moon.

Crescent (Latah). T38N R1W sec 11. An early logging community on Bedbug Creek, in SE part of the county; post office, 1895-1930. Appears on GLO map as early as 1883.

A descriptive name for the shape of open site in a wooded area.

Crescent Bay (Kootenai). T49N R4W sec 35. On the W side of Coeur d'Alene Lake 4 mi S of Mica Bay and 11 mi S of Coeur d'Alene.

A descriptive name for the shape of the bay.

Crescent Lake (Adams). T22N R2W sec 33. Located in the Six Lakes area, Hells Canyon National Recreation Area, Payette National Forest.

The uppermost lake in the basin, Crescent is just over the low divide from the head of Oxbow Creek. Its lower end is shallow, its upper end very deep. Named for its shape.

Crib Springs (Lemhi). T21N R21E sec 18. Located 1 1/2 mi W of Baldy Mountain.

John Hill built a crib here to keep the cattle from muddying the spring.

Crichton (Camas). T1N R15E. Ghost town 5 mi from Soldier, probably just W of Fairfield.

Established in 1884 by the RR company and named for a Mr. Crichton, whom the company sent to establish a townsite for a RR station. No evidence of the town remains.

Crittendon Peak (Shoshone). 6416'. T46N R7E sec 15. In the Coeur d'Alene National Forest, almost on the Idaho-Montana line.

Named for E. G. Crittendon, formerly employed on the St. Joe National Forest, who lost his life in military service in France, 15 October 1918.

Crone Gulch (Lemhi). T26N R21E sec 23. About 1 mi in length, almost directly across the valley from Hammerean Creek: enters N Fk Salmon River drainage 1 mi N of Gibbonsville.

Named for a Mr. Crone, who owned and operated a sawmill here in early days. He cut the lumber used to build the Gibbonsville schoolhouse.

Cronks Canyon (Lemhi). T16N R21E sec 18/8. On the Salmon River, about 3 mi NE of Ellis; runs about 2 mi NE.

Named for James Cronk, an early-day cattle raiser in this area. Also Royal Gorge of Idaho.

Crooked Creek (Clearwater). T37N R3E sec 15. In the SW quadrant of the county. A 3-mi tributary of Whiskey Creek from the E; Clearwater River drainage.

The creek is very crooked.

Crooked Creek (Valley). T21N R11E sec 17. Rises near the border of Idaho and Valley counties and flows 4 mi SW to Big Creek.

Named for its course.

Crooked River (Adams/Washington). T19N R3W sec 29. Rises on the N slopes of the Cuddy Mountains, Washington County, and flows NE 12 mi and W 3 1/2 mi to confluence with Bear Creek to form Wildhorse River; Snake River drainage.

A descriptive name.

Crooked River (Boise). T6N R8E sec 17. Rises in the SE part of the county and flows 22 mi SW into the N Fk Boise River at the border of Boise and Elmore counties.

Crooked River (Idaho). T29N R7E sec 24. Fourteen mi long; heads at the junction of its W and E Fks and flows N to S Fk Clearwater River 8.5 mi N of Orogrande.

Crooked Fk (Idaho). T37N R14E sec 34. Rises in Clearwater County and flows erratically S, E, and SW 15 mi to Lochsa River.

Named for their winding courses.

Crooks (Blaine). T2N R23E sec 18. A community and post office in the E part of the county on Fish Creek, 4 mi N of Fish Creek Reservoir. Post office, 1906-1920.

Named for the first postmaster, Mary Crooks, in 1906.

Crooks Corral (Idaho). T26N R1W sec 23. Corral located 5 mi W of Lucile, between the Snake and the Salmon rivers; at the head of Corral Creek, its namesake.

A man named Crooks lived at the head of this stream and had a number of placer mines here. He also trained horses in the corrals before taking them out for sale.

Crooks Hill (Latah). T41N R5W sec 18-20. A promontory between Viola and Potlatch.

Named for Bert Crooks, landowner in the area.

Crossport (Boundary). 1800′. T62N R2E sec 20/29. A flagstop on the GNRR, situated 5 mi E of Bonners Ferry.

In the late 1800s this was a rough-tough railroad town, said to be a worthy rival of Virginia City, Montana.

Named for its proximity to a ferry crossing on Kootenai River.

Crouch (Boise). 3021′. T9N R4E sec 15. Established in 1934.

Named for William Crouch.

Croy Creek (Blaine). Rises in the SW part of the county on the N slope of Richardson Summit; flows 12.5 mi NE to the Big Wood River at Hailey.

Named for C. P. Croy, who settled with his family in 1880 on land where Hailey Hot Springs is situated; he was one of the earliest settlers of the Hailey area.

Cruikshank Creek (Lemhi). T17N R27E sec 33. Heads on the Idaho-Montana border in the Beaverhead Mountains, just W of Deadman Pass, and flows W 4 1/2 mi to enter Canyon Creek 7 mi NE of Leadore; Lemhi River drainage.

Alexander Cruikshank, who scouted for the army during the Nez Perce War of 1877, patented land here in 1916. He reportedly raised Arabian horses.

Crumerine Creek (Latah). T40N R5W sec 30. A 4.1 mi stream, flows SW to Palouse River. The principal placers in

the Moscow-Troy Mining District lie along this creek.

Named for Andrew S. Crumrine (sic), who acquired 160 acres along this stream from James R. McConnell for $600 in 1883. Also Crumarine.

Crystal (Custer). 5378′. T11N R18E sec 22. Ghost town at the mouth of E Fk Salmon River in the center of the county.

Began in 1880 as a way station and vied with Challis for the county seat, but lost by 15 votes; consequently, settlers moved to Challis, and Crystal died.

Named for the quartz found in the area.

Crystal Creek (Clearwater). T37N R6E sec 11. In the central part of the county. Flows 4 mi SE into Orogrande Creek; Clearwater River drainage.

About 1893 a party found some crystals of quartz at the headwaters of the creek.

Crystal Gulch (Lemhi). T24N R19E sec 13. Approximately 1 mi N of Indianola Ranger Station, a gulch about 1 1/2 mi long, runs W and enters Indian Creek; Salmon River drainage.

Named for the Crystal mine located here.

Crystal Ice Caves (Power). T5S R28E sec 29-32. A rift cave in the NW part of the county, about 29 mi NW of American Falls; in the Kings Bowl fissure, Great Rift National Landmark. Named for ice formations within.

Crystal Lake (Adams). T22N R2W sec 26. Located in the Hells Canyon National Recreation Area, Payette National Forest, .2 mi SE of Monument Peak.

Above the timberline, this lake is hemmed in on all sides except the E with high crags, and is difficult to reach. A part of its shore is whitish granite.

Crystal Springs (Gooding). T9S R15E sec 12. In the SE extremity of the county, 1.4 mi W of the Cassia-Lincoln county line and 1 mi E of Niagara Springs.

Named for the quality of the water; it is crystal clear.

Crystal Springs (Twin Falls). T9S R15E sec 12. On Snake River, 7 mi NE of Buhl. John Blass, one of the first settlers in the area, built his cabin near these springs in the Snake River Canyon.

Named for the clarity of the spring water.

Cub Creek (Clearwater). T39N R12E sec 15. Rises in the extreme E part of the county on Hanson Ridge and flows 3 mi SW into Bear Creek; Clearwater River drainage.

This creek is part of a group name. Bear Creek was named first, then its tributaries Cub, Polar, and Kodiak creeks.

Cub Lake (Fremont). T9N R45E sec 7. In SE Fremont County; 5 mi WSW of the corner of Yellowstone National Park; located 1/2 mi from its larger neighbor, Bear Lake.

Named for its proximity to Bear Lake.

Cub River (Franklin). Rises in the extreme E part of the county, Wasatch Range, Cache National Forest; flows SW 16 mi almost parallel to Bear River, into Utah; used extensively in the Bear River-Bear Lake irrigation project.

Probably named Cub because of its nearness to Bear River and its much smaller size.

Cuddy Mountains (Adams/Washington). Located primarily in the NW part of Washington County, but extending E into Adams County and NW to the Snake River. Cuddy Mountain and Cuddy Point are the highest promontories in the range, reaching almost

8000′ and located in Washington County, W of Council. The top of this range is almost flat. To the W it breaks abruptly into Wildhorse River. To the N the mountain drops by a steep escarpment to a lava plateau; to the E it falls away to Weiser Valley, and to the S to a narrow plateau that separates it from Hitt Mountain. Glaciers left many cirques in this range, the largest being the one at the head of No Business Creek, a tributary of Wildhorse River at its mouth.

Named for John Cuddy, who settled on Cuddy Mountain in the 1880s and built the first sawmill and flourmill in the area.

Culdesac (Nez Perce). 1687′. T35N R3W sec 14. Town on Lapwai Creek 2 mi W of Jacques.

Charles S. Mellon, president of the Northern Pacific RR, gave the name Cul-de-sac to the small community, which is at the terminus of the branch line. He was supposedly going along the proposed route and remarked that this is indeed a cul-de-sac—a French term which can be roughly translated "blind alley," "the bottom of a bag," or a "place with only one outlet."

In 1900, when the railroad was being built, there were two towns: Mellon, named for President Mellon, and Culdesac, named for his remark. The citizens of the towns applied for a post office and suggested that the name Cul-de-sac be given, spelling it as a compound word. The Post Office Department refused this name, and instead gave the name Magnolia. The people petitioned in July, 1902, that the post office be named Culdesac, writing it as one word. This was granted.

Cully Moores (Clearwater). T37N R4E sec 19. Town 2 mi NE of Grangemont.

Named for homesteader Cully Mooers (sic), an early-day packer and USFS employee.

Culver (Bonner). T57N R1W sec 5. Town 3 1/2 mi NW of Sunnyside; 5 1/4 mi ENE of Sandpoint; on Pend Oreille Lake.

Named for a local resident.

Cunningham Bar (Lemhi). T23N R14E sec 1. On the Salmon River near Corn Creek.

Named for John Cunningham, who lived on the flat and placer-mined across the river. He earned a grubstake by working on a sweepboat in the 1900s.

Cup Creek (Boise). T10N R8E sec 30. Rises on Deadwood Ridge and flows E into Clear Creek 7 mi N of Lowman; Payette River drainage.

The Cup family from Valley County owned a mine on this creek.

Cuprum (Adams). T20N R3W sec 9. Formerly a copper mining town, now serves as a gateway to Black Lake and Six Lakes Basin. Located in the N part of the county at the S end of Seven Devils mining district. The town began with a teamsters' campsite, a few cabins, and Nels Swanson's wagonload of merchandise.

Named Cuprum, a Latin word meaning "copper," for the copper mines that brought it into being.

Curiosity Gulch (Latah). T42N R3W sec 32. A 2-mi tributary of Maple Creek, 2 mi N of Harvard; Palouse River drainage.

Reported in a mining notice of a gold prospect in 1894. Named by miners who were curious enough to prospect here, despite greater activity in nearby gulches.

Curlew Valley (Oneida). T15/16S R32E. Bounded on the N and E by the Sublett Range and on the W by the Black Pine Range, this slender valley extends from Utah N between the two ranges and is drained by Deep Creek; about 9 mi long. Lies in the center of Curlew National Grassland, a 34-square mile area. Formerly Holbrook Valley. Curlew Valley Reservoir, 3 mi long, is in the valley on Deep Creek, where water is impounded for irrigation.

Named for the long-billed curlews that frequented the area.

Currant Creek (Bonneville). T2S R44E sec 2. Rises in SE part of county and flows 2 mi NE into Bear Creek; just W of Palisades Reservoir; Snake River drainage.

Named for the currant, a small edible berry-like fruit common in the area. Other Bonneville County features bearing the same name include: Currant Hollow, Currant Hollow Creek, and Little Currant Hollow Creek, all in T1N R43E; Snake River drainage.

Curry (Twin Falls). 3755'. T10S R16E sec 10/15. An agricultural area in the N central part of the county, just E of Filer.

Named for an early landowner.

Curtis Creek (Bonner). T55N R4W sec 34. Heads 3/4 mi SE of Hoodoo Mountain; flows 5 1/2 mi E into Hoodoo Lake near Edgemere.

Named for a local man.

Custer County. County seat, Challis.

Custer County was created out of Alturas and Lemhi counties in 1881. Its history begins with fur traders and pathfinders as early as 1824; later, in the 1860s and 1870s, prospectors and miners came. Mining camps sprang up along Yankee Fork, Bayhorse Creek, Loon Creek, and in Stanley Basin.

Custer County contains portions of the Sawtooth, Salmon River, White Cloud, Pioneer, Lost River, and White Knob mountains. It is drained by the Salmon and Lost rivers and contains the highest peaks in the state.

Custer. T12N R15E sec 9/10. Ghost town on the Yankee Fork 2 mi N of Bonanza. The town was founded in 1878 by Justice of the Peace Samuel Halman. It reached its peak in 1888 with a population of 3500. Post office, 1879-1915.

Both the town and the county were named for the General Custer mine, which in turn honored the American general who lost his life at the Battle of the Little Bighorn.

Custer Peak (Shoshone). 6423'. T48N R5E sec 8. In the extreme E part of the county, 1 mi NW of Burke.

Named for the Custer mine at the same location.

Cutler Creek (Bannock). T8S R36E sec 2. An intermittent stream that heads 1 mi SE of Bonneville Peak and flows for about 2.5 mi SW into the Portneuf River. Alternate name: Cutter Creek, because USFS mispelled the name Cutler.

Named for a local family, who homesteaded and lived on this stream.

Cyanide Gulch (Lemhi). T26N R21E sec 36. S of Gibbonsville, 1 mi long, trends SW to N Fk Salmon River.

A cyanide process was used in the mill located at the mouth of the gulch.

D

D C Gulch (Lemhi). T17N R24E sec 24. Runs 1 mi NE to enter Lemhi River drainage 4 1/2 mi SE of Lemhi.

The gulch carries the surname initials of Mark J. David and James B. Cryder, early stockmen in this area who filed on water rights from Mill Creek in 1883 and who patented their land in 1887.

Daggett Creek (Boise). T4N R4E sec 16. Flows 8 mi SE into Mores Creek; Boise River drainage.

Named after a Mr. Daggett, who was killed in a sawmill on this creek in the 1890s; he was buried beside the creek.

Dahlonega Creek (Lemhi). T26N R21E sec 36. Heads near Morgan Mountain and flows N and W 7 mi to enter N Fk Salmon River.

The men who first took up placer ground on this creek reportedly were from Dahlonega, Georgia, and named the stream after their hometown.

Dairy (Owyhee). Townsite 15 mi S of Ballard; 22 mi SW of Silver City at the site of Camp Three Forks.

The Bachellor family had a milk ranch at this location. When the post office was granted (1887-1910), it was called Dairy.

Dairy Creek (Oneida). T12S R35E sec 5. Rises in the mountains of the N extremity of the county and flows generally S about 10 mi to Wright Creek; Malad River drainage.

Named for a dairy located here in the early 1900s.

Dairy Creek (Lemhi). T15N R24E sec 13. Forms in Lemhi Range in Dairy Lake, and flows NE 2 mi to enter Big Eightmile Creek; Lemhi River drainage. Post office, 1918-1927.

William Gray Purcell had a big dairy here in the early days.

Dairy Mountain (Idaho). 6480'. T27N R3E sec 17. In the Nezperce National Forest, 6 mi NW of Adams Ranger Station.

Named for the work of Charles Rice, dairyman on the mountain, who in early days delivered milk by pack string to persons on Salmon River.

Dalton Hill (Bonneville). 6778'. T1S R41E sec 1. In the central part of the county, about 10 mi NE of Bone.

Named for Charles Dalton, one of twenty-seven Mormon missionaries called to the area by Brigham Young to convert the Indians.

Daly Creek (Lemhi). T23N R20E sec 25. Forms 1 mi NW of Wallace Lake and flows generally N 5 mi to enter Moose Creek; Salmon River drainage.

Named for James Daly, who was elected secretary of the Summit Mining District in September, 1866.

Dan Lee Creek (Clearwater). T35N R5E sec 12. Rises in the S extremity of the county and flows 3 1/2 mi SW into Swede Creek; Clearwater River drainage. Dan Lee Ridge trends W-E 5 mi from the head of Dan Lee Creek, 5 mi SE of Pierce.

Named for a miner at Pierce who later homesteaded along the creek.

Daniels (Oneida). T12S R35E sec 18/20. In the NE part of the county, 13.5 mi N of Malad City. Apparently this was only a post office serving the area along the upper reaches of Deep Creek in the early 1900s. No community remains.

Named for the Daniels family, settlers.

Daniels (Clearwater). T38N R4E sec 10. Town 6 mi NW of Headquarters.

Named for settler Thad Daniels, who owned 40 acres here. Daniels died in the early 1950s. Post office, 1900-1929.

Danish Flat (Bear Lake). T13S R42E sec 13/14. An area 3 mi SW of Liberty. Like Copenhagen Basin and Copenhagen Canyon, it was settled by Scandinavian Mormons, mostly Danes, who continued their original ways and dress in their adopted country.

Danskin Canyon (Elmore). The canyon of S Fk Boise River from its mouth to Indian Point, a distance of 35 mi.

The walls of the canyon have several caves.

Danskin Lake. T1N R7E sec 7. Danskin Peak (6694') is about 1 mi SE of the lake.

Both the lake and the peak are named for the canyon, which in turn may have been named for Peter Danskin, settler and miner of Danskin

Creek, Boise County, 2 mi NE of Grimes Pass.

Darby Creek (Teton). T4N R45E sec 17. Rises on the W slope of the Teton Range and flows W 6 mi to Teton River. Formerly Goodfellow Creek, which see.

Darby. T4N R46E sec 6. Early settlement and post office on the bench about 4 mi SE of Driggs above Darby Creek. Settlers came between 1882 and 1902. The Darby townsite was dedicated in 1907.

Named for Jim Darby, who settled on Goodfellow Creek in 1882. Local usage of Darby Creek, because Darby lived here, replaced the original name.

Darlington (Butte). 5700'. T6N R25/26E sec 25/31. In the extreme NW part of the county on the Butte-Custer county line. Established in the 1890s as a mining town, the first shaft having been sunk at Saddle Mountain mine in 1893. There were early stores, stations, and a post office (1902-1927).

Named for Wayne Darlington, an early miner and the first postmaster.

Daveggio Creek (Shoshone). T44N R3E sec 9. In the SW part of the county. Rises in Daveggio Meadows on the W slope of Twodot Peak and flows 6.5 mi N and W to Marble Creek; St. Joe River drainage. Daveggio Knob overlooks the headwaters.

Named for John F. Daveggio, who homesteaded nearby ca. 1885.

Davis Buttes (Fremont). 6700'. T12N R40E sec 27. Two buttes W of the W boundary of Targhee National Forest. Davis Lake is 4 mi W of St. Anthony. Davis Lake Wells are 3 livestock wells 2 mi NE of Davis Buttes.

Names associated with the Davis Lake Land and Livestock Company, a sheep company that used the US Stock Driveway along which these names are found. Derived from the pioneer Davis families of St. Anthony.

Davis Canyon (Lemhi). T23N R22E sec 36. Heads S of Ajax Peak and runs SW 4 mi to Freeman Creek; Salmon River drainage.

Named for John W. Davis, an early settler in this area.

Davis Gulch (Boise). T5N R4E sec 27. A 2-mi gulch trending NE to Grimes Creek; Boise River drainage.

Sam Davis had a mining claim on this gulch.

Davis Gulch (Lemhi). T22N R19E sec 22. About 1 1/2 mi long, runs S to Arnett Creek about 3 1/2 mi up from its mouth; Salmon River drainage.

Named soon after 1866 to honor President Jefferson Davis of the Confederacy.

Dayley Creek (Cassia). T12S R23E sec 6/7/17. Rises on the NW slope of Albion Mountains in the Sawtooth National Forest, flows 2.5 mi NW and N, and disappears between Pine Knob and Antelope Hill.

Named for the Dayley family, early settlers in Marsh Basin.

Days Defile (Custer). Early name for Little Lost River Canyon.

So named by Donald Mackenzie's Snake brigade of the Northwest Company, because John Day died here 16 February 1820.

Dayton (Franklin). 4748'. T15S R38E sec 23. In the SW part of the county, 8 mi W of Preston.

Originally called Franklin Meadows because the original settlers had come from Franklin; then Five Mile Creek because of its location 5 mi from Weston and from Clifton. Then renamed Chadville, for Joseph Chadwick. Its final name, Dayton, was bestowed by Bishop William B. Preston, because he always visited the settlement by day. Post office, 1912-1931.

Dead Horse Cave (Gooding). T4S R14E sec 6. A lava tunnel cave in the N central part of the county, 1.5 mi SW of McKinney Butte; 8.5 mi NW of Gooding; one of the Mt. McKinney Butte caves.

A dead horse was found here.

Dead Mans Hole (Custer). T12N R18E sec 26. Just below Clayton.

In 1882 Lew Clawson found a skeleton here believed to be that of Isaac T. Swim.

Dead Mule Creek (Clearwater). T39N R7E sec 15. Rises on Deadhorse Mountain and flows 4 mi E into N Fk Clearwater River.

A mule was shot at the head of the creek by a hunter who mistook it for an elk. Trail locator Tom Good was adjusting the packs of the mule at the time it was shot. George Gleason is believed to have been the careless hunter.

Deadhorse Creek (Lemhi). T22N R17E sec 4. Heads in vicinity of Indian Point and flows N to converge with Lick Creek; flows 2 mi generally N to enter Clear Creek; Salmon River drainage.

Willard Rood, Sr., named this creek. A friend of his, while prospecting ca. 1879 and while endeavoring to travel through this creek drainage, lost a horse in an accident.

Deadhorse Gulch (Boise). T6N R4E sec 24. A 2 1/2-mi gulch trending W into Grimes Creek 3 mi S of New Centerville; Boise River drainage.

Named because pioneer loggers worked so many horses to death in the rough terrain.

Deadhorse Mountain (Clearwater). T39N R7E sec 7. In the central part of E Clearwater County, 7 mi SW of Canyon Ranger Station. Deadhorse Creek rises on Deadhorse Mountain and flows 4 mi SE into N Fk Clearwater River.

A horse that belonged to a Mr. Swanson, an employee of Clearwater Timber Protective Association, was found dead on the mountain slope.

Deadline Ridge (Twin Falls). T15/16N R18/19E. Along the Twin Falls-Cassia county line. In the 1890s the battle between sheepmen and cattlemen had reached such a state that cattlemen were attempting to enforce a deadline at this point, W of which they said no sheepman could graze his herd.

Deadman Creek (Bonneville). T2N R45E sec 36. Rises in the E part of the county and flows 2 mi SE into Palisades Creek; Snake River drainage.

A hunter died of exposure in this area in the early 1900s.

Deadman Creek (Bonneville). T2S R44E sec 5. Rises in central part of the county W of Palisades Reservoir and flows 4 mi NW into Bear Creek; Snake River drainage.

Named in 1901 because of the death of a French sheepherder employed by Joe Archant. He was buried at the corral SW of the top of Big Elk Mountain.

Deadman Creek (Bonner). T63N R4W sec 19. Heads at Plowboy Mountain; flows 2 1/2 mi NE into Upper Priest Lake 5 1/2 mi E of the Idaho-Washington border. Received its name from the finding of a dead man in the creek.

Deadman Creek (Idaho). T33N R8E sec 6. Rises between Frenchman Butte and Brush Hill and flows about 8 mi SE to the Lochsa River 9 mi NE of Lowell.

A skeleton was found at the mouth of this stream in 1906 by John Austin (USFS).

Deadman Flat (Elmore). T7S R10E sec 8-22. In the SE part of the county 10 mi due S of Glenns Ferry. Deadman

Creek rises on Grindstone Butte and flows about 20 mi NW to the Snake Narrows, 1 mi SE of Hammett; Snake River drainage.

Buffalo Horn and his Bannock Indian band preyed on emigrant trains and stagecoaches around King Hill and in the area S. They killed three miners on the flat. The name Deadman was transferred to the nearby stream.

Deadman Gulch (Shoshone). T46N R3E sec 4. In the SW part of the county W of Big Creek.

Six men were trapped and burned to death near this area on 20 August 1910, during the great forest fire of that summer.

Deadman Gulch (Shoshone). T48N R5E sec 25. A 2-mi gulch trending N to S to S Fk Coeur d'Alene River, in the E part of the county 1 mi E of Mullan.

A local informant accounts for the name with an unverified story of Chinese miners fighting among themselves, probably over gold.

Deadman Pass (Lemhi). T17N R28E sec 14. On the Idaho-Montana border, 1 mi N of Horse Prairie Mountain.

There are two different versions of the origin of this name: two informants say that a dead man was found here by Alexander Cruikshank during the mining activity at Nicholia in the 1880s, and no one ever identified the body. Another informant says an old prospector named Brown was crossing this pass when his saddle cinch broke and he fell from his horse and was killed.

Deadman Point (Bonner). T55N R1E sec 10. On Lake Pend Oreille, 7 1/4 mi E of Talache and 8 1/2 mi S of Hope.

Named for an Indian known as Death-on-the-Trail, who was killed in an accident.

Deadwater Gulch (Lemhi). T24N R20E sec 25. About 2 mi long; runs N to S to the Salmon River about 5 mi E of Indianola Ranger Station. Deadwater Spring (3500') is a small spring along the Salmon River road at the mouth of Deadwater Gulch, about 4 mi SW of North Fork.

At the mouth of this gulch there is a natural rock ridge that extends across the Salmon River and slows the water, giving it the appearance of stillness.

Deadwood River (Boise/Valley). T9N R7E sec 25/35. Rises in Valley County on the mountains NW of Cape Horn at an altitude of 6000' and flows about 30 mi SW to S Fk Payette River 2 1/2 mi W of Lowman. Deadwood Ridge is located W of Deadwood River and is named for the river.

Deadwood (Valley) 5635'. T13N R7E sec 11/13. Ghost town on Deadwood River in a mining district 17 mi S of Landmark, ca. 1864.

Deadwood Basin (Valley). E of Smiths Ferry, drained by Deadwood River; relatively narrow and about 20 mi long. Deadwood Summit is situated 2 mi N of the source of Deadwood River.

Probably named for the dead wood standing in the basin in the upper reaches of the river; some say for an old miner, "Deadwood" Jim, who lived on the stream.

Deary (Latah). 2960'. T40N R2W sec 14,15,22,23. An incorporated company town in the E part of the county, 12 mi NE of Troy.

Platted in 1907 by William Deary for the Weyerhaeuser Timber Company, on land homesteaded by Joe Blailock; incorporated in 1912. Early name, "Anderson," which see. Post office, 1907-.

Named for William Deary, early settler and manager for Weyerhaeuser Company, who directed construction of the lumber mill and town in 1906.

Death Creek (Clearwater). T38N R8E sec 12. Rises on Buckingham Point in the east-central part of Clearwater County and flows 3 mi SE into N Fk Clearwater River.

In the fall of 1908, a man was found dead at the head of the creek by Jack Sprague and Fred Dennison, trappers. The man, who had only a small canvas for shelter and a bow and arrows, was never identified. Jack Harlan (USFS) served as the coroner and buried the man here along the creek.

Deception Gulch (Clearwater). T40N R11E sec 6. Runs from Deception Point (5462') in the NE part of the county 2 1/2 mi SE then 2 1/2 mi N to N Fk Clearwater River.

The gulch may have gotten its name from miners in the area whose mining claim was not as good as it looked. Or it may have come from the deceptive way the gulch runs—first SE, then N.

Decker Gulch (Blaine). T4N R18E sec 35. Runs from 8 mi N of Hailey 1.5 mi S to E Fk Wood River.

Named for the family who lived at the mouth of this gulch.

Decker Peak (Custer). 9847'. T8N R13E sec 4. Just W of the Sawtooth National Forest in the Sawtooth Range. Decker Flat is about 4 mi E of Decker Peak between Salmon River and Huckleberry Creek.

Named for Ray Decker, who lived in the mining town of Custer on Yankee Fork at one time. He built a cabin on Decker Flat and lived there with his family before 1910.

Declo (Cassia). 4200'. T10S R24E sec 27/35. In the N central part of the county, on Marsh Creek 2 mi upstream from the Snake River.

Originally a Mormon settlement, founded in the late 1870s.

When the rail line from Salt Lake City, Utah, to Boise arrived at Declo in 1884, the town experienced a small boom and the number of businesses increased dramatically. Post office, 1917-.

Formerly Marshfield, which name the Post Office Department rejected because of its length. Declo, from the Dethles and Cloughly families, was acceptable.

Decorah (Adams). T21N R3W sec 25. Site of an early mining town on Garnet Creek between Landore and Helena. Post office, 1901-1922.

Named for Decorah, Iowa, which in turn was named for a Winnebago chief.

Deep Creek (Oneida). T14S R33E sec 31. Rises in the southernmost part of the county and flows N 13 mi to empty into Rock Creek; Snake River drainage. Flows through Curlew Valley in Curlew National Grassland; it has been impounded to form Curlew Valley Reservoir for irrigation.

This Deep Creek, like all others bearing the name, is unusually deep for its size.

Deep Creek (Boundary). T62N R1E sec 19. Merges with the Kootenai River 2 mi W of Bonners Ferry. A major tributary of the Kootenai River from the S.

Named by the USFS.

Deep Creek (Latah). T41N R5W sec 2. Rises in McCroskey State Park on Mineral Mountain and flows 8 mi S to the Palouse River 1.5 mi W of Potlatch; fed by West, Middle, and East forks, the system draining the E half of Townships 42 and 43.

Deep Creek 2519'. An early-day community 1 mi N of the junction of Deep Creek and the Palouse River. More than 25 sawmills were located along the creek from 1888 to 1966.

Deep Creek (Twin Falls). T9S R14E sec 10. Rises SE of Rogerson and flows NW through Deep Creek Reservoir (2 mi long) and Lower Deep Creek Reservoir (1 mi long) 31 mi NW to the Snake River. The reservoirs impound irrigation water for the area extending N, NW, W, and E of the lower reservoir.

Deep Creek Mountains (Power/Oneida). T8-15S R32/33E. Trend slightly NW to SE from near American Falls almost to Holbrook; maximum width, 12 mi.

Prominent peaks: Bannock Peak (8256') and Deep Creek Mountain (8670').

Named for the creek that flows through Curlew Valley.

Deer Creek (Caribou). T10S R45E sec 6. Rises on Dry Ridge 2 mi N of Green Mountain amd flows 12.5 mi SE to Crow Creek, Bear River drainage.

Named for the abundance of deer in the region. Huge herds were reported in 1811-12; few in the 1920s, then a great increase as late as 1926.

Deer Creek (Boise). T6N R5E sec 14. Flows 4 mi SE into Elk Creek; Boise River drainage.

Named because a Mr. Luckett of Idaho City shot a 155-pound blacktail deer on this creek in 1864.

Deer Park Creek (Lemhi). T15N R25E sec 10. Forms 2 mi NE of Devils Lake and flows 2 mi NE, just NW of Adams Creek; Lemhi River drainage.

The area contains small groves of trees, and deer are often seen here.

Deer Parks (Jefferson). A very early name for the area E of the big bend in S Fk Snake River.

Named because it afforded an ideal habitat for deer with the abundance of natural hay and of brush for winter pro-

tection. Later it was homesteaded, cleared, and turned into grazing and farmlands.

Degan Mountain (Lemhi). 8748'. T19N R20E sec 27. Five mi N of Sheephorn Mountain.

Named for Louis A. Degen (sic), a carpenter, who settled nearby and patented his land in 1924.

Dehlin (Bonneville). 6170'. T1N R40E sec 26. Townsites 26 mi SE of Idaho Falls, settled in 1910.

Named for the Dehlin family, who settled here.

DeLamar (Owyhee). 5500'. T5S R4W sec 5. Ghost town 4 1/2 mi W of Silver City. Delmar Mountain, covered with old workings of early-day miners as well as later workings, is located at the town.

The DeLamar mine was formed in 1888 by the purchase of mineral claims on DeLamar Mountain. Around the property of the mine grew the town, which was in its heyday in 1890.

Post office, 1889-1942.

Named for Joseph R. DeLamar, mining capitalist and former sea captain.

Delate Creek (Shoshone). T42N R6E sec 33. In the extreme SE part of the county, a 2-mi stream trending SE to Little N Fk Clearwater River.

Named by W. H. Daugs (USFS) in 1927. Chinook jargon De-late, "straight," suggested by the unusually straight course of the stream.

Della Basin (Bonneville). T3S R43E sec 23/24. In SE Bonneville County about 2 mi E of Herman.

Named for Della, a "shady lady" who had a cabin here during the gold rush of 1875.

Delta (Shoshone). 2517'. T49N R4E sec 10. In the E part of the county, 4 mi SW of Murray, at the mouth of Trail Creek. This was a gold camp in the late

1800s, and nuggets were panned here as late as the 1920s.

Named because of its location at the mouth of the stream.

Delyle Creek (Bonner). T54N R2E sec 1. Heads 1/2 mi NW of Summit Campground and flows 3 mi E into Twin Creek; Clark Fork River drainage. Delyle Forks is the area bounded by Twin Creek on the W, Dry Creek on the E, and Delyle Ridge on the N. Delyle Ridge extends 3 mi NE from Delyle Forks.

Named for Charlie Delyle, a settler in the 1870s.

Demming (Owyhee). T6S R3W sec 5. Townsite in the Flint and Boone Peak area. A mining camp that arose near the Demming mine.

Named for the mine's discoverer.

Democrat Gulch (Blaine). T2N R18E sec 18. In the Hailey Gold Belt, 2 mi SW of Hailey. Trends 5 mi NW to SE to Croy Creek; Big Wood River drainage.

Named for the Democrat mine at the head of this gulch.

Democrats, The (Owyhee). T2S R4W sec 36. Democrat Creek, a tributary of Jordan Creek, Owyhee River drainage, flows near The Democrats.

Town and stage station 6 mi NW of Silver City. Nothing now remains of this station on the Reynolds Creek stage route.

Some say that the station was named because Democrat wagons, light uncovered wagons with two or more seats, were built (or used) here. Others say that the owner of the station, Douglas McDonald, was an avid Democrat who took his politics very seriously; hence the name.

Dempsey (Bannock). T9S R38E sec 22. An abandoned settlement.

Named for Bob Dempsey, an early trapper.

Dempsey Creek (Camas/Gooding/ Elmore). T3S R12E sec 35. Rises in the SW corner of Camas County, and flows about 10 mi through the NW corner of Gooding County into Dry Creek, Elmore County; Snake River drainage.

At the opening of the Bannock War in 1878, Indians killed a man named Dempsey at the headwaters of this stream when they attacked white men herding hogs on the Camas Prairie, which the Bannock considered theirs to harvest for food.

Dennis Butte, East/West (Benewah). 4626'/4808'. T43N R3W sec 14/9.

Named for an early settler in this heavily timbered area.

Dent (Clearwater). 1500'. T38N R2E sec 20. Town 10 mi N of Orofino.

Named for early settler and first postmaster Charles Dent. In the 1890s it was a stopping place for persons migrating up the river.

Dent Creek (Shoshone). T47N R3E sec 28, a 2-mi tributary of Middle Fk Big Creek; St. Joe River drainage. Nine mi SW of Wallace.

Named for a local homesteader.

Denton (Bonner). 2087'. T56N R2E sec 18. Town 4 3/4 mi SE of Hope, 4 1/2 mi NW of Clark Fork. Denton Slough, 4 mi SE of the town, heads 1 mi SE of Ellisport Bay Point and flows 1 3/4 mi SE into Lake Pend Oreille.

Originally named Thornton in 1891, when a siding of the Northern Pacific RR was built. The station later moved and the town name was changed to Denton, in honor of Dennis Thorton.

Denver (Idaho). T31N R2E sec 29. In the NW part of the county. Currently a ghost town, Denver was laid out in 1890 by the Denver Land and Townsite Company, composed of realtors from Moscow.

Probably named for Denver, Colorado, as the sites were similar and hopes for the new Denver were high. Formerly called Centerville, named by its founder, B. F. Morris, for his hometown, Centerville, Missouri. Post office, 1892-1914.

Derian Creek (Lemhi). T22N R22E sec 18. Forms 2 mi E of Wallace Lake and flows E 3 1/2 mi to enter the Salmon River near Carmen.

Named for John Deriar (sic), an early settler in this region. Also Deriar Creek.

Derr Creek (Bonner). T55N R2E sec 9. Heads 2 3/4 mi S of Derr Point and flows 6 mi generally N into Johnson Creek; Clark Fork River drainage.

Derr Point (5225′), a promontory midway between Derr Creek and Johnson Creek, is 1 1/2 mi SW of the mouth of the creek. Derr Ridge extends S from Derr Point to the Bonner-Shoshone county line. Derr Island is surrounded by Middle Fk Clark Fork River on the N and S Fk on the S.

Named for Al R. Derr, a resident of Clark Fork.

Desmet (Benewah). 2560′. T44N R5W sec 24. In SW Benewah County, on the Coeur d'Alene Reservation. Post office, 1890-.

Named for Father Pierre Jean DeSmet, Belgian Jesuit who came to Idaho as a Catholic missionary in 1842 and founded a mission located first on the St. Joe River, then at Cataldo on the Coeur d'Alene River (which see), and then at this location.

Devil. Devil has been applied to several formations in Idaho. Most are alike in that they are difficult and hazardous to reach, and the scene is often much like our imaginings of the Devil's abode: desolate, rough, and characterized by bleak greyness.

Devil Creek (Twin Falls). T11S R13E sec 9. Rises near the Idaho- Utah border in SW Twin Falls County and flows 14 mi NNE to Salmon Falls Creek; Snake River drainage.

Devils Basin (Lemhi). T14N R24E sec 10. In the Lemhi Range, at the head of Big Eightmile Creek on the Lemhi side and N Fk Big Creek on Pahsimeroi side.

Named for the "devil fish" or "mud puppies" that are in abundance here.

Devils Bedstead, The (Blaine/Custer). 11,100′. T5N R19E sec 2. Third tallest peak in the Pioneer Range.

This is one of several separate granite intrusions on the eastern flank of the batholith. It consists of some 30-40 square miles of exposed granite, with The Devils Bedstead the highest peak.

Named for the shape of the mountain.

Devils Canyon (Lemhi). T15N R25E sec 7. Heads near Devils Lake, 1 mi N of Gunsight Peak, and flows N 3 mi to Big Eightmile Creek, 7 mi SW of Leadore.

Named because it is so rough and rocky.

Devils Club Creek (Shoshone). T42N R6E sec 23. A 2-mi tributary of N Fk Clearwater River at Devils Lake.

Named for the stickery plant, devils club, which grows in the area.

Devils Corral (Jerome). T9S R18E sec 32/35. In the S part of the county, between Shoshone Falls and Twin Falls on the Snake River; a natural arena where rustlers cached their stock when pursuers came too close. The rustlers were known as the Devils Corral Gang.

Devils Gorge (Shoshone). T50N R1E sec 12. A 2-mi gulch trending NE to SW, 9 mi N of Enaville; Coeur d'Alene River drainage.

Devils Kitchen (Caribou). T11S R40E sec 23. This rock formation lies at the far end of Ice Cave, 2 mi S of Grace; piles of lava occupy an extension of the corridor-like Ice Cave.

Devils Kitchen (Twin Falls). T10S R14E sec 30. A cave-like formation in a cliff near Castleford. Entrance to the room is by way of a hazardous descent down the chimney.

Devils Ladder (Adams). T21N R1W sec 3/10. Rock formation about 2 mi SW of Pollock Mountain, in the Seven Devils area.

Named because from a distance the rocks suggest rungs of a ladder giant-steps apart.

Devils Lake (Shoshone). T42N R6E sec 25. In the extreme S central part of the county; the source of Devils Club Creek.

Devils Playground (Elmore). T4S R10E sec 32. Rock formation on a flat above King Hill; an interesting scenic area of round smooth stones.

Devils Punch Bowl (Gooding). T6S R14E sec 28. A canyon opening where the headwaters of the Malad River flow down the lavas to a deep pool.

Devils Scuttle Hole (Jerome/Twin Falls).

A name given the 35-mi stretch of the Snake River below Caldron Linn (which see) where one of Wilson's Price Hunt's canoes was destroyed in 1811.

Devils Washbasin (Gooding). T6S R13E sec 25/36. The bottom of Malad Gorge, at the mouth of the Malad River on the Snake.

The water has worn the rock and eroded the basin-like formation.

Devils Washboard Falls (Twin Falls). T9S R14E sec 11. On the S side of the Snake River. A series of small falls over rock ledges and boulders.

Dewey (Owyhee). 5850′. T4S R4W sec 36. Deweys Peak, formerly Spanish Queen (before the Spanish-American War), takes its name from the town, which lies on Jordan Creek near Silver City.

The oldest settlement in Owyhee County, originally named Booneville. The mining town was founded in the summer of 1863 by J. C. Boone, for whom the town was first named. Boone was one of the original 29 discoverers of gold in Owyhee County. Post office, 1896-1911.

Colonel William Henry Dewey, for whom the town was later named, bought what remained of Booneville in 1896 and 1897, revamped the old town, and built an ornate sixty-room hotel and other buildings.

Dewey Creek (Clearwater). T36N R6E sec 33. In the SE extremity of the county. Flows S into Musselshell Creek; Clearwater River drainage.

Named for an early settler or miner.

Deweys Grove (Gem). A popular picnic area in the early 1900s. Located E of Emmett.

The 40-acre grove, east of Emmett, belonged to Mr. and Mrs. John Cyrus Dewey. It was full of cottonwood trees. In 1970 this grove was annexed to Emmett and called Deweys Addition.

Dewitt Canyon/Creek (Fremont). T9N R41E sec 11. In southcentral Fremont County; runs 4 mi S to unnamed reservoir. Creek flowing from the reservoir is named Snow Creek.

Named after one of the original homesteaders who lived in the area.

Diablo Mountain (Idaho). 7461′. T33N R15E sec 17/8. In the Clearwater National Forest, 8 mi W of the Idaho-Montana line.

"Diablo" is the Spanish word for devil.

Diamond Creek (Lemhi). T23N R22E sec 31. Forms near the S end of Jackass Ridge and flows E 4 1/2 mi to enter the Salmon River.

Reportedly named for the shape of the terrain in the creek drainage.

Diamond Creek (Twin Falls). T15S R18E sec 10. Rises near the E border of the county and flows 3 mi SW to empty into Cottonwood Creek 14 mi SE of Rogerson. Diamond Flat Spring lies 1 mi S of the mouth of the creek.

These features have their origin in the name of Diamondfield Jack Davis, hired to protect cattle ranges in south-central Idaho against sheepmen. He was tried for the murder of two sheepherders, found guilty, and sentenced to hang but was eventually pardoned and released. This area is among several where he worked for cattlemen.

Dickey (Custer). 6345'. T9N R22E sec 6. A prosperous mining center in the late 1800s. Dickey Peak (11,140') is 6 mi N of Dickey and 6 1/4 mi NW of Mt. Borah in the Lost River Range; said to be much more impressive than Mt. Borah, with its deep and symmetrical ravines. Challis National Forest, Lost River Division.

Named for the first postmaster, Joseph Dickey.

Dicks Creek (Latah). T38N R1E sec 24. Rises N of Mason Butte in the SE corner of Latah County and flows SE 5 1/2 mi to N Fk Clearwater River.

Named for a homesteader named Dix.

Dierkes Lake (Twin Falls). T9S R18E sec 31/32. In the bend of the Snake River just S of Shoshone Falls.

Named for an early settler named Dierikson (sic).

Dietrich (Lincoln). 4080'. T6S R18E sec 12. In the S part of the county, 7 mi E of Shoshone on the UPRR. Like Shoshone, this began as a RR construction camp for the OSL; unlike Shoshone, there were no saloons within a 2-mi radius. Post office 1906-.

Named for Judge Frank S. Dietrich of Boise, later of the Ninth Circuit Court in San Francisco.

Dike Lake (Custer). Lake.1 mi long, at the base of the Chinese Wall.1 mi WSW of Gunsight Lake.

There is a quartzite dike in the rock wall on the N side of the lake.

Dillinger Creek (Idaho). T25N R11E sec 9. Rises in the Meadow of Doubt and flows 6 mi NE through Dillinger Meadow to the Salmon River 6 mi E of Bargamin Creek.

Creek and meadow are named for Sam Dillinger, who arrived in Elk City in 1865, placer mined on Mallard Creek, and built the first arrastra in Dixie in 1892.

Dingle (Bear Lake). 5956'. T14S R44E sec 11/12. In the SE part of the county, 10 mi S of Montpelier.

Its first name was Dingle Bell, suggested by the tinkling bell of a lead sheep; then Cottonwood for the cottonwood trees in the area; and finally Dingle in 1881. This was a small Mormon settlement in the 1870s; some of the settlers came directly from England. Post office, 1890-.

Dingle Swamp. T14/15S R43/44E. Adjoining Bear Lake on the N and including Mud Lake; an area 3-6 mi wide and 8 mi long; contains the Bear Lake National Wildlife Refuge, sheltering thousands of ducks and geese each year.

Dip Creek (Blaine). T5N R17E sec 23. Rises 2.2 mi N of Sun Valley and flows 1.3 mi SW to the Big Wood River.

Named because there was a sheep-dipping trough on this creek.

Discovery Bar (Owyhee). T4S R4W sec 34. One mi E of DeLamar and 6 mi below Booneville.

Named by the original party of 29 men who first discovered gold at this site.

Dishrag Spring (Lemhi). T19N R19E sec 35. In Moyer Creek drainage 2 mi N of Iron Lake; Salmon River drainage.

USFS crews found a dishrag that some camper had left at the spring.

Disney (Lincoln). T5S R17E sec 31. In the SW part of the county on the UPRR, 4 mi W of Shoshone.

Named for Frank T. Disney, state senator (1921-1924) from Shoshone.

Distillery Bay (Bonner). T62N R4W sec 32. On Priest Lake, 4 1/4 mi NW of Nordman; 4 1/2 mi SE of Blacktail Mountain.

Named because a man grew potatoes here but had no market for them, so he used them to make potato whiskey (for which there was a market).

Ditch Creek (Lemhi). T25N R21E sec 8. Headwaters located in vicinity of Allan Lake, flows approximately 6 mi SE and then S to where it enters Hughes Creek; N Fk Salmon River drainage.

Named because early miners ran a ditch from here to mining operations in the area ca. 1865.

Dive Creek (Elmore). T2S R8E sec 21. Heads just W of Bennett Mountain and flows SW 4 mi to its confluence with Bennett Creek; Snake River drainage.

Named because the trail that once crossed this creek near the upper end was so steep on both sides of the creek.

Divide Creek (Lemhi). T14N R27E sec 27. Originates N of the headwaters of Mud Creek; flows W 4 mi, then NW 5 mi to enter Eighteenmile Creek; Salmon River drainage.

Named because the stream's headwaters are on the Continental Divide.

Dixie (Canyon). T4N R3W. One of the earliest settlements in Boise Valley, on the S shore of the Boise River on the lower edge of Caldwell.

Dixie Valley, a camp located near Caldwell, was mostly occupied by Missourians in about 1864.

Lower Dixie was located about 9 mi S of Caldwell.

Many of the first settlers were southern sympathizers and so named their community Dixie or, as often called, Dixie Slough.

Dixie (Idaho). 5600′. T26N R8E sec 34. In the central part of the county, 12 mi S of Orogrande; in Nezperce National Forest, Clearwater Mountains, on Crooked Creek. Founded as a mining camp in 1867 and named for an early prospector, possibly from the South, nicknamed "Dixie"; given the date of its founding, there may have been several Confederate settlers.

Dixie Creek (Washington). T13N R2W sec 27. Rises in the E central part of the county on the S and E slopes of Dixie Lookout; flows NW and W to Weiser River 1 mi E of Midvale.

Dixie, an early RR station, settlement, and post office 1 1/2 mi E of Midvale, is on this creek.

Believed to have been named by southern sympathizers.

Dodge Creek (Boise). T8N R5E sec 2. In the central part of the county. Flows NW into the S Fk Payette River 3 mi NE of Grimes Pass.

The creek was named for Leo Dodge, who homesteaded here in the 1880s.

Doe Creek (Clearwater). T39N R13E sec 31. Rises in the SE corner of the county and flows 7 mi NW into Deer Creek; Clearwater River drainage.

This may be an office name given by the USFS, since the creek is a tributary of Deer Creek. These two creeks are located near Bear, Cub, Kodiak, and Polar creeks.

Dog Lake (Idaho). T23N R2W sec 34/35. On the old Boise Trail in the Seven Devils Mountains just E of Twin Imps and Devils Farm; in the SW corner of the county. This typical alpine lake is 12 acres in extent.

One of 16 names of flora and fauna applied in the area by USFS men sent out to name every geographic feature; Dog Lake is shaped like a dog.

Dolbeer (Caribou). T8S R39E sec 14. In the SW part of the county. Apparently an early name for Bancroft (which see).

Settled in 1892 and named for A. P. Dolbeer, one of the earliest pioneers of Bancroft.

Dollar Butte (Owyhee). T9S R2E sec 35. Two mi W of Sugar Loaf Butte. The most prominent landmark between the Blue Creek drainage and Battle Creek; named because it is said to be the size of a dollar, in comparison with nearby Half Dollar Butte.

Dollar Creek (Idaho). T34N R6E sec 12. Rises on Mex Mountain in the Clearwater National Forest and flows 3.5 mi SW to Eldorado Creek; in the N central part of the county; Clearwater River drainage.

This stream was named by miners but the reason for the name is not known. Its name, however, led to the naming of Two Bit, Four Bit, and Six Bit creeks nearby.

Dollarhide Summit (Camas/Blaine). 8719'. T3N R15E sec 16. On Camas-Blaine county line 1 mi S of Dollarhide Mountain (9276'). Located between Ketchum and S Fk Boise River in the Smoky Mountains.

Both promontories are named for an early mine owner in this area, A. H. Dollarhide.

Dolomite (Nez Perce). T37N R2W sec 29. Camas Prairie RR siding on the Clearwater River 2 mi NW of Agatha.

Named for the dolomite deposits in the area.

Dome Mountain (Lemhi). T22N R17E sec 18. Approximately 5 mi NE of Goat Mountain. Dome Lake lies 2 mi N of the mountain and 1 mi E of Horse Heaven.

Named for its rounded top.

Donaldson Creek (Shoshone). T46N R3E sec 15. In the SW quadrant of the county, 8 mi NE of Calder. Rises on Cemetery Ridge and flows 2 mi SW to E Fk Big Creek; St. Joe River drainage.

A man named Donaldson homesteaded on this creek.

Doniphan (Blaine). 6333'. T1N R17E sec 19. Ghost town in the SW part of the county in the Hailey Gold Belt, 11 mi SW of Hailey. This town started in the 1880s and flourished some 20 years as the trade and postal center for the Big Camas, Tip Top, Hidden Treasure, and Black Cinder mines.

Named for the first postmaster, James Doniphan.

Donkey Creek (Shoshone). T44N R3E sec 3. In the SE part of the county, 5 mi S of Marble Creek. Rises on Pocono Hill and Huckleberry Mountain and flows 2.5 mi SE to Marble Creek; St. Joe River drainage.

Named because donkey-engine logging in the Coeur d'Alene National Forest was practiced here. A "donkey" was a steam-driven winch.

Donnelly (Valley). 4742'. T16N R3E sec 10/15. At the N end of Cascade Reservoir, 1 1/2 mi W of Roseberry.

This town was settled primarily by Finns, about 1890, but did not grow much until the RR came through in 1912.

Named for the founding family of Donnellys.

Donnelly Gulch (Lemhi). T24N R21E sec 22. Approximately 3 mi long; runs SE to the Salmon River approximately 1 mi downriver from North Fork.

Named for James Donnelly, a pioneer rancher on this stream.

Dorion Peak (Custer). 12,016′. Seven mi SE of Leatherman Peak in the Lost River Range, Challis National Forest.

The name honors the Iowa Indian woman who was the wife of Pierre Dorion, interpreter for the Wilson Price Hunt party of 1811.

Doris Butte (Clearwater). 4753′. T37N R8E sec 2/11. Six mi NE of Bungalow Ranger Station. Doris Creek rises on this butte and Fox Butte and flows 5 mi SW into Weitas Creek; Clearwater River drainage.

This name may have come from the USFS as the butte was named relatively recently, when many other female names were assigned to features in the area.

Dorsey Creek (Owyhee/Elko Co., Nevada). T15S R8E sec 14. Stream 18 mi long; heads in Nevada, flows N into Idaho to the Jarbidge River 18 mi WNW of Three Creek.

Reportedly named for John Dorsey, local horse breeder.

Doumecq Plain (Idaho). T29N R1E sec 8 to sec 31. A 5-mi long plain extending from NE to SW about 5 mi NW of White Bird.

Named for John Doumecq, native of France, who migrated to Idaho about 1863 and engaged in both mining and stock-raising. The area where his stock grazed is now called Doumecq Plain.

Dover (Bonner). 2088′. T57N R2W sec 29. Town 4 3/4 mi NE of Wrencoe; 3 mi SW of Sandpoint.

Dover was named ca. 1919 because the stockholders in the Dover Lumber Company came from either Dover, Ohio, or Dover, England, and they merely transferred the town's name. The town was first named Welty in honor of the president of the lumber company. Post office 1912-.

Downata Hot Springs (Bannock). T12S R37E sec 12. Three mi SE of Downey on US 91. Natural springs that have been developed.

Named for Downey with a Greek suffix -ata, "result of, act of."

Downey (Bannock). 4852′. T11S R37E sec 34. In the SW part of the county, 6 mi S of Virginia. Town began in 1894, when the UPRR installed standard-gauge track. Little growth until 1910 when a large irrigation canal from Portneuf River brought water. Post office, 1894-.

Named for an official of the UPRR.

Doyle Creek (Clearwater). T40N R6E sec 35. A tributary of Beaver Creek from the E; Clearwater River drainage. In the N central part of the county.

Named for Ike Doyle, one of the first clerks at Headquarters for the Clearwater Timber Company.

Drake Canyon (Teton). T3N R44E sec 12/13. Near the head of the Teton River and trending NE to the Teton at T3N R45E sec 8, about 2 mi W of Victor.

Richard Drake and his family came to this area in 1889. They are remembered because they fiddled and played the piano for many local dances.

Draney Peak (Caribou). 9131′. T8S R45E sec 11. In the E part of the county; in Caribou National Forest; 20 mi NE of Soda Springs. Draney Creek rises on the W slope of this peak and flows 6 mi first SE then E to Tygee Creek at T8S R46E sec 10.

Named for Samuel Draney, elder brother of USFS ranger Jesse E. Draney.

Dream Gulch (Shoshone). T49N R5E sec 6. One mi W of Murray in the Summit Mining District.

The Rev. Floyd M. Davis located a claim near Murray and named it Dream Gulch. He called himself a circuit-riding gospel peddler, though he never preached in the Prichard and Eagle Creek areas, where he was learning about placer mining from operators. He came to be called "Dream" Davis. He washed gold out from the gravel on his claim, but no paying quantities of gold were found on any other claims in Dream Gulch.

Drift Creek (Clearwater). T41N R8E sec 8/17. Rises on Avalanche Ridge near the N border and flows 5 mi E into Collins Creek; Clearwater River drainage.

Named for the heavy snowfall.

Driggs (Teton). 6116'. T5N R45E sec 25/26/35. County seat. Situated about 1/2 mi N of Spring Creek in the center of E Teton County. Though a few families had come earlier, the main settlement (by Mormon colonists) occurred in 1898. Originally called Alpine. The town was established in 1909. Post office, 1894-.

Driggs was named by the Post Office Department for the great number of Driggses who signed the petition for a post office.

Driscoll Ridge (Latah). 2600' to 2700'. A ridge about 3 mi long beginning 2 mi SW of Troy and running SE to Bethel Church and Cemetery between Bethel Canyon on the E and Middle Potlatch Creek on the W.

Named for the first homesteaders on the ridge, John Driscoll and his family, who came to the area in 1880.

Driveway Gulch (Blaine). T4N R19E sec 33. Ten mi NE of Hailey; trends SW to NE to Cove Creek; E Fk Wood River drainage.

Named because cattlemen and sheepmen used this gulch to drive their stock between Quigley Gulch and Cove Creek.

Drop Creek (Boise). T8N R12E sec 15. Rises on the Boise-Custer county line on Elk Peak (10,076') and flows W into the S Fk Payette River.

The stream drops over the canyon walls at one point. Will C. Barnes of the USFS named it in 1928.

Drummond (Fremont). 5603'. T8N R43E sec 23/26. Town 10 mi SE of Ashton.

Named for a construction engineer on the railroad during the building of the line from Ashton to Driggs in 1911.

Dry Bed Channel (Jefferson). A high-water channel of the Snake River formed many years ago by spring runoffs that came out of the rock canyon at the SE tip of Jefferson County.

Dry Bed is about 50 mi long, running NW almost to the Rigby area, then W by S to rejoin the main river channel 4.5 mi W of Lewisville. All that lies between Dry Bed and the Snake River is designated as an island. Current map name for what locals call the Great Feeder.

When the river receded, the channel dried up; hence the name.

Dry Buck Creek (Boise). T8N R3E sec 5. Rises in the NW corner of the county on Dry Buck Mountain (6508') and flows 8 mi SE into Payette River.

These names originated with the Dry Buck band of Shoshoni who inhabited the Horseshoe Bend area; by 1880 they were driven off. Perhaps the band of Indians were named for the nearby mountain.

Dry Canyon/Creek (Bonneville). T1N R45E sec 3. Extends 6 mi SE to NW in the E part of the county, SE of Palisades Peak; Snake River Range, Targhee National Forest. The creek flows into Palisades Reservoir; Snake River drainage. Big Dry Canyon/Creek enters about 8 mi NW of Dry Canyon.

Named because the creeks go dry in the summer. Numerous applications of the term "dry" give evidence of the aridity of the area. Additional Bonneville County features with the same name include: three Dry Canyons with their respective creeks in T2/3N R43/44E and T1S R46E; Dry Elk Canyon and its creek in T2N R45E; Dry Gulch and its creek, T1S R45E; Dry Hollow, Dry Hollow Creek, Big Dry Hollow, and Big Dry Hollow Creek in T1N R41-43E.

Dry Ridge. The ridge formed between Dry and Big Bear creeks, locally referred to as Dry Creek; running 7 mi NE to SW. Nicknamed Little Sweden from the preponderance of Swedish homesteaders, who began their settlement in the 1880s.

So named because there is no water here in the summer.

Dry Creek (Twin Falls). T11S R20E sec 6. A 5-mi stream that rises 3.5 mi S of Murtaugh Lake in Cassia County and flows N through Murtaugh Lake to empty into the Snake River. The early mining town of Drytown sprang up at the mouth of this creek in 1864. Creek was known to dry up in the summer.

Dry Diggins Ridge (Idaho). T23N R2W sec 35/26. Nine Mi W of Windy Saddle in the Seven Devils Mountains; Hells Canyon National Recreation Area; SW part of Idaho County. In 1903 Jack Hastings filed mining claims here and constructed earthen dams across several gullies in order to trap snow melt for placer mining in the summer and fall.

Dry Ridge (Caribou/Bear Lake). A ridge extending 27 mi from the juncture of Georgetown Canyon and the Left Fk Twin Creek NE and then NW between Dry Valley and Diamond Creek to the Blackfoot River.

The ridge ranges in elevation from 8300' to 8900' and contains rich deposits of phosphate. Dry Valley is a very small valley drained by Dry Creek, which rises 1.2 mi E of Green Mountain and flows 7 mi N then SW to Slug Creek; Blackfoot River drainage. An arid ridge.

Dryden Peak (Owyhee). 5731'. T1S R5W sec 24. Mountain 1 mi N of Piute Butte.

Named for the Dryden family, who lived along Reynolds Creek, near the peak.

Dual Creek (Latah). T41N R2W sec 2. A 2-mi stream flowing E to Big Sand Creek; Palouse River drainage.

Named by W. H. Daugs (USFS) because two main streams form the drainage pattern.

Dublin (Lewis). T33N R1W sec 1. Railroad station and post office (1900-1910) in the middle of the county, about 3 mi SE of Craigmont.

Named by D. H. Lowry, an Irishman, for Dublin, Ireland.

Dubois (Clark). 5149'. T10N R36E sec 21. County seat. In the S central part of the county on Beaver Creek at the foot of the Centennial and Beaverhead mountains.

Settlers came in the 1880s, among them Fred Thomas Dubois, but the settlement did not grow until the farming boom of 1910-1920. Dubois became a trade center for the area and was chosen as the county seat in 1919. The boom did not last; many farmers and townspeople moved out and most buildings were razed. Now it is the center of a large grazing area. Post office, 1892-.

Named for Fred T. Dubois, who moved to Idaho in 1880, was US Marshal from 1882 to 1886 and Idaho's US Senator 1891-1897 and 1901-1907.

Duck Creek (Lemhi). T18N R16E sec 36. Heads near Duck Creek Point and flows generally S 4 mi to enter Camas Creek; Middle Fk Salmon River drainage.

Beaver dams built at the mouth of the creek backed up water, providing good feeding ground for ducks, which were usually found here in great numbers.

Dudley (Kootenai). 2137'. T48N R1W sec 2. In the SE part of the county, 5 mi SW of Cataldo. Established as a shipping point on the Coeur d'Alene River for the lumbering industry with a store and a post office, 1907- ca.1936.

Dudley Peak (3983') lies 1.5 mi SE of the village.

Named in 1895 for the subsequent first postmaster, Amy A. Dudley.

Duffield Creek (Latah). T42N R6W sec 33. Rises 5 mi W of Potlatch and flows SW into Washington to the Palouse River.

Named for Albert M. Dufield (sic).

Dull Axe (Clearwater). 5100'. T39N R5E sec 25/36. Mountain 4 mi NE of Headquarters.

At a distance the mountain looks like the blade of an axe with a nick in it.

Dummy Creek (Lemhi). T20N R19E sec 18. A stream approximately 2 mi long; flows NW and then SE to enter Panther Creek; Salmon River drainage.

Named for a deaf-mute miner who lived briefly at the mouth of the creek before the Copper Creek (now Cobalt) Ranger Station was built.

Dummy Creek (Lemhi). T19N R21E sec 14. One mi N of Briney Creek; flows 2 mi W to empty into Salmon River.

Named because two mutes were partners in the ownership of the ranch here.

Dump Creek (Lemhi). T24N R20E sec 26. Forms near the head of Comet Creek and runs mostly N 5 mi to enter Salmon River.

Early miners transferred Moose Creek water to Dump Creek in order to mine Moose Creek. They dumped the tailings from Moose Creek placers in Dump Creek, but the dam broke, eroding the Dump Creek drainage into the Salmon River.

Duncan Creek (Owyhee). T10S R4E sec 17. Flows NE into Wickahoney Creek; Bruneau River drainage.

Named after William Duncan, one of the party who first discovered gold in the county.

Duncan Ridge (Blaine). 11,491. T5N R19E sec 13,23. Ridge trending NE to SW between Hyndman Peak and Hyndman Creek; in the Pioneer Mountains, Sawtooth National Forest.

Named for Capt. Jonathan Duncan (USFS), who was killed in action with the 10th Mountain Division in Italy in WWII.

Dunlup (Latah). T42N R6W. An early community and post office near the Washington boundary, above the Palouse River.

Named for Thankful Dunlup, the first postmaster (1907).

Dunnigan Creek (Boise). T4N R4E sec 22. Flows 4 mi NW into Mores Creek; Boise River drainage.

Named for the Dunnigan family, who operated a way station at the mouth of the gulch.

Dunnville (Franklin). T14S R39E sec 6. In the NW part of the county, 20 mi N of Franklin; a short-lived (April 1878-May 1879) railroad tent-camp.

Early name for Banida, which see.

Durfees Spring (Cassia). T15S R24E sec 25. In the central part of the county, 2 mi E of Almo; formerly called Almo Springs.

Named for the Durfee family, early settlers and cattle raisers in the Almo area.

Durkeyville (Nez Perce). Ghost town on Craig Mountains 30 mi E of Lewiston; a roadhouse or way station established by Clark W. Durkee. In 1863 it was a mining camp with a population of 200.

Dutch Flat (Latah). T39N R4W sec 3. A flat 4 mi SE of East Moscow Mountain Lookout and 3 mi W of Troy, on Little Bear Creek.

Named for the Dutch Jake mining claim, located and recorded by Henry J. Klein in 1890.

Dutch Town (Latah). T42N R3W. A mining area in 1895 between Jerome and Big creeks.

Named for the Dutch Jake mines.

Dutchler Basin (Lemhi). T24N R19E sec 4/5. Just S of Dutchler Mountain (6994') at the head of Transfer Gulch and Little Spring Creek, approximately 3 mi N of Salmon River.

Named after Herman Dutchler, who had mining property at Shoup and in this area.

Dutchman Creek (Clearwater). T35N R6E sec 10. Flows S into Lolo Creek on the SE county line; Clearwater River drainage.

The name is descriptive of the ethnic group that once mined here.

Dutchmans Hump (Lemhi). T22N R18E sec 13. Hill S of Trail Creek on Panther Creek.

Named for James H. Hockensmith, a German who had mining claims in this area and patented land in the Lemhi Valley. To the early miners, all Germans were Dutch (Deutsch). Formerly called Hockensmith Hill.

Dutchoven Creek (Lemhi). T23N R18E sec 8. About 2 1/2 mi long, runs SE from its headwaters about 1/2 mi SW of Nabob mine to empty into the Salmon River.

There are three explanations for this name: a natural rock formation that looks like a large old-fashioned oven lies at the head of the canyon; the heat in this canyon is so great in the summertime that it is like being in a huge dutch oven; and a broken dutch oven was for a long time a landmark at the mouth of the creek.

Duthie (Shoshone). 4200'. T50N R5E sec 24. About 5 mi NE of Wallace; a mining camp, located by Jack Waite in the late 1800s or early 1900s.

Named for a Mr. Duthie, former owner of the Jack Hite mine.

Dwight (Teton). T5N R44E sec 4. The UP station at Cache, which see.

Dwyer Creek (Idaho). T24N R13E sec 17. N tributary of Salmon River, 5 mi long.

Named for the Dwyer brothers, who made a Salmon River trip with Captain Harry Guleke in 1903.

E

Eagan Creek (Valley). T20N R14E sec 6. A tributary of Big Creek 2 1/2 mi W of its confluence with Middle Fk Salmon River. Eagan Point (4190′) is a promontory on Eagan Creek.

Private Harry Eagan, Co. "C," Second Infantry, was shot through both thighs in a surprise attack by Sheepeater Indians at this site 20 August 1879. Eagan died after amputation of one leg and was buried on the spot. The War Department erected a modest monument to mark his grave and the site of the engagement.

Eagan, Mount (Bonner). 5278′. T57N R1E sec 26. Located 1 1/2 mi N of Hope; 4 1/2 mi E of Sunnyside.

Named for a settler.

Eagle Bar (Adams). 1000′. T22N R3W sec 28. Remnant of a much larger bar before Hells Canyon Dam was built, located about 1 1/2 mi S of Sawpit Creek on the Snake River.

In 1926 Morrison and Knudsen Co. built a road from Ballards Landing to this bar for the Butler Ore Company, to give access to their Red Ledge copper mine. Then during construction of Hells Canyon Dam, Idaho Power used the site for offices, tool shops, and a first-aid station. The road is now under water, as is most of the original bar.

Eagle Cliff (Shoshone). 7543′. T44N R10E sec 27. On the Idaho- Montana border.

Named for the eagles that nested here.

Eagle Creek (Shoshone). T50N R4E sec 35. In the extreme E part of the county, rising on the Idaho-Montana line in East Fork (8 mi long) and West Fork (10 mi long), two forks converge 1 mi NE of the town of Eagle and flow 1 mi SW to Prichard Creek; St. Joe River drainage.

Eagle (Shoshone) 2546′. T50N R4E sec 26/35. In the NE part of the county at the mouth of Eagle Creek. A riproaring town that flourished during the early days of the Coeur d'Alene Mining District.

Named for the creek, which in turn was named by Andy J. Prichard for a large bald eagle's nest which he spotted in a dead snag while he was prospecting this stream.

Eagle Island (Ada). T4N R1W sec 14. An area between the N and S branches of Boise River to a point where the branches rejoin (T4N R1E sec 24). A livestock ranch until 1930, when it became a prison honor farm until 1974. Now it is the site of Eagle Island State Park, a 30-acre developed area with a 12- acre lake.

Eagle. T4N R1E sec 8/9. A town located 5.3 mi E of Star, 1/2 mi N of the Boise River. Post office, 1908-.

Named for the bald eagle, which used this area as habitat.

Eagle Point (Clearwater). 5709'. T40N R7E sec 23. Peak 3 mi SE of Canyon Ranger Station, in the N part of the county. Eagle Creek rises on this peak and flows 3.2 mi SE into N Fk Clearwater River.

Named for the osprey (sic) that nested here.

Eagle Rock (Bonneville). Early name for Idaho Falls, which see.

Early Creek (Shoshone). T47N R3E sec 28. In the SW quadrant of the county. Rises in the Coeur d'Alene Mountains and flows SW 3 mi to Middle Fk Big Creek 10 mi NE of Calder.

A man named Early homesteaded near this stream. He lost his life in the 1910 Idaho fire.

Easley Creek (Boise). T10N R4E sec 34. Rises in the NW corner of the county and flows 4 mi SE into the Middle Fk Payette River 3 mi N of Crouch.

John Easley was a driver with the Overland Stage Company in 1864. He later settled on this creek near Garden Valley.

Easley Peak (Blaine/Custer). 11,108'. T6N R16E sec 16. Highest peak in Boulder Mountains. On the Custer-Blaine county line.

Named for J. V. Easley, a miner of the 1880s in Easley Gulch, 6 mi S of the peak. At the mouth of this gulch is Easley Hot Springs.

East Twin Butte (Bingham). 6605'. T2N R32E sec 14. The big cinder cone about 9 mi NE of Atomic City is a familiar landmark. Middle Butte (6394') is 2.5 mi SE of E Twin Butte. These two buttes, with Big Butte in Butte County, were major landmarks for early trappers, explorers, and emigrants. The once-smooth slopes of these buttes are now trenched by deep valleys and sharp intervening ridges.

Eastport (Boundary). 2600'. T64N R2E sec 10. Port of entry between Canada and Boundary County. Post office, 1910-.

Named because this is the eastern of two ports of entry in north Idaho.

Eaton (Washington). 2104'. T11N R6W sec 20. Early RR station and post office (1916) on Warm Springs Creek, 5 1/2 mi W of Weiser.

Named for Joseph L. Eaton, an early settler.

Ebenezer Bar (Lemhi). 3100'. T23N R17E sec 30. Along the Salmon River at the mouth of 4-mi long Ebenezer Creek.

There are conflicting stories about this name. It was named for either Ebenezer Snell or Ebenezer Smith, who had a mining rocker along the river at this place.

Eccles (Fremont). T12N R44E sec 31. Railroad siding 15 mi N of Warm River community. Eccles Butte (6500') is 3 mi W of Eccles Siding; also, Black Mountain.

Named for Si Eccles, division superintendent of the UPRR when the line to West Yellowstone was built ca. 1912; afterward chairman of American Smelting and Refining Company and member of the UP board of directors.

Echo Canyon/Creek (Bonneville). T1N R43E sec 16/9. Extends about 2 mi SE to NW in E half of the county, 4 mi S of Swan Valley. The 2-mi creek empties into Fall Creek; Snake River drainage.

An echo heard in the canyon led to the name.

Echo Rock (Bonner). T55N R1W sec 23. Rock formation on Lake Pend Oreille, 3 3/4 mi SE of Talache; 5 1/4 mi N of the town of Cedar Creek.

Named because steamboat whistles were blown here, and the sound echoed.

Eckersell Spring (Lemhi). T19N R25E sec 18. On Agency Creek, 2 1/2 mi SE of Poison Gulch Spring.

Named for two brothers, Art and Jack Eckersell (sometimes spelled Eckersall), who raised large bands of sheep in this area.

Edaho Mountain (Boise). 9643′. T8N R11E sec 26. In the SW corner of the county on the Boise-Elmore county line.

Named for what was sometimes believed to be the origin of "Idaho" (which see), an imaginary Indian word said to mean "light at sunrise" or "light on the mountain."

Eddy Creek (Boise). T9N R4E sec 30. Flows 4 mi SE into the S Fk Payette River 3 1/2 mi SE of Crouch.

Named by the USFS for an eddy in this creek.

Eden (Jerome). 3900′. T9S R19E sec 27/35. In the S part of the county. The townsite was laid out in 1905; settlement began in 1907, on the completion of the UPRR. Post office, 1912-.

Named for the biblical Eden, because the beautiful valley surrounding the town suggested the Garden of Eden.

Edgemere (Bonner). 2950′. T55N R4W sec 34. Town on the SIRR and N bank of Hoodoo Lake; 8 1/2 mi SE of the town of Priest River. Settled in 1891 primarily by people from Spokane Val-

ley. Like other railroad stops in this area, it is a shipping point for lumber products.

Named for the location beside Hoodoo Lake: on the edge of a mere, "a pool of water."

Edie Creek (Clark). T12N R33E sec 4. Rises in the Targhee National Forest on the Continental Divide and flows 5 mi SW to Dry Creek; Medicine Lodge Creek system. Ten mi E of the Clark-Lemhi county line. Edie Ranch lies at the mouth of this creek.

Named for George B. Edie, 1886 homesteader and first postmaster (1906).

Edna Creek (Boise). T7N R7E sec 3. Flows 5 mi SE into Beaver Creek; Boise River drainage.

Named for Edna Ashcroft (Mrs. A. C.) Gallup by John Henry, a miner who admired her. He named his mine the Edna, and the name was later transferred to the creek.

Edna Lake (Boise). T7N R13E sec 6. In the extreme E part of the county.

Named by a fish-stocking party. Since several neighboring lakes in the area were known locally by female names, this one was called Edna.

Edwards Gulch (Camas). T1N R14E sec 9. About 2 mi long, extending from NW to SE to Soldier Creek, 4 mi N of Soldier.

Named for Carter Edwards, one of the first cattlemen on Camas Prairie, who settled here.

Edwardsburg (Valley). 5380′. T21N R9E sec 35. A ranch with an early post office serving the Big Creek country, in the N part of the county at the confluence of Government and Logan creeks with Big Creek.

William and Annie Edwards homesteaded at the mouth of Logan Creek in 1904 during the Thunder Mountain gold rush. Post office, 1909-1918.

Named for the Edwardses, founders of the town, who finally lost all they had in a mining venture on Logan Creek.

Eena Creek (Benewah). T43N R2W sec 13. Rises on Nakarna Mountain and flows 3 1/2 mi W to E Fk Charlie Creek, in the SE corner of the county; St. Maries River drainage.

Named by W. H. Daugs, USFS. The name is Chinook jargon for "beaver," which were plentiful in this stream.

Egin (Fremont). T7N R39E sec 15/16. Town 7 mi W of St. Anthony; oldest permanent settlement in the county, established by Mormons in 1879. Andrew Henry built a temporary post here where he wintered in 1810; it consisted of a few log houses. Egin Bench trends 5 mi SW to NE, adjoining the town.

Formerly Greenville; name changed by Post Office Department in 1880. Name from a Shoshoni word, ech-unt, meaning "cold."

Egypt (Franklin). T16S R40E. Early name for a farming community in the S part of the county near Franklin.

Named for the similarity settlers saw between this land, drained and watered by the Bear River, and Egypt, drained and watered by the Nile.

Eidelman Canyon (Lemhi). T12N R29E sec 27. Heads 1 mi S of the head of Willow Creek and runs SW 4 mi, then W 1 1/2 mi and about 2 mi S of Nicholia. Henry Edleman (sic) was a miner and at one time sheriff of Nicholia (ca. 1885).

The name is sometimes spelled Eidleman.

Eighteen-Mile Creek (Caribou). T7S R39E sec 8. In the NW part of the county. Rises in the Chesterfield Range 4 mi E of Hatch; flows 11.5 mi erratically NW and W to the Portneuf River.

An early settlement was made on this creek at the site of Hatch, but it no longer appears on maps.

Named for the mouth of this stream on the Portneuf River, which is 18 mi N of Lava Hot Springs.

Eighteen Mile Peak (Lemhi/Montana). 10,680′. T13N R29E sec 21. On the Continental Divide in the Bitterroot Range; Targhee National Forest. It is 18 mi SE of Leadore, where Eighteen Mile Creek empties into Lemhi River.

Eightmile Creek (Bear Lake/Caribou). T9S R42E sec 36. Rises in the N part of Bear Lake County, W of Sherman Peak, in Cache National Forest; flows N and NE about 13 mi to empty into Bear River 8 mi SE of Soda Springs.

Eightmile Creek (Bear Lake). T10S R43E sec 12. Community on Eightmile Creek, near Bear River, in the N part of Bear Lake County; an agricultural community. Now Manson (which see).

The creek was named because it is approximately eight miles SE of Soda Springs; the town, for the creek.

Eightmile Creek (Boise). T6N R6E sec 3. Flows 3 mi SE into Mores Creek; Boise River drainage.

Named because the head of this creek is eight miles up Mores Creek from Idaho City.

Eightmile Island (Bonner). T60N R4W sec 3. On the E side of Priest Lake, 6 mi SE of Nordman; 7 mi N of Coolin.

Named because it is approximately eight miles N of Coolin.

Elba (Cassia). 5000′. T13S R25E sec 32. In the central part of the county, 11 mi S of Albion.

Formerly Cassia Creek, then Beecherville, which was considered unsuitable by the Post Office Department. Settled by Mormons in 1871. Elba Valley is at the headwaters of Cassia Creek; nearly 10 mi E and W, 5 mi

N and S, 5000' elevation. On the SW is Mt. Independence (10,034') and on the NW Mt. Harrison (9285'); slopes are wooded with pine, cedar, and aspen. Cassia Creek runs through the valley to Raft River. Post office, 1881-.

Named for Napoleon's island of exile in the Mediterranean.

Elbow Canyon/Creek (Bonneville). T1S R45E sec 14. Extends about 2 mi N to S in the E part of the county, just SW of Palisades Peak.

Named because the course of the creek and its canyon resembles the crook of an elbow.

Elbow Creek (Clearwater). T38N R7E sec 32. In the S central part of the county. Flows E into Orogrande Creek; Clearwater River drainage.

The original road from Oxford Ranger Station to Orogrande Creek made a horseshoe turn or switchback over this creek; the bridge here was referred to as the Devil's Elbow Bridge, and creek name comes from this.

Eldorado Creek (Idaho). T34N R6E sec 18. Rises on Austin Ridge and flows erratically SW and NW to Lolo Creek, about 15 mi NE of Kamiah; Clearwater River drainage.

First named Fish Creek by Lewis and Clark in 1805; then renamed by miners in the 1860s, because of their belief that they had found a land rich with gold, a land of opportunity—the general meaning of "El Dorado" (the golden).

Eldorado Gulch (Boise). T6N R5E sec 12. Flows SW into Elk Creek at Idaho City; Boise River drainage.

Name transferred from the Eldorado mine, which was located on this rich gulch.

Eldorado Gulch (Latah). T42N R2W sec 1. Ninth of the ten named gulches almost parallel to each other and emp-

tying into N Fk Palouse River from the N; in St. Joe National Forest.

Named for the Eldorado Quartz Mining Co., which had claims W of this area, on Moscow Mountain, and perhaps along the N Fk Palouse River. See Banks Gulch. Ultimately the name suggests the rich desires of every prospector.

Eldridge, Mount (Valley). 9210'. T21N R8/9E sec 24/19. Lies S of Summit Road, an important route between Edwardsburg and Warren Mining District; 1 mi S of Elk Summit.

The name honors Capt. Eldridge, one of the early discoverers of gold in the area (1860s).

Elfers Creek (Idaho). T25N R1E sec 2. Flows 4 1/2 mi E to the Salmon River at Lucile.

The name honors Henry Jurgen Elfers and his wife, who lived by the Salmon River on John Day Creek.

Eli Creek (Lemhi). T21N R22E sec 32. Forms N of the head of Sevenmile Creek and flows N 3 mi; Salmon River drainage.

Named for Eli Minert, an early rancher in this region. He was also a well-known packer and tinsmith; he made many of the utensils needed by the miners and settlers.

Elip Creek (Benewah). T43N R2W sec 13. Rises on the S slope of Tyson Peak and flows SW to Eena Creek; St. Maries River drainage.

Named by W. H. Daugs, USFS. The word is Chinook jargon for "first"; this creek is the first or lowest of three tributaries of Eena Creek.

Elizabeth Lake (Idaho). T33N R10E. In The Crags, Clearwater Mountains; in Selway Country.

Named for the wife of Andy Hjort, an early-day packer and USFS employee, who contributed much to the development of the Selway country.

Variant name: Stove Lake.

Elk. As a place name Elk signifies the presence of elk in an area. Eighty-three such names appear in twenty Idaho counties on creeks, buttes, falls, flats, gulches, lakes, meadows, mountains, peaks, and springs.

Elk City (Idaho). 4200′. T29N R8E sec 23/26. In the central part of the county, on Big Elk Creek, 15 mi NE of Orogrande; S Fk Clearwater River drainage.

The oldest mining town in the county. Founded 6 August 1861, within three weeks it had a population of nearly 1,000 and 25 buildings. By 1866 the Elk City gold production reached $3,600,000. In 1888 there were 400 Chinese in the town.

The name comes from the creek on which it is situated; both the creek and the valley had previously been named for the elk that grazed in the valley and drank from the stream.

Elk Creek (Lemhi). T26N R21E sec 10. About 2 mi long; runs W into N Fk Salmon River.

During one harsh winter in the 1930s someone killed four or five elk in this drainage. Authorities never found out who did it, but the place was given this name by Mike Wilkins, conservation officer, and Al Wheeler, forest ranger, because of the event.

Elk Flat (Teton). T4N R44E sec 7/18/19. An area lying at the headwaters of Mahogany, Canyon, and Elk Flat creeks in the Big Hole Mountains.

Elk Flat Creek. T2N R44E. Rises S of Elk Flat and flows SE to Pine Creek (Bonneville County).

Named for the elk herds that roamed this area.

Elk Peak (Boise/Custer). 10,605′. T8N R12E sec 19. On the Boise-Custer county line 1.5 mi W of The Temple.

Named for the local Elk Lake.

Elk River (Clearwater). T40N R2E sec 26. Town 13 mi E of Bovill on Elk Creek.

Originally known as Trumbull, for the Trumbull Hunting and Fishing Lodge. In 1909 the Milwaukee RR from St. Maries was completed and the Potlatch Lumber Co. began extensive lumbering activities, completing its mill and millpond here in 1911. As a typical logging town, Elk River had company houses, a few homesteads, a company store, a mess hall, and tents. As workers were attracted to the area, schools, stores, hospital facilities, and frame houses were added. The spurt of growth ceased in 1927 when Clearwater Timber located in Lewiston. Post office, 1897-.

Named for Elk Creek, because of the great number of elk in the area.

Elk Summit (Valley). 8672′. T21N R8E sec 13. On the Summit Road, a major route between Edwardsburg and Warrens. A landmark for early travelers. The road lies between Elk Summit on the N and Mt. Eldrige on the S.

Named for the elk common to the area. A meadow at the foot of this peak is named Meadow Fawn, probably an office name.

Elkberry Creek (Clearwater). T40N R4E sec 28. In the NW part of the county. Rises W of Bertha Hill and flows 10 mi W into Dworshak Reservoir.

Named for the "elkberries" found along the stream.

Elkhorn Creek (Lemhi). T22N R17E sec 14. Heads in Bighorn Crags; flows generally W for 3 mi to enter Clear Creek; Salmon River drainage.

Willard and Burrel Rood, while hunting bear in this area around 1900, found a large elk horn, which they placed in a fir tree.

Elkhorn Gulch (Lemhi). T25N R22E sec 26. Runs NW 1 1/2 mi to Little Sheep Creek drainage; N Fk Salmon River drainage.

In 1920 someone put a large set of elk horns on a tree at the mouth of the gulch.

Elkhorn Peak (Oneida). 9176'/9001'. T12S R35E sec 35/36. On the Bannock-Oneida county line, in the NE part of the county. A peak with two points about 1 mi apart, in the Caribou National Forest about 6 mi SE of Daniels.

A descriptive name: the namer saw a resemblance between the contour of the peak and a pair of elk antlers.

Elkhorn Peak (Bonneville). 10,040'. T1S R46E sec 5. Lies at the head of Little Elk Creek near Palisades Dam.

Named for the elk horns found in the area.

Elliot Bay (Bonner). T56N R1E sec 17. On the W side of Lake Pend Oreille, 7 1/2 mi NE of Talache.

Named for Ed Elliott, the president of Northwest Navigation Company, which operated steamboats on the lake.

Ellis (Custer). 4648'. T16N R20E sec 31. Town in the NW section of the county on the Salmon River.

Post office, 1906-1956.

Named for George Ellis, local rancher and one-time postmaster.

Ellis Creek (Bannock). T9S R36E sec 34. Rises just SE of Tom Mountain in the Caribou National Forest and flows SE intermittently 3 mi into Birch Creek; Portneuf River drainage.

The name Ellis came from early homesteaders who farmed here.

Ellisport (Bonner). T57N R2E sec 36. A village that has now been incorporated into East Hope.

Named for a Mr. Ellisport, who was involved with one of the early lumber mills at the location.

Ells Creek (Benewah). T44N R2W sec 34. Rises S of Emida Peak and flows erratically 2 mi W to Charlie Creek; St. Maries River drainage. In the SW quadrant 5 mi N of the Benewah-Latah county line.

Named by Edd. F. Helmers, USFS ranger, in 1939 for the Ells family, homesteaders on this creek.

Elmira (Bonner). 2149'. T59N R1W sec 9/10. On the Great Northern RR and US Highway 95, 3 1/2 mi NE of Samuels. Formerly Halfway. Elmira Peak is about 1 mi NE of Elmira, for which it is named. Post office, 1892-1917.

Railroad workers are credited locally for the name Elmira, as they often named sidings after their home cities. There is an Elmira, New York.

Elmore County. County seat, Mountain Home. Established 1889, named for the Ida Elmore mines, the area's greatest silver and gold producer of the 1860s.

Elmore County is located in the SW part of Idaho, bounded on the N by Boise County; on the E by Blaine, Camas, Gooding, and Twin Falls counties; on the S by Owyhee County; on the W by Ada County. The northern section is mountainous, drained by S Fk Boise River and overshadowed by Sawtooth and Soldier mountains; the southern is on the Snake River plain. The altitude ranges from 2500' to 5500'.

Elo (Valley). 5030'. T18N R3E sec 23. In the NW quadrant. Formerly SE of McCall, now absorbed by the town. Settled by Finns in the early 1900s.

Post office, 1905-1909.

Named for the Eloheimo family, who had a store and the post office.

Emerald Creek (Benewah/Shoshone). T43N R1E sec 15. Heads at the junction of its E and W forks and flows 3 mi generally N to the St. Maries River about 4 mi SE of Fernwood and 21 mi SE of St. Maries.

Emerald Creek, East Fork (Latah). T43N R1E sec 34. Rises in the NE corner of Latah County W of Sherwin Point and flows 8.4 mi NE to its confluence with the West Fork, 8 mi long, to form Emerald Creek.

Emerald Butte (4480'). T42N R1E sec 6. In the NE corner of the county, St. Joe National Forest. Its twin, West Emerald Butte (4622'), lies 1.2 mi SW.

Named because many reddish garnets, at first thought to be emeralds, were found in the streams and gulches and on the mountains; also, the banks of the streams and the mountains are green with plants.

Emida (Benewah). 2850'. T44N R2W sec 33. Town in the S part of the county, 7 mi W of Santa.

This area was homesteaded in 1896 by three families, the Easts, Millers, and Dawsons. Emida is a combination of the three homesteading families' names. Folk etymology of the name is that the place is not worth a dime; a dime is reversed to give Emida.

Emigrant Canyon (Cassia). T16N R23/24E sec 22. In the S part of the county, just S of City of Rocks and E of Granite Pass. Heads near the juncture of the emigrant trails to Salt Lake City and California, a spot where emigrants often camped; Raft River drainage.

Emigration Creek (Bear Lake). T13S R43E sec 9. Rises in the W part of the county in the Wasatch Range, Cache National Forest; flows ESE 7 mi to Mill Creek.

So called because large companies of Mormon colonizers followed the road along this creek to travel from Cache Valley, Utah, to Franklin and Bear Lake counties in the 1860s and 1870s. A flat near the source of the stream is known as Emigration Campground, because the emigrants used this as a stopping place.

Emma Creek (Boise). T9N R8E sec 33. In the NE part of the county; flows 2 mi NW into the S Fk Payette River 4 mi E of Lowman.

Named in honor of Emma Edwards (Mrs. James) Green, who lived near this creek. She designed the state seal of Idaho.

Emmett (Gem). 3769'. T6N R1W sec 7. County seat. In the S part of the county, at the head of Payette Valley. Emmett Bench extends E and W a little NW of the town. Emmett Valley, noted for its fertile soil, is W of town and N of the bend in the Payette River.

In 1862 the first wagon train of emigrants and prospectors entered the Payette Valley by way of treacherous Freezeout Hill and crossed the river where Emmett is situated. In 1864 Jonathan Smith and Nathaniel Martin stopped here and built a roadhouse and Martins Ferry, in preference to prospecting in the Boise Basin; the ferry proved a profitable venture. The growing settlement was named Martinsville.

In 1870 Thomas Cahalan was named postmaster for a place 7 mi W of Martinsville. He named the post office Emmettsville after his son Emmett, the first white child born in the area. Six years later Cahalan moved to Boise and the post office was moved to the site of Martinsville, carrying its name with it; it was shortened to Emmett in 1885. Post office, 1868-.

Empire City (Owyhee). T5S R3W sec 20. Townsite. A mining camp named after the Empire mine on War Eagle Mountain.

Enaville (Shoshone). 2160′. T49N R2E sec 30. In the W extremity of the county, 1 mi N of Kingston; on the Coeur d'Alene River and UPRR; a lumbering town. This was first a supply station for miners and sportsmen in the 1880s.

Named for Princess Ena, daughter of Queen Victoria and later Queen of Spain.

Eneas Peak (Boundary). T64N R1W sec 20. In the Kaniksu National Forest.

Named after Eneas, a prominent Kootenai Indian, who lived near this peak for many years.

Engle Mountain (Benewah). 5412′. T47N R2W sec 30. In the N part of the county, 12 mi SW of Mt. Wiessner.

Named by John Mullan in 1859 for a member of the Mullan Expedition. This promontory was nicknamed by many children of the area "the Prophet," for its gloomy, gray appearance.

The original Mullan Trail passed over the broad dome of this peak and followed the narrow divide to the N extremity of Mt. Wiessner.

Variant name: Round Top.

Engstrom Creek (Shoshone). T44N R2E sec 4. In the SW part of the county. Rises on Blackwell Hump and flows 4 mi E to Mica Creek; St. Joe River drainage.

Albert Engstrom homesteaded near this stream.

Ennis Gulch (Lemhi). T16N R21E sec 32-34,27. Forms 2 1/2 mi NW of Red Point; runs S 3 mi, then SE 2 mi to the Pahsimeroi Valley 3 mi SE of Ellis.

Jack Ennis was an early rancher in this vicinity.

Era (Butte). 5940′. T3N R24E sec 22. Ghost town in the W part of the county, about 16 mi WSW of Arco on Champagne Creek.

This settlement began when Frank Martin discovered silver ore in 1885. By 1887 the population of the settlement had grown to 1,000 and the business district had 15 stores. The mines produced an estimated $1,000,000 in silver ore.

Named for a mining company.

Erickson Meadow (Latah). T40N R1W sec 3. A meadow 2 mi SW of Bovill.

Named for early homesteader and settler Ed Erickson (1893).

Erncliff (Cassia). T16S R25E sec 1. Site of post office (1870) in the SE part of the county, on The Narrows of Raft River 11 mi E of City of Rocks.

Appears on the 1898 Rand, McNally Pocket Map of Idaho as Earncliff. Post office, 1870-1890.

A descriptive name: ern, "eagle," plus cliff, for a cliff where eagles were seen.

Estes (Latah). T40N R5W sec 30. An early community 5 mi S of Viola and almost 3 mi N of Moscow; a RR stop on the Spokane and Inland Empire Line.

Named for Archie B. Estes, who homesteaded here in 1874.

Eugene (Nez Perce). T36N R2W sec. 23. Townsite adjoining Gifford and incorporated into the town in 1904.

A Mr. Keene named the small community after his wife.

Eureka (Ada). Early settlement and post office, near Meridian.

The name is from the Greek, meaning "I have found it."

Eureka Meadows (Clearwater). T38N R5E sec 19/20. Two mi W of Headquarters. Eureka Ridge, a 3-mi ridge trending NW to SE 3 mi N of Orofino.

Named because of the gold discoveries and placer mining here ca.1900.

Eutopia Creek (Idaho). T26N R8E sec 7. Stream 3.5 mi long, flows E to Big Creek 9 mi E of Buffalo Hump.

Named for the Eutopia (sic) mine. Utopia means "the ideal," "the perfect."

Evans Creek (Oneida). T13S R36E sec 35. Rises in the Bannock Range in Caribou National Forest; NE part of the county; flows 3.5 mi SW to empty into Devil Creek, 4 mi N of Malad; Malad River drainage.

Named for settlers on the stream.

Evans Creek (Clearwater). T39N R4E sec 32. Rises on Lewis Mountain in the NW quadrant of the county and flows 4 mi SW into N Fk Clearwater River.

Named for James Evans, a homesteader near the creek in 1904.

Evans Landing (Bonner). T55N R2W sec 28. On the W side of Lake Pend Oreille.

Named for an early resident of the area.

Evergreen (Latah). T43N R5/6W. In the NW quadrant of the county in the Pine Creek area. The settlement began in 1871.

Named for its setting among many ponderosa pines.

Everson Creek (Lemhi). T16N R25E sec 30. Originates at Everson Lake and flows NW 4 mi to enter Stroud Creek; Lemhi River drainage.

John Everson was a pioneer rancher on this creek.

Excavation Gulch (Latah). T42N R2W sec 9/16. A small canyon and stream on Strychnine Creek (which see) in the NE quadrant of Latah County; not over 2 mi long, it dries up by late spring; Palouse River drainage.

Gold was discovered here in the 1880 mining days in the Hoodoos, but white miners soon abandoned it for lack of water for sluicing. Chinese miners were allowed to move in, and with patience and persistence they dug—or excavated—ditches across the ridge to a stream that furnished adequate water for sluicing, drinking, cooking, etc.

Eyrie Canyon (Oneida). T13S R30E sec 3. A 2.2-mi canyon draining into Sublett Creek in the NW extremity of the county. Eyrie Peak (7458') lies SE of the head of this canyon.

Both features are named for an early settler.

Ezra Creek (Lemhi). T17N R21E sec 9. Forms 1 mi N of King Mountain and flows SE 3 1/2 mi to enter Salmon River.

Named for Ezra Orn, pioneer packer in this region.

Ferrell (Benewah County), Hanging Gardens, 1934.

F

Fagan Creek (Benewah). T43N R2W sec 14. Heads just E of Preston Knob (4140′) in the S part of the county and flows 2 mi NW to Charlie Creek; St. Maries River drainage.

Named in 1939 by Edd. F. Helmers of the USFS for the Fagan family, old-timers in the vicinity.

Fairfield (Camas). 5055′. T1S R14E sec 9/10. County seat. In southern Camas County, with Soldier, Smoky, and Pioneer mountains for a backdrop and Camas Prairie in the foreground.

First settlers came in 1880; construction following the Reclamation Act of 1902 made possible the complete settlement of the prairie. When the RR came through, it missed Soldier (which see), so the settlers there moved to the RR and called their new town New Soldier, later changed to Fairfield.

In 1917 old Blaine County was divided into Blaine, Butte, and Camas counties, and Fairfield was made the Camas County seat.

Named by reclamation settlers as descriptive of the vicinity.

Fairview (Franklin). 4514′. T16S R39E sec 23. In the S part of the county, 5 mi S of Preston.

A small agricultural area settled primarily by Mormons in the 1880s,

although settlers were in the area before 1870. Post office, 1883-1965.

Named early by Peter Griffith for the fair view offered by the site; some say the fair view of Cache County, but one early historian says a fair view of the Mormon temple in Logan.

Fairview (Latah). T43N R5E sec 1. An early Pine Creek community in the NW part of the county; between Silver and Cedar creeks.

Named because of the view from the top of the wooded mountainous site; as the early settlers said, "the fairest view in the world."

Fairview (Latah). T41N R1W sec 18. A lumbering community about 2 mi N of Bovill in the first decade of 1900.

The U.S. Post Office refused this name, as there was already another Fairview in Idaho. The name was changed to Slabtown, which see.

Fairview (Owyhee). T5S R3W sec 15. Ghost town on the NE slope of War Eagle Mountain; 2 mi E of Silver City.

The mining town overlooked miles of desert toward the Snake River with the Boise mountains in the background. The town was settled in 1863, destroyed by fire in 1875, and rebuilt after a quartz mine was discovered.

Named for the view from this site.

Fairview Knob (Benewah). T43N R3W sec 17. In the S central part of the county, 2 mi N of the Benewah-Latah county line.

Named by W. H. Daugs, USFS ranger. At the time of naming, this small knob had a fairly heavy stand of timber.

Fairylawn (Owyhee). T10S R6W sec 12. Town 2 mi E of the Idaho-Oregon border. Primarily a way station for the stage line and a post office. The owner installed a windmill, and with a small spring the place was kept green.

Because of the desolate surroundings, the person who settled in this area felt that it should have an imaginative, fanciful name.

Falcon (Shoshone). 3413′. T46N R6E sec 10. In the E part of the county, on N Fk St. Joe River and the Milwaukee RR; a mining town, established early in the century.

Named for falcons that nested in the area.

Falconberry Lake (Lemhi). T16N R14E sec 4. Near the head of Powder Creek. Falconberry Peak (9465′) is situated just SW of Falconberry Lake.

Named for Ned Falconberry, a rancher in the early 1900s.

Falks (Payette). 2305′. T7N R3W sec 8. On the Payette River between Emmett and Fruitland. David Bivens built and operated the first ferry here in 1862 but sold it to James Toombs in 1867. Toombs opened a store here, on the road between Boise and Payette, which he later sold to Nathan Falk, who made the place well known.

Fall Creek (Boundary). T60N R1W sec 1. A perennial stream 11 mi long flowing in a SE direction to its confluence with Deep Creek; Kootenai River drainage. In the Kaniksu National Forest.

The name Fall Creek has been in use for at least 70-some years, according to local residents. The creek has two small waterfalls. Local USFS personnel call it Fall Creek, even though their maps show the plural form.

Fall Creek (Bonneville). T1N R43E sec 4. Rises in the S central part of the county in the Caribou Range and flows about 12 mi NE into the Snake River. Also Sulphur Creek and Muddy Creek.

Fall Creek Falls drop 40′ into the Snake River.

Fall Creek (Elmore). T1N R9E sec 16. Rises in the Boise National Forest 1 mi S of Big Roaring River Lake and flows about 14 mi generally S to Anderson Ranch Reservoir; S Fk Boise River drainage.

There are two 15-foot falls on this stream, which give it its name.

Fall Creek (Idaho). T24N R4E sec 8. An 8-mi tributary of Salmon River from the S. A settlement on this stream took its name from the creek, which was named for its descent of 4500′ in 5 mi.

Falls (Franklin). 4685′. T14S R39E sec 36. In the SW part of the county on Bear River; an agricultural area.

Named for the waterfalls on the river.

Falls City (Jerome). 3838′. T9S R17E sec 1. In the W part of the county on the UPRR, 6 mi E of Jerome and 5 mi N of Pillar Falls, from which it probably takes its name. Post office, 1909-1916.

Falls Creek (Shoshone). T46N R1E sec 23. In the W part of the county, 12 mi SW of Kellogg. Rises on the Shoshone-Kootenai county line and flows 5 mi SE to the St. Joe River.

Named in 1884-1885 by Tom Jones, an Irish sailor who lived in the area, for the falls in the creek near its mouth.

Falls Creek (Lemhi). T14N R22E sec 16. Originates just W of headwaters of Patterson Creek; flows generally SW 11 mi to enter Pahsimeroi River.

Lorenzo Falls acquired ranchland here in 1873. He came to the Pahsimeroi Valley after mining in the Boise Basin; Florence; Helena, Montana; and finally Leesburg in 1867.

Falls River (Wyoming/Fremont). T8N R41E sec 14. Rises in Yellowstone National Park, enters Fremont County, flows SW to Henrys Fork.

Falls River descends 3400' in 26 mi with many waterfalls along its course. It is 45 mi long, its drainage 580 square miles. The terrain is timbered upland and plateau and lava canyon.

Fan Gulch (Lemhi). T24N R20E sec 27. About 2 mi long, drains N to enter the Salmon River about 2 mi downriver from Deadwater Spring.

There is a fairly large delta in the shape of a fan at the mouth of the creek.

Fannies Hole (Custer). T13N R17E sec 2. Stopping place on road between Bonanza City and Custer (1880s). Named for Miss Fannie Clark, the owner; formerly known as Twelve-Mile House, owned by Daniel McKay. Called Fannie Clarks Upper Hole when traveling from Challis to Bonanza City.

Fannies Lower Hole is the local name for the last station on the toll road before reaching Challis. Nickname for Greenwood.

Farber Point (Latah). 2800'. T42N R5W sec 13. Promontory between Deep and Crane creeks, 3 mi N of Onaway.

Named for a family that once lived here.

Farewell Bend (Washington). T11N R7W sec 7/17/18. About 11 mi W of Weiser on the the Snake River.

This is the place where emigrants said farewell to the Snake River, which they

had followed for 400 mi across S Idaho. Early pathfinders found this spot too and camped on it: Wilson Price Hunt, 1811; Captain Bonneville, 1834; Nathaniel Wyeth, 1834; and John C. Fremont, 1843.

Farnum (Fremont). T8N R43E sec 20/29. Town 6 mi S of Ashton.

Named for an early settler.

Farrow Mountain (Idaho). 8987'. T22N R13E sec 11. In the SE part of the county S of the Salmon River; Salmon National Forest. Farrow Creek rises on this mountain and flows 5 mi NW to Cottonwood Creek; Salmon River drainage.

The name honors Lieutenant Edward C. Farrow, who in 1879 commanded troops in the Sheepeater War.

Fawn Creek (Boise). T9N R7E sec 12. Flows SE into Clear Creek; Boise River drainage.

Named by a body of prospectors, headed by K. P. Plowman, who shot and ate a fawn that was drinking from this creek.

Feary Creek (Clearwater). T39N R4E sec 24. Rises on John Lewis Mountain in the NW part of the county and flows NE into Silver Creek; Clearwater River drainage.

Named for Al Feary, an Idaho State Land Commissioner.

Feather River (Elmore). T3N R10E sec 10. Rises in the mountains E of Rocky Bar, Boise National Forest, and flows 6 mi SE and S to S Fk Boise River.

Believed to have been named by miners for the Feather River in California.

Featherville (Elmore). 4350'. T3N R10E sec 9/10. In the NE quadrant of the county at the confluence of the Feather and S Fk Boise rivers. A former gold-mining site.

Formerly called Junction Bar and later known as Featherville Stage Station, because it was a stop on the way to Rocky Bar. It has been reported that 33,000 ounces of gold were dredged from this vicinity between 1922 and 1927. Post office, 1906-1928.

Named for the Feather River.

Fedar Creek (Bonner). T61N R5W sec 1. Flows 4 mi S to Blacktail Creek, which empties into Priest Lake.

Charles Fedar was an old trapper in this country. In 1929 he became afflicted with cancer of the stomach and was told he could live only a year or so. Rather than be a burden, he took his life in the vicinity of the drainage.

Felt (Teton). 6030'. T6N R45E sec 5/6. Town in N Teton County 5 mi NW of Tetonia, near Badger Creek.

John Felt and his brother came here in 1889 and claimed land on and near Badger Creek. Settlers and homesteaders took up almost all the land in the area by 1911, when the townsite was dedicated. Post office, 1913-.

Felton Creek (Latah). T40N R4W sec 34. Rises between East Moscow and Moscow mountains and flows 3.2 mi SE to W Fk Little Bear Creek, 3 mi NW of Troy; Potlatch River drainage.

Named by Edd. Helmers, USFS, in 1937 for J. H. Felton, who owned a ranch along the creek and had a sawmill here.

Fenn (Idaho). 3283'. T30N R2E sec 4. In the NW part of the county, 8 mi N of Grangeville. Established in 1907 as the first RR station on the Camas Prairie RR, Fenn soon became the center of a rich agricultural area. Post office 1908-.

Named for Stephen S. Fenn, territorial delegate to Congress 1874-1876 and a soldier in the Indian War of 1877.

Fenn Mountain (Idaho). 8014'. T33N R10E sec 33/34. In the Crags, Selway-Bitterroot Wilderness Area.

Named by C. K. Hjort, former deputy game warden, for Major Frank Alfred Fenn, one of the first forest supervisors in Idaho. The Fenn family settled in the Fenn area in the 1860s.

Fenster Creek (Lemhi). T22N R22E sec 18. Forms 2 mi E of U P Lake; flows E 3 1/2 mi to the Salmon River.

Named for Jacob Finstur (variously spelled as Finster, Feinsteur), who had the first livery and feed stable in Leesburg. He had a ranch here, which he patented in 1892.

Fenton Creek (Boundary/Bonner). T60N R4W sec 26. Enters Bonner County 4 mi N of Coolin; flows 2 mi W into Priest Lake at Cavanaugh Bay 9 1/2 mi SE of Nordman.

Named for Mark Fenton, who settled near the creek.

Ferdinand (Idaho). 3728'. T33N R1W sec 36. In the NW part of the county, 8 mi N of Cottonwood; on Camas Prairie RR.

Frank M. Bieker homesteaded in the area of Keuterville, and when the Nez Perce Reservation opened in 1895, he established a claim on the site of present-day Ferdinand for himself and for ten others. Post office, 1898-.

Named for the home town of Frank Bieker's mother, Ferdinand, Indiana.

Fern Creek (Latah). T42N R1W sec 20. Rises in the Hoodoo Mountains and flows 2 1/2 mi S to the Palouse River.

Named for the many ferns or bracken growing along its banks.

Fernan Lake (Kootenai). T50N R3W sec 16-19. In the foothills of the Coeur d'Alene Valley just SE of Coeur d'Alene city limits. This lake is 2.3 mi long and .5 mi wide at the greatest point.

The name has been transferred to a number of nearby features: Fernan Creek, a 7-mi stream that rises on the W end of Fernan Ridge and empties into

Fernan Lake; Fernan Saddle, 6.5 mi NE of the lake; and Fernan Dry Gulch, 2 mi SE of the lake.

Named for an early settler ca. 1888.

Fernwood (Benewah). 2707'. T44N R1E sec 31. Town in SE Benewah County on St. Maries River.

This community was founded by a Mr. Fenn, who applied in 1901 for a post office to be named Fennwood. The post office was granted, but the postal authorities misread the name as Fernwood and that name remains. The creek named for the same man now appears on maps as Finn Creek.

Ferrell (Benewah). T46N R1E sec 22. Town on the St. Joe River near the Shoshone-Benewah county line. Now St. Joe, which see.

In 1884 William W. Ferrell located a homestead on the St. Joe River later to become the site of the Elk Hotel, the Ferrell steamboat landing, and the Ferrell ranch.

Ferry Butte (Bingham). 4824'. T3S R34E sec 33. In the SW quadrant of the county 1 mi S of the confluence of the Blackfoot and Snake rivers. This was originally a meeting place for Indians.

Named because it overlooks the site of the first ferry on the Snake River in this area.

Ferry Creek (Lemhi). T17N R25E sec 31. Originates just N of the headwaters of Walter Creek; flows generally NE 6 mi to enter the Lemhi River.

Rudolph Ferry patented his land here in 1920.

Fiddle Creek (Idaho). T25N R1E sec 22. Salmon River tributary from the E.

Named for Dick Martin, rancher on the creek, who played the fiddle at all local dances and thus earned the nickname "Fiddle."

Field Creek (Clearwater). T38N R11E sec 4. Flows NW into Cayuse Creek at sec 4; Clearwater River drainage.

Named for the nearby Cayuse landing field.

Fifth Fork Rock Creek (Twin Falls). T12S R18E sec 25. Rises at Bold Hill and flows 10 mi N to Rock Creek 17 mi SE of Twin Falls; Snake River drainage.

This is the fifth tributary of Rock Creek from its mouth.

Fighting Creek (Kootenai). T47N R5W. In the SW part of the county on the Coeur d'Alene Indian Reservation; 15 mi S of Coeur d'Alene.

In 1902 when the reservation land was first opened for homesteading, the settlers had a big dance. Two of the women at the dance got into a hair-pulling, face-clawing fight. The next day during a discussion about a suitable name for the settlement, a man suggested they should name it Fighting Creek. The name is still known locally but does not appear on current maps.

Filer (Twin Falls). 3804'. T10S R16E sec 8. Four mi W of Twin Falls. Established in 1903 and incorporated in 1909.

At first there were two towns close together, Eldridge and Filer, but Eldridge was absorbed in 1919. Post office, 1907-.

Named for Walter Filer, general manager of Twin Falls Canal Company.

Filer Creek (Shoshone). T42N R2E sec 34. In the SW extremity of the county, 5 mi SE of Clarkia. Rises on the Shoshone-Clearwater county line and flows 2 mi NW to Middle Fk St. Maries River.

This name was included in a proposed system of naming smaller side streams of the Middle Fk St. Maries

River with white pine logging terminology. A filer sharpened the saws in a logging camp.

Finley Creek (Blaine). T3N R19E sec 4. Rises in the N central part of the county and flows 4.5 mi SW to Baugh Creek 9.5 mi SE of Ketchum; E Fk Wood River drainage.

Named for an old Scotsman, fondly called "Uncle Finley," who lived up the E Fk from the mouth of this stream.

Finn Creek (Benewah). T44N R1E sec 31. Rises near the Benewah-Shoshone county line in the SE quadrant and flows about 3 1/2 mi SW to Fernwood.

Like Fernwood, this creek was intended to honor an early settler named Fenn, but the map spelling erred.

Fir Grove (Camas). T2S R14E sec 34. On the S border of Camas County, 3 mi S of Mormon Reservoir.

A little grove of fir trees on the rocky side of Fir Grove Mountain (6236'). These were the only fir trees on the S side of Camas Prairie for over 20 mi. When the settlers first came in the 1880s there was a charcoal pit on this site.

Fir Grove (Kootenai). 5160'. T53N R5W sec 36. In the extreme NW part of the county, known since 1910 as Twin Lakes (which see) 6 mi N of Rathdrum.

It was known as Furst, then Fir Grove, for the fir trees surrounding it.

First Creek (Boise). T5N R7E sec 3. Rises on Hungarian Ridge and flows 3 1/2 mi SE into Rabbit Creek; Boise River drainage.

This is the "first" of a number of parallel creeks emptying into Rabbit Creek.

Firth (Bingham). 4656'. T1S R36E sec 25. In the N part of the county, 11 mi NE of Blackfoot. A Swedish settlement begun in 1885 by colonizers of the Mormon Church. Post office 1905-.

Named for Lorenzo J. Firth, English emigrant, who with William Dye swung the decision to place the RR station at Firth in 1890. Firth gave land for the section house and water tank, and the RR in turn named the station for him in 1903.

Fish. Fish appears as a place name in all areas where fish were once plentiful. The names of such lakes and streams appeared first, with Lewis and Clark being the earliest namers; then they were transferred to nearby features such as promontories and sometimes a settlement.

Fish Creek (Blaine). T1S R21E sec 16. In the SE part of the county. Rises in the Pioneer Mountains, Challis National Forest; flows SW 22 mi through Fish Creek Reservoir to Little Wood River. Tributaries: Long Canyon, Iron Mine Creek, E Fk Fish Creek, and W Fk Fish Creek; drainage 130 square miles.

Fish Haven Creek (Bear Lake). T16S R43E sec 14. Rises in the SW extremity of the county on the SW border and flows SE 7.5 mi to Bear Lake at the town of Fish Haven.

From the days of settlement the fish in the stream and Bear Lake were an important food: brown trout, lake trout, carp, perch. Earlier this was a summer campsite for Shoshoni Indians. Later it became the site of a commercial fishery operating on Bear Lake from 1900 to 1925, when both Idaho and Utah outlawed commercial fishing on Bear Lake.

Fish Haven. 5932'. T16S R43E sec 14. Town in the extreme S of the county, 3 mi N of the Utah-Idaho border on the W side of Bear Lake. Post office, 1873-.

Fish Lake (Kootenai). T52N R5W sec 2. Situated at the mouth of Fish Creek, which rises in Washington and flows E to empty into Twin Lakes. Now called

Twin Lakes Station. Post office 1909-1915.

Named for the creek on which it was located.

Fisher Creek (Shoshone). T47N R4E sec 36. In the SW part of the county, 7 mi SE of Wallace. Rises on Gibson Point and flows SW to Slate Creek; St. Joe River drainage.

In 1887 the four Fisher brothers (John, Jess, Hogue, and Joe) built the first sawmill on the St. Joe River, due N of the creek named for them.

Fisher Creek (Clearwater). T38N R9E sec 6. Flows 5 mi SE into N Fk Clearwater River, at Fourth of July Pack Bridge.

Named for Charles Fisher, Clearwater Forest Supervisor from 1911 through 1914.

Fisher Creek (Custer). T8N R14E sec 4. Heads on W slope of Patterson Peak and flows generally E to the Salmon River.

Named for Frank G. Fisher, first postmaster (1900) in the community of Fisher.

Fishfin Ridge (Lemhi). T21N R16E sec 15/16. In Bighorn Crags, runs approximately E and W, 1 1/2 mi long, just N of Wilson Lake.

Named in 1962 by Dr. Paul Dalke of the University of Idaho because this ridge looks like the large dorsal fin of a prehistoric fish.

Fishing Falls (Jerome/Twin Falls). T11S R13E sec 9. On the Snake River.

Indians originally gathered here in great numbers to fish, hence the name.

Five Lakes Butte (Shoshone). 6713'. T42N R9E sec 25. In the SE extremity of the county. Nmed for the nearness of five lakes: Heather, Silver, Gold, Copper, and Tin.

Five Mile Creek (Lewis). T35/34N R2E sec 31/5. Rises in the NE quadrant of the county 5 mi N of Nezperce and flows 7 mi NE to the Clearwater River, T35N R2E sec 16. Five Mile Canyon is situated in NE quadrant and runs to mouth of Five Mile Creek.

Sources differ about this name. Some say that Five Mile refers to the length of the road to the top of the canyon; others, that it marked the distance from an old Indian crossing on the river to the Nez Perce Prairie.

Fix Creek (Clearwater). T40N R10E sec 16. Rises in the NE part of the county on Pot Ridge and flows SE into N Fk Clearwater River.

Named for Joe Fix, an early-day trapper.

Fix Ridge (Latah). Ridge about 8 mi long beginning about 2 mi W of Juliaetta and extending NW.

Named for the area's first settler, Ebenezer Fix, who filed a homestead claim in 1878.

Flag Creek (Shoshone). T46N R3E sec 18. A 3-mi w tributary of Big Creek; St. Joe River drainage.

A man by the name of Flag homesteaded near this creek.

Flannigan Creek (Latah). T41N R5W sec 21. Rises in the Palouse Range W of Granite Point and flows NW and NE to Palouse River.

Franklin Flanagin (sic) homesteaded 160 acres drained by this creek in the 1890s. Dudley Tribble, who was among the prospectors working along this creek, is believed to have named this stream.

Flat Creek (Clearwater). T36N R5E sec 4. Flows NE into Orofino Creek 2 mi W of Pierce; Clearwater River drainage.

Named by miners for the flat land through which the creek flows.

Flat Rock (Fremont). T14N R43E sec 26. An early townsite platted in the

1920s, now absorbed in Macks Inn. Located on the banks of Henrys Fork.

Possibly named because the riverbed rocks are flat here, or after a large flat rock along the bank.

Flatiron Hill (Bonneville). 10,025′. T1N R44E sec 19. In the NE quadrant of the county in the Caribou Range near the mouth of Fall Creek. Flatiron Hollow lies in the Caribou Range SW of Irwin.

Named for the configuration of the hill; from a particular vantage, it looks like flatiron.

Flatiron Mountain (Lemhi). 11,019′. T13N R25E sec 18. Situated in the Lemhi Range, about 1 mi SE of Big Creek Peak and 10 mi W of Portland Mountain.

Named because it looks like a big flatiron.

Sometimes called Pahsimeroi Mountain.

Fleming Creek (Shoshone). T45N R4E sec 12. In the SW part of the county, 4 mi W of Avery. Rises on Boulder Divide and flows 1.5 mi E, then 4 mi N to the St. Joe River.

Named after Arthur Fleming, prospector, lumberjack, and USFS employee (beginning in 1908) in the Avery area. Fleming, an Englishman, was known for his gaudy and often comical manner of dress. He enlisted in the Canadian Princess Pat Regiment during WW I and is said to have been killed.

Fleming Point (Bonner). 3584′. T55N R1E sec 28. Located 7 1/2 mi SE of Talache; 3 1/2 mi N of Pack Saddle Mountain.

Named for the Fleming mine located near the point.

Fletcher (Lewis). T34N R1W sec 14. Abandoned town in the N part of the county about 6 mi E of Reubens. The townsite was surveyed by the govern-

ment in May 1896 and opened for filing when the surveying was completed. Simon L. Finney, homesteader, donated the land. In 1903 the population was estimated at 200. Post office, 1896-1910.

Named for a local resident.

Fletcher Creek (Camas). T4N R13E sec 33. Stream 2 1/2 mi long rising in the Sawtooth Mountains 4 mi E of the Camas-Elmore county line and flowing SE to S Fk Boise River.

Named for C. C. and W. A. Fletcher, who came to Camas Prairie in 1882. Both lived at Corral and were among those who prospered and raised their families here.

Flint (Owyhee). 5400′. T6S R4W sec 22. Town 10 mi SW of Silver City. One of the earliest mining camps in southern Idaho. Between 1860 and 1870, 1,500 people lived here.

Flint Creek flows SW into Jordan Creek; Owyhee River drainage. Flint Gulch, between Silver City and War Eagle Mountain, runs W to Jordan Creek; once called Webfoot Gulch, because a rock formation nearby resembles a beaver foot. Flint started in 1865 with the discoveries of tin and cinnabar. Post office, 1892-1914.

These locations are all named for P. J. Flint, one of the 29 prospectors who first discovered gold in the area.

Florence (Idaho). T25N R3E sec 13. In the SW part of the county, 6 mi N of Riggins, in Florence Basin. Now a ghost townsite, formerly a mining town.

Settled in 1861 with the discovery of placer mines on the SW side of the Salmon River Canyon, the town was first named Millersburg for Millers Creek, where Joaquin Miller, poet and freighter in the area, washed out $100 worth of gold in one afternoon. The name was changed to Florence City by Dr. Furber, one of the first arrivals on the site, for his adopted daughter. By 1862, 10,000 miners had found their way to Florence, and production reached $50,000 a day. Though mining decreased, the town did not cease operating until 1912. Post office, 1862-1912.

Florence Lake (Idaho). T33N R10E sec 28. In The Crags, just W of Fenn Mountain.

Named for the wife of Frank Alfred Fenn, USFS supervisor whose name is commemorated by Fenn Mountain.

Flume Creek (Shoshone). T47N R4E sec 27. In the SW quadrant of the county, 4 mi S of Wallace. A 3-mi tributary of Slate Creek from the S; St. Joe River drainage.

Named because loggers built a flume here to float logs down the mountain to Slate Creek.

Flume Creek (Lemhi). T19N R25E sec 16. Forms S of Pattee Creek and flows SW 4 mi to enter Agency Creek; Lemhi River drainage.

Named for the flume built ca. 1915 by Charles A. Carlson to get irrigation water to a farm in the area.

Fluorspar Gulch (Lemhi). SE of Fluorspar Ridge; approximately 2 mi long, runs SW to enter Camas Creek drainage; Middle Fk Salmon River drainage. Fluorspar Ridge lies SE of Duck Creek drainage.

Named in 1943 by Dr. Alfred L. Anderson of the University of Idaho when he studied the fluorspar mineral deposits in the area.

Fly Creek (Clearwater). T41N R10E sec 21. Rises on Fly Hill in the NE part of the county and flows NE into Meadow Creek; Clearwater River drainage.

There are two stories about the origin of the name: it came from the tent-flies (square pieces of canvas over poles), or from the flies that bothered surveyors working here.

Fly Creek (Lemhi). T16N R17E sec 18. Originates in vicinity of Fly Creek Point and in the area SE; flows 3 mi NE to enter Camas Creek; Middle Fk Salmon River drainage. Fly Creek Point (8984') is 2 mi S of the mouth of Fly Creek, at the head of Snowshoe Creek on the SW and Fly Creek on the NW.

Named because of the bothersome horseflies in the area.

Flynn Butte (Latah). 3604'. T42N R2W sec 13. A promontory in the NE quarter of the county, just W of Dry Fork and 3 mi N of Laird Park.

According to Jake Johnson's diary (1904), the butte was named for John Flynn, who homesteaded 160 acres about 10 mi S of the butte. Pat Flynn filed a mining claim about 3 mi E of the butte in 1896.

Flynn Creek (Idaho). T30N R3W sec 29. An E tributary of Salmon River; 4 mi long.

Charley Flynn settled on the river bank at this spot, and used the creek's water in his mining.

Flytrip Creek (Elmore). T7N R11E. In the Boise National Forest, tributary to Middle Fk Boise River from the E, heading between Glens Peak and Snowyside Mountain.

Named by a mapping party camped on this stream while fly-fishing.

Fogg Butte (Fremont). 6900'. T11N R41E sec 12. One mi NE of Crystal Butte, 20 mi NW of Ashton; a small timbered knob.

Named for Jim Fogg, an early businessman of Ashton and St. Anthony, who had a sawmill in the area and a cabin on the W side of the butte.

Fohl Creek (Clearwater). T38N R5E sec 26. S of Headquarters; flows NE into Reeds Creek; Clearwater River drainage.

Named for Theodore Fohl, a German immigrant, who was originally a timber cruiser for the Weyerhaeuser Timber Company. He later worked for the Clearwater Timber Protective Association.

Foolhen Creek (Shoshone). T47N R4E sec 27. In the SW part of the county, 5 mi S of Wallace. A 2-mi tributary of Slate Creek from the S. Foolhen Mountain (5963′) lies 1 mi SE of the source of this stream.

Named for the grouse in the area. A spruce grouse is commonly called a "fool hen" because it is such a slow bird that anyone can kill it.

Ford (Kootenai). 2560′. T48N R5W sec 20. In the SW part of the county, 4 mi W of the westernmost arm of Coeur d'Alene Lake; a logging area and post office (1911).

Probably named for the crossing on Lake Creek at this site.

Ford Creek (Lemhi). T17N R23E sec 28. Flows NE 2 mi to enter Bear Valley Creek 1 mi up from its mouth; Salmon River drainage.

Named to honor Albert H. Ford, a one-time county assessor, prospector, and well-known piano player in the area.

Forest (Lewis). 4524′. T32N R3W sec 1. Abandoned village situated SW of Westlake, Idaho County, about 12 mi S of Winchester. The old trail from Lewiston to the Pierce mining district passed through this town.

Named for the wooded area surrounding it.

Forest King Gulch (Boise). T7N R5E sec 36. Runs SW into Elk Creek at T7N R5E sec 36; Boise River drainage.

This was originally called Forest Gulch; it is situated in a wooded area. Its name was partially transposed with King-of-Lager-Beer Gulch; thus it

became Forest King and the other became Lager Beer Gulch.

Forest Siding (Bonner). T58N R1W sec 20. A railroad siding 7 1/4 mi NNE of Sandpoint; 4 mi S of Samuels.

Named because logs were hauled here and loaded on trains.

Forge Creek (Lemhi). T18N R16E sec 22. Originates near Duck Creek Point and flows W for 2 mi, then SW 1 1/2 mi to enter Camas Creek; Middle Fk Salmon River drainage. Forge Creek Hot Springs is situated about 1 mi up from the mouth of Forge Creek.

Named because a portable blacksmith forge, used to sharpen steel for drilling rock on a trail project, was located near the mouth of the creek.

Formation Cave (Caribou). T9S R41/42E sec 12/7. In the S part of the county, 2.5 mi NE of Soda Springs. An unusual cave, walled in and roofed over by lime deposits around pools.

Named for the way in which it was formed.

Forney (Lemhi). 5672′. T19N R18E sec 3. Town near the mouth of Porphyry Creek; a way station and post office, 1896-1930, named for Hank Forney, an old-timer in the area.

Fort Boise (Canyon). T6N R6W sec 25. Historic site near the confluence of Boise and Snake rivers 5 mi NE of Parma.

First built as a temporary shelter in 1813 by John Reid, of the John Jacob Astor's Pacific Fur Company, in 1813 when he wintered here. The post was eliminated when he and nine of his men were killed by Indians in 1814. Donald McKenzie established a post for the North West Company at the same site in 1819.

In 1832 Thomas McKay, of the Hudson's Bay Company, built an adobe fort on the E bank of the Snake River N of Reid's site. This became known as

Fort Boise, for the river. In 1838 McKay was joined by Francois Payette, who managed the fort for nine years. The fort served Oregon Trail travelers until 1852. The next year flood waters destroyed the adobe fort, and a new, smaller one was erected in 1854, to be destroyed in 1862 by another flood. The site was subsequently used for a ferry.

Fort Hall (Bingham). 4458'. T4S R34E sec 35.

Built by Nathaniel Wyeth in 1834 as a storage place for $3,000 worth of merchandise that fur traders Thomas Fitzpatrick and Milton Sublette had asked him to bring to the annual rendezvous in 1834, then refused to accept. His plan was to sell the merchandise from the fort to Indians. He had brought with him Jason and Daniel Lee, missionaries, with two other missionaries, an ornithologist, a naturalist, and some 60 others. He built Old Fort Hall in the form of a stockade 60' square and surrounded by a 10' wall, with stores and quarters made of poles and brush and dirt- covered. Wyeth named the fort to honor his partner and benefactor, Henry Hall. The Hudson's Bay Company bought the fort in 1836 and used it as a trading post for 20 years. Then in 1870 a military post was established on Lincoln Creek about 40 mi distant from Old Fort Hall and given the name Fort Hall. This too was abandoned, and the name was given to the place that now serves as headquarters for the Fort Hall Indian Reservation. Post office, 1866-.

Fort Hall Bottoms (Bannock). T5S R33E sec 6/8/16. Lowlands lying between the Snake River and American Falls Reservoir and bordering the NE edge of American Falls Reservoir.

Fort Lapwai (Nez Perce). 970'. T35N R4W sec 2. Military post 2 mi S of Spalding. The first military fort in Idaho;

established in the fall of 1862 to prevent disturbances between the whites and Indians on the Nez Perce Reservation. The post was built under the supervision of D. W. Porter of the First Oregon Cavalry and was 1 square mile in size. It was occupied by the US Army until 1884 and in 1904 became the site of the North Idaho Agency for the Bureau of Indian Affairs.

Named for Lapwai, the nearby mission established in 1836 by Henry Harmon Spalding.

Fort Sherman (Kootenai). T50N R4W sec 7/18. Early name for Coeur d'Alene.

Established in 1877 as a military post on the N shore of Coeur d'Alene Lake upon the recommendation of Gen. W. T. Sherman. The first garrison arrived in the spring of 1879 under Col. H. C. Merriam. First known as Fort Coeur d'Alene, but changed to Fort Sherman after the death of Gen. Sherman in 1891. A large part of the original grounds now constitutes a residential section of Coeur d'Alene.

Fossil Canyon (Bear Lake/Caribou). T9/10S R43E sec 26, 35, 36/3/8/9. Trends NE to SW about midway between Soda Springs and Georgetown.

Named for the fossils found here.

Fossil Creek (Owyhee). T3S R1E sec 35. Flows 11 mi NE into the Snake River.

In the early days of the county this creek was called Fart Creek by the men in the area; when there were women present, it was called Fossil Creek, for the number of fossils found in the area. The country between Reynolds Creek and the Bruneau River is a vast fossil bed.

Fossil Gulch (Twin Falls). T3S R1E sec 35. Along the Snake River in the NW extremity of the county, across the river from Hagerman Fossil Bed.

This is really two 1-mi gulches trending SE to Snake River, named for the fossil deposits extending 1 mi N of the named gulch and 4 mi S.

Foundation Creek (Valley). T17N R13E sec 27. Five mi SE of Hospital Bar on the Middle Fk; flows 2 mi SE.

Named for a cabin that was begun but never finished. The foundation remains near the mouth of the stream.

Fountain Creek (Lemhi). T23N R16E sec 18. Heads 1 mi W of Long Tom Lookout and runs SW for 3 mi to enter the Salmon River.

At one time there was a waterfall at the base of this creek that spewed water like a fountain. This feature no longer exists.

Four Mile Creek (Latah). Rises on the NW slope of the Palouse Mountains about 4 mi W of Moscow Mountain, flows NW 1 mi, then W into Washington.

Named because it empties into S Fk Palouse River 4 mi S of Colfax, Washington.

Four Mile. Early name for present-day Viola (which see) one of the oldest settlements in the county; located 10 mi N of Moscow on Four Mile Creek.

Fourth of July. Fourth of July appears in fifteen place names in eleven counties in Idaho. Each such name marks a particular event on the site or a date when travel is possible. There are nine Fourth of July creeks, in Adams, Caribou, Clearwater, Custer (2), Idaho, Lemhi (2), and Washington counties.

Fourth of July Canyon (Kootenai). T49N R1/2W. Historic site on the N side of I-90 commemorating the spot where Capt. John Mullan and his road-building crew celebrated July 4, 1861, at the summit of the Mullan Road by chopping the date into a huge white pine, the stump of which still stands.

Fourth of July Creek flows through the canyon, and Fourth of July Summit (3070') is 2 mi E of Mullan Tree Historic Site.

Fourth of July Creek (Clearwater). T38N R9E sec 6. Rises in the SE extremity of the county on Lookout Peak (6876') and flows 12 mi NE into N Fk Clearwater River at the Fourth of July Pack Bridge. Fourth of July Lookout is just N of the pack bridge and 6 mi SW of Kelly Forks Ranger Station.

Early-day packers and rangers considered it unsafe to ford the river near the mouth of the creek until the Fourth of July, when the water level had gone down.

Fourth of July Creek (Lemhi). T24N R21E sec 35. Heads on the Idaho-Montana border, 2 mi S of Pyramid Peak, and flows W 3 1/2 mi then SW 7 mi to enter Salmon River.

The first settlers on this creek are said to have arrived on the Fourth of July. Early settlers in this vicinity also held picnics here on the Fourth of July because of the pleasant grassy areas and stream.

Fourth of July Ridge (Bonneville). T1S R43E sec 9-36. Trends NW to SE in S part of the county; in Caribou Range. Overshadowed by Fourth of July Peak (7438').

Named to commemorate a Fourth of July party held in 1900 by Sim and Joe Raty, Charles and Cyrus Grow, Earl and Ray Anderson, John Laird, Jack Peterson, and Jack Berry, all sheepherders in the Caribou Forest. They left their bands of sheep unattended while they celebrated.

Fowler Gulch (Blaine). T3N R19E sec 4. Extends 1.5 mi NE to Cove Creek; E Fk Wood River drainage.

Named for the John Fowler family, who once grazed livestock here.

Fox Butte (Clearwater). 6375'. T37N R9E sec 4. Nine mi SE of the Bungalow Ranger Station. Fox Creek rises here on Cook Butte and flows 5 mi NW into Johnny Creek; N Fk Clearwater River drainage.

A horse named Fox belonged to a member of the party camped at Cook Mountain. The horse often wandered away and hid by what came to be known as Fox Butte.

Fox Creek (Boise). T10N R10E sec 28. Flows 4 mi SE into the S Fk Payette River 3 1/4 mi NE of Warm Springs Creek Airport.

A man named Fox, from Cascade, had a claim on this creek.

Fox Creek (Custer). T9N R18E sec 3. S tributary of E Fk Salmon River, about 4 1/2 mi long.

Named for J. C. Fox, member of a party of six from Idaho City who, in 1880, went exploring near Bonanza. Fox remained and built a sawmill on this creek.

Fox Creek/Canyon (Teton). T4N R45E sec 20. Rises in the highlands E of Chapin and flows W and NW to empty into the Teton River.

Fox Creek. A community located on the creek. Name changed to Chapin in 1896.

Named in 1872 by USGS surveyor F. V. Hayden for the number of red foxes in the area.

Fox Hills (Caribou). T7S R42/43E. In the N central part of the county, E of Wooley Valley, NE of Soda Springs. They are somewhat lower in elevation than Wooley Mountains; part of Peale Mountains.

Foxes reportedly endangered lambs from the time they were brought into this area; both red and cross fox were reported in the 1920s.

Francis Creek (Shoshone). T45N R3E sec 4. In the SW part of the county, 6 mi E of Calder. A 4-mi tributary of the St. Joe River from the N.

Named for John Francis, who had a ranch near the mouth of this stream.

Franer Gulch (Boise). T6N R6E sec 17. Flows SE into Mores Creek 3 mi NE of Idaho City; Boise River drainage.

Franer, a ditch-digger from Idaho City, owned a claim on this creek.

Frank Hall Creek (Lemhi). T17N R27E sec 35. Forms W of the headwaters of Quaking Asp Creek and flows generally W 2 1/2 mi to enter Cruikshank Creek; Lemhi River drainage.

Frank Hall was a pioneer rancher in this area.

Franklin (Franklin). 4504'. T16S R40E sec 21. In the extreme S part of the county.

This was the first permanent settlement in Idaho, founded in 1860 by Mormons who believed they were in Cache County, Utah. The area was surveyed in 1868 and the state line was found to be S of Franklin.

The first settlers came in April of 1860: 13 men with their teams and some of the families. The next day many more arrived and work started immediately to reach the proposed townsite. A bridge across Spring Creek came first, then the surveying began, a corral was built, and by May plowing was begun. Five companies of settlers followed in the 1860s. Post office, 1864-.

The townsite was named Franklin for Franklin Richards, a prominent Morman leader.

Franklin County. County seat, Preston. Created in 1913 from Oneida County and named for the first settlement in Idaho, Franklin, which in turn was named for Franklin D. Richards, Mormon apostle.

Franklin County lies in the extreme SE part of the state; bounded by Bear Lake County on the E, Utah on the S; Oneida County on the W, and Bannock and Caribou counties on the N. It is drained by the Bear and Cub rivers and their tributaries, Bear River extending from the NE to the SW into Utah. The Bannock Range lies on the W, the Portneuf on the NW, and Wasatch on the SE. The population is centered primarily along the streams.

Fraser (Clearwater). T35N R3E sec 7. Town W of Weippe.

The first postmaster, Patrick Cain (or Keam), named the town Fraser for his friend David M. Fraser, Pierce merchant, who was brutally murdered—reportedly by some Chinese—in 1885.

Fred and Mary Draw (Lemhi). T15N R21E sec 1. Runs 2 mi SE to Morgan Creek; Salmon River drainage.

Fred and Mary Horn had a water right from Morgan Creek to irrigate their ranch in this area in the late 1800s.

Freedom (Caribou). 5783′. T5S R46E sec 15. At the Idaho-Wyoming border.

An early Mormon settlement (1879), so called by the settlers who intended it as a refuge from arrest and prosecution for practicing polygamy.

Freedom (Idaho). T27N R1E sec 36. Early name for Slate Creek, which see.

There are two local explanations for the name: Josh Folkler, an early miner and property owner of Slate Creek, was a Northern man and may have named it in honor of freeing the slaves; or, named for Josh Freedom, one of the last survivors of the first Democratic convention held in Packer John Welsh's cabin on Goose Creek, near Meadows, in 1863.

Freeman Creek (Lemhi). T23N R22E sec 35. Forms near Freeman Peak and flows W 7 mi to enter Carmen Creek; Salmon River drainage. Freeman Peak is situated 1/2 mi W of the Idaho-Montana border.

Named for James Freeman, a pioneer rancher on this stream. Once called Oro Cache Creek.

Freeman Peak (Boise). 8111′. T7N R6E sec 11. In the central part of the county, 11 mi NE of Idaho City.

Named for James Freeman, who had a mining claim on the mountain.

Freeze (Latah). T42N R5W sec 22. Settlement founded in 1877.

Named for the Freeze families who homesteaded here.

Freezeout Hill (Gem). T6N R1W. A promontory on the main road in 1871 between Boise and Umatilla, Oregon. Located just S of present-day Emmett.

The name is said to have derived from an 1864 incident. Freighters on the way to the Payette Valley to winter arrived at the top of the hill and found the road icy. One of the group rough-braked his wheels and started downhill, but the wagon slipped and turned over in the gulch. Other freighters, seeing his plight, camped on the hilltop and nearly froze to death. It has been called Freezeout ever since.

Fremont County. County seat, St. Anthony. With some irregularities, lies in the NE corner of Idaho. Bounded on the N by Montana, on the E by Wyoming, on the S by Teton, Madison, and Jefferson counties, on the W by Jefferson and Clark counties. Formed in 1893, taken from the N portion of Bingham County, which had been formed in 1885.

Named for General John C. Fremont, who traversed Idaho in 1843, accompanied by 39 men, among them

Thomas Fitzpatrick and Kit Carson. However, he was never in this part of the state.

French/Frenchman. French or Frenchman in a place name appears wherever the French settled or worked in Idaho during the late 1800s. Though many French fur traders and hunters combed the area in the early 1800s, they did not leave their national name. Many French miners followed the gold rushes along streams. Once the stream was designated as French, nearby promontories and lakes assumed the name also.

French (Payette). T9N R3W sec 13. Abandoned community and former post office in the NW part of the county on Little Willow and Alkali creeks.

French Corner. T8N R2W sec 4. On Big Willow Creek at the intersection of Tucker Creek and Dry Creek roads.

Named for Burton Lee French, Congressman from Idaho, 1903 to 1911.

French Creek (Clearwater). T37N R7E sec 3. Rises on French Mountain (5324') in the SW quadrant of the county 4 mi E of Pierce and flows NE and E 13 mi to empty into Orogrande Creek, 14 mi NE of Pierce.

Named for the Frenchmen who formed a company or partnership in the early mining days and staked claims along this creek.

French Gulch (Kootenai). T50N R3W sec 8. In the central part of the county, now a SE part of Coeur d'Alene.

Named because a colony of French settled the area.

French Gulch (Lemhi). T20N R18E sec 17. About 1 mi long; runs SW to enter Musgrove Creek drainage; Salmon River drainage.

Some Frenchmen had a mine at the head of the gulch in the early days.

French John Hill (Owyhee). 4682'. T1N R5W sec 24. Mountain 3 mi N of Elephant Butte.

Named for "French" John Carrey, who built a road in the early 1870s that runs parallel to the present US Highway 95.

Friedorf Gulch (Lemhi). T26N R21E sec 26. About 2 mi long 1.4 mi NW of Gibbonsville, runs E to N Fk Salmon River drainage.

Named for Max W. Friedorf, who ran a sawmill in the vicinity. Even though this drainage was listed as Doolittle Creek on some maps, it has never been called that name by local people. The original Doolittle Gulch (not creek) was a small gulch down the N Fk from this point (Vineyard Gulch).

Frisco (Shoshone). 3200'. T48N R5E sec 8. In the E part of the county, 2 mi W of Burke. On the UPRR and Canyon Creek; an early mining camp.

Named for the Frisco mine nearby.

Fritser Creek (Valley). T20N R7E sec 8. Rises in a lake between Zeno Creek and S Fk Salmon River and flows SE to S Fk Salmon River. In the Payette National Forest.

George Fritser had a ranch here. Formerly spelled Fritzer.

Fritzer Gulch (Lemhi). T22N R18E sec 26. Two mi long; runs SW to enter Panther Creek drainage; Salmon River drainage. Fritzer Flat is S of Fritzer Gulch.

Named for Fritz Gilbert, who lived in this gulch.

Frog Meadow (Lemhi). T20N R16E sec 13. Near the head of Yellowjacket Creek just NE of Yellowjacket Lake.

Named ca. 1935, because of the many frogs found here, by the USFS crew building a ridge road to Yellowjacket Lake.

Frogtown (Idaho). T26N R6E sec 10. Site of an 1861 mining camp, now a ghost town 1 mi S of Humptown, and often considered a minor part of Humptown.

The name was probably derived from the persistent croaking of frogs in the adjacent meadows.

Frost (Custer). Ghost town about 18 mi S of Challis.

Named for the only postmaster, Charles P. Frost (1885).

Fruitland (Payette). 2226'. T8N R5W sec 27. Situated in the NW part of the county, 2 mi S of Payette. In the 1880s known as Zellers Crossing, for A. Zeller, who platted the town in 1908. Since 1900 this community has been famous for its fruit orchards. Post office, 1910-.

Fruitvale (Adams). 3083'. T17N R1W sec 10/15. Situated 6 mi N of Council. A community on the N edge of a farm area, named for the many orchards in the valley. Post office, 1904-.

Fry Creek (Latah). T41N R1E sec 32. Rises 3 mi E of Purdue and flows 3 mi S to E Fk Potlatch River.

Fry Meadow. This meadow lies at the mouth of Fry Creek in the extreme E part of the county SE of Bovill; drained by E Fk Potlatch River and Ruby Creek.

Named for John and Anna M. Frei (sic), who homesteaded on separate parts of the meadow in 1903 and 1907. Name appears as Frei Meadows on the Metsker Map, but Fry on the USGS quadrangle maps.

Frying Pan (Power). T5S R28E sec 20/21. A depression in the Great Rift 1.5 mi N of Crystal Ice Caves; .8 mi long and .3 mi wide; 29 mi NW of American Falls and 18 mi W of Aberdeen.

Locally named because the shape of the feature resembles that of a frying pan.

Furnace Creek (Custer/Lemhi). T17N R17E sec 32. Heads near Van Horn Peak in Custer County and flows W 6 1/2 mi to enter Camas Creek; Middle Fk Salmon River drainage.

The rocks in the canyon give the illusion of a fire or the view inside the open door of a furnace when the light hits it at a particular angle. Walls of the canyon are like a big furnace.

Gilmore (Lemhi County).

G

Galena (Blaine). 7294′. T6N R15E sec 11. Ghost town on the Big Wood River about 29 mi NW of Ketchum. Established in 1879, it developed into a typical mining settlement. By 1890 it was deserted. Post office, 1884-1888.

Named, according to locals, for Galena Barry, son of Martin Barry, owner of the Galena Shoe Shop. There is no explanation of why the son was named Galena. Others attribute the name to the presence of lead-silver (galena) ore in the area. The name is applied to other features in the area, including Galena Peak (11,110′), Boulder Mountains; Galena Summit (8752′), about 4 mi W of Galena Peak and named for the peak; and Galena Gulch (Custer), about 2 mi NW of Galena Peak.

Gallagher Canyon (Clark). T10N R32E sec 28. Trends 4 mi E to Chandler Canyon, 4 mi W of Emigrant Trail Road.

On 14 January 1864, three members of Henry Plummer's gang held up a stagecoach on the road between Camas and Nicholia. Two of the bandits, Haze Lyon and Jack Gallagher, were captured and hanged. It is highly likely that this canyon and Gallagher Peak, 4 mi W of the canyon, were named for the bandit Jack Gallagher.

Gallagher Gulch (Lemhi). T25N R21E sec 18/7/8. Approximately 1 1/2 mi long, runs into the Hughes Creek drainage.

Named for Thomas F. Gallagher, who had land in this area.

Gallagher Mountain (Boise). 6072′. T9N R6E sec 19/20. In the central part of the county, 10 mi NE of Pioneerville. Gallagher Pasture lies 2 mi SW of the mountain. Little and Big Gallagher creeks rise on the peak and flow S into the S Fk Payette River at Gallagher Ranger Station.

The Gallagher family came to Boise Basin in 1863 to mine; they later kept a store at Idaho City (1866).

Gamble Island (Payette). T7N R5W sec 29/30/31/32. In the Snake River in the SE part of Payette County.

Frank Gamble was the first person to live on the island, hence the name.

Gambrinus Gulch (Boise). T6N R6E sec 9. A 2-mi gulch trending SE into Washington Gulch 4 mi NE of Idaho City; Boise River drainage.

This gulch was named after the Gambrinus mine, located in it. The mine was named after Mr. Gambrinus, who was an employee of Jacob Wiegner, from New York, owner of many mines in the area.

Game Creek (Teton). T3N R46E sec 19. Rises on the S slope of Housetop Mountain and Baldy Knoll on the Teton Range in Wyoming and flows SW to Trail Creek 4 mi SE of Victor.

Named by federal surveyor F.V. Hayden in 1872, for the abundance of game.

Gamlin Lake (Bonner). T56N R1E sec 7. A lake 3/4 mi W of Glengary. Variant name is Gamble Lake.

Named for early settler Israel Gamlin, a French-Canadian whose name was originally spelled Gamblin. He resented the English pronounciation and changed it to Gamlin.

Gannett (Blaine). 4928′. T1S R19E sec 2/3/11. Center of an agricultural area in SW Blaine County; 12 mi SE of Hailey and 8 mi S of Bellevue. Established in 1916.

Named for the first early settler, Lewis E. Gannett, who owned the townsite and donated it. Post office, 1911-.

Gannett Hills (Caribou/Bear Lake). T10S R45/46E. Bounded by the Wyoming state line on the E and the Tygee, Crow, and Preuss creek valleys on the W; extend through SE Caribou Co. and NW Bear Lake Co. to Thomas Fork Valley. Elevation: 7000′ to 8000′, with the highest point in the S portion at Red Mountain.

Named for the geographer Henry Gannett.

Gant Creek (Lemhi). T22N R18E sec 22. Heads near Indian Point and flows E 3 mi to enter Panther Creek; Salmon River drainage. Gant Mountain (8276′) is 1 mi SE of Gant Creek and 1 1/2 mi NE of Indian Point. Gant Ridge, trends N of Gant Mountain N and S between Clear Creek and Rood Gulch.

Named for John Gant, early miner, who discovered Henry Ford's Redbird mine in Custer County and who later mined on this creek.

Garden City (Ada). 2660′. T3/4N R2E sec 31/5. In NW Ada Co. on the Boise River; adjoins Boise on the west.

Nicknamed "Saturday Night Town," since it was incorporated in 1949 to allow slot machines. For some time it remained primarily a night-club area. Its main street is called Chinden, for Chinese gardens, which previously occupied much of the townsite and gave it its name.

Garden City (Custer). T14N R19E sec 28. Ghost town located on Garden Creek; served as a distributing point for the Bayhorse Mining District. It was absorbed by Challis.

Named for the creek.

Garden Creek (Bannock). T10S R37E sec 7. Rises in Caribou National Forest in the Bannock Range, near the W boundary of the county; flows 14 mi generally SE to Marsh Creek; Portneuf River drainage.

Named for the garden-like spots along the stream. There was an early town named Garden Creek 3.5 mi upstream from the mouth; the name was changed to Robin before 1889.

Garden Creek (Lemhi). T23N R18E sec 19. Heads near Dome Mountain and runs NE about 8 mi to enter Panther Creek; Salmon River drainage.

The first garden on this section of the Salmon River was grown here in the early days to supply much-needed vegetables to settlers and miners.

Garden Creek (Valley). T21N R12E sec 28. Stream 2 1/2 mi long, flows S to Big Creek; Middle Fk Salmon River drainage.

Named for homesteaders Arthur (Kid) and Auntie Viola Garden, who proved-up in 1913.

Garden Gulch (Latah). T41N R3W sec 5. A small canyon and creek in the Palouse River drainage, its mouth almost 1/2 mi W of Harvard.

Named because vegetables were raised on the creek for sale to miners.

Garden Gulch (Lewis). T31N R2W sec 7. Draw in the SW corner of the county near the mouth of Maloney Creek on the Salmon River.

Mike Maloney had his garden here in the early 1900s.

Garden Valley (Boise). 3000'. T9N R4E sec 24. Town in the NW corner of the county. Post office, 1871-.

Named by early (ca. 1870) residents, mostly farmers, because the area is both fertile and scenic.

Gardena (Boise). 2670'. T7N R2E sec 2. Town located on the N Fk Payette River in the W part of the county.

Officials of the Oregon Short Line RR gave this name in 1914, probably to make the site sound attractive to would-be settlers.

Gardner Creek (Custer). T11N R16E sec 30. About 4 mi long, flowing generally S to the Salmon River. Variant name is Bell Creek.

The original creek name was Gardner Creek, after the family that homesteaded at the mouth of the creek about 1900.

Garfield (Jefferson). 4816'. T4N R38E sec 34/35. On the S border of the county, 4.5 mi SW of Rigby.

Originally a school district; organized as a Mormon Church ward in 1908 and named for President James A. Garfield.

Garnet Gulch (Latah). T42N R1E sec 7. A canyon and stream on E Fk Emerald Creek; St. Maries River drainage.

Named because of the sizable garnet deposits in this area.

Garns Mountain (Teton). 8999'. T4N R43E sec 24. In the Black Hole Mountains in the SW part of the county.

Ed Garns, owner of a herd of sheep in this area in 1914-1915, lost much of his herd because of difficulties between stockmen and sheepmen.

Garwood (Kootenai). 2200'. T52N R4W sec 25. In the NW part of the county 11 mi N of Coeur d'Alene. Established in 1905. Post office, 1905-1926.

Named for the timber products of the Ohio Match Company: The name is derived from gar "spear" + "wood," literally spearwood.

Gay (Bingham). 5640'. T4S R37E sec 27. A small mining community near Fort Hall, near the S border of the county. The Gay phosphate mine opened in 1946.

Named for the daughter of mine owner J. R. Simplot.

Gedney Creek (Idaho). T31N R9E sec 2. In the NE quadrant of the county, 13 mi E of Lowell. Rises on Louse Point (7020') and Chimney Peak and flows 12 mi generally S to Selway River. Gedney Point lies 6 mi NE of the mouth of the stream.

Named for a trapper who worked the stream.

Geertson Creek (Lemhi). T21N R23E sec 19. Forms on the Continental Divide and flows SW 10 mi to enter Lemhi River.

Named for Lars C. Geertson, a rancher and reportedly an expert horticulturist, who first came into the Salmon country in 1866 from Utah.

Gem (Shoshone). 3240'. T48N R5E sec 18. A ghost town in the extreme E part of the county, 2.5 mi SW of Burke. This is a small mining community established in 1886 when silver was discovered; original home of the Hecla and Gem mining companies.

Named for the first mine, the Gem of the Mountain.

Gem County. County seat, Emmett.

Established in 1915, this county shares the early history of Ada, Canyon, and Payette counties. In 1818 fur trappers came; in 1824 Alexander Ross explored Squaw Creek; and from 1860 on prospectors and miners crossed the area on their way to the Boise Basin. The Boise Basin-Umatilla, Oregon, trail ran through this county.

Bounded on the W by Washington and Payette counties, on the N by Adams County, on the E by Valley and Boise counties, and on the S by Ada and Canyon counties

Named for the state nickname, "Gem State."

Gem Lake (Clearwater). T38N R10E sec 33. Nine mi S of Kelly Forks Ranger Station.

The appearance of the lake is suggestive of a gem.

General, The (Custer). 10,325′. T13N R14E sec 3. A promontory in the NW part of the county in the Salmon River Mountains.

Named for its impressive appearance.

Genesee (Latah). 2677′. T37N R5W sec 14. Town in the SW part of county, 13 mi S of Moscow.

First settled in 1871 by Jacob Kambitsch. The railroad came through in 1888, missing the town by a mile; so the town moved to the railroad. The first town is now called Old Genesee. Post office, 1878-.

The valley drained by Cow Creek was named Genesee by journalist Alonzo Leland, who exclaimed upon seeing the area that it reminded him of his old home, the Genesee Valley in New York. When the town grew, it was called Genesee also.

Geneva (Bear Lake). 6000′. T12S R46E sec 22/27. In the E part of the county, 13 mi E of Montpelier.

A few families homesteaded here and established cattle ranches; Mormon colonizers came in 1879, mostly from Switzerland, and established dairy farms. Post office, 1898-.

Named by Henry Touvscher, one of the settlers, for his home town, Geneva, Switzerland.

Gentian Lake (Custer). T8N R16E sec 4. Lake 400′ long, one of the Big Boulder Lakes, .9 mi SW of Walker Lake.

Named for a species of wildflower, usually blue.

Gentian Lake (Lemhi). T21N R16E sec 10. In the Bighorn Crags, just SE of Airplane Lake and about 1/2 mi W of Mirror Lake.

Named for the flower that grows near this lake.

Gentile Valley (Caribou/Franklin). T10/11E R40E. Between the Bear River and Bear ranges; drained by Bear River; 20 mi long and 12 mi wide.

Named by Mormons because this area was partly settled by non-Mormons or "gentiles."

George Creek (Clearwater). T38N R11E sec 4. Rises in the SE part of the county on the SE slopes of Scurvy Mountain and flows SE into Cayuse Creek; Clearwater River drainage.

Named for George Gorman, one of the men who died of scurvy in this area in the winter of 1907. Both George and Gorman creeks, less than a mile apart, are named for him. See Scurvy Mountain.

George Gulch (Shoshone). T50N R4E sec 27. In the upper Burke Canyon, 2 mi N of Burke. Named for Big George, a black man who lived with a Flathead Indian about 5 mi below the source of the Coeur d'Alene River. George made a strike somewhere in the area, but he never revealed where. Some men from Wardner decided to learn the source of the gold he and the Indian showed; but upon finding their cabin, they discovered that George was dead from a bullet hole in his forehead and his Flathead partner gone. No one ever discovered his mine.

Georgetown (Bear Lake). 6006′. T11S R43E sec 12. In the N part of the county, 11 mi N of Montpelier; center of a farming community. Georgetown Creek rises in the NE corner of the county on the S slope of Green Mountain and flows 12 mi to empty into Bear River just W of Georgetown. Georgetown Summit (6283′) overlooks the town from the N.

Settlement by Mormon colonizers began in 1870, with the name Twin Lakes. Post office, 1871-. Renamed in 1873 by Brigham Young for his friend George Q. Cannon, later a delegate to Congress from Utah, who visited the colony with him.

German Gulch (Lemhi). T23N R19E sec 7. Two mi long, runs N from Copper Mountain to Pine Creek drainage; Salmon River drainage.

Named for the German who located a homestead here.

German Settlement (Nez Perce). 3200′. T36N R1W sec 31. Early community 2 mi SE of Gifford.

Named for the many Germans who settled in the area.

Getta Creek (Idaho). T28N R2W sec 23. A 9-mi tributary to Snake River from the SE; 10 mi W of Whitebird.

Named for John Getta, cattleman in the late 1870s.

Gibbonsville (Lemhi). T26N R21E sec 25. Town on N Fk Salmon River, at the mouth of Anderson Creek.

Founded in 1872 when gold was discovered on Anderson Creek; it became a town in 1877. The townsite was created by an act of Congress, July 1899,

and chartered by Judge Steele. Post office, 1878-.

Named for Colonel John Gibbon, who pursued Chief Joseph's band near this area just before the Battle of the Big Hole in 1877. Formerly Dahlongs or Gibtown.

Gibbs (Kootenai). 2140′. T50N R4W sec 10. A mill town established just W of Coeur d'Alene on the Spokane River when the Winston Lumber Company established itself here.

Named for an owner of the Stack-Gibbs Lumber Company.

Gibbs Creek (Lemhi). T24N R17E sec 14. Flows from the S for 1 mi to enter Owl Creek almost opposite the mouth of Wallace Creek; Salmon River drainage.

Named for John Gibbs, a miner on this stream.

Gibson (Bingham). 4464′. T4S R35E sec 6. Site of an Indian settlement in the central part of the county, 7 mi S of Blackfoot, within the Fort Hall Indian Reservation. First settled by Indians and named for Gibson Jack, an Indian.

Gibson Butte 4824′. T3S R34E sec 32. A massive shield volcano at the junction of the Snake and Blackfoot rivers. This was a landmark known to many pioneers as Ferry Butte, because it was here that they crossed the Snake River. The official name, however, is Gibson, named for the settlement.

Gibson Creek (Bonneville). T1N R42E sec 33. Rises in NE quadrant and flows about 3 mi SE into June Creek, 24 mi SE of Idaho Falls; Snake River drainage.

Named for Robert Gibson, one of the first cattlemen to run cattle in Fall Creek (ca. 1885).

Gibson Jack Creek (Bannock). T7S R35E sec 17. In the NW part of the county. Rises at the confluence of N and S Fks of Gibson Jack Creek and flows 2 mi NE to the Portneuf River. N Fk Gibson Jack Creek rises on the S slopes of Kinport Peak and flows SE 1.5 mi, then ENE 4 mi to converge with S Fk. S Fk rises on Gibson Mountain and flows 4 mi NE to converge with N Fk to form Gibson Jack Creek. Gibson Mountain (6773') is at the head of S Fk.

All the features are named for an Indian, who lived in the area after settlers came.

Gifford (Nez Perce). 2800'. T36N R2W sec 23/26. Town 6 mi S of Lenore, 2 mi N of Lookout.

Seth Gifford, for whom the site is named, homesteaded about 2 mi E of the present town, buying 20 acres and platting it into the townsite in 1901. The towns of Eugene and Gifford were incorported as Gifford in 1904. Many of the early settlers were German immigrants who had originally settled in Kansas before coming to Idaho. Two fires in the 1920s destroyed the town, and it was never rebuilt. Post office, 1901-1965.

Gilfillian Creek (Clearwater). T39N R9E sec 15. Rises in the E central part of the county S of Mush Saddle and flows SE into N Fk Clearwater River.

To miners, Gilfillian is the same type of folk hero Paul Bunyan is to loggers. The road builders gave his name to this section near the creek because of the difficulty of the terrain, no problem for Gilfillian.

Gilmore (Lemhi). 7086'. T13N R27E sec 17. Town in the SE part of Lemhi County, 15 mi SE of Leadore. The area is said to have produced more than $40,000,000 worth of silver and lead in its heyday.

Named for John T. (Jack) Gilmer, of the Gilmer and Salisbury Stage Company, who was a pioneer in the stagecoach business in the West. A clerk in the post office department in Washington copied the name wrong when the post office was established here in 1903.

Gilson Draw (Shoshone). T46N R1E sec 24. A 4-mi draw trending NE to SW, 4 mi W of Calder on the St. Joe River.

Named for George Gilson, an early logger who harvested timber from this area.

Gisborne Mountain (Bonner). T58N R3W sec 29. Located 9 3/4 mi SE of Coolin; 3 mi NW of Bald Mountain.

Named for Harry T. Gisborne, a USFS fire-control worker, much of whose work was done in the Priest River Experimental Forest. Controversy arose when the name of the mountain was changed from Lookinglass to Gisborne. Local residents were in favor of naming a mountain to honor Gisborne, but they did not like withdrawing the descriptive name Lookinglass.

Givens Springs (Owyhee). 2260'. T1N R3W sec 21. Town on the S bank of the Snake River; 12 mi SW of Marsing and 20 mi S of Nampa.

Milford R. Givens, who developed the site as a resort, settled here in the early 1880s and built his home near the natural hot springs.

Glade Creek (Idaho). T33N R7E sec 12. In the N part of the county, 6.5 mi NE of Lowell. Rises on the N slope of Cedar Knob in Glade Creek Meadows and flows SE 5 mi to Lochsa River.

Named for its location in a glade.

Glassford Peak (Custer). 11,500'. T7N R17E sec 28. Located on head of Lost Mine Canyon, Pass Creek, a tributary of E Fk Salmon River. In the Boulder Range.

Named for Thomas H. Glassford, a popular conductor on the Shoshone-Ketchum Branch of OSLRR, 1890s.

Glendale (Franklin). 5137'. T15S R41E sec 7. In the central part of the county on Cub River.

Named by George A. Parkinson because of its sheltered location at the foot of the Wasatch Mountains. Post office, 1895-1904.

Glengary (Bonner). 2051' T56N R1E sec 7. Town on Lake Pend Oreille, 3 3/4 mi NE of Midas; 9 mi SE of Sandpoint.

Two explanations are given for the name. Some say that owners of the first store in this community were so taken with the popular novel entitled *The Man from Glengary* that they gave the name to the town; others, that the explorer David Thompson, who had settled in Glengary, Ontario, Canada, had named the area for his home.

Glenns Ferry (Elmore). 2560'. T5S R10E sec 29/32. In SE Elmore County, on the N side of the Snake River between Gooding and Mountain Home.

Gustavus P. Glenn, for whom the town is named, operated a ferry across the Snake River here from 1865 to 1889. He and his brothers owned freight teams, and the ferry shortened the route from Kelton to Boise by 20 mi. The town was platted in 1883 by the OSLRR 1 mi W of the ferry. Post office, 1879-.

Glenwood (Idaho). T34N R5E sec 33. In the NW part of the county, 8 mi E of Kamiah, on Crocker Creek; a lumbering community. Post office, 1880-1933.

Locally believed to have been named by Sam Dean because it was located near a glen completely surrounded by timber.

Glover Creek (Clearwater). T41N R4E sec 22. Rises on White Rock, Shoshone County and flows 10 mi SE into the Little N Fk Clearwater River.

Named for Charlie Glover, a homesteader along the creek.

Glover Creek (Idaho). T32N R9E sec 32. In the NE quadrant of the county, 12 mi SE of Lowell. Rises on Round Top Mountain (6207') and Glover Saddle and flows 6 mi S to Selway River; Glover Ridge parallels the creek on the E side.

Named for Henry Clay Glover, a packer for the Sloan sheep business in this area, who spent his vacations on Glover Saddle and in its vicinity from 1918 to 1924.

Gnat Creek (Latah). T40N R5W sec 24. Rises S of East Twin, flows generally S for 2 mi to S Fk Palouse River.

Named for the swarms of gnats along the stream in the summer.

Goat. Goat as a place name occurs fifty-two times, in seventeen counties. Idaho County leads with twelve; Lemhi and Custer have five each. Wherever herds of mountain goats ranged, creeks, promontories, lakes, and springs bear that evidence in the names assigned to them.

Goat Creek (Custer). T10N R13E sec 1. Rises in Goat Lake and flows NE 6 mi to Valley Creek in Stanley Basin. Goat Lake is on a high rocky bench at the head of Goat Creek, several mi E of Sawtooth Lake.

Named for the mountain goats found in the area.

Goat Lake (Clearwater). T38N R13E sec 3/4. In the SE corner of the county, 2 mi NE of Blacklead Mountain.

Named for the mountain goats found in the area until the 1910 Idaho fire.

Goat Mountain (Valley). 9065'. T20N R9E sec 22. Located 4.4 mi SSW of Edwardsburg. Dominates the view to the S of the Big Creek-Edwardsburg area.

The name is widely used and accepted by local people and derives from the Rocky Mountain goats that are frequently seen in the area.

Goblin, The (Idaho). 8981′. T23N R2W sec 24. The easternmost peak of the Seven Devils; in the SW part of the county, in Hells Canyon National Recreation Area.

Named goblin, an evil or mischievous spirit, an elf, because it is one of the smallest of the Seven Devils.

Goddard Canyon (Clark). T9N R30E sec 4. In the SW part of the county. Trends 3.5 mi SW to Birch Creek.

The Goddard ranch lies in this canyon. George Goddard was a settler here in 1885.

Goddard Creek (Idaho). T32N R7E sec 22. Rises on the SE slope of Lookout Butte and flows 9 mi NE and N to Selway River at Goddard Bar.

The name honors a man named Goddard who located Wynkop Bar, (which now bears his name as well).

Godin Valley (Custer). T9/10N R23/24E. The first name of Lost River Valley.

Antoine Godin named this area, including the river, valley, and rugged mountains, for himself in 1823 when he explored the rough and rugged country of present-day Custer County. When his party returned several years later, they were unable to find the river and valley Godin had described, so they renamed the features Lost River and Valley.

Goff (Idaho). T24N R1E sec 10. In the SW part of the county at the mouth of Race Creek, on the Salmon River; about 2 mi N of Riggins.

A road station on the stage line between Meadows and Grangeville in 1894, established by John Levander; however, the place already bore the name of John Goff, who had occupied the

site from 1871. Levander also established a ferry at this point. Post office, 1894-1913.

Gold Creek (Clearwater). T35N R6E sec 19. Rises in the SE part of the county; flows SW into Musselshell Creek near the SE extremity; Clearwater River drainage.

Named because of placer mining here after the discovery of gold. Another Clearwater Gold Creek, tributary of Reeds Creek, T37N R4E sec 2-4, is named for the same reason. Gold features appear in all parts of Idaho where gold was found or sought.

Gold Creek (Latah). T41N R4W sec 8. Rises at the Benewah-Latah county boundary just S of Prospect Peak and flows SW 9 mi to Palouse River, 1 mi E of Potlatch; fed by E Gold Fork, Hoteling, Arson, and Nelson creeks on the E, and by Waterhole and Crane creeks on the W.

Gold discoveries are said to have been made on this creek from 1862 to 1870.

Gold Creek. A mining town with a store and post office and a population of about 120 men near the Carrico mine at the head of Gold Creek.

Gold Fork (Boise). T8N R7E sec 34. Flows SE into Beaver Creek; Boise River drainage.

Pioneer and freighter John Hailey named this creek because he found mica in the bottom of the creek and probably thought it was gold.

Goldburg (Custer). 6000′. T13N R24E sec 31. Town in the NE section of the county 25 mi NE of Dickey; a mining and livestock community settled in 1885.

When the post office was applied for, locals requested that it be named Bullsburg for the cattle industry. That name was refused and the US Post Office named the town Goldburg for the gold-mining interest in the area.

Golden (Idaho). 3463′. T29N R6E sec 35. In the central part of the county on Brown Creek at S Fk Clearwater River; 35 mi SE of Grangeville.

Founded when a claim was staked on its site in 1899, and the place named for the mineral mined here. The district also bears the name Golden. Formerly called Ten Mile Cabin, an overnight stopping place between Grangeville and Elk City, named because it was about 10 mi up the mountain from Wahl Ranch.

Golden Gate Peak (Bonneville). T1S R43E sec 26. In E part of county, in Caribou Range.

Named by transfer from the Golden Gate Bridge in California, supposedly for the open view to the west from this point, believed to be like that of the Golden Gate Bridge.

Golden Lake (Fremont). T12N R43E sec 22. Created by damming Thermon Creek on the Railroad Ranch 20 mi N of Ashton.

This lake and its neighbor, Silver Lake, were constructed as private trout-fishing lakes for Railroad Ranch guests; associative significance of the names is doubtful, as there is no gold or silver in the vicinity.

Golden Ridge (Lewis). T34N R2W sec 7. A wheat-growing area approximately 4 mi N of Winchester.

Named for the color of the crops at maturity. Said to have been named by a German settler after he had a good crop.

Golden Trout Lake (Lemhi). T21N R17E sec 31. About 1 mi SE of Cathedral Lake.

Named ca. 1940 by Lester Gutzman and a USFS crew when they planted California golden trout here.

Goldstar Gulch (Lemhi). T23N R22E sec 10. Runs 2 mi SW to Tower Creek; Salmon River drainage.

Originally called Silverstar Gulch because the Silverstar mine was located here by Wash Stapleton of Butte, one of Montana's more noted mining lawyers. It is said to be the first patented mine in Idaho. The name was changed when the USFS put up the wrong sign.

Goldstone Mountain (Lemhi). 9909′. T21N R24E sec 26. Situated 2 mi S of Goldstone Pass (9090′), at the head of Sandy Creek. Goldstone Pass is situated at the head of Pratt Creek, on the Idaho-Montana border.

Named for the Goldstone mine, which was producing gold bullion ca. 1905.

Goodenough Creek (Bannock). T9S R36E sec 22. Rises 1.5 mi SE of Scout Mountain in the W part of the county, Caribou National Forest; flows SE 6 mi into Marsh Creek; Portneuf River drainage.

Named for an early homesteader (ca. 1870) whose family still lives near McCammon.

Goodfellow Creek (Teton). Early official name for Darby Creek, which see.

Named by federal surveyor F. V. Hayden in 1872 for the cook on his expedition.

Goodheart Creek (Caribou). T9S R44E sec 5. Rises on the W side of Schmid Mountain and flows 5.5 mi generally SW to Slug Creek; Blackfoot River drainage. Goodheart Spring lies on the N side of this stream.

Named for George Goodhart (sic), who camped on this stream in 1860 and returned to homestead on it.

Gooding (Gooding). 2750′. T6S R15E sec 31/32. County seat. In the E central part of the county between Big and Little Wood rivers. First established in

1883 as a railroad station on the UPRR under the name To-po-nis, a Shoshoni word defined as both "black cherries" and "trading post."

The town name was changed in 1896 and the post office name in 1900 to Gooding for Frank Gooding, a prominent landowner and founder of the town, on whose sheep ranch the townsite was located. Gooding later became mayor of the town, governor of Idaho, and finally US Senator (1921 until his death in 1928). In 1913 the town was made the county seat.

Gooding Butte 3841' lies 3 mi SW of the town and Gooding City of Rocks lies 13 mi NW. Both features are named for the town; however, Gooding City of Rocks is a local name to distinguish it from the larger City of Rocks in Cassia County.

Gooding County. County seat, Gooding. One of the smallest counties in Idaho, with an area of 740 square miles; included successively in Alturas, Logan, Blaine, and Lincoln counties from 1865 to 1913, when it was created as a separate county from the W side of Lincoln County.

Gooding is bounded by Elmore County on the W, Camas on the N, Lincoln County on the E, and the Snake River on the S.

Named, like the county seat, for Frank R. Gooding, pioneer sheep rancher, early mayor of the city of Gooding, later Idaho governor and US Senator.

Goodrich Creek (Adams/Washington). T16N R2W sec 32. Rises on the S slope of Cuddy Mountain in Washington County and flows generally S about 3 mi into Adams County to the Weiser River E of Cambridge.

Goodrich (Adams) 2700'. T15N R2W sec 10. Town (ca. 1900) in the center of the county on the Weiser River halfway between Cambridge and Council.

Named for the Goodrich family, who settled on the creek in the 1880s and who had already given their name to Goodrich Creek.

Goose Creek (Adams). T19N R1E sec 12. Rises in the Brundage Mountains NE of Meadows and flows SW and N about 3 mi to the Little Salmon River; Salmon River drainage. An important source of irrigation water for much of the valley.

Goose Creek Falls. A series of cascades about 4 mi upstream from the McCall/New Meadows road.

Goose Lake. T20N R2E sec 1/11/12/14. A reservoir about 8 mi N of Meadows and 20 mi NW of McCall. At high water this lake is about 2 mi long.

Named for the Canada geese that formerly summered here and hatched their young. Wherever wild geese summered and nested, the name goose is common.

Goose Creek (Cassia). T10S R23E sec 21. In the NW part of the county, just NE of Burley. Rises in the mountains of Nevada at an altitude of 6500'; flows N through Goose Creek Reservoir, past Oakley, and empties into the Snake River near Burley at an altitude of 4134'; 65 mi long; drainage of 120 square miles.

Named by members of the Rocky Mountain Fur Company under Milton Sublette in 1832, for the vast number of geese that congregated upon and fed along its course.

Goose Creek. Community post office established in 1878; name changed to Thatcher.

Goose Creek Mountains (Cassia/Twin Falls). Local name for the mountains primarily because they are drained by Goose Creek on the E. Bounded by Rogerson on the W, Rock Creek on the

N, and Oakley on the E, a circular area. The long ridge running N to S down the center is known as Deadline Ridge (which see).

Goose Heaven Lake (Benewah). T46N R3W sec 1. Due E 3 1/2 mi of Lake Chatcolet, just S of the Kootenai County line. This lake covers 60 acres.

Gooseberry Creek (Boise). T9N R4E sec 15. Rises on Pyle Point and flows 5 mi SW into the Middle Fk Payette River 2 1/2 mi N of Crouch.

There are no gooseberries in this area. Residents may have mistaken unripe currants for gooseberries, because there are a few currant bushes on the creek and the plants belong to the same genus.

Gooseneck Lake (Lemhi). T21N R16E sec 10. Between Glacier Lake on the N and Crater Lake on the E, in the Bighorn Crags.

Named by Lester Gutzman, Ernest Marsing, and a USFS trail crew ca. 1940 because of its shape.

Gopher Canyon/Creek (Bonneville). T3N R44E sec 36-31. Extends 5 mi NW to SE in NE quadrant of the county. The creek flows SE into Fleming Canyon Creek; Snake River drainage.

Named for the northern pocket gopher, common in the area.

Gorley Creek (Lemhi). T21N R22E sec 30. Originates 1/2 mi SE of Baldy Mountain and flows generally E 4 1/2 mi to enter Salmon River.

Named for James Garley (sic), an early freighter and packer who lived here. Originally called Garlic Creek because of the wild garlic which grew in the area.

Gorman Creek (Clearwater). T38N R11E sec 4. Rises in the SE part of the county on the SE slopes of Scurvy Mountain and flows SW into Cayuse Creek; Clearwater River drainage. Gorman Hill (5400′) lies 4 mi NE of

the mouth of this creek and 10 mi E of Kelly Forks Ranger Station.

Named for George Gorman, one of the trappers who died of scurvy in the winter of 1907. See Scurvy Mountain.

Goshen (Bingham). 4630′. T1S R37E sec 23/26. In the NE part of the county, 9 mi E of Firth. An early Mormon settlement on a loop of the UPRR.

Named for the biblical Land of Goshen.

Gospel Peak (Idaho). 8345′. T26N R4E sec 3. In the Buffalo Hump area 12 mi W of Buffalo Hump; Wilderness Area. Gospel Lakes lie to the W of this peak, and Gospel Creek rises in the lakes and on the slopes of the peak and flows 6 mi NE to Johns Creek; S Fk Clearwater River drainage.

Named because W. N. Knox preached an impromptu sermon here in 1899. Knox had been invited to camp on this mountain with a group of surveyors, prospectors, miners, and freighters.

Gotch Creek (Boise). T8N R8E sec 29. Flows 4 mi SW into Banner Creek 1 mi S of Banner mine; Boise River drainage.

Henry Gotch ranched in this area; he raised cattle and supplied the Banner mine.

Gould Basin (Lemhi). T19N R25E sec 18. On Agency Creek; Lemhi River drainage.

Named for George Gould, who homesteaded a ranch in this area.

Governor Creek (Clearwater). T39N R7E sec 1. In the N central part of the county. Flows SE into N Fk Clearwater River.

A party of about seven men, among them Idaho Governor James Brady (1909- 1911), was on a sightseeing trip on the N Fk Clearwater River. The raft on which they were riding capsized in the rapids at the mouth of the creek.

Governor Brady was drenched and another member of the party broke his leg, but no one was drowned. Because of this incident, the rapids became known as Governor Rapids; then the creek became known by the same name.

Governors Punchbowl (Blaine). T7N R15E sec 33. Lake in the NW extremity of the county 3 mi E of Sawtooth City site.

Named by Alexander Ross in 1824, when he was exploring the area. Ross climbed to the summit of Boulder Peak to view the area. He named Mt. Simpson for Governor Sir George Simpson of the Hudson's Bay Company, and this lake Governors Punchbowl for him as well. When he returned to company headquarters from this scouting and exploring trip, he was demoted for failure to provide the information the company wanted.

Grace (Caribou). 5533'. T10S R40E sec 2/12. In the SW part of the county, 5 mi S of Alexander Reservoir on Bear River; in Gentile Valley. Post office 1894-.

Named in 1894 for Grace, wife of D. W. Standrod, then a government agent in Blackfoot, after Riverside was rejected by the Post Office Department.

Graham (Boise). T8N R10E sec 33. Early mining town and post office at the foot of Graham Peak (8823'), which lies in the extreme SE part of the county.

Named for Matt Graham, who developed the silver-mining industry in E Boise County.

Graham (Elmore). 5600'. T7N R10E sec 9. In the NE quadrant of the county on N Fk Boise River, on the Boise-Elmore line. Once a mining town. Post office, 1888-1892.

Matt Graham, a mining magnate from Boise, Hailey, and London, reported finding wide veins of ore on Silver Mountain. A road was built and a tunnel driven in 1887 and by 1888 excitement reached boom stage. The mine proved unproductive.

Grand Creek (Clearwater). T38N R7E sec 33. Flows S into Orogrande Creek; Clearwater River drainage.

The creek was named by USFS ranger W. L. Clover. It was hidden by shrubbery at the Orogrande Road and it seemed to flow from the thick vegetation.

The name is an aesthetic one.

Grand View (Owyhee). 2365'. T5S R3E sec 16/15. Town on the Snake River 24 mi S of Mountain Home; started about 1880 as a placer mining town but was not extensively settled until 1908. Post office, 1880-.

Named for the view of the valley.

Grand View Peak (Twin Falls). 7222'. T13S R18E sec 36. One mi W of the Cassia-Twin Falls county line, in the Sawtooth National Forest at the head of Fifth Fork Rock, Secesh, and Little creeks; 16 mi ESE of Hollister.

Named for the view available from its summit, some 1300' higher than the surrounding area.

Grandad Creek (Clearwater). T40N R4E sec 14. Rises in the NW quadrant of the county on Armstrong Saddle and flows NW into Dworshak Reservoir.

Named by early homesteaders for an old settler whose nickname was "Grandad."

Grandjean (Boise). 5580'. T10N R11E sec 34. Town. Grandjean Peak (9105') lies 4 mi SE of the town, and Grandjean Creek empties into the S Fk Payette River at Grandjean.

These features were named for Emil Grandjean, Supervisor of the Boise National Forest from 1908 to 1919.

Grandview Crater (Power). T7S R30E sec 1. Six mi NW of American Falls.

As one nears the summit of this crater on the way to Crystal Ice Caves, one has a good view of the surrounding area; hence the name Grandview.

Graney Creek (Boise). T9N R7E sec 27. Rises on Deadwood Ridge and flows 2 mi SE into the S Fk Payette 1 mi N of Lowman.

Thomas Graney, a saloon-keeper near the Banner mine once lived on this creek.

Grangemont (Clearwater). 3300'. T37N R3E sec 25. Town about 10 mi NE of Orofino.

Named Grangemont for the grange established there by W. W. Deal, ca. 1885.

Grangeville (Idaho). 3390'. County seat. T30N R3E sec 19. In the central part of W Idaho County, on Three-Mile Creek and Camas Prairie RR.

Organized in 1874 as Charity Grange No. 15 by farmers and stockmen who built a flour and gristmill and a grange hall on this site in 1876; from those the present town of Grangeville developed. Post office, 1876-.

Named for the grange hall, the first building on the site; land donated by John Crooks.

Granite (Bonner). 2260'. T54N R3W sec 22. Northern Pacific RR station, 2 mi SE of Kelso and 8 mi W of Lake Pend Oreille. An early way station that became more important in 1874 when gold was discovered on Lake Pend Oreille and when the railroad was completed in the 1880s.

Granite Creek rises in the Kaniksu National Forest 1/2 mi S of Granite Mountain and flows 9 mi SE to Priest River. A second Granite Creek rises on the S slope of Pack Saddle Mountain and flows in a semi-circular direction N and W to the E side of Lake Pend Oreille 1/2 mi S of Granite Point, T55N R1W sec 26.

Granite Creek (2100'). Town located at the mouth of Granite Creek at Lake Pend Oreille.

The name of these features derives from the granite outcroppings throughout Bonner County.

Granite Creek (Boise). T6N R5E sec 7. Rises 2 1/2 mi N of Granite and flows 8 mi SE into Grimes Creek 1 1/2 mi S of New Centerville; Boise River drainage. The first quartz mill in the Boise Basin, located on the creek, was built by W. W. Raymond, ca. 1864.

Granite is common near these creeks.

Granite Pass (Cassia). T16S R22E sec 34. One mi N of the Idaho-Utah border just S of the California-Salt Lake City cutoff.

Gold seekers and other travelers on the California Trail and Applegate Cutoff went through this pass, as did Salt Lake City travelers on their way to join the Oregon Trail at the mouth of Raft River.

Named for the formation in the area.

Granite Peak (Shoshone). 6815'. T49N R5E sec 25. Situated 1 mi W of the Montana line, 4 mi NE of Burke, this peak is a sharp, bare point. Granite Gulch, overlooked by the peak, trends 2 mi SE to Prichard Creek, Coeur d'Alene River drainage.

Both features are named for the Granite mine, which lies just S of the mouth of the gulch.

Grant (Jefferson). 4785'. T4N R38E sec 32. In the SE quadrant of the county on the S county line, 4 mi S of Lewisville.

Founded in 1880 by Mormons from Cache Valley, Utah, and named for Heber J. Grant, a leader in the Mormon Church, who helped organize the community. Times were hard for a long while and the place was locally known as Poverty Flats or Gravy Bend, for the thin, watery gravy they were forced to eat.

Grantsville (Lemhi). T22N R20E sec 21. Town near Leesburg on Napias Creek; Salmon River drainage.

Named in honor of General Ulysses S. Grant.

Grasmere (Owyhee). 5125′. T12S R5E sec 16. Cattle town on Louse Creek 7 mi N of Tindall. Post office, 1910-1965.

Named by Frank W. Holmquist, the first postmaster, presumably for Grasmere Lake, Westmoreland, England, the home of William Wordsworth.

Grass Creek (Boundary). T64/65N R3/4W. Tributary to Boundary Creek near the Canadian boundary; Kootenai River drainage; rises on Grass Mountain. Not Meadow Creek.

Named for the abundance of grass in the area.

Grasser Creek (Clearwater). T39N R12E sec 21. Stream 2.8 mi long in the Bitterroot Mountains, heads on Toboggan Hill, flows NNE to Kelly Creek 1.1 mi W of Kellys Thumb 40 mi SW of Missoula, Montana; Clearwater River drainage.

Named for John Adam Grasser (1885-1954), who operated an outfitter and guide service in the area from 1929 to 1952.

Grasshopper Creek (Clearwater). T35N R4E sec 15. In the SE part of the county; flows 9 mi SW into Jim Ford Creek; Clearwater River drainage.

Jim Clarke, who set up a chicken ranch about 4 mi from Weippe, sold fresh produce and poultry to the miners. In order to feed the chickens during the winter, he trapped grasshoppers and crickets in nets, killed them, and used them for chicken feed.

"Grasshopper" Jim Clarke, as he came to be called, lived near the creek that is now named for him.

Grassy Cone (Butte). 6351′. T2N R24E sec 34. Cinder cone 1 mi SW of headquarters of Craters of the Moon, adjacent to White Knob Mountains on the N.

Named for the vegetation growing on its slopes.

Grave Canyon (Custer). T7N R17E sec 12. Canyon 2.2 mi long, trends NE to East Pass Creek 20 mi N of Ketchum, T8N R18E sec 31.

Named for the grave of William Coulter, sheepherder, who was buried on 6 September 1909, in the canyon about .7 mi from the mouth of East Pass Creek.

Grave Peak (Idaho). 8267′. T35N R14E sec 8. In the NE part of the county.

Levi, an Indian, reportedly was killed on this peak by Chief Joseph's Nez Perce in 1877 and was buried here.

Grave Yard Point (Owyhee). T4N R6W sec 19. Five mi SW of Homedale.

On top of the point is a rock marker telling of emigrants who died in this area.

Graves Creek (Latah). T42N R2W sec 24. Rises on Beals Mountain and flows NW to Palouse River at Graves Meadow, which is drained by Johnson and Graves creeks.

Named by USFS ranger W. H. Daugs after an early-day homesteader near the mouth of this creek. One early diary gives Charles Graves as the namesake.

Gravey Creek (Clearwater). T38N R11E sec 33. Rises on Indian Grave Peak, Idaho County, and flows 9 mi NE into Cayuse Creek in the SE extremity of Clearwater County; Clearwater River drainage.

The creek was originally named Grave Creek, after the Indian graves near the creek in Idaho County. Since another creek nearby had the same name, this creek was renamed Gravey Creek.

Gray Creek (Bonner). T54N R1W sec 2. Sinks before reaching Whiskey Rock Point in sec 3 or is tributary to a small creek back of W Rock Spring.

Named for the A. L. Gray Lime Co., which burned lime here in 1892. It shipped lime by barge to Hope, Idaho, and then to Spokane, Washington, to help plaster houses after the Spokane fire of 1889.

Grayback Gulch (Boise). T8N R5E sec 32. Flows N into the S Fk Payette River.

Miners in this area were bothered by lice; "graybacks" is a slang term for lice.

Grayback Gulch (Boise). T6N R5E sec 33. Flows NW into Mores Creek 3 1/2 mi SE of Idaho City; Boise River drainage.

Probably named to honor (or defame) the large number of ex-Confederate soldiers in this area, who were called "graybacks" for their gray uniforms.

Grays Lake (Bonneville/Caribou). T4/5S R43E. One of the largest lakes in Idaho; a very shallow body of water, flanked by tule marshes, bogs, and meadows; hence a favorite habitat for wild ducks. Thirty mi N of Soda Springs and next to the W boundary of Caribou National Forest.

This lake and the adjoining swamp on the SW have been designated as a wildlife refuge.

Gray 6000'. T4S R43E sec 26. Village in S part of the county on the E side of Grays Lake. Settled by Mormons from Star Valley, Wyoming.

Grays Lake Outlet. T3S R43E sec 31. Creek that rises in Grays Lake and flows 39 mi NW to Willow Creek; Snake River drainage.

Named for John Gray, a half-Iroquois and half-English trapper; he discovered the lake in 1819. Name is in dispute; variant is John Days Lake. Gray appears as the name in journals during the trapping era, but later maps designate John Day. Though John Day did frequent the area, these features were first called Gray; officially called Gray by the post office in 1892 and currently called Gray.

Great Rift National Landmark (Blaine/Power). T1-7S R25-28E. Extends from Craters of the Moon SE to a point 10 mi S of Crystal Ice Caves; 46 mi long.

It is the longest exposed rift in the United States.

Green Bay (Bonner). T55N R1W sec 26. On the W side of Lake Pend Oreille 1/2 mi SE of Midas.

The name derives from the lush growth surrounding the water.

Green Canyon (Fremont). T12N R42E sec 14. In NW Fremont County; trends N-S to Island Park Reservoir; Henrys Fork system.

Said to be named for a timber operator of the area.

Green Canyon Hot Springs (Madison). T5N R43E sec 6. In the E part of the county.

Natural hot springs on Canyon Creek; originally on a limestone claim owned by John E. and James H. Pincock, who developed them as a resort and operated them under the name Pincock Hot Springs, 1903-1924. Bob Thueson bought the springs in 1924 and piped the water to a new site, setting up a new resort which he named Green Canyon Hot Springs because of the area's vegetation.

Green Creek (Boise). T9N R8E sec 32. Flows N into the S Fk Payette River 1/2 mi E of Kirkham Hot Springs.

Named for Emma (Mrs. James) Green, who designed the state seal of Idaho and lived near this creek.

Green Monarch Mountain (Bonner). 5082'. T55N R1E sec 16. Located 1 mi S of the Green Monarch mine on Lake Pend Oreille. Green Monarch Ridge consists of low-lying mountains extending 4 mi SE of Green Monarch Mountain.

There is some controversy over whether the Green Monarch mine was named for the mountain or vice versa. The latter seems to be more likely, since a 1912 USFS map lists the mine but not the mountain or the ridge. The name Green Monarch is applicable to both the mine and the mountain since the ore taken from the mine was green and the mountain is green from the many trees.

Green Mountain (Bear Lake/Caribou). 8777'. T9S R45E sec 31. In the NE corner of the county in a deep cleft on the Bear Lake-Caribou county line, about 10 mi NE of Georgetown.

A descriptive name: the mountain is covered with vegetation.

Green Pass (Bear Lake/Franklin). T13S R42E sec 20. Mountain pass on the Bear Lake-Franklin county line, about .3 mi N of Midnight Mountain. In Cache National Forest, 9 mi NW of Paris. Green Basin lies 1 mi S of the pass.

No doubt the basin was a grazing area and green with vegetation, and the pass is at least more green than the surrounding promontories.

Green Point (Clearwater). 5719'. T39N R8E sec 35. Mountain 8 mi N of Weitas Ranger Station.

The 1910 Idaho fire burned around the mountain but left a patch of green timber on the peak itself.

Greencreek (Idaho). 3136'. T32N R1E sec 13. In the NW part of the county, 7 mi E of Cottonwood. An agricultural community.

Named for Greencreek, Illinois, the native town of many of the settlers in the vicinity.

Greenhorn Gulch (Latah). T42N R2W sec 23. The second of the ten named gulches emptying into N Fk Palouse River from the N.

Site of the Greenhorn mine.

Greenleaf (Canyon). 2420'. T4N R4W sec 21. Town in central Canyon County halfway between Caldwell and Wilder. Founded in the early 1900s by a group of Quakers, who built their community around the Friends Church and the Greenleaf Academy, founded in 1908. The town incorporated in 1972. Post office, 1908-.

Named for the Quaker poet John Greenleaf Whittier.

Greentimber (Fremont). T9N R44E sec 20. Town (early 1900s) 10 mi E of Ashton.

Named for the color of the surrounding vegetation.

Greenwood (Jerome). T9/10S R20/21E sec 36/6. In the SE part of the county. An agricultural area; name first designated a school district, then transferred to the entire community.

Named for teacher and author Annie Pike Greenwood. She and her husband settled here in the early 1900s and endured numerous hardships.

Greer (Clearwater). T35N R2E sec 11. Town 11 mi W of Weippe.

Founded in 1861, when Colonel William Craig and Jacob Schultz built a ferry across the Clearwater River to accommodate the Orofino miners. In 1877,

164

John Greer, for whom the site is named, and John Molloy acquired the ferry; when the railroad came in 1899, Greer and John Dunn formed a partnership and platted a town site. The ferry was a key link from Lewiston to the mines around Pierce.

Greer Gulch (Clearwater). T36N R6E sec 32. On the SE border of W Clearwater County. Flows S into Musselshell Creek; Clearwater River drainage.

Named for a miner, Henry Greer, after the discovery of gold in Pierce in 1860.

Gregg (Idaho). T34N R4E. Abandoned town. Established in 1902 by Al Kincaid and George Gregg and named for the latter. Formerly a lumber town, but the commercial timber was exhausted in the early 1900s. Post office, 1898-1903.

Gregory Gulch (Boise). T5N R5E sec 4. Trends 2 mi SE into Mores Creek; Boise River drainage.

John Gregory, a former Californian, had a claim near this creek.

Greylock Mountain (Elmore). 9317'. T6N R11E sec 24. In the NE quadrant of the county just NE of Atlanta. Greylock Springs lie at the foot of the mountain, 3 mi above the town of Atlanta on the S side of Boise River.

Said to have been named by Chinese miners who reworked Atlanta mines. The mountain is composed of masses of grey rock, and unable to pronounce the initial letter "R," the Chinese called it Greylock.

Griffin Butte (Blaine). 8411'. T5N R17E sec 34. A rocky butte on the E end of an E-W extending ridge, between Adams Gulch and Fox Creek; 4 mi NW of the village of Sun Valley.

Named for a rancher who filed on nearby land in 1899.

Grimer Lake (Idaho). T37N R17E sec 7. A small lake in the Clearwater National Forest, 1.5 mi W of Idaho-Montana line.

Named for an old family at this site.

Grimes Creek Pass (Boise). T8N R5E sec 35. Summit. Grimes Creek rises SE of the peak on Freeman and Wilson peaks and flows NW then SW 41 mi to Mores Creek; Boise River drainage.

This creek is named for George Grimes, who with Moses Splawn traveled a circuitous route from Pierce, Idaho, and discovered gold in the Boise Basin in 1862. He was killed by Indians (or trappers who wanted his gold) in 1862.

Griswold Meadow (Latah). T42N R3W sec 36. Early name for late 19th-century Grizzle Camp.

Named for a man named Griswold, who settled in the Viola area, reportedly married a Nez Perce woman, and moved E to more primitive land as settlers increased. Grizzle is no doubt a pronunciation spelling of Griswold.

Grizzle Camp (Latah). T42N R3W sec 36. A camping site for trail packers and prospectors and the terminus of the Palouse-Grizzle Camp stagecoach line during the Hoodoo mining excitement. Within what is now Laird Park.

Freighters and stagecoaches unloaded here and mule trains carried what was unloaded to mines and miners along the 14-mi Hoodoo Trail. Apparently Griswold, for whom the area is named, moved farther and farther into primitive areas until only a few settlers remembered him and the spelling of his name became Grizzle, later Grizzly. Also Grizzly Camp and Griswold Meadow.

Grizzly Creek (Washington). T15N R2W sec 20. Rises on Grizzly Basin in the NE corner of the county and flows

6 1/2 mi generally SE to the Weiser River 5 mi NE of Cambridge.

Early settlers found so many grizzlies in the area that any mountainous area might well have been named Grizzly or Bear.

Gross (Gem). T11N R1E sec 10. An early settlement located on Squaw Creek.

There is a strong possibility that Gross was first called Squaw Creek, which was granted a post office in 1883 and located on this creek.

Named for the first postmaster, Ruth Gross.

Grouse (Custer). 6167'. T4N R24E sec 9. A community located in the extreme SE section of the county, about 20 mi S of Darlington.

Grouse is a common name throughout Idaho, indicating that the habitat of the sage, spruce, and ruffed species extended to many parts of the state. Early settlers relied on the grouse for meat, especially in the fall.

Grouse Creek (Custer). T14N R22E sec 27. Heads on the W slope of Grouse Creek Peak (11,085') and flows NE to Goldburg Creek; Salmon River system. Grouse Peak (8464') is situated 14 mi WNW of the mouth of the creek; Challis National Forest.

The creek was named for the birds that formerly were found in the area in great numbers.

Grouse Creek (Latah). T41N R4W sec 1. A 2-mi stream that flows S to Palouse River halfway between Princeton and Harvard.

Named for the blue grouse seen in great numbers in the area.

Grouse Creek (Lemhi). T18N R14E sec 29. Headwaters located near Woodtick Summit; flows 5 mi NW to enter Middle Fk Salmon River near the Tappan Ranch.

Named in 1920 by Andy Lee, homesteader at Meyers Cove, because there were numerous grouse found on the creek.

Groveland (Bingham). 4487'. T2S R38E sec 28. In the central part of the county, on Riverside Canal.

A Mormon settlement begun in 1902 and named by O. F. Smith for several local groves.

Guffey (Owyhee). T1S R2W sec 35. Town 4 mi N of Murphy and 30 mi from Silver City. Guffey Butte (3130') lies 1 mi S of Guffey. The first structure here was built in 1897 by Fred Brunzell. In 1899 it was known as Guffey Station and is presently called Riva on the maps, but most residents still refer to it as Guffey. Post office, 1897-1919.

Named for G. M. Guffey, an engineer and a friend of Colonel William Henry Dewey.

Gull Island (Washington). T10N R5W sec 26. A 5-acre patch of rock, sand, and brush in the middle of the Snake River, 7 mi SE of Weiser.

Aptly named, as both Western gulls and Canada geese use the land as a nesting place. The island has been designated part of Deer Flat, a federal refuge. More commonly known as Smith Island.

Gunbarrel Creek (Lemhi). T24N R14E sec 26. Heads 1/2 mi SW of Skunk Camp and flows SW 2 mi to empty into Salmon River.

Named because the creek is enclosed by vertical cliffs on both sides— straight as a gunbarrel. Additionally, a gun was found near a tree in the basin above the creek.

Gunnell (Cassia). T15S R28E sec 16. Early post office, now a ranch; in the SE part of the county, 7 mi E of Bridge. Six-Mile Ranch and Gunnell now occupy the same area.

Named for early settler and first post-master Frank O. Gunnell.

Gunsight Peak (Lemhi). 10,835'. T15N R25E sec 30. At the head of Adams Creek, 3 mi NW of Timber Creek Reservoir; in Lemhi Range; Salmon National Forest.

There is a notch in the top of the mountain that looks like the rear sight on a rifle. It is necessary to be at the head of Big Eightmile Creek, in the Lemhi Range, to see the feature.

Guyer Hot Springs (Blaine). 5925'. T4N R17E sec 14/13.

Named for Harry Guyer, who first operated a small smelter in Ketchum, then established this resort near Ketchum.

Gwenford (Oneida). T15S R35E sec 2. An agricultural community in the SE part of the county, 5.5 mi SW of Malad. Settled about 1890 when John Jones built a store; he later applied for a post office and named it for his daughter, Gwen. The community has been absorbed by Pleasantview.

Gyppo Creek (Clearwater). T40N R4E sec 22. Flows NW into Dworshak Reservoir just S of Grandad Creek Bridge; Clearwater River drainage.

Named for gyppo loggers, who contract with logging companies to be paid by the board foot for the timber they cut.

H

Haden (Teton). T6N R44E sec 20. Early 1900s townsite about 1 mi W of Tetonia and 3 mi E of the Teton River Bridge.

The townsite was dedicated in 1905, although the community had had a post office since 1890. The town flourished until the Union Pacific RR came through Tetonia, 1 mi E. Then most of Haden's establishments moved to Tetonia. Post office, 1890-1913.

Named by the US Postal Service to honor federal geologist and surveyor F. V. Hayden; for some reason the "Y" was omitted—probably to avoid confusion with Hayden Lake (ca. 1880).

Hager Lake (Bonner). T61N R5W sec 34. Three mi W of the Idaho-Washington border, 2 3/4 mi SW of Nordman.

Named for Swan Hager, an early homesteader.

Hagerman (Gooding). 2964′. T7S R13E sec 14. In the SW part of the county, 3.5 mi S of Malad Bridge.

This town began as a village situated by Lower Salmon Falls, where Shoshoni Indians for centuries speared migrating salmon. Once a stage station on the Oregon Trail.

In 1892 Stanley Hegeman and Jack Hess applied for a post office to be named Hess, but it was refused as there was already such a post office. It was then named for Hegeman, but the name was misspelled.

Hagerman Valley (Gooding). T65 R13E to T7S R13E. This valley is an expansion of the Snake River Canyon, cut by the river from the foot of the plain near Bliss for about 12-15 mi southward.

Hahn (Lemhi). T12N R27E sec 15. Deserted townsite near the mouth of Spring Mountain Canyon. A small mining hamlet that lasted for only two years, 1909-1911.

Named for a man from St. Louis, Missouri, who built a smelter here in 1907.

Hailey (Blaine). 5328′. T2N R18E sec 9. County seat. In the SW part of the county on the Big Wood River, 11 mi S of Ketchum. Hailey began during the Wood River boom. John Hailey (who was running the Utah, Idaho, and Oregon State Company when the boom started), J. H. Boomer, W. T. Riley, and E. S. Chase platted the town in 1881 on land Hailey donated. The town was in the center of Mineral Hill Mining District and grew rapidly. Its heyday lasted until 1889.

When John Hailey and his party platted the town they named it Marshall, but the name was quickly changed to Hailey in honor of the acknowledged founder, who was territorial delegate to Congress 1873-1875 and 1885-1887.

Hailey Creek (Boise). T9N R5E sec 11. Rises in the NW part of the county in Granite Basin and flows 2 mi S into Anderson Creek about 2 mi N of Basque Springs; Payette River drainage.

Named for John Hailey, who was one of the first packers in the area.

Hale Canyon (Fremont). T9N R43E sec 20. In S central Fremont County; runs 3 1/2 mi S to Henrys Fork, 3 mi NE of Ashton; Henrys Fork system.

Named for Frank Hale, who homesteaded the area.

Hale Gulch (Lemhi). T24N R19E sec 22. Heads just E of the head of China Gulch; runs N 2 mi to enter the Salmon River.

Named for Jim Hale, a prospector who lived in this vicinity.

Half Round Bay (Kootenai). T48N R4W sec 11/14. In the S part of the county on the E side of Coeur d'Alene Lake.

Named for the curved shoreline.

Halfmoon Point (Boise). T7N R5E sec 16. Two mi N of Centerville.

Named because there is a half-circle bend in Grimes Creek at this point.

Halfway Gulch (Lemhi). T23N R18E sec 10. One mi long, runs NW to Salmon River.

Named because it is approximately halfway between Shoup and Panther Creek on the Salmon River.

Halfway Hill (Shoshone). T45N R7E sec 20. Promontory on the N side of the St. Joe River.

The hill is halfway between Avery and Conrad Crossing.

Hall Creek (Shoshone). T46N R3E sec 15. In the SW part of the county, a 2-mi tributary of E Fk Big Creek from the NW, 9 mi SW of Wallace; St. Joe River drainage.

A man named Hall homesteaded on this creek.

Hall Creek (Boundary). T65N R1W sec 36. Rises 2 mi NW of Hall Mountain (5428') and flows NE 3 mi to Mission Creek.

Named for Hall Mountain whose derivation is unknown.

Halls Gulch (Idaho). T25N R4E sec 28-34. A 2-mi gulch emptying into Wind River from the NW; Salmon River drainage. In the Florence Mining District, 6 mi E of Florence.

Locally believed to have been named for a placer miner.

Halm Creek (Shoshone). T42N R9E sec 5. A 1-mi tributary of the St. Joe River from the E, 4 mi SW of Needle Point and 25 mi SW of Superior, Montana.

Named for Joseph B. Halm (died in 1966), USFS ranger, who was credited with saving the lives of a fire-fighting crew in the vicinity of this stream during the Idaho fire of 1910.

Halsey Meadow (Bonner). T57N R4W sec 13. Six mi NW of Wrencoe; 7 1/2 mi NE of the town of Priest River.

Named for a homesteader who lived near the meadow. Now officially called McCormick Meadow, but local residents still refer to it as Halsey Meadow.

Hamburg Siding (Canyon). T3N R2W sec 16. An early name for the community that became Caldwell. Also shortened to Hamburg.

Named for the blacksmith shop of Jack Ham, at the place which is now First or Second and Aven streets. While the shop was moved to downtown Caldwell when the new town was laid

out, the old name was still sometimes used for the townsite.

Hamer (Jefferson). 4802'. T7N R36E sec 15/22. Lies in the NE quadrant of the county 15 mi N of Roberts, on the UPRR and US 91. The community was founded by easterners; the first building was a RR section house. Mormons came, established irrigation from artesian wells, and raised grains and hay in the area. Post office, 1909-.

Named for Colonel Thomas R. Hamer, who was born in Fulton County, Illinois, in 1864; moved to Idaho in 1893; served as a state legislator; and was elected to Congress (1909-1911).

Hamilton Canyon (Lewis). T34N R3W sec 14. Extends for approximately 3 mi from 3 mi N of Winchester to T34N R3W sec 3. The N end of the canyon opens into Mission Creek 1/4 mi N of Slickpoo; Clearwater River drainage.

Named for the Hamilton family, who lived in the canyon.

Hammer Creek (Lemhi). T18N R16E sec 25. A stream 1 1/2 mi long; flows generally S to enter Camas Creek; Middle Fk Salmon River drainage.

Named by Irvin Robertson, a forest ranger, because of the creek's proximity to Forge and Anvil creeks. See Forge Creek.

Hammerean Creek (Lemhi). T26N R21E sec 18. Flows in SE direction for 3 mi to the N Fk Salmon River.

Named for "Old Man" Hammerean, who placer mined here in the 1870s.

Hammett (Elmore). 2531'. T5S R8E sec 35. In southern Elmore County on US 30, 10 mi W of Glenns Ferry. Platted in 1883 by the OSLRR, the town did not develop until about 1909. Post office, 1908-.

Named Medbury in 1883 for a Captain Medbury, believed by locals to have been connected with Boise Barracks. The name was changed to Hammett in 1909 to honor Charles Hammett, a promoter of the King Hill irrigation project.

Hammond Creek (Bear Lake). T13S R43E sec 23. Rises at Little Valley Reservoir, flows NE to Ovid Creek. 3 mi S of Ovid; Bear River drainage.

Named for Levi Hammond, who was sent by Brigham Young to Bear Lake County NW of Paris in 1874 to settle in Liberty. He built what is reputed to be the first home there.

Hampton (Latah). 2520'. T41N R4W sec 9. An early-day store and supply center; located about 2 mi E of Potlatch and 1/2 mi W of Princeton.

This place provided a stagecoach stopover between Palouse and St. Maries. Formerly Starner, which see.

Named for J. E. Hampton, who homesteaded here 1904.

Hand Meadows (Idaho). T23N R10E sec 32. Meadows, the largest of which is 1.5 mi long, along Hand Creek 20 mi SSE of Dixie.

Named for James Hand, settler and prospector around 1890 in this area.

Hangmans Gulch (Clearwater). T36N R5E sec 10. Three mi SW of Pierce.

Five Chinese, who were accused of murdering Pierce businessman D. M. Fraser, were hanged here in 1885 by a vigilante group. See Fraser.

Hanks Creek (Boise). T8N R5E sec 10. In the NW part of the county; flows S into the S Fk Payette River 1/2 mi E of Grimes Pass.

Named after Henry (Hank) Halverson, the packer for an early USFS surveying party.

Hansberg (Clearwater). T37N R2/3E sec 24/19. Town 6 mi NE of Orofino.

Named for Hans Berg, who homesteaded along the creek.

Hansen (Twin Falls). 4000'. T10S R18E sec 25. In the NE part of the county, 2 mi E of Kimberly and 10 mi SE of Twin Falls. The townsite was laid out in 1907. Post office, 1905-.

Officials of the OSLRR named the station here for John F. Hansen, 1876 settler in the area, who was active as a businessman and public official.

Hanson Creek (Clearwater). T39N R12E sec 27. Rises on Tobaggan Ridge in the NE extremity of the county and flows 3 mi N into Kelly Creek; Clearwater River drainage. Hanson Meadows lies immediately E of the mouth of the creek.

Named for the Hanson brothers, who prospected around Kelly Creek and Blacklead Mountain about 1902 to 1914.

Happy Camp (Elmore). T4N R10E. In the Feather River drainage. Site of the first gold discovery in South Boise Basin, probably established in 1863. By the fall of that year, there were 35 companies of prospectors and miners, with from one to five miners in each, averaging $25 per man per day.

Named for the mood of those early miners who had struck gold.

Happy Camp (Owyhee). One mi S of Ruby City on Jordan Creek.

So called because the 29 prospectors, the first discoverers of gold in the county, were happy upon finding numerous grains of gold on Jordan Creek.

Harbor Lake (Lemhi). T21N R16E sec 21/16. Just W of Wilson Lake in Bighorn Crags.

Named ca. 1938 by Lester Gutzman and a USFS crew because two natural rock dikes run out into the lake to form a natural harbor.

Hardpan Creek (Benewah). T43N R3W sec 29. Rises on Holaki Knob and flows 1 mi SE to Meadow Lake; Palouse River drainage.

Named by W. H. Daugs, USFS, because prospectors found an abundance of hardpan (hard clay-like strata) while prospecting for placer deposits.

Hardscrabble Pasture (Boise). T10N R5E sec 5. A flat in the NW part of the county near the N county line.

This is three acres of thin, rocky soil. One man tried in the 1860s and 1870s to garden here and went bankrupt; he called it Hardscrabble—"hard struggle to make a living."

Harlan Creek (Clearwater). T40N R6E sec 34. Rises in the N central part of the county on Micky Point and flows 3 mi SE into Beaver Creek at sec 34; Clearwater River drainage.

Named for John P. (Jack) Harlan, who settled near the creek in the early 1900s and had a cabin at the head of the stream. He was known as an historian of Clearwater County.

Harpster (Idaho). 1575′. T31N R4E sec 28/33. In the NW part of the county, 8 mi NE of Grangeville, on S Fk Clearwater River. Formerly Bridgeport and Brownsville.

In the early 1860s William Jackson built a small station and toll bridge across the river here and named it Bridgeport; it was destroyed by fire during the Nez Perce War in 1877. Loyal Brown owned the land in 1883 and sold 80 acres to the Clearwater Mining Company, which laid out a townsite and called it Brownsville for the former owner. The post office was established in 1895 as Harpster.

Named for Abraham Harpster, one of the early settlers of Idaho County and a pioneer of the gold-rush days.

Harrington Peak (Caribou). 8554′. T10S R44E sec 5. On Bear Lake-Caribou county boundary at the head of Wide Canyon, 13 mi SE of Soda Springs.

Named for an early settler.

Harrington Peak (Cassia). T14S R19E sec 2. In the W part of the county, 4 mi E of Cassia-Twin Falls county line. Harrington Fork rises on the E slope of this peak and flows 6 mi NW to Rock Creek, 21 mi SE of Twin Falls. (Not Harrington Creek.)

Named for J. E. Harrington, sheriff of Cassia County in the 1870s.

Harris (Lewis). T33N R1E sec 3/9. RR siding about 5 mi E of Craigmont and 3 mi W of Nezperce.

Named for J. A. (Johnny) Harris, farmer, ca. 1900.

Harris Creek (Boise). T7N R2E sec 34. Rises in the SW part of the county on Harris Creek Summit (5202′) and flows 11 mi NW into the Payette River 3 mi S of Horseshoe Bend.

Named for Felix Harris, a wealthy Kentuckian who settled near Horseshoe Bend in 1863. He mined and also operated a lucrative toll road to the Boise Basin mines.

Harrisburg (Idaho). T34N R3E sec 12. In the NW part of the county, 5 mi NNE of Kamiah.

Founded in 1902 by Frank Harris, who had a store and established a post office in 1902; there was also a school and a church, but now there is only a townsite.

Harrison (Kootenai). 2135′. T47N R4W sec 1. In the SW part of the county on the E side of Coeur d'Alene Lake; on the UPRR. Formerly a lumbering center for the Coeur d'Alene mining district. The first sawmill was erected here in 1889 and 10 years later Harrison was incorporated. Post office, 1891-.

Named for President Benjamin Harrison.

Harrison Lake (Boundary). T62N R3W sec 36 and T62N R2W sec 31. About 1 mi SW of Harrison Peak in the Kaniksu National Forest; 5 mi N of Chimney Rock. A glacial cirque, the largest lake in the Selkirks is in a group of lakes that form an 8-mi chain E of Priest Lake. Covers 30 acres.

Harrison Peak 7306' is located in the Kaniksu National Forest just N of Harrison Lake. This mountain is a massive, anvil-shaped rock that descends abruptly on the S into the lake. Formerly Anvil Peak.

Named for President Benjamin Harrison.

Harrison, Mount (Cassia). 9265'. T13S R24E sec 9. In the central part of the county, in Sawtooth National Forest; 7 mi S of Albion. One of the best-known mountains in S Idaho, Mt. Harrison has an excellent view from its summit.

Named by picnickers during the election of 1888 when the campaign between Benjamin Harrison and Grover Cleveland for President of the United States was in heated progress. The picnickers decided to name the mountain after the victor in the campaign and the nearby lake after the defeated candidate. Harrison won; hence the name.

Hartley Peak (Power). 8500'. T12S R30E sec 4. In the SW extremity of the county in the Sawtooth National Forest; 1 mi SW of Hartley Canyon, 3 mi long and trending NE to SW.

Named for a pioneer settler in the canyon.

Harvard (Latah). 2560'. T41N R3W sec 9. A WIM railroad station 9 mi E of Potlatch, platted and dedicated 28 May 1906. Post office, 1906-.

Named by Homer W. Canfield, who owned much land along the WIM location. For his cooperation during construction, the company proposed to honor him by naming the station Canfield. He did not consent to the proposal but assumed that he could choose a name; he chose Harvard. This set the pattern for college names along the line.

Harvey Creek (Clearwater). T37N R4E sec 22. Rises on Democrat Mountain in the SW quadrant of the county and flows SW into Cow Creek; Clearwater River drainage.

Named for an employee of the White Pine Lumber Company. Deeds indicate George Harvey settled near the head of the creek in 1911.

Haskin Creek (Bonneville). T1S R42E sec 11. Rises in the center of the county in the Caribou Range and flows NE into Fall Creek; Snake River drainage.

Named for Frank Haskins, a construction worker for the Utah Northern RR, who took up a homestead in 1879 at the point where Sand Creek branched from Willow Creek.

Haskins Flat (Latah). T39N R5W sec 10. Area E of Moscow.

Settled by Lorethus Haskins in the 1870s.

Hat Creek (Idaho). T23N R1E sec 20. A 4-mi stream that flows W to Little Salmon River at Pollock.

In the early 1890s a man tried to cross the creek when it was high and lost his hat.

Hat Creek (Lemhi). T17N R21E sec 20. Originates just W of Sheephorn Mountain and flows S 5 mi, SE 2 mi, and E 2 mi to enter Salmon River.

Charlie Matt, who was herding cows for the Shoup outfit, lost his hat in the creek during high water in the 1870s.

Hatch (Caribou). 5500'. T7S R39E sec 13. In the NW part of the county, on Eighteen-Mile Creek, 6 mi N of Bancroft. Settled in 1880 by the Hatch brothers, Mormon colonizers.

Its first name was Eighteen-Mile, for the creek on which it is located. Renamed Hatch for William Ansel Hatch, son of the first settler in this community.

Hatter Creek (Latah). T41N R4W sec 9. Flows NW for 7 mi from Basalt Hill to the Palouse River at Princeton.

Charles Hatter homesteaded 160 acres near the head of this creek in 1879. Stephen A. Hatter and his wife purchased 80 acres N of this creek from the U.S. for $50.00. Dudley Tribble, prospector, worked this creek and is said to have named it.

Hatwai Creek (Nez Perce). T35N R5W sec 25. An 8-mi stream that flows SE into the Clearwater River. The small community of Hatwai (785') is located on this stream, 2 mi S of Lewiston Hill and 1/2 mi W of Lewiston.

Hatwai is a Nez Perce Indian word meaning "place of the cactus."

Hauser (Kootenai). 2130'. T51N R5W sec 19. In the NW part of the county, one terminal of the 13-mi Spokane Falls and Idaho RR built by D. C. Corbin between 1887 and 1889 from Coeur d'Alene to Hauser Junction.

After purchase of the line by the NPRR, it was the western station of the NPRR in Idaho. It lay N of present-day Hauser Siding and 1 mi S of Hauser Lake, in the center of a logging area. Post office, 1888-1907.

Named for S. T. Hauser, one of the incorporators in 1886 of the Coeur d'Alene Railway and Navigation Company, of which D. C. Corbin was the head. Variant names (all between 1864 and 1881): Antoine Plantes Ferry, Cowleys Ferry, Spokane Bridge.

Hawkins (Bannock). 5200'. T10S R35E sec 23. Settlement in the W part of the county, 12 mi W of Arimo; settled in 1890 by Latter-day Saints and named

for pioneer W. Carl Hawkins. Post office, 1901-1922.

Hawkins Creek. T10S R37E sec 31. Rises on the E slopes of the Bannock Range, in the W extremity of the county, 11 mi SW of McCammon; flows SSE to Hawkins Reservoir, then in an easterly direction 9 mi to Marsh Creek, 1 mi W of Virginia; Portneuf River drainage.

Hawley (Blaine). 4320'. T8S R26E sec 14. A UPRR station in the S part of the county, 3 mi N of Lake Walcott.

Named for James H. Hawley, who came to Idaho in 1862 and was US Attorney, 1885-89; governor of Idaho, 1910-12.

Hawley Creek (Lemhi). T16N R26E sec 325. Flows W 9 mi to enter Eighteenmile Creek 1 mi E of Leadore; Lemhi River drainage.

Named for E. R. Hawley, whose stock ranch was a pioneer holding on this stream.

Hawley Mountain (Boise). 7301'. T8N R4E sec 31. In the NW part of the county, 8 mi E of Gardena.

Hawley Mountains (Butte). T9N R26/27E. A small range covering about 9 square miles and trending NW to SE between Little Lost River on the E and Lost River Range on the W. The highest promontory in the range is Hawley Mountain, (9752').

Hawley Peak (Custer). 12,130'. The first name placed on this peak in the Lost River Range, 4 1/2 mi E of Leatherman Peak. Now Breitenbach Mountain.

All these features honor James H. Hawley.

Hay Creek (Clearwater). T37N R4E sec 36. Flows SW into Poorman Creek 2mi SW of Jaype; Clearwater River drainage.

Named for John Hay, a miner and settler.

Hayden Creek (Lemhi). T18N R24E sec 17. Flows N 8 mi, then NE 3 mi to enter the Lemhi River. Hayden Basin lies on Basin Creek, 5 mi SE of North Basin.

Named for Jim Hayden, an early packer and freighter, who shot Bill Smith, one of the original discoverers of gold in Leesburg during December 1871, in a dispute over a card game in Salmon. Smith had fired on the unarmed Hayden, who was tried and acquitted. Along with some other freighters bringing in supplies for George L. Shoup of Salmon and Dave Wood of Leesburg in 1877, he was killed by Indians in the Birch Creek Valley.

Hayden Lake (Kootenai). T51/52N R3/4W. In the N central part of the county, 4 mi N of Coeur d'Alene. This lake is 7 mi long and from 1 to 3 mi wide; about 8 square miles.

Hayden Lake (2280′), the village, grew up on the shores of the lake. Originally a fishing and trapping village, it is now a resort town. Post office, 1907-.

Both the lake and the village owe their name to an 1878 incident. Matt Heyden (sic) and John Hager were playing cards in Hager's cabin on the lake. They decided to name the lake after the winner of a seven-up game. Heyden won.

Hayden Peak (Owyhee). T5S R3W sec 22. The peak of Cinnabar Mountain.

The peak was named after Edward Everett Hayden, a surveyor on special duty with the Smithsonian Institution in the 1880s. Old-timers in the county were annoyed that it would be named after Hayden because the surveyor was never in the area.

Haynes Creek (Lemhi). T20N R23E sec 24. Forms 2 1/2 mi E of Porcupine Spring and flows NW 9 mi to enter Lemhi River. Haynes Basin lies at the head of Haynes Creek, about 2 mi NW of Baldy Basin.

Named in honor of N. I. Haines (sic) Andrews, who had a ranch on this stream and who later ran a store in Salmon.

Hays Gulch (Bonner). T57N R2W sec 25. Heads 1 3/4 mi SW of Sourdough Point; extends 1 mi to lake Pend Oreille 2 mi SE of Sandpoint.

Named for the Hays family, who lived near here and probably prospected for gold.

Haystack Mountain (Lemhi). 8800′. T23N R20E sec 31. About 3 mi SE of Point of Rocks.

The feature is shaped like a big, loose haystack.

Hazard Creek (Adams/Idaho). T21N R1E sec 2. Rises over the ridge from the headwaters of Goose Creek in Big Hazard Lake, Idaho County, and flows 13 mi W and SW through a rugged canyon to the Little Salmon River in Adams County. Hazard Creek Falls are 4 mi from the outlet of the creek.

Hazard Lakes, Big (Idaho). T22N R3E sec 24. Twenty-eight mi NW of McCall. They vary in size from 20 to 60 acres.

Named for an old hunter and trapper who lived on the Little Salmon River near the mouth of this creek.

Hazel (Cassia). T12S R23E sec 9. An early community with a post office (1905-1904); in the N part of the county, 9 mi S of Burley.

Named for Hazel Stoddard, daughter of an early settler who was the first postmaster.

Hazelton (Jerome). 4068′. T9S R20E sec 32. In the SE part of the county, 4.1 mi E of Eden. First settled in 1905; the UPRR reached it in 1907; it began to grow immediately thereafter. The town was founded in 1911 by Joe Barlow.

Two mi SE of Hazelton is Hazelton Butte (4401').

The town was named for Hazel Barlow, daughter of the founder; the butte was named for the town.

He Devil (Idaho). 9393'. T23N R2W sec 23. This peak and She Devil mark the end of the Seven Devils, the N extremity of the Seven Devil Mountains.

He Devil Lake lies immediately W of the peak.

Head Creek (Latah). T42N R1E sec 32. Rises S of Sherwin Point and flows 1 1/2 mi SW to the Potlatch River; Clearwater River drainage.

The first appearance of this creek name on maps came as a surprise to many local people, who had always called the stream Hood Creek; a good example of how place names may change.

Headlong Creek (Latah). Head 3600', mouth 2800'. T42N R2W sec 28. A 1-mi stream flowing N to Big Sand Creek; Palouse River drainage.

The stream, less than 1 mi long, has a drop of 800'; thus the water rushes headlong to mouth of the stream.

Headquarters (Clearwater). T38N R5E sec 15.

This was a rail terminus and loggers' camp for the Potlatch Lumber Company in the area.

Headwall Lake (Custer). T9N R16E. Lake.15 mi long, one of the Boulder Chain Lakes.

There is a headwall along the SW and N shores of the lake.

Heals Island (Jefferson). Early name for Menan, which see.

Named for Israel Heal, who ran a herd of cattle here in the 1870s and is the first white man known to be in this area. The name changed to Pooles Island

after the arrival of the Poole family in 1879. See Pooles Island.

Heart Lake (Lemhi). T21N R16E sec 21. In the Bighorn Crags. About 1/2 mi S of Harbor Lake.

Named ca. 1938 by Lester Gutzman and a USFS crew because of the shape of the lake.

Heath (Washington). T16N R4W sec 1. An 1890s silver-mining town in the N part of the county, 20 mi NW of Cambridge, near the Oregon border. Post office, 1900-1930. At one time an active mining area with a smelter, which was junked during World War II for lack of labor and profitable ore prices.

Named for Thomas Heath, one of the discoverers of silver in the district.

Heath Gulch (Latah). T41N R3W sec 8. A 3-mi gulch running NE to the Palouse River SE of Harvard. One of the Gold Bug mines is at the head of this gulch on Jerome Creek.

Named for a surveyor and timber cruiser for the Potlatch Lumber Company, Bill Heath.

Heather Creek (Clearwater). T41N R8E sec 5. On the Clearwater-Shoshone county line. Flows E into Collins Creek; Clearwater River drainage.

Named for the mountain heather, a purple flower found here.

Heavens Gate (Idaho). 8429'. T23/24N R1W sec 5/32. Two mi NE of Windy Saddle Camp, trailhead for hikers in the Seven Devils; 9.5 mi SW of Riggins.

From this vantage point one can see Hells Canyon, Washington, and Oregon on the W; Montana on the E; and much of Idaho, including the clearest Idaho view of the Seven Devils.

Named in contrast to the Seven Devils area.

Heglar Canyon (Cassia). T10S R27E sec 35. Originates in the extreme NE part of the county in the Sawtooth

National Forest; trends 16 mi generally NW to Raft River.

The Heglar community is located in this canyon, about 8 mi W of its source; a small trading center in a livestock and dry-farming area. Post office, 1912-ca. 1930.

Named for early settler and sheepman Heglaer (sic), a German who brought the first sheep into the vicinity.

Heifer Creek (Lemhi). T17N R14E sec 7. Flows NW for 2 mi to enter the Middle Fk Salmon River.

Named by the Ramey brothers, who trailed cattle from their ranch in the Middle Fk area via Cow and Heifer creeks to the Andy Lee ranch at Meyers Cove.

Heise Hot Springs (Jefferson). 5000'. T4N R41E sec 31. In the extreme SE part of the county on the N side of the S Fk Snake River.

Tales of the curative powers of these springs arose from Indians and extended to the report of Capt. Charles B. Hawley, an early resident and trapper, who claimed that he saw a wounded deer cured here. Richard C. Heise, whose name the springs now bear, was an emigrant from Germany who heard these tales in 1894 and went to the area to find the springs. He homesteaded here and spent the rest of his life developing and promoting them. The spot became a popular resort even before roads and bridges facilitated travel. When Heise died, his daughter, Bertha Gavin, continued his efforts. Post office, 1900-1944.

Helena (Adams). 5800'. T21N R3W sec 12. An early-1900s copper-mining town located about 10 mi N of Cuprum on Indian Creek, in the Seven Devils area. Though prospects were promising for the town, the railroad from Weiser to

Helena was never finished and the town died. Post office, 1890-1902.

There are two accounts of the name: One source says it was named for the first girl born in the mining camp; another that I. I. Lewis and Levi Allen, owners and operators of the Peacock mine at the time, named it for their former residence, Helena, Montana.

Helende Creek (Boise). T9N R8E sec 24. Rises in the NE quadrant of the county and flows 2 1/2 mi SE into the S Fk Payette River.

Named for a Basque sheepherder who worked in this area.

Hell Roaring Creek (Custer). T7N R13E sec 5. W tributary of the Salmon River. Heads on the E slopes of the Sawtooth Range near Mt. Cramer and flows E to T8N R14E sec 17. Hell Roaring Lake lies on Hell Roaring Creek a little below the center of Sawtooth Valley.

Named for the roar of the water as it rushes from mountain to valley in 2 miles.

Hellgate Creek (Idaho). T33N R7E sec 14. A 3-mi tributary of the Lochsa River from the E.

Named for Hellgate Rapids at its mouth; these are particularly bad rapids, hence the name.

Hellroaring Creek (Bonner). T59N R2W sec 3. Rises N and NE of Flat Top and flows E and SE about 12 mi to Pack River. Hellroaring Ridge extends 3 mi E and W just S of Hellroaring Creek and is named for the creek.

Named for the noise resulting from the fast-flowing water.

Hells Canyon. The deepest and narrowest river gorge in North America. The Snake River flows through this canyon, forming the Oregon-Idaho boundary. It is 40 mi long and, averages 5500' in depth, but in some places it reaches

7900'. This gorge can be viewed from Kinney Point and Sheep Rock, both accessible by car.

In *Hells Canyon of Snake River*, Cort Conley writes: "Most old-timers knew the gorge as Box Canyon or Snake River Canyon. The first reference to Hells Canyon which the writer has been able to locate appears in an 1895 edition of McCurdy's *Marine History of the Pacific Northwest*. In discussing the voyage of the steamboat *Norma* (at the mouth of Deep Creek, just below the site of Hells Canyon Dam), the author writes: 'She then bounded off, swinging into midstream, and, like a racehorse, shot into Hell Cañon, where the river winds like a serpent and the wall rocks tower to such a height that they almost shut out the sun.' The name was twice used by the Mazama hiking club of Portland in their 1931 bulletin, though USFS maps in 1935 still labeled the area Box Canyon. It was not until the early 1950s that Hells Canyon became a popularly accepted descriptive term for the gorge — primarily because of several articles by Oregon's Senator Richard Neuberger which used the present name."

Hells Gulch (Benewah). T46/47N R2W. Extends 8 mi erratically from Eagle Mountain (5412'), Grassy Mountain (4947'), and Sharp Top in a three-part gulch.

Named because of the sharp-ridged upper reaches.

Helmer (Latah). 2820'. T40N R1W sec 21. A village 4 mi E of Deary.

Founded in 1906 on the land belonging to J. G. Liner; thrived during early years as the head of a shortcut route to homesteads in the upper reaches of the Potlatch River and Elk Creek areas. Post office, 1907-1929.

Named for early-day timber cruiser William Helmer.

Hem Creek (Clearwater). T37N R7E sec 29. Rises on the SE boundary of the county on Hemlock Butte (6057') and flows 5 mi NE into Sylvan Creek; Clearwater River drainage.

This is a shortened form of hemlock; Hemlock Creek is located nearby. The USFS may have applied this as an office name.

Heman (Fremont). T7N R39E sec 12. An agricultural town; 6 mi W of St. Anthony.

A small community named for Heman Hunter, a pioneer settler.

Hemingway Butte (Owyhee). T1S R3W sec 13/14. Located 2 1/2 mi W of Walters Ferry. Named for William S. Hemingway, who was a stage driver. The stage that Hemingway was driving to Silver City on 31 July 1878 was attacked by a small band of Indians. The driver was gravely wounded but drove the passengers to safety before he died.

Hemlock Butte (Clearwater). 6057'. T36N R7E sec 7. Seven mi W of Pierce. Nearby Hemlock Creek flows NE into Weitas Creek; Clearwater River drainage. Hemlock Ridge lies 6 mi SW of the Bungalow Ranger Station, and Hemlock Butte (5650') 5 mi N of Elk River.

Named for the stand of hemlock trees here.

Hemlock Creek (Kootenai/Shoshone). T51N R1E sec 28. Rises in Shoshone County on the E side of its namesake, Hemlock Mountain (4932'), and flows generally NW 4 mi to empty into Leiberg Creek, in Kootenai County; N Fk Coeur d'Alene River drainage.

Named for the hemlock growing in the area.

Henderson (Owyhee). Town near Homedale.

A small community named for Robert Henderson, the first postmaster and proprietor of Henderson's Ferry in the same location.

Henderson Ridge (Lemhi). From T26N R20E sec 31 S for 2 mi to T22N R20E sec 1. Between McConn Creek and the head of Indian Creek.

Named for David Henderson, who settled in this area ca. 1885.

Henry (Caribou). 6161'. T6S R42E sec 9/15. In the N part of the county, between the two NE arms of Blackfoot River Reservoir; 20 mi N of Soda Springs. Henry Mountain (8320') lies 6 1/2 mi NE of the town.

The first post office was named Omega. In 1885, renamed Henry, for Henry Schmidt, early settler and merchant.

Henry Creek (Bonneville). T1N R38E sec 21. Rises in NW quadrant and flows 6 1/2 mi NW into Taylor Canal, SE of Idaho Falls; Snake River drainage.

Henry Mountain. 8320'. T6S R43E sec 3. In the N part of the county at the head of Little Blackfoot River and Sheep, Dry, and Gravel creeks.

Named for Andrew Henry of the Missouri Fur Company, who entered the Snake River Valley in 1810 to escape Blackfoot warriors.

Henry Creek (Boise). T6N R5E sec 6. Rises in the E central part of the county. Flows SE into Grimes Creek at New Centerville; Boise River drainage.

W. W. Henry located a claim on this creek in 1862 and lived here.

Henry Creek (Clearwater). T40N R9E sec 1. Rises on Mountain Ridge in the N central part of the county and flows NE into Quartz Creek; Clearwater River drainage.

Named for an Indian miner by the name of Henry. Two other features located near the creek are also named for him: Indian Creek and Indian Henry Ridge.

Henry Creek (Lemhi). T20N R21E sec 24. Originates 2 mi NE of Lake Mountain and flows E 5 mi to enter the Salmon River.

Named for Bronco Henry V. Williams, who patented the land at the mouth of this creek on 2 Oct 1900. He was an excellent rider who rode in the first rodeo held in Madison Square Garden.

Henrys Fork River (Fremont/Madison). Bisects Fremont County N to S. Rises in Henrys Lake and at Big Springs, flows S and SW 65 mi to its juncture with S Fk Snake River in Madison County at T5N R38E.

Henrys Lake. T15N R43E. Covers 8 square miles SW of Targhee Pass.

Henrys Lake Flats, a flat meadow and rangeland E of Henrys Lake.

Henrys Lake Mountains. Mountain range running in a semi-circle on the Idaho-Montana border N and E, extending to the Madison Plateau in Yellowstone National Park. The range forms approximately 15 mi of the state border in extreme northern Fremont County.

All of these features are named for Major Andrew Henry, who built Fort Henry in 1810 about 5 mi SW of St. Anthony on Henrys Fork.

Henrys Gulch (Idaho). T26N R1E sec 12. E tributary of the Salmon River 11 mi S of White Bird.

Named for Henry Rhett, whose family settled in the John Day area about 1 mi S of this location. He is the grandson of William Rhett, for whom two Salmon tributaries are named, and one of the three sons of Elbert Rhett.

Herbert (Madison). 5593'. T4N R41E sec 5. In the S part of the county on

Lyman Creek, 6 mi N of Heise. Settlers in the 1890s immediately diverted water to their crops. Post office, 1906-1916.

According to Merrill D. Beal, Snake River Country, the community was named for Herbert Englunc (sic), the firstborn child in the community.

Herman (Bonneville). 4900'. T3S R43E sec 21. Early name for Twin Pines. Located in the S part of the county just N of Grays Lake, an agricultural area.

Named for Herman Wakeman, first postmaster and early resident of the area.

Heyburn (Minidoka). 4342'. T10S R23E sec 15. A town on the Snake River; formerly Riverton.

Platted in 1903 with the opening of the Minidoka reclamation project; originally named Riverton for its location on Snake River; the post office was named Heyburn in 1892.

All sources except post office records say that the Bureau of Reclamation named the place in 1905 for Weldon Brinton Heyburn, US Senator from Idaho. However, he lived and worked in the area in the 1890s and became in all likelihood the namesake of the post office at that time. It was not uncommon in the late 1800s and early 1900s for the post office, the community, and often the RR station to bear different names.

Heyburn Mountain (Custer). 10,880'. T9N R13E sec 17/18. In the Sawtooth Range at the S end of Redfish Lake; one of the better-known of the Sawtooth peaks.

Named for Senator Weldon Heyburn.

Heywood Creek (Clearwater). T35N R4E sec 25. Rises in Lew Hard Meadow and flows 6 mi SW into Jim Ford Creek 2 1/2 mi SE of Weippe; Clearwater River drainage.

Named for Bert Heywood, who settled here.

Hi Peak (Lemhi). 10,971'. T16N R22E sec 27. In the Lemhi Range, at the head of Bray Creek on the Lemhi side and an unnamed branch of Morgan Creek on the Pahsimeroi side. In Lemhi Range, Salmon National Forest.

Named because it is such a high mountain; the name was shortened to its present form.

Hibbard (Madison). 4845'. T6N R39E sec 10/11. Rural community in the NW quadrant, 2.5 mi W and N of Rexburg and separated from Burton by S Fk Teton River. Formerly called Island Ward because it is almost surrounded by water.

Settlement began here in 1883. Post office, 1903-1905.

Named for an early settler and first Mormon bishop of the community, George A. Hibbard.

Hida Creek (Idaho). T26N R10E sec 25. Rises on Hida Point (6756') and flows 3 mi N to Salmon River.

Named for Lee Hida, watchman for the Comstock mine for many years.

Hidden Creek (Latah). T42N R1E sec 26. Rises on NE slope of Sherwin Point and flows SE into N Fk St. Maries River, Shoshone County.

Like other creeks bearing such a name, this creek is in a deeply wooded area.

Hidden Lake (Benewah). 1800'. T47N R3W sec 36. One of a group of lakes in Heyburn Park on the Kootenai-Benewah county line, this lake covers 76 acres, with a low-water depth of 7' and a high-water depth of 35'.

Named because when the water is high the lake merges with Lakes Chatcolet and Benewah; they seem to be one lake.

Hidden Lake (Custer). T11N R11E sec 12. About 14 mi NW of Stanley.

Formerly, it had neither inlet nor outlet; but now, during high water, an outlet drains into Meadow Creek. It covers about 4 acres and is shallow, having a maximum depth of 17'.

High Creek (Clearwater). T39N R9E sec 14. Rises on Flat Mountain and flows S into the N Fk Clearwater River.

This creek was named by W. O. Clover; it was higher than the riverside trail and a slight climb was necessary to reach it while traveling either up or down the N Fk of the Clearwater River.

High Creek (Lemhi). T19N R24E sec 1. One mi long; flows W to enter Pattee Creek 1/2 mi S of Wade Creek; Lemhi River drainage.

Named because of the steepness of the terrain; the creek is higher than the creek drainages on either side of it.

Highline Creek (Latah). T42N R1W sec 13. Rises in the mountains S of Emerald Creek and flows 1 mi NE to E Fk Emerald Creek; St. Maries River drainage.

Named in 1926 by USFS ranger W. H. Daugs because the Potlatch Lumber Company removed logs from this drainage by means of a steam donkey with a highline—a log-skidding cable.

Hildebrand Creek (Clearwater). T36N R5E sec 11. Flows N into Orofino Creek at Orofino; Clearwater River drainage.

Named for a settler near Pierce who had a saloon near the creek. Hildebrand was the sheriff at Pierce.

Hill City (Camas). 5090'. T1S R12E sec 29. In SW Camas County 14 mi SW of Fairfield. A Mr. Nicklewaite founded this town when he learned that the RR was coming through. He first named it Prairie for Camas Prairie but changed it to Hill City for the Bennett

Mountain Hills nearby. Post office, 1912-.

Hills Camp (Idaho). T26N R6E sec 2. Early name for Calendar.

Named by and for the 1898 camp superintendent of Jumbo mine, Walter Hovey Hill.

Hillsdale (Jerome). T10S R19E sec 10/14. In the S part of the county, 2.2 mi SW of Eden.

This site has been eliminated with the construction of Interstate 84. Post office, 1908-1913.

Named for its location on a dale, just S of Skeleton Butte.

Hinckley (Madison). 4840'. T6N R39E sec 3. Farming community in the NW quadrant, 1 mi N of Hibbard.

Settled in 1883, when 16 Mormons came into the area. One was Ira N. Hinckley, who homesteaded here and left his name.

Hitt Peak (Washington). 7100'. T15N R5W sec 34. The highest peak in the southern Payette National Forest, on the divide between Mann and Brownlee creeks. Hitt Mountain (3314'); bounded on the S by the town of Weiser, on the W by Snake River, on the N by Cuddy Mountain, and on the E by Weiser River.

Named for the Hitt family, who homesteaded in the area.

Hiyu Creek (Boise). T9N R10E sec 34. Rises in the E part of the county and flows 2 mi N into Tenmile Creek 17 mi E of Lowman; Payette River drainage.

Hiyu is Chinook jargon for "many." The creek has many feeder streams.

Hjort Lake (Idaho). T33N R10E sec 21. In the N central part of the county; in The Crags, Clearwater Mountains.

Named for Andy Hjort, an early-day packer and USFS employee who contributed much to the development of the Selway country.

Hobo Cedar Grove (Shoshone). T43N R3E sec 7/8. In the SW part of the county, 8 mi NE of Clarkia, in the Marble Creek drainage. A 240-acre area classified on 17 February 1969 by Regional Forester Neal Rahm to protect this stand of giant cedars for scientific, botanical, and recreational uses.

Named before 1904 for the temporary shelters used by men protecting their logging claims from claim jumpers

Hodges Spring (Lemhi). T18N R23E sec 9. On McDevitt Creek, 6 mi SW of Tendoy.

Named for Art Hodges, who had a ranch in this area.

Hodson Creek (Clearwater). T38N R3E sec 27. Flows NW into Dworshak Reservoir 3 mi N of Johnson Mill.

Some say this creek was named after John Hodson, a homesteader, or that it was named for a girl who worked in the state forestry department at Boise. Also called Hudson Creek.

Hog Creek (Washington). T11N R6W sec 19. Rises in the SW quadrant of the county on a divide 12 mi NW of Weiser, and flows SE 10 mi to the Snake River 5 mi W of Weiser.

Named because hogs were pastured on the upper reaches of this stream.

Hog Heaven (Latah). A pioneer community from which the town of Moscow developed.

Said by some to be named for the herds of hogs feeding in the area, supposedly left by transients in the area before 1870; or for the availability of camas roots for the hogs that settlers raised.

Hog Hollow (Fremont). T7/8N R42/43E. In S Fremont County, halfway between Teton City and Canyon Creek just N of Newdale; N of the Teton River 5 mi E of St. Anthony. Richard (Beaver Dick) Leigh had his winter home here until his death (1865-1880s).

No verifiable information about the name. Said to be named for the hogback ridges that enclose it; or for some association with the hog-leg, a pioneer six-shooter, since the area was used by rustlers and stage robbers. Both hypotheses are folk etymologies. The area is a dry basin unsuitable for raising swine, and no local sources consulted recalled any connection with domestic animals.

Hog Meadows (Latah). T40N R1W sec 9/10,15/16. Area between the mouths of Corral and Meadow creeks just N of Helmer. Hog Meadows Creek flows 7 1/2 mi SE through Hog Meadows to the Potlatch River; Clearwater River drainage.

Hog Meadows. A half-way rest stop and store to accommodate timber cruisers, prospectors, and homesteaders; owned by Josh and Sue Lamphear, homesteaders on Hog Meadows, 1898.

Named for the numerous hogs kept here by the Galloway brothers to root out the camas bulbs.

Hogback Ridge (Kootenai). 2810'. T48N R2W sec 16/17. In the SE part of the county, between the Coeur d'Alene River and Cottonwood Peak, 8 mi E of Coeur d'Alene Lake.

Named for the geologic formation: a long, sharply crested ridge.

Holaki Knob (Benewah). T43N R3W sec 20. Promontory in the center of southern Benewah County, 1 mi N of Latah-Benewah county line.

Named by W. H. Daugs. The name is Chinook jargon for "open" or "clearing," which seemed appropriate to Daugs for the prominent, open, grassy hill.

Holbrook (Oneida). 4860'. T14S R33E sec 31. A wheat-growing community in the SE part of the county, 20 mi W of Malad.

Settled by Mormons and named for its first bishop, Heber A. Holbrook. Post office, 1901-.

Holbrook Summit (5812′) is in the S part of the county, 10 mi E of Holbrook; in the Blue Spring Hills. Named for the town.

Holbrook Island (Nez Perce). T36N R5W sec 31. Island on the Clearwater River at Lewiston.

Noyes B. Holbrook homesteaded the island in 1862 and it has since been known as Holbrook Island. Holbrook also ran the Holbrook Livery Stable in Lewiston.

Hole in the Rock (Caribou). T7S R41E sec 1/12. Lake 1.8 mi long, SW of Blackfoot Reservoir, 1.5 mi N of China Hat and 6.5 mi SW of Henry.

Named because lava rocks surrounded the area now covered by the lake.

Hole in the Rocks (Clark). T10N R36E. In the S central part of the county near Dubois.

A stage station in the 1880s. Maier Kaufman, who ran it, had earlier been express manager for Ben Holladay's stage line from Corrine, Utah, and had driven for the Fargo Express and the Gilmer and Salsbury Stage Line.

Hole-in-the-Wall Creek (Boise). T8N R6E sec 1. Flows 3 1/2 mi NE into the S Fk Payette River 1 mi SE of Pine Flat Campground.

A sheer granite wall separates this creek from the S Fk Payette River. The creek has worn a hole in this wall to drain into the river, so the USFS bestowed the name.

Holland Canyon/Creek (Bonneville). T2N R42E sec 16. Extends 2 1/2 mi NE to SW in NE quadrant, near Swan Valley. The creek flows SW into Snake River.

Named for a family who settled here in 1912.

Hollister (Twin Falls). 4500′. T12S R16E sec 28. A community founded in 1909 and named for H. L. Hollister, an early settler connected with the Twin Falls Land and Investment Company and a promoter of the Salmon Irrigation Company, 1908. This is the largest village within an area of 20 mi. Post office, 1910-1965.

Hollister Mountain (Kootenai). 4320′. T52N R3W sec 11. In the N central part of the county, 3 mi N of the upper extremity of Hayden Lake; in the Coeur d'Alene Mountains, Coeur d'Alene National Forest.

Named for three brothers, early settlers in this area.

Hollywood (Clearwater). T37N R5E sec 9/16. Town 5 mi N of Pierce.

The town developed very rapidly where Potlatch Forests, Inc. had Camp 12. As the railroad workers moved into the area, a shacktown with tents and small camps arose. The town was referred to facetiously as Hollywood.

Homedale (Owyhee). 2235′. T3N R5W sec 4. Town 7 mi S of Marsing. Homedale began when Jacob Mussell built a ferry on the Snake River in 1898. In 1912 the town was platted; it was eventually incorporated in 1920 – the first incorporated town in the county. Post office, 1900-.

The name was chosen in 1907 by a drawing. Residents of the area met and each put a name in a hat: Homedale, suggested by Jacob Mussell, was the winner.

Hood Gulch (Lemhi). T17N R27E sec 28. Originates near the Idaho- Montana border and runs E 3 mi to enter Canyon Creek drainage; Lemhi River drainage.

Named for Mark Hood, an early prospector in this area.

Hoodoo Creek (Boise). T6N R3E sec 30. Flows 3 mi SE into Mores Creek 1 1/2 mi NE of Idaho City; Boise River drainage.

A miner got "hoodooed" on this creek and sank all his money into a worthless claim.

Hoodoo Creek (Bonner). T56N R4W sec 31. Tributary of the Pend Oreille River, 21 mi long, rising in Kelso Lake and flowing NW, SW, S, and E to the Pend Oreille River. Hoodoo Lake lies 6 mi E of Hoodoo Mountain (5091'), 6 mi W of Edgemere. Hoodoo Valley extends 12 mi from the Kootenai-Bonner county line N to Pend Oreille River.

The name for these features was probably brought to this area when miners flocked to the British Columbia gold mines in the 1870s and 1880s. This is a common name applied to mining sites and mines, first noted in the California mines.

Hoodoo Creek (Lemhi). T19N R16E sec 28. Heads in Hoodoo Meadows and flows S 8 mi to enter Yellowjacket Creek; Middle Fk Salmon River drainage.

Since early miners could not find any gold in this area, they said the country was "hoodooed," meaning that there was some sort of hex on it.

Hoodoo Gulch (Latah). T42N R2W sec 23. On the NW side of the N Fk Palouse River, about 1 mi N of its mouth; site of the discovery of gold in the county, made by a Mr. Hoteling in 1860.

Hoodoo. A mining boom town and post office that existed during the peak of mining activities in the Hoodoo Mining District between 1880 and 1903. The name, and probably the location, was changed to Woodfell in 1903.

Hoodoo Mountains. A mountainous area mostly in the NE quarter of the county, marked roughly by Potlatch and Sanders on the W, Clarkia on the E, Santa on the N, and Deary on the S. They are in the St. Joe National Forest and include important tracts of timber.

The discovery of gold in this area was at the Hoodoo mine, from which first the gulch, then the mountains and finally the mining district took their names. Hoodoo may have been brought here by California miners, as the term was common there in names of gold mines and areas in the 1840s and long before that in regard to fortunes and misfortunes, whether in mining or some other activity.

Hooton Creek (Boise). T6N R6E sec 2. Flows NW into Mores Creek 7 mi NE of Idaho City; Boise River drainage.

William Hooton mined a claim on this creek in the 1860s.

Hoover Point (Lewis). 4583'. T32N R3W sec 36. In SW quadrant, about 2 mi N of the Salmon River and 12 mi S of Winchester.

Named for Joseph Huber (mispronounced Hoover by many persons), a homesteader.

Hope (Bonner). 2087'. T57N R1E sec 35. Town 16 mi E of Sandpoint. East Hope, an extension of Hope, lies 1 1/4 mi E.

The settlement began in 1882 with the construction of the NPRR. It was named for a Dr. Hope, veterinarian with the NPRR. The town was platted in 1896 and incorporated in 1903. Post office, 1887-.

Hope Creek (Latah). T42N R3W sec 5. Flows 2 mi SW to Big Creek. One of the headwater streams of Big Creek; Palouse River drainage.

Named by Edd. F. Helmers, said to be for the hope some gyppo (contract) loggers had that they would make good money along this creek. Before Helmers named this creek, there were several mining locations named Hope in this area; H. P. Bakkenson, Chas. E. Kane, and Wm. Moorehead filed such claims in 1891, 1892, and 1894.

Hopkins Creek (Boise). T8N R5E sec 11. Flows S into the S Fk Payette River 1 mi E of Grimes Pass.

William Hopkins homesteaded near the creek with his family.

Horn Creek (Boise). T8N R5E sec 7. Flows NW into the S Fk Payette River 1/2 mi E of Grimes Pass.

Named by the USFS because the area is winter range for a number of horned animals.

Hornby Creek (Bonner). T57N R2W sec 31. Heads 3 3/4 mi E of Johnny Long Mountain and flows SE to the Pend Oreille River. Named for the president of the Dover Lumber Co., who owned a residence near the mouth of the creek.

Hornby Creek (Clearwater). T39N R7E sec 20. Flows N into Washington Creek in the central part of the county; Clearwater River drainage.

Named for Lloyd G. Hornby, a USFS employee. Hornby was supervisor of the Clearwater National Forest in 1921-1922.

Hornet Creek (Adams). T16N R1W sec 15. Rises on the W slope of Cuddy Mountain and flows about 15 mi SE to the Weiser River, near the lower end of Council Valley.

Hornet Creek (Lemhi). T23N R20E sec 26. Forms about 1 mi E of Haystack Mountain and runs E 3 mi to enter Moose Creek; Salmon River drainage.

Named for the many hornet nests along the streams and valleys.

Horse Camp Creek (Shoshone). T45N R5E sec 33. A 2.5-mi tributary of Fishhook Creek from the E, 4 mi S of Avery; St. Joe River drainage.

Named by surveyors Caulkins, Jones, Pardee, and McDonald, who camped here while working with the USGS survey in 1910. A horse belonging to the party got down on a rock ledge near the campsite and could not get off. He fell from the first ledge to another, crippling himself. The party finally managed to pull the horse off the ledge with ropes and ultimately back into camp.

Horse Creek (Lemhi). T24N R14E sec 27. Large stream that flows about 21 mi in a SW direction from its headwaters near Horse Creek Pass on the Idaho-Montana border to its confluence with the Salmon River.

There are two stories of how Horse Creek got its name: In the early days the Horse Creek drainage was known as Big Sheep Creek. A man by the name of Reynolds, who had a little store in Shoup, went into the area with a halfbreed Indian by the name of Allen in 1891. They packed their supplies and traps to the big meadow of what was then Big Sheep Creek, built a cabin, and prepared to spend the winter trapping, mostly marten. They turned a herd of horses out on the south slopes of Big Sheep Creek. In the early spring the men got "cabin fever" and decided to go out to civilization. On their way to the Bitterroot Valley on snowshoes, Allen saw his chance and put his rifle to Reynolds' ear and pulled the trigger. Allen took the pelts and other valuables, but was caught and hanged before he got out of the country. This left the horses on Big Sheep Creek. They wintered on the open hillsides for several years before they were caught or died, so local people started calling the drainage Horse Creek.

The other story claims that the Gattin brothers, who had the ranch on what is now Horse Creek, were horse thieves operating in Oregon, Idaho, and Montana. They would steal horses in Oregon, bring them to their ranch on the creek, alter brands, and take them to Montana to sell. On the return trip they would steal horses in Montana, change brands at the ranch and then sell them in Oregon. This all took place in 1863 and 1864.

The rest of the horse names were given by trail and mapping crews, most of them by the men who built and manned Blue Nose Lookout.

Horse Creek Butte (8351'). T24N R17E sec 8. Approximately 3 mi NE of Long Tom Ridge Camp.

Horse Creek Hot Springs. T25N R17E sec 15. About 2 mi NE of Oreana Lookout.

Horse Creek Pass (7305'). T25N R18E sec 18. On the Idaho-Montana border, 36 mi NW of Salmon, Idaho.

Horse Heaven (Gooding). T6S R14E. A grassy plain near the source of the Malad River in the Hagerman Valley.

During stagecoach and freighting days, horses were allowed to rest and graze on the lush grass here.

Horse Heaven (Lemhi). 8086'. T22N R16E sec 1. At the head of Shell Creek about 1 1/2 mi W of Dome Lake.

Named by Mag and Bonner Bevan because of the good meadow and spring they found here for their horses, ca. 1924.

Horse Prairie Mountain (Lemhi). 10,194'. T17N R28E sec 32. On the

Idaho-Montana border 1 1/2 mi N of the headwaters of Quaking Asp Creek.

The area has excellent grass for horses and is named because it is at the head of Horse Prairie Creek in Montana.

Horsefly Gulch (Lemhi). T24N R18E sec 22. Gulch about 2 mi long; heads W of Sheepeater Point and runs E to enter the Boulder Creek drainage.

Horsefly Spring (Fremont). T10N R45E sec 16. In SE Fremont County, 3 mi W of the Yellowstone National Park border.

Horseflies were pesky in both areas.

Horsemint Spring (Fremont). T14N R42E sec 21. In N Fremont County, 1/2 mi S of Reas Point on the Idaho-Montana border.

Named for the presence of this variety of wild mint.

Horseshoe Bend (Boise). 2613'. T7N R2E sec 26. Located 28 mi N of Boise on a bend in the Payette River.

Mahlon B. Moore, said to be the first settler, arrived 1862-1863; gold mining began in 1890; and the RR came in 1910. Post office, 1867-.

Named for the river bend on which the town is situated.

Horseshoe Bend (Idaho). T27N R1E sec 14. A stretch of the Salmon River at the mouth of McKinzie Creek, 1 mi N of Slate Creek.

This is the point at which Yellow Buffalo Bull and his band of Nez Perces camped just after the beginning of the Nez Perce War of 1877.

Named for the horseshoe-like curve of the Salmon River at this point.

Horseshoe Bend Creek (Lemhi). T19N R25E sec 14. Heads on the Idaho-Montana divide and flows S 2 mi to enter Agency Creek; Lemhi River drainage.

Named because there is a bend in the Agency Creek road as it crosses the creek, and there was a horseshoe nailed above the door of the stage station located here.

This is the first creek the Lewis and Clark Expedition crossed in what is now Idaho.

Horseshoe Creek (Teton). T5N R44E sec 12. W tributary of the Teton River; rises in Packsaddle Basin and flows SE then NE to the Teton River.

F. V. Hayden named this stream in 1872 because an Indian was killed here by his horse, according to an account by Hayden's guide, Richard "Beaver Dick" Leigh.

Horstmann Peak (Custer). 10,500′. T9N R12E sec 13. In Sawtooth Range 8 mi SSW of Stanley; 3/4 mi NE of Stephens Lake and 1 mi N of Redfish Peak.

Named for Berrhard Deidrick (Dick) Horstmann, trapper and early manager of Redfish Lake recreational facilities. He homesteaded in the Sawtooth Valley in 1912 and built many trappers' cabins in this area, including one at the base of this peak.

Horton Creek (Boundary/Bonner). T60N R4W sec 3. Rises in Boundary County and flows SW into Priest Lake immediately W of Eightmile Island.

Named for Charlie Horton, who lived near the creek but later moved to Alaska when a neighbor moved next door – 6 mi away. Horton Ridge in Boundary County is also named for him.

Hospital Bar (Valley). T17N R14E sec 6. On the Middle Fk Salmon River on the W bank.

Named because of the belief that soldiers from the Sheepeater Campaign of 1879 recuperated at this spot.

Hot Springs (Owyhee) 2592′. T7S R6E sec 23/26. Resort town 6 mi SE of Bruneau.

Named for the innumerable hot springs in the area.

Hotel Creek (Fremont). T14N R42E sec 28. Flows SW to Island Park Reservoir, Island Park/Henrys Fork system.

Named for the Arangee Company Hotel, which was built on the creek in 1881. It was later sold to A. S. Trude and remained his summer home until flooded by the waters of Island Park Reservoir in the late 1930s.

Hoteling Creek (Latah). T42N R4W sec 14. A 2-mi stream that rises W of Gold Hill and flows W about 2 mi to Gold Creek; Palouse River drainage.

Named for a prospector who made the gold discovery in Hoodoo Gulch in 1860, before the Orofino strike. Hoteling prospected in various locations until 1863, when he left for newer strikes.

Hotsprings Creek (Lemhi). T23N R18E sec 28. Forms about 1 mi NW of Copper Mountain and flows SW 3 mi to enter Panther Creek; Salmon River drainage.

Named for the hot springs found on the upper part of the creek.

Houston (Custer). 5900′. T7N R24E sec 20/28. Ghost town near the site of Mackay. Established as a town in 1885, Houston proved a very prosperous community until 1901, when the RR bypassed it to run near Mackay. Most of the town was absorbed by Mackay. At its peak, Houston had a population of more than 200 and some seventy buildings. Post office, 1884-1905.

Named for the first postmaster, Martin Houston.

Howard (Lewis). T34N R1E sec 23. Abandoned town in the E part of the county about 3 mi S of Nezperce and 1 1/2 mi E of Mohler. The town was platted shortly after the Milwaukee RR did a survey of the area.

Howard Creek (Idaho/Clearwater). T38N R11E sec 36; rises in Idaho County on Moccasin Peak (6759') and flows 8 mi NE into Cayuse Creek, Clearwater County; Clearwater River drainage.

Howard Creek (Fremont). T15N R45E sec 15. Rises on the Idaho-Montana border at Howard Springs on the Montana side, enters Fremont County, and flows SW to Henrys Lake.

Howard Gulch (Nez Perce).. T36N R3W sec 7. Near the Clearwater River, 1/4 mi E of Arrow. Flows S into the Clearwater River.

All named after Major General Oliver Otis Howard (1830-1909), a Civil War hero who led US forces in the long pursuit of the nontreaty Nez Perce bands led by Looking Glass and Joseph in 1877.

Howard Creek (Latah). T40N R5W sec 35. Rises between East Twin and Paradise Point and flows 3.3 mi SE to Gnat Creek, 4 mi NE of Moscow; S Fk Palouse River drainage.

Named for Albert, Joseph S., Horace W., G. W., Alice R., and George W. Howard, who homesteaded here from 1879 to 1892. Also called Howard Gulch.

Howe (Butte). 4500'. T5N R29E sec 4/9. In E central part of the county, 23 mi NE of Arco.

The first settler in this area was E. R. Hawley, who came in the early 1880s. When a post office was applied for, the name listed was Hawley, for this settler. However, the request was refused on the grounds that Hawley and Hailey were too much alike and would cause confusion. The Postal Department suggested instead Howe. Post office, 1882-.

Howe Mountain (Bonner). T56N R2E sec 21. Located 5 3/4 mi SE of Hope.

Named for a settler who lived near the mountain.

Howell (Latah). T39N R4W sec 10. An early RR station on the NPRR line between Troy and Cornwall. Howell Creek flows 3.3 mi SE to Big Bear Creek; Potlatch River drainage.

Named for Murt Howell, settler in the area.

Howell Creek (Cassia). T11S R25E sec 28/29. Rises SE of Lake Cleveland; flows 9 mi NE to Marsh Creek NE of Albion; Snake River drainage. Howell Canyon trends 5 mi NE to empty into this stream at T12S R25E sec 29.

Both the stream and the canyon were named for a Mr. Howell, who had the first water rights in the canyon.

Hubb Butte (Twin Falls). 4611'. T11S R17E sec 32. In the NE part of the county, 9 mi S of Twin Falls.

Named for Frank Hubbs, a well known cattleman in the 1870s. Formerly Hubbs Butte.

Hubbard Gulch (Nez Perce). T37N R3W sec. 14/25. Early name for an area on Potlatch Ridge NW of Juliaetta, between Little Potlatch Creek and Middle Potlatch Creek; Clearwater River drainage.

Named for the brother of James Anderson Hubbard. Both were early settlers in the Fix Ridge area.

Huckleberry Creek (Boise). T9N R7E sec 36. Rises in the central part of the county on Bonner Ridge and flows 3 mi NW into the S Fk Payette River. Huckleberry Flat lies 3 mi W of New Centerville.

There are many huckleberry bushes in these areas.

Huckleberry Mountain (Bonner). 4365'. T55N R3W sec 35. 6 1/2 mi E of Edgemere; 2 1/2 mi NE of Careywood. Huckleberry Bay is on the W side of Priest Lake.

Name derived from the huckleberries growing throughout the county.

Huddlestons Bluff (Idaho). T29N R5E sec 27/33. A promontory just W of the mouth of 3-mi-long Huddleston Creek, on S Fk Clearwater River, 7 mi W of Golden.

Named for Cal Huddleston, among the best-known mountain men and miners in the area; Huddleston settled here.

Hudlow Creek (Kootenai). T52N R1W sec 31. Rises in the NW part of Coeur d'Alene National Forest and flows 4.5 mi SW to empty into the N Fk Coeur d'Alene River. Hudlow Mountain (3395') lies several mi W of the stream, 1 mi E of the tip of Hayden Lake.

The creek was named by forestry officials for a local settler's five sons, who hunted in the area. The mountain is probably named for the creek.

Huffman Ridge (Latah). T39N R2W sec 22-27. Extends NE to SW between Big Bear and Texas Ridge, locally considered part of eastern Big Bear.

Named for James and Joe Huffman, homesteaders.

Huffs Gulch (Latah). Early name for Troy, which see.

Hughes Creek (Lemhi). T26N R21E sec 22. Headwaters located on the Idaho-Montana divide; flows SE for approximately 10 mi to where it enters the N Fk Salmon River.

Named for Barney Hughes, one of the discoverers of the famous Alder Gulch diggings in Montana in 1863, who discovered the placers on this drainage in 1876.

Hughes Fork (Bonner). T63N R5W sec 24. Rises in the SW corner of Boundary County and flows SE into Upper Priest Lake.

Named for an early settler.

Hull Creek (Lemhi). T25N R21E sec 28/29. Stream approximately 5 mi in length, with headwaters located near Indian Peak; flows SE to where it enters N Fk Salmon River. Hull Creek Reservoir is approximately 2 1/2 mi up Hull Creek from the N Fk Salmon River.

Named for Joseph Hull, an early settler who had a ranch on this stream. It was originally called Spring Creek, but was changed to Hull Creek in 1925 by H. M. Shank, who was surveying for the USFS at that time.

Humbug Creek (Lemhi). T25N R21E sec 8. About 2 mi long; enters Hughes Creek; Salmon River drainage.

Name derived from the fact that no one could ever find the source of the gold in the creek.

Humbug Gulch (Boise). T6N R6E sec 32-30. Flows NW into Mores Creek just NE of Idaho City; Boise River drainage.

A claim on this gulch was "salted" (gold was planted in it), so the miners called it "humbug."

Humbug Gulch (Idaho). T25N R3E sec 11. In the Florence Mining District; runs into Miller Creek.

Apparently named from some disappointment in gold prospecting, though claims were filed in this gulch in 1864 after the name was established.

Hummock Lake (Custer). T9N R16E. Lake.3 mi long, one of the Boulder Chain Lakes. There is an island formed by a hummock in the lake.

Hump (Idaho). T26N R6E sec 26. In the Buffalo Hump Mining area; a mining campsite. Post office, 1899-1905.

Named for the formation that also gave the mining district its name.

Humphrey (Clark). 6526'. T13N R36E sec 4. In the N central part of the county on Beaver Creek and UPRR; 5 mi S of the Montana line.

The community began in the 1880s when it was discovered that the site was ideal for storing ice in the winter months; this occupation lasted until the early 1920s.

Named for the first postmaster, Samuel G. Humphrey, who was also manager of the Monida-Yellowstone Stage Company.

Hungry Creek (Idaho). T35N R8E sec 24. Early name for present-day Hungery Creek. Stream about 8 mi long, in the Clearwater National Forest. Formed by the junction of its headwater fks and generally flowing SE to Fish Creek; Lochsa River drainage.

Named by Lewis and Clark 16 September 1805, because their company was out of food, having killed a colt two days earlier. The name was changed to Obia Creek and appeared so on old maps, but the name (not the spelling) was restored on the recommendation of forester Ralph S. Space and the name Obia Creek was given to one of its tributaries.

Hunt (Jerome). T8S R19E sec 36. In the S central part of the county, about 6 mi NNW of Eden. A post office name for the Minidoka War Relocation Center, where 9400 Japanese Americans were held prisoner during World War II.

Named in honor of Wilson Price Hunt, the Astorian explorer of 1811.

Hunt Creek (Bonner). T60N R4W. N and S Fks rise in Boundary County and flow generally W, merging in sec 11 and emptying into Priest Lake at sec 10, 2 mi N of Cavanaugh Bay.

Named for an early-day logger. Hunt Peak and Hunt Lake in Boundary County are also named for him.

Huntz Creek/Gulch (Idaho). T24N R4E sec 2. A 2-mi SE tributary of the Salmon River at the Wind River Pack Bridge.

Named for an early settler. The original Huntz cabin was still standing in l987.

Huron Creek (Lemhi). T26N R22E sec 30. Just E of Keystone Gulch; enters Dahlonega Creek; N Fk Salmon River drainage.

Named for Old Man Huron, a miner from Gibbonsville who had claims in this area.

Hurry Back Creek (Owyhee). T10S R3W sec 9. Flows E into Deep Creek; Owyhee River drainage.

Five Silver City girls on an outing on this creek got word from town about the Bannock uprising of 1878 and therefore had to hurry back to Silver City. Five smaller creeks in the area were named for the girls: Josephine Creek, Mary Creek, Louisa Creek, Rose Creek, and Catherine Creek.

Huston (Canyon). 2518'. T3N R4W sec 11. An agricultural center located SW of Caldwell in the Deer Flat area. Post office, 1920-.

Possibly named for J.W. Huston, district attorney in 1870 and unsuccessful candidate for delegate to Congress in 1872.

Hyaak Creek (Latah). T42N R2W sec 29. Flows 1.4 mi NW to Palouse River.

Named by USFS ranger W. H. Daugs in 1927; Chinook jargon meaning "swift," for the flow of this creek.

Hyde Creek (Lemhi). T21N R22E sec 32. Stream 2 mi long; heads in the Lemhi Range, flows NNW to the Salmon River 5.5 mi S of Salmon.

Named for George W. Hyde (1837-1905), who homesteaded along this stream in 1878.

Hyndman Peak (Blaine/Custer). 12,078'. T15N R20E sec 19. Peak in the Pioneer Range on the E boundary of the Sawtooth National Forest at the head of Hyndman and Wildhorse creeks. Hyndman Lake is at the head of the Yankee Fork. It covers about 8 acres. In Challis National Forest.

This peak, as well as Hyndman Creek and Hyndman Lake, is named for Civil War veteran, lawyer, and mining man Major William Hyndman. He came to the Wood River area during the boom days of 1888 and was superintendent of the Silver King mine, Sawtooth City. He died in Ketchum in 1896.

I

Ibex Peak (Cassia). 7310′. T15S R20E sec 23. In the SW corner of the county in the Sawtooth National Forest. Ibex Hollow heads on this peak and extends 2.2 mi NE to Trapper Creek.

Named (incorrectly) for the mountain sheep that once frequented this area.

Ice Creek (Clearwater). T39N R9E sec 10. Rises on Flat Mountain in the E part of the county and flows SE into Cold Springs Creek; Clearwater River drainage.

This is a group name that came from the cold springs near Cold Lake and Cold Springs Creek.

Icehouse Creek (Fremont). T13N R41E sec 36. In NW Fremont County. Runs 7 mi S and empties into Island Park Reservoir; Island Park Reservoir/Henrys Fork system.

No known icehouse on the creek, but the water is exceptionally cold.

Idaho. Capital: Boise. Established in 1863 from the E part of Washington Territory. Idaho Territory at first included all of present-day Idaho, Montana, and Wyoming. In 1864, Montana was lopped off and in 1868 Wyoming, leaving Idaho with the boundaries it has today. Lewiston was named capital of the new territory in 1863, but in 1864 Congress approved the territorial legislature's action making the new territorial capital. Statehood came to Idaho 3 July 1890, making it the 43rd state in the union.

Idaho is a coined word. It has no origin in any known Indian language, despite the popular belief that it was originally Ee-da-how—"Light on the Mountain." This interpretation was attributed to Idaho by romanticists, and Idahoans adopted it as true. In fact, both "Gem State" and "Light on the Mountain" are common nicknames. Idaho was first applied to Idaho Springs, Colorado, in 1859; to a steamboat on the Columbia River in 1860; and to Idaho County, by the Washington Legislature, in 1862.

Idaho City (Boise). 3906'. T6N R5E sec 26. County seat.

Idaho City was founded in 1862; it was the most important mining town in the Boise Basin. It is still the county seat of Boise County. It was also known as West Bannock, 1862-1864. Once the largest city in the Northwest. Post office, 1864-.

Idaho County. County seat: Grangeville. Established in 1861 as the third county of Washington Territory, now lying in Idaho; named for the steamer that plied the Columbia River and served miners during the gold rush in N Idaho; included all the country lying N of the Salmon River and E of the Snake River. Reconstructed by the First Legislature of Idaho Territory in 1864 with reduced boundaries, it remains the largest county in the state with 5.4 million acres. Florence was named county seat in 1864, to be replaced by Mount Idaho in 1875 and by Grangeville in 1902 after a 10-year struggle between Mount Idaho and Grangeville proponents.

Bounded on the N by Nez Perce, Lewis, and Clearwater counties; on the E by Montana; and Lemhi County; on the S by Valley and Adams counties; on the W by Oregon.

Idaho Creek (Clearwater). T40N R6E sec 13. Rises on Beaver Butte in the N central part of the county and flows into Beaver Creek; Clearwater River drainage.

This is probably a group or office name given by the USFS, as this creek is located near Montana Creek.

Idaho Falls (Bonneville). 4710'. T2N R37/38E sec 18/19. County seat. Situated on the Snake River about 42 mi from the E border of Idaho.

J. M. Taylor established a ferry here in 1863, and it was followed by the toll bridge in 1866. The settlement was first called Taylors Ferry, then Taylors Bridge, or Andersons Bridge, for the co-owner of the bridge.

When the Utah and Northern RR came through, the name was changed to Eagle Rock, for the big rock in the river above the bridge where a bald eagle nested. In 1891, on the advice of Chicago developers, residents changed the name to Idaho Falls. The town was incorporated in 1900. In 1911 the town built a diversion dam for a power plant, thus creating a 20' fall and making the name truly descriptive. Post office, 1866-.

Idahome (Cassia). 4428'. T11S R26E sec 34. In the NE part of the county, 7 mi N of Malta; 1 mi W of Raft River. Post office, 1914-ca.1965.

The name is a contraction of Idaho and home.

Idavada (Twin Falls). 5345'. T16S R15E sec 25. In the S part of the county, about 1 mi N of the Idaho-Nevada line.

The name is a contraction of Idaho and Nevada.

Idlers Rest Creek. (Latah) T40N R5W sec 28. Flows 8 mi SW to Paradise Creek; Palouse River drainage. The summer home of N. L. Patten, 1910, now Idlers Rest Nature Preserve, lies along the creek.

Named for the lovely and tranquil area it drains.

Idmon (Clark). T12N R38/39E sec 13/19. In the NE part of the county just S of Kilgore, on Camas Creek.

The name is a contraction of Idaho and Montana.

Illinois Gulch (Boise). T6N R6E sec 17. Runs 3 mi SE into Mores Creek 4 mi NE of Idaho City; Boise River drainage.

Two brothers from Illinois located a claim on this gulch in 1863.

Ilo (Lewis). T34N R1W sec 31. Former town in the center of the county 1 mi W of the present site of Craigmont. Formerly Chicago.

Named for Ilo Leggett, older daughter of O. W. Leggett, general merchandise store owner and postmaster.

Incendiary Creek (Clearwater). T34N R4E sec 6. Flows SW into Lolo Creek 4 mi S of Weippe; Clearwater River drainage.

Named for the incendiary fires around the creek, set here in the 1920s.

Incline Ridge (Shoshone). T43N R2E sec 4. A mountain ridge trending NE to SW 12 mi S of Calder.

Named because of the incline RR over this ridge. A steam donkey at the ridge top would pull cars up from the Marble Creek drainage to pass over to the St. Maries drainage and vice versa.

Independence (Madison). T5N R39E sec 7. Site of a ghost town in the SW part of the county SW of Rexburg and S of Burton where Henrys Fork approaches its confluence with Snake River. Post office, 1889-1905.

Settled in the 1880s by non-Mormons and the Morrisite sect of Mormons, who chose the name to show their independence from the Latter-day Saints church.

Independence Creek (Clearwater). T39N R11E sec 4. In the central part of E Clearwater county. Rises on Moose Mountains and flows 7 mi SE into Moose Creek; Clearwater River drainage. Independence Ridge, a 4-mi ridge trending NW to SE, runs parallel to the creek on the E.

Named for the Independence mine located here.

Independence Peak (Cassia). 10,360′. T14S R24E sec 17/20. SE of Oakley in the Sawtooth National Forest. Under its E rim are four glacial lakes called Independence Lakes. The summit is very rough, with cliffs and rock slides.

The name was chosen by local residents, settlers from Utah, for Independence, Missouri.

Indian Bathtub (Owyhee). T8S R6E sec 3. Rock formation 8 mi S of Bruneau, just below Hot Creek Falls.

Indians once bathed here and put pictographs on the stone.

Indian Camp Hollow/Creek (Bonneville). T1N R42E sec 13 to T1N R43E sec 19. Extends 8 mi NW to SE in NE part of the county. The creek flows 8 mi SE into Fall Creek; Snake River drainage.

Named for an Indian camp in the valley.

Indian Cove (Owyhee). T6S R7E sec 2. Town on the Snake River; a very small community located in a cove.

At one time this area was a rendezvous site for Bannock Indians.

Indian Creek (Boundary/Bonner). T61N R4W sec 27. Rises in, Boundary County and flows 3 mi SW into Priest Lake at Indian Creek Bay.

These names, as all other topographical names that include the word "Indian," derive from the generic name for those who were the first inhabitants of the area.

Indian Creek (Clearwater). T41N R9E sec 36. Rises along the E edge of the township and flows 4 mi SW into

Quartz Creek; Clearwater River drainage. In the NE part of the county, Indian Henry Ridge trends 3 mi SW to NE about 2 mi W of the creek.

An Indian named Henry supposedly brought out some gold nuggets as large as a hen's egg. Henry Creek is also named for him.

Indian Creek (Clark). T11N R34E sec 25. Originates in the confluence of 5.5-mi E Fk and 6.5-mi W Fk Indian creeks and flows 6 mi S to Medicine Lodge Creek, 3 mi N of Small; drains the NW part of the county from the Targhee National Forest to its mouth. Indian Creek Butte (6959') lies 3.5 mi NE of the confluence of E and W Fks.

Named for the Indians who first lived in the area and then used this route as a trail to and from Montana and the buffalo grounds until the late 1800s.

Indian Creek (Elmore/Ada). T1N R5E sec 5. Rises in SW Elmore County N of Mayfield and flows 25 mi generally W through Indian Creek Reservoir and into Mora Canal at Mora, Ada County.

Named because Indians customarily held meetings along this stream.

Indian Creek (Idaho). T24N R7E sec 28. A 4.5-mi Salmon River tributary from the NE. There were Indian pictographs along this creek until they were covered by a landslide after a cloudburst in 1920.

Indian Creek (Lemhi). T24N R19E sec 24. Heads on Idaho-Montana border; runs directly S for about 12 mi to where it enters the Salmon River. Captain William Clark called this Berry Creek on 23 August 1805, because of the berries his party found here when they were running low on food.

Renamed because of a local incident, retold in *To Him that Endureth*, 205-207, by James Herndon. Three young men staked a rich claim on this

stream. The next day they returned to the claim and encountered a small band of Indians. The young men were frightened and left hurriedly. Thereafter, the stream was called Indian Creek.

Indian Creek (Valley). T15N R11E sec 26. Rises on Pistol Rock (9169'), and flows 19 mi SE to the Middle Fk Salmon River about 5 mi NE of Pistol Creek; drainage, about 70 square miles.

This name was on the land after the Sheepeater Campaign of 1879. Much later the tributaries were given Chinook jargon names and Indian names by the USFS, in harmony with the Indian motif: on the N, Mowitch, "deer"; Kiwah "crooked"; and Big Chief; on the S, Endook; Cultus "worthless"; Si-ah, "far off"; Wampum; and Papoose.

Indian Grave Creek (Idaho). T36N R11E sec 22. Rises on Indian Grave Peak (6496') and flows 5.5 mi SE to the Lochsa River. Grave Butte (6190') lies 1.6 mi W of the mouth of this stream.

Named for the grave of a 14-year old Indian boy, Albert Parsons Mullickan. The boy and his family were picking huckleberries, hunting, and fishing along the Lolo Trail in 1895 when he became ill and died. He was buried near the stream.

Indian Head Canyon (Lemhi). T11N R29E sec 26. Heads 1 mi N of Mahogany Mountain and N of Cliff Canyon; runs SW 6 mi, 1 mi SE of Reno.

Indian paintings are located at the mouth of the canyon.

Indian Meadows (Owyhee). T9S R3W. Meadow in the Nip and Tuck Creek area.

The summer camping site of Indians before the coming of the white man.

Indian Settlement. T16S R3E sec 29. Town on the Western Shoshoni and Northern Paiute (Duck Valley) Indian Reservation; hence the name.

193

Indian Point (Bonner). T55N R1E sec 8. On S side of Lake Pend Oreille, 3 mi N of Echo Rock. Named for an Indian, Death-on-the-Trail, who was killed in an avalanche near this point.

Indian Post Office (Idaho). T37N R12E sec 17. Two rock cairns in the NE extremity of the county on Lolo Trail. Named from an old story that Indians conveyed messages by piling these stones in various ways. Legend also has it that it was a spot where prospectors, warriors, and hunters left messages. The site is probably where Lewis and Clark lost their way on their return trip E in 1806.

Named in 1886 by Wellington Bird's construction crew, employed by the US Department of Interior to build a road from Lewiston, Idaho, to Virginia City, Montana.

Indian Springs (Power). 4371′. T8S R31E sec 18. Well-known commercialized springs 2 mi W of American Falls. One of the more popular of the hot mineralized springs of the state.

Indian Valley (Adams). T14N R1W sec 10-14. Located near the Washington-Adams county line, extending about 6 mi SE from just S of Goodrich.

Indian Valley (3002′). T14N R1W sec 10. Town in Indian Valley 6 mi S of Mesa and 15 mi E of Cambridge. Post office, 1873-.

The climate along the Weiser River is milder than that of other valleys in the area. Therefore the Indians of the upper reaches of the river made this valley their winter headquarters.

Ingle Butte (Latah). T39N R2W sec 29. A promontory in the NW quarter of this township.

Took its name from the David Jefferson Ingle family, homesteaders in 1884.

Initial Butte (Ada). 3240′. T1N/T1S intersects with R1E/R1W. Eighty-acre mound from the remains of an ancient lava flow and some heavy rock slabs.

A point established in 1867 by Lafayette Cartee, first surveyor general of Idaho Territory, on a volcanic hill visible for many miles. All Idaho surveyors depend upon this point in establishing land boundaries; Boise meridian runs N and S through this point.

Inkom (Bannock). 4548′. T7S R36E sec 21/27. On the Portneuf River, 7 mi SE of Pocatello. Settled in 1895; townsite laid out in 1914. Post office, 1903-.

The name is reportedly a variant of Indian Ink-um "come ahead."

Invisible Peak (Custer). 11,343′. T7N R25E sec 5. In Lost River Range 17 mi NE of Mackay; Challis National Forest.

The peak is often hidden by clouds.

Inyo Creek (Lemhi). T14N R23E sec 24. Forms on the W slope of Inyo Mountain and flows NW 3 mi NE to enter Patterson Creek 2 mi NE of Patterson; Salmon River drainage. The creek flowed near a freight trail in the slide rock, which was very treacherous at times. Inyo Mountain (10,611′) is 5 mi E and slightly S of Yellow Peak and 5 mi NW of Big Creek Peak, at the head of Mill Creek on the S; Challis National Forest.

The name reputedly means "dwelling place of the great spirit" or "something scary" in the Shoshoni tongue.

Iona (Bonneville). 4782′. T2N R39E sec 1/6/12. Village 7 mi NE of Idaho Falls. An agricultural community first known as Sands Creek. Settled in 1884 by Mormons and renamed Iona. Post office, 1892-.

Named for a small town in Israel, the meaning of which is "beautiful."

Iowa Creek (Bonneville). T3S R44E sec 24. Rises in SE quadrant. Flows N 4 mi into McCoy Creek; Snake River drainage.

Iowa Bar. 6900'. Early name for Caribou City, because of its location on Iowa Creek.

Named by settlers who came to the area from the state of Iowa.

Ipsoot Creek (Latah). T41N R2W sec 1. Heads at 4000' and flows W 1 mi to Big Sand Creek at 3200'.

Named by W. H. Daugs. Ipsoot is Chinook jargon for "to hide oneself"; here "hidden," as it lies in a dense forest.

Irish Canyon. (Lemhi). T11N R29E sec 15. SE of Italian Canyon; runs SW about 5 mi to enter the Birch Creek drainage about 1 1/2 mi NW of Reno.

Named for the Irish workers at the mining camp of Nicholia.

Irish Creek (Clearwater). T37N R6E sec 11. A short tributary of Orogrande Creek between Arnett and Oxford meadows in the S central part of the county; Clearwater River drainage.

Bob Gaffney and other Irishmen named it for themselves, ca. 1920.

Iron Creek (Custer). T10N R13E sec 4. Heads in Alpine Lake, Sawtooth Range, and flows NE to Valley Creek; about 7 mi long; Salmon River drainage. Iron Creek Springs are located at the site of the recreation area. Iron Basin lies 8 mi S of Robinson Bar.

Iron Creek (Lemhi). T18N R21E sec 15. Flows 7 mi generally SE to enter Salmon River. Iron Lake (8800') is 2 mi NE of Taylor Mountain (7766'), which is 3 mi SW of Sheephorn Mountain.

Iron Mountain (Butte/Blaine). T2N R23E sec 13. On the Butte-Blaine county line, at the S end of Pioneer Mountain Range.

Iron deposits were found on these mountains and in the waters of the streams.

Iron Mountain (Idaho). 6816'. T30N R7E sec 2. N of Newsome. Said to be composed of iron, as lightning seems to be attracted to it and strikes very often. The peak is bare; lightning-set fires have burned all growth.

Iron Springs (Adams). 6780'. T22N R2W sec 25. An abandoned mining town in the Seven Devils area about 40 mi NE of Council.

Built during the Seven Devils boom, this town had about 30 houses, a hotel, several saloons, and a livery stable. Post office, 1903-1907.

Named for the mineral springs, which taste metallic.

Irwin (Bonneville). 5326'. T1N R44E sec 21. Town in NE quadrant, in Swan Valley on the S Fk Snake River. Irwin Canyon/Creek extends 2 1/2 mi NE to SW into the Snake River. Post office, 1897-.

Locally said to be named for Joseph B. Irwin, an 1888 settler who prospected up the Snake River and found some of the best placer claims on the river.

Isabella Creek (Clearwater). T41N R4E sec 7. Rises on Elk Butte in the NW corner of the county and flows 9 mi NE into Glover Creek; Clearwater River drainage.

An old miner in this area in the 1860s had the Isabella mine, which may be the source of the derivation. However, the USFS information sheet states the Nez Perce called the stream Hisboy–"Isabella."

Island (Cassia). T13S R22E sec 6. In the NW part of the county, 4 mi N of Oakley on an island formed by two forks of Goose Creek. Post office, 1882-1916.

The name describes the feature.

Island Park (Fremont). T12N R42/43E. Valley.

Island Park Village was incorporated in the late 1940s, extending from Last Chance N approximately 15 mi to Island Park Lodge; a Swiss colony founded by the Arangee Co. Includes the resorts of Ponds Lodge, Macks Inn, Phillips Lodge, and others.

According to Charlie Pond, early resort owner, named for islands of timber on the high sagebrush plain.

Issick Creek (Benewah). T43N R4W sec 25. A tributary of Meadow Creek, in the SW quadrant near Latah county line; Palouse River drainage.

Named in 1930 by W. H. Daugs for the alder that grows profusely along this stream. Issick is Chinook jargon meaning "alder."

Italian Canyon (Lemhi). T11N R29E sec 2. Forms near Italian Peak and runs W 3 mi and then S 1 1/2 mi to enter Irish Canyon.

Italian Gulch. T16N R26E sec 24. Heads SE of Grizzly Mountain; runs 2 mi S to Canyon Creek drainage, just E of Leadore; Lemhi River drainage.

Italian Peak. 10,998'. T12N R30E sec 22. Situated on the Continental Divide about 2 mi NW of Scott Peak.

Named for the Italian workers whose labor at the charcoal kilns supplied coke for Nicholia. They lived in Italian Gulch.

Italian Creek (Boundary). T65N R2W sec 17. Stream 1.5 mi long, rises on Italian Peak (6083') and flows N to Boundary Creek 6 mi WSW of the village of Porthill. Variant: Dago Creek.

Said to have been named for Italians who worked on the GNRR in 1892. The official name was changed from Dago to Italian by the US Geographical Names Board in eliminating all derogatory place names.

Ivy (Latah). Site of early settlement about 3 mi SE of Deary and 6 mi N of Linden.

Named for a local resident. Also Ivey.

J

Jack Creek (Lemhi). T19N R14E sec 5/7. Flows W about 5 mi to enter the Middle Fk Salmon River. Jack Creek Rapids lie at the mouth of this stream,

17 mi S of the mouth of the Middle Fk Salmon River.

Named for a male mule.

Jack Lake (Clearwater). T39N R8E sec 12.

Named for Jack Sprague, a local trapper.

Jack Mountain (Idaho). 8489'. T27N R9E sec 31. Site of the highest lookout in Red River Ranger District when the 90' tower was built in 1931. Formerly Mallard Mountain.

Named for USFS ranger Jack Horner.

Jack Pine Flats (Bonner). T59N R4W sec 27. Six mi W of Atlasta Lookout; 3 mi S of Coolin.

Named for the stand of jack pine in the area.

Jack Smith Gulch (Lemhi). T16N R24E sec 15. Just S of Bates Gulch; runs NE 2 mi to Alder Creek; Lemhi River drainage.

Jack Smith owned a ranch at the mouth of Big Eightmile Creek and grazed his cattle in this area.

Jackass Creek (Shoshone). T49N R3E sec 31. In the W part of the county, just W of Kellogg. A 2.5-mi tributary of S Fk Coeur d'Alene River from the N. Named for Noah Kellogg's legendary jackass, said to have been responsible for Kellogg's rich strike because a search for the animal found it standing on the lode.

Jackass Creek (Boise). T7N R3E sec 23. Flows E into Payette River at T7N R2E sec 23.

Named for Jackass Basin, where Conrad Wertz kept a string of donkeys in 1863.

Jackknife Creek (Clearwater). T38N R8E sec 15. Flows SE into the N Fk Clearwater River. Jackknife Meadows lies 2 mi N of the creek.

Forest rangers once found a jackknife along the creek.

Jacks Creek (Owyhee). T7S R3W sec 28. Flows NE 2 mi into Little Valley Creek; Bruneau River drainage.

Named for Jack Turner, the first white settler in the Bruneau area.

Jacks Gulch (Latah). T42N R3W sec 18. Early-day mining camp located at the headwaters of Last Chance and Jerome creeks, where 150 miners lived; also referred to as Jerome Creek.

Probably named for the man who located the Gold Bug mine on Jerome Creek in 1882.

Jackson (Washington). 4568'. T16N R6W sec 23. Promontory in the NW corner of the county 2 mi E of Snake River. Jackson Gulch extends NW nearly 3 mi to Snake River.

Named for Alex Jackson, settler in 1896 from Missouri.

Jackson Bar (Idaho). T24N R8E sec 28. Situated along Salmon River near a cove where once there was hydraulic mining. About 1 mi E of Mackay Bar.

Named for Bill Jackson, a miner, who in 1929 resided here.

Jackson Creek (Owyhee). T4S R6W sec 1. Flows SW 8 mi into Cow Creek; Owyhee River drainage. Jackson Mountain lies on Jackson Creek, 3 mi W of Rooster Comb Butte.

A man named O. Jackson settled in this area.

Jackson Creek (Boise). T9N R8E sec 26. Rises in the N central part of the county on Jackson Peak (8135') and flows about 6 mi NW into S Fk Payette River.

Named for John Jackson, who packed for General George Custer at one time; he had a ranch on this creek.

Jackson Mountain (Clearwater). 4685'. T40N R1E sec 12. Five mi NW of Elk

River. Jackson Creek rises on this mountain and flows 5 mi NW into Ruby Creek, Latah County.

Named for Frank Jackson, a homesteader.

Jacobson (Clearwater). T35N R4E sec 26/35. Town 3 mi S of Weippe.

Named for the Jacobsen (sic) family, who settled here.

Jacot Creek (Benewah). T46N R1W sec 17. Rises S of St. Joe River 3 mi E of St. Maries and flows 3 mi N to St. Joe.

Named for Charles Jacot, homesteader of the late 1800s.

Jacques (Nez Perce). 1388'. T35N R3W sec 17/16. Town 6 mi E of Lapwai. Jacques Spur is a RR siding across Lapwai Creek from Jacques.

Named for Stephen Jacques, who came from France to Spokane, to Lewiston, to Camas Prairie, to Grangeville, and then settled 6 mi E of Lapwai at Jacques, ca. 1880. He operated a mercantile business here.

Jakes Canyon (Lemhi). T16N R26E sec 20. Heads at the top of Stroud Gulch; runs S 5 mi to enter the Lemhi River drainage.

Named for Jacob "Jake" Yearian, pioneer rancher and cattleman, who patented land in this area in 1887 and 1889.

Jamestown (Latah). T42N R6W sec 12. An early community and post office in the NW part of the county, N of Palouse River on Cedar Creek.

Named for its only postmaster, Lorenzo D. Jameson, an 1876 homesteader.

Jap Creek (Clearwater). T40N R12E sec 5. Rises in Bitterroot Mountains and flows W into Lake Creek; Clearwater River drainage.

This may be a group name given by the USFS since the creek flows near Siam

Creek; Siamese Lakes are located just over the Montana border.

Jarbidge River (Owyhee). T13S R7E sec 5. Rises in Nevada and flows NW 45 mi into W Fk Bruneau River. Both the river and canyon were named Jarbidge by the Shoshoni Indians.

Reportedly a Shoshoni word meaning "devil" or "monster."

Jaype (Clearwater). T37N R5E sec 21. Town 3 mi NE of Pierce. Pronounced JAY-pee.

When the RR was built, the siding was named after J. P. Weyerhaeuser Jr., onetime president of Potlatch Lumber Co. His initials were combined to form one word.

Jazz Creek (Clearwater). T38N R7E sec 35. Rises on Clarks Mountain in the S central part of the county and flows S into Orogrande Creek; Clearwater River drainage.

The creek came into the Orogrande Road over a 50' drop which was strewn with washed boulders. In the spring runoff, the water was white and was considered to be "jazzing" right along. W. O. Clover, USFS, named the creek.

Jeanne Creek (Clearwater). T39N R11E sec 18. A short tributary to Kelly Creek from the N; Clearwater River drainage.

Named for Jeanne Glaus, the daughter of a forest engineer who was locating road in that area. Joan Creek is named for another of his daughters.

Jefferson County. County seat, Rigby. Created in 1913 from the SW part of Fremont County. Bounded on the N by Clark county, on the E by Fremont and Madison counties, on the S by Bonneville and Bingham counties, and on the W by Butte county.

Named for Thomas Jefferson, third president of the United States.

Jefferson Creek (Lemhi). T22N R20E sec 20. Two mi long; runs SE to Napias

Creek SW of Leesburg; Salmon River drainage.

Named for Jefferson Davis, president of the Confederacy.

Jefferson, Mount (Fremont). 10,196'. T14N R42E sec 4. At NW end of Henrys Lake Mountains, two peaks in the Centennial Mountains, 8 mi SW of Henrys lake.

Assumed to be named for Thomas Jefferson.

Jenkins Creek (Washington). T11N R6W sec 36. Rises 10 mi N of Weiser and flows 11 mi SE and SW to Weiser River.

A man by the name of Jenkins had a small dairy where the road crosses this stream and sold his dairy products to travelers.

Jenness (Gem). T6N R2W sec 30. An early RR station on the UPRR 2 mi NW of Emmett.

Named for Ned Jenness, former postmaster of Nampa 1924-1932.

Jenny Creek (Lemhi). T19N R16E sec 33. Heads about 1 1/2 mi SW of Middle Fork Peak; runs SW 2 mi to enter Yellowjacket Creek, 1 mi NE of Buckhorn Bridge; Middle Fk Salmon River drainage.

Named for the jenny, or female mule. Many pack trains passed through here in the early days.

Jensen Creek (Bonneville). T3S R45E sec 11. Rises in the SE quadrant and flows 2.3 mi into McCoy Creek, W of Palisades Reservoir; Snake River drainage; drains Jensen Meadow.

Named for Michael Jensen, an early freighter in the area.

Jepson Canyon (Butte). T7N R26E sec 31. Canyon 1.7 mi long, trends W to open out in Big Lost River Valley 5 mi NE of Leslie.

Named for a homesteader in the area.

Jericho (Clearwater). 4334'. T39N R3E sec 17. Peak 5 mi SE of Elk River.

Named for the Jericho mine.

Jerome (Jerome). 3669'. T8S R16E sec 13/19. County seat. In the W part of the county, 4 mi E of the Gooding-Jerome line. The town was platted in 1907 when this was still sagebrush country; settlement began in 1908; the village was incorporated in 1909 and became the county seat in 1919, when Jerome County was created.

Named for Jerome Kuhn, son of a Pittsburgh financier who with I. B. Perrine and S. B. Milner was influential in getting the North Side Canal Project under way and thus opened up this land to settlement; some reports say the name was for Jerome Hill, grandfather of Jerome Kuhn.

Post office, 1907-.

Jerome County. County seat, Jerome. Created by an act of the state legislature in 1919 from the S part of Lincoln County, the SW part of Minidoka, and the E part of Gooding; bounded on the S by Twin Falls County, with Snake River forming the S border. Originally a part of Alturas County.

Three sources for the name are commonly given: Jerome Hill, one of the developers of North Side Irrigation Project; his grandson, Jerome Kuhn, Jr.; or his son-in-law, Jerome Kuhn. All were important to the growth of the county.

Jerry Johnson Hot Springs (Idaho). T36N R13E sec 7. In the NE part of the county. 2 mi S of Lochsa River; on US 12.

Named for an early-day trapper, miner, and outdoorsman.

Jerusalem Valley (Boise). T7N R3/2E sec 5,6/1,2. In the W part of the county just E of Gardena.

Named by the Rev. Fred Faull, an English minister, in 1864 for the city of Jerusalem.

Post office, 1885-1888.

Jesse Creek (Lemhi). T22N R22E sec 31. Originates SW of U P Lake; runs SW 3 mi, then E 3 1/2 mi to Salmon River.

Named in honor of Captain Jesse McCaleb, a Confederate Civil War veteran of 36 battles, who was killed by Indians in the Lost River country when he led a group to defend a wagon train of supplies belonging to him and George L. Shoup after it had been attacked. A onetime clerk-recorder and later sheriff of Lemhi County, McCaleb was also elected to the Idaho legislature. He was born in Tennessee and mined in Virginia City, Montana, before coming to Leesburg in 1867.

Jim Brown Creek (Clearwater). T35N R5E sec 25. Rises 3 mi S of Pierce and flows 11 mi S into Musselshell Creek; Clearwater River drainage.

Named for Jim Brown, a prospector in the early days of Pierce.

Jim Byrns Slough (Lincoln). T4S R19E sec 25. Ditch 16 mi long, heads at Richfield Canal, trends SSE to Little Wood River 1 mi SE of Richfield.

Named for an early homesteader and rancher.

Jim Ford Creek (Clearwater). T36N R2E sec 28. Rises 5 mi SE of Weippe and flows NW 18 mi into Clearwater River at Orofino.

Named for a Lewiston merchant who cut trees on the creek and rafted them to Lewiston to sell.

Jim McGary Meadow (Latah). T40N R1W sec 24. Area about 2 mi W of McGary Butte.

Named for James D. McGary, who homesteaded in the area in 1905.

Joan Creek (Clearwater). T39N R10E sec 14. In the NE part of the county 5 mi E of Kelly Forks Ranger Station; flows S into Kelly Creek; Clearwater River drainage.

Named for Joan Glaus, the daughter of a forest engineer locating road routes in the area. Jeanne Creek is named for her sister.

Joe Moore Creek (Lemhi). T20N R23E sec 19. Forms 2 1/2 mi E of Sal Mountain and 2 mi NW of K Mountain; flows N 2 mi to enter Withington Creek 2 mi SW of Baker; Lemhi River drainage.

Joseph M. Moore had a sawmill at the mouth of this creek ca. 1900-1905.

Joe Rich Springs (Bear Lake). On the W shore of Bear Lake, these springs were long utilized as a health resort.

Named for Joseph Rich, considered the oldest of the early Mormon settlers in Bear Lake, being 78 in 1864 when he helped settle Paris.

Joel (Latah). 2614′. T39N R4W sec 19. A community 6 mi E of Moscow on State Highway 8.

Post office, 1892-1893.

Joel Station, a NPRR station, was established in 1891.

Named for Joel Kaufmann, a local resident.

Joes Gulch (Custer). T11N R13E sec 35. N tributary to Salmon River, below Stanley.

Named for an early miner, Joe Garadine, in the 1880 gold rush in this area.

John Creek (Benewah). T45N R2W sec 29. A 9-mi stream that flows NE and N to St. Maries River 7 mi S of St. Maries. It runs SE of John Point (3200′).

John A. Raywalt homesteaded near this creek in the late 1800s.

John Creek (Clearwater). T41N R7E sec 9. Flows S into Isabella Creek at sec 9; Clearwater River drainage.

Named for John Durant, USFS, who served as ranger at Musselshell from 1906 to 1912.

John Day Creek (Custer). Early name for Little Lost River, which see.

John Day Creek (Idaho). T26N R1E sec 23. An 8-mi tributary of Salmon River from the SE, 4 mi S of White Bird. John Day Bar and Gulch are at the mouth of this stream and John Day Mountain (7424') lies at the head of its S Fk.

John Day, freighter and miner, lived at this site in the early 1860s, building John Day House and running it as a stopping place on the way to Salmon River diggings. Post office, 1862-1885. Philip Cleary built and operated a ferry here, in 1877, and the settlement grew large enough to support a 3-month school the same year. John Day House burned in 1926 and all other signs of a settlement are gone.

John Lewis Mountain (Clearwater). 4218'. T39N R4E sec 27. Eight mi NW of Headquarters.

Named for John Lewis, who homesteaded near the mountain and worked for the Clearwater Timber Protective Association as a lookout.

Johnagan Creek (Clearwater). T37N R9E sec 30. Flows SW into Weitas Creek; Clearwater River drainage. Johnagan Mountain (4460') is 5.5 mi SW of the mouth of the creek and 9 mi SE of Bungalow Ranger Station. Johnagan Ridge trends 2 mi NE to SW between the mouth of the creek and the mountain; 10 mi SE of the Bungalow Ranger Station.

Named for a trail foreman for the USFS.

Johnny Creek (Clearwater). T38N R8E sec 27. Rises in the SE part of the county on Bee Butte and flows 7 mi W into Weitas Creek; Clearwater River drain-

age. Johnny Butte lies 5 mi W of the creek.

Named for John Durant, ranger at Musselshell from 1906 to 1912.

Johnny Long Mountain (Bonner). 4704'. T57N R3W sec 17. Four mi NNW of Wrencoe; 8 1/4 mi WNW of Sandpoint.

Named for an early trapper, Johnny Long, who disappeared in the area. Also known as Bonnet Top Mountain.

Johnny Woods Gulch (Boise). T5N R5E sec 7. A 3-mi gulch trending W and NW to Mores Creek 5 mi SW of Idaho City; Boise River drainage.

Johnny Woods was a placer miner who lived and mined on this gulch.

Johnson (Clearwater). T37N R3E sec 4. Town 9 mi NE of Orofino.

Bill Johnson established a mill here. Also known as Johnson Mill.

Johnson (Clearwater). T36N R4E sec 26. Town 3 mi N of Weippe.

Named for Hjalmer Johnson, who settled here.

Johnson Creek (Bonner). T55N R2E sec 5. Heads 3 3/4 mi SE of Fleming Point; flows 6 1/4 mi into Clark Fork River 2 1/4 mi SW of Clark Fork. Johnson Peak (4478') is located at the mouth of Johnson Creek.

Named for R. Johnson, who owned land at the mouth of Johnson Creek.

Johnson Creek (Idaho). T25N R5E sec 33. A 1/2 mi tributary of Salmon River from the N. Rises between Johnson Butte (5097') and Black Butte (6731') and flows S.

Named for Graf Johnson, a USFS district ranger.

Johnson Creek (Latah). T42N R1W sec 19. Stream 2.4 mi long, flows NE to Palouse River.

Named for the Jake Johnsons, who homesteaded here and whose cows pastured along this stream. Johnson freighted from Laird Park to the Hoodoo mines and established and served as postmaster for Hoodoo and Woodfell post offices.

Johnson Creek (Valley). T19N R8E sec 29. Rises in Payette National Forest, flows 22 mi N to empty into E Fk of the S Fk Salmon River near Yellow Pine.

Named for H. W. Johnson, an early local trapper.

Johnson Gulch (Lemhi). T26N R21E sec 23. Directly N of Fire Gulch; runs E 3 mi to N Fk Salmon River drainage.

Named by North Fork forest ranger Al Wheeler; derivation unknown. Once called Penstock Gulch when the Penstock family lived here. Also known as Placer Creek at one time because of the number of placer mines found in the drainage.

Johnson Hill (Camas). T1/2S R13E sec 32/4. Just S of Camas Creek, 7 mi SW of Fairfield.

The Johnson brothers, George, Gustavis, Lester, Bert, and Lou, and two sisters, Zena and Mrs. Monroe, were among the first of the settlers in 1885.

Johnson, Mount (Bonner). T57N R2E sec 30. Near Hope.

Named for the chief engineer of the Northern Pacific Railway in the 1870s and 1880s.

Johnstone Creek (Blaine). T4N R19E sec 16. Rises 6 mi E of Ketchum and flows 3 mi S to Hyndman Creek; E Fk Wood River drainage.

Named for an old miner who had a little ranch at the fork of Johnstone and Hyndman creeks.

Jones Creek (Cassia). T15S R19E sec 17. Rises in the SW part of the county in Jones Spring and flows 2.5 mi SW to empty into Goose Creek.

Both features were named for the Jones brothers, who settled in the area in 1879 and raised cattle.

Jones Gulch (Camas). T3N R13E sec 4. A 1 1/2-mi gulch on the W side of S Fk Boise River, 20 mi N of Corral.

Joe Jones settled on a hot springs farm in this gulch in 1879.

Jordan Creek (Owyhee). Rises in the mountains near Silver City at an altitude of 5000' and flows N, then W, then S, then W, and then N to enter Oregon. Its length is 55 mi; drainage, 100 square miles. Jordan Valley is drained by Jordan Creek and Jordan River.

Named for Michael M. Jordan, who discovered gold here in May 1863. He was killed in an Indian fight in the Owyhee country in 1864.

Jordan, Mount (Custer). 10,054'. T13N R14E sec 11/12. In Salmon River Mountains in the center of Challis National Forest. Jordan Creek rises on this mountain and flows 19 mi S to Yankee Fork.

Named for Sylvester Jordan, early-day miner on the Yankee Fork, who discovered gold on Jordan Creek in 1870.

Joseph (Idaho). T28N R1W sec 5. A town in the W part of the county, 17 mi W of White Bird. The post office opened in 1906. Named Joseph for Chief Joseph of the Nez Perces, whose Indian name was Hinmaton "The thunder that passes through earth and water." Joseph was a baptismal name given to his father by the Reverend Henry H. Spalding.

Joseph (Nez Perce). 807'. T36N R4W sec 22. Town within 1/2 mi of Spalding, 11 mi SE of Lewiston at the mouth of Lapwai Creek.

Joseph was named for the famous leader of a band of Nez Perce Indians during the war of 1877. Joseph was born near the mouth of the Imnaha River (Oregon) in June 1837, and died at

Nespelem, Washington, on the Colville Indian Reservation, 21 Sept 1904.

Josephine Creek (Owyhee). T7S R3W sec 16. Flows 6 mi NE into Rock Creek; Owyhee River drainage.

Named after a Silver City girl. See Hurry Back Creek.

Josie Creek (Boise). T9N R7E sec 8. Rises in the NW part of the county on Deadwood Lookout (7575') and flows 3 mi E into Deadwood River 5 air mi NW of Lowman; Payette River drainage.

Named for Josie Joshua, a lookout for the USFS.

Juliaetta (Latah). 1075'. T37N R3W sec 4. On S border of the county on Potlatch River. Founded and platted by homesteader Rupert Schupfer in 1878 and named Schupferville. Post office, 1882-.

Named for first postmaster Charles Snyder's two daughters, Julia and Etta.

Julie Creek (Boise). T9N R7E sec 5. Flows S into the Deadwood River 6 mi NW of Lowman; Payette River drainage.

Named by an unknown miner for his favorite mule, Julie.

Jumbo (Idaho). T26N R6E sec 26. Ghost town 4 mi S of Buffalo Hump.

Grew up around the Jumbo mine in 1898.

Jump Creek (Owyhee). T3N R5W sec 14. Flows 20 mi NW through Jump Creek Canyon into the Snake River. Jump Creek Falls are on Jump Creek 6 mi SW of Marsing.

The name derives from the 35' falls. The stream itself is very small, but the falls and the canyon are unusual.

Jump-off Canyon (Fremont). T9N R42E sec 13. Three mi N of Ashton. Run S to Shows Creek; Henrys Fork system.

A series of lava terraces on the canyon floor used as a winter road for hauling logs on sleighs. Even snow did not prevent sleighs from "jumping off" from terrace to terrace.

Junction (Lemhi). T16N R26E sec 21. Town about 1 mi N of Leadore. Founded by A. M. Stephenson, who ran a hotel here for a number of years.

Post office, 1874-1919.

Named because it was at the junction of the Bannock Road from the E and the Mormon Road from the S.

Junction Creek (Cassia). T16S R23E sec 34. Rises 1 mi E of Lyman Pass, flows W, then S to the Idaho-Utah border; 7.5 mi long.

It flows through Junction Valley, which extends N between Albion and Middle mountains. Both the creek and the valley are named from the junction of Salt Lake City and California Cutoff trails, which lies just E of the creek.

Junction Creek (Clearwater). T39N R10E sec 17. Flows 6 mi NE into N Fk Clearwater. Junction Creek Pack Bridge lies at the mouth of the creek, 1 mi W of Kelly Forks Ranger Station. Junction Lake is 3 mi S of the ranger station, and Junction Mountain is 2 mi SW the ranger station.

Trails form a junction in this vicinity.

Junction Peak (Lemhi). 10,608'. T14N R25E sec 29. Situated 1 mi SE of Yellow Peak, and 4 1/2 mi W of Sheephorn Peak, Salmon National Forest.

Named for the community of Junction, which it overlooks.

Juniper (Oneida). 4725'. T15S R30E sec 6/8. An agricultural area in the SW part of the county, 16 mi W of Holbrook; on Interstate 80 and 1 mi W of the Cassia-Oneida line. Founded by Mormons in 1889.

Post office, 1914-1918, 1919-ca. 1965.

Named for the juniper trees growing in the vicinity.

Juniper Butte (Owyhee). 5475'. T13S R9/10E sec 25/30. Three mi N of Mosquito Lake Butte.

A large area of the county is covered with a dense forest of juniper, one of the largest such forests in the world. Other features in Owyhee County bearing this name are Juniper Basin; Juniper Basin Reservoir; and three Juniper Creeks, two tributaries of Owyhee River and one of Snake River. Located mostly near the Nevada boundary.

Juniper Buttes (Fremont). This prominent group of hills, composed of gently sloping lava, is NW of St. Anthony, beyond the sand dunes.

Junipers, The (Fremont). T8/9N R39E sec 33/34. Ridge in SW part of county; 14 mi W of St. Anthony.

Junipers, The 6400'. T11N R39E. Two buttes in W central Fremont County, 10 mi WSW of Antelope Flat.

Named for the junipers on the slopes.

K

K Mountain (Lemhi). 8063'. T19N R23E sec 5. At the head of Kadletz Creek on the N and Price Creek on the NE.

Named because of the natural K formed on the mountain by a big patch of sliderock.

Kadletz Creek (Lemhi). T20N R23E sec 15. Forms N of K Mountain and flows NW 4 mi to enter Lemhi River.

Kadletz Creek (Lemhi). T17N R23E sec 29. Forms S of the headwaters of Wright Creek; flows NE parallel to Wright Creek 4 mi to enter Bear Valley Creek; Lemhi River drainage. Pronounced CAT-lits or CAD-lits.

Named for Johnny and Bill Kadletz, who were ranchers and government blacksmiths at the Lemhi Indian Agency. Johnny had a ranch near the mouth of the first stream.

Kalispell Bay (Bonner). T60N R4W sec 7/18 and T60N R5W sec 12. A bay in the western part of Priest Lake; in Kaniksu National Forest. After 1844, this was a base for Jesuit missions to the Pend Oreille Indians, who were taught farming and health care.

Kalispell Creek. T60N R5W sec 12. A stream that rises in or near T36N R45E sec 17, Willamette meridian, Pend Oreille County, Washington, and flows SE, entering Priest Lake. Kalispell Island lies in the W part of Priest Lake, NE of Kalispell Bay.

Kalispel is the Indian name for the Pend Oreilles, which see, and in English means "Canoe" or "Boat People"; they used canoes on Pend Oreille Lake and on Clarks Fork below the lake.

Kamiah (Lewis). 1200′. T33N R3E sec 1. Town in Kamiah Valley on the Clearwater River about 65 mi upstream from Lewiston, Idaho, in the extreme E part of the county. Pronounced KAM-ee-eye.

Kamiah was a camping ground of the Nez Perce, where they manufactured ropes out of strong hemp bark. It was here that Lewis and Clark camped for several weeks in the spring of 1806, waiting for the snow to melt. Kamiah Valley surrounds the town of Kamiah.

Post office, 1878-.

Named for the stream that Lewis and Clark called Comearp (now Lawyers Creek), from which Kamiah is derived. The Nez Perce word Kamia—"ropes"—led to the name Kamiah, "place of rope litters."

Kanaka Flat (Gooding). T9S R14E sec 2. Early name for Clear Lakes.

Named for a family of Kanakas (Hawaiians) who mined the area in the 1870s.

Kaniksu Mountain (Boundary). T65N R4W sec 7/18. Just S of the Canadian boundary in Kaniksu National Forest.

Kaniksu is the Coeur d'Alene Indian word for "black robe"—that is, referring to the Jesuit missionaries who worked in the area.

Kathryn, Lake (Custer). T8N R12E sec 10. Lake .3 mi long, one of the Upper Redfish lakes, located 2.6 mi SSE of Warbonnet Peak.

Proposed by Glenn E. Mills in 1976 to commemorate his daughter Kathryn Mills Jones (1925-1967), who, between 1956 and 1966, spent her summers hiking and climbing in this area.

Katsuck Creek (Benewah). T43N R1W sec 18. A 2-mi N tributary of Eena Creek; St. Maries River drainage, in SE Benewah County near the S border.

Named by W. H. Daugs, USFS ranger, in 1929 because this is the middle of three tributaries of Eena Creek. Katsuck is Chinook jargon for "middle."

Kauder Creek (Latah). T38N R1W sec 22. Rises on Norwegian Ridge and flows SW 3 1/2 mi to Cedar Creek; Clearwater River drainage.

Named for the Kauder family, who lived in the area; Minnie Kauder owned 260 acres above the headwaters of the creek in 1937.

Kaufman (Clark). T10N R30E sec 32. In the W part of the county at the site of present-day Blue Dome, on Birch Creek.

Post office, 1899-1915.

Named for Maier Kaufman, a German emigrant, who came to this area, and for his wife, Katie, who served as the first postmaster.

Kaufman Saddle (Clearwater). T40N R6E sec 9. Six mi W of Canyon Ranger Station.

Named for Sam Kaufman, a lookout in 1922.

Keating Ridge (Idaho). T24/25N R2E. A N-S-trending ridge about 5 mi long, on the N side of Salmon river, 30 mi S of Grangeville and 6 mi E of Riggins; bounded on the E by Van and Spring creeks and on the W by Allison Creek.

Named for Gus Keating, who was terribly burned while firefighting along Allison Creek during the 1910 Idaho fire.

Keeler Creek (Shoshone). T50N R4E sec 6. A 1-mi tributary of Coeur d'Alene River from the N, 3 mi N of Prichard.

Bull Keeler, a mountain man, prospected with Andy Prichard along Prichard Creek.

Appears on some maps as Keller.

Keeler Creek (Clearwater/Shoshone). T42N R1E sec 27. Rises in the NW corner of Clearwater County and flows N into W Fk St. Maries River, Shoshone County.

Named for a man named Keeler, who was the head engineer for the Milwaukee RR survey.

Keg Creek (Fremont). T13N R41E sec 3. In NW Fremont County; runs 5 mi S to Willow Creek just inside the Clark County border. Island Park Reservoir/Henrys Fork system.

Said to be named for a moonshining cabin located along the creek during Prohibition.

Keg Gulch (Lemhi). T11N R29E sec 27. Heads near Lemhi-Butte county line; runs N 2 mi, NE 2 mi, E 3 mi, and finally S 2 mi to enter Birch Creek drainage. Keg Spring lies in Keg Gulch, 2 mi NE of Sagebrush Spring.

One informant says an old moonshiner lived here. Another says kegs were put in the springs to collect water.

Keithley Creek (Washington). T13N R3W sec 5. Rises on the S and E slopes of Hitt Peak and flows generally SE 13 mi to Weiser River a short distance above Midvale.

Named for the first settlers in the area, Levi and John Keithley.

Kelley Canyon (Jefferson). T3N R41E sec 28/32/33. In the SE extremity of the county.

A rock canyon that bears the name of its first settler and homesteader, Peter Kelley, who located near the mouth of the canyon. Noted from the 1880s for its abundant supply of timber.

Kelley Mountain (Jefferson). 6664'. T3N R41E sec 33. Just S of the E end of Kelley Canyon and named for it.

Kelley Rock (Jefferson). T3N R41E sec 31. A huge rock formation at the W end of Kelley Canyon, 45' high and 60' long, which was blasted into the river channel to divert the water into the Great Feeder Canal for irrigation purposes. Two additional rock formations in this area were named for the daughters of Richard C. Heise, Bertha and Blanche.

Kelley Creek (Shoshone). T45N R5E sec 15. A 4-mi tributary of the St. Joe River; enters river from the S at Avery.

Named for Spike Kelley and his brother, Bill, who established a store at Avery. Spike built a cable bridge and a handsome residence on this creek, which was named for him in 1909.

Kellogg (Shoshone). 2309'. T48N R3E sec 6. In the W part of the county on I-90 and the UPRR, 12 mi NW of Wallace. The town was laid out by Robert and Jonathan Ingalls and named Milo for Milo Creek, where Noah Kellogg found a vein of ore. The name was changed to Kellogg in 1887 to honor Noah Kellogg. Post office, 1891-.

Kellogg Peak (6291') lies 3 mi S of Kellogg and .6 mi E of Wardner Peak (6198'). Named for the town.

Kelly Creek (Shoshone). T46N R7E sec 7. In the extreme E part of the county. Rises on Bald Mountain and flows 3 mi S to Loop Creek, 9 mi NE of Avery; St. Joe River drainage.

Named by Tom Eagen, owner of the Kelly mine on this creek. He and Jack Purcell lived at the head of the creek for many years.

Kelly Creek (Clearwater). T39N R10E sec 18. Rises in the confluence of N Fk and Middle Fk Kelly creeks in the Bitterroot Mountains and flows W 26 mi to N Fk Clearwater River.

Kelly Lake and the mountains, Kellys Finger (7845'), Kellys Sister, and Kellys Thumb (5461'), are situated in the upper reaches of the creek 3 to 9 mi N of Blacklead Mountain.

Named for John Kelly, an early-day miner.

Kelly Creek (Idaho). T24N R3E sec 18. Rises on the N side of Lookingglass Butte and flows 6 mi SW to Salmon River, 9 mi E of Riggins. Kelly Mountain lies 1 mi SE of the mouth of the stream.

Both features were named for Bill "Old Poker" Kelly, who came from the Florence mines to settle at the mouth of the stream, 1 mi E of Riggins Hot Springs, 1884-86. He died in 1898 and is buried here.

Kelly Gulch (Boise). T4N R3E sec 24. A 2-mi gulch that runs SW into N Fk Robie Creek; Boise River drainage.

Named for Michael Kelly, who had a mining claim on this gulch.

Kelso (Bonner). T54N R3W sec 20. Two mi NW of Granite and 4 1/2 mi SW of Careywood.

Kelso Lake is located just S of the community of Kelso.

Named for an early pioneer in this area.

Kelso (Cassia). T15S R27E sec 33. In the SE part of the county 3.5 mi SE of Bridge and 5 mi N of Naf; at the mouth of Kelsaw (sic) Canyon and of Clear Creek. Kelsaw Canyon originates on War Eagle Peak in the Black Pine Mountains

and trends WSW 9 mi; mouth at Round Mountain Creek, .2 mi E of mouth of Clear Creek.

Post office, 1880-1885.

Named for J. W. Kelso, a local farmer in the 1870s and 1880s.

Kendrick (Latah). 1242'. T38N R3W sec 24. Incorporated town in the southern part of the county on the Potlatch River 3.4 mi N of Juliaetta.

Founded as Latah in 1888 by John Kirby, first postmaster; named changed in 1890 to Kendrick for the chief engineer of the NPRR upon the guarantee that the railroad would build a line through the town.

Kennedy Ford (Latah). T41N R5W sec 4. An early-day ford on the route from Walla Walla to Coeur d'Alene.

First used by Indians, then later as the only wagon crossing of the upper Palouse River for freighting supplies from Walla Walla to the mines along the upper Palouse River. After 1880, settlers held camp meetings here.

Named for a family who lived here in the 1880s.

Kenney Creek (Fremont). T15N R43E sec 17. In N Fremont County, runs NE 8 mi to Henrys Lake.

Earlier called Hope Creek for original homesteader. Name changed by the USFS for the T.E. Kenney ranch.

Kenney Creek (Lemhi). T20N R24E sec 3. Heads on the Idaho-Montana border in the Beaverhead Mountains; flows SW 9 mi to enter Lemhi River.

Named for Dr. George Alexander Kenney, who had a ranch on this stream. Dr. Kenney came to the Lemhi Valley in April 1874 and became the first physician on the Lemhi Indian Agency in 1875. He was born in 1837 in Bernardston, Massachusetts, and died in Salmon, Idaho, in 1931. He served with the Union Army, Minnesota Volunteer Infantry, Company G, 1st Regiment, during the Civil War. The Kenney ranch was an early stage stop 17 mi from Salmon on the run from Salmon to Montana, and was known as the Seventeen Mile Ranch.

The stream was first known as Lewis Creek after Frank Lewis, who moved from here to the mouth of Carmen Creek on the Salmon River.

Kent Peak (Boundary). 7000'. T62N R3W sec 11. Kent Lake is about 1/2 mi SE of Kent Peak, and Kent Creek rises 1 mi W of Kent Lake and flows N to Lion Creek, between the Challis and Sawtooth national forests.

Named for an old trapper, who was once lost in this area.

Kent Peak (Custer). 11,700'. T6N R18E sec 31. On the boundary between Challis and Sawtooth national forests about .8 mi SE of Ryan Peak and about 15 mi N of Ketchum.

Named for Kent Easton Lake (1930-1959), a local mountain climber.

Kentuck (Shoshone). T48N R2/3E sec 12/7. Early name for Wardner, which see.

Kenyon (Cassia). 4290'. T11S R22E sec 34. A UPRR siding and site of a labor camp in the N part of the county, 2.5 mi W of Burley.

Post office, 1911-1919.

Named for the first postmaster, William D. Kenyon.

Kepros Mountain (Ada). 5428'. T3N R4E sec 35. In the Danskin Mountains 2 mi SSW of Arrowrock Reservoir and 32 mi NNW of Mountain Home.

Named for George N. Kepros (d.1973), a rancher who homesteaded in the area in 1909.

Kerr Canyon (Fremont). T9N R42E sec 3-15. In S central Fremont County, runs N-S to Ashton Reservoir; Henrys Fork system. Three mi NW of Ashton.

Named for Joe Kerr, who had a ranch on the creek.

Kerr Creek (Lemhi). T15N R16E sec 34. Heads near Parker Mountain; flows 1 1/2 mi SW to enter Warm Spring Creek; Middle Fk Salmon River drainage.

Named for Jim Kerr, pioneer rancher in this area.

Kerr Lake (Bonner). T61N R5W sec 12. Located 4° 1/2 mi E of Idaho-Washington border; 1 1/2 mi SW of Watson Mountain.

Named for Thomas Kerr, who owned property near the lake.

Kessler Creek (Idaho). T24N R1E sec 6. A 4-mi tributary of Race Creek from the NW, 3 mi W of Riggins; Salmon River drainage.

Named for a pioneer settler on the stream ca. 1890.

Ketchum (Blaine). 5600'. T4N R17E sec 13/18. In the NW part of the county on Big Wood River; 10 mi N of Hailey. Formerly Leadville. David Ketchum, for whom the town is named, built his cabin here in 1879. The town was established in 1880 as Leadville and in 1881 an application was filed for a post office. Since there were already several Leadvilles, the US Post Office Department denied the name. The name was changed to honor the first settler.

Post office, 1880-.

Kettle Butte (Bonneville). 5571'. T3N R35E sec 17. In the N part of the county, 18 mi NW of Idaho Falls.

Named because the butte has the configuration of a kettle.

Kettles, The (Custer). T9N R16E sec 18. Topographical depressions. The larger depression is 250' wide.

Named because the depressions look like huge kettles.

Keuterville (Idaho). 3960′. T31N R1W sec 10/15. In the NW part of the county, 4.5 mi W of Cottonwood.

Settled in 1883 by four families from Kansas. Henry Kuther built the store and applied for the post office, naming it Kutherville to preserve his name, as he had no sons. However, the Post Office Department misread the name and in 1888 granted the post office as Keuterville.

Keystone Gulch (Blaine). T4N R18E sec 16. In the mining area just E of Ketchum; a 2.2-mi long gulch that empties into Parker Gulch; Big Wood River drainage.

Named for a mining claim in the gulch.

Keystone Gulch (Lemhi). T26N R22E sec 30. Approximately 1 1/2 mi long; runs directly S to Dahlonega Creek; N Fk Salmon River drainage.

Named because one of the mines in the gulch had a tunnel that went through the mountain and then up into a stope shaped like a key.

Kid Lake (Clearwater). T40N R13E sec 27. Nine mi N of Blacklead Mountain. Kid Lake Creek rises in the lake and flows S into Middle Fk Kelly Creek; Clearwater River drainage.

Named for the goats seen here.

Kidder Ridge (Idaho). T33N R4E sec 1/11/14. A NE-SW trending ridge about 5 mi long, 8 mi E of Kamiah.

Named for three brothers, Charles, Eugene, and Cy Kidder, who came W from Missouri and settled on this ridge. At one time it had its own post office (discontinued before 1913), a sawmill, and a store.

Kilgore (Clark). 6000′. T13N R39E sec 32. In the NW part of the county 14.5 mi E of Spencer on Camas Creek. Settled in 1885 for agricultural purposes. Post office, 1892-1965.

Named for General James Kilgore, an active participant in the Nez Perce War of 1877.

Killarney Lake (Kootenai). T48N R2W sec 10/11/14/15. One of the 9 lakes formed by overflows of the Coeur d'Alene River; in the SE part of the county, 10 mi E of the Coeur d'Alene Lake and .5 mi N of the river.

The name is Irish, probably given because of its nearness to O'Gara Bay, named for Irish settlers.

Killum Point (Idaho). 5914′. T24N R14E sec 34. Situated on the E side of Salmon River between Gunbarrel Rapids and Wheat Creek; in the Bitterroot National Forest; in SW Idaho County.

Named for the Jack Killam (sic) family who lived here.

Kilroy Bay (Bonner). T55N R1W sec 13. On Lake Pend Oreille, 3 1/2 mi E of Blacktail and 7 mi N of the town of Cedar Creek. Kilroy Creek heads at Kilroy Lakes and flows 2 mi S and SW into Lake Pend Oreille.

A man named Kilroy, a newspaperman from Butte, built a summer home on the bay.

Kimama (Lincoln). 4272′. T7S R23E sec 5. In the SE part of the county, 15 mi W of Minidoka. Kimama Butte is on the Lincoln-Minidoka county line 6 mi SW of Kimama.

Settled primarily in the early 1900s, when people from the Palouse country, E Washington, the Midwest, and the South came to homestead on newly irrigated lands in Idaho.

Post office, 1886-1929.

Named by officials of the OSLRR; reputedly an Indian word which they believed meant "butterfly."

Kimball (Bingham). 4565′. T2S R36E sec 3. In the central part of the county, 9 mi N of Blackfoot.

Named for Elijah Kimball, a rancher in the vicinity of Blackfoot, who settled in the area in 1896.

Kimberly (Twin Falls). 3911'. T10S R18E sec 20/28. In the NE corner of the county, 6 mi E of Twin Falls.

Founded in 1906, the settlement was named for Peter Kimberly, one of the financiers of the Twin Falls South Side irrigation project. The center of a rich agricultural area, the town boasted the first electric flour mill and alfalfa mill in the state.

Post office, 1905-.

Kimta Creek (Benewah). T43N R1W sec 18. An eastern tributary of Eena Creek, St. Maries River drainage, in the SE quadrant near the Benewah-Latah county line.

Named by USFS ranger W. H. Daugs in 1929 because it is the last of the three tributaries of Eena Creek. Kimta is Chinook jargon for "last."

King Hill (Elmore). 2529'. T5S R10/11E sec 12/7. In the SE quadrant, on Snake River 7 mi E of Glenns Ferry on US 30. King Hill Creek rises in Bennett Hills N of King Hill at 5500' and flows 25 mi generally southward to Snake River below the town at 2497'; drainage, 300 square mi.

The site of the town was originally a mi E of its present site, nearer the big hill for which it is believed to be named. It was moved to make it more centrally located in the King Hill irrigation project. Post office, 1908-.

It is believed that the name derives from the hill, which freighters found the most difficult on the stage road between Kelton, Utah, and Boise. The hill, which looks something like a crown, was dubbed King Hill and the settlement adopted it. Charles Walgamott, however, believed that the name came from a Mr.

King of the Big Wood Irrigation Company.

King Mountain (Lemhi). 7956'. T17N R20E sec 1. About 4 mi SE of Iron Mountain, at the head of Shep Creek.

Named for Horace B. "Deddie" (or "Deddy") King, who patented a ranch here in 1929.

Kings Bowl (Power). T5S R28E sec 32. A fissure in the Great Rift National Landmark, in which Crystal Ice Caves are located; in the W part of the county. An enlarged portion of the rift through which lava and other materials have been ejected.

A descriptive name.

Kings Landing (Latah). T41N R4W sec 7/8. A log-holding pond and lumber skid on the Palouse River, 1892-1932.

Wilson W. King homesteaded 80 acres here and worked for Potlatch Lumber Company, with holdings E and N of the Palouse River. King made a place to cross the river on the N side just W of Hampton. Logs were decked on the N side of the river.

Kinney Creek (Clearwater). T38N R6E sec 5. Flows SE into Scofield Creek. In the central part of the county; Clearwater River drainage.

Named for Tom Kinney, logging superintendent for Potlatch Forests, Inc., at Headquarters.

Kinnikinnic Creek (Custer). T11N R17E sec 25. N tributary of Salmon River at Clayton. About 7 mi long, this creek was the scene of much prospecting.

Named for a plant growing in the area from which Indians and pioneers secured dried leaves and the inner bark to use as tobacco; probably related to the sumac. This is an Algonquian word meaning "that which is mixed"—a mixture of bark and leaves for smoking.

Kinport (Bannock). 7207'. T7S R34E sec 16. Promontory overlooking Pocatello from the SW; 5 mi SW of Pocatello, 1 mi E of the Power-Bannock County line.

Named for Harry Kinport, said to have been the first white man to climb this peak. He came to the area in 1885 and was known as a businessman and a great hunter; he accompanied President Theodore Roosevelt on a hunting trip.

Kinzie Butte (Lincoln). 4900'. T4S R18E sec 9. A landmark 10.5 mi N of Shoshone. Said to be named for a Mr. Kinsey (sic), who herded goats in this area in the 1880s.

Kippen (Lewis). 3550'. T34N R2W sec 11. Abandoned town in N part of the county 3 mi S of Reubens.

The town started in 1896, when the Erickson sawmill began operations in the area, and was incorporated in 1907. At that time it was a trading center for a farm community. The town began to decline when the RR placed a depot in Reubens instead of Kippen.

Post office, 1896-1905.

Named for the first postmaster, David A. Kippen.

Kirby (Latah). T38N R3W sec 25. Early name for P.O. of Latah.

The post office was applied for by Thomas Kirby in 1888, when it was called Latah, and established in 1889 with Kirby as postmaster; name changed to Kendrick in 1890, with Kirby as postmaster.

Kirkham Creek (Boise). T9N R8E sec 32. Flows 4 mi S into S Fk Payette River 3 mi E of Lowman. Kirkham Hot Springs lie at the mouth of this stream.

Named for a man who came from Chicago in 1911 and settled at the springs.

Kirkwood Creek (Idaho). T26N R1W sec 30. Rises along Snake River on Camel Ridge and flows 6 mi NW to Snake River.

Named for Dr. J. W. Kirkwood, who settled here about 1902. He had practiced medicine in Lewiston as early as 1883.

Kirtley Creek (Lemhi). T21N R22E sec 9. Originates about 3 mi S of Freeman Creek, flows about 7 mi to Lemhi River.

Named for James L. Kirtley, a pioneer rancher on this stream.

Kitty Gulch (Lemhi). T25N R20E sec 31. Approximately 1 mi long; runs SE into Indian Creek near Ulysses; Salmon River drainage.

Named because the Kitty (Kittie) Burton mine was located in this gulch.

Kiwa Creek (Latah). T42N R2W sec 18. Stream 1 1/2 mi long that flows SW to Dry Fk Strychnine Creek; Palouse River drainage.

Named by USFS ranger W. H. Daugs; the Chinook jargon word means "crooked," for the winding bed of this creek. Daugs spelled the word Kywa and it appears so on some maps.

Klawa Creek (Latah). T41N R2W sec 6. Flows .9 mi W to Little Sand Creek; Palouse River drainage.

Named by W. H. Daugs; the Chinook jargon word means "slow," suggested by the slow flow of the stream.

Klockmann (Boundary). T65N R5W sec 36.

A community named for Albert Klockmann, organizer of the Idaho Continental Company.

Post office, 1916-?

Klootch Mountain (Boundary). T62N R3W sec 17. In Kaniksu National Forest.

Said to be Chinook jargon for "squaw," perhaps because the shape resembles a woman.

211

Klop Gulch (Lemhi). T25N R21E sec 7. Located between Gallagher Gulch and W Fk Hughes Creek; enters Hughes Creek drainage; Salmon River drainage.

Name comes from a shortened form of Klupenger, the name of a man who had a mining claim here.

Knoll (Clark). 7467'. T14N R35E sec 16. Promontory on the Idaho-Montana line about the center of the county.

Named for its rounded summit; a descriptive name.

Knox (Valley). 5192'. T15N R6E sec 1. On Warm Lake Creek in the SW quadrant; some 22 mi NE of Cascade, 3 mi above Warm Lake. Originally a way station established by a man named Knox on the old Boise-Thunder Mountain Trail. It was abandoned and reestablished by Dan Drake as Drakes Hotel.

Named for the first owner of the way station.

Kodiak Creek (Clearwater). T39N R12E sec 16. Flows SW into Bear Creek in the E extremity of the county; Clearwater River drainage.

This creek is part of a group name. Bear Creek was named first, then by analogy the tributaries Cub, Polar, and Kodiak creeks followed.

Konkolville (Clearwater). T36N R2E sec 3. Town 4 mi E of Orofino on State Highway 9.

Named for Andrew Konkol, who homesteaded here.

Kooskia (Idaho). 1235'. T32N R4E sec 5. In the NW part of the county at the junction of Middle and S Fks Clearwater River; on US 12 and State 13. Pronounced KOOS-kee.

The town was laid out in 1895 upon the opening of the Nez Perce Reservation for settlement and named Stuart for James Stuart, a Nez Perce surveyor who later became a merchant in Kooskia. When the Camas Prairie RR came through in 1899, the name became Kooskia, as there was already a Stuart on its line. Post office, 1890-.

The name originates in the Nez Perce Kooskooskia, which Lewis and Clark misinterpeted as "clear water." Lewis and Clark had to work through interpreters, who first translated from Nez Perce into Shoshonean, then into French, and finally into English; thus there was room for much error. The truth is that the Nez Perce did not name streams in the manner now known. Nevertheless, what was believed to be a true Indian word with a definite meaning remains as Kooskia, "where the waters join."

Kootenai County. County seat, Coeur d'Alene. Created by the Second Territorial Legislature in 1864 with Seneaquoteen, a trading post below Lake Pend Oreille, as the county seat. Rathdrum replaced Seneaquoteen in 1881 and Coeur d'Alene replaced Rathdrum in 1908.

Bounded on the N by Bonner County; on the E by Shoshone County; on the S by Benewah County; on the W by the state of Washington.

Kootenai (Bonner). T57N R2W sec 12. Town 1 1/2 mi SW of Boyer and 2 3/4 mi NE of Sandpoint. The town was laid out as early as 1885, and an NPRR station was established in 1889. First a lumbering center; now a mill and pole yard. Post office, 1885-.

Kootenai Peak (Kootenai) 5054'. T47N R1W sec 15. About 9 mi NE of St. Maries.

Kootenai Point (Bonner). T57N R1W sec 8. On Lake Pend Oreille 2 mi SE of the town of Kootenai and 3 1/2 mi NE of Sandpoint.

Kootenai River. Rises in Canada, flows into Montana and Idaho and back into Canada; divides Cabinet and Purcell mountains.

Kootenai is derived from a Kutenai tribal word meaning "water people"—the Indians who occupied the area until the coming of the white man. Tribal headquarters today are near Bonners Ferry, Boundary County. The Kutenai are a remote Algonquin group who were once buffalo hunters but left the plains for the forested area of what is now Kootenai County.

Koppes Creek (Boise). T10N R4E sec 26. Flows W into Middle Fk Payette River 4 1/2 mi N of Crouch. Pronounced KOP-us.

Named for the first settler in the area, John Koppes. He was first a miner, later a farmer.

Kriley Creek (Lemhi). T23N R21E sec 1. Just S of Fourth of July Creek; flows 3 mi SW to enter Salmon River drainage 7 mi N of Carmen. Lewis and Clark camped here 31 Aug 1805 and named the stream Salmon Creek for the many salmon here. The drainage was originally

known as Bear Gulch because a man roped a bear here and killed it. In 1918 the name was Boyle Creek.

Mathias M. Kriley ranched on this land (ca. 1919).

Kuna (Ada). 2690'. T2N R1W sec 23/25. Town located at the W boundary of the county, originally a railroad stop, 1884. Kuna Butte (3236'), an immense irregular hill 4 mi in basal diameter and 375' above the plain, is 3 mi S of the town.

In 1905 Mr. and Mrs. F. H. Teed filed a 200-acre claim under the Desert Land Act, where Kuna now stands. Persons largely from Iowa and Missouri settled in the area later.

There is some difference of opinion about what "kuna" means. Some say that E. P. Vining chose the name from a Shoshoni dictionary, believing the word means "snow"; others say it means "the end"; and still others, "green leaf" or "good to smoke."

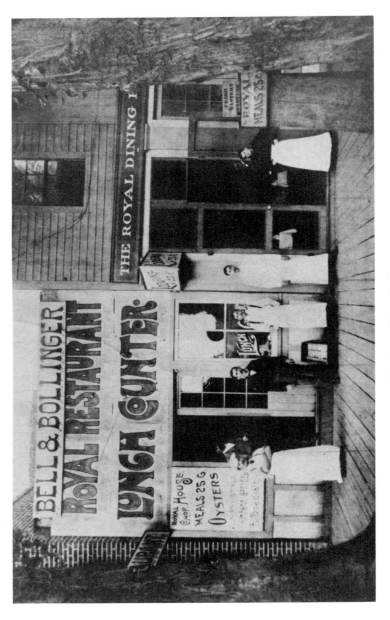

Old Bell & Bollinger Restaurant, Lewiston (Nez Perce County).

L

Labelle (Jefferson). 4880′. T4N R39E sec 3. In the SE quadrant of the county 3 mi E of Rigby and 1 mi W of S Fk Snake River. Pronounced luh-BELL.

Settled by Mormons in the early 1880s and named Cleveland for President Grover Cleveland. Government agents used the name against the community during the period of disfranchisement and the Mormon leaders suggested it be renamed for a Mormon bishop, Winslow F. Walker. Walker refused but, when requested to suggest a new label for the community, said, "That's it. Labelle will do."

Post office, 1906-.

Laclede (Bonner). 2088′. T56N R3W sec 31. Town 7 mi E of the town of Priest River and 5 mi SW of Wrencoe; formerly called Markham.

The town was named by the Great Northern Railway in honor of a French engineer.

Lacy Creek (Benewah). T43N R2W sec 14. A 2-mi creek from the SE to Charlie Creek, St. Maries River drainage; near the Benewah-Latah county line.

Named by Edd. F. Helmers, 1939, for Jesse B. Lacy, homesteader in the area.

Ladder Creek (Idaho). T25N R1E sec 22. A 2-mi tributary from the W to Salmon River, 2 mi S of Lucile.

A descriptive name. The stream flows through a canyon that looks like a 50′-wide stone building with the roof gone and the front wall crumbled; the back wall slopes like a ladder.

Named before 1910.

Ladds Creek (Clearwater). T38N R3E sec 22. Flows S into Dworshak Reservoir 4 mi N of Johnson Mill.

Named for homesteader Charlie Ladds. Also known as Ladd Creek.

Lady Face Falls (Custer). T11N R12E sec 33. On the inlet to Stanley Lake, 2 mi from the mouth.

Some people see the profile of a woman's face in these falls.

Lager Beer Gulch (Boise). T6N R5E sec 1. Flows SW into Elk Creek 5 mi N of Idaho City; Boise River drainage.

Originally named King of Lager Beer Gulch, it was named for a mine of the same name.

Lago (Caribou). 5095'. T11S R41E sec 23. In the SW part of the county, on Trout Creek. Settled by trappers in 1870 and named Trout Creek, for the stream on which it is located; later settled by Mormons from Utah.

Post office, 1887-ca.1965.

There is uncertainty about whether the name is derived from Italian lago "lake" or from an Indian word.

Laguna Creek (Latah). T42N R1W sec 36. Stream 2.5 mi long flowing S to Feather Creek; W Fk Potlatch River drainage.

Named by USFS ranger W. H. Daugs with an Italian word meaning "swampy," which is descriptive of this area.

Lake (Fremont). 6700'. T16N R43E sec 33. Town on the NE side of Henrys Lake; a community with a post office as late as the 1930s.

Named by Joseph Sherwood, ca. 1889, for Henrys Lake.

Lake Canyon (Bonneville). T1N R45E sec 27-9. In NE quadrant; extends SE to NW. Lake Canyon Creek flows NW into Palisades Creek; Snake River drainage.

Named for a lake that was once in this canyon.

Lake Creek (Clearwater). T41N R11E sec 28. Rises in Fish Lake in the Bitterroots and flows 11 mi NW into N Fk Clearwater River.

Lake Creek (Idaho). T22N R5E sec 7. Rises on Marshall Mountain (8443') and flows W through Marshall Lake, then S to Secesh River 1.5 mi SE of Burgdorf; 12.5 mi long.

Lake Creek (Lemhi). T23N R17E sec 30. Headwaters located near Dome Mountain; runs N 4 mi to empty into Salmon River 2 1/2 mi E of the mouth of Middle Fk.

Lake Fork (Valley). 4900'. T17N R3E sec 3/10. Trading post in W Valley County, 5 mi S of the heart of McCall, on Lake Fork. A post office and trading post established by Dave Collender in 1931, but now a part of McCall. Lake Fork rises in Payette National Forest 7 mi E of N extremity of Payette Lake and flows 2 mi NW, then 11 mi SW and W through Cruikshank Reservoir and 13 mi SW and S into Cascade Reservoir; a 26-mi tributary of N Fk Payette River.

These names are descriptive: the streams rise in or flow through lakes.

Lake Mountain (Lemhi). 9274'. T20N R20E sec 34. About 5 mi N of Degan Mountain and 6 1/2 mi NE of Moyer Peak.

Named because it overlooks Lake Williams.

Lakeview (Bonner). 2260'. T53N R1W sec 3. Town on the E shore of the S end of Lake Pend Oreille. Lakeview Mountain (3988') overlooks the town from the E; situated on a small plateau between N and S Gold creeks.

Settled around 1888 and first known as Chloride because of the influence of the mining industry in the area. Now it is a resort town with summer homes, accessible by boat from Bayview or by road from Athol. Post office, 1892-1965+.

Named for the beautiful view.

Lamb Creek (Bonner). T59N R4W sec 6. Enters Bonner County 7 3/4 mi SW of Nordman; flows 1 mi SE, 1/2 mi ENE, 3 1/4 mi ESE, then 3 mi SE into Priest River near Outlet Bay of Priest Lake.

Named for the sheep raised by a settler in the area. Also called Allenand, by Fr. Pierre Jean deSmet.

Lamb Creek (Latah). T42N R1E sec 32. A stream .8 mi long that flows S to Potlatch River.

Named for early homesteader Harvey T. Lamb, ca. 1894. Perhaps this name set the pattern for names of other creeks in the area: Sheep, Porcupine, and Wolf appear along that segment of Potlatch River.

Lamont (Fremont). T7/8N R44E sec 36/1. Siding and community 16 mi SE of Ashton. Post office, 1915-1965.

Named by George Ferney for L. A. Lamont, who settled on the N side of Biche Creek in 1907.

Lanark (Bear Lake). 5900′. T13S R43E sec 13. In the W part of the county, 3 mi NW of Paris and 3 mi S of Liberty.

Originally called South Liberty, but wanting to be independent the settlers renamed the place Freedom. Renamed Lanark in 1883 by William Budge for his birthplace in Scotland. Budge and the Henry Parker and John Bunn families established homestead farms here, 1874-1878, as a Mormon colony.

Post office, 1894-1896.

Land Creek (Cassia). T13S R24E sec 7. Heads in a spring about 1 mi S of Mount Harrison; trends N and NE for 6 mi. Partially in Sawtooth National Forest.

Named for Sam Lann (sic), a homesteader in the area whose name was pronounced LAND.

Landmark Rock (Valley). 8433′. T15N R7E sec 22. At the head of Landmark Creek 1 1/4 mi S of Warm Lake Summit Campground.

Landmark (6617′) is a mountain junction at the intersection of Burnt Log, Landmark-Stanley, and Warm Lake roads, on the mouth of Landmark Creek.

The name is descriptive. Miners and prospectors used the rock as a landmark to find their way to Yellow Pine, Big Creek, and Warm Lake.

Landore (Adams). 5332′. T21N R2W sec 30. Ghost town, formerly a mining town, located 35 mi NW of Council on Indian Creek.

Established in 1898; Post office, 1901-1920.

Locally said to have been named for Landore, Glamorgan, Wales.

Landslide Creek (Bonneville). T2S R45E sec 3. Rises in SE quadrant, and flows 1 mi NE into Palisades Reservoir; Snake River drainage.

Named to commemorate a landslide that occurred in the area.

Lane (Kootenai). 2513′. T48N R2W sec 14. In the SE part of the county, on Coeur d'Alene River and State Highway 3. Established as a lumber town in the 1880s. Post office, 1891-1930.

Named for a logger in the area, ca. 1880.

Lanes Creek (Caribou). T7S R44E sec 10. In the NE part of the county, in Rassmussen Valley. Rises on N slope of Stump Peak and flows about 14 mi NW then SW and S to Blackfoot River. Lanes Butte lies 4 mi W of the upper portion of Lanes Creek, from which it takes its name.

Named for J. W. Lane, an emigrant attached to a wagon train, whose grave is on the creek. Named before 1858.

Lanes Gulch (Cassia/Power). T10S R28E sec 18. Originates in the NW corner of Cassia County and runs N into Power County to empty into the Snake River. Post office, 1880.

Named for an early settler, dry farmer, and cattleman, who came here in 1879.

Lantz Bar (Idaho). T24N R13E sec 16. At the mouth of Squaw Creek, tributary of Salmon River.

Several owners occupied this bar in the early 1900s before Frank Lantz, for whom it is named, moved here in 1925. He worked for the USFS for 27 years.

Lapwai (Nez Perce). 970'. T35N R4W sec 2. Nez Perce village 11 mi E of Lewiston on Lapwai Creek, a tributary of Clearwater River from the SE flowing through Lapwai Valley. In 1805 Lewis and Clark named this stream Cottonwood for the trees on its banks. Pronounced LAP-way.

Site of US Army's Fort Lapwai and Indian Agency by that name. Colonel Wm. Craig, the first Indian agent and first permanent resident in what is now Idaho, was buried near Lapwai in 1869. This is the administrative and cultural center for the Nez Perce Reservation. Post office, 1868-.

There are two versions of the meaning of the Nez Perce word "lapwai." One is "the place of the butterflies," used because there were always many butterflies in the area of the mill and pond built by Reverend Henry H. Spalding when he established his mission in this location in 1836. Lapwai is formed by the Nez Perce words lap-lap, for "butterfly" and wai, for "stream." This location was sometimes called Butterfly Valley.

Yellow Wolf, a Nez Perce Indian, said concerning the name: "In 1926 Many Wounds said to me: 'I will show you the true name of Lapwai.' Leading the way to a partially dried-up quagmire lying between the Spalding Mission site and the mouth of Lapwai Creek, he pointed to the myriads of butterflies settled on the black mud, and demonstrating with his hands the slow fanning of their wings, explained: "that winging is laplap. The Indians knew this spot by that name. The whites changed it to Lapwai, and so called the entire creek."

Lewis and Clark said that the word lapwai was from Nez Perce Lap-pit, "two," and waitash, "country," meaning a boundary line. The creek actually was a boundary that separated the territory of the Upper Nez Perce Indians from that of the Lower Nez Perce.

Laraway Gulch (Boise). T6N R5E sec 26. Flows NE into Mores Creek at Idaho City; Boise River drainage.

A Mr. Laraway, from Idaho City, had the first claim on this gulch, ca. 1862.

Larch Butte (Clearwater). 5539'. T37N R7E sec 23/24. Six mi S of Bungalow Ranger Station. Larch Creek rises on the butte and flows W into Hemlock Creek; Clearwater River drainage.

Named for the larch trees (or tamarack) here.

Lardo (Valley). 5030'. T18N R3E sec 8. In the NW quadrant of the county. Founded S of Payette Lakes, where mining began in 1886. On exhaustion of the gold mines, the town was moved to the mouth of Payette Lake on the W side of N Fk Payette River and later was absorbed by McCall.

Post office 1889-1917.

Named for a local incident. A load of flour and lard burst as the wagon went over rough roads. When the driver unloaded and saw the spilled flour and lard, he exclaimed, "Lard, Oh Lardo!" Hence the name Lardo. Formerly Eugene.

Large Bar (Idaho). T27N R1E sec 24. Along Salmon River, 7 mi S of White Bird.

Sam Large, for whom it was named, and Harry Cone mined this area beginning in 1875.

Larson Creek (Clearwater). T40N R8E sec 31. Flows 4 mi N into N Fk Clearwater River. Larson Point (5133'), a peak, is 2 mi SE of the mouth of the creek and 7 mi N of the Bungalow Ranger Station.

Named for homesteader John Larson, who often ran the river on rafts.

Last Chance (Fremont). T12N R43E sec 8. Town 25 mi N of Ashton.

Formerly: Dewiner Inn, Ripleys Ford.

Named because it was the last resort going S on Hwy 191 until Ashton, some 40 mi away.

Latah (Latah). 1242′. T38N R3W sec 24/25. Former name for Kendrick, which see.

Latah County. County seat, Moscow. Created in 1864 as Lah-Toh County with Coeur d'Alene as the county seat; later actions dropped the name Lah-Toh and in 1867 put all of present-day Latah County into Nez Perce County. In 1888 Congress created the county as we know it, the 16th Idaho county and the only county to be created by Congress. Moscow was named the county seat.

The county is named for Latah Creek, which drains the NW corner. The name is Nez Perce and means "the place of pine trees and pestle," because the Indians found stones here suitable for pulverizing camas roots and shade under the pine trees in which to work.

The county is drained by the Potlatch and Palouse river drainages. Palouse range divides the county and the Hoodoos dominate the NE corner. Between the mountainous areas lie the fertile rolling Palouse hills. Bounded on the W by Washington state, on the N by Benewah County, on the E by Shoshone and Clearwater counties, and on the S by Nez Perce and Lewis counties.

Latour Baldy (Kootenai). 6232′. T48N R1E sec 32. In the SE extremity of the county in the Twin Crags area; 5.5 mi S of the Mission of the Sacred Heart near Cataldo. A dome of rock projecting above the surrounding timber, it is visible from I-90. Latour Peak (6408′) lies 2 mi S of Latour Baldy and serves as a lookout. Latour Creek rises on Reeds Baldy in Benewah County and flows NW 6 mi, then 9 mi NE to Coeur d'Alene at Cataldo.

Named for one of the French settlers who came to the area in the 1880s.

Lava (Jefferson). 4816′. T8N R36E sec 21/22. Early name for Camas, which see.

Lava Butte (Idaho). 8318′. T23N R3E sec 32. In the SW part of the county, midway between Burgdorf and Pollock. Lava Lakes lie .5 mi S of the butte.

Named for its composition.

Lava Creek (Bonneville). T2S R42E sec 18. Rises in S part of county and flows SW 4 1/2 mi to Grays Lake Outlet; Grays Lake system.

Named for the lava that lines the bed of this creek.

Lava Hot Springs (Bannock). 5060′. T9S R38E sec 22. On the Portneuf River in the E part of the county, 10 mi SE of McCammon. A health resort; originally named Dempsey; a number of hot springs gush from the lava. Post office, 1895-.

Indians paid tribute to the Great Spirit for the curative powers of these waters and the area was set aside to be used by all tribes in peace.

Named for the geologic composition of the area.

Lava Lake (Blaine). T1N R23E sec 27/28/33. In the SE part of the county, 4 mi NW of Craters of the Moon at the edge of and partly surrounded by lava beds. Feeders: three creeks that rise on the W slopes of Pioneer Mountains, Copper, Cottonwood, and an unnamed stream.

Named for the lava beds.

Lawrence Creek (Bannock). T9S R36E sec 27. Rises in the SW part of the county in Caribou National Forest and flows SE 3 mi then NE 3 mi into Marsh Creek.

Named for homesteaders who farmed the land drained by this stream.

Lawrence Creek (Camas). T2N R14E sec 32. Rises on W side of Elk Ridge and flows 3 mi SW to Soldier Creek, as Camas Creek tributary; Big Wood River drainage.

In 1883 Frank and Nettie Laurence (sic) lived on Soldier Creek and had a home here. They are buried near the homeplace.

Lawyers Creek (Lewis). T31N R2W sec 2. Forms the principal boundary between Lewis and Idaho counties, and flows NE and E to Clearwater River in T33N R4E sec 8. Approximate length within the county is 39 mi; Clearwater River drainage. Also Lawyer Creek.

Lawyers Creek flows through Lawyers Canyon, formerly Comearp.

Named for Lawyer, a Nez Perce Indian leader from 1848 to 1871, who lived near the lower end of Lawyers Canyon. He received his name from early fur traders because of his talents in languages and oratory. A friend of the whites, he helped the missionaries prepare dictionaries and translate the Bible into Nez Perce and played an important role in treaty negotiations. He died in 1876. He was the son of Twisted Hair, who was a friend of Lewis and Clark.

Leacock Point (Lemhi). 7237′. T21N R19E sec 29. About 1 mi W of the mouth of Deep Creek.

Named for Abner C. Leacock, who patented the ranch at the mouth of Napias Creek in 1917. The ranch was a stage stop during the boom days of the Yellowjacket mines.

Leadore (Lemhi). 5989′. T16N R26E sec 23. Town located in the E part of the county near the confluence of Texas and Eighteen Mile creeks. Leadore Hill (8453′) overlooks the town from the S; situated 6 mi N of Sheephorn Peak and 7 mi E of Gunsight Peak.

Post office, 1911-.

Named for the lead-silver ore in the area that brought the mining town into being.

Leadville (Lemhi). 6400′. T16N R26E sec 24. Town about 1/2 mi W of the mouth of Italian Gulch.

Named because of a lead mine located near here in early days. The town no longer exists.

Lean Creek (Clearwater). T37N R8E sec 3. Heads on Lean-to Point and flows NE into Weitas Creek; Clearwater River drainage.

This is a shortened form of Lean-to, as the creek heads at Lean-to Point.

Lean-to Point (Clearwater). 5078′. T37N R8E sec 27/28. Peak 8 mi SE of Bungalow Ranger Station. Lean-to Ridge trends 4 mi NE-SW; 8 mi SE of Bungalow Ranger Station.

A trapper's lean-to was located here but burned in a forest fire in 1919.

Leatherman Peak (Custer). 12,230′. T9N R23E sec 26/27. In the Lost River Range 10 mi SE of Mount Borah in Challis National Forest. So far as is known, this is the second-highest peak in Idaho.

Named for Henry Leatherman, early-day hunter and trapper in the Lost River Valley.

Ledge Creek (Bonner/Boundary). T63N R5W sec 6. Heads near S section line and milepost 166 of Idaho-Washington state line survey and flows NE into Jackson Creek near center of T64N R5W sec 32. (Not Quartz Creek.)

New name, Ledge Creek, given to avoid duplication, suggested by large rock outcroppings near head of stream.

Leduc (Blaine). T1S R20E sec 22. In the S central part of the county 2 mi N of Picabo.

Established in Alturas County, 21 May 1886, with Peter LeDuc as postmaster. LeDuc remained postmaster until 1900, when the name was changed to Picabo and the site moved 2 mi S. See Picabo.

Lee Creek (Bonner). Heads 1 mi W of Sundance Lookout; flows 2 1/2 mi W into a marsh 1 3/4 mi N of Chase Lake.

Named for a settler who homesteaded here.

Lee Creek (Lemhi). T16N R25E sec 3. Originates 2 mi E of Mill Lake; flows NE 8 1/2 mi to enter Lemhi River drainage about 6 mi NW of Leadore.

Charley Lee was an early rancher on this stream.

Leesburg (Lemhi). 6950'. T22N R20E sec 21. Town in the center of the county on Napias Creek, about 5 1/2 mi NW of Phelan Mountain and 6 mi NE of Jureano Mountain.

Platted in 1866 by southerners who named it to honor General Robert E. Lee. Most of the early miners in the vicinity had fought on the Confederate side during the Civil War. A rival town called Grantsville was established by northern sympathizers, but was eventually absorbed by Leesburg, since the streets of the two towns were continuous. Leesburg is said to have had a population of 7000 people at one time, but now only a few buildings remain.

Post office, 1869-1930+.

Legend Creek (Idaho). T24N R14E sec 29. N tributary of Salmon River at the E extremity of the county. In the Bitterroot National Forest.

So called because Indian pictographs on the bluff above the high-water mark depict figures on horseback; believed to have been drawn after 1750.

Leigh (Teton). Original name for Clawson, which see.

Named for Leigh Creek, on which it was located.

Leland (Nez Perce). 2140'. T37N R2W sec 5. A community in an agricultural area 3 mi N of Dolomite on Potlatch Ridge. Post office, 1888-1943.

Named for Alonzo Leland, a prominent citizen of Lewiston, a member of the first territorial legislature of Idaho, and the founder of the *Lewiston Teller* with his son, C. F. Leland.

Lem Peak (Lemhi). 10,985'. T17N R22E sec 7. One of three peaks in Lemhi Range over 10,000' in elevation; Salmon National Forest.

The name is short for Lemhi, a companion name to Hi Peak.

Lemhi County. County seat, Salmon. Established 1869. Bounded on the N by Montana, on the E by Montana and Clark County, on the S by Clark, Butte and Custer counties, and on the W by Idaho and Valley counties.

Named for Fort Lemhi, the Mormon Salmon River Mission, which in turn took the name of a character (Limhi) in the Book of Mormon.

Lemhi, Fort (Lemhi). T19N R24E sec 20. Historic site near the Lemhi River near the mouth of Pattee Creek.

Post office 1870-1907; Nathaniel J. Hall, first postmaster. Name changed to Hover (for postmaster Lucy Hover) in 1902.

Named by Mormon settlers in 1855 after Limhi (sic), a character in the Book of Mormon. Part of the old mud walls of the fort is still visible.

All the Lemhi features that follow received their names directly or indirectly from Fort Lemhi.

Lemhi (Lemhi). 5100'. T18N R24E sec 33. Town on the Lemhi River. Post office, 1911-.

Lemhi Bar (Idaho). T25N R9E sec 31/32. Along Salmon River, just below Lemhi Creek. Both features derive their names from Harry "Lemhi" Serrin, who survived being lost in Lemhi Mountains in winter and the Rains Massacre at the mouth of S Fk Salmon River, 1879. Formerly called China Bar for the extensive mining carried on by Chinese miners, 1882-1884.

Lemhi Pass (Lemhi). 7373'. T19N R25E sec 14. On the Continental Divide 26 mi SE of Salmon. Lewis and Clark crossed the Rocky Mountains seven times at six places. This is the only pass over the main range used by them twice.

Lemhi Range (Lemhi/Butte). Running from Salmon Mountain SE for about 48 mi, separating Lemhi Valley from the Salmon River and Pahsimeroi valleys. Among the higher elevations of this range are Sheep Saddle, Bell, Flatiron, and Mogg mountains and Lem Peak, all over 10,000' in elevation.

Lemhi River (Lemhi). T22N R22E sec 32. Forms near Leadore and flows NE 14 mi to the town of Lemhi, N 12 mi, thence NW 12 mi to empty into the Salmon River.

Lemhi-Union Gulch (Lemhi). T13N R27E sec 33. Heads near Sheep Mountain and runs NE 4 mi to enter Birch Creek Valley. Named for the Lemhi-Union Mining Company of St. Anthony, Idaho, which owned mining interests in this gulch.

Lemhi Valley (Lemhi). One of the larger valleys in Idaho, it lies between the Beaverhead Range on the E and the Salmon River Mountains and Lemhi Range on the NW. It is broad and open, bordered by precipitous walls that continue as the sides of Birch Creek Valley. The elevation ranges from 4000 to 5000'. About 70 mi long, at the widest 20 mi, the valley is drained by the Lemhi River. Gilmore is the division point

between Lemhi Valley and Birch Creek Valley.

Lemman Creek (Latah). T41N R4W sec 9. A 4.2-mi stream flowing SW to Palouse River, 2.5 mi SE of Potlatch.

Named for Charlie Lemman, a homesteader in this area. Formerly Grouse Creek and Hamilton Creek.

Lemoosh Creek (Benewah). T43N R1W sec 30. One mi N of the Benewah-Latah county line in the SE quadrant. An E tributary of Charlie Creek; St. Maries River drainage.

Named by USFS ranger W. H. Daugs, in 1923; Chinook jargon for "flies." Nothing about the creek suggested a name, so this name was submitted.

LeMoyne Creek (Blaine). T3N R20E sec 2. Rises in the NE part of the county and flows 1.5 mi ENE to Little Wood River 15 mi NE of Hailey.

Named for Harry and Charles LeMoyne, who owned a ranch in the area around 1900.

Lemp (Canyon). 2150'. T4N R2W sec 3. An old BVTRR station in NW Canyon County on Smith Prairie. Post office, 1901-1904.

Named for Boise businessman John Lemp, who was an active supporter and builder of irrigation ditches.

Len Landing (Kootenai). 2150'. T48N R4W sec 3. In the SW part of the county on the W shore of Coeur d'Alene Lake, 4 mi S of Mica Bay and 11 mi S of Coeur d'Alene. Post office, 1897-1905.

Landing site originally owned and developed by Leonard "Len" H. Nichols, who applied for and was granted a post office under the name of Lenlanding with himself as postmaster.

Lenore (Nez Perce). 914'. T37N R2W sec 35. Town 1 mi W of Leland and on the Clearwater R 16 mi below Orofino.

Lewis and Clark camped here 7 Oct 1805 opposite Jacks Creek. Post office, 1900-. Named by the GNRR, but for whom is not known.

Lenville (Latah). T38N R4W sec 16. An early trading center S of Joel and about 13 mi SE of Moscow, originally a general store established by first postmaster Leonard "Len" Nichols, for whom the site was named, and a school established in 1890. Post office, 1894-1901.

Leonia (Boundary). T61N R3E sec 22. A railroad station on the Kootenai River. The town had a store, hotel, and post office before 1923.

Believed locally to have been named for his home town by an Italian worker on the GNRR in 1891.

Leopold Creek (Latah). T39N R1W sec 35. About 5 mi long; in SE Latah County; flows SW into Cedar Creek.

Named after an old settler who lived on its bank; also called Lepo and Lepold.

Leroux Creek (Blaine). T5N R17E sec 10. Rises in the N part of the county and flows 2.5 mi SW to Big Wood River 7 mi N of Ketchum.

Named for a French miner who had a small farm on this stream.

Leslies Canyon (Owyhee). In W Owyhee County, this canyon, commonly called Leslie Gulch, is beautifully sculptured with bluffs and pinnacles.

Named for Hiram Leslie, a Silver City photographer.

Letha (Gem). 2285'. T7N R3W sec 36. Town situated on the UPRR and the Enterprise Canal, in the SE part of the county, 8 mi W of Emmett. Post office, 1912-.

Named for Letha Wilton, only daughter of W. W. Wilton, railroad official, who, with Col. Barnard, sponsored the New Plymouth RR extension to Emmett.

Level (Jefferson). T7N R34E sec 32. An irrigated agricultural community in the early 1900s, 3 mi W of Mud Lake. Post office, 1915-1935.

Named for the flat, level terrain.

Lewis County. County seat, Nezperce. Created in 1911 from the E part of Nez Perce County; located in the NW part of the state, containing 478 square miles.

The Nez Perce Indians made this area their home and knew no whites until the coming of Lewis and Clark, whose expedition was welcomed here on its return from the Pacific Coast (in 1806) and remained for a month. Though miners passed through the area, none stopped until the Nez Perce Indian Reservation was open to settlement.

Bounded on the north by Latah County; on the E by Clearwater and Lewis counties; on the S by Lewis County; and on the W by Oregon and Washington.

Named for Meriwether Lewis of the Lewis and Clark Expedition.

Lewis Creek (Clearwater). T39N R4E sec 32. A 3-mi tributary of N Fk Clearwater River. John Lewis homesteaded near here in 1910.

Lewiston (Nez Perce). 741'. T35/36N R6/5W sec 1/31. County seat. Located in the W part of the county at the confluence of the Clearwater and Snake rivers. The first incorporated town in Idaho, the first capital of Idaho Territory, the only seaport in Idaho.

The townsite was platted in 1861; the Territory of Idaho was created by Congress in 1863 and Lewiston named as the capital. Lewiston was incorporated by the Territorial Legislature in 1866. The capital was removed to Boise in 1864. Post office, 1863-.

Named officially for Meriwether Lewis.

Lewiston Orchards 1440'. T35N R5W sec 14. Adjoins Lewiston on the SE. Laid out in 1905 when irrigated tracts for planting apple orchards were being offered in all sections of the NW. Originally contained 4,200 acres. At first an apple orchard, then cherries, English walnuts, filberts, chestnuts, and grapes were added.

Lewisville (Jefferson). 4790'. T4N R38E sec 8. A Mormon community.

Lewisville Knolls (4912'-4924') are three promontories within 2 mi WSW of Lewisville. Settled in 1882. Post office, 1886-.

Named for Meriwether Lewis of the Lewis and Clark Expedition.

Liberty (Bear Lake). 6000'. T13S R43E sec 5. In the center of the county, 4 mi NW of Ovid (an early Mormon settlement); settled in 1864. Liberty Creek heads in Copenhagen Canyon near Franklin-Bear Lake county line and flows 6 mi NE to Mill Creek, 2 mi W of the town.

This was the first community in Bear Lake County to adopt cooperative farming practices; residents watered their gardens and fields by irrigation from nearby Mill Creek. Post office, 1873-1920.

Mormon settlers, frustrated by governmental restrictions, named their new town Liberty.

Liberty Gulch (Blaine). T2N R17E sec 33. Trends 1 mi SE to Croy Creek; Big Wood River drainage.

Named for Liberty Gem mine. 5 mi up this gulch.

Lice Creek (Boise). T9N R7E sec 34. Flows NW into S Fk Payette River just SW of Lowman.

Named for the abundance of lice among the miners in the area.

Lick Creek (Clearwater). T40N R11E sec 6. A 7-mi tributary of N Fk Clearwater River from the N.

Named for the deer and elk lick here.

Lick Creek (Lemhi). T21N R17E sec 1. Forms near the head of Deadhorse Creek; flows 1 1/2 mi SE to enter Big Deer Creek; Salmon River drainage.

Game licks are found at mineralized springs along Big Deer Creek, near the mouths of Lick and Mudlick creeks.

Lick Creek (Lemhi). T25N R21E sec 2. Heads 2 mi W of Morgan Mountain and flows W 3 mi to enter N Fk Salmon River.

Mountain sheep obtained natural salt on a low pass between Sheep Creek and Lick Creek.

Lidy Hot Springs (Clark). T9N R33E sec 11. Once a resort site 2 mi SW of Winsper.

Named for Bob Lidy, who was a regular freighter to the Gilmore-Hahn mines until a freighting accident left him a cripple and he settled near these springs.

Lidyville (Latah). T38N R4W sec 35. A small pioneer community near Genesee: Post office, 1879-1883.

Said locally to have been named by a settler.

Lightning Creek (Shoshone). T43N R7E sec 32. Rises NE of Snow Peak and flows 2.6 mi S to Canyon Creek; N Fk Clearwater River drainage. Lightning Ridge extends NW to SE 3 mi between Lightning and Buck creeks.

Name suggested in 1923 by Will C. Barnes, because lightning had set many fires on the ridge.

Lightning Creek (Boise). T10N R4E sec 13. Rises on the NE slopes of Lightning Creek Rocks (7831') and flows 13 mi SW and W into Payette River 5 1/2 mi N of Crouch.

Named by the USFS because this area has an extraordinary number of lightning-caused fires.

Lightning Creek (Bonner). T55N R2E sec 3. Heads 1 1/2 mi SW of Smith Lookout in Lake Darling, flows 20 mi into the Clark Fork River 1/2 mi SW of Lightning Creek.

"Lightning" is derived from the nature of the creek: the source is near 6500' and the mouth approximately 2000', hence rapid flow and the name.

Lightning Creek (Clearwater). T40N R6E sec 27. A 2-mi tributary of Haran Creek from the NE; Clearwater River drainage.

Thunder and lightning storms led to this name. Thunder Mountain (now Bertha Hill) and Camp Thunder were other nearby features named for the same reason.

Lightning Creek (Idaho). T24N R2W sec 1. Rises in SW Idaho County on The Narrows and flows 3.5 mi NW to Sheep Creek, 2.7 mi SSW of Stormy Point and 38 mi SW of Grangeville; Snake River drainage.

Named because of the frequency of lightning strikes in this vicinity.

Lightning Points (Clearwater). 4230'. T39N R4E sec 1/2/11. Nine mi NW of Headquarters.

Named after the thunder and lightning storms common to the area. The iron deposits in the ground might attract the lightning.

Lignite (Bonner). 2116'. T56N R2W sec 2. Town 2 mi NNE of Sagle; 3 1/2 mi SSE of Sandpoint.

Named for a small amount of lignite coal found on a nearby mountain.

Lime Creek (Lemhi). T18N R21E sec 3. S of Waddington Creek; flows 2 1/2 mi W to enter Salmon River 16 mi S of Salmon.

W. W. Schultz had a kiln on this creek to produce lime for sale in Salmon.

Lime Mountain (Custer). 11,179'. T6N R23E sec 17. In the SE part of the county, 8 mi SW of Mackay; in Challis National Forest.

Named for the limestone deposits on its surface.

Lime Point (Adams). T20N R3W sec 11. Point of land on the Snake River about 3 mi W of Cuprum.

At one time the Portland Cement Company had a tunnel here and there were several buildings. The company built the first unit of the plant, intending to produce a million barrels of cement a day, but transportation facilities were inadequate. Limepoint Creek rises 2 mi W of Cuprum and flows 2 mi W to Snake River, 3 mi SE of Lime Point.

Named for limestone found on the point.

Limekiln Canyon (Madison). In the SE extremity of the county, in Targhee National Forest.

A canyon where limestone deposits were developed and lime produced for construction work. The Pinnock brothers developed a limestone claim about 8 mi N on Canyon Creek.

Limekiln Gulch (Blaine). T3N R17E sec 14. In the W part of the county 3 mi W of Gimlet; extends SSE to Greenhorn Gulch; Big Wood River drainage.

Named because Jack Shipman operated a lime kiln here for many years during the late 1800s.

Limekiln Rapids (Nez Perce). Rapids 2000' long 1/2 mi SE up river from the junction of Grande Ronde River with the Snake River.

Named for the limestone formations on either side of the Snake River. A kiln was planned but never constructed. Name came into use in the early 1880s.

225

Limerock Mountain (Caribou). 7475'. T5S R41E sec 2. Just S of Bingham-Caribou county line and about 4 mi E of N arm of Blackfoot River Reservoir.

W. R. Chenoweth, United States Geological Survey, established a triangulation station on this point in 1912 and named the station Limerock for the limestone deposits here.

Lincoln (Bonneville). 4754'. T2N R38E sec 10. Town 4 mi NE of Idaho Falls.

Said locally to have been named for Abraham Lincoln.

Lincoln County. County seat, Shoshone. Lincoln County was created in 1895 from a corner of Blaine County, formerly a part of Alturas County.

In 1889 Elmore and Logan counties were created from parts of Alturas, but they were temporarily combined into Blaine County in 1895, two weeks before Lincoln County was created. Lincoln was much larger originally, containing within its borders what are now Gooding, Jerome, and Minidoka counties. In 1913 Gooding and Minidoka took about half the original Lincoln County; after the creation of Jerome in 1919, Lincoln was left with only the N central section of its original area, with 1208 square miles.

Bounded by the N by Camas and Blaine Counties; on the E by Minidoka County; on the S by Jerome County; and on the W by Gooding County.

Named for President Abraham Lincoln, under whose administration Idaho Territory was established.

Linden (Latah). T38N R1W sec 6. A community in the SE part of the county in Cedar Creek area, which experienced a gold rush in 1879. Post office, 1889-1929.

Named for Linden, Missouri.

Lindsayville (Bear Lake). 6000'. T11S R43E sec 34. In the NW part of the county, on Stauffer Creek, 3 mi S of Nounan, in Nounan Valley.

Edgar Monroe Lindsay, for whose family the site was named, homesteaded near Nounan in 1880 and was bishop of the Nounan LDS Ward, 1897-1918. Lindsay and a relative, George Edwin Lindsay, worked in a sawmill in N. Canyon.

Line Gulch (Lemhi). T23N R17E sec 24. Heads 1 mi NE of Sagebrush Lookout; runs NE 2 mi to meet Garden Creek; Salmon River drainage.

Named because the telephone line to Sagebrush Lookout ran up this gulch.

Linfor (Shoshone). 2215'. T49N R2E sec 8. In the W part of the county, an early mining town and post office, 3 mi N of Enaville on the Coeur d'Alene River. Post office, 1916-1925.

A descriptive Gaelic name meaning "pool beneath a waterfall." There is a waterfall at the junction of N Fk and Coeur d'Alene rivers.

Linn Gulch (Latah). T42N R2W sec 22. Canyon and stream on Palouse River between Poorman and N Fk Palouse.

Named for a prospector; name known in the 1880s.

Lionhead (Fremont). 9574'. T16N R43E sec 12. Mountain 4 mi NE of Targhee Pass on the Idaho-Montana border.

Named for its shape, resembling a crouching lion when seen from the E.

Lions Head (Boundary). 7300'. T63N R3W sec 27. A rock formation that resembles a massive, shaggy lion head against the skyline; located due E of Upper Priest Lake in Kaniksu National Forest. Lion Creek heads on the W of Lions Head and flows SW into Bonner Co. and into Priest Lake.

A descriptive name.

Little Bald Mountain (Latah). 4800'. T42N R2W sec 3. A promontory in St.

Joe National Forest, in the Hoodoo Mountains about 1 mi S of Bald Mountain and 21 mi S of St. Maries.

Earlier name: Little Baldy. As with Bald Mountain, there is reportedly little growth on the summit.

Little Baldy (Idaho). 5363', T30N R6E sec 14/15. A promontory in the N central part of the county, in the Nezperce National Forest and Clearwater Mountains, N of the Elk City Wagon Road; 3 mi SE of Baldy Mountain (6613').

The summit was once bare but is now forested.

Little Basin (Cassia). T13S R23E sec 33. Early name for Basin. Area between Mt. Harrison and Mt. Independence, 6 mi E of Oakley.

A Mormon settlement was established here in 1878 and called Little Basin, a descriptive name.

Little Bear Creek (Latah). T38N R3W sec 22. Originates at the confluence of Nora and Spring Valley creeks 3 mi E of Troy and flows SE 8 mi to empty into Big Creek at Kendrick; Potlatch River drainage. W Fk Little Bear is 14 mi long and converges with Little Bear 4 mi upstream from its mouth.

Salmon in quantity could be speared here in 1878, and there was enough flow in the 1890s to float logs on the stream to Harvard, where they were transported to Lewiston by RR.

Little Bear Ridge. About 9 mi long and runs between and parallel to Nora and Little Bear creeks on the W and Dry and Big Bear creeks on the E. Trends NW to SE.

Said to have been named by a pioneer named Prather, who saw a small bear in this area. See Big Bear Ridge.

Little Boulder Creek (Latah). T40N R1W sec 33. Flows W 3 mi and empties into E Fk Potlatch River. In heavily timbered land in St. Joe National Forest.

The creek was discovered after nearby Boulder Creek was named; both streams are tributaries of E Fk Potlatch River.

Named for boulders along the stream.

Little Camp Creek (Boise). T9N R6E sec 16. Flows 2 mi SW into Big Pine Creek; Payette River drainage.

Andy Little, a sheep rancher, had a sheep camp on this creek.

Little Crater (Caribou). 6540'. T6S R41E sec 34. In the N part of the county, just W of the S end of Blackfoot River Reservoir, 3 mi NE of Broken Crater.

Name proposed by G. R. Mansfield, geologist, with the U.S. Geological Survey, in 1917; a descriptive name.

Little Fall Creek (Boise). T9N R6E sec 33. Flows N into S Fk Payette River 6 air mi E of Grimes Pass.

The creek was named by the USFS for the falls at its mouth.

Little Grass Mountain (Bonner). 5727'. T63N R5W sec 31. Located 1/2 mi E of Idaho-Washington border; 6 1/2 mi SW of Upper Priest Lake.

Named for its grassy slopes.

Little Joe Mountain (Shoshone). 7052'. T44N R10E sec 18. On the Idaho-Montana border in the Bitterroot Mountains.

Overlooks the headwaters of St. Joe River. Named in 1923 by USFS for administrative purposes.

Little Lost River. Heads NE of Mt. Borah in Lemhi Range, flows generally S 5 mi to form Lemhi-Custer county line for 10 mi, enters Custer County at T11N R26E sec 35, cuts the corner of the county, and enters Butte County, where it flows generally SE to T15N R30E to Lost River Sinks, E of Arco.

So named because the river goes completely underground in several places and at various times of the year. Antoine Godin is credited with naming the feature in 1823, when he returned to the area where he had discovered a river and found that it had disappeared.

Little Lost River Valley (Custer/ Butte). 55 mi long, 6-11 mi wide. On Little Lost River; between Lemhi and Lost River ranges; S end enters Snake River Plain. See Godin Valley.

Little Salmon Meadows (Adams). T19N R1E sec 2/11/14. On the headwaters of Little Salmon River with Mud Creek on the W and Little Salmon River on the E; Salmon River drainage.

Communities of Meadows and New Meadows lie here. Today the area is commonly referred to as The Meadows or as Meadows Valley.

Named before 1884 for Little Salmon River.

Little Salmon River (Adams/Idaho). T24N R1E sec 15. Rises in Adams, flows generally N and NW into Idaho County, and empties into Salmon River at Riggins; 40 mi long. The source is near New Meadows at an altitude of 5000'; it drops to 1730'. Its drainage is 578 square miles through timbered mountains and its canyon. Named for Salmon River.

Little Silver Creek (Clearwater). T39N R4E sec 4. Flows 4 mi W into Silver Creek; Clearwater River drainage.

Named for Silver Creek, to which it is a tributary.

Little Sweden (Latah). T39W 4D2 sec 1/2. Nickname for Dry Ridge.

So named for the many Swedish homesteaders in the area. It has been reported that school teachers had hard work to teach their Swedish-speaking pupils in English.

Little Wood River (Blaine). T5S R14E sec 33. Rises in Pioneer Mountains in the NE extremity of Blaine County and flows S and SE through Carey Lake, through the NW corner of Lincoln County, and across Gooding County to Big Wood River; about 90 mi long.

Named in the early 1800s for the woods along its banks.

Lizard Butte (Canyon). 2634'. T3N R4W sec 35. An erosion remnant left over a volcanic vent; an historic landmark just E of Snake River and Marsing, Owyhee County, and W of Deer Flat Reservoir.

So named because it looks like a giant lizard with extended legs and reared head. When viewed from the W there is also a tail.

Lloyd Lake (Idaho). T33N R10E sec 21. In the Selway-Bitterroot Wilderness Area, in The Crags; 1 mi NNW of Fenn Mountain, 0.2 mi across.

Named for Lloyd Fenn, son of Major F. A. Fenn, an early USFS ranger and supervisor.

Lochsa River (Idaho). T32N R7E sec 4. Heads high in the Bitterroots on Lolo Pass; formed by the conjunction of Crooked and White Sand creeks and flows 65 mi SW, partly through a 4000'-deep canyon in rugged, forested mountains, to its confluence with Selway River to form Middle Fk Clearwater River at Lowell; drainage, 1880 square miles; the largest tributary of Middle Fk. This river roughly parallels the Lolo Trail, the historic route of Lewis and Clark.

Lochsa is a Flathead Indian word meaning "rough water."

Lodgepole Lake (Custer). T9N R16E. Lake.2 mi long, one of the Boulder Chain Lakes.

Named for lodgepole pine surrounding the lake.

Lodi (Fremont). T9N R42E sec 23. School and post office, no longer extant, in S central Fremont County, 1 1/2 mi N of Ashton.

According to tradition in the family of the first postmaster, named for a character or place in the Book of Mormon, but no indices of that book refer to Lodi, nor do qualified members of the church consulted recognize it. Possibly a transfer name from Lodi, California, which derives from Lodi, Italy.

Loening, Mount (Custer). 10,012'. T13N R13E sec 13. In the Salmon River Mountains 16.5 mi N of Stanley.

Named for Michael Loening (1932-1977), Idaho back-country pilot whose flying included forest-fire assistance, fire patrol, and outdoor-recreation support. Earlier name, Tango Peak.

Lolo Pass (Idaho). 5233'. T38N R15E sec 16. The highest point on US 12; on the crest of the Bitterroot Mountain Range that marks the border between Montana and Idaho.

Lolo Creek (Clearwater). T35N R2E sec 14. Flows about 40 mi SW then NW into the Clearwater River.

Two explanations have been given for the name Lolo: (1) the Flathead pronunciation for Lawrence, a trapper; (2) a corruption of the French name Le Louis, the name French trappers gave the stream and pass to honor Meriwether Lewis.

Lone Pine (Clark). T10N R29E sec 24. In the SW part of the county on Birch Creek; on an early stage line to the Upper Birch Creek mines in Lemhi County.

The name is descriptive: a pine served as an early landmark for travelers before there were roads here.

Lone Pine Peak (Custer). 9652'. T12N R19E sec 25/26. W of Grandview Canyon and E of Salmon River. Lone Pine Creek heads on slopes of Lone Pine Peak and flows generally N and NW about 10 mi to Warm Springs Creek.

Lone Pine was an early stage stop near the summit of this peak, on a freight line beginning in Utah and ending in Challis. The route follows present-day US 93 fairly closely, with the Lone Pine stop about 4 mi W of US 93.

The peak was a landmark for early travelers, for it was a prominent single peak with a pine tree at its summit; hence the name Lone Pine Peak, from which the creek and stage stop take their name.

Lone Rock Creek (Cassia). T15S R24E sec 22. Rises in the S central part of the county on Graham Peak and flows SE to Almo Creek.6 mi W of the town of Almo; 4 mi long.

Named for the large rock at the head of this drainage.

Long Creek (Boise). T9N R7E sec 12. Flows 4 1/2 mi SE into Clear Creek at 4 mi NE of Lowman; Payette River drainage.

Named for John Long, a carpenter, who lived on the creek. He helped build the church and the high school at Garden Valley.

Long Creek (Latah). T41N R4W sec 34.. Heads on Granite Point and flows 4.1 mi NE to Hatter Creek; Palouse River drainage.

N. B. Long recorded his homestead 8 June 1894.

Long Hollow Creek (Lewis). T34N R1E sec 13. Rises in the center of the county 3 mi SE of Craigmont and flows E to Nezperce and then NNW to Holes Creek; Clearwater River drainage.

Originally called Cow Creek. The name Long Hollow Creek has been used only since 1965. It is believed to have been named by the Army Corps of Engineers as part of a flood control survey. The creek passes through a long hollow rather than a canyon.

Long Liz Creek (Shoshone). T46N R6E sec 7. Rises on Long Liz Point (4811') and flows 2.3 mi W to N Fk St. Joe River.

Said to have been named for a Wallace prostitute, whose pimp was a river poleman.

Long Meadow (Latah). T39N R1E sec 4-9. A meadow running to the Latah-Clearwater boundary approximately 4 mi long by 1/2 mi wide.

Characterized by its shape, from which the name is derived.

Long Meadow Creek. Flows 7 mi E and empties into Elk Creek; Clearwater River drainage. Some maps show this as Lone Creek, perhaps a clerical error; on USFS maps, Thompson Creek and Meadow, for the original homesteaders.

Long Tom Creek (Idaho). T25N R5E sec 31. A 3-mi tributary of Salmon River from the S; on Long Tom Bar.

Named for the Long Tom mine at its source, operated 1906-1910. A long tom is a combination of a rocker and a sluice box.

Long Tom Creek (Lemhi). 3100'. T23N R16E sec 27. Heads W of Long Tom Lookout; runs S 3 1/2 mi to enter Salmon River about 1/2 mi E of the mouth of Middle Fk.

Named because a mining implement called a long tom, which is a combination of a rocker and a sluice box, was found at the mouth of the creek; transferred to nearby features. A bit of folklore grew out of a local incident. A man named Joe "Tom" Lockland drowned in Pine Creek Rapids and was found at the mouth of this creek. His body was packed up to Shoup by Wallace St. Clair. A coffin that had been made in Salmon

for him was waiting in Shoup, but when they tried to put Tom in, he was too tall for the coffin; so Wallace St. Clair cut the cords under the dead man's knees, bent the legs up over the thighs, nailed the lid down, and packed him out to Salmon. Since Tom was too long for the coffin, the place became known as Long Tom Creek.

Long Valley (Valley). T12-20N R3E. Extending N about 50 mi from below Cascade to the Upper Payette Lake, separated from Round Valley by a low ridge. Drained by N Fk Payette River; a part of the N-S depression that extends from Payette Lakes. Cascade, the county seat, is located at the S end of this valley.

Named for its length.

Longfellow Gulch (Latah). T38N R1W sec 17. A tributary of S Fk Cedar Creek 1.5 mi SE of Linden, in SE part of the county.

Alphonso W. Longfellow patented a homestead in this gulch 23 Feb 1889. He also ran a sawmill, and his wife, Emma S. Lyons Longfellow, was postmaster of Linden.

Longs Creek (Boise). T8N R4E sec 15. Rises in the W part of the county on Charters Mountain and flows 3 mi E into Alder Creek 5 1/2 mi S of Garden Valley; Payette River drainage.

John Long homesteaded at the head of this creek.

Looking Glass Butte (Idaho). 6465'. T25N R3E sec 35. 13 mi ENE of Riggins and 3 mi S of Florence. Looking Glass Creek rises in the S slope of this butte and flows 3 mi SW to Kelly Creek; Salmon River drainage.

Named for a Nez Perce chief who joined the nontreaty Nez Perces after his village was attacked by soldiers. His father was a friend of Lewis and Clark.

Lookout (Nez Perce). 3378'. T35N R2W sec 2. Town 6 mi NW of Culdesac. Founded by Abe Schenkley, a butcher, who donated the land for Lookout and laid out the town in 1902. Post office, 1901-1916.

Named for the view.

Lookout Butte (Idaho). 5869'. T31N R6E sec 12. In the N central part of the county, 6 mi SW of Lowell.

This promontory reputedly served as an Indian lookout point.

Lookout Canyon (Boise). T9N R6E sec 5. Rises in the NW part of the county on Scott Mountain (8215') and flows 2 1/2 mi S into E Fk Anderson Creek; Payette River drainage.

The USFS named this canyon because the Scott Mountain Lookout directly overlooks the canyon.

Loon Creek (Custer). T15N R14E sec 10. Tributary of Warm Springs Creek. Heads in the lakes W of Custer at an altitude of 8000'. Altitude at its confluence with Warm Springs Creek is 4005'; hence its flow through a deep canyon is steep. There was much prospecting and mining along this stream.

Loon Creek (Custer). Ghost town; a mining camp founded in 1869 and abandoned by 1873.

Loon Creek Summit (Custer) 8687'. T13N R14E sec 8/9. A mountain pass N of Bonanza at the head of Mayfield Creek.

Nathan Smith, a California pioneer, prospected Loon Creek in 1869. He named the stream from a bird of that species found on the stream.

Loon Creek (Valley). T21N R5E sec 11. Rises in a small lake 2 mi SW of South Loon Mountain and flows NE 9 mi through Loon Lake to empty in Secesh River; S Fk Salmon River drainage. During the Sheepeater Campaign, Captain Reuben Bernard's men crossed this creek on the way to the army campsite on E Fk of S Fk Salmon River.

Loon Lake is situated about 1 mi up from the mouth of Loon Creek; covers 30 acres. Loon Mountain, South and North, are promontories on a ridge on the E side of the upper reaches of Loon Creek.

Named for the loons that occasionally reside on the lake.

Loon Creek (Lemhi/Custer). T17N R14E sec 18. Rises in Custer County and flows into Lemhi County, generally NE and NW 30 mi, then N 2 1/2 mi to enter Middle Fk Salmon River. Post office, 1872-ca.1900.

Named for the loons found on the nearby lake.

Loop Creek (Shoshone). T46N R6E sec 7. In the E part of the county, rising in the Bitterroot Mountains and first flowing W, then describing a northward arc to N Fk St. Joe River.

Named by the USFS because the stream follows the Milwaukee RR in its big loop up to the point where it tunnels through the Bitterroot Mountains.

Lorena (Idaho). R32N R4E sec 5. A 1902 name for the Kooskia post office. At the time, when a new postmaster was appointed he had the privilege of choosing a new name. Charles A. Palmer was appointed postmaster 4 Mar 1902 and promptly renamed the post office for his girlfriend, who had just jilted him. He tired of the office in two years and a Mr. Turner was appointed. Turner changed the name to Kupro for the traces of copper in the nearby mining field.

Lorenzo (Jefferson). 4862'. T5N R39E sec 33. In the SE part of the county on the US Highway 20, the UPRR, and the S Fk Snake River, 2 mi E of Menan. Post office, 1901-.

Settled in 1880 and named for Lorenzo Snow, a one-time president of the Church of Jesus Christ of Latter-day Saints. The Yellowstone Branch of OSLRR had bridged Snake River at this point by 1900.

Lost Basin (Adams). T17/18N R4/3W sec 2/36 and 30. In the Payette National Forest along the southern border between Adams and Washington counties.

So named because "Crazy Horse" Smith got lost in this area in a fog.

Lost Creek (Bonner). T59N R3W sec 9. Heads on the E slopes of Cabinet Mountains in Lake Estelle and flows NW to S Calchan Creek.

Named because it is in large part hidden by the forest.

Lost Creek (Bonner). T59N R4W sec 25. Heads on SE slopes of Sundance Lookout and W slope of Lost Creek Lookout; flows generally SW 6 mi into Chase Lake; 2 1/4 mi SW of Coolin.

So named because the creek sinks into the ground about 3/4 mi from Chase Lake.

Lost Knife Meadows (Idaho). T35N R12E sec 14. In the NE part of the county between the upper drainages of Warm Springs and Bear Mountain creeks; N of the N part of the Selway-Bitterroot Wilderness Area.

W. E. Parry, founder of Lowell, and his wife were at this site with their cattle during the 1910 Idaho fire; Mr. Parry lost his knife in the meadow.

Lost Lake (Bonner). T56N R1E sec 19. Two mi E of Garfield Bay on Lake Pend Oreille.

The forest comes to the W edge of this lake and partially conceals it.

Lost Lake (Lemhi). T21N R16E sec 29. Near Puddin Mountain on the SW.

Named in 1963 by USFS and Coast and Geodetic Survey. There was no trail

to this lake, making it very hard to find, and USFS personnel were lost for a time while trying to locate it.

Lost Mine Creek (Kootenai). T51N R2W sec 15. Rises on the SE slope of Huckleberry Mountain and flows 1 mi NE to Lone Cabin Creek; .5 mi E of Hayden Lake; Coeur d'Alene River drainage.

Named for J. P. Breen's discovery claim in 1889. Breen brought gold nuggets into Coeur d'Alene to find someone to grant him a grubstake, but he did not reveal where the mine was. N. R. Palmeter and Jack Osier, both prominent businessmen, agreed to back him. That night Breen went to a saloon to celebrate, followed by would-be friends offering to buy him drinks in hopes he would reveal the location. Palmeter and Osier in an attempt to protect Breen had him jailed until he sobered. Subsequently Breen set fire to the jail and perished. Many searched for the mine N and E of Hayden Lake, but no find was ever reported.

Lost Packer Meadows (Lemhi). T25N R14E sec 29/30. About 1/2 mi SE of Lost Packer Peak on the Idaho-Lemhi border. Lost Packer Lake lies 1 mi SE of Lost Packer Peak and 3 1/2 mi NW of West Horse Lookout.

Since the trail that crosses the meadows is difficult to locate, and a packer bringing a load of timber out got lost, the place was always referred to as Lost Packer Meadows.

Lost Pete Creek (Clearwater). T40N R7E sec 3. In the N part of the county 2 mi E of Headquarters. Flows 3 mi SW into N Fk Clearwater River.

Named for Pete Olson, a trail man who got lost here in 1921; he was a member of the crew building a trail near the creek. It was named for him after his death in 1922 or 1923.

Lost River Range (Custer/Butte). This range lies between Pahsimeroi and Little Lost rivers on the E, and Salmon River, Warm Spring Creek, and Big Lost River on the W, including at the southern end Howe Peak, in T5N R20E.

The crest of this 100-mi range is above 10,000' with several peaks over 11,000'.

Named for the Little and Big Lost rivers, which lie on either side.

Lost Spring Canyon/Creek (Bonneville). T2N R45E sec 36. In NE quadrant in Snake River Range, Targhee National Forest. The creek flows NW to empty into Palisades Creek; Snake River drainage.

Named because the canyon contains a "lost" springs – one that goes underground.

Lost Trail Pass (Lemhi). 7100'. T27N R21E sec 11. One mi NW of Chief Joseph Pass.

The name originated in 1805 with the Lewis and Clark Expedition. When they hired Old Toby, a Shoshoni, to guide them, he went up the W Fk of the North Fork by mistake and got on the wrong trail. Sometimes confused with Gibbons Pass to Wisdom, Montana, which is located farther N.

Louise Creek (Boise). T7N R9E sec 5. Flows NW into the Bear River; Boise River drainage.

Named for Louise (Mrs. Selwin) West.

Lovell Valley (Benewah). T45N R5/6W. Extends 5 mi NE from the Idaho-Washington line through the Coeur d'Alene Indian Reservation within 6 mi of Plummer, forming a canyon for Little Hangman Creek.

Named for a man who was wounded in the Plateau Indian war of 1858 and nursed by an Indian woman, whom he later married.

Loveridge Island (Owyhee). T6S R6E sec 3/2. On the Snake River, 6 mi NE of Bruneau. Loveridge Gulch, an intermittent stream, runs N 10 mi, stopping short of Bruneau River, 3 mi S of Bruneau.

Named for the Loveridge family, who settled near Bruneau.

Lowe (Idaho). 3282'. T32N R3E sec 8. Early name for Winona, which see.

Lowell (Idaho). 1500'. T32N R7E sec 4. In the NW part of the county, at the confluence of the Lochsa and Selway rivers; in the Clearwater National Forest.

Established in 1903, 18 mi E of Kooskia, with 21 inhabitants. Lowell became an important stopping place for travelers and workers to and from the construction site of US 12 and as a headquarters for the work crew. Its nearness to a prison camp, to Fenn Ranger Station, and to the O'Hara CCC Camp up the Selway contributed to its importance. William Parry, a New Englander, is credited with being the founder. It was he who found half-starved Henry Lowell in the canyon of Lochsa River and succeeded in reviving him and nursing him back to health. When Parry applied for a post office, he named Henry Lowell as postmaster.

Named for Henry Lowell, the first postmaster.

Lower Boise (Canyon). T6N R6W Early settlement and post office on N side of Boise River, beginning about where Notus is and continuing down the valley to the mouth of the Boise River. Boise Ferry was established here before 1864: Post office, 1869-1901, when the name was changed to Lemp.

The site of Lower Boise was destroyed by flood twice and each time was reestablished with a different name.

It has at different times been called Lemp, Parma, and Notus, which see.

Lower Goose Lake (Fremont). T9N R45E sec 22. In SE Fremont County, 1/4 mi long, SW of the SW corner of Yellowstone National Park. One-half-mi-long Upper Goose Lake is 1 mi SW of Lower Goose Lake.

Named for the migrating geese that use the lake as a stopping place.

Lower Mesa Falls (Fremont). See Mesa Falls.

Lower Rock Creek (Bannock). T7S R36E sec 35. Stream 4 mi long, flows W to the Portneuf River 2.5 mi SE of Inkom.

Named because of a large rocky outcrop at its head.

Lower Salmon Falls (Gooding/Twin Falls). T7S R13E sec 2. Near the mouth of Billingsley Creek where it empties into Snake River, 2 mi N of Hagerman.

The falls were known to trappers as Fishing Falls and appear thus on maps until the 1870s.

Named because salmon were seen attempting to jump the falls.

Lower Twin Creek (Clearwater). T40N R7E sec 1. Flows SW into N Fk Clearwater River at T40N R7E sec 1.

Upper Twin Creek enters N Fk Clearwater River right beside this creek. The two creeks were called Twin Creeks since they were so close together; then Upper and Lower were added to distinguish between the two.

Lowman (Boise). 8380′. T9N R7E sec 27. Town in N central Boise County on S Fk Payette River.

Named for the first owner of the townsite, Nathaniel Lowman, who homesteaded this spot.

Luby Bay (Bonner). T60N R5W sec 24. A resort area on the W side of Priest Lake about 1 mi NE of Vans Corner.

Named for M. J. Luby, a Spokane attorney who built the first permanent summer home here in 1912.

Lucile (Idaho). 1689′. T25N R1E sec 2. In the SW part of the county, 15 mi S of White Bird and 9 mi N of Riggins. Post office, 1899-.

In 1896 a group of placer miners in this vicinity petitioned for a post office, with the support of Judge James Ailshie. When the miners failed to name the post office, Judge Ailshie supplied the name of his baby daughter, Lucile.

Lucky Peak (Ada). 5908′. T3N R3E sec 11. Seven mi E of Boise in Boise National Forest.

Named for Lucky mine.

Ludwig Gulch (Lemhi). T20N R18E sec 1. Source near head of Ostrander Creek; runs NE 2 mi to enter Blackbird Creek drainage 3 mi W of Cobalt; Salmon River drainage.

Arthur Ludwig, prospector and USFS worker, lived at the mouth of this gulch.

Lunch Peak (Bonner). 6414′. T58N R2E sec 15. Three mi SW of Mount Pend Oreille at the head of Lunch Creek.

Named because members of a roadbuilding crew ate their lunch at this location.

Lund (Caribou). 5485′. T9S R39E sec 15. In the SW part of the county, 5 mi S of Bancroft. A farming, dairying, and sheep-raising community settled in 1893. Post office, 1910-ca.1965. Formerly Hawley.

Named for Carl Johan Lundren, the first settler.

Lunde Creek (Clearwater). T38N R11E sec 4. Flows NW into Cayuse Creek at sec 4; Clearwater River drainage; 4 mi S of Kelly Creek Work Center. Lunde Peak (6367′) is 3 mi S. Lunde Ridge lies 5 mi SE.

Named for a United States Geological Survey topographer.

Luther (Kootenai). T49N R4W sec 11. A resort area on the N side of Mica Bay, W shore of Coeur d'Alene Lake. Post office, 1904-1909.

Named for the founder and only postmaster, Luther P. Faber.

Lykow Flat (Boise). T6N R5/6E sec 12/7. Pronounced LIE-ko.

Mr. Lykow, a woodcutter from Idaho City, raised a tent on this flat, which then was given his name.

Lyman (Madison). 4885'. T5N R39E sec 25. In the W part of the county, at the mouth of Lyman Creek, 1.2 mi S of Thornton. Lyman Creek rises on Buckskin Morgan Ridge near Kelly Mountain and flows in a meander about 14 mi to empty into Snake River at the community of Lyman. Post office, 1887-1914.

Settled first by Theodore K. Lyman in 1879 and named for him. Formerly Lyon Creek.

Lyman Pass (Cassia). 6196'. T15S R23E sec 28. In the S central part of the county, 2 mi W of City of Rocks and 4 mi NW of Twin Sisters.

Named for Goose Creek stage driver Marion Lyman, 1881.

Lyndale Landing (Kootenai). T49N R4W sec 9. A point and a campground at the W end of Mica Bay, on Coeur d'Alene lake; originated as Lyondale. Post office, 1906-1910.

Named for the steamboat *Lyondale*, which plied the waters of Coeur d'Alene Lake and River in 1906.

Lyon Creek (Madison). Early name for Lyman Creek, which see.

In 1871 John Albert Lyon and his sons, Albert and Johnnie, settled on this creek.

Lyon Creek (Idaho). T27N R1E sec 15. Rises on Riverview Saddle and flows 2.5 mi NE to Salmon River 2 mi N of Slate Creek.

Named for Mark Lyons, who carried mail in 1946 and 1947 to Orogrande from Elk City and afterwards ran a stage to Dixie three times weekly.

Mohler (Lewis County) before 1910.

M

Macarte Creek (Lemhi). T18N R14E sec 24. Heads about 1 mi NW of Martin Mountain; flows N 2 1/2 mi to enter Camas Creek; Middle Fk Salmon River drainage. Pronounced muh-CART-ee.

A macarte is a Mexican rope, one end of which is tied to a horse's neck by the rider, who then tucks the other end in his belt so that if he is bucked off he can grab the end of the macarte and keep his horse from running off.

Named by Frank Bradley and a construction crew when they built this section of the Camas Trail in the 1920s.

Mace (Shoshone). 3600′. T48N R5E sec 9. An early mining camp in the E part of the county, near Burke and on a narrow grade from Wallace to Burke. Post office, 1899-1922.

Named for Amasa B. "Mace" Campbell. He and John A. Finch were managers of the Standard mine, where most of the inhabitants of the camp worked.

Mackay (Custer). 5900′. T7N R24E sec 20/28. In SE part of Custer County on US 93, with Lost River Range on the E and White Knobs on the W. Pronounced MACK-ee.

Area opened in 1884-85 when copper was discovered and mining began. In 1901 George Mackay, an Irish immigrant, built a smelter and platted a townsite just below the Mackay mine, and named it Mackay. Though the mine failed, the town remained, consolidated with Carbonate and Houston. Post office, 1901-.

Mackay Peak (Custer). 10,273′. T9N R23E sec 34. In the E part of the White Knobs, about 5 mi SW of the town of Mackay, for which it is named.

Mackay Bar (Idaho). T24N R8E sec 28/29/31/32. On Salmon River at junction of S Fk Salmon River and Salmon River.

Named for Wm. B. Mackay, first white settler, about 1900.

Macks Inn (Fremont). T14N R43E sec 35. Town 31 mi N of Ashton.

Named for W. H. Mack, who founded the resort in 1921 and was first postmaster in 1923.

Macumber Meadow (Latah). T42N R3W sec 15/16. A small area defined on the N by Smith Marsh, on the E by Meadow Creek, and on the W by Big Creek; in St. Joe National Forest.

A claim by Ora Macomber (sic) of the Gold Bug Mining Co. was filed 26 Sept 1904. Also Macomber Meadow.

MacDonald Creek (Boise). T9N R9E sec 14. Rises in the E part of the county on Tenmile Ridge and flows 4 mi NE into the S Fk Payette River 13 air mi E of Lowman.

Named for John MacDonald, who worked for his uncle, Alex MacPhereson, a sheep rancher.

MacGregor (Valley). 4850'. T16N R3E sec 27. Three mi S of Donnelly on Cascade Reservoir. Founded in 1936 by the Boise Payette Lumber Company. From 1936 to 1944 there was a population of 225 and the village had a number of large shops, a post office, store, and community building, and its own power and water systems. Now a part of Donnelly.

Named for the superintendent of the lumber company, Gordon MacGregor.

Maddens (Canyon). 2439'. T4N R2W sec 29. A RR station on the UPRR. A farming community.

Named for a prominent local farm family important in the early history of Caldwell, the Ross W. Maddens.

Madison (Kootenai). T55N R3W sec 33. Early name of Corbin, which see.

Madison County. County seat, Rexburg. Established in 1913 from the S part of Fremont; named for President James Madison; diminished in 1915, when Teton County was created. Bounded on the N by Fremont County, on the E by Teton, on the S by Bonneville, and on the W by Jefferson.

Magic (Camas). 4822'. T2S R17E sec 12/13. In the SE part of the county on the W side of Magic Reservoir. A resort area that extends along the reservoir about 2 mi. Post office, 1913-1921.

Named by analogy to Magic Valley.

Magic Hot Springs (Twin Falls). T16S R17E sec 25. In the extreme S part of the county, 38 mi S of Twin Falls. Long commercialized, these springs are charged with radium and other minerals; they were a favorite with Indians for their curative powers.

Named for Magic Valley, in which it is located.

Magic Valley. The irrigated area along the Snake River, in south-central Idaho, including Cassia, Gooding, Jerome, Lincoln, Minidoka, and Twin Falls counties. I. B. Perrine, called the father of irrigation in Idaho, dreamed of turning the dusty sagebrush areas N and S of Snake River into a garden of Eden. Almost single-handedly he enlisted the interest of eastern and Salt Lake financiers, who also caught a glimpse of Perrine's vision. The names of these developers and investors are preserved in the names of communities throughout Magic Valley.

Named by developers who turned desert lands into gardens, "as if by magic."

Magpie Canyon (Lemhi). T24N R22E sec 29. Runs S 2 mi to enter Cottonwood Creek, Fourth of July Creek; Salmon River drainage.

Named for the magpie, which is usually plentiful in the area.

Magruder Mountain (Idaho). 7482'. T27N R13E sec 3. In the Bitterroot Range, 16 mi W of the Montana-Idaho line. Magruder Creek rises on this mountain and flows 5 mi NE to Selway River. Magruder Corridor, the pack-train route Lloyd Magruder followed from the confluence of S Fk Clearwater and Red rivers E to the Montana line, passed through River of No Return Wilderness; about 70 mi long.

Named for Lloyd Magruder, Lewiston packer who with his companions was murdered near this stream 16 Oct 1863. Magruder had sold merchandise in Virginia City and was returning with about $20,000 when the outlaws murdered the party and shot their mules. They were subsequently tried for their crime.

Erroneously written McGruder on some maps.

Mahogany (Owyhee). Town in the W part of the county in the lower drainage of Jordan Creek. Post office, 1907-1921.

Named for the mountain mahogany in the area.

Mahogany Creek (Teton). T5N R45E sec 31. Rises in the Big Hole Mountains and flows about 8 mi NE to empty into Teton River.

Named by Dr. F. V. Hayden, USGS, in 1872 for the scrubby mountain mahogany trees here.

Mahogany Creek (Lemhi). T14N R23E sec 17. Originates 4 mi N of Patterson, between Falls Creek on the NW, and Patterson Creek on the SE; flows SW 3 mi to Patterson Creek drainage; Pahsimeroi River drainage. Mahogany Creek heads near the source of Mammoth Canyon on Lemhi side; flows SW 2 1/2 mi, then S 3 mi to Little Lost River drainage. Mahogany Mountain (10,095') is at the head of Cliff Canyon 2 mi W of Lemhi-Clark county line on the E.

Named for the mountain mahogany trees in the area.

Mahogany Ridge (Bonneville). 7200'. T1N R42E sec 35 to T1S R43E sec 17. Extends 5 1/2 mi NW to SE in the NW quadrant, in Caribou Range.

Named for the mountain mahogany, which was used for fuel by the settlers.

Mahoney Creek (Valley). T16N R13E sec 6. Rises in Boise National Forest on Mahoney Creek Lookout (7862'), and flows 2 mi SE to Middle Fk Salmon River.

Named for Ray Mahoney, who raised orchard fruits on the bench above the river.

Mahoney Creek (Lemhi). T15N R16E sec 8. Flows SW 3 1/2 mi to enter Warm Spring Creek; Middle Fk Salmon River drainage.

There are several different versions of the source of this name. One informant says it was named for Al Mahoney, prospector; another says for Ezra Mahoney, early-day packer who followed this stream during the season of the Thunder Mountain boom of 1903. Still another says Elzie Mahoney took up a ranch here and built a cabin in 1889. All could easily be related.

Maiden Rock (Bonner). T55N R2W sec 24. Rock formation on W side of Lake Pend Oreille, 3 1/2 mi SW of Talache. Maiden Creek begins 3/4 mi SW of Blacktail Mountain and flows into Lake Pend Oreille at Maiden Rock.

Named because the rock has the contour of a woman when seen from a certain place on the lake.

Mains Ridge (Boise/Custer). T11N R11E sec 12/13. Two mi long, extends ESE from Bull Trout Point.

Named for Guy B. Mains (1878-1958), superintendent of Payette and Boise national forests.

Malad City (Oneida). 4700'. T14S R36E sec 21/22. County seat. In the center of the county, 13 mi N of the Utah line.

Settled in 1864 by a number of Latter-day Saints from Utah, it was soon a booming frontier town. It was in the center of a prosperous farming area and became the most important commercial center between Salt Lake City, Utah, and Butte, Montana. Prosperity lapsed in 1868 when the U and N RR came through and took away its freighting business. Then in 1906 the UPRR built a branch from Brigham City, Utah, and the town got a new lease on life. Post office, 1865-.

Named for Malad River, tributary of Bear River.

Malad River. Stream about 50 mi long, heading in a series of reservoirs about 5 mi N of Malad City, and flowing generally SSE to the Bear River in Utah about 7 mi NW of Brigham City.

The main tributary is Little Malad River (Oneida/Power), which rises in Power County (T12S R34E sec 14), and flows generally SE to the Malad River 5 mi SW of Malad City. (T15S R36E sec 18). About 22 mi long.

Malad Range (Oneida/Franklin/Utah). Located in the Caribou National Forest in the SE corner of Oneida County and the SW corner of Franklin County, running generally S on the W side of Malad River into Utah.

Malad Valley. A fertile valley drained by Malad and Little Malad rivers, about 20 mi long and 8 mi wide, located between Blue Springs Hills and Malad Range; trends S into Utah.

All the Malad features were named for Malad River, which in turn received its name from incidents involving early fur trappers and explorers.

See Malad River (Gooding County) for derivation.

Malad River (Gooding). T6S R13E sec 34. Heads in Snake River Canyon springs SE of Bliss and flows 2.5 mi W to empty into Snake River. Said to be the shortest river in the world.

This river was named by Donald McKenzie in 1819 because his men became ill on this stream after eating beaver, malade in French meaning "sick." In 1824 Alexander Ross had the same experience and believed the beaver had eaten water hemlock; he named the stream Riviere Malades. John Work reported the same circumstances with his men in 1830, and named the stream 'Sickly River.'

In 1862 emigrants named the Big and Little Wood Rivers for the great number of poplars growing along their banks. These rivers join near Gooding, but the stream below their confluence and The

Narrows retains the name given it in 1819, Malad.

Malad Gorge. T6S R13E. About 7.5 mi SE of Bliss at the head of Malad River. Rugged chasm with cascading waterfalls.

Malamute Creek (Shoshone). T44N R4E sec 3. In the SW part of the county, a 5-mi tributary of Boulder Creek from the SE; St. Joe River drainage.

Named in 1919, on the recommendation of Acting Forester R. H. Rutledge, for a stray malamute found in the woods here. The name had been established for some time before this recommendation.

Malin Creek (Shoshone). T45N R7E sec 21. In the SE part of the county, rising on Malin Point (5145') and flowing 3 mi S to St. Joe River at Halfway Hill.

A halfway cabin was built on this creek for overnight stops of pack strings and the creek was named after the man in charge of the cabin. R. H. Rutledge, supervisor of the St. Joe National Forest, recorded this story from Con Faircloth, an old-time prospector.

Mallard Creek, Big (Idaho). T25N R10E sec 6. Rises in Magruder Corridor and on Jack Mountain and flows SW, then SE 15 mi to Salmon River below Bargamin Creek.

Named for prospector Pete Mallard, an early comer to the region, ca.1870.

Mallard Peak (Shoshone). 6870'. T42N R7E sec 36. In the extreme S part of the county in the Mallard-Larkins Pioneer Area. Mallard Lake lies to the immediate E of the peak.

Named by forester Will C. Barnes in 1927 for the mallard ducks that frequented the lake in the fall.

Mallory Creek (Clearwater). T41N R1E sec 20. Flows S into E Fk Potlatch River at T41N R1E sec 20.

Named for Frank Mallory, early settler, ca.1880.

Maloney Creek (Lewis). T31N R2W sec 7. A 10-mi Salmon River tributary from the N, 8 mi S of Winchester.

Named for Mike Maloney, an early Irish miner, who in 1900 settled along this creek and grew produce.

Malta (Cassia). 4600'. T13S R26E sec 12. In the E part of the county, 12 mi NE of Elba in the middle of Raft River Valley; long a trading center of a livestock area.

Founded in 1890. In 1912 T. E. Anderson installed the first pump 8 mi N of Malta to demonstrate feasibility of pumping underground water for irrigation in the Raft River area. Post office, 1883-.

Named by Sara Condit, a teacher from Iowa, for the Isle of Malta in the Mediterranean Sea, because of the euphony of the name.

Mammoth (Butte). 9360'. T6N R23E sec 10. Ghost town; a small mining operation with a small mill. Only a few cabins were built.

Named for the first mine in the area.

Mammoth Cave (Lincoln). T4S R17E sec 14. Eight mi N of Shoshone; 1.5 mi W of State Highway 75. A lava tube discovered in 1902.

A descriptive name for the size of the cave.

Mammoth Mountain (Idaho). 6560'. T25N R8E sec 33. 1.2 mi long, in the Clearwater Mountains 25 mi SSW of Elk City.

Reported to have been named for the Mammoth mine.

Mammoth Soda Spring (Caribou). The largest of the springs at Soda Springs.

A descriptive name.

Mann Creek (Shoshone). T43N R2E sec 23. In the SE corner of the county; a 3-mi tributary of Merry Creek 5 mi NE of Clarkia; St. Maries River drainage.

Named for an early schoolteacher in the Clarkia area.

Mann Creek (Washington). T10N R4W sec 6. Rises on the S side of Hitt Mountain and flows S 26 mi to Weiser River, 4 mi E of Weiser.

In 1811 Wilson Price Hunt and his party ascended Mann Creek to Monroe Creek and crossed the head of Wolf Creek, then followed the Snake River.

Named for Jack Mann, an early settler who lived in a dugout a mile or two above the mouth of this stream. Also known as Mans, Man's, Mann's and Man Creek.

Mannering Creek (Latah). T42N R3W sec 12. Rises NW of Three Tree Butte and flows S 6.2 mi to Meadow Creek; Palouse River drainage.

Named for John Mannaring (sic), who homesteaded here in 1891.

Manuel (Idaho). T28N R1E sec 24. An early post office on Baker Creek, where the Manuel family lived in 1877 during the Nez Perce War. The Manuels were with James Baker when the Indians attacked and killed him on Baker Creek. Henry Manuel applied for a post office, which was granted in 1864, and became the first and only postmaster. It was closed in 1878.

Named for Manuel.

Maple Creek (Latah). T41N R3W sec 9. Flows 5.1 mi SE to a point just E of Harvard.

Named for Maple placer mine, located in 1895.

Mapleton (Franklin). 4808'. T15S R40E sec 26/35. In the SE part of the county, on Maple Creek.

A Mormon settlement, 1875-1899, first known as St. Joseph, for Joseph Thomas Perkins, the first settler; then Mapleton in 1898. Post office, 1898-1906.

Named for the creek, which in turn is named for the maple trees in the area.

Marble Creek (Shoshone). T45N R3E sec 13. Rises on Crater Peak and Orphan Point and flows NNW and NE for 25 mi to St. Joe River at the logging community of Marble Creek.

Marble Creek post office, 1916-1927.

Named for the quartzite and granite in the stream bed and along its banks.

Marble Creek (Valley). T18N R12E sec 8. Rises on Lookout Mountain Ridge 2 mi NE of Thunder Mountain and flows 19 mi SE to Middle Fk Salmon River.

Marble City, near the source of Marble Creek, was a log and tent town below Sunnyside mine, primarily a stopping place on the road from Challis, Salmon, and Ketchum to the Dewey mine and Roosevelt. Now a ghost town.

Named for the rock formations.

Marcus Cook Peak (Shoshone). 5570'. T46N R5E sec 5. In the W part of the county, 7 mi N of Avery.

Named for Marcus Cook, a former employee of the USFS who lost his life in Tuscania, Italy, in 1918 in WW I.

Margaret, Mount (Latah). 3770'. T41N R3W sec 13. Promontory 3 mi SE of Harvard between the headwaters of E Fk Flat and Ruby Creeks with an E-W axis of approximately 2 mi.

Named for an early pioneer woman who lived in the area, whose last name is now unknown.

Maria, Mount (Boise). 3472'. T7N R2E sec 11. Pronounced muh-RYE- ah.

Mount Maria was named in 1864 by Fred Faull, an English minister. It commemorates Mt. Moriah (sic), which

guarded the entrance to Biblical Jerusalem, as Mt. Maria guards the entrance to the Jerusalem Valley in Boise County.

Marion (Cassia). T13S R22E sec 17/18. In the central part of the county, 4 mi NW of Oakley.

A Mormon community settled in 1881 and named in 1885 when a post office was applied for. Post office, 1885-1918.

Named for Francis Marion Lyman, a local Mormon apostle, whose surname was given to Lyman Pass.

Marion, Mount (Bonner). T57N R1E sec 22. Near Hope.

Named for Marion Canfield, a settler.

Market Lake (Jefferson). T5N R37E sec 8. A small lake SE of Mud Lake and 3 mi N of Roberts.

In 1833 Captain Bonneville and his party camped on the flats here and feasted on fresh game—as the Indians had done for centuries, for this was a favorite Indian campground. In 1853 floodwaters from Snake River formed a lake here. In 1855 Brigham Young led 142 of his people by this lake and camped here, on their way to Fort Lemhi; he called the place Lava Lake. Hunters, trappers, travelers, and early settlers have all commented on the great abundance of game.

Some sources say Bonneville bestowed the name Market Lake; others that hunters referred to "going to market" for game, and still others that the great flocks of wild geese and ducks were slaughtered and sold here.

Market Lake 4773'. T5N R37E sec 32. An early community established by William J. and John Adams, the first settlers in present-day Jefferson County, in 1868, and named for the lake. Post office, 1868-1910.

Marlin Spring (Lemhi). T25N R19E sec 17. About 1 mi SE of Saddle Spring, at the head of Squaw Creek near the Idaho-Montana border.

Part of an old rifle (possibly with the brand name Marlin) was found by the spring.

Marquette Creek (Clearwater). T41N R6E sec 25. In the NE part of the county near the Shoshone County border. Flows S into N Fk Clearwater River.

Named for Frank Marquette, who had a mining claim here. He settled along the creek in 1906.

Marsh (Gem). T7N R1E sec 27. Early post office and stage station, at the mouth of Stagecoach Canyon at the present site of Montour. Post office, 1889-1906.

This post office was first established at the mouth of Squaw Creek in 1870 and named Squaw Creek. On 14 June 1889 the name was changed to Marsh for the new postmaster, Edson Marsh.

Marsh Creek (Bannock). T7S R36E sec 21. A major stream, 42 mi long; heads at the junction of its Right and Left Hand fks and flows NW to Portneuf River at Inkom. Left Hand Fork Marsh Creek rises 8 mi NE of Downey, flows SSW 6 mi to join Right Hand Fork to form Birch Creek. The source is in the mountains E and S of Downey at an altitude of 7000'; the drainage is 500 square miles.

Marsh Valley 4760'. T10S R37E sec 29. A Mormon settlement established in the late 1870s.

Both the creek and the settlement were named for the marshy ground.

Marsh Creek (Cassia). T10S R24E sec 30. Rises in Albion Mountains; flows about 30 mi NE and W to empty into Snake River 2 mi W of Declo; drains Marsh Basin, in which Albion is located.

Colonizing of the basin began in 1873, primarily by stockmen. In 1881 George S. Sucas filed a notice of intention to appropriate water for irrigation purposes from Marsh Creek. He dammed the creek, forming a reservoir to service his ditch. Thus the area was under irrigation very early.

Named for the appearance of the creek; it is muddy and marshy.

Marshall Lake (Idaho). T24N R5E sec 31. S of Salmon River, between California and Lake creeks. Marshall Mountain (8443') lies 2 mi E of this lake.

Marshall Lake District is one of the mining districts NE of Warren. Lisfe Holte discovered gold ore in the area 25 Dec 1915; the mine was known as Holte mine until 1929, when it was sold to the Golden Anchor Mine Company.

Named for Jim Marshall, miner and trapper, who built a mountain house on the lake as a stopping place on the trail between Florence and Warren.

Marsing (Owyhee). 2249'. T2/3N R4W sec 33/4. Town in the northmost part of the county. Earl Q. Marsing and Mark Marsing settled in the area in 1913. The Marsings and C. A. Johnson bought 44 acres, had it platted into town lots, and offered them for sale. They called the town Butte because of Lizard Butte, which is across the river and E 1 mi.

The first settler in the town was Frank E. Volkmer, who came in 1921. He applied for a post office and his son, Walter Volkmer, was appointed the first postmaster in March, 1922. The post office objected to the town name because there were already number of post offices called Butte. Therefore the name was changed to Marsing, for Earl O. and Mark Marsing.

In 1922 the railroad was built into Marsing and the railroad placed the name Erb on the depot. This helped add to the confusion. Erb was named for George E. Erb, who was a member of the Public Utilities Commission of the state of Idaho and who may have had some part in having the railroad built into Marsing.

To people who lived outside Marsing, the town was also known as Claytonia. All four names were in use at the same time. Butte was dropped as the most common name, but to this day if one buys a town lot in Marsing, the title comes from Butte. The name Claytonia was eventually dropped, and on 15 Oct 1937 Erb was dropped.

Marten Creek (Clearwater). T37N R11E sec 5. A 7-mi tributary of Cayuse Creek from the W; Clearwater River drainage. Marten Hill (5805') lies at the head of the creek, 12 mi SE of Kelly Forks Ranger Station.

Named for Bill Marten, a homesteader.

Martin (Butte). 5605'. T2N R24E sec 11. Ghost town near Lava Creek 1 mi N of Blizzard Mountain. A mining settlement near Park and Elkhorn mines, where Jack Hood and Fred Winterhoff made their discoveries. The population reached 700-800, and about 250 men worked in the mines and mill. Post office, 1882-1938.

Named for the first postmaster, Samuel Martin, 1882.

Martin Bay (Bonner). T56N R1E sec 5. On W side of Lake Pend Oreille, 1/2 mi N of Glengary, 3 1/2 mi WSW of Hope.

Named for Johnny Martin, who lived here and who drowned in the lake.

Martin Creek (Clearwater). T40N R8E sec 8. Flows NE into N Fk Clearwater River at sec 8.

Named for Bill Martin, an early settler.

Martin Mountain (Lemhi). 9423'. T17N R15E sec 2/3. Located 4 1/2 mi E of Hospital Bar.

Named by Charles Metz, homesteader of the Goat Creek Ranch on Camas Creek. Metz was a trapper and named the mountain because trappers took more marten (sic) from this area than any other place in the area.

Martindale Creek (Lemhi). T17N R16E sec 11. Flows S 4 mi to enter W Fk Camas Creek; Middle Fk Salmon River drainage.

Named for Tommy Martindale, who came into the vicinity prospecting for the Lost Cleveland mine. He reportedly was killed by a horse at the Three Forks Ranch at Meyers Cove.

Martindale Spring (Cassia). T13S R19E sec 34. Located .5 mi ENE of Cow Spring and 25 mi SE of Twin Falls.

Named for a cattleman who grazed cattle in the area about 1910.

Martins Flat (Bonneville). T2N R39E sec 8. A benchland E of Iona in the NW quadrant.

Named for Charles Martin.

Martinsville (Gem). Early name of Emmett, which see.

Marys Creek (Owyhee). T13S R6E sec 5. Rises E of Duck Valley Indian Reservation and flows NE 28 mi to Sheep Creek; Bruneau River drainage.

Named for one of five girls from Silver City who were warned to hurry back because of a reported Indian raid in 1878. See Hurry Back Creek.

Marysville (Fremont). T9N R43E sec 30/31. Town 1 mi E of Ashton.

Said to be named for Mary Baker (first postmaster, 1891), Mary Dorcheus, Mary Patlow, Mary Spratling, and Mary Smith, all residents in the community when it was founded; thus the name is a plural rather than a possessive.

Mashburn (Benewah). 2580'. T44N R1W sec 8. An old RR siding.

Named for homesteaders Lee and Luther Mashburn, who had ranches here.

Mason Butte (Lewis). 4639'. T33N R2W sec 15. About 7 mi SE of Craigmont.

Mason Prairie. SE of Lewiston, covers appoximately 300 square miles. It is located E of Waha Prairie and is bounded on the N by the Clearwater River, on the S by the Salmon River, and on the E by the Camas Prairie. It includes Mason Butte.

Named for Mr. and Mrs. Thomas Mason, early settlers who operated a way station on Mason Prairie from about 1866 to 1876, when the Indians drove them away.

Mason Butte (Latah). 3745'. T38N R1E sec 11. A lookout in the SE corner of the county, just S of Mason Meadows.

Also named for Thomas Mason, father-in-law of James DeHaven, homesteader of Genesee.

Mason Prairie (Nez Perce). Early name for Westlake, which see.

Masonia (Shoshone). 2756'. T48N R2E sec 34. In the W central part of the county; an old mining camp on E Fk Pine Creek, 14 mi SW of Kellogg. Post office, 1916-1925.

Named for Peter Mason, the first postmaster and an early settler.

Massacre Flat (Custer). T6N 416E. Near Easley Peak, where the USFS supervisor of 1914 put up a series of Burma Shave-type signs in an effort to prevent forest fires: Kill Fire, Butcher Blazes, Douse Coals, Put Out Sparks, and others; hence the name Massacre.

Massacre Mountain (Custer). 10,924'. T8N R24E sec 1. In the S.E. part of the county 8 mi NNE of Mackay; Challis National Forest.

Named in memory of the 1878 battle between Bannock Indians and Joe Skelton's freight train, when four men lost their lives.

Massacre Rocks (Power). 4249'. T9S R30E sec 6. In the W part of the county on Snake River, 9 mi SW of American Falls; on US 15.

A massacre occurred near here 10 Aug 1862, when a train of 11 ox-drawn wagons carrying 25 families from Iowa was attacked by Indians. Wagons were plundered and burned, teams driven off; 5 men and 1 woman were slain.

Mastodon Mountain (Shoshone). 5909'. T46N R4E sec 4/5. Eight mi S of Wallace.

Named by regional Forester R. H. Rutledge for the Mastodon mine, situated near the top of the mountain.

Matchwood (Bonner). T58N R1W sec 22/29. An area near Selle.

Named for the small trees here that have little value.

Maxwell Gulch (Lemhi). T24N R21E sec 27. Heads near Napoleon Ridge; runs NE 2 mi to enter Salmon River drainage, almost directly across from the mouth of Wagonhammer Creek.

Dave Maxwell, who made saddles in Salmon, lived here for a time.

May (Lemhi). 5068'. T15N R21E sec 25. Town in the S part of the county in the Pahsimeroi Valley. This is a farming district. Post office, 1897- .

The wife of postmaster Rudolph Wright chose the name May because the government had requested a short name and the application was made in the month of May.

May Mountain (Lemhi). 10,971'. T16N R22E sec 34. Located 6 mi NE of May and 6 mi W of Mogg Mountain; Salmon National Forest. Named for the town of May, which it overlooks.

Mayfield (Elmore). T1N R5E sec 18. In the W part of the county, 28 mi NW of Mountain Home and 3 mi E of the Boise line. A dry-farming area. Originally named Corder, for a pioneer family who ran a stage station from 1865 to 1887 about 6 mi NE of the present site. Post office, 1883-.

Renamed Mayfield 1887, for the second postmaster, Arthur Mayfield.

Mayflower Gulch (Lemhi). T23N R18E sec 36. Runs 1 mi N to Beaver Creek drainage; Salmon River drainage.

The Mayflower mine was located just across Beaver Creek from this gulch.

McArthur (Boundary). T60N R1W sec 27. A railroad stop on Great Northern and UPRRs; on Highway 95 and Deep Creek. McArthur Lake is situated on Deep Creek, adjoining the settlement.

A railroad name.

McCaleb, Mount (Custer). 11,599′. T8N R24E sec 28. About 6 mi N of Mackay in the Lost River Range.

Named for Jesse McCaleb, a Mackay freighter in the 1870s, who was killed by Indians near this peak in 1878.

McCall (Valley). 5021′. T18N R3E sec 9. In the NW quadrant on Lower Payette Lake, at the head of picturesque Long Valley. The center of one of the chief resort areas in the state.

McCall was born when an 1899 caravan of wagons camped on the shore of Lake Payette and the McCall family decided to stay. Thomas McCall bought the E part of present-day McCall from Sam Devers. The townsite was platted in 1901. When the UPRR came through, the station was named Lakeport, but that name was unsatisfactory to the residents and McCall replaced it. Post office, 1901, 1905-.

Named for the earliest settler, Thomas McCall.

McCalla Creek (Idaho). T24N R12E sec 33. Rises in the Payette National Forest and flows 7 mi N to Whimstick Creek; Salmon River drainage.

Named for a local rancher.

McCammon (Bannock). 4719′. T9S R36E sec 12. In the central part of the county on Portneuf River, at the junction of two branches of the UPRR. In 1873 Congress granted a right of way to John W. Young, son of Brigham Young, for the construction of the Utah and Northern RR to enter Idaho Territory along Bear River Valley, through Soda Springs, up the Snake River Valley, and across Montana to a junction point with the NPRR. In July 1882, Congress officially ratified an agreement made at Fort Hall between the Shoshone and Bannock Indians and J. H. McCammon (the town's namesake) and several RR officers, by which promoters secured a right-of-way through the reservation. These railroads gave the first great impetus to settlement and development of SE Idaho.

Post office, 1883-.

McCan Gulch (Camas). T1N R14E sec 29. A 4-mi gulch flowing SE into Three Mile Creek, a Camas Creek tributary; Big Wood River drainage..

Named for the William McCann (sic) family, pioneers of the 1890s, who homesteaded about 1 1/2 mi from Soldier.

McCarthy (Shoshone). 2925′. T48N R4E sec 23. On the NPRR and Ninemile Creek. A mining siding 1 mi N of Wallace; later the site of a slaughterhouse.

Named for James F. McCarthy, a developer for the Hecla Mining Company in the 1890s.

McComas Meadows (Idaho). T30N R4E sec 35. On Meadow Creek, 20 mi S of Stites.

Named for Jess McComas, who came W in 1898 and ranched along the Snake River for 40 years. He also owned this meadow, where he grazed his livestock. In 1944, Potlatch Forests, Inc., had a logging camp here and harvested 20M board feet of timber from January to November.

McConn Creek (Lemhi). T25N R20E sec 18. Heads in the area between Muleshoe Springs and Saddle Spring; runs E, then SE to empty into Indian Creek; Salmon River drainage.

Named in honor of James W. McConn, Co. C, 12th West Virginia Infantry, who was a soldier during the Indian campaigns in the Salmon River country in the 1870s. He is buried in a marked and fenced-in grave on the grounds of the Indianola Ranger Station.

McConnel Island (Canyon). T5N R5W sec 22. Island S of Parma, in Boise River, settled by the four McConnel brothers; afforded pasturage and forage for cattle and horses when this was stock country.

McConnell Mountain (Idaho). 7415'. T35N R12E sec 23. In the NE part of the county and the N part of Selway-Bitterroot Wilderness Area.

Named for Oliver W. McConnell (USFS), who planted fish in Gospel Mountain Lakes and other lakes in the wilderness areas.

McCoy Canyon (Lemhi). T11N R28E sec 16. Heads about 1 1/2 mi NE of head of Meadow Canyon; runs NE 3 mi to UC Gulch, 4 mi SE of Charcoal Kilns. McCoy Spring is in McCoy Canyon 2 1/2 mi SE of Coal Kiln Spring.

Named for Al McCoy, a rancher in this area.

McCoy Creek (Bonneville). T3S R46E sec 6. Rises in SE quadrant and flows 8 1/2 mi into Palisades Reservoir; Snake River drainage.

Named for F. McCoy, one of the discoverers of gold in Caribou Basin in 1870.

McCoy Gulch (Latah). T41N R4W sec 11. Extends S between Grouse and Lemman creeks and empties into Palouse River 4 mi E of Potlatch, 1 mi NE of Princeton.

Named for early settlers in the area: Hamlin McCoy, who bought a home in 1888, and his wife Phoebe.

McCully Gulch (Idaho). T29N R1E sec 35. A 2-mi gulch trending NW to SE to Salmon River, 4 mi N of White Bird.

Homer and Helen McCully had a ranch at the head of the creek ca.1880; they raised 12 children here.

McDevitt Creek (Lemhi). T19N R24E sec 32. Forms in the area just E of North Basin; flows generally E 9 mi to Lemhi River 1 mi S of Tendoy; Lemhi River drainage.

Named in honor of Neil McDevitt, an early settler and rancher who patented his land here in 1897.

McDonald Gulch (Lemhi). T20N R18E sec 25. About 1 1/2 mi long; runs SE into Panther Creek drainage, 2 1/2 mi SW of Cobalt Ranger Station; Salmon River drainage.

Archie "Horse Thief" McDonald, an old trapper and miner who earned his nickname by being sent to prison for stealing horses, lived at the mouth of the gulch.

McDonald Lake (Custer). T8N R14E sec 19. Just SW of Yellow Belly Lake.

Named for James McDonald, who owned a summer home on Pettit Lake.

McDonald Point (Bonner). T49N R4W sec 26. On E side of Lake Pend Oreille, near the mouth of the Clark Fork River.

Named for Angus McDonald, a member of the Hudson's Bay Company, ca.1810.

McEleny Mountain (Lemhi). 8938′. T20N R16E sec 25. About 5 mi SW of Quartzite Mountain and 6 mi NW of Red Rock Peak. Pronounced MACK-uh-lane-ee.

One informant says it was named for an old prospector who had a mining claim here. Another says that McEleny was a sheepherder who ran sheep near here because of the flat ground for grazing.

McFadden (Custer). A mine and post office located on Jordan Creek after 1880. Post office, 1900-1901.

Named for the only postmaster, Caroline F. McFadden.

McGary Butte (Latah). 4451′. T40N R1E sec 29. Promontory at headwaters of three southern tributaries of Ruby Creek; 6 mi SE of Bovill. McGary Creek, tributary of Long Meadow Creek, rises on this butte.

Named for J. S. McGary, homesteader and timber cruiser in the area, ca.1910.

McGinty Creek (Lemhi). T13N R27E sec 2. Forms N of the head of Divide Creek; flows NW 6 mi to enter Divide Creek; 4 mi NE of Gilmore; Lemhi River drainage.

A man named Edward McRea lived near this stream; the local people called him Ed McGinty.

McGowan Basin (Lemhi). T19N R18E sec 16/2. NW of Moyer Basin and SW of Treloar Gulch; on Panther Creek 11 mi SE of Cobalt.

George McGowan had a slaughterhouse here ca.1870 and sold beef to the people of Yellowjacket.

McGowan Peak (Custer). Approximately 10,000′. T10N R12E sec 8. In the Sawtooth Range, overlooking Stanley Lake.

Named for George L. McGowan, who was among the first to settle in the Stanley Basin country in the early 1860s.

McGregor Creek (Idaho). T27N R16E sec 6. Rises in the Bitterroot Range at the Idaho-Montana boundary and flows 1.6 mi generally SSE to Deep Creek about 3.7 mi SE of Nez Perce Peak.

Named for Charles A. MacGregor (1887-1953), who, as a USFS ranger in this area from 1917 to 1947, played a constructive part in the building and protection of natural resources.

McGuire, Mount (Lemhi). 10,082′. T21N R16E sec 4. Located 1 1/2 mi NE of Ship Island Lake.

Named for Dan McGuire, a mining engineer and geologist.

McKay Creek (Custer). T13N R16E sec 2. SE tributary of Yankee Fork.

There was an early waystation at the confluence of the creek with Yankee Fork, owned and operated by Daniel McKay, for whom it is named. He later sold to Fannie Clark, and it became Fannies Hole.

McKay Creek (Elmore). T8N R10E sec 24. In Boise National Forest in the extreme N end of the county. A 2-mi stream, tributary to N Fk Boise River from the E, between Ballantyne and Bayhorse creeks. Pronounced ma-KI.

Named for a pioneer sheep rancher.

McKay Creek (Lemhi). T24N R19E sec 30. SE of Boulder Basin and SW of Spring Creek; runs 1 mi SE to enter Salmon River, about 1 mi NE of Shoup.

Named for Johnnie McKay, who wintered in a cabin at the mouth of the creek because he wrecked his boat near here. He was a millwright who built a flatboat and worked placers along the river. Local tradition says the place should have been named James Creek because a cousin of Frank and Jessie James built the cabin.

McKenzie (Owyhee). T8S R5W. Town S of Silver City on South Mountain.

Named for George S. McKenzie, the only postmaster, 1881.

McKey Creek (Custer). T5N R23E sec 25. Flows NE for about 2 mi to a confluence with Cherry Creek at T5N R23E sec 25.

Named for Elizabeth McKey, who homesteaded in the area between Poison and McKey creeks in 1907.

McKim Creek (Lemhi). T17N R21E sec 17. Heads near Bear Valley Lakes; flows W 5 mi to enter Salmon River 26 mi S of Salmon.

Named for David McKim, pioneer rancher on this stream, ca.1880.

McKinley Gulch (Boise). T5N R4E sec 3. Flows SE into Mores Creek 6 mi SW of Idaho City; Boise River drainage.

Named for the McKinley mine, which was located on the gulch.

McKinnon (Clearwater). T41N R6E sec 28. Settlement 6 mi NW of Canyon Ranger Station.

Named for George McKinnon, a Potlatch Forests, Inc., camp boss who had a cabin here.

McKinzie Creek (Boise). T8N R4E sec 10. Rises in SW part of the county and flows 2 1/4 mi NE into Alder Creek 5 mi S of Crouch; Payette River drainage. Pronounced m-KIN-zee.

Named for Roy McKinzie, an early settler in the Garden Valley area, ca.1865.

McKinzie Creek (Idaho). T27N R1E sec 24. A 3-mi long creek, N of Slate Creek, that flows SW to the Salmon River 7 mi S of White Bird.

Named for an early resident of the area.

McLeod Creek (Elmore). T8N R9E sec 5. In extreme NE Elmore County. Flows 4 mi NW to N Fk Boise River.

Named for an early sheep man.

McNutt Creek (Boise). T7N R9E sec 23. Rises in the SE extremity of the county and flows 2 mi SE into N Fk Boise River 6 mi NE of Deer Park campground.

Named by a Mr. McNutt, who built a great many trails through what became the Boise National Forest; he was the boss of a road crew.

McNutt Creek (Lemhi). T18N R23E sec 32. Forms 1 1/2 mi NE of Bear Valley Lakes; flows 3 mi E to enter Basin Creek; Lemhi River drainage.

Named for David McNutt, who with his partner, Fred Phillips, is said to have opened the first general store at Leesburg in the fall of 1866.

McPherson Creek (Elmore). T8N R11E sec 4. In extreme NE Elmore County between Arrastra and McLeod creeks. Flows 3 mi NW and W to N Fk Boise River.

Named for a man who grazed sheep here 20 years.

Meade Peak (Bear Lake/Caribou). 9953'. T11S R45E sec 1. On the Bear Lake-Caribou county line in the NE extremity of Bear Lake County. This is the tallest peak in Bear Lake County; in Preuss Range; Caribou National Forest. Meade Basin (Caribou). Lies just E of Meade Peak in Caribou County.

Named for Civil War General George C. Meade. Formerly named Preuss Peak/Mt. Preuss for a topographer with John C. Fremont's expedition, 1842-44. Renamed for Meade in 1877.

Meadow Creek (Boundary).. T63N R2E sec 11. An early camp on the Moyie River used by David Thompson. From 1902 to 1918 it was the center of logging operations. Post office, 1913-1920.

Named for the meadow through which the stream runs.

Meadow Creek (Bingham/Caribou). T6S R42E sec 3. Rises in Blackfoot Mountains and flows some 25 mi SE into Blackfoot River Reservoir.

Named for the meadows it drains.

Meadow Creek Mountain (Bingham) 7425'. R4S R41E sec 33. In the SE extremity of the county, about 2.5 mi NE of the N tip of Blackfoot River Reservoir.

Name proposed by USGS geologist G. R. Mansfield geologist for its proximity to Meadow Creek.

Meadow Creek (Idaho). T25N R4E sec 26. Heads at the confluence of its E and W fks and flows about 7 mi generally SE to Wind River about 32 mi SSE of Grangeville; Salmon River drainage. Post office, 1866-1867. Formerly Florence City.

Named for Rhett Meadows, source of the creek.

Meadows (Adams). 3860'. T19N R2E sec 29. Town in the E part of the county 11 mi NW of McCall.

A farming and livestock community. Its early prosperity was cut short when the RR station was located about 1 1/2 mi W of this town, and many businesses moved to the RR site, called New Meadows. Post office, 1883-.

Named for the natural meadows that are crisscrossed by many streams.

Meagher Bay (Bonner). On Lake Pend Oreille, at its southern extremity.

Named for General Thomas F. Meagher, first governor of Montana.

Mearney Creek (Lemhi). T16N R14E sec 20. Heads SE of Falconberry Peak; flows SW 3 1/2 mi to enter Loon Creek; Salmon River drainage.

Informants say the creek was named for Dan McNearney (sic) or Dan McNirney (sic), a pioneer rancher and trapper of the Upper Middle Fork Valley.

Medicine Creek (Shoshone). T43N R10E sec 36. In the extreme SE part of the county; a 3-mi tributary in the headwaters of St. Joe River.

Named by Tom Buggy and his partner, thought to be the first men to locate claims on the St. Joe River. They christened the mouth of the stream Shamrock City, where they built a saloon. Reason for the name is not known.

Medicine Lake (Kootenai). T48N R2W sec 34/33. One of the 9 lakes in the area formed by overflows from floodwaters of Coeur d'Alene River. In the SE part of the county, barely separated from Cave Lake on its E.

The town of Medimont lies about 1 mi NW of the lake and serves residents and sportsmen on the lake with supplies and mail.

Named for nearby Medicine Mountain, where Indians are said to have held rituals.

Medicine Lodge Creek (Clark). Rises in the area of Bannock Pass and along the Continental Divide in the NW extremity of the county, flows SE 35 mi, and dissipates into the terrain 9 mi SW of Small. Post office, 1880. This was the home of Sam Clark, an early settler for whom the county was named; Clark went into the sheep business but sold out to Ben Hunsaker in 1889.

Named for the Indian sweat house, or medicine lodge; applied to this stream by early settlers because of the number of sweat houses found here. In 1820 it was called Cotes Defile for a French Canadian member of Donald McKenzie's party. It was part of an

Indian trail from Montana across Medicine Lodge Pass; traveled by Lt. John Mullan in 1853.

Medimont (Kootenai). 2140′. T48N R2W sec 29/28. In the S part of the county, 11 mi NE of Harrison; a supply center for ranchers, farmers, and sportsmen. Post office, 1891-.

Named for nearby Medicine Mountain.

Melakwa Creek (Benewah). T43N R1W sec 19. A 2-mi southern tributary of E Fk Charlie Creek; St. Maries River drainage. In the SE quadrant near Benewah-Latah county line.

Named by W. H. Daugs, USFS ranger, for the many mosquitoes along the stream. Melakwa is Chinook jargon for "mosquito."

Melba (Canyon). 2652′. T1N R2W sec 36. Town on the UPRR in the SE part of the county, the center of a grain area. Post office, 1912-.

Settled in 1912 as the Boise Project made water available to the area.

Named for Melba Todd, daughter of C. C. Todd, the founder.

Melder Draw (Bonner). T54N R5W sec 28. Heads 2 mi W of Pitz Mountain; extends 3/4 mi NW to a point 1 1/4 mi SE of Blanchard.

Named for an early settler.

Melville Creek (Lemhi). T17N R16E sec 21. Flows generally N 3 mi to enter W Fk Camas Creek; Middle Fk Salmon River drainage.

Bob Melville cleared the trails in this area for many years.

Memaloose Island (Bonner). T56N R1E sec 14. On E side of Lake Pend Oreille, 3 1/4 mi SE of Hope.

Named because the Kalispel Indians buried their dead on the island. The word Memaloose is Chinook jargon for "dead." Also Mam-a-Loos.

Menan (Jefferson). 4798′. T5N R38E sec 33. Below the mouth of Henrys Fork on the island between the main channel of Snake River and Dry Bed, now Great Feeder canal, of the river; an agricultural area. Post office, 1885-.

Formerly called Heals Island, Pooles Island, Cedar Butte, and Platt. In 1879 John R. Poole and Austin R. Green and their families moved to the area and formed the first LDS settlement in what is now Jefferson County. The name was changed to Menan in 1885.

Menan is reportedly a Shoshoni word that means "many waters."

Menan Buttes (Madison). 5619′/5289′. T5N R38E sec 23/22. Just E of Jefferson-Madison county line. Buttes about 3 mi apart that were landmarks to early travelers between Rexburg and Roberts.

Menan is Shoshoni for "many waters," for their location at the confluence of Henry's Fork with Snake River.

Mennecke Creek (Elmore). T1N R7E sec 23. Rises in Boise National Forest about 12 mi NE of Mountain Home and flows 2 1/2 mi NE to S Fk Boise River.

Named for early settler Henry Mennecke.

Meridian (Ada). 2607′. T3N R1W/1E sec 12/7. An incorporated town 6 mi W of Boise. Founded in 1898 as Hunter.

The first sizable building constructed here was an I.O.O.F. Lodge, known as the Meridian Lodge, for the base meridian of the Boise survey, which passed through this spot. The city incorporated in 1909 and, though the lodge burned in 1923, the name Meridian remained. Post office, 1898-.

Meridian Peak (Custer). 10,285′. T7N R18E sec 10. In the S central part of the county, 7 mi SE of Bowery Peak; Challis National Forest.

Named for its location midway between 4th and 5th Auxiliary Meridians East.

Merkley Lake (Bear Lake). T14S R44E sec 26. On the E edge of Dingle Swamp in SE part of the county.

A small lake named for a family that used to live at the S end of the lake many years ago. It has been misspelled on some maps as Meckley.

Merriam Peak (Custer). 10,920′. T8N R24E sec 10. Located .9 mi N of Castle Peak.

Named for Dr. John Hollingsworth Merriam (d. 1973), founder and first president of the Greater Sawtooth Preservation Council.

Mesa (Adams). 3234′. T15N R1W sec 15/22. Town 8 mi S of Council on US 95. Mesa was the home of one of the largest privately owned apple orchards in the world. The town originated to provide homes and services for the employees of this orchard. Post office, 1905-.

Probably named for the RR siding N of the town, which RR officials named Mesa.

Mesa Falls (Lemhi). The Upper Fall on Henrys Fork of Snake River has a drop of 114′. With an enormous volume of water plunging over its escarpment, it is one of the more impressive falls in the state. The Lower Fall, just downstream, and visible from an observation point on US 191, has a drop of 65′.

Mesa, Spanish for "table", as a place name applies to a high tableland with sharply eroded sides.

Meyers Cove (Lemhi). T17N R17E sec 6. Located 2 1/2 mi W of Meyers Cove Point, a take-off point into the River of No Return Wilderness.

Meyers Cove Point (7590′) lies 2 1/2 mi E of Meyers Cove. Post office, 1906-1924.

Named for B. F. Meyers, of Pennsylvania, who took up the land ca.1896. He also had mines on Arrastra Creek. Formerly known as Three Forks because Silver Creek, Camas Creek, and W Fk Camas Creek meet here.

Mica Creek (Shoshone). T45N R3E sec 7. In the SW part of the county. A 14-mi stream flowing from the Clearwater Mountains NE to St. Joe River 3.5 mi E of Calder.

Named by Bill Gleason for mica deposits found near the lower reaches of the creek. Gleason was a miner who later became justice of peace and postmaster at St. Joe City in 1904-05.

Mica Mountain (Latah). 4400′. T41N R2W sec 15. About 4 mi N of Avon between the headwaters of Little Sand and Big Sand creeks.

Named for the deposits of mica. The first mica mine was discovered about 30 mi from Moscow by J. T. Woody and named the Infelice; Muscovite, San Jacinto, and Lawrence mines were also located on Mica Mountain before 1892. Commercial mining continued intermittently through World War II.

Micaville. T41N R2W sec 15. A mining village that grew up around the Muscovite mica mine.

Mica Peak (Kootenai). 5241′. T49N R5W sec 4. In the SW part of the county near the Idaho-Washington line, 6 mi W of Mica on US 95.

Mica Bay, one of the more popular resort areas on Coeur d'Alene Lake, lies 1 mi S of the village, and Mica Flats lie just above the village. Post office, 1899-1928.

Named for the mica deposits in the area.

Micky Point (Clearwater). T40N R6E sec 17/20. In the NW part of the county, 8 mi SW of Canyon Ranger Station.

Micky was the first name of a timberman who worked for the Clearwater Timber Protective Association. His last name may have been Koppang.

Midas (Bonner). T56N R1W sec 22. A resort town on W side of Lake Pend Oreille, 1/2 mi W of Garfield Bay and 8 mi SE of Sandpoint.

Named for the Midas mining interest that operated in the area, 1909-1914. Midas was the name of a legendary Greek, the king with the golden touch.

Middle Creek (Clark). T11N R34E sec 24. Rises in the NW quadrant of the county in the Centennial Mountains; flows 15.5 mi generally SE to its confluence with Medicine Lodge Creek.

Middle Creek Butte. 7966'. T13N R33/34E sec 36. About midway between Dry Creek on the W and Poison Creek on the E, both tributaries of Middle Creek; in Targhee National Forest.

Named for its position midway between the main streams of Medicine Lodge and Indian creeks.

Middle Creek (Lemhi). T13N R28E sec 36. Flows S 1 1/2 mi to enter Cottonwood Creek.

This stream marks the dividing line between the Lemhi Valley and the Birch Creek Valley; hence the name.

Middle Mountains (Cassia). T14/15/16S R22E. A northerly extending prong of the Goose Creek Mountains of NW Utah and NE Nevada. They end S of Oakley about 12 mi from the Utah border.

The angular crest of the two sections attains a height above 8000', which is about 2000' above the narrow basin that separates it from Albion Mountains.

Appears as Middle Creek Southern Mountains on some maps, for its location between Junction and Goose creeks.

Middle Valley (Washington). Early name for Midvale, which see.

Middleton (Canyon). 2398'. T4N R2W sec 6/7. Town in the NE part of the county halfway between Boise and Keeneys Ferry, near the junction of Boise and Snake rivers. A prominent stopping place on the Oregon Trail; the townsite was filed in 1865, one of the older settlements in the state. Post office, 1866-.

Middleton Creek (Clearwater). T38N R6E sec 5. In the NW part of the county. A 4-mi stream that flows S into Scofield Creek; Clearwater River drainage.

Named for Art Middleton, a land commissioner for the state of Idaho.

Midvale (Washington). 2552'. T13N R3W sec 7/17. Located halfway between Weiser and Salubria valleys, on Weiser River. Formerly Middle Valley. Settlement began at this site in the 1860s and 1870s. Post office, 1871-.

Named for its location, the middle valley, contracted to Midvale in 1903.

Midway (Bingham). T1N R31E sec 3. In the NW extremity of the county.

Named because it was midway between Arco and Blackfoot; changed to Atomic City, which see, in 1950.

Midway (Jefferson). 4795'. T4N R38E sec 4. In the S part of the county, about 7 mi NW of Rigby. Settled in 1900; the West Branch of UPRR came through in 1914 and 1915.

Named for its position midway between Lewisville and Roberts.

Miesen Draw (Benewah). T46N R1W sec 13. In the NE quadrant canyon and stream, NE tributary to St. Joe River, 6 mi E of St. Maries. Post office, until 1931.

Named for the first postmaster, Larrabee R. Miesen, who homesteaded here.

Mike White Creek (Idaho). T35N R6E sec 32. In the NW part of the county, 12 mi NW of Lowell; flows SW 2 mi to Lolo Creek; Clearwater River drainage.

Named for Mike White, who had a placer mine on Lolo Creek near the mouth of this creek.

Miles Creek (Clearwater). T34N R4E sec 25. A 4-mi stream in the SW part of the county that flows NW into Jim Ford Creek; Clearwater River drainage.

Named for the Miles family, who settled near the creek.

Milk Creek (Clearwater). T41N R6E sec 28. A stream in the NW part of the county that flows 3 mi S into N Fk Clearwater River; Clearwater National Forest.

Named for the milky water, which is caused by the clay along the creek.

Milk Ranch Gulch (Boise). T5N R4E sec 24. Rims SE into Mores Creek 3 mi E of Holcomb Guard Station; Boise River drainage.

This was the site of an early dairy ranch.

Mill Canyon/Creek (Bonneville). T2N R44E sec 26. Extends 6 mi SE to NW in NW quadrant; parallel to Swan Valley on the NE. The creek flows NW to empty into Rainey Creek; Snake River drainage.

Named for the lumber mill once located in the canyon.

Mill Creek (Adams). T17N R1W sec 34. Rises on the slopes of Council Mountain and flows W 6 mi to Weiser River.

M. L. Wilkerson built the first sawmill in Council Valley on this creek in the 1880s.

Mill Creek (Bear Lake). T13S R43E sec 27. Rises 1.5 mi SE of Midnight Mountain near the W border of the county and flows 8 mi NE then SE to join North Creek to form Ovid Creek 2.5 mi NW of Ovid. Flows to the bottom of Mill Canyon.

The name comes from a sawmill on the creek in the 1890s.

Mill Creek (Fremont). T13N R43E sec 18. In N central Fremont County. Runs 3 mi SW to Henrys Fork 1 mi upstream from main body of Island Park Reservoir.

There are many old sawmill sites in this area.

Mill Creek (Lemhi). T17N R25E sec 29. Heads in vicinity of Mill Lake; flows NE 4 1/2 mi then N 1 1/2 mi then NE 4 mi to enter Lemhi River.

This creek has been the site of sawmills since the turn of the century. An informant says that Vern Tingley had the first sawmill on the creek and named it Mill Creek.

Mill Mountain (Lemhi). 10,792'. T16N R24E sec 30. In the E part of the county at the head of Mill Creek; 14 mi W of Leadore; Salmon National Forest.

Named for Mill Creek.

Miller Creek (Shoshone). T45N R5E sec 1. A 2-mi tributary of N Fk St. Joe River from the E; 1.5 mi N of Avery.

Named for Jack "Blackjack" Miller, a miner who had several prospects in this vicinity, as well as Miller mine on Loop Creek.

Miller Peak (Shoshone). 6012'. T43N R5E sec 25. In the SW part of the county; St. Joe National Forest; 13 mi S of Avery.

Named in 1932 for Gust Miller, for many years a valued employee of the St. Joe National Forest, who spent many seasons as a smoke-chaser in the vicinity of this peak.

Miller River (Bear Lake). Early name for Bear River.

Named for Joseph Miller, member of an 1811-12 trapping party credited with being the first white men to view the river.

Millers Creek (Idaho). T25N R3E sec 34. A S tributary of Little Slate Creek that flows between the headwaters of Slate and Meadow creeks; the discovery site of the Florence gold mines.

Millers Camp grew up between Miller Creek and Warren about 6 mi NE of Burgdorf. It flourished in 1866 but had disappeared by 1936 except for the recorder's office.

Named for J. M. Miller, whose first panful of dirt from the creek yielded $25 in gold. Also called Millers Gulch.

Millersburg (Idaho). T25N R3E sec 13. Early name of Florence, which see.

Milligan Gulch (Blaine). T4N R19E sec 30. Heads E of Ketchum and extends 4.5 mi S to E Fk Wood River.

Named for the Milligan mine, owned by an Irishman whose name has been lost.

Milltown (Benewah). T46N R2W sec 14. One mi NE of St. Maries.

A lumberman named Herrick built a sawmill at St. Maries on the shores of Swan Lake and used the lake waters for log storage. Milltown, named for the sawmills, was built on the adjacent low hills to the E and to the S.

Milner (Twin Falls) 4200'. T10S R21E sec 29. A village on Snake River that grew with the construction of Milner Dam; reached a population of 1500, housed partly in tents during construction days. Formerly called the Cedars

and Cedars, for the cedars growing here, the only trees for miles around. Post office, 1903-.

Named for Stanley B. Milner, a major financial backer of Magic Valley irrigation projects.

Mineral (Washington). 3500'. T14N R6W sec 9. Early mining community 19 mi W of Cambridge. Post office, 1884-1909.

Named for the minerals that brought the community into being.

Mineral Mountain (Boise). T8N R5E sec 29.

Named by the USFS. The mountain contains many different minerals.

Mineral Point (Bonner). T56N R1E sec 30. On W side of Lake Pend Oreille, 2 mi E of Garfield Bay.

Named for the copper ore that was found here.

Minerva Ridge (Bonner). T54N R1E/1W. Approximately 6 mi long and extending in a semicircle from Pack Saddle Mountain to 1/2 mi E of Lake Pend Oreille. Minerva Peak is the highest promontory on Minerva Ridge.

Named for the Minerva mine, on the W end of the ridge, T55N R1W sec 36.

Minidoka County. County seat, Rupert. Established in 1913; named directly for the first settlement, Minidoka.

The UPRR came through in 1884 and made the first permanent settlement at Minidoka, a RR siding.

Bounded on the N and E by Blaine County, on the S by Cassia County, and on the W by Elmore and Lincoln counties.

Minidoka (Minidoka). T8S R25E sec 1. The first permanent settlement in Minidoka County. Established as a siding in 1884 by the UPRR. Post office, 1883-.

The name Minidoka is undoubtedly Indian, but the exact meaning is in dispute. The UPRR made it a practice to name sidings and stations with names that are presumably Indian in order to avoid duplication with existing names. Some say Minidoka means "well, spring"; there was no source of water such as a well or spring until 1946, but there was certainly great need for both. Others say the word is Shoshoni and means "broad expanse," because the broadest portion of the Snake River Plain lies here. The latter seems more logical.

Mink Creek (Franklin). T14S R40E sec 22. Rises on the border of Franklin and Bear Lake counties; flows 15 mi SW to Bear River, 6.5 mi NE of Preston.

Mink. T14S R41E sec 6/7. Settlement in the NE quadrant of the county, on Mink Creek. Settled in 1873 by Mormons. Post office, 1878-.

The creek was named during fur-trapping days for the mink found here. The town was named for the creek.

Minneha Creek (Boise). T5N R4E sec 35. Flows 4 1/2 mi NW into Mores Creek 8 1/2 mi SW of Idaho City; Boise River drainage.

Name was once Minnehaha, but somehow the final syllable was dropped. The gulch was the site of the Minnehaha way station, operated by F. Cooper in 1863. Minnehaha is Siouan, "waterfall."

Minnetonka (Bear Lake). 7500′. T14S R43E sec 26. The most impressive of the formation caves known in the state, located in the St. Charles Canyon SW of Paris. Discovered in 1907 by a grouse hunter from Paris.

Name derived from Siouan minne "water" and tonka "big."

Mire Creek (Idaho). T37N R11E sec 18. Rises on Monroe Butte and flows 7 mi E to Gravey Creek; N Fk Clearwater system.

Named because the greater portion of the creek bottom consists of bogs.

Mirror Lake (Bonner). T56N R1W sec 30/31 and T56N R2W sec 25. Eight mi SE of Sandpoint and 6 1/2 mi NE of Cocolalla. Mirror Creek heads at Mirror Lake and flows 2 1/4 mi Lake Pend Oreille at Talache Landing.

The mile-long lake derives its name from its surface reflection.

Mirror Lake (Kootenai). T47N R1E sec 8. In the SE extremity of the county, lying somewhat between Mt. Wiessner and Twin Crags.

A descriptive name.

Mirror Lake (Lemhi). T21N R16E sec 15. In Bighorn Crags, about 3/4 mi S of Big Clear Lake.

The lake reflects the trees and mountain peaks surrounding it.

Mission Creek (Lewis). T32N R3W sec 14. Rises 9 mi SW of Winchester and flows to Lapwai Creek in T34N R3W sec 20 in Nez Perce County; Clearwater River drainage. Forms boundary line between Lewis and Nez Perce counties beginning 3.3 mi W of Winchester for approximately 7 mi; leaves Lewis County 1 mi N of St. Josephs Mission. Approximate length 24 mi.

Takes its name from St. Joseph's Mission.

Mission Falls (Bonner). T59N R5W sec 36. Located 3 1/4 mi NW of Whitetail Butte and 3 1/2 mi N of Cottonwood Lookout.

Named for the headquarters of the 19th-century Jesuit missionaries on Kalispell Bay.

Mission Flats (Kootenai). T49N R1W/1E sec 25/30, 29, 32. On the Coeur d'Alene River just W of Cataldo Mission.

The name was proposed by the USFS and gave rise to the name Mission

Gulch, which runs 1.5 mi NE to SW at the E end of the flats.

Mission Point (Benewah). T44N R1W. The original site of the Catholic Mission of the Sacred Heart of Jesus, earliest in Idaho, established by Father Nicholas Point, S.J., and Bro. Charles Huets; 7 mi below St. Maries on the N side of the river near Santa.

Mission Mountain 4324'. T43N R5W sec 15. Lies at the head of Mission Creek in McCroskey State Park, overlooking DeSmet Mission 5 mi N.

Mission Spring (Latah). T40N R5W sec 17. On the early Nez Perce Trail between Lapwai and Spokane 4 mi N of Moscow on the E side of US 95.

This was a customary stopping place between mission stations; the Protestant missionaries, Spalding, Whitman, Gray, Eels, Walker, and others traveled this route, 1836-48, and stopped at the spring. Father Cataldo recorded a meeting here with Spalding in 1864.

Missouri Flat (Latah). T40N R6W sec 35/36 to R5W sec 19/30/31. An area 2 mi by 2 1/2 mi W of US 95 and 1 1/2 mi N of Moscow. Drained by Missouri Flat Creek, 14 mi long and flowing SW to S Fk Palouse River at Pullman, Washington.

Settled in the 1880s and 1890s by Missourians.

Missouri Gulch (Lemhi). T21N R19E sec 12. Stream 1/2 mi long; runs SE to enter Napias Creek drainage, just SW of California Bar; Salmon River drainage.

Prospectors from Missouri owned placer claims here.

Missouri Ridge (Lewis). T34N R2W sec 7. Ridge in the general area of 4 mi N of Winchester.

A transfer name from the state of Missouri, given by settlers who came from there. Many of the area's early homesteaders after 1895 came from Missouri.

Mitchell (Bingham). 4640'. T1N R37E sec 21/28. A farming area in the NE part of the county, 1 mi NE of Shelley.

Named for James Mitchell, Sr., who came to Bingham County in 1887 and homesteaded 320 acres; he was one of the builders of Cedar Point irrigation canal.

Mitchell Creek (Lewis). T33N R2W sec 17. Rises about 2 mi SE of Nezperce and flows E to Lawyer Creek, T33N R2E sec 13; Clearwater River drainage. Approximate length, 4 mi.

Named for the Henry Mitchell family, landowners.

Mizpah Creek (Latah). T42N R1W sec 19. Flows 3 mi S to Palouse River; in the Hoodoo Mining District.

Named by Edd. F. Helmers for the Mizpah mine, a lode mine located on the upper end of this stream.

Moe Lake (Idaho). T32N R15E sec 23. In the extreme E part of the county in the Bitterroot Range; Nezperce National Forest, 4 mi W of the Montana line. Moe Peak lies 1 mi S.

Named for Martin Moe, who homesteaded at the mouth of Running Creek on Selway River and trapped in the vicinity.

Mogg Creek (Lemhi). T16N R23E sec 21. Originates near Mogg Mountain; flows N 3 mi to enter W Fk Hayden Creek; Lemhi River drainage. Mogg Mountain (10,573') is in the Lemhi Range, 2 1/2 mi SW of Mill Mountain and 6 1/2 mi SE of Hi Peak.

Frederick W. Mogg homesteaded land near here and also patented land in the Lemhi Valley in 1917.

Moh, Mount (Bannock). 6245'. T9S R38E sec 27. One mi S of Lava Hot Springs. Noted for its building stone, said by engineers to be light and hard.

Named for Friedrich Mohs (1773-1839), a German mineralogist who developed the Mohs scale, in which the hardness of a mineral is determined by its ability to scratch or be scratched by specific minerals.

Mohler (Lewis). 3300′. T34N R1E sec 24. Town 8 mi NW of Nezperce. The village began in 1889 with a general store and prospered until 1908, when the RR established a station at Nezperce. Pronounced MOLE-er. Post office, in the name of Hanlon, for Thomas Hanlon, 1898. Renamed Mohler in 1900.

Named for President A. L. Mohler of the Oregon RR and Navigation Company, who investigated the possibility of a RR passage up Little Canyon to Grangeville.

Mollies Gulch (Lemhi). T16N R25E sec 11. Heads SW of Little Eightmile Creek; runs SW 4 mi to enter Lemhi River drainage.

Named for Mollie Yearian, whose family owned a large amount of land in this area.

Monazite Gulch (Boise). T6N R4E sec 13. Runs SW to Grimes Creek 2 1/2 mi S of Centerville; Boise River drainage.

Named for the monazite (a mineral) found in its water.

Monida Pass (Clark). 6823′. T14N R35E sec 11. In the N part of the county on the Montana-Idaho line; US 91, I-15, and UPRR.

A blend name, combining Montana and Idaho.

Monroe Butte (Clearwater). 6513′. T37N R10E sec 17. Twelve mi S of Kelly Forks Ranger Station. Monroe Creek rises on Monroe Butte (6513′) and flows 9 mi NE into Cayuse Creek; Clearwater River drainage; Clearwater National Forest. Monroe Lake lies near the headwaters of this stream, 12 mi S of Kelly Forks Ranger Station.

Named for Roy Monroe, a USFS ranger who was the Cook Mountain ranger 1912- 1913.

Monroe Creek (Washington). T11N R5W sec 28. Rises in the mountains W of Midvale and flows generally S and SE 20 mi to Mann Creek, at the town of Weiser; Weiser River drainage. Monroe Butte is located at the head of Monroe Creek, 20 mi N of Weiser.

Named for John Monroe Phillips, an 1880s pioneer who preferred to be called Jack Monroe.

Montana Canyon (Lemhi). T12N R29E sec 3. Heads S of Eighteenmile Peak; runs S 2 1/4 mi to enter Willow Creek drainage.

Named because of its closeness to the Idaho-Montana border.

Monte Verita (Boise). 9000′. T9N R12E sec 34. Mountain in Boise National Forest about.5 mi SE of Warbonnet Peak and about 19 mi NNE of Atlanta.

Named for a fictional mountain in a Daphne DuMaurier novel; the USFS feels that name is not out of place because of the variety of names in the area. Monte Verita means Mount Truth.

Monteview (Jefferson). 4805′. T8N R33E sec 32. A stock-raising and farming area irrigated by wells in the NW part of the county, 8 mi NW of Mud Lake. Post office, 1915-.

Named by Mabel E. Ellis, postmaster, because the settlement has an excellent view of the distant Gilmore Mountains.

Montour (Gem). 2508′. T7N R2E sec 22/27. Town situated on Payette River and the UPRR in the SE part of the county, 7 mi W of Horseshoe Bend. Formerly Marsh. Post office, 1912-.

The valley was first used as a range for livestock. Then when the RR came in 1912, the townsite was platted by Col. William Dewey, Jr., on the old Edson Marsh-John Ireton ranch, an 1860 way station for Boise Basin traffic.

Named by the secretary of Colonel Wm. Dewey, who thought the word expressed the magnificent view from this point. However, the word in French means "a frame" or "a setting".

Montpelier (Bear Lake). 5941'. T13S R44E sec 4/3. In the central part of the county, 5 1/2 mi NE of Ovid; on US 30 and State 89. Montpelier Creek rises 8 mi E of town and flows 9 mi to empty into Bear River SW of the town and is an important tributary to the Bear Lake-Bear River irrigation and power project.

Settled in 1864 by a group of Latter-day Saints, including the first bishop, John Cozzens. Post office, 1873-.

Named by Brigham Young for the capital of his native state, Vermont.

Monument Gulch (Lemhi). T25N R21E sec 29. Approximately 1 mi long; runs directly S to Hull Creek drainage; N Fk Salmon River drainage.

Named for a natural spiral rock formation about 30' high, which looks like a monument.

Monument Mountain (Kootenai). 5101'. T51N R1W sec 34.

The name refers to a number of Indian rock piles and a USGS monument on this summit; named in 1917.

Monument Peak (Adams). 8957'. T22N R2W sec 22. At the S end of the Seven Devils in the Hells Canyon National Recreation Area.

The highest point in Payette National Forest, it is a rugged lava outcrop that looks like a monument.

Monument Peak (Lemhi). 10,323'. T22N R23E sec 2. Located 1 mi SW of Freeman Peak, near the head of E Fk Kirtley Creek on the Montana border.

Originally called McGarvey Peak after John McGarvey, who came to the Lemhi Valley from Bannock, Montana. Renamed for its resemblance to a large monument.

Monumental Creek (Valley). T21N R11E sec 17. Rises between Monumental Summit and Murphy Peak (9288') in the River of No Return Wilderness and flows 23 mi generally NE to Big Creek; Middle Fk Salmon River.

Named for the rock formation at the head of the creek, a 70' column only 3' in diameter at its base and with a large boulder resting on top of the column. The formation was named Monumental Summit and the stream Monumental Creek.

Moody Island (Bonner). On E side of Lake Pend Oreille, near Hope.

Named for Z. F. Moody, the builder of the first steamboat on the lake.

Moolock Creek (Benewah). T43N R2W sec 13. A 3-mi stream that flows S to E Fk Charlie Creek; In the SE quadrant just N of Benewah-Latah county line; St. Maries River drainage.

Named by USFS ranger W. H. Daugs in 1932, for the only elk Daugs ever saw in the Palouse Ranger District. Moolock is Chinook jargon for "elk."

Moon Hill (Latah). 3145'. T41N R3W sec 16. Promontory just W of Flat Creek and about 2 mi SE of Harvard.

Named for John Moon, who owned the area 1 mi N of the hill.

Moore (Butte). 5472'. T5N R26E sec 28. An incorporated city in the W part of the county 6 mi S of Darlington. On US 93 and UPRR.

Founded in the early 1880s as a livestock area. Post office, 1901-.

Named for the first postmaster and owner of the townsite.

Moore Creek (Bonner). T57N R5W sec 5. Heads 1/2 mi S of Gleason Ranger

Station; flows 6 mi S into Lower W Branch of Priest River 9 1/2 mi NNW of the town of Priest River. Also Moores Creek.

Named for the Moore family, who settled near the creek.

Moores Lake (Idaho). T26N R4E sec 1. One of the Gospel Mountain Lakes; about 20 acres, formerly used as a storage reservoir. Moores Creek rises on the E slope of Buffalo Hump and flows 7 mi NE through Moores Lake to Johns Creek; S Fk Clearwater River drainage; Big Moores Creek, 5 mi long, is the main tributary of Moores Creek from the S.

Named for Charley Moore, who ran a way station near the lake during the Buffalo Hump gold boom of the 1890s.

Moose Creek (Clearwater). T39N R11E sec 16. Rises on Moose Creek Buttes and flows 6 mi SE into Kelly Creek; Clearwater River drainage. Model Mountain (6602'), formerly Moose Mountain, lies at the head of Moose Creek, 5 mi NW of Kelly Forks Ranger Station.

Moose Mountains trend NE to SW about 8 mi and lie at the headwaters of the creek 5 mi NW of Kelly Forks Ranger Station; they include the butte and mountain just named.

Named for the number of moose in the area. Old Moose City was named first and the name was later transferred to geographic features.

Moose Creek (Fremont). T14N R44E sec 32. Runs 6 mi NW to Henrys Fork SW of Moose Creek Plateau; Henrys Fork system.

Moose Creek. T10N R44E sec 16. Flows 5 mi S to Warm River 8 mi N of Warm River community; Warm River drainage.

The second Moose Creek described was named by Dr. F. V. Hayden of the US Geological Survey Expedition of 1872 for the numerous moose observed.

Moose Creek (Teton). T3N R46E sec 19. Rises in Moose Lake, Wyoming, and flows W and NW to empty into Teton River.

Named by USGS surveyor Dr. F. V. Hayden in 1872 for the abundance of moose in the area.

Moose Creek (Lemhi). T24N R20E sec 34/27. Heads near headwaters of Daly Creek, about 2 mi SW of Racetrack Meadows; runs generally N about 9 mi to enter Salmon River.

Named for the moose and old moose antlers found in the area.

Moose Meadow (Latah). 3115'. Tr1N R1W sec 15/16/20/21. Located N of Moose Creek and W of Potlatch River in the Collins-Purdue area.

This meadow is drained by Moose Creek, 7 mi long and flowing SE to Potlatch River.

Named for the moose transplanted from Yellowstone National Park to this area.

Mora (Ada). 2760'. T1N R1E sec 4. Former UPRR station, about 4 mi SE of Kuna. Post office, 1909-1918.

Mora is said to be an Indian word meaning "mule."

Moran Creek (Blaine). T3N R19E sec 10. Rises 9 mi SE of Ketchum and flows 2 mi NE to Cove Creek; E Fk Wood River drainage.

Named for Joe Moran, a pioneer cattleman in the area.

Moreland (Bingham). 4465'. T2S R34E sec 26. In the central part of the county, 7 mi NW of Blackfoot; formerly Keever. Post office, 1916-.

A new name was suggested by John England, one of the first settlers in 1894, because he found more land available for homesteading here than elsewhere.

Mores Creek (Boise). T4N R4E sec 33. Rises in the SE part of the county on the W slope of Mores Creek Summit and flows SW into Boise River 3 mi N of Lucky Peak State Park; Boise River drainage. An important mining area, 1862-1866. Mores Mountain (7237') is 12 mi NW of the mouth of Mores Creek.

Named for J. Marion More, a mine owner in this area in the 1860s. He was murdered in Silver City in 1868 as the result of a dispute over a mining venture.

Morgan Creek (Lemhi). T15N R21E sec 15. Forms just SW of Red Point; flows 4 mi S, where it disperses into several smaller branches that enter the Pahsimeroi River.

There are two sources for this name: George E. Morgan lived about 1 1/2 mi E of Morgan Creek Canyon and sold vegetables to the first settlers in this vicinity; John Morgan ranched on this creek and took the first water from the stream to irrigate his land.

Morgan Mountain (Lemhi). T25N R22E sec 3. On the Idaho-Montana border at the head of Dahlonega Creek.

Named for Morgan Jones, a Welsh miner who mined in Pennsylvania, Colorado, and New Mexico and served as a scout for the Santa Fe RR during its construction before coming to Gibbonsville in 1888 to mine. During the boom years of the camp he was known as the "Silver King."

Morgans Gulch (Clearwater). T38N R7E sec 11. Trends 4 mi E into N Fk Clearwater River near Castle Rock.

A man named Morgan had a timber claim along the gulch.

Mormon Canyon (Bannock). T9S R35/36E sec 13/18,7,8. In the SW quadrant of the county, in Caribou National Forest. Trends from SW to NE

and ends in Goodenough Creek; about 4 mi long.

Named for Mormon settlers who came to the area in the 1870s and 1880s.

Mormon Canyon (Lemhi). T18N R23E sec 4. Heads at Bull Spring; runs NE 2 1/2 mi to McDevitt Creek drainage 1 mi E of the mouth of Sawmill Canyon; Lemhi River drainage.

Mormon prospectors had a mine in this canyon, ca. 1870.

Mormon Mountain (Valley). 9545'. T19N R13E sec 4. On the line between Salmon and Payette national forests. It overlooks Middle Fk Salmon River and Mormon Ranch on the E side.

Named for Mormon settlers in the area.

Mormon Ranch (Lemhi). T19N R14E sec 34. On Middle Fk Salmon River, about 1/2 mi S of Bernard Bridge Ranch.

A Mormon, George T. Broadbent, owned the ranch and supplied vegetables, which were very scarce in 1900, to miners and residents of Thunder Mountain.

Morris Creek (Bonner). T56N R3E sec 7. Heads at Goat Mountain; flows 1 mi NE, then 2 1/4 mi NW into Lightning Creek 6 mi NNE of Clark Fork.

The creek was first given the name Blind Creek by Sam Morris because it disappears underground. It was later renamed for him.

Morris Creek (Clearwater). T40N R2E sec 3. Rises on the N slope of Shattuck Butte and flows 3 mi E into Elk Creek 4 mi N of the town of Elk River; Clearwater River drainage.

Named for Bill Morris, who cut cedar in the area and rafted it down the river.

Morrissey (Latah). T41N R3W sec 6. RR siding on WIM about 1 mi W of Harvard.

Named for J. D. Morrissey, superintendent of the WIMRR and owner of

160 acres adjoining the siding. Morrissey's land is drained by Morrissey Creek, 2 mi long and flowing N to Palouse River.

Morrow (Lewis). 4140'. T32N R2W sec 12. Abandoned town 1/2 mi from the county line and 1.2 mi from Westlake, Idaho County. The town was first exploited by W. L. Thompson, postmaster and M.B. Morrow's trustee. Post office, 1905.

Named for M. B. Morrow, sheep-raiser, who filed a preemption claim on this site. Also called Morrowtown.

Morse Creek (Lemhi). T14N R22E sec 5. Forms just S of Mogg Mountain in the Lemhi Range; flows SW 11 mi then SE 2 mi and seems to dissipate in sec 5.

Morse, Post office, 1889-1905.

One informant says the creek was named for B. F. Morse, rancher, another that it was named for J. E. Morris, who built the first ditch taking water out of this stream.

Morton (Bonner). 1300'. T56N R3W sec 15. This farming community lies between the towns of Priest River and Sandpoint. Morton Slough, a sluggish, marshy stream, heads 3 1/4 mi N of Morton and flows 1 1/4 mi SW into Pend Oreille River. Post office, 1907.

Named for George Morton, a settler.

Moscow (Latah). 2600'. T39N R5W sec 18/8. County seat; in the SW quadrant of Latah County in the heart of the Palouse country; home of the University of Idaho; center of the Northern Idaho pea industry. Pronounced mahs-koe.

Almon Asbury Lieuallen, the first permanent settler and founder of the town, arrived in 1871. Nez Perce Indians had called the place Tat-Kin-Mah "place of the spotted deer." When Lieuallen came it was called Hog Heaven, for the roots of the camas that had earlier furnished food for the Nez Perce and would now furnish food for hogs. Then in 1873 a post office was granted as Paradise Valley.

Named for Moscow, Pennsylvania, and Moscow, Iowa, first home towns of S.M. Neff, who completed the post office application. Moscow is from the Finnic tongue signifying "place for washing"; the term means "to wash clothes."

Moscow Bar (Clearwater). T40N R8E sec 29. About one third the SE part of this township; including a mountain and a ridge of the same name; about 8 mi SE of Canyon Ranger Station.

People from Moscow, Idaho, staked out mining claims on the bar and the name of the town of Moscow was transferred to the mining location.

Moscow Gulch (Latah). T42N R2W sec 1. Eighth of the 10 named gulches running parallel to each other and emptying into N Fk Palouse River from the N; St. Joe National Forest. Named for and by the early prospectors in the area who were originally from Moscow. See Banks Gulch.

Moscow Mountain (Latah). 5000'. T40N R4W sec 9/17. The highest peak in the Palouse Range, locally called Moscow Mountains, about 8 mi NE of Moscow.

Moscow Mountains (Latah). Local name for Palouse Range, formerly Thatuna Hills, which see. A range of low-lying promontories N of Moscow, extending E about 15 mi, with maximum width of 8 mi. Clearly visible from Moscow.

Moses Creek (Clearwater). T41N R12E sec 30. Rises on the Bitterroot Mountains and flows W into Goose Creek; Clearwater River drainage.

Named for a Nez Perce Indian called Moses.

Mosquito Creek (Clearwater). T35N R5E sec 23. In the SW extremity of the county; flows 3 mi SE into Jim Brown Creek at sec 23; 5 mi E of Weippe; Clearwater River drainage.

Named because of the many mosquitoes at a CCC camp near the creek.

Mosquito Creek (Idaho). T33N R7E sec 11.

Lewis and Clark so named this stream because the area was infested with swarms of mosquitos (1806). Now, Canyon Creek.

Moss (Canyon). T3N R2W sec 8. A community about midway between Caldwell and Nampa on US 30.

Named for A. B. Moss, a local rancher.

Moughmer Point (Idaho). 4163'. T30N R1W sec 14. A promontory in NW Idaho County, Nezperce National Forest, 8 mi SW of Cottonwood.

The Moughmer family had a ranch here, running their cattle on Joseph and Doumecq plains. They built a ferry across Salmon River at Keuterville, 6 mi N of their ranch, to transport their herds across the river to new pastures.

Moulton (Cassia). T16S R23E sec 21/27. In the S part of the county, at the confluence of Junction and Cottonwood creeks. Post office, 1910-1930.

Named for the first postmaster.

Mount Bennett Hills (Elmore/Camas/Gooding). T1/2S R7-14. Beginning with Bennett Mountain (7465') and Teapot Dome (4712') NE of Mountain Home, Elmore County, and extending about 50 mi E into Gooding and Camas counties. Mormon Reservoir and Thorn Creek mark the E boundary.

Named for Dick and Fred Bennett, sheepmen in the early 1900s.

Mount Deary Creek (Latah). T40N R2W sec 21. Rises at 4017' on Potato Hill (at one time locally called Mt. Deary) and flows 3 mi SW to Big Bear Creek (2611'); Potlatch River drainage.

Named for the promontory.

Mount Idaho (Idaho). 3649'. T30N R3E sec 28/27. 4 mi SE of Grangeville; the first settlement on the road from Lewiston to the Florence mines was made at the foot of a mountain by this name and named for it in 1862 by Loyal P. Brown, the first postmaster. A famous hotel was built here by Brown, and the little town became the county seat in 1865, to be replaced by Grangeville in 1902. Post office, 1863-1922.

Mountain Gulch (Latah). T42N R2W sec 1. Northernmost of the 10 named gulches (all listed under Banks Gulch), running somewhat parallel to each other and emptying into N Fk Palouse River from the N; St. Joe National Forest.

Named from its proximity to Bald and Little Bald mountains, which it lies between.

Mountain Home (Elmore). T3S R6E sec 25. County seat. In the SW corner of the county.

Mountain Home was originally a station for the old Overland Stage Line; called Rattlesnake for Rattlesnake Creek, on which it was located. Then Mrs. John Lemmon, wife of the first postmaster and district agent of the stage line, changed the name to Mountain Home, as it was a home to travelers and was located in the mountains. The UPRR came through in 1883. J. A. Tutwiler, stagecoach driver, set up a tent town for construction workers on the RR and called it Tuttville. Post office, 1875-.

Mountain Home (Latah). T43N R5W sec 35. Pioneer community 3 mi S of

SE corner of McCroskey State Park, 7 mi N of Potlatch.

Named before 1900 for its location near the mountains forming the northern boundary of the county.

Moyer Creek (Lemhi). T20N R18E sec 35. Forms just W of Iron Lake; flows N 3 mi, W 3 mi, and then N 5 mi to enter Panther Creek; Salmon River drainage. Moyer Basin lies between Moyer and Panther creeks at the head of Treloar Gulch. Moyer Peak (8681') is situated 3 mi E of the creek about 3 mi SW of Swan Peak and 2 mi NW of Squawboard Meadow.

Named for an old prospector, Charles Moyer, who was killed in a gambling dispute and was supposedly buried on the E side of Moyer Creek in 1900.

Moyie River (Boundary). T62N R2E sec 22. Flows through a spectacular canyon; located in NE corner of the county; empties into Kootenai River 9 mi E of Bonners Ferry. Moyie Falls, on Moyie River, visible from the bridge on US 2.

Moyie Springs. T62N R2E sec 10/11. Resort town 9 mi E of Bonners Ferry on US 2 at the mouth of Moyie River. This site was mentioned in David Thompson's Journal in 1811 and was maintained as a trappers' camp from 1832 to 1850. Post office, 1920-.

Moyie Valley is drained by Moyie River.

Moyie is a transfer name from British Columbia and stems from the name of a quartz.

Mud Creek (Twin Falls). T9S R14E sec 11. In the N part of the county. Rises 2.5 mi S of Buhl and flows 10 mi generally NNW to empty into Snake River.

Mudbarville, an 1870 gold mining settlement, grew up at the mouth of this stream on Snake River.

Named for the muddy stream.

Mud Lake (Bear Lake). T15S R44E sec 3/4/9/10/11. A triangle-shaped lake just N of Bear Lake within Dingle Swamp. It is connected with Bear Lake by an artificial channel and now serves with Bear Lake as a storage reservoir for the Bear River-Bear Lake irrigation and power project. About 4 square miles.

Named for the muddy shore.

Mud Lake (Jefferson). T6/7N R34/35E. Lake in the NW quadrant of the county resulting from a perched water table; fed by Camas Creek and with no natural outlet.

In 1864 this lake at high water did not cover more than a few hundred acres and practically dried up by late summer. Irrigation started on Egin Bench in 1895 raised the water table at Mud Lake, which was used for irrigation. In the 1920s the water level became alarmingly low, so wells were drilled to increase the storage capacity of Mud Lake and make more irrigation water available to W Jefferson County.

Named by early cattlemen for the muddy water available to their herds in late summer.

Mud Lake. 4270'. T6N R34E sec 17/21. A community 1 mi W of Terreton and 2.5 mi SW of the lake for which it is named.

Mud Springs (Lewis). 4110'. T33N R2W sec 16. On the W side of the base of Mason Butte, 4 mi SE of Winchester. Mud Springs Reservoir (4050') is located .6 mi S of Mud Springs.

Named for the boggy springs in the vicinity by the Colwell brothers, who drove cattle through this meadow area in the early 1900s.

Muldoon (Blaine). 6000'. T2N R21E sec 3. Ghost town in the central part of the county on the upper reaches of Muldoon Creek, 17 mi E of Bellevue.

At its peak, Muldoon had a population of 1500, but the settlement lasted only 5-6 years. Post office, 1882-ca.1934.

Muldoon Creek (Blaine). T2N R20E sec 22. Rises on Muldoon Ridge near the NE of the Custer-Blaine county line and flows 15 mi SW to Little Wood River 3 mi N of Little Wood River Reservoir.

Muldoon Ridge. T3/4N R21/22E. Low-lying promontories extending 5 mi N to S with Scorpion Mountain (10,545') near the N end and Smelter Butte marking the S end. Source of Muldoon Creek.

All Muldoon names transferred from the Muldoon mine, which in turn was named for a champion wrestler of the period.

Mule Creek (Valley). T16N R11E sec 19. Rises 2 mi N of Thunder Mountain and flows 1 1/2 mi NW to empty into Monumental Creek; Middle Fk Salmon River drainage. One mi N of Dewey mine.

Named for the lost mule the Caswell brothers were looking for when they made the original gold discovery in the Thunder Mountain Mining District. See Monumental Creek.

Muleshoe Spring (Lemhi). T26N R19E sec 32. Near the Idaho-Montana border.

An old mule shoe hanging in a tree near this spring led to the name.

Mulkey Creek (Lemhi). T21N R23E sec 30. Heads 1 mi N of the headwaters of Tenmile Creek; flows N 4 mi then NE 1 mi to the Lemhi River drainage.

Named for Elijah Mulkey, who with F. B. Sharkey, Joe Rapp, Ward Girton, and Bill Smith, came from what is now Deer Lodge, Montana, to find gold at Leesburg in 1866.

Mulkey Mountain (Lemhi). T24N R22E sec 14. Between the head of N Fk Tower Creek on the S and Fourth of July Creek on the N.

Daniel Johanna Mulcihy patented a ranch at the foot of the mountain in 1910.

Mulcihy was confused with Mulkey, a common name in the area, hence the name Mulkey Mountain.

Mulkey Slough (Lemhi). T20N R23E sec 11. Crosses State 28 about 1 1/2 mi SE of Baker.

William Leytner Mulkey, sheriff of Lemhi County 1907-09, purchased the ranch here from I. Johnson about 1875.

Mullan (Shoshone). 3276'. T48N R5E sec 27/26/34/35. In the E part of the county, on I-90, NPRR, and S Fk Coeur d'Alene River; 5 mi E of Wallace. A mining camp, located in 1884 on the military road built by Lt. John Mullan, grew near the gold, silver, and lead mines. The town was platted in 1888 and named for John Mullan. In 1889 the NPRR built a station here and named it Ryan for a RR official, but the citizens preferred the name Mullan. Post office, 1886-.

Murphy (Owyhee). 2768'. T2S R2W sec 27. County seat. Located 14 mi NE of Silver City. The South Alternate of the Oregon Trail passed through this townsite.

In 1891 cattle raisers established the town and in 1892 the UPRR built a branch line to transport livestock and bring in supplies. Murphy replaced Silver City as the county seat in 1934. Post office, 1899-.

Named at the time the railroad was completed in 1892. Locally, it is believed the name honors Pat Murphy, an engineer with a mining company at Silver

City and a personal friend of Col. William Dewey, the motivator for building the railroad.

Murray (Shoshone). 2880'. T49N R5E sec 6. In the E part of the county, 10 mi NNE of Wallace; on Prichard Creek; a gold-silver mining area. The village was laid out in 1884 and named Curry, then Murraysville, for George Murray, a miner and part owner of one of the claims on which the town was built. In 1885 the name had been shortened to Murray and the town was made county seat of Shoshone County. Post office, 1884-.

Murray Peak (5934') overlooks the town from the N.

Murtaugh (Twin Falls). 4630'. T11S R20E sec 6. In the NE part of the county on US 30, 16 mi E of Twin Falls. Drytown formerly occupied this site following the discovery of gold on Snake River in 1869. Jack Fuller, cattleman, homesteaded on Dry Creek S of Murtaugh, and Henry Shodde, a cattleman, above Starrhs Ferry. Post office, 1905-ca.1930.

Murtaugh Lake. Three mi SE of the town of Murtaugh, 2 mi long.

Named for Mark Murtaugh, assistant superintendent of construction of the South Side Irrigation Project.

Musgrove Creek (Lemhi). T20N R18E sec 35. Heads near the headwaters of Big Deer Creek, SW of Blackbird Mountain; flows SE approximately 8 mi to enter Panther Creek; Salmon River drainage.

Named for Major H. P. Musgrove, a Civil War veteran and an early miner in this region.

Mush Saddle (Clearwater). T39N R9E sec 5/6. In the NE part of the county, 5 mi NW of Kelly Forks Ranger Station. Mush Lake is 7 mi NW of Kelly Forks Ranger Station, and Mush Point, 6 mi.

A party camped in the area ran very low on food. Because they had mainly mush to eat, they began to call their camp Mush Camp; eventually the name was applied to the saddle and then other nearby features.

Muskrat Lake (Bonner). T57N R3W sec 35. Located 3 3/4 mi NE of Morton and 3 mi W of Dover.

Named for the muskrats seen near this lake.

Musselshell Creek (Clearwater). T34N R6E sec 6. In the SE part of the county, rises 5 mi SE of Pierce and flows 10 mi SE into Lolo Creek; Clearwater River drainage.

Named for the freshwater mussels found in the creek. Nez Perce Indians named the creek for the food found here, and the name was translated into English and kept.

Mutton Gulch (Clearwater). T36N R5E sec 11. Flows N into Orofino Creek 1 mi SE of Orofino; Clearwater River drainage.

There are four possible origins of the name. The name may have come from the slaughtering of sheep to supply meat for Pierce residents (1860s). The driveway in taking sheep to the summer range was near here. The population of Oro Fino exceeded that of Pierce by June of 1861, and the Pierce nickname for Oro Fino was Muttonville. A man and his wife named Button ran a restaurant at the mouth of the creek in the early days of Oro Fino; their name was given to the gulch but time corrupted the name of Button to Mutton.

Myers Cove (Lemhi). Early mining town and post office, 1906-1928.

Named for a man from Pittsburgh, Pennsylvania, who financed a local mining property.

Myers Creek (Idaho). T26N R10E sec 28. Rises in the River of No Return Wilderness and flows 5 mi SE to the Salmon River 1.5 mi W of Bargamin Creek.

Named for Sam Myers, veteran of the Civil War campaign with General Sherman in Georgia. He placer mined and kept a herd of horses here for 40 years.

Myrtle Creek (Boundary). T62N R2W sec 32. Flows N and E to Deep Creek at T62N R1W sec 24; Kootenai River drainage.

Named for the wild periwinkle, locally called myrtle, growing in the area.

N

Naf (Cassia). T16S R27E sec 22/27. A Mormon community in the SE part of the county, 4 mi W of Strevell 1 mi N of the Utah-Cassia county line; on Clear Creek. Post office, 1898-.

Named for early settler, farmer, and first postmaster of the community, John Naf.

Nahneke Mountain (Elmore). 9578'. T7N R11E sec 35. In Boise National Forest, W part of Sawtooth Wilderness 6 1/2 mi N of Atlanta, between Queen and Little Queen rivers.

Shoshoni Indian word for "swaybacked," descriptive of the top of this mountain.

Nakarna Mountain (Benewah). 4995'. T43N R1W sec 20. In St. Joe National Forest 1 mi N of the Benewah-Latah county line.

The US Geographic Names Board chose the name arbitrarily. This feature is a high, prominent point and Nakarna is a Clatsop Indian word for "The Great Spirit Mountain."

Nampa (Canyon). 2484'. T3N R2W sec 22/27. The largest city in Canyon County. Located on Indian Creek, US 30, UPRR.

Nampa began in 1885 when developer and first postmaster Alexander Duffes filed on land that includes the present site of Nampa.

The town incorporated in 1890. Post office, 1887-.

Once called New Jerusalem. Its official name, Nampa, derives from the name of a renegade Shoshoni, so-called Namp "foot", Puh "big."

Nanny Creek (Elmore). T7N R12E sec 31. In W extremity of Sawtooth Wilderness Area, 6 mi N of Atlanta. Flows 1 mi NW to Queen River.

Two female mountain goats were killed at the head of this stream.

Napias Creek (Lemhi). T21N R19E sec 21. Forms 1 mi W of Wallace Lake; flows 10 mi SW to enter Panther Creek 1 mi N of Leacock Point; Salmon River drainage.

Believed to be a Shoshoni Indian word that means "money." Discoverers of placer gold in 1866 at Leesburg named this creek for the rich strike.

Naples (Lincoln). T5/65 R17E sec 35/2. Early name for Shoshone, which see. Earlier Bottoms, which the UPRR officials changed to Naples in 1882, and to Shoshone in 1883. Established as a construction camp by the RR in 1882. Post office, 1882-.

Naples (Boundary). 2031'. T60N R1E/1W sec 7/12. Town on US 95 and US 2 in southern Boundary Co., 12 mi S of Bonners Ferry and 22 mi N of Sandpoint; a farming, livestock, and lumber area; uranium deposits E of Naples. Post office, 1892-1913.

Named by the Italians working as construction crews on the GNRR in 1892 for Naples, Italy.

Napo Canyon (Lemhi). T18N R24E sec 16. Heads 1 mi N of Ramsey Mountain; runs generally W 2 mi to Lemhi River drainage. Pronounced NAP-o.

An old Indian called Napo lived here and reportedly planted some apple trees in this area ca.1890.

Napoleon Gulch (Lemhi). T24N R21E sec 35. Forms near the head of Sawmill Gulch; runs NE 3 mi to enter Salmon River drainage. Napoleon Hill (7433') is at the head of Napoleon Gulch. Napo-

leon Ridge runs N and S for about 2 mi and at the head of Maxwell, Bobcat, and Napoleon gulches.

Named for Napoleon LaVarre, an early settler in this area, ca.1880.

Nashville (Franklin). T16S R40E sec 8. In the S part of the county, just N of Franklin.

A small agricultural community settled by Preston Thomas and James Packer, later a presiding elder, in 1877 and named for Nashville, Tennessee.

Nat Brown Creek (Latah). T41N R1E sec 18. Rises between Collins and Bovill and flows 3.2 mi SW to W Fk Potlatch River.

Named for Nat Brown, son of C. O. Brown, lumberman and discoverer of the white pine timber stands in Latah County. The younger Brown was a timber cruiser, homesteader, operator of a sawmill, agent of the Clearwater Timber Company (1902-08), and president of Clearwater Timber Protective Association. The creek runs through his homestead.

Nat-Soo-Pah Warm Spring (Twin Falls). T12S R17E sec 31. In the central part of the county, 3.5 mi E of Hollister and 15 mi S of Twin Falls.

The name is reputedly an Indian word meaning "health" or "life-giving water." Its use in this form dates from 1892. Not Nah Supah Hot Spring, Natsoopah Springs.

Nats Canyon (Bannock). T10S R37E sec 22. Trends S and in a westerly direction 3.5 mi to its mouth at Arkansas Creek; Portneuf River drainage.

The US Board of Geographic Names found that a Jonathon Heaton had taken up two parcels of land near this canyon in the late 1800s. Nat may be a nickname for Jonathon.

Navarre Creek (Custer). T7N R23E sec 17. Begins at the junction of E Fk

Navarre Creek and Middle Fk Navarre Creek in T7N R23E sec 17 and flows N to Warm Springs Creek in T7N R23E sec 5.

The creek was named for Steven D. Navarre, a Frenchman who settled at the mouth of Navarre Creek in 1879.

Neal (Ada). T2N R4E sec 29. Ghost town.

Arthur Neal discovered gold here in 1889, just over the summit from the Upper Blacks Creek Road. The mine dumps are at the head of the valley.

Ned Creek (Lemhi). T17N R14E sec 28 to sec 19. Flows NW 2 1/2 mi to enter Loon Creek; Salmon River drainage.

Named to honor Ned Falconberry, who had a ranch in this area.

Needle Peak (Bonneville). 9445′. T1S R46E sec 21/22. On the Idaho-Wyoming line in the E part of Bonneville County.

Name derives from the shape of the peak, thin and sharp.

Neeley (Power). 4371′. T8S R30E sec 11/14. In the central part of the county, 2.6 mi SW of American Falls on Warm Creek, between Snake River and I-86. Named Neelyville for William Neeley, the first settler here, and shortened to Neely (sic) by the US Post office, Department, but appears on all maps as Neeley. Post office, 1886-1888.

Negro Creek (Clearwater). T39N R12E sec 25. See Rhodes Creek.

Neinmeyer Creek (Elmore). T5N R7E sec 24. A 2-mi stream flowing SW to Middle Fk Boise River 2 mi E of the Boise-Elmore county line.

Named for the Neinmeyer mine in the area. Neinmeyer Springs is on this stream.

Nelson Creek (Latah). T42N R4W sec 33. Heads S of Gold Hill and flows 4 mi SW to Gold Creek; Palouse River drainage; St. Joe National Forest.

Named for the Nelson family. Mary, A. J., N. A., and Marg E. Nelson recorded homesteads in the area just S of the mouth of this creek between 1894 and 1896.

Nelson Creek (Bonneville). T3N R42E sec 31/32. Rises in the NE quadrant and flows 2 mi N into Antelope Creek; Snake River drainage.

Said locally to be named for Antone Nelson, an early resident of Swan Valley.

Nelson Creek (Boise). T8N R5E sec 5. Flows 2 mi S into the S Fk Payette River 2 mi W of Grimes Pass.

This area was homesteaded by the Charles Nelson family from Norway.

Nelson Spring (Twin Falls). T14S R17E sec 23. In the SE part of the county, in Sawtooth National Forest; 9 mi E of Rogerson.

The Nelson brothers, Al and Tudoll, herded cattle here. Tudoll was said to be the best rider that ever straddled a horse in the Snake River Valley. Both rode the range S of Snake River in the Rogerson area and in Cassia and Owyhee counties.

Nettle Creek (Clearwater). T39N R11E sec 15. In the NE extremity of the county. Rises on Gorman Hill (5400′) and flows 1/2 mi N into Kelly Creek at sec 15; Clearwater River drainage.

Named for the nettles growing here.

Neva (Clearwater). T40N R1E sec 23. Settlement 5 mi W of Elk River. Post office, 1916-1918.

Named by the Milwaukee Railroad surveyors, perhaps for a girlfriend of one of the workers.

Never Creek (Clearwater). T38N R11E sec 8. Flows SE into Cayuse Creek 8 mi SE of Kelly Forks Ranger Station; Clearwater River system. Never Again

Ridge trends NW to SE parallel to the creek, SE of the lower stretch. Never Again Flats lie across Cayuse Creek.

Named for the difficult trail that followed along the creek.

New Meadows (Adams). 3865′. T19N R1E sec 24. Town just W of Meadows on US 95. Begun in 1910 as the N terminus for the Pacific and Idaho Northern RR. Plans originally were to make the terminus at Meadows, but there was a disagreement between Meadows officials and Col. E. M. Heighho, president of the RR company, so the line was built 1 1/2 mi E of Meadows and the terminus named New Meadows. Settled in 1864; Post office, 1911–.

Named for the lovely meadows in which the town is located; called New Meadows because there was already Meadows. In 1878 the place was called Whites Mail Station.

New Plymouth (Payette). 2300′. T7N R4W sec 4. Town in the center of the county about 1 1/2 mi SW of the Payette River. A colony planned under the aegis of the National Irrigation Congress in Chicago in 1894. The purpose was to promote irrigation projects and to prove the feasibility of making small farming communities in arid regions. Enthusiastic people from Boston and the Midwest banded together and secured 250 heads of families, who came W in 1895 and established New Plymouth. Post office, 1896–.

Said to have been named for Plymouth Colony; the name was chosen by the founders. A planned community laid out in the shape of an arch.

New Soldier (Camas). T1S R14E sec 9/10. Early name for Fairfield, as the residents of Soldier (which see) moved here to be on the RR.

New Sweden (Bingham/Bonneville). T3N R13/14E. Farming area in NW

quadrant of Bonneville County and the NE quadrant of Bingham County. The area includes all the land served by the New Sweden Irrigation Company.

The area was settled by Swedes and named for their native country.

New York Summit (Owyhee). T4S R3W sec 32. In the NW part of the county, 1 mi NE of Silver City.

The New York Company had a quartz mill on War Eagle Mountain. The summit received its name from this company.

Newdale (Fremont). 5065′. T7N R41E sec 34. Community 7 mi SE of St. Anthony. Post office, 1916–.

Presumably named because of its location in a dale.

Newman (Bonner). T56N R1W sec 10 Town on a crossroad 1 mi SE of Bottle Bay.

Named for Jimmy Newman, who settled here.

Newport Hill Lookout (Bonner). 4100′. T56N R5W sec 5. Three mi SE of Stone Johnny Lookout and 5 1/4 mi NW of the town of Priest River.

This is a transfer name from the nearby town of Newport, Washington.

Newsome (Idaho). 4006′. T30N R7E sec 30. A ghost town in the NW part of the county, on the Old Elk City Road; 18 mi S of Lowell and about 30 mi E of Grangeville; on Newsome Creek.

This is an old mining area, opened with John Newsome's mining claim near the site sometime in 1861. Post Office, 1896–ca.1924.

Named for John Newsome.

Nez Perce County. County seat, Lewiston. Established by the Territorial Legislature of Washington in 1861 and named for the Nez Perce Indians who occupied the area.

This was one of the four original counties in 1863 from which all 44 have been carved. The present boundaries were set in 1911: Snake River on the W and Salmon River on the S; Latah County on the N; Clearwater and Idaho counties on the E.

Nez Perce Creek (Lemhi). Two creeks by this name are located on the Nez Perce Trail and are so named because the Nez Perce followed these streams and camped on their banks; one is tributary to Texas Creek (Lemhi River drainage) and the other to Dahlonega Creek (Salmon River drainage).

Nez Perce Lake (Lemhi). T14N R26E. 1 mi E of Sheephorn Peak, overlooking the Texas Creek tributary of the same name.

Nez Perce Pass (Lemhi) 6587'. T27N R16E. At the summit of Bitterroot Mountains on the Nez Perce Trail.

Nez Perce Peak (Idaho) 7531'. T28N R15E sec 26. In Bitterroot National Forest, about 4 mi WNW of Nez Perce Pass and 42 mi SW of Hamilton. The Nez Perce Trail passed just S of this promontory.

Nez Perce Prairie (Lewis). Extends practically the entire length of the county. A rich land with the capacity for producing wheat and other cereals. Productivity was undeveloped until 1895 when the area (which is part of the Nez Perce Indian Reservation) was opened for homesteading.

Niagara Springs (Gooding/Twin Falls). T9S R15E sec 11. In the SE extremity of the county in Snake River Canyon, 4 mi E of Clear Lakes.

Named for Niagara Falls, because of the way the springs gush.

Nicholia (Lemhi). 6800'. T12N R29E sec 21. Mining town at the mouth of Smelter Gulch in the SE part of the county. Begun in the early 1880s and platted in 1885; Post office, 1884-1916.

Named for Ralph Nichols, manager of a local mining company, who in 1886 was appointed the third postmaster.

Nickleplate Mountain (Bonner). T61N R5W sec 10/15. Located 2 3/4 mi E of Idaho-Washington state border; 1 1/2 mi NW of Nordman.

Named for the nearby Nickleplate mine.

Nicks Creek (Latah).

Named for Nick Harper, who filed his Old Nick mining claim in 1892.

Nigger Brown Hill (Benewah). T46N R3W sec 14. At the S tip of Benewah Lake, about 4 mi W of St. Maries.

Named for a black man who mined here and lost his life in a mining accident.

Nigger Creek (Lemhi). T14N R26E sec 14. Heads 2 mi N of Nigger Peak (10,571'); flows NE 5 mi to enter Texas Creek; Lemhi River drainage.

Two blacks, Jerry and Greene, drove George Yearian's ox teams to haul supplies for his general merchandise store at Junction, for the Indian Agency and for Salmon City. On one such trip, Greene froze both his feet and died as a result. The creek and peak are named for him.

Also called Nigger Green Creek; renamed Negro Creek/Peak.

Niter (Caribou). 5405'. T10/11S R40E sec 36/1. In the SW part of the county, 5 mi S of Grace. Settled in 1895 by Mormons and named Hanna, which was changed in 1904 to Niter, for the mineral deposit nearby. Post office, 1902-1918.

Nixon Creek (Idaho). T25N R11E sec 14. Rises in the Nezperce National Forest on Bear Point (7975') and flows S to Salmon River.

Named for Bert Nixon, who worked for the USFS as a lookout. Rumor that he had died in Weiser led to the naming of this stream for him; the rumor proved false.

No Cut Timber Canyon/Creek (Bonneville). T3N R43E sec 35 to T2N R44E sec 6. Extends 3 mi NW to SE. In the NE quadrant in Snake River Range, Targhee National Forest. The creek flows 3 mi SE into Pine Creek; Snake River drainage.

Named because the canyon contained timber that had not been cut, an unusual occurrence in this area in the 1880s.

Noble Creek (Idaho). T26N R9E sec 26. Rises on Dixie Summit and Jack Mountain and flows about 8 mi SE to Mallard Creek; Salmon River drainage.

Named for William Noble, a former employee of Nezperce National Forest at Grangeville. He and his family were killed in a car accident in 1924 at Three Devils Camp on Middle Fk Clearwater.

Noble Gulch (Boise). T6N R5E sec 35. A 1-mi gulch that flows N into Mores Creek at Idaho City; Boise River drainage.

Named for Doc Noble, who was an early, wealthy miner and doctor from Idaho City (1860s and 1870s).

Noe Creek (Clearwater). T39N R9E sec 32. Flows S into N Fk Clearwater River.

Named for a trail man, a one-time employee of the USFS. Noe operated road-building equipment above the Bungalow Ranger Station.

Noisy Lake (Custer). T8/9N R16E sec 4/33. A 17-acre lake in the glacial deposits of the White Cloud Peaks at 8997′ elevation.

A small stream of water, caused by melting snowbanks, flows over a ledge onto rock at the shore of the lake, causing enough noise to suggest the name.

Nora (Latah). T40N R3W sec 34. A small trading center about 5 mi NE of

Troy. Nora Creek rises 2 mi E of Spring Valley Reservoir and flows 4 mi S to converge with Spring Valley Creek, forming Little Bear Creek; Potlatch River drainage. Established in 1892. Post office, 1900-1906.

Name honors Nora Johnson, daughter of the first postmaster.

Nordman (Bonner). 2500′. T61N R5W sec 14. This is a resort and logging area 4 mi E of the Idaho-Washington state border and 2 mi W of Priest Lake.

Post office, 1915-.

Named for John Nordman, an early settler.

North Basin (Lemhi). T19N R22E sec 34. At the head of Twelvemile Creek.

Named because it is the basin farthest N of those in the Hayden Creek drainage. Antone Swartz had a small ranch here ca.1925.

North Cone (Caribou). T7N R42E sec 8. In the N part of the county, 1 mi NE of Middle Cone. A dome-type cinder cone; named for its northernmost location of three such cones near the S shore of Blackfoot River Reservoir. See China Hat.

North Crater (Butte). 6338′. T1N R24E sec 35. Cinder cone about .5 mi SW of the entrance to Craters of the Moon. The N wall of this crater broke into pieces and lava carried away the masses of red tuff. The North Crater flow covers an area 1.5 square miles, 1.5 mi NE of the crater.

Named for its location N of the other large eruptive craters.

North Fork (Lemhi). T24N R21E sec 16. Located where N Fk Salmon River meets the main Salmon River.

Named because of its location at the mouth of the N Fk Salmon River. Lewis and Clark called the stream Fish Creek on 1 Sept 1805, when they followed it to its source and crossed the divide of the Bitterroot Mountains.

North Jump Creek (Lemhi). T12N R28E sec 13. Flows 3 mi S to Birch Creek Valley.

Named for an incident: Jed Noble jumped another man's claim and tried to settle on it. When the owner returned home, he kicked Jed all the way to Nicholia to get him off his land, and he had to jump over two creeks to get there.

North Laidlaw Butte (Blaine). 5912'. T1S R25E sec 7. Located 22.5 mi SW of Arco.

Named for Andy Laidlaw, who was the first man to run sheep in this area (ca.1900).

North Lake (Jefferson). T7N R34/35E sec 24/19. Located 1/2 mi N of Mud Lake.

Northernmost of several shallow lakes in the area that lie above a perched water table.

North Leigh Creek (Teton). T6N R45E sec 27. Stream, 14 mi long, heads in the Teton Range, Wyoming, and flows WSW into Idaho to Spring Creek, 1 mi E of Tetonia.

Named by Dr. F. V. Hayden, USGS surveyor, in 1872 for his guide, Richard "Beaver Dick" Leigh.

North Pine Gulch (Latah). T42N R4W sec 15. Tributary of Gold Creek; NW of Gold Hill between E Fk Gold and Hoteling creeks; St. Joe National Forest; Palouse River drainage.

Named for the heavy stand of pine in the area.

North Promontory Range (Oneida). T15/16S R33E. This is a Utah range extending about 12 mi N into Idaho and ending just E of Holbrook.

A descriptive name. Variant: Hansel Mountains.

North Putnam Mountain (Bannock). 8989'. T5S R37E sec 30. The S end of a sharp rocky ridge approximately 1 mi in length, which runs N and S.

Named for Captain James E. Putnam, who was in command of the detachment that established Fort Hall Military Post on Lincoln Creek in 1870. See South Putnam Mountain.

Norton Creek (Valley). T17N R14E sec 7. Rises on Norton Ridge (8426'), and in Norton Lake and flows 8 mi SE to empty into Middle Fk Salmon River; drainage, 18 square miles.

Named for Charlie Norton, who survived being mauled by a grizzly bear.

Norton Peak (Blaine). 10,285'. T5N R15E sec 15. In the Smoky Mountains in NW part of the county.

Named for W. A. Norton, miner, who made the first quartz-gold strike on Yankee Fork, 1875; he named his mine the Charles Dickens.

Norwegian Ridge (Latah). T38N R1W sec 5/7/8. An area E and SE of Linden in SE Latah County. The highest point in this ridge is called Gold Hill.

Named for the ethnic background of settlers here.

Noseeum Lake (Shoshone). T43N R5E sec 36. In the extreme SW part of St. Joe National Forest.

Named for the great number of gnats or biting midges around the lake. Named officially in 1919 by R. H. Rutledge, USFS, though the name was well established before that.

Notch Butte (Lincoln). 4240'. T6S R17E sec 22. In the SW part of the county, 3 mi S of Shoshone and .5 mi E of US 93.

The name is descriptive: the butte is the remnant of a volcano with its shallow summit crater collapsed in the middle.

Notus (Canyon). 2308'. T5N R4W sec 34. Town 8.1 mi SE of Parma on the Boise River; originally known as Lower Boise.

The name Notus was assigned by the Oregon Short Line when it came through; the OSL namer thought it was an Indian word meaning "it's all right." Locals say that the name arises from an Oregon Trail incident. Some of the travelers decided to stay and homestead at the river crossing. When asked if they were ready for the last lap to Oregon, they replied, "Not us." A third story says it derives from an ancient city of North Africa, but how it got to Idaho is a mystery. It is also said to be a Greek word meaning "south wind."

Nounan (Bear Lake). 6000'. T11S R43E sec 8/17. In the N part of the county, 3 mi W of Georgetown.

Named in 1878 for a trapper and already inhabited by the John Cozzens family in 1863, Nounan was not really founded until the 1870s, when Mormon colonizers arrived. A Swiss family, the Frederick Bartschis, arrived in 1889 by way of Emigration and Stauffer canyons. Post office, 1883-.

Nub Creek (Clearwater). T40N R8E sec 4. In the NE part of the county. Rises on The Nub (6924') and flows 3.5 mi SE into Skull Creek; Clearwater River drainage; 5 mi NE of Canyon Ranger Station. Nub Lakes lie at the head of the stream.

Named for the small, thimble-like peak on the top of the promontory. The Nub is now unforested.

Nucrag (Lewis). 2675'. T34N R2W sec 9. RR siding and spur 2 1/4 mi SW of Reubens.

Named for two workers on the Camas Prairie RR: a Mr. Newton, a conductor, and a Mr. Craig, an engineer.

Nugget Creek (Idaho). T29N R7E sec 5. Rises on Nugget Point and flows 2 1/2 mi SW to Newsome Creek.

Both the creek and the gulch in this vicinity were placer-mined for gold by Chinese and whites, side by side.

Nugget Creek (Shoshone). T45N R7E sec 27. A 6-mi tributary of St. Joe River from the S, in the E part of the county.

Con Faircloth and another prospector panned the creeks around this area for gold in the 1800s but could find no color. Upon breaking camp, they decided to name this creek Nugget Creek, as they agreed it would be a good place to find nuggets if there were any here. They blazed the name on a tree, and it found its way onto maps.

Nut Basin Lake (Idaho). T25N R2E sec 1. In the SW part of the county 7 mi E of Lucile.

Named for the pine nuts, probably those of the yellow pine.

O

O'Gara Bay (Kootenai). T47N R3W sec 20. In the S part of the county on the lower E side of Coeur d'Alene Lake.

The village of O'Gara grew up on the E extremity of the bay and O'Gara Gulch empties into the bay.

All the features were named for early settlers from County Cork, Ireland. Ultimately three of the family's daughters (Anna, Margaret, and Mary O'Gara) opened a rooming house in St. Maries and bootlegged on the side. The women were said to be very adept at separating miners and loggers from their money.

O'Hara Creek (Idaho). T32N R7E sec 25. Rises on O'Hara Saddle and flows 10 mi N to Selway River, 6 mi SE of Lowell.

Named for Pat O'Hara, a prospector who had a mining claim on this stream in 1885.

O'Mill (Clearwater). T36N R4E sec 3. Settlement 6 mi W of Pierce.

This is an abbreviation for Olson Mill, previously called Hayley.

O'Neil Basin (Twin Falls/Elko County, Nevada). T16S R13E sec 13,24. In the SW extremity of the county. A 30-mi long basin that trends into Idaho, 13 mi W of Contact, Nevada.

Named for the O'Neils, the first settlers in the area in the early 1880s.

O'Neil Creek (Clearwater). T38N R3E sec 29. Flows S into N Fk Clearwater River 3.5 mi E of Dent Bridge.

Named for homesteader Patrick O'Neil.

O'Rourke Bay (Kootenai). T51N R3W sec 15/16/21.

On the E side of Hayden Lake. Named for Phil O'Rourke, man-about-town, teller of tall tales, pseudo-miner, and gambler, about whom legends arose throughout the Coeur d'Alene Mining District. Some credit him with having made the great Bunker Hill discovery with Noah Kellogg. Others say that Kellogg induced him to file the claim in order to welch on indebtedness to his backers.

Oakden Canyon/Creek (Bonneville). T2N R44E sec 27-30. In the N quadrant; extends 6 mi NE to SW. The creek flows 6 mi SW to empty into Snake River.

Named for Robert Oakden, early resident of Swan Valley and first postmaster of Irwin (1897).

Oakley (Cassia). 4191'. T13/14S R22E sec 33/4. In the central part of the county, on Goose Creek, 24 mi S of Burley.

Once called Goose Creek Crossing, later named Oakley for stage station operator Thomas Oakley.

Settled by Mormon families from Tooele, Utah, in 1878-1880, when Goose Creek Ward was founded. Post office, 1876-.

Obia Creek (Idaho). T3TN R8E sec 7. Rises on Rocky Ridge and flows 3 1/2 mi S to Hungry Creek; Lochsa River drainage.

Two hunters, one a Russian as the story goes, found two elk cows here. The Russian called out, "I got obia" meaning "two." Hence the name. Changed to Hungry Creek, the name bestowed by Lewis and Clark in 1805.

Obsidian (Custer). 6640'. T8N R14E sec 21. Town, formerly Pierson, in SW Custer County just E of State Highway 78. Post office, 1916-.

Named for a glassy material of volcanic origin used by Indians for weapons and tools.

Ocalkens Lake (Custer). T9N R15E sec 12. A lake near the headwaters of Slate Creek and approximately 4 mi E of The Meadows. Also Calkins Lake.

Named after a pioneer resident.

Ogre, The (Idaho). 9210'. T23N R2W sec 24. A peak in the Seven Devils Mountains; Nezperce National Forest; about 1 mi ESE of He Devil and 12.5 mi SW of Riggins. Formerly, Mount Apollyon.

Named by analogy with other names of the Seven Devils Mountains, which suggest utter destruction or a devilish destroyer.

Ohio Gulch (Blaine). T3N R18E sec 20. Extends 10 mi NE to SW to Big Wood River, 1.5 mi S of Gimlet.

Named for a mining claim up the gulch which in turn was named for the state of Ohio.

Old Ilo (Lewis). Abandoned town 1 mi W of the present site of Craigmont. See Craigmont and Ilo.

Old Man Creek (Idaho). T34N R8E sec 36. Rises in The Crags and flows about 18 mi to Lochsa River 9 1/2 mi E of Lowell. Old Man Point (5012') lies 2 mi NE of the mouth of the creek. Old Man Lake is in The Crags at the head of the stream. The Old Man Rock lies some 15 mi E of the source of the creek; it is perfectly square.

Local legend has it that older Indian men who could not travel far stopped here on this rock and waited for their party to return. But there is no agreement on the source of the name. The story of the older Indian men using the rock as a stopping place seems plausible. Andy Hjort (USFS) says that a mammoth-sized grizzly bear made his home at Old Man Lake for many years. Another informant says that there is a representation of the face of an old man on the cliff.

Old Moose City (Clearwater). T40N R11E sec 29. Townsite 4 mi N of Kelly Creek Work Center.

The town thrived from the early 1860s to the 1870s, after rich gold discoveries brought an influx of miners, prospectors, and settlers. The diggings failed in the 1870s and the town was abandoned.

Named for the many moose in the area.

Old Tom Mountain (Bannock). 7810'. T9S R35E sec 23/24. A large N- S-bearing mountain in the W part of the county entirely within the Caribou

National Forest. Variant name: Tom Mountain.

Named for a lame cougar that lived years ago on the mountain.

Old Williamsburg (Caribou). 6317'. T5S R44E sec 31. See Williamsburg.

Olds Ferry (Washington). T11N R7W sec 17. On Snake River 12 mi W of present-day Weiser and 1 3/4 mi S of Farewell Bend. Formerly Indian Crossing.

A Mr. Abernathy built a store here in 1862 and sold it in 1863 to Reuben P. Olds, who added a ferry to his holdings. He operated the ferry for years, transporting Oregon-bound emigrants and other travelers. A little community grew up around the ferry and the whole area was called Olds Ferry. The UPRR kept the name for its station here.

Named for the operator of the ferry.

Olevan Creek (Latah). T42N R3W sec 8. Stream 1.8 mi long that flows NE to Big Creek; Palouse River drainage.

Named by USFS ranger W. H. Daugs, with a phonetic spelling of "au le vent," a French term meaning "to the east," or "eastward," the general course of this creek.

Olson (Clearwater). T36N R4E sec 9. Settlement 6 mi N of Weippe. Olson Creek rises E of the settlement and flows 2 mi NW into Orofino Creek; Clearwater River drainage.

Lawrence Olson owned a sawmill here.

Onaway (Latah). 2480'. T41N R4W sec 6. Incorporated town just NE of Potlatch.

Formerly Bulltown, for the pioneer Bull family. Onaway was a stage stop on the Wells Fargo line from Palouse to Grizzle Camp in the 1880s.

Named for Onaway, New York, the home of some early settlers.

Oneida County. County seat, Malad City. The sixth county; created in 1864 with Soda Springs as the county seat. The seat was changed to Malad City in 1866, because of its rapid growth and its location on the stagecoach line and freight road between Corinne, Utah, and the mines in Butte, Montana.

Bounded on the N by Power County, on the NE and E by Bannock County, on the SE by Franklin County, on the S by Box Elder and Cache counties (Utah), and on the W by Cassia County.

Named for Lake Oneida, New York, in the area from which most of the early settlers had come.

Opal Creek (Lemhi). T18N R18E sec 14. Flows generally NW 3 mi then SW 1 mi to enter Panther Creek; Salmon River drainage. Opal Lake is situated about 2 mi up from the mouth of Opal Creek.

Named because opals were found in the gravel near the mouth of the creek.

Ophir Creek (Boise). T7N R4E sec 23. Rises W of Pioneerville and flows 5 mi SW into Woof Creek 2 mi S of Placerville; Boise River drainage.

Named for the Ophir mine, which was located near the creek. Ophir was a land of riches in the Bible.

Ora (Fremont). T9N R42E sec 30. Community and farming area 2 mi W of Ashton. Formerly: Sand Creek, Arcadia.

Named Ora in 1890 by the Post Office Department for the first postmaster, Ola N. Kerr, SInce there was already an Ola P.O. in Idaho, the name was changed.

Orchard (Ada). 3152'. T1S R4E sec 19. An early UPRR station located in eastern Ada County 28 mi SE of Boise. Post office, 1893-. Orchard Gulch rises in Boise National Forest at the Ada-Boise line and flows SW to Cottonwood Creek at T4N R3E sec 34; Boise River drainage.

At one time there was a large orchard here, irrigated with water from Indian Creek. The place was named for the orchard.

Formerly Bisuka, a name applied by the OSLRR, believed to be of Indian origin meaing "not a large place."

Orchard Homes (Latah). T38N R3W sec 32. An early community about 2 mi NE of Genesee and directly N of Juliaetta.

Named for the fruit orchards here.

Oreana (Owyhee). 2828'. T4S R1E/1W sec 24/30. Town in N part of the county, 11 mi SE of Murphy. Pronounced ore-ee-AN-uh.

The first use of the small community was as a headquarters for cattlemen. Michael Hyde, an early-day Owyhee cattle rancher, founded and named the settlement in the early 1860s. Post office, 1885-.

Oreana is a Spanish word meaning "an unbranded but earmarked calf."

Oregon Butte (Idaho). 8463'. T25N R6E sec 12. In the SW part of the county 7 mi S of Buffalo Hump. Oregon Lake lies 1/2 mi S of the butte.

Named for the clear view of Oregon's Wallowa Mountains from the lookout on this butte.

Oro (Owyhee). T6S R5W sec 20. Mining town in the Flint Mining District. Pronounced ORE-oh. Post office, 1866-1869.

"Oro" is the Spanish word for gold.

Oro Fino (Clearwater). T36N R5E sec 11. Ghost town 1 mi S of Pierce.

This mining town sprang up in 1861 when gold dust was discovered here. The settlement served as a supply point for gold diggings on Canal Gulch and Rhodes Creek. Post office, 1863-.

California miners, who invaded the area on the discovery of gold at Pierce, named the place Oro Fino (Spanish for "fine gold") for the gold dust they found. The name was transferred to Orofino Creek and then to other features.

Orofino (Clearwater). T36N R2E sec 7. County seat. Located near the confluence of S and Middle Fks of Clearwater River and the Dworshak Dam and Reservoir, on Orofino Creek. The Clearwater gold rush occurred on Orofino Creek at present-day Pierce and Gold Hill.

The town originated in 1895 when the Nez Perce Reservation opened to settlement and Clifford Fuller established a trading post amd also set up the Clearwater Improvement Co., which laid out the town and established a ferry in 1896. Post office, 1901-.

Named directly from Orofino Creek, indirectly from Oro Fino, the ghost town.

Orogrande (Custer). T14N R14E sec 33. Ghost town on a high bar W of Loon Creek. A mining camp hampered by the scarcity and high cost of lumber. In 1870-71, the population was about 200, of which 60-70 were Chinese. By 1879, only five Chinese remained.

Derived from the Spanish for "big gold," in contrast to Orofino.

Orogrande (Idaho). 4100'. T27N R7E sec 1. A ghost town in the central part of the county 10 mi SW of Elk City. Placer mined many years before settlement was established in 1899. It became a center for trade during the Hump Boom, 1898-1913. Post office, ca.1900-ca.1934.

Orogrande Creek (Clearwater). T38N R8E sec 18. Rises in the N central part of the county and flows 7 mi NE into

N Fk Clearwater River 4 mi W of Weitas campground.

William F. Basset, a miner from Oro Fino, discovered gold E of Orofino Creek; from the nature of the gold, the diggings were named Oro Grande. The name then was given to Orogrande Creek.

Osborne Butte (Fremont). 6310'. T11N R43E sec 8. E of Osborne Ranch and Osborne Bridge across Henrys Fork. Osborne Bridge is 18 mi.N of Ashton.

Said to be named for Robert Osborne; who had a fishing resort here in 1906.

Osburn (Shoshone). 2350'. T48N R4E sec 18. In the central part of the county on I-90, UPRR, and S Fk Coeur d'Alene River; 5 mi SE of Kellogg. Site of a construction camp for the Mullan Road, then abandoned. Later Bill Osborne built a trading post here and the place was known as Bill Osborne's (sic) Trading Post. The town was platted when the UPRR came through, and it was named Georgetown for Lee George, one of the owners of the townsite. But that name was not acceptable to the Post Office Department, as there was another Georgetown in Idaho Territory; so the name was changed to Osborne for the storekeeper and the first postmaster in 1887.

In 1890 Osburn replaced Murray as the county seat, but it lost out to Wallace in 1893.

Osgood (Bonneville). 4788'. T3N R37E sec 27. Village in the NW part of the county about 10 mi N of Idaho Falls.

Named for a pioneer family.

Osier Creek (Clearwater). T39N R11E sec 9. Rises in the NE extremity of the county on Osier Ridge (6115') and flows 10 mi SW into Moose Creek; Clearwater River drainage.

Said to be named for early-day miners from the Hoosier state, Indiana. The derivation is uncertain. Osier is a variant name for a variety of willows.

Ostrander Creek (Lemhi). T20N R18E sec 28. Headwaters near the head of Ludwig Gulch; runs SW 1 1/2 mi to enter Musgrove Creek; Salmon River drainage.

Named for Horace E. Ostrander, the discoverer of gold on Musgrove Creek, who patented the land here in 1893.

Otter Creek (Lemhi). T18N R18E sec 25. Heads 1 mi SW of Hat Creek Lakes; flows W 2 1/2 mi to enter Panther Creek; Salmon River drainage.

Named because of the number of otter found here. Originally called Cow Creek because a hundred head of cows died here when they were trapped in a box canyon in the late fall. Name was changed because there were so many other Cow Creeks.

Otto (Latah). T39N R4W see 19. A community on the Bronta Cabin place about 6 mi E of Moscow, 1886; named for Moscowite Otto Fries, a partner with Joe Niederstadt in the Moscow Brewery. Subsequently Fries sold out to Mason Cornwall, who built a general store, applied for a post office, and changed the name to Cornwall in 1887.

Otto Creek (Idaho). T28N R1E sec 10. A 3-mi stream flowing SE to Salmon River, 2 mi NW of White Bird.

Named for early rancher Newt Otto.

Outlaw Creek (Shoshone). T44N R4E sec 24. A tiny tributary of Fishhook Creek S of Avery.

Named for 9 "outlaws" from the mining war between union and non-union workers at Gem, who are said to have taken refuge in a cabin on this stream.

Outlet Bay (Bonner). T59N R4W sec 5. On SW extremity of Priest Lake where Priest River heads. Outlet Mountain is 1 mi S of Outlet Bay, for which it is named.

Named because the water flows into Priest River at this point.

Outlet Valley (Bonneville). T3S R42E sec 26-30. Trends 6.7 mi NW to SE, on Grays Lake Outlet between the Caribou Range on the NE and Outlet Ridge and Pine Mountains on the SW.

Named for Grays Lake Outlet.

Oviatt Creek (Clearwater). T39N R2E sec 18. Rises in the NW corner of the county on Neva Hill and flows 5.5 mi SE into Long Meadow Creek, N of Elk Creek arm of Dworshak Reservoir; Clearwater River drainage.

Named for a homesteader.

Ovid (Bear Lake). 5993'. T13S R43E sec 23. In the center of the county, 4 mi S of Bern and 6 mi N of Bloomington on US 89 and State 36. Post office, 1873-.

Named for a town in New York by Charles Rich; first settled by Mormons, primarily Danes, in the spring of 1864.

Owens Bay (Bonner). T56N R1E sec 13/23. On the E side of Lake Pend Oreille 2 mi S of Hope.

Named for Sam Owens, who settled just N of this bay in 1898.

Owinza (Lincoln). 2200'. T6S R20E sec 15. A UPRR siding 10 mi E of Dietrich. Post office, 1916-1924.

Named by UPRR officials for what they believed to be an Indian word meaning "to make a bed of" or "to use as a bed."

Owl Creek (Lemhi). T23N R17E sec 15. Northern tributary of the Salmon River. Owl Creek Hot Springs is 2 mi upstream from the mouth of Owl Creek.

Named for the owls that roosted in a large pine grove about 4 mi upstream.

Owyhee County. County seat, Murphy. Established in 1863.

Located in the SW corner of the state, this is one of the largest counties in the United States. It is topographically rough, with an elevation ranging from 2000' to 6000', with peaks in the N, Owyhee Mountains in the W, and spectacular Bruneau Canyon in the E half of the county. Bounded on the N by Elmore, Ada, and Canyon counties; on the E by Elmore and Twin Falls counties; on the S by Nevada; and on the W by Oregon.

Owyhee is the word used by British and American traders during the early 19th century in referring to natives of the Hawaiian Islands, called Sandwich Islands then. When missionaries went to the islands in 1820, they devised a phonetic alphabet for writing the native language. The word spelled "Owyhee" in English became Hawaii in the missionary alphabet.

After trading posts were established on the Pacific Coast, Donald McKenzie sent three Owyhees with other trappers into the area in the winter of 1819 to trap for beaver on the river, to trade, and to penetrate the Snake River country for the North West Company. The Owyhees were primarily hired for the purposes of carrying on a more successful trade with Bannock and Shoshoni Indians. These three Owyhees left the main party and went to explore the unknown terrain. They never returned and it was believed they had been killed by Indians. Because of their disappearance, the British fur trappers called the entire region and the river Owyhee. In 1826 Peter Skene Ogden knew the stream as the Owyhee or Sandwich Island River.

All the other features bearing this name are directly or indirectly based on the name of the river and arise from this incident.

Owyhee (Ada) 2963'. T1N R2E sec 15. UPRR station in the central part of Ada County about 13 mi SE of Kuna. Post office, 1910-1919.

Owyhee Heights (Owyhee) 2387'. T3N R5/6W sec 1/6. Situated 1 mi N of Homedale.

Owyhee Highlands (Owyhee). T9/10S R1/2/3W. Mountain range.

Owyhee Mountains (Owyhee). T1N R5W. This range extends from Oregon into Owyhee County in a SW direction for about 60 mi, varying in width from 10 to 35 mi. Florida, War Eagle, and Cinnebar mountains are in this range.

Owyhee River (Owyhee). T9S R4W. Flows W into the Snake River in Oregon. S Fk Owyhee and its tributary Little Owyhee River rise in Nevada and flow generally N where they converge with Owyhee River.

Oxbow Creek (Adams). T22N R3W sec 15. Located in the NW part of the county about 1 mi N of Hells Canyon Dam; rises in Oxbow Spring and flows generally W to Snake River; 8 mi long.

Named because the creek has an oxbow-shaped bend in it about 1 mi upstream from the mouth. The spring takes its name from the creek.

Oxbow, The (Adams). T19N R4W sec 16/17/20/21.

An oxbow-shaped bend in the Snake River.

Oxford Creek (Franklin). T13S R38E sec 28. Rises in Bannock Range in the W extremity of the county and empties in Oxford Slough.

Named when hunters found oxen tracks at the ford of this stream and therefore named it Oxford. The town and topographical features that follow are named for the creek.

Oxford (Franklin) 4748'. T16S R38E sec 28. A Mormon vilage 4 mi N of Clifton, in the N part of the county on Oxford Creek. Post office, 1872-.

Oxford Peak (Franklin/Oneida). 9281'. T13S R37E sec 23/26. Near the head of Oxford Creek on Franklin-Oneida county line; in Caribou National Forest.

Oxford Slough. T13/14S R38E. Marsh in the NW part of the county adjoining the town of Oxford and 12 mi NW of Preston; 4 mi long. Variant: Round Valley Marsh.

Ozone (Bonneville). 5800'. T1N R39E sec 14. Village in the NW quadrant, 15 1/2 mi SE of Idaho Falls. Post office, 1911-1925.

Named because of the high elevation.

Peck Ferry, Peck (Nez Perce County).

P

Pack River (Bonner/Boundary). The source of this river is the divide between Kootenai and Priest rivers; rises in Boundary County and flows generally SE to empty in Lake Pend Oreille at T58N R1E sec 6. It flows directly across the Purcell Trench and cuts off a mass of hills from the main Cabinet Range.

Pack River Flats is 9 mi NE of Sandpoint and 4 mi NW of Hope, S of the mouth of Pack River. Packer Meadows lies between the Idaho-Washington state boundary and W Fk Packer Creek. Packer Creek rises on the SE slope of Boulder Mountain and flows SW to Granite Creek, feeder of Priest Lake.

Named because loaded supply boats ascended the river, and loggers packing their supplies walked along the river to the logging camps in the area. Early pack trails usually went through the meadows drained by the creeks; thus the area was given the name of Packer, which was transferred to the creek that drains it.

Pack Saddle Mountain (Bonner). 6414'. T54N R1E sec 17. Located 2 1/2 mi SE of Minerva Peak and 6 mi NE of Lakeview. Also Packsaddle Mountain. Packsaddle Creek heads on the N slopes of Pack Saddle Mountain and flows 2 1/4 mi NE into Granite Creek, W feeder of Lake Pend Oreille.

Named because its two small peaks give the impression that it is shaped like a saddle.

Packer John (Boise). 7055'. T10N R3E sec 11. Mountain.

Named for John Welch, an early packer in what is now the Boise National Forest. He was a Fenian politician.

Packer Meadows (Idaho). T38N R15E sec 14/15. A beautiful stopping place atop the Bitterroot Mountains near Lolo Pass where Lewis and Clark camped; a favorite camping site for Indians traveling across the mountains. A man built a cabin here and planned to homestead the land but dropped the plan when the NPRR Company got a large part of the meadow. The Indian name for this meadow was Quamash Glade.

Presumably used by packers as a campsite.

Packer Spring (Boise). T10N R5E sec 18. In the NW part of the county 1 mi E of Middle Fork Payette River.

Named by the USFS. This spring is located in a rough, mountainous area. Until 1934 everything had to be packed into the area because there were no roads; this was the only water on the trail.

Packrat Lake (Boise). T8N R12E sec 10. On the SE Boise-Custer county line.

Packrat Peak (10,600′) lies 1 mi N of Packrat Creek on the SE county line.

Named by the USFS in 1928 because a packrat was sighted on the mountain.

Packsaddle Basin (Teton). T5N R43E sec 25/26/35/36. Lies between the headwaters of Packsaddle, Calamity, and Warm creeks NW of the Big Hole Mountains. Packsaddle Creek rises in Packsaddle Basin and flows about 10 mi NE to Teton River. Packsaddle Lake is a 20-acre lake on the Teton River watershed. It forms the headwaters of N Fk Packsaddle Creek.

Named by Dr. F. V. Hayden, USGS surveyor, in 1872 for the packsaddles discovered in the basin.

Packsaddle Creek (Boise). T10N R6E sec 2. In the N central part of the county; flows E into Scott Creek of Deadwood River; Payette River drainage.

Named by the USFS because they had to pack supplies into the area; there were no roads.

Page (Shoshone). 2600′. T48N R2E sec 9. A mining and milling village situated 6 mi W of Kellogg.

Named for the Page mine, owned by the Federal Mining and Smelting Company of Wallace. In 1927 an attempt to change the name to Burbidge, for the general manager of the company, failed. Post office, 1927-1965.

Pahsimeroi River (Custer/Lemhi). T16N R21E sec 26. Rises on E and W slopes of Leatherman Peak and flows NW to Salmon River. Pahsimeroi Mountains lie NW to NE, N of Lost River Range and almost parallel to Pahsimeroi River on the W; greatest elevation is Grouse Creek Mountain (11,085′). Pahsimeroi Valley lies between Pahsimeroi and Upper Lemhi mountain ranges; an arid plain divided at the upper end by Donkey Hills, drained by Pahsimeroi River; about 30 mi in length and 6-15 mi in width. Pronounced puh-SIM-uh-roy.

According to John E. Rees, Pahsimeroi is of Shoshoni origin: pah, "water"; sima, "one"; roi, "grove." There was one grove of conifers by the Pahsimeroi River, miles from any other trees; hence the name.

Paint Canyon (Lemhi). T11N R29E sec 13. S of Scotts Canyon; runs mostly W 3 mi, about 2 mi NE of Reno.

Named for the Indian paintings, which look like fish, on the rocks at the mouth of the canyon.

Painter Bar (Idaho). T24N R8E sec 15. At the junction of Jersey Creek and the Salmon River 28 mi S of Elk City.

Named for John R. Painter, who settled on the land and was granted a patent in 1929. He is buried here.

Palisades (Bonneville). 5346′. T1N R4YE sec 35. Town on the Palisades dam site, situated at the mouth of Palisades Creek. The stream rises in the E part of the county and flows 19 1/2 mi SW into Snake River.

Palisades Peak (9780′) is 12 mi S of Victor; overlooks Upper Palisades Lake from the E. Little Palisades Peak lies 1 mi S.

Named for the cliffs that line the Snake River in this area, now beneath the water of Palisades Reservoir.

Palmer Butte (Latah). 3166′. T43N R5W sec 18. Hill in the NW corner of the county about 2 mi W of McCroskey State Park.

Named for homesteaders Earl A., Katherine A., Asher H., Chas. W., Sarah M., Loretta D., and E. P. Palmer. All settled in the area of this butte. Formerly Stratton Butte and Queeners Butte, for earlier settlers.

Palouse. The source of this term as a place name has long been in dispute.

The most commonly accepted explanation is that it derives from French pelouse—"grassy spot" or "lawn"—and was bestowed by French trappers because it describes the area. However, there seems to be a more plausible explanation for the name. It may have come from the name of the major village of the Palouse Indians. The Saehaptin Indian word for the village, Palus, meant "something sticking down in the water." The village was located at the confluence of the Palouse and Snake rivers, and the "something sticking down in the water" was a large rock. The Palouse believed the rock to be a solidified heart of Beaver, who played an important role in their religious beliefs. The Nez Perce believed the rock to be the canoe of Coyote, who played an important part in their religion. The derivation from Indian "Palus" has the support of Deward Walker and Roderick Sprague, anthropologists, based on extensive research. (See "The Meaning of Palouse," *Idaho Yesterdays*, Vol. 12, No. 2[Spring, 1968].)

Palouse River (Latah). Heads in the NE corner of Latah County in the Hoodoo Mountains at an altitude of 5000′, and flows W to Snake River in Washington at an altitutde of 480′. North Fork Palouse is 8.9 mi long and flows SW to Palouse River 4 mi E of Laird Park; famous for extensive prospecting and gold mining. South Fork Palouse is 18.3 mi long, rises on the S slope of Moscow Mountain and flows SW into Washington to the Palouse River.

Originally named by explorers Lewis and Clark for George Drewyer, a member of their expedition. French Canadian trappers changed the name to Pavion and then to Pavillion because of the temporary Indian tent camps along its banks. Finally the name was changed

to Palouse. The following "Palouse" names derive from the name of the river.

Palouse Bridge. An early settlement on the Palouse River just E of Washington-Idaho boundary upstream from Palouse City, Washington. Post office, 1873-1975.

Palouse Range. Low-lying mountains S of Palouse River and N and NE of Moscow; though locally called Moscow Mountains, the US Geographic Names Board says this is not the official name, nor is Moscow Hill, Thatuna Hills, or Thatuna Mountains. Includes Moscow, E Moscow, Twin, and W Twin Mountains; Turnbow, Paradise, and Stanford points; and Basalt Hill; extends approximately 15 mi E and W, from 3-6 mi N and S.

Pamas Creek (Benewah). T43N R2W sec 10. Near the southern county line; a 4-mi stream, tributary of Charlie Creek from the NE; St. Maries River drainage.

Named by USFS ranger W. H. Daugs in 1929 for traces of gold along the creek. Pamas is Chinook jargon for "gold."

Panther Creek (Lemhi). T23N R18E sec 19. A long stream that heads on Morgan Creek Summit; flows generally N for about 40 mi to empty into Salmon River.

Originally called Big Creek, but the name was changed because local authorities thought there were too many creeks with the same name. Renamed Panther for the numerous cougars in the area.

Papoose Creek (Idaho). T37N R13E sec 36. Rises on Papoose Saddle 1 mi S of the Clearwater-Idaho county line and flows 5 mi S to Lochsa River, 34 mi NW of Hamilton, Montana.

Named for an incident of the 1879 Sheepeater War on the headwaters of this creek, when Lt. Farrow captured two Indian women and a baby. He sent the mother after her people and kept the baby to insure her return, much to the discomfort of his men who could not sleep because of the vociferous crying of the baby.

Papoose Creek (Lemhi). T24N R19E sec 14. Tributary of Squaw Creek; forms about 2 mi E of Dutchler Mountain and runs S 2 1/2 mi to enter Squaw Creek 5 mi E of Shoup; Salmon River drainage.

Named because it is a small tributary to Squaw Creek.

Papoose Island (Bonner). T60N R4W sec 17. Midway between Kalispell and Bartoo islands in Priest Lake.

Named because it is small like a papoose and looks as if it is riding on the back of Kalispell Island.

Paradise (Adams). T22N R2W sec 22. A mining community adjoining Iron Springs; located on Paradise Creek.

There are several "paradise" features in the Seven Devils area, usually characterized by green growth and life in contrast to stark boulders and overpowering promontories. Among such are Paradise Creek, which rises in Crystal Lake and flows 6 mi SE and E to Rapid River; Paradise Flat, drained by Paradise Creek; Paradise Cabin, at the mouth of Paradise Creek, Rapid River tributary; and Paradise Flat, in the bend of Crooked River, T19N R3W sec 28/33.

Paradise Valley (Latah). T39N 5RW sec 18/8. Early name for Moscow. The local story is that when settlers first came to the area, the place was called Hog Heaven; the women objected to Hog Heaven and it was renamed Paradise Valley from its natural beauty and in direct contrast to Hog Heaven. The name Paradise transferred to other features in the area.

Paradise Creek (Latah). T39N R6W sec 1. Stream 12.1 mi long, heads 2 mi W of Paradise Point and flows generally S through Moscow to S Fk Palouse just S of Moscow.

Paradise Point (Latah) 4356'. T40N R5W sec 10. Peak in Palouse Range 3 mi NW of Moscow Mountain, 6 mi N of Moscow.

Paradise Ridge. T39N R4W sec 28/29/32-34. Low-lying hills SE of Moscow and including the SE edge of the city. Transfer name from Paradise Valley.

Paradise Valley. An L-shaped area extending E from the mouth of Paradise Creek near Pullman, Wn., to Moscow, and turning N to the ridge W of Moscow Mountain. Also called Palouse Hills, Palouse Country, or Palouse Prairie. Named for the town Paradise Valley.

Paradise Valley (Boundary). T61N R1E. A part of Kootenai River Valley.

Named by migrants from the Dust Bowl who found refuge here after 1936 and settled in the area.

Paragon Lake (Lemhi). T20N R16E sec 8. Just SE of Wilson Mountain in the Bighorn Crags.

Named in 1963 by USFS surveyors because they thought this beautiful little lake was a model of perfection.

Parallel Creek (Clearwater). T38N R5E sec 8. Rises in the NW quarter of the county on Silver Butte (4680') and flows 5 mi SW into Alder Creek 2 mi NW of Headquarters; Clearwater River drainage.

The creek runs parallel to Casey Creek and not far from it, so came to be known as Parallel Creek.

Pardee (Idaho). 1139'. T34N R3E sec 7. In the NW part of the county on the Clearwater River 7 mi S of Greer.

Established in the 1890s with a post office and backed by A. D. Pardee, a Philadelphia capitalist who owned the townsite and was interested in developing the mineral deposits along the Clearwater River.

Named for Alfred Day Pardee, the developer and owner of the townsite.

Pardus Creek (Latah). T41N R2W sec 11. Stream 1 1/2 mi long, flows W to Triplet Creek; Palouse River drainage.

Named by USFS ranger W. H. Daugs, with a French word meaning "lost." The stream is well hidden by dense forest and is not readily noticeable, according to Daugs (15 Jan 1931). Originally Perdus Creek, closer to the correct spelling of the French word.

Paris (Bear Lake). 5966'. T14S R43E sec 3/11. County seat. In the SE part of the county on US 89, 2 mi N of Bloomington. Paris Creek rises in Paris Spring on the slopes of Paris Peak (9572') and flows 9 1/2 mi through Paris Canyon to Bear Lake Outlet.

Settled and developed by leaders of the LDS Church, who scouted and prepared the area for a town that would serve well a hundred years hence: the streets were 40 yards wide, the city blocks divided into suitable lots, and public buildings planned for convenience and permanence. A great influx of families came from all parts of Europe, mostly England, and the East Coast in 1864. Post office, 1873-.

Named for Frederick Perris, who platted the townsite.

Park (Latah). T39N R1W sec 9/16. A former trading center 18 mi E of Troy and 4 mi SE of Deary. Post office, 1886-1930.

The grassy area and beautiful trees reminded early settlers of eastern parks they had left behind.

Park Creek (Lemhi). T17N R20E sec 34. Originates about 1 1/2 mi S of Wards Butte; flows SE 5 mi to enter Little Hat Creek about 1 mi N of Lemhi- Custer county line; Salmon River drainage.

Named for the series of quaking aspen parks in the vicinity.

Parke Canyon (Oneida). T13S R30E sec 15. In the NW corner of the county, 7.5 mi SW of Roy; 1.5 mi long; trends E to Pine Creek.

Named for the Parke family, who settled in this area in 1867.

Parker (Fremont). 4971'. T7N R40E sec 5/9. Town 4 mi W of St. Anthony. Formerly: Garden Grove (community); Egin (post office).

Said to be named for Wyman Parker, presiding bishop of the Mormon community and later postmaster. A later postmaster (1900) was Isac Parker and the first postmaster at Egin was Adelbert Parker (1880). Apparently the community of Greenville acquired a post office called Egin under postmaster Adelbert F. Parker. The community of Garden Grove, becoming somewhat larger, acquired the post office, moved from Egin and renamed it Parker. The two communities were and are separate places.

Parker Creek (Lemhi). T15N R16E sec 21. Headwaters located 1 1/2 mi NE of Parker Mountain (9151'); flows N 2 mi and then SW 2 mi to enter Warm Spring Creek; Salmon River drainage.

Named for Old Man Parker, assayer and prospector of Challis, Idaho.

Parker Mountain (Lemhi). 8053'. T25N R16E sec 30. At the head of Bronco Creek approximately 1/2 mi from the Idaho-Lemhi county line.

Named by the US Board of Geographic Names in 1965 in honor of the Reverend Samuel Parker, who camped near here in 1835, though some say after A. F. Parker, who was a scout during the Sheepeater Campaign of 1879 and who later owned the Idaho Free Press at Grangeville.

Parkinson (Madison). 5200'. T6N R41E sec 31. A farming community in the NE quadrant, on the UPRR, 5 mi E of Rexburg.

Named for the Parkinson brothers, local farmers.

Parks Peak (Blaine Custer). 10,208'. T7N R13E sec 4. On the Blaine-Custer county line, 2.5 mi NE of Snowyside; Sawtooth Wilderness Area.

Said to be named for Samuel B. Parks, judge of later Boise County, appointed in 1863 by the Territorial Legislature.

Parma (Canyon). 2245'. T5N R5W sec 9. Town situated in the NW part of the county and known as Lower Boise until 1882. Settlers arrived here perhaps as early as 1862-63 and the town was incorporated in 1904. Post office, 1884-.

Frank Fouch, who originally operated a post office across the Snake River, decided to open one at Parma when the railroad was built. The RR officials wanted a short name. Fouch was a student of history, so he chose the name Parma, for Parma, Italy.

Parrot Creek (Lemhi). T21N R14E sec 26. Heads in vicinity of Parrot Lake and flows NW 3 mi to enter Middle Fk Salmon River. Parrot Lake lies at the mouth of this stream, 1 mi NW of Mount McGuire.

Named for a recluse, Earl K. Parrott, who lived more than 25 years up on a slope above the MF of the Salmon River.

Partridge Creek (Clearwater). T40N R2E sec 23. Rises in the NW corner of the county at Diamond Match Camp and flows 4 mi W into Elk Creek just N of the town of Elk River; Clearwater River drainage.

Named for the Hungarian or gray partridges here.

Partridge Creek/Butte (Idaho). T24N R3E sec 19. A 10-mi stream rising in Partridge Creek Lakes and flowing N to Salmon River, 8 mi E of Riggins. Partridge Creek Bridge is situated here.

Named for an early miner who lived on the creek.

Pasture Creek (Latah). T42N R1E sec 32. Stream 1 1/2 mi long, flows W to Potlatch River.

It appears among a group of creeks bearing animal names; a USFS office name.

Pattee Creek (Lemhi). T19N R24E sec 17. Forms on the Continental Divide; flows W 4 mi, S 3 1/2 mi, and finally W 3 1/2 mi to enter Lemhi River just S of Sacajawea Monument. Pronounced Pat-TEE.

Named for Joseph B. Pattee, who first came into the valley as an employee of the American Fur Company and who later settled on land at the mouth of this stream.

Patterson Creek (Lemhi). Originates in Lemhi Range; 2 1/2 mi SE of Mogg Mountain; flows S 6 mi, SW 2 mi to Patterson; NW 13 1/2 mi to enter Pahsimeroi River; Salmon River drainage.

Patterson (6050'). T14N R23E sec 22. Town in Pahsimeroi Valley, on Patterson Creek about 11 mi SE of May. Post office, 1900-1924.

Named for John Patterson, who found a silver ledge in this drainage in 1879.

Patterson Peak (Blaine). 8350'. T2N R19E sec 5. In the Pioneer Mountains 4.5 mi ENE of Hailey.

Named for Grant Alma Patterson (1921-1982), local civic leader, postmaster for Hailey from 1968 to 1982, and former Hailey city councilman.

Paul (Minidoka). 4200'. T9S R23E sec 30/32. In the S part of the county, 6 mi W of Rupert. A UPRR station, platted by the US Bureau of Reclamation in 1905 as a town. Post office, 1913-.

Named for C. H. Paul, a reclamation engineer.

Pauline (Power). 5146'. T10S R33E sec 12. In the SE part of the county, at the junction of Arbon Valley Highway and Crystal-Pocatello Road; on Bannock Creek; about 38 mi SE of American Falls. Settled in 1890. Post office, 1911-1920.

Formerly Meadow, for the meadow-like nature of the area. Changed to Pauline for the mother of Mormon bishop Kornwalles, one of the first settlers.

Pauls Gulch (Boise). T7N R5E sec 16. Runs SE into Grimes Creek 2 mi N of Centerville.

The Paul family homesteaded in the area of this gulch.

Payette (Payette). T9N R5W sec 33/34. County seat. Located at the confluence of Payette and Snake rivers in the NW corner of the county. Its first name Payettenville, then Payette. Post office, 1864-.

Named for Payette River, which see.

Payette Lakes (Valley). Upper Payette (T21N R314E sec 25, 36/14/30) is 19 mi N of McCall on the McCall-Warren road. It has an area of about 80 acres, with green meadows or timber surrounding it. Lower Payette, (T18/19N R3E) at McCall, is about 7 mi long, 40 mi in circumference, with a maximum depth of at least 300'. The S half is surrounded by lodgepole and yellow pine, the upper half by Douglas and white fir. Little Payette is located E of McCall in T18N R3E sec 1/2/11/12/13.

Payette Peaks (Boise/Custer). 10,211'. T28N R13E sec 30. On the Boise-Custer county line; in the

Sawtooth Range; Sawtooth National Forest.

Named for Payette River, which see.

Payette Valley (Payette/Gem/Valley). A rich area of bottomland extending from Snake River to the mountains in the E.

Named for Payette River, which see.

Payette County. County seat, Payette. Established in 1917 after having been a part of Ada County for 26 years and a part of Canyon County after that. It lies in W Idaho, includes Lower Valley of the Payette River, with a total of 410.9 square miles, and with an elevation of 2147'. The Snake River forms the W border; separating it from Oregon; Washington County, the N; Gem County, the E; and Canyon County, the S.

Named for Payette River, which see.

Payette River (Payette/Gem/Valley/Boise). T8N R5W sec 29. Tributary of the Snake River from the W, just W of Payette; approximately 55 mi long; its drainage is 3300 square miles. It has three important forks: N Fk, 55 mi long, drains W Valley County; Middle Fk, 45 mi long, drains the NW corner of Boise County and a portion of S Valley County; S Fk, 60 mi long, drains N Boise County. Payette River proper, with its major tributaries Big and Little Willow creeks, drains Payette County.

Named for Francois Payette, a Canadian fur trapper and explorer with the North West Company, who came to this country in 1818. He was the first white man in the area and brought the first cattle.

Payne (Bonneville). 4745'. T3N R39E sec 29. Village in NW quadrant about 9 mi W of Osgood in the St. Leon area. Post office, 1903-1904.

Named for Joseph Payne, one of the early settlers.

Payne Creek (Lemhi). T17N R23E sec 27. Flows 1 1/2 mi NE to Bear Valley Creek, 1 1/2 mi up from the latter's mouth; Lemhi River drainage.

Named for Ed Payne, an early settler of this region.

Peale Mountains (Bear Lake/Caribou). A large group of mountains in the SE part of the state, trending NW to SE and including several divisions: Aspen, Preuss, and Webster ranges; Schmid and Dry ridges; and Fox and Gannett hills. Length, about 65 mi; width, 25 mi maximum; occupy the extreme SE area except for Bear River Ridge. This area is also called the Middle Rocky Province.

Named for geologist A. C. Peale.

Pearl (Gem). 4340'. T6N R1E sec 15. An old mining town in the SE part of Gem County about 11 mi E of Emmett.

Once a bustling gold camp that existed more than 50 years. Gold-bearing quartz was discovered on Willow Creek in 1867 and the area continued to be worked after the 1893 panic and from 1903 to 1907. Post office, 1915-1926.

First named De Lava, for the first prospector to strike pay ore, then Pearl, for the Pearl mine.

Pearl Island (Bonner). T56N R1E sec 10. In Lake Pend Oreille, 2 1/2 mi SW of Hope and 2 mi E of Glengary.

Named for Joe Child's daughter Pearl. Previously known as Twin Island.

Pearson (Shoshone). T46N R6E sec 7. A station on the Milwaukee RR at the mouth of Trap Creek, 7 mi NE of Avery.

A RR spur was built from this point up the N Fk St. Joe River in 1910-1911 and the station was named Bogle for Mike Bogle, who was logging there in 1911. Later the station was renamed Pearson for Harry and Morris Pearson, head men of the Lucky Swede mine, later known as Pearson Mining Company.

Peavey (Twin Falls). 3740'. T10S R15E sec 2. In the N part of the county halfway between Buhl and Filer; a UPRR siding.

Named for Arthur J. Peavey, Twin Falls, who owned the land where the siding is located.

Peck (Nez Perce). 926'. T36N R1W sec 11. Community 6 mi NW of Gifford at the mouth of Big Canyon Creek, 35 mi E of Lewiston. Homesteaded in 1896 and the village established in 1899, when the RR was built. Post office, 1896-. The principal industry is agriculture.

Named for George Peck, a RR official.

Peck Spring (Jefferson). T8N R36E sec 15. A spring near the town of Camas.

Named for Jared G. and George W. Peck, who sold their homestead as a site for Camas, 1883.

Pee Wee Gulch (Latah). T42N R1E sec 18. Canyon and stream 1.3 mi long, flows SE to E Fk Emerald Creek; St. Maries River drainage.

Named for a prospector from Fernwood who found a large garnet crystal in this gulch; his nickname was Pee Wee.

Peel Tree Basin (Lemhi). T18N R20E sec 11, 12. One mi N of Sheephorn Mountain.

A porcupine infestation in the area peeled the bark from almost all the trees.

Peep A Day Ridge (Bonner). T55N R1E sec 28. Extends 3 1/2 mi NW from a point 2 1/2 mi NE of Pack Saddle Mountain to Fleming Point.

Named for its location in regard to the rising sun.

Peer Canyon (Lewis). A side canyon to the canyon through which Lapwai Creek flows. Located W of Winchester.

Named for a local family.

Pegram (Bear Lake). 6036'. T15S R46E sec 6. In the SE part of the county, on Bear River and the OSLRR, 7 mi E of Bear Lake. Settlement at this site dates from 1883. Post office, 1901-1940.

Named for an engineer.

Pelican Ridge (Caribou). T5S R41/42E. In the N part of the county NE of Blackfoot River Reservoir outlet. Extends NW to SE from Limerock Mountain to Camp Peak and lies NW of Pelican Slough, from which it takes its name.

Pelicans are attracted to the marshy area.

Pen Basin (Valley). T15N R8E sec 17/18. Lies at the mouth of Johnson Creek about 1 mi S of Landmark.

Named for a trappers' pen or storage stockade built in the basin S of the mouth of Whiskey Creek prior to the development of large-scale mining in the vicinity in the late 1800s.

Pence Butte (Owyhee). 3714'. T8S R7E sec 1. Located 7 1/2 mi NE of Soldier Cap Butte. Pence Hot Spring is in the Roberson Cave area near Bruneau.

Named for the Pence family, who lived around Three Creek and Bruneau.

Pend Oreille, Lake (Bonner/Kootenai). The largest lake in Idaho and one of the largest freshwater lakes in the US, with an area of 180 square miles. The extreme length is 65 mi, extreme width 15 miles, and shoreline 300 miles. Soundings are said to have been made to a depth of 1225'. Warren Island, 160 acres, is the largest of the islands in the lake. The chief tributary of Lake Pend Oreille is Clark Fork; the chief outlet, Pend Oreille River.

Pend Oreille, Mount (Bonner). 6785'. T59N R2E sec 35. Located 5

3/4 mi W of Idaho-Montana state border and 1 3/4 mi S of Mount Willard.

Pend d'Oreille (Bonner). T57N R2W sec 22. Post office, 1867-1893, when the name was changed to Sandpoint.

Pend Oreille River (Bonner/Pend Oreille Co., Wn./British Columbia). T57N R2W sec 31. River 115 mi long, heads in Lake Pend Oreille and flows W then N into Washington and across the international boundary into British Columbia to the Columbia River 10 mi NE of Newport, Washington. The Canadian form of the name is Pend d'Oreille River.

Variant names: Bitter Root River, Bitterroot River, Clarke Fork, Clarkes Fork, Clark Fork, Clarks Fork, Clark's Fork, Deer Lodge River, Hell Gate River, Missoula River, Pend d'Oreille River, Silver Bow River. The name is derived from an Indian tribe called Pend Oreilles by early French trappers, some say because they wore ornaments in their ear lobes, which anthropologists deny. The widespread use of the word generally indicates the area occupied by the Pend Oreilles.

Pepper Creek (Lemhi). T20N R20E sec 18. Flows 3 mi to enter Deep Creek. Peppercreek Ridge is located in the area from the mouth of Pepper Creek northward, about 3 1/2 mi E of Cobalt.

Named for the weed locally known as "pepper plant," which is abundant in this area.

Perjue Canyon (Owyhee). T7S R2E sec 13. Located 7 1/2 mi E of Chalk Hills on Shoo Fly Creek.

Named for the Perjue family who lived in the Bruneau area.

Perk Canyon (Lemhi). T15N R28E sec 31. Runs 2 mi S to Powderhorn Gulch, 13 mi SE of Leadore.

Named for an old prospector, Marshal "Perk" Perkins, who lived in this canyon.

Perkins (Ada). T3N R2E sec 11. UPRR station, E of Julia Davis Park and NE of Boise State University.

Named for a local farmer, Simon P. Perkins.

Perreau Creek (Lemhi). T20N R30E sec 31. Forms near Crib Spring; flows S 2 mi and E 7 mi to enter Salmon River. Pronounced PROE.

Named for John Perreau, an old Frenchman who mined in this area in the 1870s.

Perrine (Jerome). 3870'. T9S R18E sec 11. In the central part of the county, 7 mi NW of Eden; a farming area on the UPRR.

Named by RR officials for I. B. Perrine, who brought the area to life by promoting and raising the money to irrigate it.

Perrine Coulee Falls (Twin Falls). T9S R17E sec 33. In the NE part of the county, about 3 mi NE of Twin Falls at the head of Perrine Coulee, a 12-mi drain extending SE from Snake River. The falls form a long, slender drop of nearly 200' from an overflow of the irrigated terrain N.

Pete and Charlie Creek (Clearwater). T34N R5E sec 21. Rises on Brown Creek Ridge in the SW part of the county and flows 3 mi SW into Lolo Creek 7 mi SE of Weippe; Clearwater River drainage.

Named for homesteaders. It is uncertain whether the names were Pete Lewis and Charlie Holbrook or the Car brothers.

Pete Creek (Idaho). T26N R7E sec 5/8. Stream 2.2 mi long, flows SW to Fish Lake 4 mi ESE of Buffalo Hump.

Named for Pete Johnson, miner and packer who lived at the mouth of this stream.

Pete King Creek (Idaho). T33N R7E sec 28. Rises on Woodrat Mountain

(4983') and flows 11 mi SE to Lochsa River 1.5 mi N of Lowell.

Named for Pete King, who had a mining claim here in the 1880s. King spent $2000 in an unsuccessful attempt to divert the creek from its original channel. Named by the USFS.

Pete Ott Creek (Clearwater). T39N R10E sec 5. Rises in the NE quadrant of the county in Pete Ott Lake and flows 3.5 mi SE into N Fk Clearwater River, 2.5 mi N of Kelly Forks campground.

Named for a trail foreman.

Petersen Creek (Boise). T9N R2E sec 36. Flows 3 1/2 mi SW into Dry Buck Creek 2 mi W of Banks; Payette River drainage.

Named for Anthony Petersen, an early Norwegian pioneer who settled near the creek.

Peterson (Bingham). 4499'. T2S R35E sec 16. In the N part of the county, 4 mi N of Blackfoot.

This was an UPRR station, named by RR officials for Ebbe Peterson, first owner of the site of Shelley; an old-timer and prospector and prime mover in the development of the Snake River Valley and Cedar Point irrigation canals.

Peterson Canyon (Clark). T9N R31E sec 13. Rises on Scott Butte and trends 5 mi NE, 8 mi SE of Blue Dome.

William Peterson had a ranch here; said to be the last of the big stockmen to run continuously on the open range without storing winter feed.

Peterson Creek (Lemhi). T17N R25E sec 30. Originates N of East and West Peak; flows SW 6 mi to enter Lemhi River.

Named for William "Billy" Peterson, a native of the Bornholm Islands, Denmark, who came to Leesburg during the early gold rush and then settled on a ranch on this creek. He was also an early Montana pioneer and was reportedly one of the small party to explore and announce the discovery of land now in Yellowstone Park.

Petes Gulch (Lemhi). T19N R18E sec 12. N of Salt Creek; runs 3 mi W to enter Moyer Creek in Salmon River drainage.

One informant says it was named for Pete Rood, a cowboy for the Shenon Land and Livestock Company. Another says it was named for Pete Washey, a German who lived here.

Pettibone Creek (Idaho). T31N R13E sec 9. Rises on Wapoo Peak (7681') in the Bitterroots and flows 13 mi SW to Selway River. Pettibone Ridge, 14 mi long, trends NE to SW south of the creek and roughly parallel to it.

The ridge and the stream commemorate Henry Pettibone, who lived for many years in this vicinity; named before 1921.

Pettit Lake (Blaine). T8N R14E sec 25. In the NW extremity of the county NW of Alturas Lake.

Some say it was named for W. H. Pettit, early manager of Monarch mine, Atlanta, Elmore County; others, that it was named for Tom Pettit, a noted early-day stage driver, who drove a party from Boise into this country and camped on this lake in the early 1870s.

Phelan Creek (Lemhi). T21N R19E sec 12. Forms 1 mi W of Baldy Mountain; flows generally W 5 1/2 mi to enter Napias Creek; Salmon River drainage. Phelan Mountain is near the head of S Fk Phelan Creek, and Phelan Ridge runs NE in the area between Phelan Creek and Pony Creek. Pronounced FEE- lin.

Named for Lawrence W. Phelan, who located placer mines on this stream. He was born in New York and came west in the early 1860s, coming to the Leesburg Basin from Virginia City, Montana, in the fall of 1866.

Phi Kappa Mountain (Custer). 10,516'. T6N R19E sec 26/33. 32 mi S of Phi Kappa mine at the head of Phi Kappa Creek; in Pioneer Mountains; Challis National Forest.

Both the creek and the peak are named for Phi Kappa mine.

Phillips Creek (Camas). T1N R14E sec 5. Rises on Monument Peak about 9 mi NW of Soldier and flows 7 mi SE to Soldier Creek, tributary of Camas Creek; Big Wood River drainage.

John and Bert Phillips settled on upper Soldier Creek in 1884. John Phillips remained on Camas Prairie the rest of his life.

Piah Creek (Latah). T43N R3W sec 36. Stream 4 mi long, flows SW to E Fk Meadow Creek; Palouse River drainage; north central part of the county.

Named by USFS ranger W. H. Daugs; the Chinook jargon word Piah means "where the timber has been burned off," as was true in this area.

Picabo (Blaine). 4832'. T1S R20E sec 27. In the SW part of the county on Silver Creek, 6 mi W of Carey. Pronounced PEEK-uh-BOO. This is a trading post and shipping point for a livestock area; also a fishing area. Post office, 1902-.

Picabo Hills. T2S R19E. Between the town of Picabo on the E and Magic Reservoir on the W, bounded on the N by Silver Creek and on the S by Snake River Plain. Not: Resurrection.

The name is believed to be an Indian word for "come in"; some say, for "silver water."

Picard Point (Bonner). T56N R1E sec 17. On W side of Lake Pend Oreille, 1/2 mi SE of Glengary.

Named for a railroad worker who built a stone house on the point.

Piccolo Creek (Latah). T42N R2W sec 35. Stream.6 mi long, flows E to Big Sand Creek; Palouse River drainage.

USFS ranger W. H. Daugs is credited with naming nine of the eleven short tributaries of Big Sand Creek in 1928. Piccolo lies between Torpid and Yakala, and the name has the mark of Daugs' thumbprint if not his signature, though its origin has not been determined.

Picket Corral (Gem). T7N R1W sec 33. An 1860s robber and rustler rendezvous 2 mi above Emmett on Payette River. Also called Robbers Den. This is a natural box canyon near the Payette River, a perfect place to pen stolen horses. A group of outlaws used the place and stole from Boise Basin travelers.

Adjoining the corral was the stockade, a structure built with picket walls, from which the name comes.

Pickett Creek (Owyhee). T4/5S R1/2W. A drain running NE beginning between Cinnebar Mountain and Quicksilver Mountain approximately 13 mi toward State Highway 45.

Named Pickett Creek for a man who lived here.

Pickles Butte (Canyon). 3088'. T2N R3W sec 29. Four mi S of Lake Lowell, just S of Lizard Butte.

Named for the dog of a local rancher's small son, which he called "Pickle."

Pie Creek (Clearwater). T39N R10E sec 16. Rises in the NE quadrant of the county and flows SW into Kelly Creek; Clearwater River drainage.

An analogical name made up by the USFS, since the creek is located near Bacon and Coffee creeks.

Piedmont Plain (Owyhee). From an elevation of nearly 6000' at the Idaho-Nevada line, this plain descends N in a long gentle slope to approximately 3500' at the rim of the lower basin of Bruneau River, and extends N to the Snake River Plain.

A generic name from French, "foot of the mountains."

Pierce (Ada). T4N R2E sec 30. An old BVTRR station. Pierce Gulch is located near the station in sec 19/20/21.

Named for W. E. Pierce, a railroad official and Boise businessman and mayor.

Pierce (Clearwater). 3100'. T36N R5E sec 2. Town between the headwaters of Orofino and Orogrande creeks, some 24 mi E of Orofino. Pierce Creek lies just E of the town, a short tributary of Rhodes Creek; Clearwater River drainage. Post office, 1863-.

Named for Captain Elias D. Pierce, a prospector from California who discovered gold in the area in 1860 and later helped found the town.

Pierce Canyon (Lemhi). T11N R30E sec 34. Runs SW 2 mi, near the Lemhi-Clark county line on the S.

Named for an old miner and prospector who lived here in the early days.

Pierce Creek (Lemhi). T27N R21E sec 34. Heads on Idaho-Montana border; flows SW 3 mi to enter N Fk Salmon River.

Named for an early placer miner and homesteader, John Pierce.

Pierres Hole (Teton). T4-7N R44/45E. Early name for Teton Valley/Basin.

Named for an Iroquois Indian trapper whose Canadian name was Pierre Tevanitabon, an employee of North West Company. He trapped here frequently, and it was given his name by contemporary fur trappers. He was killed by Blackfoot Indians in 1827.

In 1832 Pierres Hole was the site of the annual trappers' rendezvous, when

Rocky Mountain and American Fur companies were in competition.

Pierson Creek (Clearwater). T35N R5E sec 14. Flows 2.5 mi SW into Jim Brown Creek at Peterson Corners; Clearwater River drainage.

Named for a homesteader who logged for the Blackwell Lumber Company.

Pigeon Hollow (Latah). T44N R6W sec 25/36, T44N R5W sec 29-32, T43N R5W sec 5/6. A Pine Creek community in the NW corner of Latah County.

Named for the flocks of wild pigeons that nested in barns and trees in the area.

Pillar Butte (Power). T6S R28E sec 20. In the W part of the county, 4 mi S of Crystal Ice Caves; in the Great Rift. Formed by constant lava eruptions; the source of flows that resulted in Crystal Ice Caves.

A descriptive name: the butte is shaped like a pillar.

Pillar Falls (Jerome). T9S R17E sec 35. On Snake River between Perrine Memorial Bridge and Shoshone Falls.

A descriptive name; water flows over and splits around pillars of basalt, forming many channels.

Pilot Knob (Idaho). 7135'. T30N R6E sec 28. In the NW quadrant of the county 19 mi E of Grangeville; Clearwater Mountains.

This was the highest point visible from the Nez Perce Trail, presumably a landmark for travelers.

Pinch Gulch (Boise). T8N R6E sec 17. Flows N into Grimes Creek 5 mi SE of Grimes Pass; Boise River drainage.

The Pinch family lived on this gulch and tried to mine but went broke and left.

Pinchot Creek (Boise). T8N R12E sec 7. Rises on the W boundary of the SE extremity of the county; flows 5 mi N into the Payette River 1 mi NW of Fern Falls. Pronounced PIN-show. Pinchot Mountain (9542') lies 1 1/2 mi S of the mouth of the creek.

Named by the USFS in honor of Gifford Pinchot, chief of the Division of Forestry, U.S. Department of Interior. He visited Idaho in 1905.

Pincock Hot Springs (Madison). T5N R43E sec 6. An early resort, with swimming pool; in the E part of the county on Canyon Creek.

Named for John E. and James H. Pincock, on whose limestone claim the springs are located. The Pincocks operated the resort 1903-1924. Currently named Green Canyon Hot Springs.

Pine (Elmore). 4172'. T2N R10E sec 31. An early stage station on S Fk Boise River; at N extremity of Anderson Ranch Reservoir, 8 mi S of Featherville. Formerly Pine Grove. Post office, 1888-1929.

When Anderson Ranch Dam was completed, Pine Grove was inundated. Some of the buildings were moved upstream to the present village of Pine, others to higher ground near the Franklin mine. Mine dumps are still visible.

Named for the heavy stand of yellow pine in this location.

Pine Creek (Latah). A community in the NW corner of the county in the area drained by Pine Creek; Palouse River. The first homestead was registered in 1872 by Lyman Davenport.

Post office, 1873-1884.

Named for the creek, which in turn was named for the pine forest in the area.

Pine Creek (Lemhi). T24N R18E sec 36. Forms near Haystack Mountain; flows NW 9 mi to enter Salmon River, about 1 mi downriver from Shoup. Pine Creek Rapids are on Salmon River just below the mouth of Pine Creek. Pine Creek Ridge runs NW to SE on the NE side of the stream, about 1 mi N of Haystack Mountain for about 3 mi to Stormy Peak.

Sam James and Pat O'Hara, two miners from the Big Creek country, came to this area in 1881 and named the drainage for the beautiful pine trees they found here.

Pinehurst (Shoshone). 2119'. T48N R2E sec 5. In the W part of the county, 5 mi W of Kellogg; on I-90, UPRR, and Pine Creek. A mining village. Post office, 1865-. Founded in the 1880s.

Named for the pine forest in which it was located and Pine Creek.

Pingree (Bingham). 4450'. T3S R33E sec 33. In the SW part of the county, 17 mi SW of Blackfoot.

John Pingree, of Salt Lake City, financed the platting and development of this townsite, with plans to sell homes to Mormon settlers. Post office, 1909-1930.

Pinnacle Ridge (Shoshone). T44N R7E sec 16-19. A 3-mi ridge trending NE to SW on the W border of Red Ives Ranger District between Thor Mountain and Whistling Peak.

Officially named in 1930 by the USFS for the high rock pinnacles along the ridge that can be seen from a great distance.

Pinnacles, The (Valley). 9270'. T20N R9E sec 34. Mountain having two distinct peaks similar in shape and size, in Payette National Forest at the N end of the Missouri Ridge, about 7 mi S of the settlement of Big Creek and 40 mi ENE of McCall. Not: The Pinnacle, Pinnacle, Pinnacle Peak.

A descriptive name.

Pinney Creek (Boise). T10N R4E sec 22. Flows 2 1/4 mi S into Scriver Creek 4 1/2 mi N of Crouch; Payette River drainage. Pronounced Pie-nee.

Named for Idaho City merchant Jason Pinney; he had a placer mine on this creek.

Pioneer (Latah). T41N R4W. A primitive settlement of the 1880s and 1890s, twelve mi E of Palouse, Washington, on Rock Creek.

Named for the pioneer settlers. Also called Pioneer Mill.

Pioneer Butte (Gooding). 3372'. T5S R12E sec 17. In the W part of the county, 1.8 mi E of the Elmore-Gooding line. Pioneer Reservoir lies 1/2 mi SW of the butte on Clover Creek.

The butte was named for the first whites in the vicinity, and the reservoir for the butte.

Pioneer Gulch (Clearwater). T40N R11E sec 21. Runs E into Osier Creek; Clearwater River drainage.

Named for the Pioneer mine.

Pioneer Mountains (Blaine/Custer). Adjoin the White Knob Mountains on the E, the Boulder Mountains on the N, the Big Wood River on the W, and Snake River Plain on the S.

Bisected by Little Wood River, the E ridge of this group was formerly known as Antelope Mountains; and the W ridge, between Little Wood and Big Wood Rivers S of Hailey, is now known locally as Rock Creek Mountains.

The group has been named Pioneer to honor early settlers of southern Idaho.

Pioneerville (Boise). T7N R5E sec 3. Village 7.1 mi N of Centerville.

This was a mining camp, founded October 1862 by members of the Splawn- Grimes propecting party. One of the first important mining camps in the Boise Basin, it was early nicknamed

Fort Hogem when newly arrived miners found the ground already staked. Post office, 1864-.

Named for the pioneer miners here.

Pipe Creek (Bonneville). T1N R41E sec 7. Rises in NE quadrant in Caribou Range and flows 8 mi SW into Tex Creek; Snake River drainage.

Named for water pipe used in irrigation.

Pistol Rock (Valley). 9169'. T17N R9E sec 20/29. At the head of Indian and Pistol creeks at the N extremity of Pistol Ridge, in Boise National Forest. This is an area just S of the major skirmishes of the Sheepeater War, which in all probability affected the name of the peak, regarded as a landmark to prospectors after 1879.

Pistol Creek (Valley). T16N R11E sec 17. Rises on Pistol Creek Ridge and flows NE and E to Middle Fk Salmon River. The main stream is about 16 mi long; its main tributary, Little Pistol, 13 mi long; the drainage of Pistol Creek system, 86 square miles.

The creek took its name from Pistol Rock, a landmark for late-19th- and early-20th-century travelers. The tributaries named by the USFS in recognition of the skirmishes with Sheepeater Indians are all names of weapons, mostly guns. They must have been named after World War I as Luger, a German weapon, appears on one of the creeks. The names of main Pistol Creek tributaries are Thirty-two, Twenty-five, Forty-five (Shrapnel and Grenade), Popgun, Twenty-two, Forty-four, and Luger; names of Little Pistol Creek tributaries are Foresight, Colt, Trigger, Savage, Remington, Winchester, Stevens, Springfield, Marlin, and Twenty-eight.

Pistol Lake lies in the mountainous area of Pistol Ridge, just S of Lake Mountain, and rugged Pistol Ridge extends from Pistol Rock SW, S, SE,

E, and NE in a circular fashion some 35 mi around the Pistol Creek drainage.

The names of all these features derive from the first name given, Pistol Rock. They reinforce the memory of the Sheepeater Indian War of 1879.

An interesting sidelight to the naming process can be seen in names of features on Middle Fk just S of Pistol Creek. These are Canon, Mortar, Cap, and Artillery creeks and Artillery Lake and Rapids.

Pitch Fork Creek (Boise). T8N R12E sec 17. Rises in the SE extremity of the county and flows N into the S Fk Payette River at Fern Falls.

Named by the USFS in 1928 for the shape of the creek.

Pittsburg Landing (Idaho). T26N R1W sec 4. On the Snake River 1 mi S of Pittsburg Bar and 6 mi SW of Pittsburg Saddle. A road from White Bird to Pittsburg Saddle was completed in 1900; from it one can view Salmon River and Snake River canyons; the road continues to Pittsburg Landing. This road opened up the area to settlement. A ferry operated at Pittsburg Landing from 1891 to 1933.

According to Cort Conley, Pittsburg Landing is likely a transfer name from Pittsburg Landing on the west bank of the Tennessee River in Tennessee, site of the Battle of Shiloh, Mar.-Apr. 1862. The name appears in the Lewiston "Golden Age" in Mar. 1863 and would have been given by the Stubadore party (Levi Allen) at the location Apr/May 1862.

Pittwood Creek (Latah). T42N R1W sec 17. In the NE quarter of the county; St. Joe National Forest; a tributary of Fern Creek; Palouse River drainage.

Named by W. H. Daugs, USFS ranger, after an early-day miner of that name.

Pivash Creek (Clearwater). T41N R1E sec 35. Flows 3 mi NW into E Fk Potlatch River.

Named for gyppo logger Sam Pivash.

Placer Creek (Shoshone). T48N R4E sec 27. In the E part of the county. Rises on the St. Joe Mountains and flows 7 mi NW and N to S Fk Coeur d'Alene River at Wallace. Placer Peak (5200') lies at the headwaters of this stream.

Placer Center. Early name for Wallace, bestowed by Col. Wardner who in 1884 named it for the nearby creek. But as the settlement grew, the name was changed to Wallace, which see.

Named for the many placer mines in the area.

Placer Creek (Clearwater). T36N R4E sec 2. Flows 2 mi NW into Orofino Creek; Clearwater River drainage.

Named for the extensive hand placering done along the creek bottom.

Placer Creek (Latah). T40N R1E sec 17. Rises on the N slope of Mt. McGary and flows 2 mi N to empty into Ruby Creek; Potlatch River drainage.

Henry Ables worked profitable placers here up to the 1920s.

Placerville (Boise). T7N R4E sec 14. Ghost town 6.1 mi NW of New Centerville.

Founded 1 Dec 1862 by men from California; placer mining could be seen everywhere from Main Street. The settlement increased to 3200 by September, 1863. Post office, 1863-.

Plank Creek (Bonner). T59N R2E sec 8. Heads 1 mi E of Grouse Mountain and flows 1 1/2 mi SE into Grouse Creek; Pack River drainage.

Probably an office name. It lies between Flume and Chute creeks, tributaries of Grouse Creek. "Plank" is in harmony with other logging/lumbering names in the area.

Plano (Madison). 4845'. T7N R39E sec 32. Community in the NW part of the county, 7 mi W of Sugar City. Settled in 1884 by Mormons.

In the late 1890s named Plain, descriptive of the topography. However, the post office was granted in 1899 with the name Plano.

Also Hiatt and Plain.

Plateau Lake (Lemhi). T20N R16E sec 7. About 1 1/2 mi W of Paragon Lake and about 1 mi NE of South Fork Lake.

Named by USFS in cooperation with US Coast and Geodetic Survey in 1963, because the lake is located on a glacial bench.

Pleasant Valley (Ada). T1N R2E sec 5/6. An area SE of Kuna and Mora lying between N Indian and Ten Mile creeks.

Early recognized for its pleasant grassy terrain.

Pleasantview (Oneida). T14/15S R35E sec 35/2. An agricultural area in the SE part of the county, 5 mi SW of Malad City. Post office, 1899-1907.

A Mormon community so named because it commands a fine view of Malad Valley. Gwenford once occupied part of this site, but it has been absorbed by Pleasantview. Variant: Pleasant View, Gwenford.

Pleasantview Warm Springs. A tourist and recreational attraction that lies at the SW edge of the town.

Plowman Gulch (Latah). T41N R4W sec 12. Canyon and stream between Morrissey and Turnbow creeks; trends S 1.2 mi N of Palouse River.

Henrietta Plowman owned the land drained by this creek.

Plummer (Benewah). 2722'. T46N R4W sec 18. In the NW part of the county in the heart of the Coeur d'Alene

Indian Reservation. The town was incorporated in 1911. Post office, 1910-.

Claimed widely to have been named for the outlaw Henry Plummer, who had a hideout near the present townsite. Some local informants say the name comes from a Mrs. Plummer, who reputedly bought the first lot in 1910; highly doubtful, as the name was on a 1909 map.

Pocatello (Bannock). 4471'. T6S R34E sec 26. County seat. Second-largest city in Idaho; gateway into Idaho from the S and E; on Portneuf River; in the extreme NW part of the county.

A stage station was established here in 1864 and named Pocatello; the Utah and Northern RR came through in 1879; and it came to be known as Pocatello Junction in 1884 when the UPRR station was completed, because it became a junction for railroads and highways branching in all directions. It was organized as a village in 1889. In 1905 more reservation land was opened to settlement, resulting in a rush of homesteaders. Post office, 1883-.

Named for a Northwestern Shoshoni chief, who was called Pocatello. The meaning of the name is obscure.

Poe (Latah). T40N R6W sec 12/13. Railroad stop between Estes and Viola on the Spokane and Inland Empire Railroad.

Named for Plosa P. Powe (sic), whose property the railroad crossed, and who operated a gravel pit nearby.

Poe Creek (Idaho). T27N R1E sec 4. Rises on Howard Ridge and flows 3 mi SE to join Howard Creek; Salmon River drainage. Four mi SW of White Bird.

Named for Frank Poe, the original homesteader who worked in Warren and Slaughter Creek mines during the gold-boom days.

Poirier Creek (Bonner/Kootenai). T54N R5W sec 28. Stream 4 mi long, heads in Kootenai Co. and flows N to Blanchard Lake .4 mi SE of Blanchard.

Named for Lewis Poirier, an early settler. Variant spelling: Poirrier Creek.

Poison Creek (Bonneville). T3N R44E sec 29. Rises in NE quadrant in Caribou Range and flows 3 mi NW into Pine Creek; Snake River drainage.

Named because several head of sheep and cattle died in this area from larkspur poisoning.

Poison Creek (Lemhi). T16N R28E sec 33. Originates on the Idaho-Montana border; flows S 2 1/2 mi to enter Big Bear Creek; Lemhi River drainage. Poison Peak. T18N R22E sec 17. 2 mi W of Watson Peak.

Named for the larkspur and death camas located here. The roots of these plants are poisonous to livestock.

Other features in Lemhi County characterized by poison larkspur and death camas are Poison Creek, of Salmon River, named by Steve Mahaffey, Sr., who lost cattle here by poisoning; Poison Creek, T14/15N R28E; and Poison Gulch Spring, T19N R24E.

Poker Peak (Bonneville). 8435'. T2S R45E sec 16. In SE quadrant just W of the Palisades Reservoir.

Named by Thomas, Doc, and Joe Rowberry, brothers, in 1900 for a game of poker they enjoyed at this site.

Polar Creek (Clearwater). T39N R12E sec 16. Flows 2 mi SE into Bear Creek; Clearwater River drainage.

This is part of a group name developing from Bear Creek. Its tributaries were named Cub, Polar, and Kodiak creeks.

Pole Camp Creek (Twin Falls). T14S R17E sec 12. Rises in the E central part of the county in Sawtooth National Forest and flows 4 mi SW to Shoshone

Creek, 10 mi E of Rogerson. Pole Camp Springs lies near the head of this stream.

Named for the lodgepole pine in the area.

Pole Creek (Lemhi). T17N R16E sec 21. Heads about 3/4 mi NW of Rock Lakes; flows NE 5 mi to enter W Fk Camas Creek; Middle Fk Salmon River drainage.

There are good stands of lodgepole pine growing here, which ranchers use to make fence poles.

Pollard Canyon (Lemhi). T21N R22E sec 6. Rises near the headwaters of Pony Creek; runs E 7 mi to enter Salmon River drainage.

Named for Frank M. Pollard, who had a very productive coal mine in this canyon.

Pollock (Idaho). 2353'. T23N R1E sec 20. In the SW part of the county, on Little Salmon River, 7 mi S of Riggins and 60 mi SE of Grangeville.

First settled in 1872, Pollock served a mining area nearby and became a prosperous trading point by 1904.

Sometime between 1914 and 1919, the townsite was moved 4 mi S. Post office, 1893-.

Named for Thomas Pollock, on whose land the old Pollock townsite was laid out and who was the second postmaster.

Pollock Creek (Clearwater). T40N R11E sec 25. Flows 4 mi SW into Swamp Creek; Clearwater River drainage. Pollock Hill (5503') is situated 5 mi NE of the mouth of the creek. Pollock Ridge trends NE-SW on the S side of the creek, 3 mi NE of Kelly Creek Work Center.

Named for George Pollock, a firefighter in the USFS.

Polly Creek (Idaho). T24N R6E sec 12. A 3.2-mi stream flowing N to Salmon River about 30 mi E of Riggins.

Named for Polly Bemis, the Chinese wife of Charlie Bemis, who secured her freedom from indenture, married her, and moved (1894) to the mouth of this tributary of the Salmon River.

Pollywog Lake (Lemhi). T21N R16E sec 6. In Bighorn Crags about 1/2 mi due E of Parrot Lake.

Named by Lester Gutzman, Ernest Marsing, and USFS crew ca.1938 for the pollywogs found in the lake when they planted it with fish.

Ponderay (Bonner). T57N R2W sec 12. Town 3/4 mi WSW of Kootenai and 2 mi NE of Sandpoint.

Post office, 1907-.

A respelling of Pend Oreille, for which it is named.

Pony Creek (Clearwater). T38N R11E sec 7. Flows 3 mi SE into Cayuse Creek; Clearwater River drainage. Drains Pony Flats; 5 mi SW of Kelly Creek Work Center.

This is a group name, with Pony Creek being a tributary of Cayuse Creek.

Pony Creek (Lemhi). T22N R20E sec 32. Forms near the NE end of Phelan Ridge; flows W 4 mi to enter Napias Creek; Salmon River drainage.

Lawrence Phelan and James A. MacNab kept a large herd of saddle and pack horses in this area during the Leesburg gold rush (1860s and 1870s).

Pony Lake (Lemhi). T21N R20E sec 4. About 2 mi E of California Bar.

The California Bar Placer Company built an artificial reservoir here in the early days.

Named for Pony Creek (Lemhi).

Pooles Island (Jefferson). T5N R38E sec 33. Probably the best known of the early names for Menan. In 1879 John R. Poole and Austin R. Green and their families moved to the island known as

Heals Island at that time. The new families formed a nucleus for an LDS settlement, the first in the area encompassed by Jefferson County today.

When a post office was applied for, it was granted 18 Mar 1880, with the name of Cedar Butte, which see.

Poorman Creek (Clearwater). T37N R4E sec 36. Flows 5 mi S into Orofino Creek; Clearwater River drainage.

The miners named this creek for their lack of success in getting gold; it was thought to be a poor prospect in comparison with others.

Poorman Creek (Latah). T42N R2W sec 22. Tributary of Palouse River; rises S of Little Bald Mountain and flows S 3.9 mi to Palouse River, St. Joe National Forest.

Placer mining was said to be so difficult that it literally made a man poor to work the area. However, Lonnie Wilkins, miner, said the vein actually played out and it did not pay to work it. Arthur A. Hughes located Poorman's Pocket in Rocke Gulch (sic), a tributary of Poorman Creek, 8 Aug 1894.

Poplar (Bonneville). 5025'. T3N R40N sec 1. Farming community in the NE quadrant 4 mi E of Ririe. Settled by Mormons in the 1880s. Post office, 1894-1910.

Named for a nearby poplar grove.

Porcupine Canyon (Fremont). T12N R41E sec 16. Empties into Island Park Reservoir; Henrys Fork system.

Porcupine Creek. T9N R44E sec 25. Flows 6 mi S to Rock Creek thence to Robinson Creek, 12 mi E of Ashton; Warm River drainage. Porcupine Lake is 3 mi SE of Porcupine Ranger Station, which is 13 mi E of Ashton.

Named for the frequent appearance of porcupines in the area.

Porcupine Creek (Latah). T41N R1E sec 6. Flows 2.6 mi SE to Potlatch River.

Three creeks within .5 mi have names of animals; Sheep is most westerly, followed by Porcupine and its tributary Wolf, perhaps all office names given by USFS personnel.

Porphyry Creek (Lemhi). T19N R18E sec 3. Heads just NE of Quartzite Mountain; flows SE 5 1/2 mi to enter Panther Creek; Salmon River drainage. Porphyry Ridge runs parallel to Porphyry Creek in the area between Porphyry Creek and Musgrove Creek, generally from NW to SE. Pronounced PORE-fri.

Named for the mineral. The area is mostly schist, but porphyry ridges come up through the schist.

Porphyry Peak (Custer). 10,087'. T7N R21E. In the White Knob Mountains; Challis National Forest.

Named for the composition of the rocky surface: it consists of feldspar crystals embedded in a compact dark red or purple ground mass.

Porthill (Boundary). 1797'. T65N R1W sec 8. Located 24 mi NW of Bonners Ferry; established in 1893 as one of two ports of entry on the Canadian border.

Some say the name derives from Charles Hill, a postmaster; others that the first postmaster, James Barnes, named it because it was a port of entry. Previously known as Ockanook.

Portland Mountain (Lemhi). 10,820'. T13N R26E sec 14. About 3 mi SE of Negro Peak; Salmon National Forest.

The Portland Mining Company of Butte, Montana, had mining property in the area N of this mountain.

Portneuf River (Bannock). T5S R33E sec 23. 75 mi long; drainage, 1700 square miles; terrain, timbered upland river valley and plain. Rises between the Chesterfield and Portneuf ranges in lower Bingham County; flows S through Portneuf Reservoir and Portneuf Valley,

SW across a gap in Portneuf Range into Bannock County, then W and NW between Portneuf Range and Bannock Mountains to empty into American Falls Reservoir in the NW extremity of Bannock County; before the reservoir was built, Portneuf River emptied into Snake River.

Fur trappers worked this stream as early as the 1820s, and travelers' followed the same route.

Named for a member of Peter Skene Ogden's trapping party, who was killed by Indians on this stream in 1825. All the other Portneuf names are derived from Portneuf River.

Portneuf 4490'. T7S R35E sec 22. Town in the NW part of the county, 7 mi SE of Pocatello in the Portneuf Canyon. This was originally in the Fort Hall Indian Reservation and there was an Indian school about 1 mi S called Black Rock. There is still a Black Rock Canyon. This site is also near the Black Rock Stage Station, which served stage routes prior to the railroad in 1880. Post office, 1917-1918.

Portneuf Range. The largest range in SE Idaho, extending roughly from Blackfoot to a point a few mi N of Preston between a bend in Portneuf Canyon on the W and Portneuf and Bear River valleys on the E; about midway, Portneuf River cuts a gorge through the range. Through the early 1920s was used mostly for grazing.

Portneuf Valley (Caribou). Lies between the Chesterfield Range on the E and Portneuf Mountains on the W, this winding valley is drained by the Portneuf River. Named in 1825.

Post Falls (Kootenai). 2172'. T50N R5W sec 4. In the W part of the county, on Spokane River, 3.8 mi E of the state line.

Established on the Upper Falls of Spokane River in 1871 by Frederick Post, who built a mill here, earlier known as Marshall, but renamed to honor its founder. He also dammed the three channels of Spokane River and raised the Spokane Falls, which powered his lumber mill. Post office, 1887-.

Pot Lake (Clearwater). T39N R8E sec 12. Seven mi NW of Kelly Forks Ranger Station, 1 mi W of Pot Mountain (7139'). Pot Creek, 6 mi long, flows NW from Pot Mountain into Lightning Creek; Clearwater River drainage. Pot Mountain Ridge entends NE 8 mi from Pot Mountain to Saddle Lake, 5 mi N of Kelly Forks Ranger Station.

The shape of the mountain with its steep sides suggests the name.

Potato Hill (Latah). 4017'. T40N R2W sec 14. A promontory 1 mi N of Deary.

Named for its general shape. Also Spud Hill and Mt. Deary.

Pothole Lake (Lemhi). T21N R16E sec 10. In Bighorn Crags, just W of Big Clear Lake.

Named by Lester Gutzman, Ernest Marsing, and USFS trail crew ca.1940 because the lake reminded them of a big pothole in a road.

Potlatch. The name Potlatch, as nearly as can be determined, is Chinook jargon referring to a ceremonial gathering of one or more tribes held each spring. Loosely translated, the word has come to mean an exchange of gifts in the spirit of good fellowship. Indian chiefs always exchanged gifts during a potlatch or destroyed them, though many accounts have the chiefs returning the gifts to the original giver at the end of the potlatch. The name transferred from this creek to the river, to other large tributaries of the river, to the general area, and finally to the first large lumber company in the area.

Potlatch (Latah). 2775′. T41N R5W sec 1. Incorporated lumber company town about 16 mi NE of Moscow.

Established and named by the Potlatch Lumber Co. (present-day Potlatch Corp.) in 1905. Formerly a large sawmill center. The company owned all the real estate, the houses, schools, churches, and stores. Nothing was owned privately until 1952. The mill was dismantled in 1985.

Post office, 1904-.

Potlatch Creek (Clearwater/Latah). Flows SW into Latah County.

The creek was named by the early miners for an incident that took place here. A Nez Perce Indian, Shacklatumna Hi Hi, had a pony for miners to use in crossing the creek. One day the water was high and the miners who were crossing were quite large; one was an Irishman of 200 pounds. The miners were dumped into the river when the horse stumbled, but all made it to shore safely. The Indian shouted across to the miners on the opposite side, "Potlatch two bits," meaning "give me a quarter," but the miners wouldn't pay. The creek is also called the E Fk Potlatch River. Formerly called Yaka "black bear" Creek; then Colter Creek, for Private John Colter, Lewis and Clark Expedition.

Potlatch River (Latah). Heads in the mountains around Bovill at an altitude of 5500′ and flows SW 42.6 mi to Clearwater River in Nez Perce County. The drainage basin is 625 square miles; terrain is rolling forested foothills, canyon, and valley. N and W fks rise in the NE corner of the county below Emerald Creek drainage; E Fk rises in Clearwater County and empties into the main stream 3 mi N of Bovill; S Fk rises just above the SE corner of Latah County and empties into Potlatch River. Clearwater River drainage.

Little Potlatch Creek rises 1 mi S of Tomer Butte; flows 15 mi generally SE; enters Nez Perce County 14 mi SW of Juliaetta; tributary of Potlatch River.

Middle Potlatch Creek rises 4 mi W of Troy; flows SE 15 mi parallel to Little Potlatch Creek; empties into Potlatch River at Juliaetta.

Potosi Peak (Owyhee). T5S R3W. Near Silver City. Pronounced puh-TOE-see.

Named after the Potosi mine located near Silver City. A transfer name from Potosi, Bolivia, a rich silver mining area.

Poverty Flat (Lemhi). T23N R17E sec 17. Two mi E of Colson Creek Cabin, on the N side of Salmon River.

Named because nothing would grow on the poor soil here.

Powder Gulch (Lemhi). T25N R21E sec 1. Runs NW 1 mi to enter Lick Creek drainage; N Fk Salmon River drainage.

The Civilian Conservation Corps had a powder house in this gulch in the 1930s.

Powderhorn Gulch (Lemhi). T15N R27E sec 36. Originates 1/2 mi W of Mountain Baldy; runs 2 mi S then 4 1/2 mi S and W.

Named because the gulch is shaped somewhat like an old powderhorn.

Powderhouse Gulch (Boise). T10N R5E sec 6. In the NE extremity of the county; flows SE into the Payette River.

Named by the USFS because they stored dynamite here in a shack at the head of the gulch.

Powell Creek (Camas). T1S R15E sec 28. Rises S of Cannonball Mountain and flows about 5 mi SW, then SE to Camas Creek; Big Wood River drainage.

The Powell family had a log home in the quarter section where the Soldier Creek Cemetery is located.

Power County. County seat, American Falls. Created in 1913 from parts of Bingham, Blaine, Cassia, and Oneida counties; named for the American Falls power plant.

Located in the SE part of Idaho, it is drained from S to N by Rock, Rattlesnake, and Bannock creeks, with American Falls Reservoir and Snake River stretching from NE to SW across the county.

Bounded on the N by Blaine, Bingham and Bannock counties; on the E by Bannock County; on the S by Oneida County; on the W by Cassia and Blaine counties.

Prairie (Elmore). 4650'. T2N R7E sec 13. In the center of Elmore County, 13 mi W of Pine and 22 mi N of Mountain Home on Smith Creek; S Fk Boise River. Called Smiths Prairie in 1900, then Lenox and Fall Creek, and finally Prairie, which is descriptive of the area. Post office, 1909-ca.1934.

Prater Creek (Bonner). T57N R4W sec 5. Heads 1/2 mi NW of Prater Mountain; flows 2 1/4 mi NW into Priest River 10 mi N of the town of Priest River. Prater Mountain (4622'), at the head of Prater Creek, is 4 mi SW of Gisborne Mountain.

These features were named for James Prater, an early pioneer (ca.1870).

Preachers Cove (Custer). T12N R13E sec 20. Homesite of a man named Foster, a short distance S of Bonanza City.

So called because Foster organized a Sunday school in Custer and people started calling him "Preacher."

Presto (Bingham). T1S R37E sec 3/4/9/10. Bench S and E of Firth; a pass over which most of the stock of N Bingham County must go; irrigated from Blackfoot River. Post office, 1889-1907.

Named for Presto Burrell, early settler in the area, first to build a diversion dam on Blackfoot River and irrigate his land.

Preston (Franklin). 4714'. T15S R39E sec 22/26. County seat. In the central part of the county, about 10 mi N of the Idaho-Utah line.

Founded in 1866 by William Head. Settlers located along Worm Creek and called their settlement Worm Creek. In 1878 the RR came through; the town was not platted until 1885, after the settlement had been renamed Preston for William B. Preston, a prominent Mormon. Post office, 1882-.

Preston Creek (Benewah). T43N R2W sec 10. Rises on Preston Knob (4140') and flows NW to Charlie Creek; St. Maries River drainage. Two mi N of Benewah-Latah county line.

Gilbert E. Preston homesteaded near this creek and patented his land in 1905.

Price Creek (Lemhi). T20N R23E sec 23. Originates 1 1/2 mi NE of K Mountain; flows NE 3 mi then NW 1 mi to enter Lemhi River.

B. F. Price, who first brought cattle into the Lemhi Valley in 1867, had a ranch on this stream.

Prichard Creek (Shoshone). T50N R4E sec 29. In the NE part of the county, rising on Bitterroot Mountains on the Idaho-Montana line and flowing 15 mi NW to Coeur d'Alene River at the town of Prichard. Prichard Peak lies 2 mi NE of the village. Post office, 1910-ca.1934.

All the features above are named for Andrew J. Prichard, who discovered gold on the stream in 1881.

Priest (Blaine). 4800'. T2S R20E sec 1. UPRR station in the W part of the county, 3 mi SE of Picabo. Post office, 1920-.

Named for Joel Priest, traffic agent for the UPRR at Boise for many years.

Priest Lake (Bonner). T59-62N R4W. Situated 22 mi W of Sandpoint, Priest Lake, with its islands and its forest backdrop, is 24 mi long by 14 wide; the upper part is 8 mi by 5 1/2; in Kaniksu National Forest.

Named in honor of Father John Roothaan, superior of the Society of Jesus, whose members did missionary work in Washington and Idaho. Fr. Pierre-Jean De Sonef, best known of the missionaries, originally called it Lake Roothaan. It was renamed Priest Lake in 1890 in conjunction with the building of the GNRR through the area.

Priest River (Bonner/Boundary/British Columbia). T56N R4W sec 30. Stream about 70 mi long, heading in British Columbia and flowing generally S across the international boundary and through Upper Priest Lake and Priest Lake to the Pend Oreille River about 20 mi W of Pend Oreille Lake; the lower course of the stream is in Kaniksu National Forest. Not: Upper Priest River (name sometimes applied to the upper course of the stream).

Priest River (Bonner). T56N R5W sec 24. Town 6 1/4 mi E of Idaho-Washington border; 17 1/2 mi WSW of Sandpoint. Post office, 1890-.

In 1888 settlers moved to an area 1 mi E of the present site of Priest River, but they were forced to move to the present location to escape regular flooding. The GNRR was completed in the area in 1891-1892, and the town was named Valencia on their maps. The name was later changed to Priest River because another town was also known as Valencia.

Prince Peak (Shoshone). 5333'. T46N R4E sec 30. In the SW part of the county, 12 mi S of Wallace, at the head of Black Prince Creek, formerly Prince Creek, for which it was named.

Named officially in 1919 by forester R. H. Rutledge, though the name had existed long before that.

Princeton (Latah). 2417'. T41N R4W sec 9/10. One of 8 WIM stations bearing the names of colleges; 4 mi E of Potlatch. Post office, 1894-.

Founded in 1896 and named by Orville Clough, prominent lumber man and donor of the school site, for his hometown of Princeton, Minnesota. When construction on WIM began, Princeton was already a town with a post office, hotel, and a stage stop for the Palouse-Hoodoo stagecoach.

Profile Gap (Valley). 8500'. T20N R9E sec 18/19. Mountain pass NW of Yellow Pine, on Big Creek. Profile Creek rises on Profile Summit (7606') just S of Profile Gap and flows 9 mi S to empty into E Fk of S Fk Salmon River. Profile Lake and Peak lie 3 1/2 mi N of Profile Gap.

Profile post office, in N part of the county at Profile Gap, 1914-1931.

There was gold prospecting on the creek and the slopes of the promontories, and the gap was a major route between Edwardsburg and Yellow Pine. Profile Gap from a particular vantage point resembles a human profile, hence the name that has been transferred to nearby features.

Prospect Creek (Bonner). T53N R1W sec 33. Heads 1/2 mi N of Prospect Peak; flows 1 mi SE into Honey Creek 5 mi SW of Lakeview.

There was much prospecting for gold in this area, hence the name.

Prospect Peak (Gem). 4874'. T6N R1E sec 23.

Located in the Pearl mining district, where there was widespread prospecting.

Prospect Peak (Latah). 4138'. T43N R4W sec 35. Peak in the St. Joe

National Forest. Prospect Creek rises on the E slopes of Prospect Peak and flows 2.1 mi NE to Meadow Creek; Palouse River system.

Named when a Mr. Moore and a doctor from Palouse found where a Mr. Carrico had tunneled into the hill. They filed on it, calling the claim Lost Wheelbarrow mine, because they had found an old wheelbarrow and a gun here.

Prospect Peak (Madison). 8023'. T4N R43E sec 20. In the SE extremity of the county in Targhee National Forest. Miners prospected in this area; the Morning Glory mine is 4 mi W of the promontory.

Pruvan Creek (Lemhi). T25N R22E sec 14. Forms near Pyramid Peak; flows NW 3 1/2 mi to enter N Fk Sheep Creek; N Fk Salmon River drainage. Pronounced PRO-van.

Named for an old prospector and Civil War veteran, John Pruvan, who lived on this stream.

Puddin Mountain (Lemhi). 9684'. T21N R16E sec 31/32. Three mi SE of Aggipah Mountain, and 2 mi NW of Wilson Mountain.

Named for "Puddin River" Wilson, who ran a saloon in Yellowjacket when it was a booming mining town.

Pulaski, Mount (Shoshone). 5480'. T48N R4E sec 32/33. In the E central part of the county 3 mi SW of Wallace.

Named for Ed Pulaski, USFS, who in the fire of 1910 saved the lives of some 40 men by leading them into an old mining tunnel and keeping some of the heat out with blankets soaked in water.

Punggo Creek (Boise). T8N R9E sec 1. Rises in the extreme E part of the county and flows N into Tenmile Creek; Payette River drainage. Pronounced PUNKTH.

This is the Bannock Indian word for "horse" and was assigned by the USFS.

Purcell Spring (Lemhi). T14N R26E sec 10. One mi SW of Cold Spring.

Charles Purcell was an early rancher in this vicinity.

Purdue (Latah). 2891'. T41N R1W sec 24. Two mi N of Bovill; originally a WIM terminus on an extension to Potlatch Logging Camp 8. Purdue Creek, 3.7 mi long, empties into Potlatch River about 1 mi SE of Purdue.

One of 8 WIM stations bearing college names. Later this terminus became a stop on the Chicago, Milwaukee, and St. Paul Railroad.

Purdy Gulch (Owyhee). T5S R3W sec 18. E of Fairview, on the W side of War Eagle Mountain.

Named for Oliver Hazard Purdy, one of the party that first discovered gold in Owyhee County. He was killed in the Bannock Indian War in 1878.

Purgatory Lake (Idaho). T23N R2W sec 23. In the Hells Canyon National Recreation Area between Mt. Belial and He Devil Peaks.

The name suggests the theological, "place of punishment" between heaven and hell.

Putney Canyon (Fremont). T9N R42E sec 14. In SW Fremont County. Trends 4 mi N to S into Ashton Reservoir; Henrys Fork system.

Named for "Old Man" Putney, who had a ranch in the area.

Pyramid Mountain (Idaho). 8650'. T23N R2W sec 34. In the Seven Devils Mountains, Nezperce National Forest, just SW of Slide Rock Lake and 2.7 SSW of He Devil.

Two other pyramid promontories lie in Idaho County: Pyramid Peak (8369') in the Gospel Hump area, Nezperce National Forest; and Pyramid Mountain (7768') in the Bitterroot National Forest, E of the Selway River.

A descriptive name applied to features that slope to a pyramidal shape.

Pyramid Peak (Custer). 11,626'. T5N R21E sec 5. Situated about 2 mi SW of Big Black Dome at the head of Newell, Belles, and Betty lakes and canyons; Challis National Forest.

Named because it is shaped like a pyramid.

Q

Quaking Asp Creek (Lemhi). T16N R28E sec 29. Forms 1/2 mi S of Horse Prairie Mountain; flows 4 mi S to enter Reservoir Creek; Lemhi River drainage.

Named for the aspens found along the creek.

Quarles Peak (Shoshone). 6565'. T46N R7E sec 35. In the NE part of the county on the Idaho-Montana line, 14 mi NE of Avery.

Forester R. H. Rutledge made the name official in 1919, after it had been accepted for many years, with no known reason for the name.

Quartz Creek (Bonner). T58N R2E sec 26. Heads 2 1/4 mi NNW of Trestle Peak; flows 3/4 mi ENE, then 1 1/4 mi ESE into Lightning Creek 1 1/2 mi SE of Lunch Peak. Another Quartz Creek, WSW of this one, heads 1 mi W of Cot-

tonwood Lookout and flows 5 1/2 mi SSE into Priest River about 2 mi N of McAbee Falls. Quartz Mountain (4062') lies about 1 1/2 mi SW of Quartz Creek.

Quartz Creek (Clearwater). T37N R5E sec 34. Rises in the SW quadrant of the county at Headquarters and flows 6 mi SE into Orofino Creek just S of Jaype; Clearwater River drainage. Named in the earliest days of Pierce: on 26 Apr 1861 William Moore and Company recorded a claim for a sawmill location on the creek.

Named for the quartz found in these areas.

Quartzburg (Boise). 4200'. T7N R4E sec 9. Ghost town.

This camp was located in 1864. There was a great deal of hard-rock

307

mining in the region. Post office, 1874-1940.

Queener Creek (Latah). T41N R3W sec 31. Flows 4 mi NW to E Fk Flat Creek; Palouse River drainage.

Named in 1938 by Edd. F. Helmers after Peyton and Jack Queener, among the first loggers in the area.

Queeners Butte (Latah). T43N R5W sec 18. Early name for what is now Palmer Butte.

So called for the Thomas Queener family, settlers in the Pine Creek area in the 1870s.

Quicksilver Mountain (Owyhee). 8406'. T5S R3W sec 31. The highest peak near Silver City, located 7 1/2 mi SE of Silver City.

Named because it was within a mining district in which there was a quicksilver mine.

Quiet Lake (Custer). 9242'. T8N R16E sec 5. A 35-acre lake in the glacial deposits of the White Cloud Peaks. It is .3 mi long; 1.2 mi NE of Patterson Peak.

Located in a tranquil setting, for which it is named.

Quigley (Power). 4447'. T8S R29E sec 9. In the W part of the county, about 15 mi W of American Falls in Pleasant Valley. A farming community settled by Russians about 1890. Post office, 1913-1921.

Quigley Creek (Blaine). T2N R18E sec 16. Rises 9 mi NE of Hailey and flows 10 mi SW to Big Wood River 1 mi S of Hailey.

Named for William Quigley, early-day miner in Blaine County and later a resident of Power Co.

Quigley Creek (Lemhi). T12N R26E sec 6. Flows 1 1/2 mi W to meet Main Fk Little Lost River.

Edgar E. Quigley patented land on this creek on 19 Jan 1918.

R

Rabbit Creek (Owyhee). T1S R2W sec 34. Flows NE into the Snake River at T2S R2W sec 26; 16 mi long; drainage 110 square miles.

Rabbit Creek (Lemhi). T22N R20E sec 29. Originates near the head of Turner Gulch; flows W 4 mi to enter Napias Creek; Salmon River drainage.

Named for the whitetail and blacktail jackrabbits often seen in these areas.

Race Creek (Idaho). T24N R1E sec 10. A 10-mi stream flowing E to Salmon River, 1 mi N of Riggins.

Named for Patrick Race Hickey, a Florence miner and packer who settled on the creek with a partner, named McLee.

Racetrack Meadows (Lemhi). T23N R20E sec 25. On Daly Creek, just E of Coffee Gulch.

Miners from Moose Creek and Leesburg would gather at the racetrack here on the Fourth of July to bet on the races.

Rae Creek (Boise). T8N R5E sec 1. Rises in the NW part of the county 10 1/2 mi W of Lowman and flows NW into the S Fk Payette River 2 1/2 mi NE of Grimes Pass.

Named for Jacques "Scotty" Rae, a Scots immigrant who homesteaded on this creek.

Raft River (Cassia). T9S R27E sec 25. Rises in the Raft River Mountains in Utah at an altitude of 8000'; collects its waters from Green, Sublette, and Cache creeks, and flows through Cassia County from S to N to empty into Snake River 22 mi NE of Albion.

Named Raft because it was a deep, muddy stream that inconvenienced trappers and later travelers on the Oregon Trail who had to cross it on rafts.

Railroad Canyon (Lemhi). T16N R27E sec 24. Follows Canyon Creek, beginning 1 mi E of Leadore; runs N 5 mi to the head of Canyon Creek.

Formerly called Cruikshank Canyon; the canyon was renamed when the Gilmore and Pittsburgh RR came in through the drainage in 1910.

Rainbold Ridge (Idaho). T28N R5E sec 2/10/11. A ridge about 1 mi S of S

Fk Clearwater River between Huddleson and Wing Creeks.

Named for a Mr. Rainbold who used to prospect in this area.

Rainbow Falls (Bonneville). T1N R45E sec 12. In NE quadrant of county; lies E of Swan Valley, 1 mi E of Upper Palisades Lake in the Targhee National Forest.

Named for the rainbow seen at the waterfall on a sunny day.

Rainbow Lake (Idaho). T27N R7E sec 19. In the Gospel Hump Wilderness Area.

Rainbow trout were planted very early by people from Orogrande, hence the change of name from Crooked River Lake.

Rainbow Peak (Valley). 9329'. T19N R10E sec 27. In Payette National Forest about 3 1/2 mi W of the Dewey mine in Thunder Mountain territory. Rainbow Creek rises on the S slope of Rainbow Peak, for which it is named, and flows 2 mi SE to empty into Monumental Creek; Salmon River drainage.

The peak takes its name from the many strata of various colors that in sunlight look like a rainbow.

Rainey Creek (Bonneville). T1N R43E sec 3. Rises in NE quadrant and flows 12 mi SW into Snake River just S of Swan Valley.

Named for Alex Rainey, who first settled a ranch at the mouth of Indian Creek.

Rakers, The (Boise). T8N R12E sec 30. Two mountain peaks, South Rakers (9988') and North Rakers (9943'). In the SE extremity of the county near the Boise-Elmore line.

The USFS named these peaks for their resemblance to the raker teeth of a crosscut saw.

Rammell Hollow (Teton). T6N R44E sec 26. A small canyon (hollow), about 2 mi long.

Named after Harley S. Rammell, who homesteaded at the mouth of the hollow.

Ramsey (Kootenai). 2322'. T52N R4W sec 11. In the NW part of the county, 6 mi NE of Rathdrum; formerly a shipping point on the NPRR, now an agricultural area. Post office, 1898-1911.

Named by NPRR officials, though for whom is unknown.

Ramsey Canyon (Lemhi). T12N R29E sec 4. Runs S 2 1/2 mi to Willow Creek drainage. About 2 1/2 mi N of Nicholia and 1/2 mi W of Montana Canyon; Lemhi River drainage.

A man named Ramsey lived in the canyon.

Ramsey Mountain (Lemhi). 8171'. T18N R24E sec 23. Two mi NE of Lemhi.

Named for Lewis T. "Tom" Ramsey, an early owner of the Lemhi Store, who patented land in this area in 1913.

Ramshorn Lake (Lemhi). T20N R16E sec 8. In the Bighorn Crags just NE of Paragon Lake.

Named by USFS and US Coast and Geodetic Survey personnel in 1963 when they found a bighorn mountain sheep horn with a full curl on the shore.

Ramskull Creek (Benewah). T43N R2W sec 6. A 3-mi stream that flows NE to Santa Creek; St. Maries River drainage. In St. Joe National Forest in SE quadrant of Benewah County, 1 mi SW of Emida.

Named by USFS ranger W. H. Daugs, for a dead ram found near the head of this stream.

Rancherio Creek (Lemhi). T22N R17E sec 12. Originates in the area NE of Sagebrush Lookout; flows 2 mi SW to enter Clear Creek; Salmon River drainage. Pronounced RANCH-uh-ree-o.

Named by a Spanish prospector and trapper who lived in the Clear Creek area about 1875, perhaps because it appeared to be a good location for a ranch.

Randall Butte (Latah). 3316'. T41N R5W sec 19. Promontory in southern part of Viola Ridge, 2 mi N of Viola and 9 1/2 mi N of Moscow.

Dora F. Randall's homestead in 1885 included this butte.

Ranger Creek (Boise). T4N R5E sec 35. Rises near the S border of the county and flows SE into Cottonwood Creek at Cottonwood Ranger Station; Boise River drainage.

Named by the USFS in honor of its rangers.

Ransack Creek (Lemhi). T25N R21E sec 17. Stream approximately 3 1/2 mi long; flows W then S to Hughes Creek; Salmon River drainage.

This area was heavily placer-mined in the early days. The creek was "ransacked" for gold. Spelled Ramsack Creek on USFS 1938 map.

Rapid Creek (Bannock). T7S R36E sec 21. In E part of the county, the mouth on the E edge of Inkom. Rises in Portneuf Range on the E and Camelback Mountain on the W; flows 12 mi generally E, then SW to Portneuf River at Inkom.

Named for the swiftness of the stream, rising at 6500' and emptying at 4500'.

Rapid Creek (Teton). T4N R45E sec 3. Rises on W slope of Teton Range, Wyoming, and flows generally SW to Teton Creek about 3 mi SE of Driggs.

The source of this creek is a spring, from which arises its variant name, Spring Creek. Named for the swift current.

Rapid Lightning Creek (Bonner). T57/58/59N R1/2E. Rises on the W slopes of Cabinet Mountains, flows SW to Pack River at T58N R1W sec 24.

Named for the rapid flow of the stream, which rises at more than 6000' and empties at little more than 2000'.

Rapid River (Adams/Idaho). T24N R1E sec 32. Rises in the center of N Adams County and flows 16.5 mi generally NNE to its confluence with W Fk Rapid River, then 6 mi NE to Little Salmon River, 3 mi S of Riggins.

The name is descriptive: it flows rapidly.

Rapps Creek (Lemhi). T22N R19E sec 25. Forms 2 mi SW of Haystack Mountain; flows mostly S 5 mi to enter Arnett Creek; Salmon River drainage.

Named for Joseph Rapp, one of the original discoverers of gold in the Leesburg Basin in 1866.

Raspberry Butte (Clearwater). 6381'. T38N R10E sec 36. Raspberry Creek flows 3 mi NW from the butte into Cayuse Creek; Clearwater River drainage.

Wild raspberries grow in the area.

Rathburn Gulch (Lemhi). T25N R21E sec 33. One mi S of Bills Canyon; runs W 1 mi to enter N Fk Salmon River drainage.

"Dad" Rathbun had a store here in the early 1920s and called it Purl (or Pearl) for his daughter. The name was altered for the gulch to Rathburn.

Rathdrum (Kootenai). 2196'. T52N R5/4W sec 36/31. In the NW part of the county, 17 mi NW of Coeur d'Alene, NPRR, and Rathdrum Creek; an agricultural area; formerly Westwood for pioneer citizen Charles Wesley Wood, a mail carrier from Bonners Ferry. Post office, 1881-.

When a post office was applied for in the name of Westwood, the US Postal Department objected because there were already too many Westwoods. So the Irish birthplace of an elderly resident was chosen.

Rathdrum Mountain (5003') is 3.5 mi NW of Rathdrum, in the Selkirk Mountains, and about 13 mi NW of Coeur d'Alene. Earlier names: Old Baldy, Rathdrum Bald, Rathdrum Baldy, and Storm King Mountain. Rathdrum Prairie (2200') is an agricultural valley 5-15 mi wide that extends NE from Spokane for 50 mi.

Rattle Creek (Bonner). T58N R2E sec 35. Heads 1 mi SE of Rattle Mountain; flows 4 mi NW into Lightning Creek 1 3/4 mi ENE of Trestle Peak. Rattle Mountain is located 1 1/2 mi W of the Idaho-Montana border.

The creek was named for the noise the fast water makes, probably carrying rocks in its flow. The other features bear transfer names from the creek.

Rattlesnake Creek (Fremont). T9N R42E sec 15. In SW Fremont County. Flows S through lava rock and sagebrush to Ashton Reservoir, 4 mi NW of Ashton; Henrys Fork system. Rattlesnakes are frequently encountered here.

Rattlesnake as part of a place name indicates that such snakes are common. Among the many features bearing this name are creeks, gulches, and promontories in Boise, Clark, Elmore, Nez Perce, and Power counties.

Raumaker Butte (Jefferson). T7N R37E sec 5. Near the Fremont-Jefferson county line, 4.2 mi NE of Hamer.

Named for Pete Raumaker, mail carrier from Hamer to Owsley, 1910-1916.

Raymond (Bear Lake). 6300'. T13S R46E sec 22. In the E part of the county, 6 mi S of Geneva. An agricultural community, named Thomas Fork from its beginning in 1873 until 1900. Settled by Mormon colonizers who had first settled in Montpelier and moved to this area. Post office, 1900-.

Variant names: Thomas Fork, Corinth.

Named for the first permanent settler, Grandison Raymond, whose father was an immigrant from England.

Raymond (Idaho). T28N R9E sec 7. In the central part of the county, a mining camp 5 mi SE of Elk City, on Red River. Post office, 1892-1898.

Named for Raymond Driver, the son of developer C. O. Gavin's financial backer in Chicago.

Raymond (Teton). Early name for Victor, which see.

Raynolds Pass (Fremont). 6900'. T16N R42E sec 14. On the Continental Divide between Idaho and Montana about 5 mi NW of Henrys Lake.

Named for Captain William F. Raynolds, who led an army surveying party through this pass in 1860. Entering over Teton Pass and guided by Jim Bridger, this party crossed the county from S to N in midwinter. The pass was discovered by Jim Bridger, a guide with the Raynolds expedition.

Rea (Fremont). 6300'. T13N R42E sec 13. Town at the E end of Island Park Reservoir, 5 mi W of Highway 20 on the Kilgore Road. Reas Pass (7000') is 7 mi NE of Big Springs. Reas Pass Creek flows 6 mi W to Henrys Fork, 5 mi N of Big Springs; Henrys Fork system. Reas Point is a mountain on the Idaho-Montana border about 3 mi SE of Mount Jefferson.

Arangee was the first name for this place, and the first post office was established with Arangee as its name in 1891. The name was officially changed to Rea in 1898 when George W. Rea was appointed postmaster.

Named for George Rea, local trapper, settler, and scout for General Oliver O. Howard during the Nez Perce War, and postmaster in 1898.

Red Conglomerate Peaks (Clark). 10,106'. T14N R33E sec 4. On the Continental Divide at the Idaho-Montana line.

Named for the color and composition of the formation.

Red Elephant Gulch (Blaine). T2N R17E sec 34. Trends 3 mi SE from an elevation of 7527' to Croy Creek; Big Wood River drainage.

Named for the Red Elephant mine at the head of this gulch.

Red Mountain (Custer). 9387'. T13N R14E sec 31. In Salmon River Mts. about 13 mi N of Stanley.

Named for its brilliant color.

Red Mountain (Idaho). T37N R12E. A divide near Indian Post Office where Lewis and Clark camped on their E journey, 27 June 1806.

The Nez Perce called it Mansum Ilpilp "Red Mountain" for the dock (genus Rumex) here, which turns red in the fall.

Redbird Mountain (Custer). 11,273'. T6N R23E sec 21. 7 mi SW of Mackay in the White Knob Mountains; Challis National Forest.

Named for the Redbird mine.

Redfish Lake (Custer). T9N R13E sec 2/3/10/15/16/21/22. Average length, 4 1/2 mi; width, 3/4 mi; largest body of water in Sawtooth area; S of Stanley between Salmon River and Sawtooth Mountains. Little Redfish Lake is about 1 mi N of Redfish Lake, NE of Mount Heyburn and draining into Salmon River. Redfish Lake Creek heads on N slope of Sevy Peak, Mount Cramer, and Elk Peak, and flows about 6 1/2 mi NW and NE to Redfish Lake. Redfish Lake Mountain (10,689') overlooks the lakes.

Named for the sockeye salmon found here.

Reeder Bay (Bonner). T61N R4W sec 20. On W side of Priest Lake about 4 mi NE of Kalispell Bay. Reeder Creek heads 3/4 mi S of Reeder Mountain (4728') and flows 7 mi S and E into Reeder Bay.

Named for an early settler on the bay.

Reeds Creek (Clearwater). T38N R4E sec 19. Rises at Headquarters and flows 1 mi SW and W into Dworshak Reservoir.

Named for Samuel B. Reed, a miner who accompanied Elias Pierce's first party to Canal Creek and Pierce, 1860.

Reeds Gulch (Benewah). T46/47N R1E sec 19. A 4-mi canyon and creek on St. Joe River in St. Joe National Forest, 9 mi E of St. Maries and heading on Reeds Baldy (6153').

Named for homesteader Albert D. Reid (sic).

Reeds River. T6N R6W sec 35. An 1813 name for Boise River, which see.

Reese Creek (Lemhi). T17N R24E sec 14. Originates on the Idaho-Montana border, S of S Fk Yearian Creek; flows SW 5 mi to enter Lemhi River.

Named for Robert Gilahand Rees, a pioneer settler who patented his land in 1886.

Reflection Lake (Lemhi). T20N R16E sec 4. In Bighorn Crags about 1/4 mi due N of Twin Cove Lake.

Named by USFS in cooperation with the US Coast and Geodetic Survey in 1963; a descriptive name.

Regan Bend (Gem). T7N R1E sec 16/17. A bend in Payette River. Regan Butte (3310') is situated S of Regan Bend and across the river from Daniel Regan's homestead.

Named for Daniel Regan, cattleman, who homesteaded here in 1874. He believed the land would soon be overgrazed, so he sold and moved.

Register Rock (Power). T9S R29E sec 12. Two mi SW of Massacre Rocks State Park. A 20' high stone on which the autographs of early travelers appear. In 1849 some of the names were carved into the rock, and some were painted on with black axle grease.

Relay Ridge (Teton). T4N R43E sec 1/2 and T5N R43E sec 34/35. Ridge 2.3 mi long, in the Big Hole Mountains 11 mi SW of Tetonia.

A radio relay station is located on the ridge.

Remenclau Saddle (Lemhi). 7864'. Pass in the Salmon River Mountains 3 mi SW of Blackbird Mountain.

Named for a miner and trapper who lived in this area in 1897.

Renfro Creek (Benewah). T44N R1W sec 27. Stream about 8 mi long heading at Renfro Peak and flowing SW and W to its confluence with St. Maries River at the village of Santa.

Named for Sarah Renfro, a widow, who homesteaded on this creek with her children. After a short stay she sold to a Mr. Haviland. Mistakenly written Renfrew on some maps.

Reno (Lemhi). 6560'. T11N R29E sec 22. Community in the SE part of the county 2 1/2 mi N of the Lemhi-Butte county line and SE of Gilmore. Settled in 1885 or 1886; Post office, 1899-ca.1935.

Named for the Reno family. Some say for Frank Reno, an early settler and rancher, and some for the first postmaster, Agnes B. Reno.

Reno Gulch (Clark). T9N R31E sec 14. A 5-mi gulch trending SE to NW and N in the SW part of the county.

Frank Reno, postmaster for the entire area in 1880 and a mail carrier from Nicholia to Camas, bought land in this area and in adjoining Butte County; he established irrigation ditches in each place he bought.

Rescue Creek (Clearwater). T36N R6E sec 16. Rises in the S central part of the county and flows generally W 5 mi to Orofino Creek 4 mi SE of Pierce; Clearwater River drainage.

Gus Mosher, prospecting near this creek, failed to return to his hotel in Pierce. A search party found him with a frozen foot in a cabin along the creek and rescued him.

Reservoir Creek (Latah). T42N R4W sec 15. Rises on E Gold Hill and flows to Gold Creek between E Fk Gold Creek and Hoteling Creek; Palouse River drainage.

Lonnie Wilkins, Potlatch, prospected along this creek; he said the name was derived from the slough above the creek that held a lot of water, a slough left by an earlier volcanic eruption that blew boulders all around the depression.

Resort (Idaho). T22N R4E sec 1. Early name for Burgdorf, which see.

Rettig Creek (Clearwater). T39N R6E sec 34. Rises in the N central part of the county and flows S into Scofield Creek just above Moose Creek Lodge; Clearwater River drainage.

Named for Potlatch Forests official E. C. Rettig, a vice president and general manager at PFI in the 1950s.

Reubens (Lewis). 3498'. T34N R2W sec 2. About 6.5 mi NW of Craigmont. Pronounced RU-binz.

Reubens absorbed Kippen and Chesley when it was established in 1907 on the completion of the Camas Prairie RR. Post office, 1906-.

Named for James Reubens, a Nez Perce Indian who fought with United States troops in the war of 1877 and later served as a government interpreter.

Reward Peak (Boise). 10,115'. T8N R12E sec 15.

USFS officers found a piece of paper on this peak with the statement: "$25.00 reward for the return of this paper."

Rexburg (Madison). 3264'. T6N R40E sec 19/29. County seat. In the N part of the county, 12 mi NE of Rigby; the home of Ricks College.

President John Taylor, L.D.S. Church, directed Thomas Ricks to establish a colony in the upper Snake country. Ricks went to the area from Logan in 1882, taking his four sons and seven others with him. The townsite was laid out under the supervision of William Preston, president of the Cache Valley Stake, and named Rexburg (the Latin Root of Ricks' surname), honoring Thomas Ricks. Post office, 1882-.

Reynolds Creek (Owyhee). T4S R4W sec 15. Rises N of Silver City and flows NE into the Snake River at T1S R3W sec 1. The town of Reynolds (3000') is situated 9 mi W of Murphy on Reynolds Creek; once a stage station. Post office, 1877-1943.

Renamed Brunzel, 1884-1915.

Named for John Reynolds, from Walla Walla, Washington, who was a member of the party that first discovered gold in Owyhee County. Reynolds, known as the laziest man in the party, sat in camp while the rest of the party gathered wood. The wood gatherers named the creek Reynolds because neither their lazy comrade nor the creek was doing anything.

Reynolds Creek (Lemhi). T25N R16E sec 23. Heads on the Idaho-Montana border NE of Squaw Peak; runs S about 4 mi to enter Horse Creek; Salmon River drainage.

A trapper named Jess Reynolds built a lean-to here and also mined in the area.

Rhett Creek (Idaho). T25N R9E sec 30. On the N side of Salmon River in the Nezperce National Forest; River of No Return Wilderness.

Named for former medical student William Rhett, a Virginian, who fled his home when caught with two other students exhuming a cadaver. He took refuge for several years in the Salmon River Canyon and was a pioneer in Florence and Warren.

Rhett Creek (Idaho). T27N R1E sec 35. A 2.2-mi stream flowing E to Salmon River, just S of Slate Creek Ranger Station.

Named for William Rhett (see previous Rhett Creek). Henry Creek, 2 mi S across the river, is named for his grandson, Henry Rhett.

Rhoda Creek (Idaho). T33N R12E sec 4. Rises in the NW part of the Selway-Bitterroot Wilderness Area in Crystal and Shasta lakes and flows 12 mi SE to N Fk Moose Creek; Selway River drainage.

Named for the oldest daughter of Major Frank A. Fenn; Rhoda was also the name of Mrs. Stephen S. Fenn, wife of a pioneer legislator.

Rhodes Creek (Clearwater). T36N R5E sec 11. Rises just E of Pierce and flows 3 mi SW into Orofino Creek; Clearwater River drainage.

Named for William "Billy" Rhodes, a mulatto prospector in the early days of Pierce. Rhodes was one of the big money makers at the time; he found gold on the creek and staked a claim here, taking out perhaps $80,000. He was buried in the Blacklead area not far from Rhodes Peak (7940'), where he staked another claim. Formerly Negro Creek; name changed in 1968 because of derogatory term.

Rice Creek (Cassia). T13S R26E sec 18. Rises 4 mi W of Malta in Cotterel Mountains and flows about 3 mi S to Cassia Creek; at the junction of Hudspeth Cutoff and the California Trail. Rice Canyon heads on the S slopes of the Black Pine Mountains and runs S 5 mi to the Utah border and 1 mi into Box Elder County, Utah, T16N R29E sec 30.

Named for Del Rice, an early settler who grazed cattle from Cassia Creek south.

Rice Creek (Idaho). T30N R1W sec 26. A stream rising on Rose Lewis Point and flowing 5.5 mi N to Salmon River, in the NW part of the county.

Said to be named for the staple food of the Chinese who worked on the irrigation ditch here.

Rice Peak (Valley). 8900'. T14N R7E sec 32. In the Boise National Forest near the head of S Fk Salmon River about 21 mi E of Cascade. Variant name: Blue Point Peak. Rice Creek rises on the N and W slope of Rice Peak in Rice Lake and flows 6.5 mi WNW to empty into S Fk Salmon River 18 mi ENE of Cascade. Not: Blue Point Creek.

Named for William B. "Ben" Rice, who worked for almost 40 years as a member of the USFS in Idaho and Utah.

Rich (Bingham). Early community near Blackfoot. Named for Heber C. Rich, early settler and president and director of Peoples Canal for many years. Sam Rich owned the land at the end of the canal just W of Aberdeen Junction; a school was established in 1898. Post office, 1896-1904.

Named for the first postmaster, Heber C. Rich. Variant name: McKinley, for President Wm. McKinley, 1904.

Richard Butte (Butte). T7N R31E sec 4. Just S of the Butte-Clark county line. John Richards had a ranch here in the

1880s, which he sold to Frank Reno in the early 1890s. Reno moved water to the ranch and stocked it with sheep and cattle.

Named for the original owner, John Richards.

Richardson Creek (Idaho). T25N R10E sec 5. A 5-mi stream rising on Burnt Knob (7352') and flowing 5 mi N to Salmon River. Named for early-day packer Harlan Richardson.

The main tributary of this stream bears the name Harlan, and the area between Harlan and Richardson creeks is named Harlan Meadow.

Richfield (Lincoln). 4280'. T4S R19E sec 25/26. In the N central part of the county, 18 mi NE of Shoshone; on the UPRR, US 93, and Little Wood River. Town in a farming area; Post office, 1908-.

Richfield began as an irrigation project and was called Alberta for Alberta Strunk, the first child born at the new townsite. When the New York firm of White and Co. bought the project, the new owners changed the name to Richfield, because the name suggested richness of the land and induced prospective buyers to the area.

Richmond (Idaho). T22N R6E. One of two rival towns established near Warren Creek Mining District after the discovery of gold (1862), one was called Washington by Union sympathizers and the other Richmond in honor of the Confederate states. By 1884 only a slaughterhouse remained of the two settlements. It was reported that Union and Confederate sympathizers mined side by side in the daytime and refought the Civil War every night.

Rickman Creek (Idaho). T31N R2W sec 28. In the NW extremity of the county; a 1.5-mi stream flowing E to Salmon River.

Bobby Rickman owned a ranch here before he was dragged to death by a horse.

Riddle (Owyhee). 5350'. T14S R3E sec 28. Post office 2 mi N of the N border of the Duck Valley Indian Reservation. Post office, 1898-1963.

Named for Frank W. and Grant Riddle, who had a ranch in the area.

Ridgedale (Oneida). T16S R34E sec 16/22. In the S part of the county, 16 mi SW of Malad City. Settled in 1914.

Named because the first settlers located on a ridge above the spring in the dale.

Post office, 1915-1929.

Rigby (Jefferson). 4858'. T4N R39E sec 18/19. County Seat. In the SE quadrant of the county, 3 mi E of Lewisville. Post office, 1889-.

Rigby was named by LDS church President John W. Taylor for William Rigby of Driggs, a church leader who had assisted in the organization of the community.

Riggins (Idaho). 1800'. T24N R1E sec 15. In SW Idaho County at the confluence of Little Salmon and Salmon rivers; on US 95.

Founded in the early 1900s as the center of stock-raising country and a trade and mail center for mining camps. Post office, 1901-.

Named for Richard L. "Dick" Riggins, one of the town's most prominent businessmen; also the first postmaster.

Riley Creek (Bonner). T56N R4W sec 36. Heads 3 1/4 mi SW of Johnny Long Mountain; flows 7 mi S into the Pend Oreille River 1 1/2 mi WSW of Laclede.

Named for John Riley, who owned a farm bordering on the creek.

Riley Creek (Gooding). T8S R13E sec 1. Rises in Riley Creek Springs of Thousand Springs and flows in a horseshoe-shaped route N about 2 mi to empty into Snake River.

Named for a Mr. Riley, who homesteaded a ranch in the area.

Ringle Creek (Lemhi). T18N R21E sec 33. Forms near the headwaters of Cabin Creek; flows SE 4 mi to enter Salmon River.

Named for William Ringle, who patented the land in this area in 1936.

Ripley Butte (Fremont). 6464′. T12N R43E sec 23. In central Fremont County. Ripleys Ford is a town 3 mi SE of the butte.

Named for Charlie Ripley, who had a homestead 2 mi W of the butte around 1910. There apparently was some kind of resort or settlement connected with Ripleys Ford, since local sources talk of it as a stopping place on the road to West Yellowstone.

Ririe (Jefferson). 4965′. T4N R40E sec 32. In the extreme SE corner of Jefferson County on the Bonneville-Jefferson county line; one of the most recently organized towns in the county, having been founded in 1915. Post office, 1916-.

Named for David Ririe of the Latter-day Saints Church, who was an early settler and the motivating force behind securing right-of-way for the OSLRR. The RR company honored him by naming the station and the town for him. When the LDS ward was organized, Ririe was made bishop and the ward named for him.

Riser Creek (Bonner). T56N R1E sec 1. Heads 1 1/4 mi S of Roundtop; flows 1 3/4 mi SW, then 1 mi WSW into Lake Pend Oreille at Ellisport Bay.

Named for an early (ca. 1870) miner.

Rising Butte (Fremont). 6675′. T9N R45E sec 2. In SE Fremont County, just W of the SW corner of Yellowstone National Park. Rising Creek runs 3 mi

S to confluence with Porcupine Creek; Warm River drainage.

Named for Fred Rising, an early buffalo hunter, trapper, and alleged poacher, already in the area when first settlers arrived. Local old-timers also refer to the butte as Freds Butte and Fred Rising Butte.

River of No Return. Nickname for Salmon River, which see.

Riverdale (Franklin). 4685′. T14S R39E sec 36. In the SW part of the county, in a narrow valley through which Bear River flows. Settled in 1875 by Joseph Nelson. Post office, 1882-1908.

Named for its location on the river in a valley.

Riverside (Bingham). 4457′. T2/3S R34E sec 35/1. Two mi W of Blackfoot on the right side of Snake River.

Mormons founded this town in 1885 and named it for its location on the river. Post office, 1879-1905.

Riverside (Bonner). 2160′. T56N R3W sec 30. Town on NW side of Lake Pend Oreille 1/2 mi N of Laclede. Post office, 1910-1915.

Named for the Riverside Lumber Co., which had a sawmill and RR siding here. The name is doubly appropriate because it is located on the river. Formerly Gerich.

Riverside (Canyon). 2290′. T2N R4W sec 13/24. Town, formerly Lower Boise, Keeneys Ferry, and McDowells Ferry, including some 400 acres of land on the N bank of lower Boise River.

Post office, 1879 (as lower Boise), 1882-1886.

Riverton (Bingham). 4465′. T3S R34E sec 23. In the S part of the county, 6 mi SW of Blackfoot; between the Snake and Blackfoot rivers.

Once a Mormon community.

Named for its location between two rivers.

Roaring Creek (Lemhi). T22N R16E
sec 7. Heads in area from Mount
McGuire NE to Roaring Creek lakes;
flows generally NW 6 mi to empty into
Middle Fk Salmon River.

Named because the steepness of the
terrain makes the water roar.

Robber Gulch (Idaho). T27N R1E sec
14. A 1.5-mi stream flowing W to
Salmon River; on Horseshoe Bend.

So named for an incident: a Mr.
Atkinson, who carried the mail, was
accosted by a robber. Atkinson galloped
by him and the robber ran up the gulch.
A posse formed and unsuccessfully
attempted to catch him.

Robbers Roost Creek (Bannock). T8S
R36E sec 23. Rises in the extreme E
part of the county on the S slope of
Haystack Mountain, on the Caribou-
Bannock county line; flows WSW 5.5
mi to Portneuf River, 3.5 mi N of
McCammon.

Named for the refuge of road agents,
or robbers, in a recess of Portneuf Canyon near the present site of McCammon; a place where travelers were
robbed at gunpoint and which served
as a hiding place, for robbers could not
be tracked over lava rocks or found in
the recesses of the canyon.

Roberts (Jefferson). 4773'. T5N R37E
sec 32. At the S end of Market Lake
Slough. Formerly Market Lake, which
see.

Robertson Spring (Lemhi). T13N
R27E sec 22. Located 1/2 mi S of
Slaughterhouse Spring.

Chauncey Robertson had a ranch in
this area (1870s and 1880s).

Robie Creek (Boise). T3N R4E sec 5.
Rises in the SW extremity of the county
and flows 7 1/2 mi SE into Mores Creek.
Boise River drainage. Pronounced ROE-
bee or RU-bee.

Albert Robie started logging operation on these creeks in 1863.

Robin (Bannock). 4800'. T10S R36E
sec 4/10. In western Bannock County,
6 mi SW of McCammon; settled in the
1870s.

Named Garden Creek, but the name
was not acceptable to the US Post Office
Department, and Joseph Calbe, a leader
of the community, suggested Robin, for
the birds that frequent the area.

Post office, 1899-1929.

Robinson Creek (Fremont). T9N R43E
sec 13. In SE Fremont County. Rises
in Yellowstone National Park, enters
Fremont County and flows about 14
mi SW to Warm River at Warm River
community; Warm River drainage. Dry
Robinson Creek flows S to a confluence
with Robinson Creek 2 mi W of the
Yellowstone National Park border 1 mi
N of Rising Butte.

Possibly named for Edward
Robinson, a member of Major Andrew
Henry's party at Fort Henry, 1810-11,
who remained after the party left.

Rochat Creek (Benewah). T46N R1W
sec 9. Rises on the SW slopes of Rochat
Peak, 5643', in the NE corner of the
county and flows 5 mi generally S to
St. Joe River, 4 mi E of St. Maries. Pronounced ro-SHAY.

Named for Henri Rochat, a Swiss settler who homesteaded on the St. Joe
River in 1885. He and his sons, Paul
and William, acquired title to about a
section of fine river bottom and timber-
land.

Rock Creek (Clearwater). T40N R8E
sec 29. Rises in the N central part of
the county on Mush Point and flows
4.5 mi NW into N Fk Clearwater River.

Named for the rough, rocky country. It was originally called Bull Creek
because of the many bull elk that came

to the lick about 3/4 mi up from the mouth of the creek.

Rock Creek (Latah). T41N R4W sec 6. Heads at the junction of its E and W Fks and flows N 1.8 mi into Palouse River just SE of Potlatch. E Fk heads on the NE side of Rocky Point and flows 3.8 mi NNW to join W Fk 2 mi SSE of Potlatch. W Fk Rock Creek is 3.5 mi long and heads on the N side of Rocky Point.

The area up and down this stream was under contract by the Potlatch Lumber Company for timber harvest in the early 1900s, but residents occupied the stream banks completely.

The name of the creek comes partly from its origin on Rocky Point and partly from its rocky stream bed.

Rock Creek (Twin Falls). T9S R16E sec 25. Rises at 6000′ in the Sawtooth National Forest and flows 45 mi N and W to empty into Snake River 3.5 mi NW of Twin Falls. A short distance above Twin Falls it has cut a canyon through lava and in a 3-mi stretch falls several hundred feet to 2992′.

Rock Creek Stage Station was established on this stream in 1865 by James Bascom. It became a stopping place for emigrants on the Oregon Trail, because this was the first water after leaving Snake River, about 20 mi away.

Rock Creek village grew up around Herman Stricker's homesite, and in 1929 a rock crusher was moved in or built to produce gravel for roadbuilding. Post office, 1871-1925.

Named by early trappers and emigrants for the rocks found along the stream.

Rock Garden (Clearwater). 7115′. T38N R12E sec 29. Peak 5 mi SW of Blacklead Mountain. Rock Garden Creek rises on this peak and flows N

into Toboggan Creek; Clearwater River drainage.

Named for the rocks arranged in a series of benches or levels.

Rocker Gulch (Boise). T6N R6E sec 20. A 2-mi gulch trending S into Mores Creek 3 mi NE of Idaho City; Boise River drainage.

Many rockers were in operation on this gulch, a relatively cheap form of mining.

Rockford Bay (Kootenai). 2160′. T48N R4W sec 17/18. In the SW part of the county on the W side of Coeur d'Alene Lake, 18 mi SW of Coeur d'Alene. Between 1837 and 1852, this area was an Indian village. Post office, 1911-.

Believed to have been named for Rockford, Spokane County, Washington.

Rockland (Power). 4671′. T10S R31E sec 6/7. In the W part of the county, 16 mi S of American Falls. First settled in 1876 and named by Mormon settlers in 1879 for Rock Creek and the rocky surroundings. Post office, 1886-.

Rockland Valley lies to the W of Rockland and is drained by Rock Creek; about 6 mi long.

Rockville (Owyhee). T1S R6W sec 17. Stage station and town 1 mi E of the Idaho-Oregon line. Post office, 1885-1908.

A stage station on the Boise-Silver City stage road located here. Named for the many rock formations in the area.

Rocky Bar (Elmore). 5050′. T4N R10E sec 17. A mining ghost town 8 mi N of Featherville. Second county seat of Alturas County, but became part of Elmore County when it was carved out of Alturas in 1889. Post office, 1868-1927.

The town was laid out in 1864 after a major gold discovery was made in S Fk Boise Basin in 1863.

Rocky Peak (Lemhi). 10,551'. T14N R25E sec 16. In the S central part of the county 2 mi N of Junction Peak and at the head of Rocky Creek, for which it is named.

Rocky Gulch (Boise). T5N R5E sec 8. A 2 1/2-mi gulch trending NE into Mores Creek 6 mi SW of Idaho City; Boise River drainage.

This gulch was named by stage drivers who drove past it, because it was rough and rocky.

Rocky Run (Shoshone). T43N R5E sec 15. In the S part of the county, rising on S Butte and flowing 4 mi N to N Fk St. Joe River; overlooked by Rocky Run Point (4980') on the W side of the stream, near its mouth.

Officially named by forester W. B. Greeley in 1917, for the rocky bed of the stream.

Formerly Moose Creek, Stony Creek, Stoney Creek, Alex Creek.

Rogers Creek (Clearwater). T41N R1E sec 35. In the NW extremity of the county. Flows S into E Fk Potlatch River 1 mi W of Lewis Mills.

Asa Rodgers settled here in 1904.

Rogers Creek (Shoshone). T46N R3E sec 15. In the SW part of the county, 6 mi NE of Calder. Rises on Cemetery Ridge and flows 2 mi NW to E Fk Big Creek; St. Joe River drainage.

A man named Rogers homesteaded on this stream.

Rogerson (Twin Falls). 4895'. T14S R16E sec 8/16. On US 93 and a branch of the UPRR, 24 mi S of Twin Falls. Homesteaded in 1880, this village was first known as Deep Creek Meadows, then renamed Terminal City by RR officials in 1909, when the line from Twin Falls was completed, because this was the terminal; then it was renamed Rogerson when a post office was applied

for in 1910. The center of the region's livestock business. Post office, 1910-.

Named for Robert Rogerson, pioneer settler, stockman, and landowner in this area, credited with having platted the townsite on his property.

Rogue Mountain (Boundary). T65N R2E sec 15. Topographic feature approximately 1 mi in length.

Howard Monks, who has settled here since 1906, claims to have known the old prospector and homesteader which the mountain was named after and says the correct spelling was O'Hogue.

Roman Nose (Boundary). 7300'. T61N R2W sec 21. A well-known promontory in the Selkirk Mountains on the E side of upper Pack River drainage.

Roman Nose is a prominent feature that has been used as a landmark for many years; never known as mountain or peak. The name refers to the apparent feature of a person's face with an enormous nose, with the person lying face up.

Rood Gulch (Lemhi). T22N R18E sec 3. Heads 1 1/2 mi NE of Gant Mountain; runs NE 1 1/2 mi to enter Panther Creek drainage; Salmon River drainage.

Named for Willard Rood, Sr., who patented the land here in 1914.

Rooker Basin (Lemhi). T19N R18E sec 34. Two mi S of McGowan Basin.

Named for either Jack Rooker, sheepherder, or Frank Rooker, homesteader.

Roosevelt (Valley). T19N R10E sec 24. Ghost town on Monumental Creek in the Thunder Mountain area.

Settled during the gold fever following discovery on Thunder Mountain, it lay along a big gully near Thunder Mountain, 50 mi from Payette Lakes. In 1909 a big landslide completely dammed Monumental Creek and submerged Roosevelt.

There is some disagreement about how the settlement came to be named Roosevelt. Some say the name is for Alice Roosevelt because the nearby rock formation on the creek seemed to resemble her: woman's face, wasp waist, and flowing skirts. Others, that it was named for Teddy Roosevelt, her father and President of the US at the time of settlement here.

Rooster Comb Butte (Owyhee). 6390'. T3S R4W sec 28. Located 1 1/2 mi S of Whiskey Mountain.

Shaped like a rooster comb. Also known as Rooster Comb Peak.

Roothaan Mountain (Boundary). T61N R3W sec 27. In Kaniksu National Forest, 6 mi E of Priest Lake.

Named for Father John Roothaan, the Dutch Superior General of the Society of Jesus in the late 1840s and early 1850s.

Rose Creek (Owyhee). T7S R3W sec 28. In the NW part of the county; flows 8 mi NE into Rock Creek and eventually into the Owyhee River into Oregon.

Named for a girl from Silver City who was warned to hurry back home on notice of an impending Indian raid. See Hurry Back Creek.

Rose Gulch (Lemhi). T24N R21E sec 18. Runs 1 mi NW to enter the Salmon River drainage.

Augustus Fred and Charles H. Rose, brothers, ranched on land at the mouth of the gulch that they patented in 1910.

Rose Lake (Kootenai). T49N R1W sec 33 and T48N R1W sec 4/5/8/9. There are 2 lakes by this name, separated by Coeur d'Alene River. The lake N of the river is 1 mi long and .5 mi wide; the one on the S is about .25 mi in diameter.

The town of Rose Lake (2125') is on the smaller lake, S of the river, 8 mi W of Cataldo, and named for the lake. Post office, 1905-ca.1930.

The name is a corruption of Rows Lake, so named for an early settler. A 4-mi tributary of Coeur d'Alene River from the N bears the same name.

Roseberry (Valley). 4873'. T16N R3E sec 11/13. In Long Valley 1.2 mi E of Donnelly. Post office, 1891-1930.

Named for the first postmaster.

Rosebud Creek (Clearwater). T36N R6E sec 16. Rises on French Mountain Saddle near the SE border of the county and flows 3 mi SW into Orofino Creek 3 mi E of Pierce; Clearwater River drainage.

Named for the Rosebud mine, which is situated at the head of the creek.

Roseworth (Twin Falls). T12S R13E sec 22. In the SW part of the county near Pig Tail Butte, 6 mi N of Cedar Creek Reservoir. Village in cattle country, settled in the 1890s. Post office, 1896-ca.1936.

Named for a local resident.

Ross Fork (Bannock). T5S R33E sec 14. Rises in the Caribou Mountains in E Bannock County, flows NW through the S boundary of Bingham County, SW back into Bannock to empty into Clear Creek; Snake River drainage; 30 mi long.

Ross Fork (Bingham). T4S R36E sec 31. Site of an early RR station and Indian school on the S border of the county on Ross Fork Creek, 2 mi E of the Fort Hall Agency. Post office, 1870-1911, when name changed to Fort Hall.

Ross Peak (Bonneville). 7935'. T2N R44E sec 21. In NE quadrant in Targhee National Forest about 6 mi N of Irwin.

Ross Peak (Camas). 9773'. T5N R12E sec 36. A prominent peak in the Smoky Mountain Range, Sawtooth

National Forest. Ross Creek, W tributary of S Fk Boise River, is about 12 mi long.

Named for Alexander Ross, early Hudson's Bay trapper and explorer of the Sawtooths, who kept meticulous notes of his travels throughout the area.

Roswell (Canyon). 2250′. T5N R5W sec 20/29. Town in NW Canyon County, S of Parma. Permanent settlement began in 1889 when the Methodist Ditch on the bench where it is located was completed. Post office, 1893-.

The US Post Office Department misread the application for a post office. Rosewell was the name requested, but the "e" was omitted. However, some still believe it was intended to honor W. H. Lowell and J. H. Ross, irrigation developers.

Rough Canyon (Bannock). T10S R37E sec 15. Trends 2.4 mi NE to SW, with the mouth at Arkansas Creek, 2.5 mi SE of Arimo.

Named by Heber Chatterton because of the rough terrain.

Rough Canyon (Lemhi). T17N R27E sec 34. Heads S of Deadman Pass; runs W 3 mi to enter Cruikshank Creek; Lemhi River drainage.

The name is descriptive of this rough, rocky canyon.

Round Lake (Bonner). T56N R3W sec 36. A 58-acre lake 2 1/2 mi WNW of Westmond.

Named for its circular shape.

Round Top (Shoshone). Early name for Engels Peak, a landmark on the Mullan Road.

The top of this promontory is rounded with quartz and thick bear grass.

Roundhouse Gulch (Shoshone). T45N R5E sec 16. A 2-mi gulch trending S to N to St. Joe River at Avery.

So called because there was a RR roundhouse at the mouth of this feature. Officially named by USFS in 1919, though this name had been applied to the gulch since the Milwaukee RR was built in 1910.

Erroneously named Roughhouse Gulch on some maps.

Roy (Power). 5102′. T12S R31E sec 21/22. In the S part of the county, 14 mi S of Rockland, almost on the S borderline of the county. A farming community. Post office, 1912-ca.1936.

Named for the first postmaster.

Ruby City (Owyhee). T5S R3W sec 6. Town 1/4 mi N of Silver City on Jordan Creek. The second mining camp of Owyhee County, Ruby City was founded in 1863 and was named county seat, 1864 to 1866. Absorbed by Silver City in 1867.

Named for the red-tinted silver ore found in the area.

Ruby Creek (Boundary). T61N R1W sec 25. Rises on Roman Nose, flows generally E to Deep Creek; Kootenai River drainage. Ruby Ridge lies S of Ruby Creek.

There was much prospecting for precious gems and metals in this area in the 1890s. It has been suggested that there may have been garnets, which at first were thought to be rubies, hence the name.

Ruby Creek (Clearwater). T39N R11E sec 9. Flows SE into Moose Creek; Clearwater River drainage.

Garnets were found in the creek; the old-timers called them rubies because of their red color.

Ruby Creek (Latah). T41N R3W sec 3. Flows 4.1 mi NW to Palouse River.

Named for Ruby Canfield, whose father was an early developer of Potlatch Forests, Inc.

Reported locally that garnets found in the stream were believed to be rubies, but the name was assigned before interest in garnets was widespread.

Rudo (Clearwater). T36N R4E sec 6. Settlement 10 mi E of Orofino. Rudo Creek empties into Orofino Creek at this site; Clearwater River drainage.

Named for a Mr. Rudo, who mined around here in 1897-1898 and discovered a sulfur spring.

Rudy (Jefferson). T4N R39E sec 23. In the SE quadrant of the county 3 mi N of Ririe and 3 mi E of Rigby. Formerly Clark. Post office, 1892- 1906.

Settled in 1884 by Mormons, who named the community for Jesse E. Clark, a Mormon bishop. When the application for a post office was processed, during the Mormon disfranchisement the government assigned the name Rudy.

Rue (Latah). 2720′. T40N R2W sec 8. One of the names for the post office Avon and the railroad station Vassar. The original village was called Avon, which see.

When the WIMRR came through the area, the town moved to it and was renamed Rue for the man who laid out the new site in 1907.

Rupert (Minidoka). 4200′. T9S R24E sec 29. County seat. In the S part of the county, 7 mi NE of Heyburn. Platted by the US Bureau of Reclamation in 1905 as a model town with a city park; incorporated in 1906.

Post office, 1905-.

Locally believed to have been named for a reclamation engineer, but oldtimers say the name existed before the townsite survey by the Bureau of Reclamation. Their story is that one day the name Rupert appeared on the mailbag dropped off by a trainman and that the practice continued: a man named Rupert

brought all the mail to the area. In time he left, but his name stayed on. The family of John Henry Rupert, early-day miner and trainman, believe he is that early-day mail carrier.

Rush Creek (Washington). T14N R3W sec 2. Rises in the NW quadrant of the county in the Cuddy Mountains, Payette National Forest, and flows 12 mi S and SE to Weiser River in Cambridge. John Cuddy built the first sawmill and flour mill in the area on this stream, the waters furnishing power for the mill.

Additional Rush features are Rush Lake, at the head of the creek; Rush Falls, 2 sets located on the upper reaches of the creek; and Rush Peak (7614′), located in the W part of Payette National Forest at the end of Cuddy Mountain.

Named for the rushes that once grew along the stream and edges of the lake.

Russell (Lewis). 3047′. T35N R1E sec 12. Abandoned town in NE quadrant about 12 mi N of Nezperce.

By 1896 Russell had several stores; and there was a good business, because this was the only trading center for settlers between Nezperce and Orofino.

Post office, 1896-1922.

Named for a local rancher.

Russell Bar (Idaho). T27N R1E sec 23. A gravel bar along the E bank of Salmon River 2 mi NW of Slate Creek.

Originally called Robie Bar for the Robie family, who had a homestead and mining claim here during the placer era. Descendants of the Robie family lived here later and the bar became widely known as Russell Bar, for their surname. Though the owner, George R. Russell, preferred the original name for his ancestors, Russell Bar was firmly established and the US Board on Geographic Names confirmed it.

Russell Creek (Boise). T8N R5E sec 10. Rises in the NW part of the county and flows S into the S Fk Payette River at Grimes Pass.

Clarence Russell homesteaded on this creek.

Russell Creek (Bonneville). T1S R44E sec 23. Flows 5 mi NE into Snake River just above Palisades Dam.

Named for the Russell family who lived at the mouth of this creek in 1905.

Ruthberg (Washington). T16N R4W. Ghost town in the NW corner of the county on Brownlee Creek.

Silver was discovered here in 1875 by Jim Ruth and Thomas Heath, who freighted in a small mill to grind their ore. After the mining ventures, Ruth worked as a carpenter-developer, founding Ruthberg. Post office, 1881-1901.

Named for the founder of the town.

Rutledge Creek (Shoshone). T43N R6E sec 18. In the S central part of the county, rising on Hilo Peak (5760') and flowing 4 mi S to N Fk Clearwater River.

The Rutledge mines are situated at the head of this stream; hence the name. Made official by forester R. H. Rutledge in 1919.

Ryan Peak (Blaine/Custer). 11,900'. T7N R17E. On the Custer- Blaine county line, in the Boulder Mountains, SE of Glassford Peak and 15 mi N of Ketchum.

Named for Mike Ryan, an early Wood River freighter.

Sun Valley (Blaine County).

S

Sacajewea Hot Springs (Boise). T10N R11E sec 33. In the E extremity of the county near Grandjean.

Named for Sacajewea, a Shoshoni woman who traveled with the Lewis and Clark Expedition.

Saddle Creek (Clearwater). T40N R9E sec 4. Rises in the NE quadrant of the county in Saddle Lake and flows 3 mi NW into Quartz Creek; Clearwater River drainage.

Named for the mountain saddle there.

Saddle Mountain (Butte). 10,795'. T7N R29E sec 13. In Targhee National Forest in the SE part of the county.

A descriptive name: a ridge connecting two higher elevations.

Sage Creek (Lemhi). T24N R20E sec 20. Flows SW 3 mi to enter Salmon River.

In the early days sagebrush grew in these areas.

Sage Hen Creek (Gem). T12N R2E sec 27. Rises in Boise National Forest in the NE part of Gem County; E Fk flows SW and S Fk flows N; empties in Squaw Creek.

Named for the sage grouse (*Centrocercus urophasianus*) in the area.

Sagebrush Mountain (Lemhi). 7147'. T22N R17E sec 3. Near the head of Rancherio Creek. Sagebrush Spring is just S of Sagebrush Mountain.

Named for the patch of sagebrush growing on the S side, near the spring, at a much higher altitude than it usually grows.

Sagehen Gulch (Owyhee). T4S R3W sec 32. Near Wagontown; flows S into Soda Creek.

Named for the sage grouse, a large grayish grouse of open country. The gulch is also called Sagehen Creek.

Sagle (Bonner). 2100'. T56N R2W sec 15. Town 5 mi S of Sandpoint and 1 1/2 mi NE of Algoma; on the NPRR. Once this was an important gateway to the Glengary Ferry and as a transfer point for passengers and freight. Post office, 1900-.

A Mr. Powell applied for a post office named Eagle, but there was already one town so named in Idaho and he was asked to choose another name. He simply substituted S for E, and the name became Sagle.

Sailor Cap Butte (Owyhee). 1096'. T8S R9E sec 18. Located 17 mi SSW of Glenns Ferry. Named for a rock formation that looks like a sailor's cap from a distance.

Saint Anthony (Fremont). 4956'. T7N 44 sec 6. County seat. Six mi NE of the county line. Post office, 1888-.

Transfer name. Named by a local homesteader and first postmaster, Charles H. Moon, for St. Anthony Falls on the Mississippi River in Minnesota, because he saw a resemblance to them in the local cascades on Henrys Fork. Moon built a bridge and a store there in 1887.

Saint Louis Canyon (Butte). T3N R24E sec 15. Heads just S of Era and extends SE for about 1 mi to where it joins Champagne Creek.

Name derived from the nearby St. Louis mine.

Saint Paul (Canyon). An 1880 RR construction camp 1 1/2 mi from the site of two proposed RR bridges across the Snake River. As soon as the bridges were completed in 1883, the camp folded its tents and moved to Parma.

Named for St. Paul, Minnesota.

Sal Mountain (Lemhi). 9592'. T20N R22E sec 34. About 11 mi S of Salmon.

This mountain was a triangulation point for base maps when the country was surveyed, and the name is a shortened form of Salmon, given for identification purposes.

Salem (Madison). 2435'. T6N R40E sec 5. An agricultural community 2 mi W of Sugar City.

Founded in 1883 by Mormons. Located on what was then called Teton Island, for it was bounded on N and W by N Fk Teton River and on the S by S Fk. Post office, 1893-1916.

Named by LSD President Thomas Ricks. Two explanations have been reported: for Salem, Massachusetts, perhaps out of sympathy for those persecuted; for the biblical Salem, city of Melchizedek, the more likely explanation.

Salmon (Lemhi). 4004'. T21N R22E sec 6. County seat. In the NE part of the county, about 1/2 mi SW of the confluence of Lemhi and Salmon rivers. Post office, 1869-.

Situated on the Lewis and Clark Trail, the townsite of Salmon was originally a supply point for mines in the Leesburg Basin in 1866. The town was called Salmon City until 1869 when Lemhi County was created and Salmon became the county seat. George L. Shoup, the first governor of Idaho, and his associates were responsible for planning the townsite of Salmon in 1867.

Named for the salmon found in the Salmon River.

Salmon Falls, Upper/Lower (Twin Falls/Gooding). T8S R13E sec 2, T7S R13E sec 10. Waterfalls on the Snake River, about 40 mi W of Shoshone Falls, Upper Salmon Falls being at the mouth of Salmon Falls Creek; Lower Salmon Falls about 5 mi downstream from Upper.

Salmon Falls was established on the S side of the river at the upper falls in 1879. Post office, 1879-1896.

Salmon Falls Creek (Twin Falls). T8S R13E sec 2. Heads in Nevada at an altitude of 7500' and cuts 90 mi through Twin Falls County to empty into Snake River. This stream flows through Salmon Canyon Gorge in the NW corner of the county, NW of Buhl.

Salmon River. T29N R3W sec 10. The Salmon River is the longest river in the contiguous US that is completely contained within the boundaries of one state. Its source is the mountains of central Idaho above 8000' and it empties into the Snake River in Lewis County at an altitude of 803'. The terrain it drains is rugged, mountainous, heavily timbered land. The main drainage is 14,100 square miles. E Fk has a drainage of 600 square miles and a length of 35 mi. Middle Fk is 111 miles long, rising in the mountains in W central Idaho and flowing N through a deep, picturesque canyon; its altitude at the source is 7000' and at its mouth, 3908'. The N Fk rises in the Continental Divide at 8500' and empties at 3596'.

William Clark called this stream Lewis River when he arrived at the junction of the Lemhi and Salmon rivers on 21 Aug 1805 because Meriwether Lewis was the first white man to visit its waters. The stream was later nicknamed "River of No Return," because it was possible to float or row downstream, but not upstream. In this day of jet-propelled boats, travel upstream is possible.

Major tributaries: Little Salmon, Lemhi, and Pahsimeroi rivers and Yankee Fork.

The name of the stream has been changed from Lewis to Salmon River because of the salmon found here. All the names in the following cluster are named for the Salmon River.

Salmon Hot Springs (Lemhi). T20N R22E sec 3. At the head of Hot Springs Creek.

Salmon River Canyon. The canyon through which the Salmon River flows. It is second in depth to Hells Canyon.

Salmon River Mountains (Custer). In central Idaho within the great bend of the Salmon River from Stanley Basin to the S Fk of that river. Peaks 10,000' and above in this range are Twin, General, Bald, Jordon, and Tango.

Salubria (Washington). T14N R3W sec 11. Formerly Upper Valley; now a ghost town. Just SE of Cambridge. Settled in the late 1860s. There were enough people to merit a post office in 1874. John Cuddy built his grist mill in 1870 above this site, but the community had grown so rapidly by 1890 that he moved his business to Salubria. Post office, 1824-1916.

Because a Mrs. Miller held out for an exorbitant price for her property when the RR was buying right-of-way for the proposed line and station, the RR changed its plans and built on the opposite side of the Weiser River, thus stifling Salubria and fostering Cambridge.

Named for the balmy atmosphere and lush valley, which one visitor described as "salubrious, health-giving."

Salzer Creek (Lemhi). T26N R20E sec 24. Flows 2 mi S and enters N Fk Hughes Creek; Salmon River drainage.

A man named Salzer had a placer mine and cabin near the mouth of the creek.

Sam (Teton). T5N R44E sec 31. Ghost town in the SW part of the county in the Big Hole Mountains; formerly Talbot for R. S. Talbot, organizer of Idaho Coal Mines Co., 1917.

High-grade coal was discovered here in the 1890s by Charles H. Rammell. F. H. Samuels became the owner after Talbot but was beset by bad luck, labor problems, and a fire that destroyed the tipple. In 1935 he was financially in ruin and the mine closed. Post office, 1925-1934.

Named for F. H. Samuels, who owned the mine in the late 1920s and 1930s.

Samaria (Oneida). 4375'. T15S R35E sec 14. In the SE part of the county, 8 mi SW of Malad City. Post office, 1881-1983.

Settled in 1868 by several Mormon familes and named for Samaria in Palestine. The settlers, mostly from Wales, are said to have become known as Good Samaritans for their good will toward one another.

Samowen Park (Bonner). T56N R1E sec 11. On Lake Pend Oreille, 2 1/4 mi SSE of Hope.

Named for Sam Owen, who settled near this location in 1898. See Owens Bay.

Sampson Creek (Camas). T1N R14E sec 9. Rises on Cannonball Mountain and flows 6 mi SW to Soldier Creek, tributary of Camas Creek; Big Wood River drainage.

The Sampson family settled on this creek and operated a sawmill here in 1879.

Samuels (Bonner). 2137' T59N R1W sec 32. Town 11 mi NE of Sandpoint and 2 1/4 mi NE of Colburn. Post office, 1914-.

The town was known as Iola, but later named Samuels in honor of Henry F. Samuels, who purchased a ranch here in 1913. It was Samuels who attempted to get the first post office, and when it was established it was named for him.

Sand Butte (Lincoln). 4974'. T3S R22E sec 28/33. Hill. Volcanic cone in the NE part of the county, 44 mi SW of Arco and 16 mi NE of Richfield.

So named because the rim of the cone consists of sand-like material.

Also Twin Buttes.

Sand Creek (Fremont). T8N R41E sec 12. Flows 6 mi S through unnamed reservoir and ends 10 mi NW of Ashton. Sand Creek is an early name for Ora, which see.

Sand Dunes run NE to SW for 16 mi, 2 mi NE of St. Anthony. The dunes are Idaho's miniature Sahara, the largest dune area in the state. The creek runs along the edge.

Sand Dunes Lake (Owyhee). T6S R6E sec 13/24. S of Snake River in the Bruneau Sand Dunes. A lake formed by the change in water flow caused by C. J. Strike Dam.

Named for its location in the sand dunes.

Sand Hole (Jefferson). 4802'. T7N R36E sec 15/22. Early name for Hamer. Maier Kaufman established and ran a stage station here in the late 1860s, one of several on the route from Utah to Butte, Montana, by way of Fort Lemhi. Kaufman operated several such stations, the last two being Sand Hole and Hole in the Wall (near Dubois).

Named for the sandy soil and hole "hollow."

Sandhole Lake. T7N R36E sec 16/20. A lake in the SE part of Camas National Wildlife Refuge and 1.5 mi W of present-day Hamer. Some early irrigation projects were worked here.

Name for the town.

Sand Springs (Gooding). T8S R14E sec 20. In the SE part of the county in Snake River Canyon; 2 mi WNW of Banbury Springs.

Named for the abundance of clean sand in the vicinity.

Sanders (Benewah). 2600'. T43/44N R4W sec 35/2. In SW Benewah County in the Coeur d'Alene Indian Reservation. Post office, 1901-.

The name Sanders appeared on the GLO Plat in 1909, and the timbered land was opened to homesteaders in 1910.

Named for the first postmaster.

Sandpoint (Bonner). 2086'. T57N R2W sec 22. County seat. Located in the center of Bonner County. Sandpoint Creek flows 9 mi W and S and empties into Lake Pend Oreille at Sandpoint. Post office, 1895-.

In 1809, David Thompson mentions a point of sand in his journal, and it is that point for which Sandpoint was named. The settlement here dates back to 1880, when Robert Weeks opened the first general store.

Sands Basin (Owyhee). T1N R6/5W sec 24/18/17. In the N part of the county, 3 mi W of French John Hill.

Named for A. J. Sands, who was one of the discoverers of the Orofino mine on War Eagle Mountain. He was also in the cattle business and his cattle grazed in this basin.

Sandy Creek (Lemhi). T20N R23E sec 24. Heads near Goldstone Mountain; flows SW 8 mi then NW 4 mi to enter Lemhi River.

Named for Alexander "Sandy" Barrack, who had a grist mill built on his ranch in this vicinity in 1872. He patented the land in 1885.

Santa (Benewah). 2681'. T44N R1W sec 22. In E Benewah County on St. Maries River 11 mi SE of the town of St. Maries.

Named for Santa Anna Creek, which was later shortened to Santa Creek. Post office, 1887-.

Santa Creek (Benewah). T44N R1W sec 8. Rises in the hills E of Sanders and flows 14 mi erratically NE to its confluence with St. Maries River 2 mi above present-day Santa.

Named Santa Anna creek by Jesuits in this country.

Sarilda (Fremont). T9N R41E sec 13. Town 7 mi NW of Ashton.

Named for Sarilda Sadoris Moon, daughter of Samuel Sadoris, the first postmaster, appointed in 1894.

Satan Lake (Adams). T22N R2W sec 35. Located 1 mi N of Black Lake in Payette National Forest, Hells Canyon National Recreation Area.

The name follows the pattern set by the Seven Devils.

Sawlog Creek (Lemhi). T17N R17E sec 21. Heads SW of headwaters of Pole Creek; flows W 2 mi to enter Camas Creek; Middle Fk Salmon River drainage.

Sawlog Gulch. T24N R19E sec 23. Heads about 2 mi E of Stormy Peak; runs N 3 1/2 mi to enter Salmon River drainage.

Trees cut in these drainages were floated down to Shoup to be sawn into lumber, which was then used for timbering in the mines.

Sawmill Canyon (Lemhi). T19N R23E sec 32. Heads near Andrews Spring; runs NE 1 1/2 mi to meet McDevitt Creek drainage; Lemhi River drainage. Named for Murdock M. McNicoll's sawmill, 1929 or 1930.

Sawmill Creek (Bonneville). T2S R43E sec 19. Rises in the S part of the county in Caribou Range and flows 3 mi SE into Brockman Creek; Grays Lake system. Named for Jack Dehlin's sawmill, 1920.

Sawmill Creek (Boise). T8N R8E sec 29. Rises in the NE part of the county on Banner Ridge and flows 5 1/2 mi SE into Banner Creek 6 mi SE of Lowman; Boise River drainage. Named for the sawmill for the Banner mine.

Sawmill Creek (Boise). T6N R5E sec 33. Flows 2 mi SE into Mores Creek 2 mi SW of Idaho City; Boise River drainage. Named for sawmill, 1864.

Sawmill Creek (Clearwater). T36N R6E sec 33. In the SE extremity of the county. Flows S into Musselshell Creek at sec 33, Clearwater River drainage. Named for USFS sawmill for the Bungalow Ranger Station.

Sawmill Gulch (Lemhi). T23N R19E sec 7. Heads near Point of Rocks; runs N 1 mi, NW 2 mi and then SW 2 1/2 mi to enter Pine Creek drainage; Salmon River drainage. Named for Herb St. Clair's sawmill for mines at Shoup and Pine Creek.

Sawmill Gulch (Lemhi). T19N R18E sec 3. Runs NW 2 1/2 mi to enter Panther Creek; Salmon River drainage. Named for Eli Minert's sawmill.

Sawtell Peak (Fremont). 10,500'. T14N R42E sec 1. Five mi S of Henrys Lake. Most of Targhee National Forest and part of southern Montana are visible from the top of this peak.

Named for Gilman Sawtell, French trapper and early settler on the slopes of the mountain ca. 1870. He attempted unsuccessfully to raise cattle here.

Sawtooth (Blaine). 7346'. T7N R14E sec 29/32. Ghost townsite situated at the foot of Sawtooth Mountains from which it takes its name. Post office, 1880-1896.

Located on Beaver Creek, this mining settlement grew out of additional discoveries N of the Vienna mine. Sawtooth mine, discovered 2 July 1878, marked the beginning of mining in this area at the head of Salmon River; a boisterous camp, 1880-1886.

Named for the mine.

Sawtooth Mountains. These include the ranges and masses around the heads of Salmon River, the S Fk Boise River, and Big Wood River. The most magnificent group of mountains in Idaho.

Roughly, the S boundary is the Snake River Plain between Bellevue and Pine; the W is an irregular line from Pine to Cape Horn, with Rocky Bar and Atlanta as contacts; the N is Stanley Basin and the Salmon River; and the E is State Highway 78 from Bellevue to Galena Summit, and from the summit to Salmon River, the E boundary of Boulder Mountains.

Named for the rugged peaks that from a distance look like the serrated teeth of a saw. The features that follow take their names from these mountains.

Sawtooth City (Custer). A town in the Stanley Basin in 1881; 60 mi N of the Yankee Fork mining district.

Sawtooth Lakes (Custer). 8 mi SW of Stanley. Upper and Lower: The upper has a maximum depth of about 250' and covers about 300 acres. It is reached by trail along Iron Creek or Stanley Lake. A stream, full of waterfalls, connects it with the lower lake, which cov-

ers only an acre and has a maximum depth of not more than 15'.

Sawtooth Range (Boise/Custer). A series of beautiful spires from Cape Horn to Alturas Lake. From the Salmon River side they rise abruptly from a broad valley floor 7000' in elevation to heights of 9000' and 10,000'. As seen from the N, the crest is exceedingly serrated and bears a striking resemblance to the teeth of a saw; but from the S the summits blend with others of the highland areas and give the impression of being parts of a dissected plateau.

Sawyer (Bonner). 2100'. T55N R3W sec 6. Town 7 1/2 mi ESE of the town of Priest River. Post office, 1909-1930.

Named for the first postmaster, Louis Sawyer, and his brother, John, both early settlers.

Schafer Gulch (Bonner). T55N R1E sec 30. Heads at Schafer Lookout (5250') and extends 1 1/4 mi S to Granite Creek.

Named for the Schafer Brothers mine nearby.

Scherrer (Minidoka). T9S R24E sec 1. First name of Acequia, which see. Post office, 1905-1907.

Named for the first postmaster, Frank K. Scherrer.

Schiller (Power). 4428'. T6S R32E sec 24. A dry-farming community and RR siding in the NE part of the county, 12 mi NE of American Falls. This siding was made a loading point for grain about 1910.

Named for J. C. Schiller, a RR supervisor.

Schlieght Lake (Bonner). T55N R3E sec 16. Lake located 1 1/2 mi N of Cabinet; 5 1/4 mi ESE of Clark Fork. Pronounced SHLIT.

Named for Henry Schlieght, an early settler.

Schmid Range (Caribou). T8/9S R43/44E. In the NE part of the county, extending NW to SE from Blackfoot River to the headwaters of Slug Creek; 15 mi long, maximum width 2.5 mi, maximum elevation 7923'; numerous springs; rich in phosphate beds; part of Peale Mountains. Schmid Mountain (8994') lies 2 mi E of the N part of the range.

Named for the Schmid Ranch.

Schmidt Creek (Clearwater). T35N R3E sec 23. In the SW extremity of the county. Flows W into Lolo Creek 12 mi SE of Orofino; Clearwater River drainage.

A man named Schmidt had a sawmill at the head of this stream.

Schoolhouse Gulch (Boise). T9N R4E sec 26. Three mi SE of Crouch, this was the site of the first schoolhouse in Garden Valley; it was a log cabin.

Schoolhouse Hill (Boise). T7N R4E sec 15.

The sites of early schoolhouses.

Schupferville (Latah). T37N R3W sec 4/3. Early name for Juliaetta, which see.

Schwartz Creek (Latah). T40N R2W sec 4. Flows 4.1 mi S to E Fk Big Bear Creek; Potlatch River drainage.

Named by Edd. F. Helmers in 1938 for rancher J. J. Schwartz, who owned and operated a farm about midway up the stream.

Schweitzer Basin (Bonner). T58N R2W sec 17/20. A ski resort area with ski, lodging, and service facilities 7 1/4 mi NW of Sandpoint. Schweitzer Creek rises N of Schweitzer Basin and flows SE to Sandpoint Creek.

Named for an old Swiss soldier who had a cabin near the creek.

Scofield Creek (Clearwater). T39N R6E sec 31 and T38N R6E sec 6/7. Flows NE into Washington Creek at T39N R6E sec 35.

Scofield was a timber owner and locater for timber claims who settled in the area. He was supposedly a former Governor of Wisconsin who invested a great deal of money (about $600,000) in 1913 to acquire the timbered land.

Scotchman Peak (Bonner). 7009'. T56N R3E sec 21. Located 7 1/2 mi ESE of Denton, 5 1/2 mi NE of Clark Fork. Scotchman No. 2 (6989') is 2 mi NE of Scotchman Peak, for which it is named.

Name derived from the shape: it looks like a Scotchman complete with ruffled shirt and tam-o'-shanter.

Scott Creek (Boise). T10N R7E sec 5. Rises NW of Lowman just S at the Boise-Valley county line on Scott Mountain Lookout (8215') and flows NE 7 mi into Deadwood River; Payette River drainage. Scott Mountain Spring lies just S of the lookout.

Named for the Scott family who homesteaded on the main creek; they later moved to Idaho City.

Scott Creek (Washington). T11N R6W sec 20. Rises in the mountains N of Weiser and W of Midvale, 2 mi S of Randall Lookout, T12N R6W sec 2, and flows S and W 13 mi to Snake River at the site of Porters Ferry.

Named for Scott Shaw, who, when he was young, herded his father's hogs in Indian Grove at the headwaters of this stream.

Scott Saddle (Idaho). T24N R4E sec 5. A bench on the N side of Salmon River, 16 mi E of Riggins.

Sylvester Scott bought a place a mi above the bench in 1894 and moved there with his wife and 21 children. The Scotts raised livestock and produce for the mines, irrigating their land from Robbins Creek.

Scotts Canyon (Lemhi). T11N R29E sec 15. Heads W of Scott Peak (11,393'); runs 8 mi SW to Birch Creek 1/2 mi N of Reno.

Scotsmen sawed wood in this canyon to make charcoal for Nicholia, hence the name Scott(s).

Scout, The (Boundary). 6300'. T64N R3E sec 22. Mountain on the border between Boundary County and Montana. Mining claims were staked here in 1895.

A figurative name; the mountain towered above the area as if "scouting" the land.

Scree Lake (Custer). 9550'. T9N R16E sec 32. An 8-acre lake in the glacial deposits of the White Cloud Peaks.

The deposit of scree or rocky debris at the S side of the lake suggests the name.

Scriver Creek (Boise). T10N R4E sec 27. Rises in Valley County, on N Fk Range and flows 4 1/2 mi into the Payette River in the NW extremity of the county.

Named for Frederick Griffin Scriver, who came to Horseshoe Bend in 1878.

Scurvy Mountain (Clearwater). 6691'. T39N R10E sec 25 and T39N R11E sec 30. Scurvy Creek rises on the E slope of this mountain and flows 2 mi NW into Kelly Creek; Clearwater River drainage. Scurvy Lake lies 3 mi SW of Kelly Creek Work Center, and Scurvy Saddle 4 mi SW of Kelly Creek Work Center.

In the fall of 1907, two men from Montana, George Gorman and Clayton Shoecraft, came into the area around Cayuse Creek. They lived in a small cabin, killing two elk for food and establishing a trap line up Cayuse Creek. In midwinter they began to suffer from a disease which they believed to be rheumatism; according to a diary they kept, the disease had all the symptoms of scurvy. In the last diary entry, one man reported that his partner was dead and that he could no longer get out of bed. In the spring the Hansen brothers reported the two men were missing, and later found them in their cabin. They buried them in a common grave near what is now called Scurvy Mountain. These features are named for the incident.

Seafoam (Custer). T14N R12E sec 24. Ghost town; mining town founded about 1886. Post office, 1927-1928.

Seafoam Creek heads in Seafoam Lake and flows NE where it converges with Baldwin and Vanity creeks and empties into the S side of Rapid River.

The town was named for the Seafoam mine, and nearby features were named for the town.

Secesh Basin (Idaho). T21/22N R5E. Mining area at the headwaters of Secesh River in Payette National Forest, between Warren and Burgdorf, NE of Upper Payette Lake and Squaw Meadow. The high peaks of Marshall Mountain, War Eagle, Ruby Mountain, Diamond Rocks, and Bear Pete, all over 8000', encircle this basin.

Secesh River (Idaho/Valley). T20N R6E sec 34. Rises in the mountains above Burgdorf and Warren and flows about 30 mi SE into Valley County to empty into S Fk Salmon River.

So named because miners from the Confederate States worked here. They were called "Secesh Doctrinaires" (as in "secessionist") and gave their name to the basin and river.

Secunda Creek (Latah). T42N R2W sec 35. Flows 1-2 mi NE to Big Sand Creek; Palouse River drainage.

So named by USFS ranger W. H. Daugs, because this creek is the second side stream up Big Sand Creek; he submitted this name for lack of a better in 1931.

Selkirk Mountains. Range extending from NE Washington and Canada into northern Idaho to lower end of Lake

Coeur d'Alene and E to the Purcell Trench. Peaks: Mt. Casey (6735'), Smith (7650'); characterized by moderate ruggedness at the boundaries, but gently rounded summits S of the Spokane River; area covered by Kaniksu National Forest.

First called Nelson Mountains by David Thompson, geographer and astronomer to the North West and Hudsons Bay companies, on maps 1812-1814; Palliser's map (1860) and Arrowsmith's (1963) and Trutch's (1970) show Selkirk, with no reference to reason or time of change, but believed that Thompson made the change after 1821, when Hudsons Bay Company absorbed the North West Company, to honor Thomas Douglas, Earl of Selkirk, the founder of Selkirk colony on the Red River (in present-day Manitoba) and one of the most enterprising patrons of the Hudsons Bay Company.

Sellars Creek (Bingham). T2S R40E sec 3. Rises on the E slope of Blackfoot Mountains and flows 10 mi ENE into Willow Creek; Snake River drainage. In the NE extremity of the county. Sellars Creek flows through a wide meadow, narrows through a canyon over a steep, rock-strewn bed, and merges with Willow Creek; a rugged stream.

Named for Kellerance Sellars, the first settler in the area. He established squatter's rights between 1887 and 1891 and operated a ranch here. Also Cellars Creek.

Selle (Bonner). T58N R1W sec 29. Town 6 1/4 mi NNE of Sandpoint.

Named for Charles and Robert Selle, two early settlers. Formerly Matchwood.

Selway River (Idaho). T32N R7E sec 4. Rises at an altitude of 6000' on the W slopes of the Bitterroot Range and flows 75 mi first N then NW and W to its confluence with Lochsa River to form

Middle Fk Clearwater at Lowell (1250'); drainage, 1510 square miles; terrain, rugged, forested mountains and a narrow valley.

Selway-Bitterroot Wilderness Area includes the drainage area between the Selway and Lochsa rivers.

There was an effort to create Selway County in 1917, with Kooskia as county seat, to include parts of Idaho and Lewis counties; a referendum of it that year failed.

Selway Falls, 50' high, lie 19 mi upriver from Lowell.

The name has generally been accepted as a Nez Perce word meaning "smooth water"; however, the water is not smooth and should there be such a Nez Perce word, it is purely coincidental. The river was named for Thomas Selway, sheepman from Beaverhead County, Montana, who ran large herds in the Selway country from the 1890s into early 1900s. His cabin was intact on the Selway River as late as 1970.

Seneaquoteen (Bonner). T56N R3W sec 31. Town on Pend Oreille River, 3/4 mi NE of Sawyer and 13 mi SW of Sandpoint; in Kaniksu National Forest.

One of the earliest settlements in the county, first begun as a Hudsons Bay Company trading post. It was for a short time the county seat of Kootenai County in 1864.

The name Seneaquoteen is derived from the Indian "crossing of the waters" and refers to an early river crossing at that point. Also Sineacateen, Seneaguoteen, and Seneacquoteen.

Serrate Ridge (Custer). T9N R16E. A prominent ridge extending from Castle Peak for approximately 1/4 mi N, 1/2 mi NE, and 3/4 mi E for a distance of 1 1/2 mi.

Name given because of the serrated, rugged, barren rocky ridge capped by tooth-shaped rocks; can be seen from many different angles and locations in the surrounding area.

Setters (Kootenai). 2582'. T48N R5W sec 32. In the SW extremity of the county, 7 mi NW of Worley, on US 95 and the Milwaukee RR; once a RR station and a post office. Post office, 1916-1924.

Named for the Setters family who lived here, one of whom was the first postmaster.

Setzer Creek (Shoshone). T45N R5E sec 8. In the central part of the county, a 2-mi tributary of the St. Joe River from the N; 2.2 mi W of Avery.

Originally this creek was called Coon Creek after the mail carrier and dispatcher for the RR engineers in 1906. Later, Lee Sezter homesteaded at the mouth of the creek, and the name was changed to Setzer Creek.

Seven Devils (Idaho). The N cluster of peaks in the Seven Devils Mountain Range, in SW Idaho County, in Hells Canyon National Recreation Area; lie in a semicircle.

The peaks in this group give the entire range of Seven Devils Mountains their name. They are, from the greatest elevation down: He Devil, She Devil, Devils Throne, Mt. Belial, The Ogre, Twin Imps, and The Goblin.

There are some 20 named lakes in this area and numerous creeks, rock formations, and rapids. The names all spring from the original demonic names of the peaks or from their opposites, such as Heavens Gate and Paradise Meadows.

Seven Devils Lake lies just E of Devils Tooth.

Seven Devils Mountains extend from Heavens Gate in Idaho County, trending NE to SW for about 30 mi. The range includes the Seven Devils and lies between Snake and Little Salmon riv-

ers, with White Bird Mountain to the N and Cuddy Mountains to the S. The extreme N and S portions of this range are high rounded hills. The central elongated dome is from 8 to 10 mi wide.

John Rees says that the Hudson's Bay Company named the seven high peaks in the early 1800s because they are mysterious and weird and must be associated with the devil. The USFS says that the name springs from an Indian legend. As the story goes, a lost Indian was surprised by a devil in this area, and as he ran away he encountered six more devils. Upon his return to his tribe, he told of the seven devils who scared him. From this, the name Seven Devils was derived.

Sevy Peak (Custer). T8N R13E sec 18. In the Sawtooth Range.

Named for John Sevy, early USFS Supervisor of Bridger National Forest and later Sawtooth National Forest, 1957-1963.

Shafer Creek (Boise). T7N R2E sec 34. Rises in the SW extremity of the county on Shafer Butte (7582') and flows 14 mi NW into Harris Creek 3 mi S of Horseshoe Bend; Payette River drainage. Post office, 1882-1888.

Named for Jacob K. Shafer, Idaho Territory's representative to the Forty-first Congress, 1869-1871; he lived in Idaho City.

Shake Creek (Clearwater). T38N R7E sec 33. Flows S into Orogrande Creek at sec 32; Clearwater River drainage.

The "shakes" (shingles) for the old Oxford Ranger Station were obtained here.

Shake Meadow Creek (Clearwater). T35N R4E sec 5. Flows S into Jim Ford Creek at T35N R4E sec 5; Clearwater River drainage.

Named for the cedar timber from which the cedar shakes were obtained.

Shanghai Creek (Clearwater). T37N R6E sec 31. Rises near SE Clearwater-Idaho county line on Shanghai Divide and flows 6 mi SW into Rhodes Creek E of Pierce; Clearwater River drainage.

Named for the Chinese who came into the area as prospectors and reworked the diggings after the white men had originally placered a stream. Because of their later predominance, the stream was named Shanghai. Ah Fong lived near where the lookout is located, which was called Shanghai Summit after his native city in China. He was the last Chinese to remain around Pierce; he lived in a single cabin situated among the tumbledown dwellings left from the Chinese settlement on the summit. He was murdered in 1932.

Share (Owyhee). T3S R4W sec 12. Stage station 1 mi S of Reynolds, 11 mi N of Silver City, to Silver City. Founded in 1877 and named for its owner, Charles Edward Share.

Sharkey Creek (Lemhi). T22N R20E sec 21. Flows generally W 3 mi to enter Napias Creek, near the mouth of Wards Gulch; Salmon River drainage.

Sharkey Creek. T19N R24E sec 25. Forms on the Idaho-Montana border, N of the head of Cow Creek; flows NW 2 mi to enter Agency Creek; Lemhi River drainage. Sharkey Hot Springs are on Warm Springs Creek 4 mi NE of Tendoy.

Named for Frank Burnett Sharkey, leader of the original party that discovered gold in the Leesburg Basin in 1866.

Sharon (Bear Lake). 6301'. T12S R43E sec 30. Town in the NW part of the county, 9 mi W of Montpelier on US 89. Post office, 1901-1915.

A Mormon settlement named in 1897 for Sharon, Vermont, the birthplace of Joseph Smith, the prophet of the LDS Church.

Shasta Butte (Kootenai). 4877'. T50N R5W sec 31. In the extreme W part of the county, 11 mi W of Coeur d'Alene. A large outcropping of rock used as a lookout and signal point by Indians. Also called locally Big Rock.

Probably named for a supposed resemblance to Mt. Shasta, California.

Shattuck Butte (Clearwater). T40N R2E sec 5. Four mi NW of Elk River. Shattuck Creek rises on the S slope of this butte and flows 4 mi S into Bull Run Creek 2 mi W of Elk River; Clearwater River drainage.

Named for a homesteader.

Shaw Hollow (Bannock). T7S R36E sec 14. An intermittent drainage that trends 2 mi W to Rapid Creek, 1 mi NE of Inkom.

Named for early homesteaders.

Shaws Gulch (Boise). T6N R5E sec 34. A 3-mi gulch trending NW into Mores Creek 1 mi SW of Idaho City; Boise River drainage. Post office, 1880.

Named for a miner who had claims here.

She Devil (Idaho). 9280'. T23N R2W sec 23. One of the Seven Devils in the Seven Devils Mountains, in Nezperce National Forest, just S of Sheep Lake and E of He Devil. Formerly, Mount Lucifer.

Shea Meadow (Latah). 3020'. T41N R1W sec 33. Area drained by Meadow and Corral creeks, just N of Helmer.

Tom and Pete Shea were early settlers in this township.

Shears Creek (Lemhi). T121N R28E sec 2. Forms near the headwaters of Cabin Creek; flows 2 mi SW, then 1 1/2 mi S to meet Cottonwood Creek; Lemhi River drainage.

Named for three Shear brothers, Al, Pete, and Jake. Alfred F. Shear patented the ground in 1917.

Sheep Creek (Fremont). T13N R42E sec 14. Flows 6 mi SE to an unnamed reservoir and a convergence with Hotel Creek 2 mi from Island Park Reservoir; Island Park Reservoir/Henrys Fork system.

Sheep Falls. T10N R43E sec 9. On Henrys Fork 5 mi upstream from Big Falls SE of Lookout Butte.

Sheep Falls. T9N R45E sec 26. 5 mi S of Cave Falls Highway, 18 mi E of Ashton on Falls River.

Sheep Point 10,609′. T16N R43E sec 4.

All of the above names indicate the presence of herds of sheep, either being driven through the area to summer pasture, or the feature itself is in summer-pasture areas.

Sheep Creek (Lemhi). T25N R21E sec 14. Heads 1 mi N of Eagle Mountain; flows W 5 1/2 mi to enter N Fk Salmon River. Sheep Mountain (9841′) is situated on the Continental Divide at the head of N Fk Sheep Creek.

Named for the great number of Rocky Mountain sheep skulls found in the drainage. There are still numerous sheep found here. Sheep Creek, tributary of Camas Creek, is also named for the Rocky Mountain sheep in the area.

Sheep Horn Peak (Lemhi). 10,456′. Situated at the head of Alder Creek, in sec 30. In Lemhi Mountains; Salmon National Forest.

Old-timers hunted mountain sheep in this vicinity.

Sheep Mountain (Bingham). 7450′. T2S R41E sec 32. In the E part of the county, between Long Valley and Cranes creeks. A. J. Stanger and his son Frank homesteaded the E slope of this mountain in 1922 and established a claim to it in 1927.

Used for grazing sheep; hence the name.

Sheep Mountain (Custer). 10,910′. T9N R18E sec 32. About 1 mi N of Bowery Peak and 13 1/2 mi SSE of Clayton.

Named for the Rocky Mountain bighorn sheep.

Sheepherder Point (Bonner). T56N R1E sec 24. On Lake Pend Oreille 5 mi NW of Clark Fork.

Named because owners had a large corral on the point.

Sheephorn Mountain (Lemhi). 8159′. T18N R20E sec 15/22. Six mi E of Taylor Mountain.

Named for the bighorn sheep horns found here.

Sheldon Creek (Lemhi). T16N R16E sec 14. Heads near Sheldon Peak; flows NE 2 mi to Camas Creek; Middle Fk Salmon River drainage.

Named for R. K. Sheldon, of New York, who mined in this area in the early days and was vice president of Goldhill Mining and Milling Company.

Shelf Lake (Custer). T9N R16E. Lake.15 mi long, one of the Boulder Chain Lakes; a rock shelf extends around the S and W shores.

Shell Creek (Lemhi). T23N R16E sec 25. Heads near Horse Heaven; runs N 2 1/2 mi to enter Salmon River.

Named for Ebenezer Snell, who mined in this area. The name was altered to Shell.

Shelley (Bingham). 4629′. T1N R37E sec 29/33. In the NE part of the county, 10 mi S of Idaho Falls. An agricultural area, with potatoes the most important crop, though sugar beets brought the first food-processing plant, the Utah-Idaho Sugar Company, to the area in 1914. Post office, 1893-.

Settled in 1884 by Mormons, and named by UPRR officials for John F. Shelley, early settler, owner of the first store, first postmaster, and Mormon bishop.

Shep Creek (Lemhi). T17N R20E sec 17. Originates near King Mountain; flows 1 1/2 mi SE to enter Salmon River.

Named for Warren Shepherd, who floated cedar logs from here down the Salmon River.

Shepard Peak (Boise). 8785'. T7N R10E sec 6.

Named by the USFS for Boise National Forest supervisor E. C. Shepard.

Shepherd Lake (Bonner). T56N R2W sec 23. Located 6 1/2 mi SSE of Sandpoint.

Named for the Sheperd (sic) family. The lake is sometimes referred to as Griffith Lake in honor of a Griffith family who lived near it.

Sherman Creek (Idaho). T35N R9E sec 27. Rises on Sherman Peak (6696'), 2 mi E of Sherman Saddle, and flows 6 mi S to Lochsa River, about 25 mi E of Lowell by river.

Named by the Truax party in 1868 for General William T. Sherman. Major Truax was a US Army officer in charge of laying out a military road W from Lolo Pass.

Sherwin (Latah). 3212'. T42N R1E sec 33. A RR siding on the Chicago, Milwaukee, and St. Paul RR. Sherwin Point (4074') lies 1.2 mi NW of Sherwin.

Named for homesteader Edwin R. Sherwin.

Sherwin Bar (Idaho). T26N R1E sec 13/14. A mining area along Salmon River; extending about 1 mi.

Named for Ed Sherwin, one of the first to reach the Warren Mining District.

Sherwood Beach (Bonner). T60N R4W sec 34. Cove on Priest Lake, 1 1/2 mi N of Coolin.

Named for a Captain Sherwood, who commanded a group of soldiers that once camped in the area.

Shewag Creek (Lemhi). T25N R22E sec 22. Heads about 1 mi SE of Stein Mountain; flows NE 2 1/2 mi to enter Sheep Creek; N Fk Salmon River drainage. Shewag Lake lies at the head of this stream. Pronounced SHE-wag.

Since the creek heads near the divide between Sheep Creek and Wagonhammer Creek, the name is a combination of both Sheep and Wagonhammer. It was named by USFS ranger Al Wheeler about 1924.

Shilling Creek (Boise). T8N R4E sec 11. Flows 2 1/2 mi E into Alder Creek 3 mi S of Garden Valley; Payette River drainage.

The Shilling family homesteaded near the head of this creek.

Shining Butte (Idaho). T26N R6E sec 29/28. In the Buffalo Hump area. Shining Lake lies 1/2 mi E of the butte.

Named for the glittering character of the rock on the mountain and transferred to the lake.

Ship Island Lake (Lemhi). T21N R16E sec 16. About 1 mi NE of Aggipah Mountain. Ship Island Creek heads in Bighorn Crags and is the main source for Ship Island Lake; runs W 4 1/2 mi to enter Middle Fk Salmon River.

Named because the lake itself is shaped somewhat like a boat or ship and it contains an island that from a distance looks like a ship with tree masts.

Shirley Creek (Cassia). T12S R27E sec 16. In the NE quadrant of the county. Rises in Quaking Aspen Spring at T12S R29E sec 17; flows W and NW 9 mi and becomes intermittent for 5 mi to Raft River.

Named for one of the earliest cattlemen in the area (1878), J. Q. Shirley.

Shoban Lake (Lemhi). T21N R16E sec 17. In Bighorn Crags 1/2 mi SW of Airplane Lake and 3/4 mi W of Birdbill Lake.

Named in 1964 by USFS in cooperation with the Coast and Geodetic Survey, to honor the Shoban (contraction of Shoshoni-Bannock) firefighters who fought many fires in this general area.

Shoecraft Creek (Clearwater). T38N R11E sec 4. Flows SW into Cayuse Creek at sec 4; Clearwater River drainage.

Named for Clayton Shoecraft, one of the men who died of scurvy in 1907 while trapping along Cayuse Creek. See Scurvy Mountain.

Shonip Creek (Boise). T8N R9E sec 15. Rises in the SE part of the county on Wolf Mountain (8876′) and flows N into the Crooked River; Boise River drainage.

Shonip is the Shoshoni Indian word for "grass." There is a grassy flat at the head of the creek. The USFS named this creek.

Shoo Fly Creek (Owyhee). T5S R3E sec 16/15. In N central Owyhee County; flows NE into the Snake River just E of Grand View. Shoo Fly Ranch is in the area of Shoo Fly Creek.

These locations are believed to have been named for the Civil War song, "Shoo Fly." Many of the miners in the county were southerners.

Shoshone (Lincoln). 3970′. T5/6S R17E sec 35/2. County seat. In the SW part of the county, 7 mi W of Dietrich and on Little Wood River, the UPRR, at the intersection of US 201 and US 93. Post office, 1870-.

When settlers began to drift into the area, they named the place Bottoms. The RR came in 1882 to start construction and applied for a post office in the name of Naples, which was also the name of the RR station. Then in 1883 both the post office and the RR station reverted to the earliest name, Shoshone.

Shoshone County. County seat: Wallace. The first organized unit of government within Idaho boundaries, created and named for the Shoshoni Indians in 1858 by Washington Territorial Legislature as part of Washington, effective in 1861: reorganized as part of Idaho Territory by Idaho Territorial Legislature in 1864, which included all of present-day Shoshone and Clearwater counties, with Pierce City as the county seat. Murray was named county seat in 1885, Osburn in 1890, and Wallace in 1893. It was reduced to its present size in 1904.

Mining, first gold strikes and then silver and lead, put Shoshone County on the map.

Three mountain ranges (the Coeur d'Alenes, St. Joe, and Clearwater Mountains) dominate the terrain. And three streams drain the county from E to W: St. Joe River, S Fk Coeur d'Alene River, and Gold Center Creek. The county is bounded by the Bitterroot Mountains on the E; Kootenai, Benewah, and Latah counties on the W; Clearwater on the S; and Bonner on the N.

Named for the Shoshoni Indians.

Shoshone Falls (Jerome/Twin Falls). T10S R18E sec 32. On Snake River N of Twin Falls. Higher than Niagara Falls at 212′, but now reduced in summer months by use of upstream water for irrigation and power. First discovered by white men in 1811 and a major attraction until it was harnessed; still an attraction in the spring before the irrigation season. Named Canadian Falls by Hudsons Bay trappers in 1811; renamed Shoshone Falls in 1849 by Major Osborne Cross, head of a military scouting expedition from Leavenworth to Fort Vancouver.

340

Shoshone Falls (Jerome). T10S R18E sec 31. Early community; Post office, 1884-1896.

Shot Creek (Clearwater). T38N R9E sec 14. Rises in the E part of the county 3.5 mi SE of Kelly Forks and flows 5 mi W into Fourth of July Creek; Clearwater River drainage.

Named for Eugene "Deadshot" Smith, who trapped in the area. Deadshot was a nickname given to him because, although he talked about his ability to shoot, he was really a poor shot. A one-time engineer in the East, he worked on roads and helped fight forest fires, as well as trapping around the Pierce area. He died in 1928.

Shotgun Valley (Fremont). T13N R41/42E. Runs E and W approximately 8 mi from head of Island Park Reservoir to Icehouse Creek.

Shotgun Creek. Settled by Army Scout George Rea, after his term with the army. A mountain and a post office were named for him.

Named by George Rea, an army scout who after a term with the army against the Nez Perce, settled here. He lost a shotgun in the area. Most of the valley Rea knew has been flooded by Island Park Reservoir.

Shoup (Lemhi). 3384'. T24N R19E sec 30. Town in the N part of the county on Salmon River, at the mouth of Boulder Creek. The discovery of the Grunter gold lode in 1881 led to the settlement of Shoup, which was once a prosperous mining town with a population of 600. Post office, 1883-.

Named for George L. Shoup, last territorial governor and first state governor of Idaho. He was an early merchant in Salmon, which he surveyed and platted.

Shovel Creek (Lemhi). T19N R17E sec 4. Heads about 1 mi SE of Quartzite Mountain; flows 4 mi SW to enter

Yellowjacket Creek; Salmon River drainage.

Named ca. 1934 by Mr. and Mrs. Lester Gutzman because they found a rusty old shovel here when they were surveying for a USFS road.

Shuck Creek (Idaho). T28N R1E sec 22. A 3-mi tributary of Salmon River from the W.

Named for Wm. A. Shuck, who homesteaded here in 1894, supporting his wife and five children by raising livestock, fruit, and vegetables.

Shurtliff Canyon/Creek (Bonneville). T2N R44E sec 20-31. Extends 5 1/2 mi NE to SW in NE quadrant between Irwin and Swan Valley. The creek flows 3 mi SW into Snake River.

Named for the William Shurtleff (sic) family, who drove cattle from Star Valley.

Siam Creek (Clearwater). T40N R12E sec 5. Rises on Bitterroot Mountains and flows 3 mi SW into Lake Creek; Clearwater River drainage.

This name was probably given by the USFS, since the creek flows near Jap Creek and heads by Siamese Lakes in Montana.

Siberia Creek (Clearwater). T35N R6E sec 9. On the SE Idaho-Clearwater county line. Flows 2 mi S into Lolo Creek; Clearwater River drainage.

Named by USFS crews who were working on opening the Lolo Trail. They started work in the spring and, while camped along the trail, were hit by a snowstorm. It was so cold they named the nearby creek Siberia.

Siegel Creek (Idaho). T28N R9E sec 7. In the Elk City area; rises on Black Hawk Mountain (6091') and flows 7 mi SW to Red River about 4 mi SE of Elk City.

Named for Dutch Siegel, an early-day miner. Formerly misspelled Seigel Creek.

Silent Cone (Butte). 6346'. T1N R24E sec 2. Cinder cone 1.4 mi S of head-quarters of Craters of the Moon, adjacent to White Knob Mountains on the N. One of the cones produced during the oldest period of volcanic eruptions.

Named because it is no longer active.

Silge Creek (Idaho). T26N R10E sec 32. A 3-mi tributary of Salmon River from the S.

Named for Fred Silge, whose father brought him to America from Germany to keep him from being drafted in the German army.

He ran the Campbell Ferry until he drowned in the river after a cable accident.

Silver Beach (Kootenai). T50N R3W sec 19/30. On the E shore of Coeur d'Alene Lake, just S of the town of Coeur d'Alene.

Named because at times the silver-fish (minnows) are so numerous, the beach looks silvery.

Silver Butte (Clearwater). 4680'. T39N R5E sec 22. Six mi N of

Headquarters. Silver Creek rises W of Silver Butte and flows 5 mi SW and 4 mi NW into Dworshak Reservoir.

Named for its appearance, as no silver was ever found here. During the winter the snow shines through a hole in the timber and looks like silver.

Silver City (Owyhee). 6129'. T5S R3W sec 6. Ghost town 15 mi E of the Idaho-Oregon line, in the W central section of the county. Silver City Mountains include all of the mountains around Silver City. Post office, 1863-1943.

The third mining camp in Owyhee County; gold and silver were discovered here in 1863. Silver City was platted 20 Mar 1865 by W. H. Dewey, Amos Springer, and Pete Donnely. It was named county seat in 1866 and remained so until 1935.

Named Silver City by the townsite platters in 1865 for the silver discovered here. Local residents refer to the town as Silver.

Silver Creek (Latah). T43N R6/5W sec 36/29, 30, 31. In the NW corner of Latah County. Flows W 3.7 mi into Washington State.

The first white men to reach this area were prospectors, who began looking for gold and silver along this stream. They found none and moved on after naming the creek.

Silver Creek (Lemhi). T17N R17E sec 6. Heads 2 mi W of Rooker Basin; flows SW, following the main road to Meyers Cove for about 10 mi to enter Camas Creek at Meyers Cove; Middle Fk Salmon River drainage.

Named for the silver ore and mines in the vicinity.

Silver King (Shoshone). T48N R2E sec 2. Community W of Kellogg where Bunker Hill Company had its lead and zinc smelters. Post office, 1900-1907.

Named for the lodes in the area.

Silver Moon Gulch (Lemhi). T13N R27E sec 29. Runs 2 mi S of Gilmore.

The gulch itself is shaped like a half moon and there was a silver mine located here, which was owned and operated by the Silvermoon Mining Company.

Silver Mountain (Boise). 8573'. T7N R10E sec 6/7.

Silver mines in this mountain were not productive.

Silver Rule Creek (Custer). T10N R16E sec 8. In the Challis National Forest; flows NW to Slate Creek.

The creek was named for a mine of the same name located nearby.

Silver Star (Franklin). T15S R38E sec 25/31. An agricultural community NNE of Weston, in the SW part of the county. Settled in the 1890s; schoolhouse built in 1897.

Named in 1904 because a schoolgirl wore a silvery star that had been cut out of lead.

Silvertip Creek (Bonner). T57N R3E sec 19. Heads 1/2 mi W of Lightning Mountain and flows 2 mi SW into Lightning Creek 8 1/2 mi ENE of Hope.

Named for the silvertip grizzly bears in the area.

Silverton (Shoshone). 2617'. T48N R4E sec 21/22. First known as West Wallace, for its nearness to Wallace; the name was changed in 1941 for the ore mined here. Post office, 1940-.

Sinker Creek (Owyhee). T4S R3W sec 29. Stream 20 mi long, flows NE into Snake River at T3S R1E in the vicinity of Sinker Creek Butte; Snake River drainage.

Named before the 1860s. The creek was named because it sinks out of sight in dry spots and comes up again.

Also called Burnt Creek, perhaps because there is no grass along the banks.

Sinker. T3S R1E sec 7. Town and stage station on Sinker Creek. Post office, 1888-1909.

Six Mile Canyon (Lewis). T34N R3E sec 7. Lies in the SE quadrant; heads 1 mi N of Nezperce and goes to the mouth of Six Mile Creek. Six Mile Creek flows approximately 7 1/2 mi through this canyon to Clearwater River 7 mi NW of Kamiah.

Informants differ on the source of the name. Some say that Six Mile refers to the length of the road to the top of the canyon; and others that it marked the distance from an old Indian cross-

ing on the river to the Nez Perce Prairie.

Skeleton Butte (Jerome). 4400'. T10S R19E sec 4. In the S part of the county, 1.5 mi SW of Eden.

Named because in the early 1880s the skeleton of Lew Landers was found at its top. Landers was a gambler, who had come to Shoshone during the building of the UPRR; he was down on his luck and desperate after learning that his home in Hailey had burned and his wife had died in the fire.

He decided to recover some stolen horses and mules for his friend Smith, of the firm of Smith and White Butchers. Smith staked him to a horse, saddle, and bridle. Landers knew the stolen horses were being held in Devils Corral and started in that direction and was never heard of again.

A year later hunters found the skeleton and reported it. When it was found and examined, the authorities learned that he had been shot through the heart. The last letter he received from his wife was in his vest pocket. Some still believe he committed suicide from grief over his wife; others that rustlers discovered his plan to recover stolen horses and mules and shot him.

Skeleton Creek (Idaho). T30N R3W sec 6. A 2-mi tributary of Salmon River from the SE; in the NW extremity of the county.

Seth "Sourdough" Jones and his son, Asa, had a herd of cattle here that starved to death during a severe winter; hence the name.

Skid Road Creek (Boise). T10N R4E sec 13. Rises in the NW extremity of the county and flows SE into Middle Fk Payette River 7 mi NE of Crouch; Payette River drainage.

A great deal of logging was done in this area. Often the flow of the creek was not adequate to float the logs, so they had to be skidded out with horses.

Skinner Creek (Bear Lake). T11S R43E sec 29. Rises on the slopes of Sherman Mountain and flows generally NE and N to Bear River 4 mi N of Nounan.

Settled in 1875 by John and Jane Skinner, LDS converts from England who homesteaded 300 acres near Nounan, built a home, established a small cheese factory, and raised cattle and sheep. He became the first bishop of Nounan.

Skitwish Peak (Kootenai). 4900'. T50N R1W sec 8. In the E part of the county, 11 mi E of Coeur d'Alene; in the Coeur d'Alene Mountains; Coeur d'Alene National Forest. Skitwish Creek rises on this peak and flows 4.5 mi SW to empty into Maries Creek; Coeur d'Alene River drainage.

These features are located in an area where the Coeur d'Alene Indians hunted and fished. The name is a corruption of Indian "Skitswish," which the Coeur d'Alene Indians called their nation. French trappers renamed the tribe.

Skookum Creek (Kootenai). T51N R1W sec 28. A 3-mi stream rising in the Coeur d'Alene Forest 13 mi E of Coeur d'Alene and flowing NW to N Fk Coeur d'Alene River.

The name is Chinook jargon for "strong" or "powerful." The tributaries of this stream are named for prospectors McMahan, Knight, and McCauley. The stream rises and flows between two promontories having significance to Indians in the area, Monument and Skitwish mountains.

Skookumchuck Creek (Idaho). T27N R1E sec 31. A 10-mi tributary of Salmon River from the E, 4 mi S of White Bird.

Characterized by rapids at this point. The name derives from Chinook jargon: chuck "rapid" and skookum "strong."

Skull Canyon (Clark). T10N R30E sec 29. In the W extremity of the county; extends 5 mi SE from Birch Creek.

Maier Kaufman and his family settled here in the 1890s, established a ranch, and opened a post office. Ben Lyons, who lived with the Kaufmans as a foster son, explored the canyon and found a cave with human skulls in it, perhaps Indian.

Skull Creek (Clearwater). T40N R8E sec 8. Rises on Pot Mountain Ridge near the N county line and flows about 14 mi SW into N Fk Clearwater River 3 mi N of Moscow Bar.

Charles Peter, an old trapper, told of finding a human skull near the mouth of the creek.

Skull Gulch (Lemhi). T23N R17E sec 16. Northern drainage of Salmon River.

Two explanations are given for the name: A Sheepeater Indian skeleton was found here by CCC workers; Dan Hurley confessed before his death in 1932 that he and two other miners had killed him. There is (or was) a natural formation on the hillside that looks like a skull, a patch of white dirt with two trees growing in it that look like eyes, and rocks that look like the mouth.

Skyhigh Lake (Lemhi). T21N R16E sec 32. In Bighorn Crags, about 3/4 mi NE of Lost Lake.

Named in 1963 by USFS in cooperation with the Coast and Geodetic Survey. Said to be the highest lake in The Crags.

Slabtown (Latah). T41N R1W sec 36. A community of settlers and loggers 1 mi N of Bovill. Formerly Fairview, which see.

Slate Creek (Idaho). T27N R1E sec 6. Rises in the Nezperce National Forest at the confluence of Little Slate and Deadhorse creeks and flows 12 mi N and W to Salmon River.

Slate Creek post office and settlement lie at the mouth of this stream. During the Nez Perce War settlers built a stockade here. Post office, 1863-1879.

Named because early miners discovered there was no placer gravel in the stream, only slate.

Slater Creek (Elmore). T1N R4E sec 23. Begins at convergence of 5- mi long W Fk and 4-mi long E Fk 1.8 mi NW of Mayfield, and flows 2 mi in a southerly direction to Indian Creek.

Named for an early settler.

Slaterville (Nez Perce). Town 12 mi below the mouth of N Fk Clearwater River.

Founded by and named for S. S. Slater in May, 1861. When Lewiston was located the following June, Slaterville was abandoned.

Slaughter Creek (Idaho). T22N R6E sec 12. In the S part of the county, at Warren.

Named for the use to which the area was put, slaughtering cattle and sheep to feed miners and prospectors.

Slaughter House Gulch (Owyhee). T5S R3/4W. Near Silver City. Cattle were driven into the area and slaughtered. Since there was a market for fresh meat, almost every mining camp had a "Slaughter House Gulch" nearby.

Sleeping Deer Mountain (Lemhi). 9881'. T17N R14/15E sec 36/31. At the headwaters of Cache Creek on the W and Camas Creek on the E.

From a distance, the mountain looks like a resting mule deer.

Sleeping Dutchman (Lemhi). T25N R21E sec 21. Rock formation along US Highway 93, near the mouth of Hughes Creek.

When viewed from the mouth of Hughes Creek, the rock formation looks like a man sleeping on top of the ridge.

Sleeping Lady (Lemhi). T22N R23E sec 12. Peaks located on the Continental Divide, NE of Salmon, SE of Freeman Peak.

At certain times of the year, the snow on the peaks here gives the appearance of a woman lying on her back.

Sleight Canyon (Bear Lake). Heads in T14S R42E sec 1 and extends E 3.5 mi to Bear Lake Valley, about 1 mi NW of Paris.

Named for Thomas Sleight, one of the nine original Mormon settlers in Paris. He had a homestead near the head of this canyon.

Sleppy Creek (Idaho). T27N R1E sec 24. A 4-mi tributary of Salmon River from the E, 1.5 mi N of Slate Creek.

Named for an early miner, Peter Sleppy, who had his cabin, and now probably his grave, here. The name appears as Slippy on the 1972 Nezperce National Forest map.

Slickenside Creek (Custer). T8N R16E sec 3. A small tributary of Little Boulder Creek approximately 2 mi in length flowing SE through glacial formations. Its bed is in a narrow canyon with nearly vertical walls, which show signs of large expanses of slickensides, clearly demonstrating the action of glaciers moving through the area.

Slickenside is a geological term for a smooth, striated, polished surface produced on rock by friction.

Slickpoo (Nez Perce). T34N R3W sec 4. Town 3 mi S of Jacques; 26 mi from Lewiston. Post office, 1898-1926.

Slickpoo is a Nez Perce Indian family name. The place was named in honor of Josue Zimckilixpusse (Anglicized to Slickpoo), who was the first chief of the tribe to become Catholic. St. Joseph's

Mission was established here in 1874 by Father Joseph M. Cataldo, S.J., the first Roman Catholic missionary among the Nez Perce.

Slide Creek (Lemhi). T18N R21E sec 7. Heads near Sheephorn Mountain; flows N 2 mi to enter Iron Creek; Salmon River drainage. Named for snow- and landslides.

Slide Gulch (Boise). T8N R5E sec 11. Runs N into the S Fk Payette River 1 mi E of Grimes Pass. The ground, mostly clay, tends to slide when wet.

Slide Hill (Custer). T12N R15E. Site of an avalanche that in 1888 took several lives and crushed buildings. Located between Bonanza and Custer.

Slide Peak (Clark). 10,200'. T14N R39E sec 9. In the Centennial Mountains on the Continental Divide 11 mi N of Kilgore. Rock slides extend from the summit to the base on the SW side.

Slim Creek (Boise). T9N R7E sec 20. Flows 3 1/2 mi SE into Deadwood River 2 3/4 mi NW of Lowman; Payette River drainage.

Named by the USFS for Slim Joshua, employed as a lookout.

Slippery Creek (Lemhi). T21N R18E sec 34. Runs W 1 mi to enter Blackbird Creek; Salmon River drainage.

Was originally called Slipper Creek because a lady's slipper was found on the road near the creek. Name changed through usage.

Slocum (Clearwater). T37N R3E sec 12. Settlement 4 mi N of Grangemont.

Named for homesteader Frank Slocum and his wife, Clara, who settled here in 1906.

Small (Clark). 5178'. T10N R35E sec 6/7. A livestock area in the S part of the county 8 1/2 mi W of Dubois on Medicine Lodge Creek. Small post office, formerly Medicine Lodge post office, 1890-1959.

Named for the owner of an 1890s lodge.

Smead Canyon (Fremont). T12N R41E sec 124. In N central Fremont County. Runs N to Island Park Reservoir 2 mi from the W end; Henrys Fork system.

Named for Sam Smead, a local lumberman in the 1920s and 1930s.

Smelter Butte (Blaine). T3N R21E sec 23/24. At the confluence of Muldoon and Copper creeks, 20 mi NE of Hailey.

Named for the smelter built here to serve the Muldoon mine.

Smelter Gulch (Lemhi). T12N R29E sec 21. Heads just S of the mouth of Milo Canyon on Willow Creek; runs SW 3 mi to the Birch Creek Valley at Nicholia.

When Nicholia was an active mining town, there was a smelter located in this gulch.

Smelterville (Shoshone). 2219'. T48N R2E sec 2. In the W part of the county, 2.5 mi W of Kellogg; originally it was considered part of Kellogg, but a settlement grew up around the operations of the Bunker Hill mine, with its own stores, post office, and lead/zinc smelters.

Smiley Creek (Blaine). T7N R14E sec 27. Rises on the E slope of Soldier Mountains on the NW county border and flows 9 mi NE to Salmon Camp Creek.

Smiley Mountain (Custer). 11,506'. T4N R22E sec 2. At the head of Lake, Smiley, Iron Bog and Grasshopper creeks. Smiley Creek, tributary of Big Creek, heads on SE slope of Smiley Mountain. Smiley Meadows lie SE of Smiley Mountain between the headwaters of Smiley and Dry creeks.

Named for Levi Smiley, who opened mining in the Salmon River that led to the establishment of the Sawtooth and Vienna mining districts in the 1880s.

Smith Canyon (Idaho). T24N R3E sec 14. In the S part of the county near the Florence gold mines; a 2-mi feature draining S into Salmon River, 4 mi SE of Florence.

S. S. "Three-Finger" Smith, a veteran of the Modoc War of 1872-73 and the Sheepeater War of 1878-79, discovered gold in Smith Canyon.

Smith Creek (Boise). T9N R4E sec 3. Flows 3 1/2 mi W into the Middle Fk Payette River 2 1/2 mi N of Crouch.

Named for P. V. "Dirty Shirt" Smith, who homesteaded on this creek.

Smith Creek (Boise). T10N R6E sec 11. Rises on the NE slope of Scott Mountain (8215') and flows 4 mi NE into Scott Creek 1 1/2 mi S of Boise-Valley county line; Payette River drainage.

Named for George "Potato" Smith, one of the few farmers in the Boise Basin.

Smith Creek (Elmore). T2N R6E sec 12. Rises in the mountains of S Fk Boise River at an altitude of 7000' and flows 14 mi SW to E Fk Boise River. The community of Smiths Prairie, now Prairie, was located on this stream, and the area at the mouth of the stream is still named Smiths Prairie.

Named for the original settler.

Smith Creek (Valley). T21N R9E sec 13. Rises on Mount Eldridge and flows about 8 mi NE then SE to empty into Big Creek.

Named for Frank Smith, who had a ranch at the mouth of this creek and during the Sheepeater War (1878-79) raised garden stuff for miners in the Warren, Secesh Basin, and Burgdorf areas. He was a distant cousin of "Three-Finger" Smith.

Smith Island (Washington). T10N R5W sec 17. In Snake River in the SW

extremity of the county, 2 mi S of Weiser.

Charles H. Smith settled in Weiser in 1881 and Mrs. Fannie M. Smith in 1884.

Smith Lake (Boundary). T63N R2E sec 30. Lake 6 mi N of Bonners Ferry. Smith Creek flows NW and NE to the Kootenai River. Smith Peak (7650') is a benchmark in the Kaniksu National Forest NE of Upper Priest Lake; overlooks Smith Creek on the S and W.

Named for Charles Smith, on whose land the lake was located.

Smith Marsh (Latah). T42N R3W sec 11/14. In the N part of St. Joe National Forest just N of Macumber Meadow between Meadow and Big creeks.

Charles F. Smith held a homestead just S of Smith Meadows, filed in 1891.

Smith Meadows (Latah). T40/41N R2W sec 1/36. A meadow between Vassar and Tee meadows, drained by Corral and Meadow creeks.

Thomas W. and Elbert E. Smith each held a homestead here.

Smith Ridge (Clearwater). T41N R5/6E. A 6-mi ridge trending E-W through the middle of these townships; highest point (5455') at the W end. Nine mi N of Bertha Hill.

Named for Charlie Smith, a homesteader here.

Smith Spring (Lemhi). T19N R23E sec 22. On Baldy Creek 3 mi NW of Tendoy.

Named in honor of George Smith, who ranched near here.

Smiths Ferry (Valley). 4500'. T11N R3E sec 10. In the SW quadrant 18 mi S of Cascade. Post office, 1910-1960s.

This community takes its name from the man who ran a ferry on N Fk Payette River as early as 1891, E. J. Smith of Caldwell.

Smithville (Lemhi). T22N R20E sec 21. A village 2 mi E of Leesburg, near the mouth of Smith Gulch, which runs S to Napias Creek about 2 mi NE of Leesburg; Salmon River drainage.

Named for William Smith, a native of South Carolina, one of the original discoverers of gold at Leesburg. He was killed in a gunfight with Jim Hayden in Salmon City in 1870.

Smithy Creek (Lemhi). T26N R22E sec 20. Originates near the head of Keystone Gulch; flows S 2 mi to enter Dahlonega Creek; N Fk Salmon River drainage.

A placer miner by the name of Dennis Smith lived near here.

Smoky Creek, Big (Camas). T3N R13E sec 9. Rises in the Smoky Mountains 18 mi E of Atlanta in NE Camas County and flows about 19 mi generally S and SW to S Fk Boise River. Little Smoky Creek is its principal tributary at T3N R13E sec 12. It rises in Smoky Mountains NW of Hailey and flows 15 mi SW and then NW.

The drop on Big Smoky is 65′ per mile for the 10 mi above its confluence with S Fk Boise River; that of Little Smoky ranges from 57 1/2′ to 72′ to the mile. Both streams take their names from the Smoky Mountains.

Smoky Mountains (Blaine/Camas). NW-SE trending mountain group about 50 mi long and 15 mi wide with elevations above 9000′, just SE of Sawtooth Range, E of the Boise and Soldier mountains, W of Boulder and Pioneer mountains, and N of Camas Prairie; it is bounded on the E by the Big Wood River and on the W by the N Fk Ross Fork, Ross Fk, S Fk Boise River, Little Smoky Creek, and Willow Creek; forms the divide between Big Wood and S Fk Boise rivers. The chief promontories in this range are Big Ross and Norton peaks

and Dollarhide and Buttercup mountains.

Named for the haze over the summit of the range from the frequent forest fires in the 1880s.

Smorgasboard Creek (Bonner). T58N R2E sec 21. Heads 1 1/4 mi W of Lunch Peak; flows 1 1/4 mi SE into Quartz Creek, a tributary of Lightning Creek; Clark Fork River drainage.

Probably an office name. It is one of three W tributaries to Lightning Creek, the other two being Garden and Lunch.

Smout Creek (Lemhi). T23N R23E sec 31. Forms on the Idaho-Montana border, in the Beaverhead Mountains 1 mi SE of Ajax Peak; flows SW 4 mi to enter Freeman Creek; Salmon River drainage. Pronounced SMOOT.

Named for Winslow T. Smout, who settled in the area ca. 1898.

Snake Creek (Clearwater). T38N R4E sec 21. Rises 3.5 mi N of Jaype and flows 8 mi NW to Reeds Creek; Clearwater River drainage.

There are snakes in the area.

Snake River. One of the largest rivers in the United States, nearly 1000 mi long. It rises in the mountainous area W of Yellowstone National Park at an altitude of 7000′ and drops to less than 1000′ by the time it leaves Idaho at Lewiston. The river flows from the Idaho line down N Fk N of Rigby through valleys and canyons, describing a great arc across southern Idaho. Then it gradually turns northward, entering Oregon W of Wilder, forms the border between Idaho and Oregon from Weiser to Lewiston. This system forms 42 percent of the Columbia River drainage. Principal tributaries in Idaho: Henrys Fork, Blackfoot, Portneuf, Raft, Big Wood, Bruneau, Boise, Owyhee, Payette, Weiser, Salmon, and Clearwater rivers, the last at Lewiston.

The Snake River is the primary producer of electricity in Idaho. All the rivers in the system are important for irrigation.

Snake River Butte (Fremont): 6000'. One mi W of Henrys Fork 2 mi N of Warm River community.

Snake River, Henrys Fork (Fremont), rises in Henrys Lake and at Big Springs, flows 65 mi S to its confluence with S Fk.

Snake River Range (Bonneville) lies NE of Snake River extending NW to SE. Peaks of greatest elevation in this range are Stouts Mountain (8616') and Palisades Peaks (9780').

Snake River Valley, the largest of all Idaho valleys, lies across southern Idaho and varies in width from a few to more than 100 mi, including the Snake River Plain. It begins at Warm River on N Fk in eastern Idaho and widens southwestward. It extends westward from Pocatello, filling the area between mountains N and S of the river. From Twin Falls it narrows westward and is known as Hagerman Valley. From Bliss to Oregon, it becomes a canyon except for occasional widening, as at Marsing, to valley proportions. Properly speaking it includes Boise Valley and plains at Mountain Home. In general, however, Snake River Valley refers to that area between Ashton and Pocatello.

Named for the Snake tribe of the Shoshoni Indians. This tribe was called Snake by their plains neighbors to the E, and by trappers either because they reputedly used snake heads painted on sticks to terrify their enemies or because they used a sinuous motion of their hand to signify that they were from "the place where salmon spawn." Also known as Lewis River, Sho-sho-nepah, Mad River.

Sneak Creek (Clearwater). T40N R7E sec 2. Rises on Sneak Point and flows 4 mi NW into N Fk Clearwater River 6 mi NW of Moscow Bar.

Named for the unexpected rapids near the mouth of the creek; the water runs smooth until the rapids.

Snoden Creek (Clearwater). T39N R7E sec 26. Flows SW into N Fk Clearwater River.

Named for Snoden Snyder, who was a member of the telephone crew working here in 1919; along with the other crew members, he went swimming after supper but he suffered cramps and drowned in N Fk Clearwater River.

Snow Cap Mountain (Latah). T42N R1W sec 6. Promontory in St. Joe National Forest less than a mile SE of Baby Grand Mountain.

Descriptive title, as the snow usually does not melt until early summer.

Snow Creek (Fremont). T9N R44E sec 18. Flows 8 mi SW and S. Also: Dewitt Canyon.

Snow Creek. T9N R44E sec 1. Flows 13 mi SW to Robinson Creek 1/2 mi N of Huckleberry Ridge; Warm River drainage.

Snow Creek Butte 7600'. T11N R45E sec 22. 1 mi SE of Big Grassy just W of Yellowstone Park border.

Snowshoe Butte 6791'. T11N R41E sec 19. At the SW end of Antelope Flat.

All of these names testify to the heavy snowfall of Fremont County, especially on these creeks where elevation averages 7000' at the source. Snowshoe Butte may be somewhat different, however. Folk etymology explains that the name comes from a snowshoe cabin, probably for a trapper or herder. The butte is located on the sheep range.

Snow Peak (Shoshone). 6762'. T43N R7E sec 30. In the S central part of the county, about 30 mi E of Clarkia, in the St. Joe National Forest.

Named before the county was mapped or surveyed, from the great quantity of white rock resembling snow on top of the mountain.

Also Goat Peak.

Snowshoe Creek (Lemhi). T15N R16E sec 6. Heads in the vicinity of Fly Creek Point; flows SW 3 1/2 mi to enter Warm Spring Creek; Salmon River drainage.

Named for "Snowshoe" Johnson, an early miner in Wilson Creek country.

Snowy Summit (Idaho). 6040'. T36N R7E sec 28. In the NW part of the county, 3 mi SE of Hemlock Butte and 10 mi SE of Pierce.

Named by Wellington Bird's construction crew in 1866. Bird was chief engineer of a US Department of Interior crew building a road from Lewiston, Idaho, to Virginia City, Montana.

A descriptive name.

Snowyside Peak (Custer/Boise/Blaine). 10,659'. T7N R13E sec 17. A commanding peak NW of Alturas Lake in the Stanley Basin, Sawtooth Mountains.

Thirty-six lakes are visible from this peak. On the NE slope is a 2-mi cirque 1500' deep containing 3 Snowyside lakes; Pettit Lake lies 5 mi below these. On the S slope lie 19 small lakes that feed the inlet of Alturas Lake. And on the W slope is a mile-wide cirque 800' deep with 9 small lakes at the head of Middle Fk Boise River.

A descriptive name.

Snyder Creek (Idaho). T34N R5E sec 36. A 2-mi tributary of Lolo Creek from the E.

Named for USFS ranger H. R. "Bob" Snider (sic).

Soards Gulch (Idaho). T28N R1E sec 10. A tributary of Salmon River from the E, 2 mi N of White Bird.

Named for Henry Soards, who grazed sheep upstream from the gulch in cattle country. He was killed and his home destroyed by a bomb placed on his doorstep by a cattleman.

Soda Creek (Lemhi). T18N R15E sec 14. Forms near the head of Aparejo Creek; runs S 2 1/2 mi to enter Camas Creek; Middle Fk Salmon River drainage.

Named because of the slight taste of soda found in the water.

Soda Springs (Caribou). 5773'. T9S R41/42E sec 12/7. County seat.

In the S part of the county, on Bear River. In an area of many mineral springs and peculiar rock formations. The location was called Beer Springs by Wyeth in 1832 and by John C. Fremont in 1843, but it appears as Soda Springs on the Dixon 1859 map. In 1864 it became the county seat of Oneida County; then as county seat of Caribou in 1919 when it was established. Post office, 1865-.

First settled in 1863 as the result of the Morrisite Rebellion, led by Joseph Morris, who was rebuked by Mormon church leader Brigham Young when he shared certain revelations with Young regarding theological error. Therefore Morris and 160 followers withdrew first to General Patrick Connor's Camp Douglas in 1862 and then in 1863 to Soda Springs, near Camp Connor. By June the detachment of soldiers had cleared a road from Franklin to Soda Springs.

Named for soda deposits in the area.

Soda Peak 8921'. T10S R41E sec 26. On the Bear Lake-Caribou county line in the SW part of the county.

Soda Point. T9S R41E sec 7. Formerly Sheep Rock, 8 mi SE of Bancroft and 6 mi W of Soda Springs at a point where the California Trail separated from the Old Oregon Trail; on Bear River. This is a noted landmark on the Oregon Trail, a 2-3 day journey from Fort

Hall. Later, waters of Soda Point Reservoir overflowed the old Soda Springs townsite.

Soda Springs Hills. T8S R40E. Extends NW to SE from Tenmile Pass to the bend of Bear River W of Soda Springs; 10 mi long. These rocky hills comprise the S member of the series of Peale Mountains.

Named for soda deposits in the area.

Soldier (Camas). T1N R14E sec 33. Ghost town in the center of the county 2 mi N of present-day Fairfield on Camas Prairie, on Soldier Creek. Post office, 1882-1919.

The town seemed secure until the OSL bypassed it, going 2 mi S. Almost overnight it became a ghost town as residents and businesses moved to the RR and named their location New Soldier, later changing it to Fairfield.

Soldier Creek. T1S R14E sec 35. Rises in Soldier Mountains in W Camas County and flows SE 20 mi to Camas Creek 4 mi SE of Fairfield.

Soldier Mountains (Camas/Elmore). E-W-trending mountain range about 38 mi long and 13 mi wide with elevations above 9000', just SE of the Boise Mountains and SW of the Smoky Mountains; it is bounded on the S by Camas Prairie, on the W and N by the S Fk Boise River, and on the NE and E by Little Smoky Creek and Willow Creek.

Named for the soldiers stationed here in the Bannock War of 1878.

Soldier Bar (Valley). T20N R14E sec 6. On Big Creek 3 mi upstream from Middle Fk Salmon River. Soldier Creek rises in Salmon National Forest on Mormon Mountain (9545') and Lewis Peak (9252') and flows 9 mi NE and E to Middle Fk Salmon River.

Named because Private Harry Eagan, veteran of the Sheepeater Indian War, was killed and buried on the bar. The US War Department provided a marker here to honor him.

Soldier Cap (Owyhee). 5430'. T2S R4W sec 1. One mi S of Horse Race Ridge.

Local residents dispute whether Soldier Cap is shaped like a Civil War cap or a World War I helmet.

Soldier Creek (Benewah). T44N R1W sec 8. Rises in St. Joe National Forest SW of Pettis Peak and flows SW to St. Maries River at Mashburn.

Originally called Trail Creek, this stream was commonly known as (Old) Soldier Creek, after a bachelor veteran who homesteaded here.

Soldier Creek (Bonner/Boundary). T59N R4W sec 3. Rises in the SW corner of Boundary County and flows 3 mi SW into Priest Lake.

Named for a group of soldiers under the direction of a Captain Sherwood who were camped in the area.

Soldiers Canyon (Nez Perce). T35N R4W sec 35. Near Lapwai; runs E into Lapwai Creek. Soldiers Meadow Dam is 5 mi S of Lake Waha, at Soldiers Meadow Reservoir; near Webb Creek.

The soldiers from Fort Lapwai cut wild hay for their horses early in the 1870s in this location, giving the meadows and the other surrounding features the name Soldiers.

Solomon Mountain (Boundary). T63N R3E sec 20. Five mi NE of Moyie Springs. Overlooks Solomon Lake 1/2 mi N; a small, narrow, crescent-shaped lake on a tributary of Deer Creek in the Kaniksu National Forest, 2 mi SE of the Meadow Creek Ranger Station.

Named for the Solomon brothers, on whose land it was located.

Sommer Camp Mountain (Owyhee). T5S R5W sec 6. Twelve mi W of Silver City. Sommer Camp Basin is on Cow Creek. Sommer Camp T1N R4W sec l4. Town in the French John Carrey Hill area, in the NW part of the county.

These three locations were named for William F. Sommercamp, an early cattle king of Owyhee County who had a cattle ranch in this area. In 1890 Sommercamp was killed by a fall in a mine shaft on Sommer Camp Mountain.

Sonna (Ada). T3N R1W sec 11. An early Union Pacific RR siding located in W Ada County. A subdivision currently bears this name, located in the same township, sec 9.

Named for a Boise businessman, Peter Sonna.

Sotin Creek (Idaho). T28N R1E sec 27. A 3.5-mi tributary of Salmon River from the W, 3 mi S of White Bird.

Named for the first white settlers in the area, Marieyee and Izora Sotin.

Sourdough Creek (Clearwater). T40N R6E sec 13. In the N central part of the county. Flows 2.5 mi W into Beaver Creek; Clearwater River drainage.

Named for "Sourdough Jack" John Pons, who lived around Pierce and served as a lookout on Sheep Mountain for many years. Sourdough Jack, or "Calico Jack" as he was also called, arrived in Pierce in the 1890s, having ridden as a cowboy in Nevada before homesteading on Brown Creek and working as a smokechaser for the USFS.

Sourdough Creek (Lemhi). T24N R17E sec 11. Heads near the NE end of Long Tom Ridge; runs SE about 2 mi where it empties into Owl Creek; Salmon River drainage.

A miner popularly known as "Sourdough" had a cabin and mining claim in this area.

Sourdough Gulch (Lemhi). T14N R27E sec 31. Runs 2 mi E to Texas Creek drainage, 3 mi N of Gilmore; Lemhi River drainage.

Emil Gravelspatcher owned some mining claims in this gulch, and since he was well-known for his sourdough bread, the place became known as Sourdough Gulch.

Sourdough Peak (Idaho). 6800′. T28N R5E sec 34. In the Nezperce National Forest between Johns and Twentymile creeks, 10 mi NW of Buffalo Hump.

Named for the "sourdoughs," prospectors who lived on sourdough bread, in the area.

Sourdough Point (Bonner). T57N R1W sec 29. On Lake Pend Oreille 4 1/4 mi SE across the lake from Sandpoint.

Named because fishermen would camp at this point and, after fishing on the frozen lake, eat their sourdough pancakes.

Sousie Creek (Clearwater). T40N R6E sec 24. Flows 2 mi NW into Beaver Creek; Clearwater River drainage.

Named for a Frenchman, Felix Sousie, who ran a sawmill here.

South Boise (Ada). T3N R2E sec 24/25. An early community and post office just SE of present-day Boise. Post office, 1907-1915.

Named for its location.

South Butte (Shoshone). 6970′. T42N R5E sec 3. In the S part of the county. One of 3 peaks on a prominent ridge known as Monumental Butte. The peaks are distinctly separated from each other and are referred to as North, South, and East buttes.

Named in 1919 by Forester R. H. Rutledge.

South Leigh Creek (Teton). T6N R44E sec 35. Stream 19 mi long, heads in the Teton Range of Wyoming and flows W into Idaho to the Teton River, 3 mi WSW of Tetonia.

Named in 1872 by USGS surveyor Dr. F. V. Hayden for his guide, Richard "Beaver Dick" Leigh.

South Mountain (Owyhee). 7806'. T8S R5W sec 10. Eight mi NE of Cliffs. So called because it is S of Silver City. Even though it is not in the Owyhee Mountain Range, South Mountain was once known as Owyhee Mountain. South Mountain Creek rises on South Mountain and flows 10 mi NE into Boulder Creek; Owyhee River drainage. South Mountain Range is in the area of and includes South Mountain.

South Mountain is a ghost town on South Mountain. Post office, 1872-1905.

An earlier name of the mining town was Bullion City, for the gold and silver mined in the area. The name was changed to South Mountain because its citizens did not think that two towns in the area should have "city" in their names.

South Putnam Mountain (Bannock/Caribou). 8989'. T5S R37E sec 34. On the Caribou-Bannock county line in the NE extremity of Bannock County; 2 mi SE of N Putnam Mountain.

Named for Captain James E. Putnam, 12th Infantry, who was in command of the detachment that established the Fort Hall military post on Lincoln Creek in 1870.

Southwick (Nez Perce). 2967'. T38N R1W sec 29. Community in the NE part of the county 4 mi W of Cameron. Post office, 1888-.

Named for the first postmaster, who settled here in 1882.

Spalding (Nez Perce). 800'. T36N R4W sec 22. Town in the N part of the county, 10 mi E of Lewiston. Originated in 1895 and named for the Reverend Henry Harmon Spalding, a Presbyterian missionary from New England, who established a mission in 1836 on Lapwai Creek near this location among the Nez Perce Indians.

After Spalding taught the Indians irrigated farming, it was the first agricultural settlement in Idaho. The first mission was actually located about 12 mi from where Lewiston now stands, 2 mi above the mouth of Lapwai Creek. In 1838, it was moved to the present location of Spalding at the mouth of Lapwai Creek. At that time it was called Lapwai.

Post office, 1897-.

Spangle Lake (Boise). T7N R12E sec 3. In the southernmost point of SE Boise County.

Named by T. C. Hoyt, USFS, because when viewed from the surrounding peaks, this lake reminds one of a cluster of gems.

Spanish Fork (Boise). T6N R5E sec 23. Flows 3 mi SE into Elk Creek 1 mi N of Idaho City; Boise River drainage.

Probably named for Spanish Rose, a prostitute in Idaho City; the Rose was dropped.

Spanish Town (Elmore). T4N R8N sec 3. Site of a mining tent camp; name given to a settlement on Elk Creek near the mouth of East Fork, 6 mi N of Featherville. Believed by some to have been the nickname of Esmeralda.

Named because miners in 1863 found old mining equipment and other evidence that they though indicated that early Spanish or Mexican miners had preceded them.

Spencer (Clark). 5883'. T12N R36E sec 23. In central part of the county, 16 mi N of Dubois. Post office, 1897-.

When the Utah and Northern RR came through in 1879 the station was named for Hiram H. Spencer, a shipper in the area at the time of RR construction.

Spion Kop (Shoshone). 5308'. T53N R3E sec 28-34. In the NE part of the county, this series of castle-like rocks lies in the Shoshone Mountains. Pronounced SPEE-on KOP.

Named for Spion Kop, Natal, Union of South Africa, near Ladysmith. Kop means hill.

Named for Spirit Lake in Kootenai County from which it flows.

Spirit Creek (Bonner/Kootenai). T54N R5W sec 21. Rises in Spirit Lake (Kootenai Co.), enters Bonner Co. 2 mi S of Blanchard, and flows into Fish Lake 1/2 mi SE of Blanchard.

Spirit Lake (Kootenai). T53N R4/5W. In the NW extremity of the county, on State Highway 41, 13 mi NW of the village of Hayden Lake. This lake is 7 mi long and 1 mi wide at its greatest; it has an area of 2377 acres.

Spirit Lake (2567') town was settled near the lake in 1884, settlers said to have been attracted by the beauty of the lake. Lumbering was the chief occupation at its settlement. Post office, 1903-.

The town was named for the lake on which it is situated, and the name of the lake is said to have been a translation of the Indian word Tesemini "Spirit Lake." A widely circulated Indian myth accounts for this name.

Chief Hyas-Tyee-Skokum-Tum-Tum, whose tribe inhabited the area, had a daughter who was loved by a young warrior in the tribe. However, Chief Pu-Pu-Mox-Mox threatened war if she were not given to him as a bride. The father agreed, but the young lovers thwarted the plan: They bound their wrists together with rushes and jumped into the lake. Indians said that Tesemini, the spirit of the waters, had claimed the pair in anger. Thereafter, they called the lake Tesemini, "Lake of the Spirits," which was gradually modified to Spirit Lake.

Spletts Creek (Lemhi). T17N R17E sec 11. Heads about 3 1/2 mi W of Woods Peak; flows NW 2 mi to enter Castle Creek; Middle Fk Salmon River drainage.

Named for a German, Ernest Splettstosser, who homesteaded a ranch in this area on 17 July 1919.

Split Butte (Blaine). 4585'. T1S R25E sec 3/4. Crater in the SE part of the county in Craters of the Moon National Monument. The outer tuff ring is about 90'-145' high and 1800' in diameter. Its tephra ring enclosed a lake of lava formed when basaltic magma erupted through ground water.

A descriptive name.

Split Butte (Fremont). 6252'. T11N R40E sec 34. In NW Fremont County, W of Antelope Flat near the W boundary of the county.

The butte has a split top.

Split Creek. T12N R44E sec 23. Rises in NE Fremont County and flows SW approximately 20 mi to Baker Draw, 4 mi SW of Island Park Siding.

The creek has at least 4 forks.

Split Road Lake (Minidoka). T6S R25E sec 13/24. In the SE part of the county, on the Minidoka-Arco Road, which splits this lake from Dug Reservoir just N.

Spokane River. The source of this river is Coeur d'Alene Lake. It flows W into Washington State, then NW to empty into the Columbia River near Spokane. It is a little over 100 mi long and drops from 2100' at its source to 1050' at its mouth. Its average flow is 7000 cubic second-feet; its drainage, 6640 square miles.

Named for the Spokane Indians.

Spori Canyon (Madison). T4N R42E sec 21. A canyon 1 mi long that trends S into Long Hollow. In the SE corner of the county in Targhee National Forest.

Named for Jacob Spori, who had a farm here and who was in 1888 principal of the school at Rexburg that became Ricks College.

Spotted Louis Creek (Shoshone). T43N R6E sec 27. In the S central part of the county; a 7-mi tributary of N Fk Clearwater River from the E.

Named by Forester W. B. Greeley in 1917 for an Indian who frequented the area for many years.

Spout Creek (Boise). T8N R9E sec 9/10. Rises in the E part of the county just N of Jennie Lake and flows NE into Crooked River 12 1/2 mi SE of Lowman; Boise River drainage.

A tributary of this stream seems to gush (spout) from the wall of the canyon.

Sprague Creek (Clearwater). T38N R8E sec 17. Rises on Chateau Rock and flows 3 1/2 mi S into N Fk Clearwater River.

Named for Jack Sprague, a trapper for the Hudson's Bay Company.

Spring Basin (Cassia). T13S R23E sec 36. A Mormon community 6 mi E of Oakley. Settled in the 1870s with H. D. Haight as bishop.

Named for Spring Creek, by which it is drained and which has a spring as its source.

Spring Creek (Lemhi). T24N R19E sec 20. Heads near Valliet Spring; runs S 6 1/2 mi to where it enters Salmon River.

Named for the springs at its head.

Spring Creek (Franklin). T16S R40E sec 29. Rises just NE of Franklin and flows SE 3.5 mi into Cache County, Utah.

Named by the first settlers of Franklin in 1860. Pioneer families first saw this stream in the spring, when it was high and roaring with melting snows

of spring, and thus named it Spring Creek.

Spring Creek (Jefferson). T5N R37E sec 35. Rises 1 mi W of Little Buttes and flows erratically 12 mi W to empty into the Snake River 2 mi E of Roberts. The area near the mouth of this stream was an early winter campground for Bannock-Shoshoni Indians. Early settlers reported as many as 75-100 Indian lodges between the creek and Snake River bend.

Named for the springs at the source of the stream.

Spring Creek (Washington). T14N R5W sec 9. Rises on the S slope of Hitt Peak, Payette National Forest, 11 mi W of Cambridge, and flows SSW to confluence with Mann Creek; Weiser River drainage.

Named because the creek rises in a spring.

Additional spring features in the county that derive from the same source include: Spring Creek, Snake River tributary S of Heath; Spring Creek, 13-mi Weiser River tributary 3 mi E of Weiser; Thousand Springs, in S part of T13N R4W; Spring Creek, 7-mi tributary of Weiser River at Salubria; and the post office, Spring, at the head of this creek. Post office, 1885-1898.

Spring Valley Creek (Latah). T39N R3W sec 30. A spring-fed stream that flows 7.2 mi SE to Little Bear Creek and converges with Nora Creek N and E of Troy to form Little Bear Creek; Potlatch River drainage.

Named for the spring at its source.

Springfield (Bingham). 4425'. T4S R32E sec 14. In the SE part of the county, 25 mi SW of Blackfoot and N of American Falls Reservoir. An early RR stop in a rich agricultural area. Post office, 1905-.

Believed to have been named in 1905 by Mormon settlers for Springfield, Illinois.

Springtown (Franklin). T14S R38E. An early Mormon settlement of homesteads that stretched between Oxford and Clifton, each with 300' of frontage on US 91 and the UPRR.

Named for the large spring nearby that breaks out from under the wall rock.

Springtown (Twin Falls). 3560'. T10S R18E sec 11. In the Snake River Canyon downstream from Hansen Bridge; named for the springs in the canyon wall.

This is the site of a mining camp that sprang up in the 1860s on the discovery of gold in the sands of Snake River. Local historian Charles Shirley Walgamott worked for a while at the Springtown store, which he described as being located a few feet back from the river's edge under the rock wall. The particular spring from which the place took its name was just above the store, flowing from under the rock.

Spud Butte (Lincoln). T3S R22E sec 10/15. An isolated butte in an area of broken lava.

Named for the shape of the butte, which suggests a huge potato.

Spud Hill (Latah). Early community later known as "Anderson" then "Deary;" owned by Joe and Lou Wells, blacks, who ran a waystation on the road to the forestland at Bovill.

Named for its location at the base of Potato Hill, locally called Spud Hill.

Square Top Mountain (Lemhi). 8402'. T25N R14E sec 36. About 1/2 mi NW of Parker Mountain.

Named because of its flat top.

Squaw Butte (Gem). 5906'. T8N R1W sec 25. Promontory landmark in S central part of the county. Travelers to and

from Boise Basin sighted their course by this feature.

Some locals say that it was named for Indian mothers and their babies who were murdered by whites while Indian men were away on a hunting trip. Regardless of local accounts, from some viewpoints the profile of the butte looks like a reclining woman. From another view there is a profile with nose and mouth.

Squaw Creek. T7N R1E sec 17. Rises in Boise National Forest and flows 45 mi SW and S to Payette River, 8 mi NE of Black Canyon Dam and 3 mi E of Squaw Butte, from which it takes its name. Its principal tributary is Little Squaw Creek, rising in Boise National Forest and flowing about 12 mi SE to empty into Squaw Creek.

At the mouth of this creek was Ezekiel Sweet's homestead, which was granted Squaw Creek post office in 1883 with Sweet as postmaster. The name was promptly changed to Sweet (which see) by the Post Office Department.

Squaw Camp Creek (Lemhi). T22N R19E sec 22. Heads just E of Gant Mountain; flows 2 mi E to enter Panther Creek; Salmon River drainage. Squaw Gulch, about 9 mi NW of the creek, runs 2 mi NE to meet Panther Creek.

Originally called Squaw Tit Creek because of a natural rock formation in the drainage, but the name was changed by the US Board on Geographic Names.

Squaw Meadows (Owyhee). T12S R1W sec 30/29. Located 10 1/2 mi E of Brace Brothers Ranch. Squaw Creek, Owyhee River drainage, drains this meadow, and Squaw Butte (6740') lies at its headwaters.

While Indian women, children, and old men were camped here, white men came to attack and kill the men and to abuse the women. Since then this location has been called Squaw Meadows.

Squawboard Meadow (Lemhi). T19N R19/20E sec 25/19. Near the headwaters of Goodluck Creek.

The old Thunder Mountain trail passed through here; a cradle board was found where Indians used to camp.

Squirrel (Fremont). T8N R44E sec 8. Town 8 mi SE of Ashton. Squirrel Creek rises in Wyoming, enters Fremont County and flows W to Conant Creek just N of Drummond; Falls River drainage. Post office, 1900-.

The community and the creek were named for the many ground squirrels that inhabited the area.

St. Charles (Bear Lake). 5985'. T15S R43E sec 14/23. In the SW part of the county, at the NW end of Bear Lake. St. Charles Creek rises in the Wasatch Mountains at the extreme SW border of the county and flows 12 mi ENE to Bear Lake just N of St. Charles. Post office, 1892-.

Settled in 1864 by Mormons from Cache Valley, Utah, and from Soda Springs. Apostle Charles C. Rich was sent by Brigham Young to colonize Bear Lake Valley. Settlers came in great numbers.

Named for Charles C. Rich.

St. Joe River (Benewah/Shoshone). T47N R3W sec 30. A roughly 94-mi stream extending from the Idaho-Montana line across S Shoshone County and N Benewah County through Lake Chatcolet and N into the S end of Coeur d'Alene Lake; navigable about 50 mi; noted for its recreational and economic value, and nicknamed "The Shadowy St. Joe."

Named St. Joseph in 1842 by Father Pierre-Jean DeSmet, a Catholic who established a mission here. Now St. Joe.

The features that follow are named for this stream.

St. Joe (Benewah). T46N R1E sec 20/29. Lumber town on the St. Joe River at the Benewah-Shoshone county line. A logging community. Post office, 1888-1927.

St. Joe Mountains (Benewah/Kootenai/Shoshone). E-W-trending mountain group about 45 mi long and 15 mi wide, comprising, with the Coeur d'Alene Mountains, the NW part of the Bitterroot Range; they are bound on the N by the Coeur d'Alene River and its S Fork; on the E by Willow Creek and its E Fork, Champion Creek, and N Fk St. Joe River; and on the W by Coeur d'Alene Lake.

St. Maries (Benewah). 9216'. T46N R2W sec 23. County seat. Situated at the confluence of the St. Joe and St. Maries rivers. Father Pierre-Jean DeSmet founded a mission near here in 1842 for the Coeur d'Alene Indians. In 1888 Joe Fisher filed a claim on land now included in the townsite of St. Maries, and he and his brothers built the first sawmill. With the coming of the railroad and the establishment of freight and passenger service by waterway from Coeur d'Alene Lake by the St. Joe River, a modern town sprang up. St. Maries was incorporated in 1902. Post office, 1889-.

In 1842 Father DeSmet named St. Maries, pronounced St. Mary's, because "So many favors have induced us unanimously to give her name to our new residence." This name was transferred to other features nearby.

St. Maries River. Rises in the mountains of SW Shoshone Co., NE Latah County, and NW Clearwater County; flows generally W to the St. Joe River in Benewah County at St. Maries. Valuable for floating logs to mills and shipping points.

St. Maries Peak. Just NE of St. Maries.

Stacy (Owyhee). T3N R5W sec 13. Three mi SE of Homedale.

Named for William Stacy, who came to Silver City in 1865 or 1866 and served as superintendent of schools of Owyhee County 1873-1874.

Stalker Creek (Blaine). T1S R19E sec 26. Stream 6 mi long, flows SE to join Grove Creek to form Silver Creek 16 mi SE of Hailey.

Named for James T. Stalker (1859-1940), who ranched in the area.

Standhope Peak (Custer). 11,878. A misnomer for Starhope Peak, which see.

Standing Rock Pass (Oneida/ Franklin). T15S R37E sec 15. On the Utah border in the SE part of the county, 11 mi SE of present-day Malad City.

In 1843 John C. Fremont, on his way to Salt Lake City, discovered and named this pass between the Bannock and Malad ranges. An upright rock marked the path for later travelers.

Standrod (Cassia). T16S R26E sec 34. An early farming community in the southernmost part of the county 4 mi W of Naf. Originally believed to be in Box Elder County, Utah, until the state line was determined by survey. Post office, 1890-1919.

Named for Judge D. W. Standrod of Pocatello, who was involved with water litigation in Cassia County.

Stanford (Latah). 2746'. T40N R3/2W sec 1/6. Located 2.5 mi SE of Yale; one of 8 WIM stations bearing names of colleges.

The Ivy League colleges had already been well represented on the line; so it is believed that the name of a western college, Stanford, was chosen for this point. However, it is entirely possible that the name is for Inman A. Stanford, who homesteaded about 4 mi S of

Standford Point, a promontory 2 mi SW of the RR station.

Stanley Basin (Custer). T10/11N R13E. Depression in SW part of Custer County extending S and W from the confluence of the upper portion of the Salmon River and Valley Creek; Challis National Forest.

Named for John Stanley, the oldest man in an 1863 prospecting party, who struck pay dirt in this area. The name has been transferred to other features in the area.

Stanley 6196'. T10N R13E sec 4/10. Town in the W part of the county, 34 mi W of Clayton, in Stanley Basin; the southern gateway to the Sawtooth Wilderness Area and to regions E and W. It lies at the foot of the Sawtooths. Post office, 1892-.

Stanley Lake is 8 mi NW of Stanley. It has an approximate area of 136 acres, extreme depth of 90'.

Stanton Creek (Clearwater). T41N R4E sec 23. Rises on Stocking Meadow Ridge on the N border of the county and flows 4 mi S into the Little N Fk Clearwater River.

Named for a settler, who was also a trapper.

Stanton Crossing (Blaine). 4880'. T1S R18E sec 22. Ghost town in the W part of the county, on Big Wood River, 10 mi S of Bellevue. Post office, 1884-1914.

Star (Ada). 2400'. T4N R1W sec 7/17. A town dating from the early 1860s in the NW part of the county about halfway between Boise and Caldwell.

The first irrigation ditches in Boise Valley were built here, and the first orchard was planted in 1867 by David W. Fouch.

Named because the first schoolhouse had a large star nailed on its door.

Star Butte (Washington). 4134′. T12N R3W sec 15. Three mi W of Crane Creek Reservoir. Star Butte Creek rises S of Star Butte and 5 mi W of Crane Creek Reservoir, and flows SE to Crane Creek; Weiser River drainage.

Named for early settler J. L. Starr, who came to the area in 1874 from Cornwall, England.

Star Lake (Lincoln). T7S R19E sec 11/12. In the extreme S central part of the county.

The lake has 5 arms and roughly suggests the shape of a star.

Starhope Peak (Custer). 11,878′. T5N R21E sec 6/7. A prominent mountain about .5 mi N of Goat Lake, .6 mi W of Betty Lake and .7 mi N of the Custer County boundary and the main divide of the Pioneer Mountains. Appears as Standhope on some maps.

Named for the Starhope mine.

Starkey (Adams). 3075′. T18N R1W sec 34. Formerly a resort (now private) 9 mi N of Council on US 95. Originally a fishing site for the Nez Perce Indians, named Quasnemah "place of many fish." Starkey Hot Springs. Post office, 1905-ca.1936.

Named for the founder of the resort and the first postmaster, Dr. Richard S. Starkey. Formerly Evergreen, from the trees in the area.

Starrhs Ferry (Cassia). T10S R22E sec 21. In the NW part of the county, on the Snake River 4 mi W of Burley. Established by George Starrh in 1880. A farming community grew up around the ferry known at first as Jessie, which was granted a post office operating under that name from 1882 to 1905. Starrh post office, 1909-1912.

Named for George Starrh, builder and operator of the ferry.

State Creek (Lemhi). T27N R21E sec 34. SW of Cool Gulch; runs SE 1 1/2 mi to N Fk Salmon River.

Formerly called Lick Creek because of natural salt licks here, but the name was changed when Idaho State Department of Transportation built maintenance sheds near the stream.

Station Creek (Boise). T9N R4E sec 36. Flows SW into the S Fk Payette River.

Named by the USFS because the Garden Valley Ranger Station is at its mouth.

Station Creek (Clearwater). T37N R8E sec 15. Flows NE into Weitas Creek; Clearwater River drainage.

The creek flows into the site of Weitas Ranger Station; hence the name.

Stauffer Creek (Bear Lake). T11S R43E sec 11. Rises near the W border of the county 1.5 mi SE of Sherman Peak; flows 9 mi E then 5.5 mi N to Bear River at Nounan.

Named for Frederick Stauffer, a Swiss who was brought to America when he was 12 by Charles C. Rich, Mormon missionary to Switzerland. Stauffer owned a beautiful ranch in this area.

Steakhouse Hill (Latah). T40N R5W sec 20. On US 95 4 mi N of Moscow.

Named for a restaurant located on the W side of the highway at the crest of the hill.

Steamboat Spring (Caribou). T9S R41E sec 10. A spouting spring in the bank of Bear River at Soda Springs.

John C. Fremont renamed this spring in 1834, not knowing an earlier passerby had already so named it. This was a small cone about 2′ in diameter, and the opening was coated with a bright red deposit of iron. The escape of carbonic acid gas agitated the water so violently that it appeared to be boiling, and the geyser-like boiling was accompanied by a subterranean noise, from which its name was derived. Now covered by Soda Point Reservoir.

Steele (Lewis). T36N R1E. Abandoned town in the N part of the county. Major J. Steele and his brother, Robert H. Steele, came W from Randolph County, Missouri, in 1892 and settled on Central Ridge, Lewis County, in 1896. Robert had a general merchandise establishment and took a pre-emption on land. Major homesteaded 240 acres. Post office, 1896-1923.

Named for its first postmaster.

Steep Creek (Boise). T7N R7E sec 35. Rises on the N slope of Sunset Mountain (7869') and flows 2 mi E into Crooked River 5 mi upstream; Boise River drainage.

This creek has an exceptionally steep grade from head to mouth.

Steep Lakes (Clearwater). T41N R12E sec 21/22. Twelve mi NE of Kelly Creek Work Center. Steep Creek rises in Steep Lakes and flows 2 mi NW into Goose Creek, in the NE corner of the county; Clearwater River drainage.

Named because of the extremely steep country. There is a large cliff on one side of the lakes.

Stein Gulch (Lemhi). T25N R21E sec 13. Heads W of Stein Mountain (8535'); runs NW 2 mi then N 1 3/4 mi to enter Sheep Creek drainage; N Fk Salmon River drainage.

Named for Henry Stein, a prospector of this area. Formerly known as N Mountain for an N-shaped patch of sliderock on one side of the mountain.

Stella Vista (Canyon). Another name for Roswell, which see.

Named by and for an early settler, a school teacher, who dreamed of founding a town in that spot.

Stephens Creek (Latah). T42N R1W sec 19. Flows 2 mi S to Palouse River

Named for an early settler in the area.

Sterling (Bingham). 4372'. T4S R32E sec 29/33. In the SW extremity of the county, 4 1/2 mi NE of Aberdeen on the NW shore of American Falls Reservoir. An agricultural community settled in 1910 by Mormons. Post office, 1911-.

Named by Thomas L. Jones, one of the settlers, for the sterling qualities of the soil.

Stevens Creek (Shoshone). T44N R8E sec 14. A 3.5 mi tributary of St. Joe River from the NE near the Montana border. Stevens Peak is 1/2 mi W of the Montana border; 1/2 mi S of Lower and Upper Stevens lakes, in a high basin and covering 2 and 5 acres, respectively.

These features were named for I. I. Stevens, early surveyor and Governor of Washington Territory.

Stevens Spring (Latah). T38N R5W sec 6. On the E side of US 95 up a draw toward Paradise Ridge, about 4 mi S of Moscow.

In 1855 Isaac I. Stevens, Governor of Washington Territory and Superintendent of Indian Affairs, camped overnight at this spring and recorded the stop in his diary. He is the first white person to visit the Moscow area and record it.

Stewart Creek (Elmore/Camas). T2N R12E sec 31. Rises on Soldier Mountains 3 mi E of Camas-Elmore county line and flows 3 1/2 mi SW to Middle Fk Lime Creek; S Fk Boise River drainage.

Named for Malcom Stewart, who came with his wife to Camas Prairie in the 1880s; had three or four young children; remained a few years and moved to Washington, D.C.

Stibnite (Valley). 6520'. T18N R9E sec 15/14. A profitable mining town that produced ore from 1932 to 1952.

Named for the stibnite (antimony ore) in the area.

Sticker Mountain (Kootenai). 4439'. T49N R3W sec 23. Early name for Coeur d'Alene Mountain. So called by forest rangers because dead trees on the summit gave the appearance of stickers. Recommended by forester W. B. Greeley in 1917.

Alternate names: Bald Mountain, Huckleberry Mountain, and currently Coeur d'Alene Mountain.

Stiens Creek (Cassia). T15S R24E sec 16. Heads in the canyon between Stiens Pass and Graham Peak, between Castle Rocks and Castle Rock and flows 5 mi to its confluence with Almo Creek.

This creek, as well as Stiens Pass at the head of the stream, was named after a Mr. Stien, who homesteaded a portion of land through which this stream flows. The stream has been known by his name for more than 100 years. Not Stines Creek, which is a misspelling.

Stierman Gulch (Boise). T5N R4E sec 23-25. Empties into Mores Creek 7 1/2 mi SW of Idaho City; Boise River drainage.

Named for the Stierman family, who ran a way station at the mouth of this gulch in the 1860s.

Stinking Creek (Lemhi). T13N R24E sec 18. Originates 1 mi S of Inyo Mountain; flows S 3 1/2 mi to Big Creek; Salmon River drainage.

The stream is hard to cross, and it has an odor, possibly because of sulphur.

Stinson Creek (Kootenai). T48N R4W sec 4. A 5-mi stream that empties into Loffs Bay, on the W shore of Coeur d'Alene Lake, 9 mi S of Coeur d'Alene. A small settlement grew up at the mouth of this stream. Post office, 1904-.

Named for the first postmaster.

Stites (Idaho). 1245'. T32N R4E sec 20/29. In the NW part of the county, 4 1/2 mi up S Fk Clearwater from Kooskia and 22 mi E of Grangeville. It is on State Highway 13 and was the terminus of the Clearwater Branch of Camas Prairie RR, a loading point for logs from Meadow Creek area.

Until the opening of the Nez Perce Reservation for settlement in 1895, this was Indian territory and remained unclaimed until Jacob Stites, the town's namesake, homesteaded a tract on which the townsite was laid out. Post office, 1900-.

Stocking Meadows (Clearwater). T41N R4E sec 1. Thirteen mi NW of Bertha Hill.

Named for Theodore Fohl's horse, called "Stocking," which was found dead near the meadow.

Stoddard Creek (Idaho). T22N R15E sec 13. A 7-mi stream rising on Stoddard Creek Lookout and flowing E to Middle Fk Salmon River. Stoddard Lake is near the headwaters and Stoddard Bar at the mouth of this stream.

Said to have been named for early relatives of Smith Stoddard, a Middle Fk back-country pilot.

Stone (Oneida). 4600'. T16S R32E sec 22/23. In the SW part of the county, 2 mi N of the Oneida-Utah line; on Deep Creek. A Mormon community. Post office, 1910-.

Named for a Malad City lawyer.

Stone Johnny Lookout (Bonner). T57N R6W sec 25. Located 1 1/4 mi E of Idaho-Washington state border; 8 1/4 mi NW of the town of Priest River.

Named for an early resident.

Stormy Peak (Lemhi). 7943'. T23N R19E sec 3. About 2 1/2 mi NW of Point of Rocks.

Named because of the rough weather and lightning storms that cross this peak.

Stratton Butte (Latah). 3166'. T43N R5W sec 18. Hill about 1.8 mi S of Farmington and 24 mi NE of Pullman in NW quarter of Latah County.

Named for Hiram Stratton, who lived here before 1900. His name appears in A. A. Lieuallen's account book for his store in Moscow. Name changed to Palmer Butte. Formerly Queeners Butte, named for the Queener brothers, who settled in the area in the 1870s.

Strawberry Creek (Bonner). T59N R1E sec 24. Heads 1/2 mi E of Mount Willard and flows 4 1/4 mi NW into Grouse Creek; Pack River drainage. Strawberry Mountain (5684') overlooks Strawberry Creek.

The origin of the name is subject to dispute. Some say wild strawberries grow in the area, but others say it is an office name in harmony with Garden, Lunch, and Smorgasbord creeks.

Street Creek (Benewah). T46N R1W sec 17. Rises between Rochat and Engle mountains in the St. Joe Mountains and flows 4 mi S to St. Joe River 4 mi E of St. Maries. Named for Joe Streit (sic), who homesteaded here. Formerly Strait Creek.

Strevell (Cassia). 5270'. T16S R28E sec 20/29. In the southernmost part of the county, 4 mi E of Naf. Once the center of a farming community.

Post office, 1913-1924.

Named for a Salt Lake City promoter under the Carey Act.

Stria Gulch (Latah). T42N R3W sec 11. Flows S 1 mi to Meadow Creek; Palouse River drainage.

Named by USFS ranger W. H. Daugs; Chinook jargon word means "small channel," which is characteristic of this stream except during the rainy season.

Stricker (Twin Falls). T11S R18E sec 23. In the NE part of the county on Rock Creek, 11 mi SE of Twin Falls.

Herman Stricker bought a store here from James Bascom, and built a permanent residence above it. After a stage stop was established here, a small village grew up around it. The Stricker Station served emigrants en route to Oregon and other passers-by. Post office, 1904-1910.

Named for Herman Stricker, the proprietor of the Stricker Stage Station and the first permanent settler in Twin Falls County.

String, The (Teton). T3N R45E sec 13/14. An early colony 2 mi S of Victor and 9 mi S of Driggs along Trail Creek.

Named because the emigrants to Teton County from Cache Valley, Utah, located on the S banks of Trail Creek in 1889, strung their farms out from the mouth of Trail Creek to near Piney Pass.

Stringtown (Latah). T42N R6W sec 4. Local name for an early settlement in Cedar Creek area later called Almeda, when the post office was granted in that name.

Opal Lambert Ross suggests that the name derived from the row of houses strung out along the road between Cedar Creek and Yellow Dog.

Strode Basin (Owyhee). T2N R6W sec 23/24/11/12/13/14. Large basin, extends SW about 2 mi. Variant spelling is Strod Basin.

Named after settler John Strode.

Strong Canyon (Fremont). T9N R43E sec 18. In S central Fremont County. Runs S to Henrys Fork 3 mi NE of Ashton.

Named for Joe Strong, who built a cabin on the creek.

Strong Creek (Bonner). T57N R1E sec 35. Heads on W slope of Roundtop and flows 3 mi SW into Lake Pend Oreille at East Hope.

Named for J. J. Strong, superintendent of the Northern Pacific Railway's dining-car division, or for his son Sam, who lived in the area.

Stroud Creek (Lemhi). T16N R25E sec 30. Flows NE 5 1/2 mi to enter Lee Creek; Lemhi River drainage. Stroud Gulch, 5 1/2 mi NE of the creek, heads NW of Mineral Hill and runs S 3 mi to Lemhi River drainage just 1 mi S of Mineral Hill.

Named for Elijah Lige Stroud, who had a ranch in the vicinity of the stream and the gulch.

Struggle Gulch (Lemhi). T17N R24E sec 22. Located 1/2 mi N of Zeph Creek; runs NE 2 1/2 mi to enter Zeph Creek; Lemhi River drainage.

Named because the Daley family, who homesteaded in the gulch, had a struggle to make a living here.

Strychnine Creek (Latah). T42N R2W sec 31. Rises SW of Bald Mountain, flows 6 mi SW to Palouse River.

According to an account by a Mr. Pankey before 1905, named from the strychnine poisoning of the stream to eliminate Chinese miners. White miners had abandoned the area and let the Chinese enter. The Chinese worked the area successfully by ditching water from Strychnine Creek across the ridge for their sluicing and for personal use. White miners poisoned the Chinese with strychnine in the water, but never found the gold that had been cached.

Strychnine Ridge. T42N R2W sec 16/21/20. Ridge lying between and drained by Strychnine Creek on the W and Poorman Creek on the E. The location is described as "on the divide between poorman (sic) and stricknen (sic) creeks and adjoins Tenner Placer."

Stuart (Idaho). Early name for Kooskia. Post office, 1896-1900, when the name officially changed to Kooskia.

Named for James Stuart, Indian surveyor who worked along Middle Fk Clearwater River and who represented the Nez Perces in settling claims with the US government.

Stump Creek (Caribou). T65 R45E sec 27. Rises on the Idaho-Wyoming line just S of the Old Salt Works and flows 14 mi NW. The Lander Road followed the course of this stream.

Named for J. H. Stump, manager of the Old Salt mine. When F. W. Lander was surveying for a road in 1858 the stream was called Smoky Creek; in 1870, Scotts Fork.

Sublett Creek (Cassia). T12/13S R28/29E. Rises in the SW part of former Minidoka Forest and flows in an arc through ranges 28 and 29 to a point 5 mi E of Malta. A dam forming Sublett Reservoir was built in 1902 and the creek empties into the reservoir.

Sublett (Cassia) 5002'. T12S R28E sec 34. A village on Warm Creek settled by ranchers in 1865 and by Mormons in 1877; at the historic junction of the Oregon Trail with the Sublett Cutoff to California. Post office, 1880-ca.1936.

Sublett Range (Cassia/Power/Oneida). About half this range lies in NE Cassia and the remainder in Power and Oneida counties. It ends on the N by merging with Snake River Plain and extends S to the Utah border. This range is lower than surrounding ranges with only a few peaks over 7500'. Characterized by steep slopes and long, narrow valleys.

All these features were named directly or indirectly for Milton Sublette (sic), who guided the first band of fur trappers over the Sublett Cutoff in 1832. Sublette was a partner in the Rocky

Mountain Fur Company and worked this area.

Succor Creek (Owyhee). T3N R5W sec 3. Stream 50 mi long, heads in Idaho in the Owyhee Mountains, flows NW 20 mi into Oregon, then 40 mi back into Idaho to the Snake River 1 mi NW of Homedale. Name preferred by locals is Sucker, though all government maps and documents record Succor.

Succor derives from an incident on the Oregon Trail 9 Sept 1860, known as the Otter massacre. Forty-four emigrants from Wisconsin on the way to Willamette River, Oregon, were attacked by Shoshonis. There were 12 survivors. Those who had settled along the southern route of the Oregon Trail gave succor to the survivors.

Sucker derives from the fact that there were suckers in the creek.

Sugar City (Madison). 4891'. T6N R40E sec 4. In the N part of the county, 4 mi NE of Rexburg, on Teton River.

In 1883 settlers began homesteading the land where Sugar City is located. Then in 1903 a group of businessmen in Salt Lake City organized the Sugar City Townsite Company and laid out a townsite already occupied by the pioneers and established a beet-sugar company. The company bought the homesteads and built the factory and worker's residences at a cost of nearly $1 million. Post office, 1904-.

Sugarloaf Mountain (Lemhi). 9045'. T20N R16E sec 15. Stands about 2 mi SE of Wilson Mountain and 3 mi NE of McEleny Mountain.

Named by USFS employees ca.1932 because the mountain is shaped like a conical loaf of concentrated sugar.

Sulphur Spring (Latah). T40N R3W sec 7. A spring about 3 mi SE of Yale, just W of Middle Fk Little Bear Creek,

1 mi N of its convergence with Howell Creek.

Named because the water of the spring has a high mineral content, earlier believed to be sulphur, because wood and metal exposed to the water turn yellow. Locally known as "The Waterhole."

Sulphur Springs (Caribou). T9S R42E sec 12. In the S part of the county, 4 mi E of Soda Springs, up Sulphur Canyon; a very cold spring so highly charged with sulphur that the rock around it will burn with a steady flame.

Sulphur Peak lies 3 mi E of the springs, and Sulphur Canyon originates in N, Middle, and S Sulphur canyons, extends 8 mi to its mouth at Bear River, 1 mi N of the Bear Lake-Caribou line.

Summit (Nez Perce). 2608'. T36N R2W sec 10. Agricultural community in the NE part of the county, 2 mi N of Gifford. Post office, 1900- 1937.

Named because it was located on the highest ridge in the area.

Summit City (Lemhi). T23N R20E sec 25. Town 6 mi E of Leesburg where Sierra Gulch (now called Coffee Gulch) meets Daly Creek. During the spring of 1867, James Glendenning surveyed and mapped the townsite, which is said to have had a population of about 400 persons for several years.

Named for its elevation, 1996'.

Sun Valley (Blaine). T4N R18E sec 7. Famous ski area just N of Ketchum. In 1936 on the recommendation of Count Felix Schaffgotsch, the UPRR bought 3888 acres from rancher Ernest F. Brass. Development began immediately; it has become a year-round resort. Named for the pleasant climate.

Sunbeam (Custer). 7065'. T11N R15E sec 20. Early mining settlement at the mouth of Yankee Fork. Sunbeam Hot Springs are about 1 mi SW of the settlement. Post office, 1907-1912.

Ebenezer E. Cunningham attempted to placer mine gold here by diverting water from a nearby stream. He named the point at which the ditch was to have been completed "Junction," but his venture was too expensive and he sold to the Sunbeam Mine Co., for which it is named.

Sunnydell (Madison). 4960'. T4N R40E sec 5/6. A community in the S part of the county, 9 mi S of Rexburg; the center of an agricultural area. Post office, 1900-1922.

Named because it is in a little cove in the hills. Only a local canal still carries the name.

Sunnyside (Bonner). 2070'. T57N R1W sec 14. Resort town on N shore of Lake Pend Oreille, 7 mi E of Sandpoint. Sunnyside Mountain is about 2 mi NW of Sunnyside.

Named because the area is exposed to the sun during most of the day.

Sunnyside (Elmore). 2300'. T2S R4E sec 2. A UPRR station just E of Ada-Elmore county line. Post office, 1907-1930.

Named for its sunny, warm climate.

Sunrise Bay (Bonner). T57N R1E sec 31. On W shore of Lake Pend Oreille, across the lake 2 3/4 mi SSE of Sunnyside.

Named because the sun can be seen rising from here better than from other places in the area.

Sunset (Shoshone). 5750'. T49N R5E sec 29/28. In the NE part of the county, 3 mi N of Burke on Sunset Peak (6424'); a mining settlement that grew up around Sunset mine. Post office, 1888-1929.

Named for Sunset Peak, which in turn was named because it caught the last rays of the sun.

Sunset Creek (Boise). T7N R7E sec 35. Rises on the E slope of Sunset Mountain (7869') and flows NE into Crooked River in the central part of the county; Boise River drainage.

The creek's name is transferred from Sunset Peak. Sunset Peak was named in 1858 by Hudson's Bay trappers. It was the last peak lit by the sunset.

Sunset Peak (Butte). 10,693'. T8N R26E sec 33. Three mi E of the NW county line, 11 mi N of Darlington; Challis National Forest.

Named for the view of the sunset.

Suttler Creek (Idaho). T32N R5E sec 4. In the NW part of the county. Rises on Woodrat Mountain (4983') and flows 6 mi SW to Middle Fk Clearwater River, 7 mi E of Kooskia.

Named for Charley Suttler, an 1875 homesteader.

Suzie Creek (Lewis). T33N R2E sec 8. Rises 1.3 mi S of Nezperce and flows NE, then SE to Lawyer Creek in T33N R3E sec 7. Approximate length, 10 mi.

Named for an Indian woman who lived close to the mouth of the creek.

Swamp Creek (Lemhi). T24N R17E sec 33. Tributary of Owl Creek; heads near Swamp Camp (Long Tom Ridge Camp) and flows SE 3 1/2 mi to enter Owl Creek; Salmon River.

There are many boggy, swamp-like places along the ridge at the head of this creek.

Swan Basin (Lemhi). T14/15N R25/26E sec 1/60. In the Big Timber Creek drainage.

In 1875 a man named Swan, who had a ranch in the vicinity, grazed his stock in this basin.

Swan Falls (Ada). T2S R1E sec 18. Located on the E side of Snake River within Snake River Birds of Prey Natural Area.

Originally named for swans that wintered in the area.

Swan Lake (Bannock). T13S R38E sec 11/13/14. Lake in the SE extremity of the county, 4 mi SE of Red Rock Junction. Swan Lake Creek, 6 1/2 mi long, rises SW of Cottonwood Peak and empties into Swan Lake. Named for the swans that nest and summer here.

Swan Lake (4779'). T13S R38E sec 10. A Mormon village named for the lake; settled in the 1870s. Post office, 1880-.

Swan Lake (Fremont). T11N R42E sec 11. Lake 15 mi N of Ashton. Another Swan Lake lies 1/2 mi S of Cave Falls Road 2 mi from the Wyoming border.

Named for the presence of swans in the area. The first-named lake commemorates the presence of a pair of nesting trumpeter swans which regularly returned to the lake during the summers of the 1960s until one was shot.

Swan Peak (Lemhi). 8416'. T20N R19E sec 35. About 3 mi NE of Moyer Peak.

Billy Swan, an early forest ranger and miner, had a cabin at the base of the peak.

Swan Point (Clearwater). T40N R6E sec 2. Peak 4 mi W of Canyon Ranger Station.

Named for Hershall Swan, who worked for the Clearwater Timber Protective Association as a cruiser. He was killed in World War II, and the peak was named for him after his death.

Swan Valley (Bonneville). 5276'. T1/2N R43/44E. In the NE quadrant on the S Fk of Snake River between Snake River Range and Caribou Range; NW of Palisades Reservoir; 12 mi long. Bounded on the N and E by Big Hole Mountains. Also Swan Basin.

Swan Valley 5277'. T2N R43E. Town in the valley of the same name in the NE quadrant at the head of Rainey Creek, 36 mi E of Idaho Falls. Surveyed for a townsite in 1886. Post office, 1916-.

Named because the area was once a haven for whistling swans.

Swanner Creek (Teton). T7N R45E sec 18. In Targhee National Forest in NE Teton County; rises in the E foothills and flows about 6.5 mi NW to Bitch Creek.

In 1891 Samuel Swanner (early settler, sheriff of Tetonia, explorer) found a gold pan and packsaddle in a cave in the mountains near Bitch Creek. They looked as if they were 100 years old.

Swanson Creek (Clearwater). T39N R7E sec 10. Rises on Swanson Saddle and flows 4 mi SE into Little Washington Creek; Clearwater River drainage.

Named for John Swanson, a trail foreman and cruiser.

Swanson Gulch (Lemhi). T17N R24E sec 25. Runs 2 mi NE to Lemhi River Valley.

Named for two brothers, Gus and Oscar Swanson, who mined at Gilmore and bought the ranch of John W. Snook, Sr., in 1913.

Swartz Creek (Lemhi). T17N R24E sec 34. Flows E 2 mi, then N 1 mi to enter Zeph Creek; Lemhi River drainage.

There are two different attributions for this name: for Antone Swartz; or for Horatio Swartz, who lived here ca. 1887.

Swede Creek (Clearwater). T35N R5E sec 14. A 4-mi stream flows SW into Jim Brown Creek between Peterson Corners and Brown Creek Mill; Clearwater River drainage.

A group of Swedes settled in the area. Pete Peterson was one of the more famous of the Swedes who lived near the creek. Similar communities with this name occur in Bonner and Clearwater counties.

Sweet (Gem). 2548'. T7N R1E sec 3. Town at the mouth of Squaw Creek in E part of the county, 16 mi NE of Emmett. First served as a way station for freighters into the Buffalo Hump mining district. Ezekiel Sweet came from Ohio to the valley in 1877. In 1884 he opened the second post office in the area and called it Squaw Creek, but the Post Office Department objected to a two-word name.

Named for the first postmaster, Ezekiel Sweet.

Sweet Sage (Butte). T6N R30E sec 19/30. An early settlement formerly in Jefferson County. Post office, 1910-1918.

Named for the abundance of sweet sage growing in the area.

Sweetwater Creek (Nez Perce). Flows NE into Lapwai Creek and eventually into the Clearwater River.

So called because a mule loaded with two sacks of sugar lay or fell down in the creek near the Craig homestead. The mule was owned by Grostein and Binnard, who operated lengthy pack trains from Lewiston to the gold mines. This may be a folk etymology. See next entry.

Sweetwater. 1085'. T35N R4W sec 14. Village in the center of the county, 2 mi S of Lapwai on Sweetwater Creek. This settlement is said to be one of the oldest in Idaho, with the inhabitants both Indian and white.

Sweetwater is an English translation of Nez Perce "che-chu-kus-koos."

Switchback Gulch (Boise). T4N R5E sec 10. Flows E into Thorn Creek 5 1/2 mi upstream; Boise River drainage.

There was an almost impassable road with many switchbacks along this gulch.

Switchback Hill (Clearwater). 6422'. T38N R10E sec 11. Six mi SE of Kelly Forks Ranger Station.

The hill was named because the trail leading to the top had many switchbacks.

Sypah Creek (Latah). T41N R2W sec 6. Flows 2.1 mi SW to Little Sand Creek; Palouse River drainage.

Named Sypah by USFS ranger W. H. Daugs; Chinook jargon for "straight," which is descriptive of this stream channel.

Syringa (Idaho). T33/32N R6E sec 32/5. A early-twentieth-century ghost town in the county, 17 mi upstream from the Middle Fk Clearwater River, 17 mi from Kooskia and 6 mi W of Lowell. Post office, 1896-1908.

Named for the shrub that grows in the area and is the state flower.

Syron Draw (Lewis). T33N R2E sec 10. Extends to T33N R2E sec 13, 2 mi SE of Nezperce. Mitchell Creek runs through this draw.

Named in recent years for Freeman Syron, owner of the land (ca.1930).

T

T-Bone Creek (Idaho). T24N R6E sec 6. N tributary of Salmon River, 24 mi E of Riggins.

Probably an office name, by analogy with Bull Creek, 2 mi E of this stream.

Taber (Bingham). 4575′. T1S R32E sec 23. In the NW part of the county, l0 mi SE of Atomic city.

Originally a RR stopping place, named for a RR employee. This stop was intended to service an irrigated area, and land was sold mostly to Chicago investors. A few families came to the area and built homes, but irrigation never materialized.

Table Butte (Jefferson). 5235′. T8N R35E sec 27. Six mi NE of Mud Lake and 4 mi W of the N extremity of Camas National Wildlife Refuge.

A descriptive name; the butte has a flat top.

Table Rock (Ada). (3600′). T3N R3E sec 18. One thousand feet above the surrounding terrain, it stands like a huge platform.

The Indians called this place ala-kush-pa or "the place to build fires at certain times." It was the meeting place of several tribes.

Table Rock is a descriptive name: it is flat.

Tackobe Mountain (Elmore). 9318′. T7N R11E sec 15. In the N extremity of the county between Little Queen River and Black Warrior Creek.

The name is a Shoshoni Indian word for "snow." This peak is usually the first one with considerable snow in the area.

Tahoe Ridge (Idaho). T32N R4/5E. A ridge 3 mi E of Kooskia, trending 5 mi SE from Middle Fk Clearwater River. Listed in Polk's Directory of Idaho County, 1913-1914, as a village 15 mi NE of Grangeville and 4 mi E of Stites. This description of the location puts the settlement on what is today called Tahoe Ridge. Post office, 1894-1912.

A transfer name from Lake Tahoe in California and Nevada, which in turn comes from Washo Tahoe, "big waters."

Talache (Bonner). 2056′. T55N R1W sec 6. Resort town on the W shore of lower Lake Pend Oreille 5 1/4 mi E of Westmond. Talache Creek rises on E slopes of Butler Mountain and flows E to Mirror Creek at the town of Talache. Talache Landing is on the W shore of Lake Pend Oreille at the mouth of Talache Creek. Post office, 1917-.

Name derived from the Talache mine, which is nearby. Talache is an Aztec word for a tiny one-handed silver pick that the Indians used to get silver from small veins.

Talapus Creek (Latah). T41N R1W sec 4. Flows 2.1 mi SE to W Fk Potlatch

River. Named by USFS ranger W. H. Daugs; Chinook jargon for "coyote." According to Daugs, this drainage seemed to be a favorite hunting spot for coyotes.

Talmage (Caribou). 5584′. T8S R40E sec 33. In the W part of the county, 8 mi WNW of Soda Springs. Settled in 1890 and named Way until after 1921, when the name was changed to Talmage. Post office, 1910-1921.

Named for a Mormon bishop.

Tama Creek (Clearwater). T37N R7E sec 3. Flows E into Orogrande Creek; Clearwater River drainage.

This is a shortened form of tamarack: Tamarack Creek enters Orogrande Creek near the mouth of Tama Creek.

Tamarack (Adams). 4104′. T19N R1E sec 30. An early settlement and sawmill site located 8 mi SW of New Meadows. This was a RR station on the PIN line, whose officials probably named the site. Post office, 1911-.

Named for the abundance of western larch, locally called tamarack, that grew here.

Tamarack Creek (Clearwater). T37N R7E sec 3. Flows 3.5 mi N into Orogrande Creek in E Clearwater County; Clearwater River drainage. Tamarack Ridge trends NW 3 mi from the head of the creek.

Named for the tamarack or larch trees here.

Taney (Latah). T38N R2W sec 35. Pioneer settlement 6 mi E of Troy. Post office, 1885-1907.

Said locally to have been named by first postmaster Roger Drury for Chief Justice Roger Brooke Taney, U.S. Supreme Court 1836-64, whom he admired.

Tango Peak (Custer). Early name for Loening Mountain, which see.

Targhee Creek (Fremont). T12S R3E sec 33. Targhee Creek runs SW to Henrys Fork, 3 mi below Henrys Lake outlet, and Targhee Creek Basin runs NW/SW on the Continental Divide 8 mi E of Henrys Lake. West Targhee Creek flows SW to convergence with the main creek. Targhee Pass (7075′) is on the NE Idaho-Montana state border. Targhee Peak (10,040′) is on the Idaho-Montana border 5 mi NE of Raynolds Pass.

All the above features are named for a Bannock chief notorious as a warrior, killed by Crows in 1871-1872. Spelled Ty-gee, later Ti-ge, then Tar-ghee. Pronounced TAR-gee, g as in gulch.

Tater Creek (Lemhi). T14N R22E sec 7. Heads 2 mi S of Hi Peak; flow SSW 3 mi, W 2 mi then S 5 1/2 mi to enter Patterson Creek; Salmon River.

John Morgan raised the first potatoes in the valley with the water from this creek. Originally called Spud Creek.

Tavern Creek (Bonner). T59N R2W sec 11. Heads 3 1/2 mi WNW of Elmira; flows 2 1/4 mi SW into Pack River 5 1/2 mi N of Colburn.

Named because it flows near a tavern.

Taylor (Jefferson). 4790′. T4N R38E sec 8. First post office name for Lewisville, which see. Lewisville applied for a post office and it was granted in 1890 as Taylor. People were dissatisfied with the name and petitioned for a change to Lewisville; it was granted in 1893.

Named for President John Taylor of the Latter-day Saints Church.

Taylor Canyon (Blaine). T5N R18E sec 30. Trends 2 mi N to S to Lake Creek; Big Wood River drainage; 3 mi N of Sun Valley.

Named for an early miner in this canyon.

Taylor Creek (Boise). T7N R9E sec 24/25. Rises in the SE extremity of the county N of Goat Mountain (8835′) and flows 4 1/2 mi S into N Fk Boise River.

The creek was named by the USFS for USFS ranger Warren Taylor.

Taylor, Mount (Bingham). 7414′. T1S R39E sec 29. In Blackfoot Mountains in the NE part of the county, 12 mi E of Firth. Taylor post office, 1890-1905.

Earlier named Blackfoot Peak by the Hayden Survey, but now called Mt. Taylor, after Colonel Sam Taylor, an early resident of this area.

Taylor Mountain (Lemhi). 9960′. T18N R19E sec 15. Near the head of S Fk Moyer Creek on the W and N Fk Hat Creek on the E.

Named for Robert Taylor, horse raiser in the 1870s, who pastured about 700 head of his own horses, as well as horses for miners and other people, in this area during the summer months.

Taylors Bridge (Bonneville). A village forerunner of Idaho Falls, which see.

Taylorville (Bonneville). 4657′. T1N R38E sec 30. Village in the SW quadrant 8 mi S of present-day Idaho Falls.

Probably named for Sam Taylor, esteemed Kentucky-born sheriff of Bingham County and originally a rancher; might also be named for his cousin Matt Taylor.

Teachers Bay (Bonner). T62N R4W sec 21. On Priest Lake, 8 mi E of Idaho-Washington state border and 3/4 mi S of Tripod Point.

Named because several teachers came to the area for recreation.

Teakean (Clearwater). 2993′. T37N R1E sec 18. Town 8 mi NW of Orofino. Teakean Butte (4140′) lies 2 mi W of the town and 10 mi NW of Orofino.

A Nez Perce word, Teakean means a series of little meadows; thus the name is descriptive. Post office, 1898-1927.

Telcher Creek (Idaho). T30N R1W sec 3/4. A 5-mi tributary to the Salmon River from the N, in the NW extremity of the county.

Named for a German immigrant, Dedrick Telcher, who settled land on Camas Prairie. He became county commissioner, county assessor, and road commissioner for the Grangeville-Meadows Valley road.

Telegraph Hill (Owyhee). T5S R3W. First name of Knob Hill; near Silver City.

From Telegraph Hill one could see travelers on their way to Silver City, and a signal for visitors was sent to Silver City; hence telegraph.

Telephone Pole Springs (Lemhi). T24N R18E sec 17. At the head of E Fk Owl Creek, just SE of Beartrap Ridge, about 5 mi W of Shoup.

Named by a USFS line crew when they built the telephone line to Sheepeater Point Lookout. The line ran by this spring.

Temple, The (Boise/Custer). 10,716′. T8N R13E sec 19. Peak on the Boise-Custer county boundary in the Sawtooth Range.

From a distance this peak looks like a temple.

Templeman Lake (Boundary). T63N R1E sec 24. Eight mi N of Bonners Ferry.

Named for a squatter who lived on the shore of the lake for years.

Ten Mile Creek (Boise). T7N R6E sec 35. Flows 4 1/2 mi SE into Mores Creek; Boise River drainage.

Named because its mouth is close to ten miles up Mores Creek from Idaho City.

Tendoy (Lemhi). T19N R24E sec 20. Town near the mouth of Agency Creek on Lemhi River.

Named for the chief of the Lemhis whose sandstone monument, erected by his white friends, stands on a hill 2 mi E of the RR station. He was born on the Boise River about 1834 and succeeded his uncle, Chief Snagg, as chief in 1863. His name means "he likes broth," from his excessive fondness for this food as a boy. He died from exposure near the narrows on Agency Creek in 1907.

Tenlake Creek (Boise). T8N R12E sec 27. Rises in the SE extremity of the county and flows 3 1/2 mi NW into S Fk Payette River at Smith Falls.

The stream drains ten lakes.

Tenmile Creek (Idaho). T29N R6E sec 35. Rises in the Gospel Hump Wilderness Area on Buffalo Hump and flows 15 mi N to S Fk Clearwater River, at Golden.

Named because its mouth is 10 mi E of Clearwater Station.

Tenmile Creek (Lemhi). T20N R22E sec 30. Forms 1 mi NW of Sal Mountain; flows NW 3 mi to enter Salmon River.

It is 10 mi from Salmon.

Tensed (Benewah). 2557′. T44N R5W sec 14. On US 95 in SW Benewah County 14 mi S of Plummer, this town was called DeSmet for the Jesuit missionary until residents applied for a post office. The name was unacceptable to postal authorities as there was already one DeSmet, so the residents reapplied for a post office as Temsed (DeSmet reversed), but clerical error resulted in the name as Tensed. Post office, 1914-.

Tepee Creek (Clearwater). T39N R7E sec 30. Flows 2 mi S into Washington Creek, 1 mi E of Tepee Rock; Clearwater River drainage.

Named for T. P. Jones, a timber cruiser.

Terrace Canyon (Caribou). T5S R44E. SE of Stump Peak. A site along the Lander Cutoff, where a steep, narrow, rocky passage was made passable by laying up rock ledges to form a roadbed on the lower side and hewing away the rock face on the upper side. Mormon settlers were paid $1 a day to do this difficult work. The terraces can still be seen in some places.

Terrace Lakes (Lemhi). T21N R16E sec 20/21. About 3/4 mi W of Heart Lake.

Named by Lester Gutzman and a USFS crew ca.1938 because the 3 or 4 lakes all looked like they had been terraced by a landscape.

Terreton (Jefferson). 4787′. T6N R34E sec 22. In the center of the county 2 mi SW of Mud Lake (the lake itself) and 2 mi E of the town of Mud Lake. Post office, 1920-.

Named for Marshal M. Terry, who established and ran the first store and who served as the first postmaster.

Teton County. County seat, Driggs. Established in 1915; created from part of Madison County.

Settlement began in 1888 with colonization of Driggs by a group of Mormons from Salt Lake City. Victor was settled by a group from Cache Valley, Utah, the same year, and by 1891 the entire valley was dotted with sawmills, dairies, and farms. The UPRR completed a branch to Driggs in 1912.

Teton County is bounded by Teton Range on the E, Bonneville County on the S, Madison County on the W, and Fremont County on the N. It is drained entirely by the Teton River and its tributaries.

Named for the Teton Range, which is derived from French teton, "breast."

Teton River. T6N R39E. Heads in Teton Peaks, Wyoming, and flows NW through the entire length of Teton

County, W along the Teton-Fremont county line, and SW to empty into the N Fk Snake River 6 mi W of Rexburg. Teton River is 60 mi long; its drainage, 1000 square miles.

Teton (Fremont) 4949'. T7N R41E sec 36. Town 6 mi S of St. Anthony. Post office, 1885-.

Tetonia (Teton). T6N R45E sec 29/28. Town 8 mi NW of Driggs at the foot of the big bluff in the center of the N end of Teton Valley. Settlement began in 1881. The townsite was dedicated in 1910, but significant growth did not occur until the UPRR came through in 1912. Post office, 1913-.

This cluster of names comes from the Teton Peaks, Wyoming, which overshadow the entire area. The peaks in turn had a descriptive name, which French fur trappers assigned, meaning "breast."

Tex Creek (Bonneville). T1N R40E sec 11. Rises in the NE quadrant and flows 9.1 mi NW into Willow Creek, about 12 mi E of Idaho Falls; Snake River drainage.

Named for Tex Turner, reportedly invited from Texas by local cattle rustlers to kill Old Dutch John in 1892. John was supposedly shot and killed by Turner, who himself was later reported killed in 1898 near Lost River for rustling horses.

Texas Creek (Clearwater). T35N R3E sec 22. Flows 5.5 mi SW into Lolo Creek 4 mi SE of Fraser; Clearwater River drainage.

Named for Tex or Old Tex, the operator of the Texas Ranch, which was a stopover place for the miners going to Pierce. The trail from Greer to Weippe went by his ranch.

Texas Creek (Lemhi). T16N R26E sec 28. Originates near Slaughterhouse Spring, 1 mi N of Gilmore Summit; flows 7 mi NW, then 10 mi N to meet Canyon and Big Timber creeks to form the Lemhi River.

A local story says that some men from Texas took up the first mining claims in this district, which is also the Texas Mining District.

Texas Ridge (Latah). 2874'. T40N R2W sec 25-36. Just S of Deary, between Pine Creek on the W and Potlatch River on the E; the Texas Ridge Road is about 10 mi long, extending from Deary to 1 mi E of Kendrick.

Texas Bager owned land on this ridge about 4 mi S of Deary, which may have influenced its name.

Texas Slough (Madison). T5N R39E sec 31-36.

This slough was named for Tex Parker, trapper, who wintered S of Rexburg, 1860s and 1870s.

Thama (Bonner). 2082'. T56N R4W sec 33. Town on Pend Oreille River 3 mi SE of the town of Priest River. Pronounced THEY-muh.

Named for settlers who once ran a ferry at this place.

Thatcher (Franklin). 4897'. T12S R40E sec 1. In the extreme N part of the county on State Highway 34 and Bear River.

An 1870 Mormon settlement. Post office, 1900-.

Named for John B. Thatcher, a Mormon bishop who became a state senator.

Therriault Creek (Shoshone). T45N R5E sec 15. A 2-mi tributary of the St. Joe River from the S at Avery.

Therriault Lake (Shoshone). T44N R3E sec 13. Ten mi SW of the source of Therriault Creek.

Named for Therriault family, who first came to St. Joe City in 1900. In 1908 they established the Mountain View Hotel in Avery.

Thiard (Shoshone). 2850'. T49N R4E sec 11. In the N part of the county, 3 mi SW of Murray on Trail Creek; a mining community. Post office, 1895-1908.

Originally called Myrtle for the daughter of one of the owners of the Myrtle claim. Since there was already a post office of that name in the state, the name was changed to Thiard for a local pioneer.

Thiessen Gulch (Nez Perce). T34N R4W sec 19. Flows N into Lapwai Creek; 4 mi N of Culdesac Hill.

Named for J. D. C. Thiessen, who had a ranch at the foot of Culdesac Grade near Thiessen Gulch. Thiessen raised sheep. He came to Lewiston in 1876 and served as deputy sheriff of Nez Perce County in 1885.

Thomas (Bingham). 4440'. T3S R34E sec 5/8. In the SW part of the county, 11 mi W of Blackfoot. A farming community, settled about 1880 and named in 1902 for Lorenzo R. Thomas, a prominent Mormon settler and bishop. Post office, 1898-.

Thomas Creek (Benewah). T46N R2W sec 12. Rises on Engle Mountain and flows S to St. Joe River.

Named for John R. Thomas, an Englishman who homesteaded at the mouth of this creek in the late 1880s.

Thomas Fork Creek (Bear Lake). T14S R46E sec 10. Heads at the Wyoming-Idaho line and flows 17 mi S to Bear River 2.3 mi NW of Border, Wyoming; the continuation of this stream in Wyoming is known as Salt Creek.

Named for a trapper. All the following Thomas Fork names are derived from this stream.

Thomas Fork. 6300'. T13S R46E sec 26. Settlement, now Raymond. First settled by Mormons in 1876 and named for Thomas Fork Creek. Post office, 1889-1900.

Thomas Fork Valley. T12/13S R46E. Between Preuss Range on the W and Wyoming on the E; length, 15 mi; width, 3 mi maximum; elevation, 6250' in the N and 6100' in the S.

Thomas Gulch (Boise). T6N R5E sec 25. Trends SW into Mores Creek just N of Idaho City; Boise River drainage.

The Thomas family lived on this gulch near Idaho City in the 1860s and 1870s.

Thompson Butte (Clearwater). T40N R6E sec 22. Five mi SW of Canyon Ranger Station. Thompson Creek flows N to Clearwater River 2 mi N of the butte, and Thompson Point is 2 mi S of the butte.

Named for a woodsman, Henry Thompson, who served as a fire lookout. He worked for the Clearwater Timber Protective Association and for survey crews.

Thompson Creek (Boise). T7N R5E sec 28. Flows 3 1/2 mi SW into Grimes Creek at Centerville; Boise River drainage.

Three Thompson children died at the mouth of this gulch when their house burned in the 1890s.

Thompson Gulch (Lemhi). T26N R22E sec 28. Runs W 2 mi to enter Dahlonega Creek drainage; N Fk Salmon River drainage.

A man named Thompson, a freighter from Gibbonsville, was also the first gold prospector on this tributary.

Thompson Gulch (Lemhi). T16N R26E sec 27. Runs about 4 mi S to Canyon Creek, just W of Baby Joe Gulch; 1 mi E of Leadore; Lemhi River drainage.

Named for Elmer E. Thompson, an early settler in this area.

Thompson Lake (Kootenai). T48N R3W sec 20/21. In the SE part of the county, 4 mi W of Coeur d'Alene Lake, just N of the river. One of the 9 lakes formed by overflows from Coeur d'Alene River.

Named for an early settler.

Thompson Peak (Boise/Custer). 10,776'. T9N R12E sec 1. On the Boise-Custer county line in the Sawtooth Range.

Named by the USFS in 1916 after old-timer John Thompson, a rancher and miner of the area, who claimed to be the first man to climb the mountain.

Thorn Creek (Boise). T5N R4E sec 25. Originates in the confluences of N, Middle, and S fks and flows 4 mi W into Mores Creek; Boise River drainage. Thorn Creek Butte (7550') lies at the head of Middle Fk Thorn Creek.

This area is thick with thorny underbrush.

Thorn Creek (Latah). T12N R46E sec 5, Whitman County, Washington. Rises 5 mi S of Moscow and flows 15.2 mi into Washington State.

Thorn Creek. T38N R5W sec 19. An early community a few mi W of Genesee on Thorn Creek. Post office, 1873-1883.

Thorn Valley. T38N R5W sec 23. An early community W of Genesee; area drained by Thorn Creek. Post office, 1878-1879.

Thornton (Madison). 4857'. T5N R39E sec 15/14. In the SW part of the county, 6 mi SW of Rexburg. Established about 1887. When the OSL was constructed across S Fk Snake River and into Madison County, this community became a RR siding named Texas Siding, for Texas Slough, an important shipping point. The name was changed to Thornton in 1904.

Named for the first postmaster.

Thousand Springs (Gooding). T8S R14E sec 8. A valley on the Snake River near Hagerman; said to be the outlet of Lost River some 150 mi NE of the springs.

These springs were a landmark to emigrants on the Oregon Trail. They are a feature of one of the larger groundwater systems in the world, which is recharged by precipitation, percolation, and irrigation over an area of several thousand acres.

Thrasher Creek (Clearwater). T41N R6E sec 30. Rises on Smith Ridge near the N boundary of the county and flows 2.5 mi SW into N Fk Clearwater River.

Named for George Thrasher, a settler and USFS employee.

Three Bear Creek (Latah). T39N R1E sec 14. Flows 7 mi NE to Long Creek; Clearwater River drainage.

Named by analogy to Little and Big Bear creeks. It is in bear country and a simple Bear Creek would not do.

Three Blaze Meadow (Idaho). T23N R9/10E sec 34/31. Along Red Top Creek 16 mi SE of Dixie.

Named for the nearby Three Blaze Trail.

Three Creek (Owyhee). 5860'. T15S R11E sec 34. Town 5 mi N of the Idaho-Nevada line; 5 1/2 mi W of Twin Falls county border. Joe Scott was the first settler, 1870s, and gave the name Seventy-one to the town, after his cattle brand. Post office, 1887-1949.

Named because of a figure 3 on a nearby canyon wall.

Three Island Crossing (Elmore). T5S R10E sec 31. About 1 mi SW of Glenns Ferry on the Snake River.

The major crossing of Snake River on the Oregon Trail. Three islands in the river at this point made it easier to get wagons across.

Three Links Lakes (Idaho). T33N R10E sec 27/28. In The Crags, River of No Return Wilderness Area. Three

Links Creek rises in these lakes and flows through Three Links Meadow 15 mi SE to Selway River; Clearwater River drainage.

Named for a carving of three links found on a large spruce tree along the stream in 1890.

Three Sisters Peaks (Bonner). T54N R2W sec 10/11/14. Three peaks equally spaced in a row parallel to the W shore of lower Lake Pend Oreille. Three Sisters Creek rises on the W slope of two peaks of Three Sisters and flows W and N to Kreiger Creek.

Named by analogy to three sisters side by side.

Threemile Creek (Clearwater). T37N R5E sec 27. Flows 2 mi SW into Quartz Creek at Jaype; Clearwater River drainage.

Named by Frank Froemelt, who logged and built a railroad spur here, because it was three miles from Jaype.

Three-Mile Creek (Lemhi). T26N R22E sec 28. Heads on the county line between Lemhi County, Idaho, and Beaverhead County, Montana; flows S 4 mi to enter Dahlonega Creek; N Fk Salmon River drainage.

The stream enters Dahlonega Creek approximately 3 mi from Gibbonsville.

Thunder Hill (Nez Perce). T36N R4W sec 34. Mountain 1 1/2 mi N of Lapwai.

Named because the Nez Perce Indian Big Thunder, was buried at its top. Hinmah-tute-ke-kaikt, better known as "Thunder Strikes," "Thunder Eyes," or "Big Thunder," was a village head at Lapwai. He fought with Reverend H. H. Spalding because Spalding built a mission on Big Thunder's grounds.

Thunder Mountain (Valley). T19N R11E sec 29. A volcanic promontory between Monumental and Marble creeks S of Lookout Mountain Ridge.

The name stems from Indian fears and superstitions. They claimed that angry gods were responsible for slopes where thunder rolled down the mountain from cloudless skies. Supposedly, the reverberations were from falling rocks—slides were common here.

Thunder City (Valley). T14/13N R3E sec 36/6. Ghost town 6 mi from present-day Cascade. Founded in 1900 as a way station and outfitting post on the wagon road to the Thunder Mountain mines, the town died when the RR established a station at Cascade in 1913. Named for Thunder Mountain.

Thunder Mountain City. T19N R11E sec 8. Ghost town about 3 mi down Monumental Creek from Roosevelt. Established in 1902. Named for Thunder Mountain.

Thurman Mill (Ada). T4N R1E sec 23. Site of an important mill and slough, located just NW of Boise City, on Boise River.

By 1865 Thurmans Slough was used for irrigation and the mill used by many settlers. The mill and slough were originally owned by William Thurmond, then by W. H. Ridenbaugh beginning in 1872; he began his own canal in 1877. Post office, 1878-1879.

Apparently the Post Office Department misread the name Thurmond and granted the post office as Thurman, which appears currently on a Boise street.

Thurmon Creek (Fremont). T12N R43E sec 35. In central Fremont County. Flows 3 mi SW to Golden Lake, then 2 mi S to Silver Lake thence 2 mi SE to Henrys Fork.

Named for a settler who lived in the area that is now Railroad Ranch (Harriman State Park).

Tie Bend (Jefferson). T4N R40E sec 25/36. The big bend of the Snake River that loops through the SE part of the county.

So called for the railroad ties and logs floated down from Kelley Canyon country and removed from the river at this point.

Tie Creek (Boise). T10N R5E sec 7. Flows E into Payette River near the N county line; nearby are Boom, Powerhouse, and Skid Road creeks, all named with logging terms.

A great deal of logging was done in this portion of Garden Valley. Much of the lumber was made into railroad ties.

Tiger Gulch (Shoshone). T49N R5E sec 6. A 1-mi gulch trending S to N to Prichard Creek at Murray; Coeur d'Alene River drainage. Tiger Peak (6625') is situated 5 mi S of the source of this creek.

Both features were named for the Tiger mine, located by Carter and Seymol in 1883 – the first mine in the Burke District.

Tikura (Blaine). 4650'. T2S R20/21E sec 25/30. UPRR siding. Post office, 1883-1919.

Named for a RR worker who helped to build the siding in 1880.

Timber Creek (Caribou). T8S R45E sec 27. Rises on Webster Range in the E part of the county; flows 5 mi SW to Diamond Creek; Blackfoot River drainage.

Named for the timber land drained by the stream.

Timber Creek Peak (Lemhi). 10,553'. T14N R26E sec 31. In the Lemhi Range 3 mi NE Timber Creek Pass and at the headwaters of Big Timber Creek; Salmon National Forest.

Named for Big Timber Creek.

Timber Gulch (Lincoln). T4S R16E sec 18. Heads on Twin Oaks, a promontory in the NW corner of the county, and extends 6.5 mi S to Preacher Creek

1 mi E of the Gooding-Lincoln county line.

Apparently there is timber in this area, unlike other parts of Lincoln County.

Timmerman Hills (Blaine). T1S R18E sec 22-25. Promontories 10 mi S of Bellevue. Extremities of these hills are marked by Ditto Hill (5361') on the W and an unnamed promontory (5642') on the SE.

Named for John L. Timmerman, a Wood River Country resident in the 1880s. He established his residence on the N slope of one of these hills and lived here until his death in 1906.

Timpa Creek (Elmore). T7N R12E sec 22. Rises on Plummer Peak on the Custer-Elmore county line and in Timpa Lake, and flows SW 3 mi to Rock Creek; Middle Fk Boise River drainage.

Timpa is a Shoshoni Indian word for "rock"; the stream has rocky banks and bed.

Tincan Spring (Lemhi). T26N R20E sec 30. At the head of Indian Creek, near the Idaho-Montana border, about 2 mi NE of Irishmans Rock. Tincup Hill, T25N R18E sec 30, is located at the head of Wallace Creek, 2 1/2 mi S of Horse Creek Pass on the Idaho-Montana border.

Named for the Tincup mine, which was located in the vicinity.

Tindall (Owyhee). T13S R5E sec 28. Town 18 mi N of the Idaho-Nevada line. Post office, 1907-.

Named for the Tindall family, who had a ranch in the area.

Tipton (Cassia). T13S R28E sec 22. In the extreme E part of the county on Meadow Creek, 10 mi ESE of Malta. Post office, 1911-1914.

Named for the first postmaster.

Tiptop Lake (Lemhi). T20N R16E sec 5. In the Bighorn Crags; about 1 1/2 mi NE of Wilson Mountain.

Named by USFS and Coast and Geodetic Survey in 1963 because of its high elevation: 8361'.

Tobias Creek (Lemhi). T16N R23E sec 3. Originates 1 1/2 mi NW of Mill Mountain; flows N 2 mi then W 1 1/2 mi to enter Hayden Creek; Lemhi River system. Pronounced tuh-BI-us.

Solon S. Tobias and Sigel F. Tobias were pioneer ranchers on this stream, arriving about 1896.

Toboggan Ridge (Clearwater) T38-40N R11/12E. A 9-mi ridge in the extreme E part of the county; trends NW-SE, with Toboggan Hill marking the NW extremity and Blacklead Mountain (7525') the SE. Toboggan Creek, 8 mi long, parallels the ridge on the W side; it flows NW and empties into Cayuse Creek.

Named for the toboggan built by the Hanson brothers in order to carry supplies down the ridge to the end of the snow line.

Togo Gulch (Bonner). T63N R5W sec 24. Heads 2 mi SE of Gold Peak; extends 1 1/2 mi NE to Upper Priest River. Pronounced tuh-GO.

The name is derived from the directions "to go."

Tollgate Gulch (Boise). T6N R5E sec 33. A 3 1/2-mi gulch trending 1 mi SW of Idaho City; runs into Mores Creek; Boise River drainage.

There was a tollgate at the head of this gulch operated by John Casner.

Tolo Lake (Idaho). T30N R2E sec 29. In the NW part of the county 5 mi N of White Bird Hill and 4 mi due W from US 95.

Named for a Nez Perce woman who befriended the whites during the Nez Perce War of 1877. Her name was Alabernot, called by white settlers Tolo (Nez Perce "Too-lah"). When the Nez Perce reservation was opened for settlement, she received an allotment under the name of Tola-Tsonmy.

Tom Beall Creek (Nez Perce). T36N R4W sec 36. Formed by the junction of N Fk Tom Beall Creek (7.3 mi long and heading in T36N R3W sec 15) and S Fk Tom Beall Creek (7.1 mi long and heading in T36N R3W sec 23). Flows SW for 1.2 mi to its confluence with Lapwai Creek.

Named for Thomas B. Beall, a pioneer in this area who married an Indian woman. Their son took an Indian land allotment.

Tomer Butte (Latah). 3466'. T39N R5W sec 23. About 2.5 mi SE of Moscow.

Named for George Washington Tomer, who arrived here in 1871 and homesteaded on the slopes of this butte.

Toms Creek (Fremont). T13N R43E sec 22. Flows NW to Buffalo River 1/2 mi upstream from Ponds Lodge.

Named by George Rea for his brother, Tom, who overturned a canoe on this stream.

Topance Creek (Caribou). T6S R39E sec 31. Rises on Portneuf Range in the NW corner of the county; flows SE to Portneuf River.

Named in 1863 for Alexander Topance, who owned cattle and freight outfits in Utah and Idaho.

Topaz (Bannock). 4929'. T9S R37E sec 23/24. In the E part of the county on Portneuf River. A Mormon settlement named for a local formation resembling topaz in color. Post office, 1911-1912.

Toponis (Gooding). Early name for Gooding, which see. The word is reputedly of Indian origin; see Bisuka.

Torelle Falls (Bonner). T57N R5W sec 16. Three mi E of Idaho-Washington border; 7 3/4 mi NNW of the town of Priest River and on Priest River.

Believed to be named for Bill Torelle, a former surveyor of the NPRR.

Tormay Creek (Lemhi). T21N R21E sec 34. Originates S of Spring Creek; flows E 2 mi to enter Perreau Creek; Salmon River drainage.

Named for John Tormey (sic), who located a mine in this area.

Torpid Creek (Latah). T42N R2W sec 35. Flows .9 mi W to Big Sand Creek; Palouse River drainage.

Named by USFS ranger W. H. Daugs, because the water is slow and muddy in the dry season.

Tosoiba (Caribou). Shoshoni name for Soda Springs, which see. The word means "sparkling waters."

Tower Creek (Lemhi). T23N R22E sec 18. Forms S of Goldstar Gulch; flows W 3 mi, then SW 1 1/2 mi to enter Salmon River.

Named by Lewis and Clark in 1805 for curiously shaped rocks in the area, which from a distance look like spires and towers of a city. The Rev. Samuel Parker described these objects as he passed them on 6 Sept 1835.

For many years called Boyle Creek, after Thomas Boyle, who settled here in the 1870s, but through efforts of the Lemhi Historical Society the name given by Lewis and Clark was restored.

Also called Cherry Creek at one time.

Town Creek (Blaine). T3N R20E sec 19. Flows 2.7 mi ENE to Baugh Creek; Big Wood River drainage; 10 mi NE of Hailey.

Named because cattlemen drove their cattle up the creek and over the summit into town. Variant: Towne Creek.

Township Butte (Clearwater). 4836'. T39/40N R4/5E. In the NW quadrant of the county, 5 mi W of Bertha Hill.

Named because townships corner on the butte.

Trail Canyon (Cassia/Power). T12S R29-31. Heads just W of Roy and extends WSW 6 mi into Cassia County to Sublett Creek.

Named because the canyon was used to trail herds of cattle and sheep from Rockland Valley to Malta Valley.

Trail Creek (Bonneville). T4S R45E sec 27. Rises in the extreme SE corner of the county and flows 6 mi SE into Jackknife Creek; Salt River, Wyoming, drainage.

Named for the nearby trail that often follows the creekbank. Trail is a popular name for streams that are a part of established trails, Indian or otherwise. Another Trail Creek empties into Indian Fork of Tex Creek; Snake River drainage.

Trail Creek (Clearwater). T39N R9E sec 32. In the NE quadrant of the county. Rises on Mush Saddle and flows 4 mi S into N Fk Clearwater River.

Either an Indian trail or a surveyor's trail follows the creek; the trail led from The Bungalow and passed not far from Pot Mountain.

Trail Creek (Lemhi). T22N R18E sec 11. Forms E of Jureano Lookout; flows 4 mi NW then 2 mi W to enter Panther Creek; Salmon River drainage.

The old trail from Big Creek (now Panther Creek) to the Leesburg Basin followed this creek. An attempt was made at one time to call this Dan Davis Creek, after a pioneer miner.

Other Lemhi County features bearing this name are Trail Creek, Yellowjacket Creek tributary; Trail Creek, Basin Creek; Trail Creek, Lake

Creek; Trail Gulch, Salmon River; and Trail Peak (10,589').

Trail Creek (Teton). T4N R45E sec 32. Stream 16 mi long, heads in Wyoming and flows W into Idaho to the Teton River 7 mi SW of Driggs.

Named in 1873 by Captain William A. Jones of the US Army Corps of Civil Engineers because there was an elk trail along this stream. Formerly called Pass Creek.

Trail Gulch (Twin Falls). T13S R18E sec 10/14. A ravine .8 mi long, trending NW to Fifth Fk Rock Creek, 4 mi NNW of Grand View Peak and 18.5 mi SSE of Twin Falls.

This was formerly the route for livestock to and from summer pastureland; hence the name.

Trailton (Bingham). 5557'. T3S R39E sec 29. In the SE part of the county, at the mouth of Trail Creek about 20 mi SE of Blackfoot. Settled about 1910, but is now deserted. Post office, 1916-1921.

Tram Creek (Benewah). T44N R1W sec 15. Rises in St. Joe National Forest, E central Benewah County, between Renfro and Dago creeks and flows 2 mi SW to St. Maries River.

Named for the tram constructed here to transport timber to the mill on the creek.

Transfer Gulch (Lemhi). T24N R19E sec 21. Gulch 1 1/2 mi long; heads in S part of Dutchler Basin and runs S to its mouth on Salmon River road.

In the early days the wagon road ended at the mouth of the gulch and supplies for mines at Shoup had to be transferred to pack string or boat.

Trapper Flat (Lemhi). T21N R19E sec 12. Located 1/2 mi E of Trapper Gulch, just W of the mouth of Little Jureano Creek.

Trappers wintered in the area because of rich fur harvests.

Other Trapper features in Lemhi County are: Trapper Gulch, Panther Creek drainage; Trapper Gulch, N Fk Salmon River; and Trapper Ridge, SE of Fritzer Flat. Trapper features occur along streams of the SE and N parts of the state.

Treasure Gulch (Latah). T42N R4W sec 11. Runs 1 1/2 mi S to Gold Creek; Palouse River drainage; in St. Joe National Forest at head of Gold Creek; an early gold-prospecting area.

Named by USFS ranger W. H. Daugs in 1931 for the gold that miner W. Carrico buried in tin cans, which he was never able to find because he lost his sight in an explosion. A local story claims "greenhorn" prospectors were sent here to get them out of the way of successful miners, because there was no gold in this gulch.

Treasure Valley (Canyon/Ada/Malhuer [Oregon]). Nickname for Canyon County, which see. Popular name for the agricultural area that stretches west from Boise into Oregon, because of its abundant agriculture and food-processing plants.

Treasureton (Franklin). 5019'. T13S R39E sec 25. In the NW part of the county, on Battle Creek, 16 mi N of Preston on State Highway 34.

Settled in 1868 by Mormons; the first church was erected in 1906 and the first school in 1909. Post office, 1881-ca.1940.

Named for early settler and first postmaster.

Treloar Gulch (Lemhi). T19N R18E sec 10. Heads E of McGowan Basin; runs N 1 1/2 mi to enter Panther Creek drainage; Salmon River drainage. Pronounced TREE-lor.

Named for Edward P. Treloar, a Frenchman who homesteaded a ranch and ran a hotel here in the 1860s and 1870s.

Trestle Creek (Bonner). T57N R1E sec 21. Heads 2 1/4 mi SW of Lunch Peak on Trestle Peak (6320') and flows 8 mi SW into Lake Pend Oreille 3 mi NW of Hope.

Named for a long NPRR trestle that ran near the mouth of the creek before the railroad was relocated.

Triangle (Owyhee). 5280'. T7S R2W sec 30. Town 18 mi S of Silver City and 10 mi SE of Flint. Post office, 1912-1954.

Named for the cattle brand of the Triangle Ranch, owned by Earl Bachman. The tract on which the ranch is located is triangular, located between small streams.

Triplet Creek (Latah). T41N R2W sec 12. Flows 1 mi NE to Big Sand Creek; Palouse River drainage.

Named by USFS ranger W. H. Daugs because the stream has three distinct forks; mining claims were staked on this creek in 1889. Apparently the creek was called Triplet locally long before Daugs put the name on the maps in 1931.

Tripod Point (Bonner). T62N R4W sec 16. On Priest Lake, 3/4 mi E of Canoe Point and 7 mi NE of Nordman.

Named in 1933 because it was used as a triangulation point for aerial-survey mapping.

Triumph (Blaine). T4N R18E sec 25. Abandoned town, probably no more than a mining camp established to support the Triumph mine, for which it was named. Post office, 1889-ca.1900.

Triumph Gulch, named for Triumph mine, lies 5.5 mi ESE of Ketchum; empties into E Fk Wood River. Old Triumph and North Star mines lie near the source of this gulch.

Trout Creek (Bonneville). T3S R46E sec 16. Rises in the SE quadrant and flows 4 mi NE into Palisades Reservoir; Snake River drainage.

Named for the trout in these waters.

Troy (Latah). 2460'. T39N R3W sec 7. Town 14 mi E of Moscow.

Known in 1885 as Huffs Gulch, in 1890 as Vollmer, and in 1897 as Troy. Post office, 1898-.

The community became disenchanted with the founder-banker, John P. Vollmer, who foreclosed on notes during the 1893 depression, and decided to hold an election to choose a new name. As the story goes, a Greek working for the railroad set up a barrel of liquor at the poll site and offered all the liquor one wanted if he voted for Troy, the most illustrious name in history and literature. The results were 29 votes for Troy and 9 for Vollmer.

Trude Junction (Fremont). T13N R43E sec 15. No longer extant.

Named for A. S. Trude, a judge from Chicago, who arrived in the area in 1888.

Tubbs Hill (Kootenai). T50N R4W sec 24. On the N side of Coeur d'Alene Lake, directly south of Coeur d'Alene.

Named for Tony A. Tubbs, who arrived at Coeur d'Alene Lake in 1883 and proved-up his homestead, which he carved into lots and sold during the development of Coeur d'Alene. He built the first hotel, Hotel d'Landing.

Tule Lake (Fremont). T9N R45E sec 27/34. Six mi SW of Porcupine Ranger Station. Named for the swamp grass and willows that grow around it. In Fremont County, tules may be any kind of watergrowth.

Tule Lake (Lemhi). T19N R23E sec 7. On Haynes Creek, about 2 mi SW of K

Mountain. Originally a small pond formed by beaverdams in the creek, this feature is generally known as Haynes Lake or Fish Lake by locals.

Named because of the cattails, sometimes called tules, that are found in the pond.

Tumble Creek (Lemhi). T22N R14E sec 25. Heads near McGuire Lake; flows NW 3 mi to enter Middle Fk Salmon River.

The water seems to tumble as it flows down the mountain.

Turkey Head Butte (Gooding). 3950'. T4S R15E sec 21/22. In the NE part of the county, 7 mi N of Gooding.

A descriptive name: the configuration of the butte resembles a turkey's head. Both wild and domestic turkeys were once important to the area. Turkey Lake is .4 mi E of the butte. Turkey Creek rises on the butte and flows 5 mi S to Big Wood River.

Turnbow Gulch (Latah). T41N R4W sec 11. Heads approximately .5 mi N of Turnbow Point, about 5 mi SW of Harvard, and runs N for approximately 2.8 mi to its confluence with Palouse River.

Named for Lon Turnbow, an early-day settler and homesteader in the area.

Turner (Caribou). 5471'. T10S R40E sec 6/8. In the SW part of the county, 5 mi W of Grace. A Mormon settlement founded in 1898. Post office, 1900-1927.

Named for Theodore Turner, an early settler who became land commissioner in Pocatello.

Turner Gulch (Lemhi). T22N R21E sec 30. Flows 3 mi E to enter Jesse Creek drainage; 3 mi W of Salmon; Salmon River drainage.

Captain Nathaniel L. Turner, a Civil War veteran whose pen name for old newspaper articles was "Driftwood," had mining property in this gulch.

Turntable Summit (Owyhee). Promontory W of Cinnebar Mountain and E of War Eagle Mountain.

In the early days of the county when timber was very important, loggers went up to the summit to turn their wagons around after they had gotten the lumber; hence the name.

Turquoise Lake (Lemhi). T21N R16E sec 32. In Bighorn Crags, just NW of Echo Lake.

Named by USFS and Coast and Geodetic Survey in 1963 because of the sky reflected from the water.

Tuttle (Gooding). 2309'. T6S R14E sec 31. In the SW part of the county, 3 mi NE of Hagerman on the UPRR and State Highway 25. A shipping point for Hagerman Valley. Near its site was the old stage station, and N of that was Horse Heaven, where stagecoach horses rested. Post office, 1915-ca.1965.

Named for Daniel S. Tuttle, Episcopal missionary bishop in Idaho from 1867 to 1886.

Twelvemile Creek (Boise). T7N R6E sec 25. A 2-mi stream flowing SE into Mores Creek; Boise River drainage.

Named because it is 12 mi from Idaho City.

Twin Buttes (Lincoln). 4645'. T3S R22E sec 28/33. In broken lava beds of the NE part of the county.

A descriptive name: there are two distinct summits and a common base.

Twin Cabin Creek (Clearwater). T41N R9E sec 34. In the NE part of the county. Flows SW into Quartz Creek; Clearwater River drainage; 7 mi NE of Mush Saddle.

Named for the two cabins built here by Jack Sprague.

Twin Falls (Twin Falls/Jerome). T9S R18E sec 31. NE of the city of Twin Falls and 2 mi upstream from Shoshone Falls. One of the two falls has now been appropriated by a power company; the cataract is less impressive than it used to be. Both Twin Falls County and the county seat were named for this cataract.

Twin Falls (Twin Falls). 3745'. T10S R17E sec 15. County seat. In the N part of the county, at the intersection of US 30 and US 93, on Rock Creek; 5 mi W of the waterfalls of the same name on Snake River; the heart of Magic Valley, produced by one of the most successful of the Carey Act irrigation projects.

Founded in 1903 by I. B. Perrine, a promoter of the Twin Falls Investment Company, Twin Falls was laid out in 1904 and incorporated in 1905. The city grew so rapidly it was nicknamed "Magic City." Most of the settlers were businessmen and farmers from the Midwest. Post office, 1904-.

Twin Falls County. County seat, Twin Falls. Created in 1907 by Idaho State Legislature from the W part of Cassia County, after a county division committee of the Commercial Club, Twin Falls, had engaged in a year-long campaign to divide Cassia County into two counties. Like the county seat, the county was named for the Twin Falls in Snake River.

Twin Falls County is bounded by Snake River on the N, its parent county of Cassia on the E, Nevada on the S, and Owyhee County on the W.

Twin Groves (Fremont). T7/8N R41E sec 4/32. Town 3 mi NE of St. Anthony; a Mormon settlement. The name was suggested by two islands in nearby Henrys Fork, covered by cottonwood and aspen.

Twin Imps (Idaho). 9000'. T23N R2W sec 27. Two peaks in the Seven Devils with approximately the same elevation; in Nezperce National Forest, SW part of Idaho County. Just NE of Devils Farm, NW of Dog Lake, and 1.8 mi SSW of He Devil.

Named by A. H. Marshall. Not: She Devil.

Twin Knobs (Bannock). 7768'. T10S R39E sec 7. In the E extremity of the county in the Portneuf Range, .2 mi N of Windy Pass and 11 mi SSW of Bancroft.

Named because it is the only prominent double-knobbed feature in this part of the Portneuf Range.

Twin Lakes (Kootenai). T52/53N R4/5. Two lakes joined by a channel, in the NW part of the county, 3 mi N of Rathdrum. The 2 lakes are 5.5 mi long, the upper one 1 mi wide and the lower .5 mi wide; 75' deep at the extreme.

The earliest name for the settlement that grew up here was Furst; then Fir Grove, for the firs surrounding the lakes; and finally Twin Lakes, for the lakes whose name is descriptive. Post office, 1911-1917.

Twin Oaks (Lincoln). 5895'. T3S R16E sec 16. The highest point in Lincoln County, in the NW corner.

Named for two similar oaks on the promontory.

Twin Peaks (Custer/Lemhi). 10,196'/10,328'. T15N R17E sec 28/29 and 30. In the Challis National Forest between the headwaters of Challis and Warm Spring creeks.

Two similar bare granite peaks, with a third almost as high to the W, are visible from US 93 between Challis and Pahsimeroi Valley. So called because the peaks are adjacent to each other and approximately the same elevation.

Another Twin Peak is located in T19N R21E sec 15 and 21 between Camp and Rattlesnake creeks.

Twisted Draw (Fremont). T10N R44E sec 21. In E central Fremont County. Runs E to W.

The draw is very crooked.

Twodot Peak (Shoshone). 6503'. T44N R4E sec 17. In the SW part of the county, 10 mi SW of Avery.

Named in 1917 by Forester R. H. Rutledge, because of the characteristic appearance when seen from a distance. Like a large cattle brand, two large dots mark its side.

Tyee Mountain (Boise). 8761'. T8N R10E sec 20. Three mi W of the Sawtooth National Recreation Area in the E part of the county.

Tyee is the Shoshoni word for "chief." This is a USFS name.

Tygee Creek (Caribou). T7S R46E sec 27. Rises N of Buck Mountain and flows N 7 mi to Stump Creek, along the Wyoming border E of Caribou National Forest. Tygee Ridge extends E of the creek barely W of the Wyoming border. In 1958 the creek was (according to F. W. Lander) called Red Willow Creek.

The name is a variant of Bannock "Tyhee", the name of a chief.

Tyhee (Bannock). 4458'. T5S R34E sec 27/34. Village in the N part of the county, on UPRR, 4.5 mi S of the Fort Hall Reservation. Post office, 1909-1910. An Indian school was opened here in the early 1900s, serving some 200 students; both academic and vocational subjects were taught.

Named for a Bannock chief; the term means "swift."

Tylers Ridge (Shoshone). T44N R2E sec 16/17/20. A 3-mi ridge trending NE to SW in the W part of the county, 8 mi S of Calder.

Named for Eugene Tyler, who was killed in 1904 by parties unknown during the era of claim-jumping in the Marble Creek area.

Tyrannis Creek (Camas). T3N R14E sec 25. Stream 2 mi long, flows SW to Carrie Creek 16 mi N of Fairfield.

Named for the Tyrannis mine located nearby; Tyrannus was a scholar at Ephesus in whose school the apostle Paul argued in behalf of Christianity.

Tyson Creek (Benewah). T44N R1W sec 26. Rises E of Tyson Peak, (4745'), in the St. Joe National Forest, and flows 6 mi NE to St. Maries River 1 1/2 mi upstream from Santa.

Named for James Henry and George Tyson, miners and owners of the Tyson Mining Co. mill, who applied for a land patent in this area in 1904. Early maps show a town of Tyson on the creek, and at one time the town had a population of more than 100 people. Post office, 1901-1918.

U

U P Lake (Lemhi). T22N R21E sec 17. One mi SW of Wallace Lake.

Named for the Union Pacific Mining Company, which had holdings near here, a branch of the UPRR.

Ucon (Bonneville). 4808'. T3N R38E sec 14/15. Town in the NW quadrant 8 mi N of Idaho Falls. An agricultural center and shipping point, Ucon was homesteaded by Mormons in 1885. The railroad came in 1904 and the town was moved 7 mi W to take advantage of it. Ucon Post office, 1901-.

Originally known as Willow Creek, from the stream on which it lies; name changed to Elba; Post Office Department requested a change because another post office was named Elba. The Post Office submitted a list of suggested names, and citizens chose Ucon. Also informally known as Hard Scrabble.

Ulysses (Lemhi). 3990'. T25N R20E sec 31. Town near Kitty Gulch on Indian Creek. Post office, 1902-1929.

Ulysses Mountain (7649') overlooks the town and is about 2 mi NE of Indianola Ranger Station. Named for the town it overlooks.

There are conflicting stories about the origin of this name. One informant says one of the locaters named the town for his hometown in Pennsylvania; another that it was named for Ulysses S. Grant; and still another, that it was named for a mine, which in turn was named for the Greek hero.

Upper Mesa Falls (Fremont). T10N R43E sec 13. A drop of 114' on Henrys Fork 10 mi NE of Ashton. Located 1.5 mi N of Lower Mesa Falls. See Mesa Falls.

Upper Priest Falls (Boundary). T65N R5W sec 13. On Upper Priest River in the Kaniksu National Forest about 1/2 mi from the Canadian border. Formerly American Falls. See Priest Lake.

Upper Red Top Meadow (Idaho). T23N R9E sec 11/12. Meadow.8 mi long, along Chamberlain Creek, 16 mi SSE of Dixie.

Named for the color of the grass in the fall.

Upper Salmon Falls (Gooding/Twin Falls). T8S R13E sec 2/3. Three mi S of Hagerman and 1 mi W of Owsley Bridge. See Salmon Falls.

Urquhart Gulch (Shoshone). T46N R1E sec 22. In the extreme E part of the county, 16 mi SE of Kellogg.

Named for a Mr. Urquhart, who homesteaded near this area.

Ustick (Ada). T4/3N R1E sec 34/3. Town 7 1/2 mi W of Boise.

The town was founded in 1908, when the Boise Valley Railway—an interurban line—built from Boise through this farming area. Post office, 1908-1958.

Named for Dr. Harlan Page Ustick, who founded the town.

UC Gulch (Lemhi). T11N R28E sec 15. Runs 1 mi N to McCoy Canyon; Lemhi River drainage.

Named for the Utah Construction Company, which ran several bands of sheep on this range.

Valley County. County seat, Cascade. Established in 1917; named for the outstanding topographical feature of the area, Long Valley.

Bounded on the N by Idaho County, on the E by Lemhi and Custer counties, on the S by Boise County, and on the W by Adams County.

Valliet Spring (Lemhi). T25N R18E sec 34. At the head of Spring Creek on the Idaho-Montana border, 2 mi SE of Blue Nose. Pronounced VAL-ee-ay.

Named for a Frenchman who mined here in the early days; once incorrectly called LaFayette Spring.

Van Horn Gulch (Lemhi). T19N R16E sec 13. Located 2 1/2 mi W of Yellowjacket Ranger Station and 2 mi E of Hoodoo Creek; enters Yellowjacket Creek; Salmon River drainage.

Henry Van Horn, of Challis, had mining claims in this area, some of which he sold in 1882.

Van Wyck (Valley). 4778′. T14N R3E sec 26. Originally W of Cascade. One of the first settlements in the area, probably as early as 1866 when there was a Van Wyck mill at this site. By 1882 it was still a small settlement, but it was established as a town in 1913 and later merged with Crawford and Cascade to form Cascade. Post office, 1888-1917.

Believed by locals to have been named for the Van Wyck mill.

Vassar (Latah). 2720′. T40N R2W sec 8. Situated 3 mi NW of Deary; founded as a WIM station; laid out in 1907 by a Mr. Rue, with the name Rue, though the post office was called Avon as long as it operated, and road maps called it Vassar.

One of 8 WIM stations bearing names of colleges. This point was named by Huntington Taylor, son of the president of Vassar, in recognition of women's colleges. The fact that Civil War veteran James R. Vassar homesteaded nearby may also have influenced the choice. Local informants say that Vassar Meadows, about 2 mi NE of Vassar, was named for the homesteader before the railroad was built, and Vasser and W. E. Grimes filed mining claims on the headwaters of Bear Creek, in Vassar Meadows, in 1894. It is much more likely that Vassar was named for Vassar Meadows.

Vay (Bonner). 1980′. T55N R4W sec 13. Town 3 3/4 mi NE of Edgemere. Formerly Valley; later Seneaquoteen, which see. Post office, 1902-ca.1930.

A contraction of the earlier name Valley; named for the valley where it is located.

Vernoni Lake (Boise). T7N R12E sec 12. In the SE extremity of the county.

Named after a member of a fish-planting party that helped stock the lake.

Victor (Teton). 6207′. T3N R45E sec 11. Town on a branch of the UPRR 8 mi S of Driggs, in the SE part of the county. Post office, 1892-.

First called Raymond, for the first Mormon bishop of the Raymond Ward, David Raymond Sinclair. It was platted and dedicated as Raymond in 1901, also formerly known as Fox.

George Victor Sherwood, mail carrier from Raymond to Jackson, Wyoming, courageously delivered the mail through an Indian scare despite great danger. His name was consequently chosen as the name for the post office and town.

Vienna (Blaine). 7500′. T6N R14E sec 32. Ghost town in the NW extremity of the county on Smiley Creek. Post office, 1882-1887.

Named for Vienna mine.

View (Cassia). T11S R24E sec 19. In the N part of the county, 7 mi SE of Burley. Post office, 1910-1911.

A man named Burgess applied for a post office for this community with the name of Burgessville, but the Post Office Department would not grant an office unless a shorter name was chosen. The community chose View, which it has.

Vine Creek (Lemhi). T26N R21E sec 3. Runs SE 4 mi to N Fk Salmon River.

Many bushes and vines along the creek made passage difficult.

Vinegar Hill (Valley). T21N R13E sec 13/14/23/24. One mi N of Big Creek between Cove and Cabin creeks; in the NE corner of the county.

During the Sheepeaters War, on 9 July 1878, Lt. Henry Catley and 60 mounted men of the 2nd Infantry were counter-attacked and surrounded by Indians for 14 hours on this ridge. They had no water and became so thirsty they drank the barrel of vinegar from their supplies.

Viola (Latah). 2676′. T40N R6W sec 1. About 8 mi N of Moscow, formerly called Four Mile; established in 1878, one of the oldest settlements in the county; a former station on the Spokane and Inland Empire RR. Low-lying Viola Ridge lies about 4 mi NE of the town. Post office, 1878-.

Named for a woman important to the Viola school. Two stories are current: the woman was the first child born here and she was the first teacher; her father, the first postmaster, gave land for the school provided it bore her name, Viola.

Earlier name, Four Mile.

Viola Gulch (Lemhi). T12N R29E sec 21. Gulch 1 1/2 mi long; runs SW just E of Nicholia. Pronounced Vi-o-luh.

Named for the Viola mine, which was discovered in the gulch in 1880 by William McKay, who tended stock for the Gilmer and Salisbury Stage Company. Bill Crawford and a man named Cummings were partners in the deal, and they named the mine Viola after the sweetheart of one of the discoverers.

Violet Gulch (Boise). T7N R5E sec 21-22. Flows E into Grimes Creek at T7N R5E sec 21; Boise River drainage.

A miner found some wild violets growing on the banks of the gulch and named his claim after the flowers. The name was transferred to the gulch.

Virginia (Bannock). 4809'. T11S R37E sec 5. In the S part of the county, 4 mi S of Arimo, on US 91/I15.

Settled in 1885 and named Thatcher; a Mormon community organized a ward here in 1912 under the name of North Cambridge because of its ecclesiastical dependence upon Cambridge, which see. The name was changed to Virginia, possibly because some of the settlers were Mormon converts from the state of Virginia. Post office, 1910-.

Vocquelin Gulch (Boise). T4N R4E sec 28. A 3 1/2-mi gulch trending W to

Mores Creek 1 mi upstream; Boise River drainage. Pronounced VOK-we-lin.

Named for the Vocquelin family, who once lived in the area.

Vollmer (Latah). Early name for Troy, which see.

Named for J. P. Vollmer, a Lewiston banker, who founded the town of Vollmer and induced the Northern Pacific Railroad to extend its line through the community in 1890. Post office, 1890-1893, when the name was changed to Troy.

Vollmer (Lewis). T34N R1W sec 33. Former town. See Craigmont.

The town of Vollmer was established on the E side of the Camas Prairie RR when the RR was completed through the region in 1908. Ilo was on the W side. The two towns were absorbed by Craigmont. Vollmer Post office, 1907-1920.

Named for John P. Vollmer.

Votler Creek (Lemhi). T26N R21E sec 36. Heads E of Granite Mountain; flows E 2 mi to empty into N Fk Salmon River.

Named for Gus Votler, who mined here until the early 1920s, when he disappeared one winter and was never found. Local people believed he was trapped in one of his mines.

Vulcan Hot Springs (Valley). T14N R6E sec 11. On S Fk Salmon River 5 mi S of Warm Lake. This is the largest spring in the Payette National Forest.

Named for Vulcan, the Roman god of fire.

W

Wabaningo Mountain (Bonner). 4282'. T61N R5W sec 26. Five mi E of Idaho-Washington state border; 2 1/2 mi SSE of Nordman. Also Mount Wabaning.

This name was assigned in 1927 and honors an Indian chief of the Chippewa tribe. There is no local connection. Before 1927 it was known as Hager Mountain.

Waddington Creek (Lemhi). T19N R21E sec 34. Just S of Lost Creek; flows 2 mi W to enter Salmon River.

Nels Watts Waddington had a ranch on this stream.

Wade Creek (Lemhi). T19N R24E sec 1. Originates just S of Pattee Creek; runs W 4 mi to enter Pattee Creek; Lemhi River drainage.

Henry Wade raised horses in this vicinity.

Wades Gulch (Owyhee). Ravine near War Eagle Mountain, runs N into Jordan Creek.

Named for H. R. Wade, one of the party that first discovered gold in Owyhee County. He was the first county treasurer. He died in Silver City in 1865.

Wagner Gulch (Latah). T42N R2W sec 26. Flows 1.8 mi SW to Palouse River.

Named by Edd. F. Helmers in 1936 for a homesteader of that name near the mouth of the gulch.

Wagon Road Gulch (Lemhi). T23N R19E sec 31. Forms near the head of Arrastra Gulch on Pine Creek; runs SW 2 mi to Beaver Creek drainage; Salmon River drainage.

In the early days, supplies were brought by wagon from Salmon to Panther Creek by coming through this gulch. At one point the wagons had to be lowered by cable to continue the journey.

Wagon Town Hill (Latah). T40N R1W sec 23. Early station in area just W of Eustler Meadow, 2 mi E of Helmer, where roads become impassable. Those going to Ruby Creek mines and other points E unloaded their wagons here and went by pack train.

Wagonhammer Creek (Lemhi). T24N R21E sec 27. Forms just S of Stein

Mountain; flows SW 5 1/2 mi to empty into Salmon River near Wagonhammer Spring (3850'), about 2 mi SE of North Fork.

Miners driving teams to the Florence gold fields left iron hardware near the stream.

Wagontown (Owyhee). T4S R4W sec 32. Stage station 1 mi W of DeLamar, on the stage line running from Silver City to Winnemucca, Nevada.

Named for freight wagons.

Waha (Nez Perce). 2400'. T33N R4W sec 9. At the foot of Craig Mountain 19 mi SE of Lewiston, on Lake Waha. Formerly a stage station established by Charles Faunce in 1882. Post office, 1890-1965.

Waha Valley/Prairie. Extends from Lewiston to Craig Mountain, E of Snake River for some distance, and consists of plateaus that rise as steps. Site of the former town of Waha and Lake Waha.

Waha is believed to be an Indian word meaning "subterranean water" or "beautiful," both appropriate to the place.

Walcott, Lake (Blaine/Cassia/Minidoka/Power). T9S R25E sec 1. Reservoir 25 mi long formed by damming the Snake River 10 mi ENE of Rupert.

Named for Charles Doolittle Walcott (1850-1927), who as the Director of the US Geological Survey in 1907 administered the Reclamation Service project, which built the dam creating the reservoir.

Walde Mountain (Idaho). 5221'. T34N R7E sec 31. In the N central part of the county, 7 mi N of Lowell.

Named for a forest ranger.

Walker Hollow (Cassia). T14S R21E sec 19-24. In SW part of the county; originates in Sawtooth National Forest and trends 6 mi E to Goose Creek Reservoir.

Named for David Walker, an early settler on Goose Creek (ca.1870s).

Wall Creek (Clearwater). T40N R9E sec 18. In the NE part of the county. Heads on Wallow Mountain and flows 2 mi SE into Quartz Creek. Clearwater River drainage, 5 mi N of Mush Saddle.

This may be a shortened form of Wallow, since the creek heads at Wallow Mountain.

Wall Point (Idaho). 5620'. T30N R5E sec 5. In the N central part of the county, 14 mi SE of Kooskia. Wall Creek rises on Wall Point and Corral Hill (5968') and flows 6 1/2 mi NW to Sally Ann Creek; S Fk Clearwater River drainage.

Named for a local settler.

Walla Walla Gulch (Boise). T6N R6E sec 30. A 2-mi gulch trending S into Mores Creek 2 mi E of Idaho City; Boise River drainage.

It was named by Adam Lind, of Walla Walla, Washington, in 1864 for his old home town. Originally he had a claim on it.

Wallace (Shoshone). 2744'. T48N R4E sec 27/35. County seat. In the E central part of the county on S Fk Coeur d'Alene River, at the confluence of Canyon, Placer, and Ninemile creeks with S Fk Coeur d'Alene River; I-90 and the NPRR; a mining town. Post office, 1886-.

Originally called Cedar Swamp, because it was located in a swamp and had a heavy stand of cedars. In 1884 it was named Placer Center, for the spate of placer mining in the area. Then it was incorporated in 1888 and named for Colonel W. R. Wallace, owner of the site and member of the first city council.

Wallace Creek (Lemhi). T22N R22E sec 6. Originates in the vicinity of Wallace Lake (8800'); flows NE 2 mi then E 2 1/2 mi to enter Salmon River.

Named for William Wallace, who discovered the Shoo Fly mine in this area in 1871.

Wallace Creek (Lemhi). T24N R17E sec 11. About 4 mi long; heads about 1 mi W of Tincup Hill and runs S to enter Owl Creek; Salmon River drainage.

Named for Wallace St. Clair, who had mining claims in this area.

Wallow Mountain (Clearwater). 6015′. T40N R8E sec 1. Ten mi NW of Kelly Creek Work Center.

Named for the bear wallows here.

Walo Creek (Shoshone). T44N R8E sec 36. In the SE part of the county, a 2-mi W tributary of the St. Joe River. Walo Point is at the head of this stream. Pronounced WAY-low.

Named because the point is literally way-low (wa-lo) on the St. Joe River.

Walter Creek (Lemhi). T17N R25E sec 32. Forms 3 1/2 mi NE of Mill Lake; flows generally NE 5 mi to Lemhi River drainage just SE of the mouth of Ferry Creek; Lemhi River drainage.

Walter Pyeatt ran a small dairy on this creek.

Walters Ferry (Canyon/Owyhee). T1S R2W sec 17. Nine mi NW of Murphy. An important crossing for the southern alternate to the Oregon Trail. Walters Butte (2938′) lies 2 mi E of Walters Ferry. Locally known as Lower Ferry to distinguish it from another ferry in Owyhee County. Post office, 1893-1899.

Emigrants who did not cross Snake River at Three Island Crossing followed the S bank of Snake River to Walters Ferry. It affforded the most direct route between Boise Basin and the Owyhee mines, as well as between San Francisco and Boise. The ferry was operated first by John Fruit and a partner, 1863-1868. Lewellyn and Augusta Walter bought the rights to the ferry and operated it until 1921, when a concrete and steel bridge replaced it.

Named for the last owner of the ferry.

Walters Spring (Lemhi). T14N R28E sec 35. Just N of Eighteenmile Creek.

Named for Ed Walters, who ranched and prospected in this area.

Wapello (Bingham). 4537′. T2S R36E sec 16/17. In the central part of the county, 6 mi N of Blackfoot. An 1890 Mormon settlement that had a school and a post office in the early 1900s.

Named for a Fox Indian chief, Wapello; the name means "light," "dawn," "he is of the morning."

Wapi (Blaine). T8S R28E sec 21. A UPRR station in the SE extremity of the county almost on the Blaine-Power county line. Post office, 1892-1908.

Named by the OSLRR; supposedly an Algonquin word. See Bisuka.

Wapito Point (Clearwater). 6396′. T40N R12E sec 22. Two mi W of the Montana-Idaho line and 8 mi NW of Kelly Creek Work Center. Wapito Creek rises on this point and flows S into Moose Creek; Clearwater River drainage.

The name might come from the Indian term for wild potatoes (arrowroot).

Wapshilla Creek (Idaho). T30N R3W sec 18. On the Salmon River, 6.5 mi above its confluence with Snake River.

The Wapshela (sic) family, Nez Perces, lived on this stream for many years.

War Eagle Mountain (Owyhee). 8000′. T5S R2W sec 18. Two mi S of Silver City. Named for the War Eagle mine, which was located on its slopes. It has been known as Orofino Mountain and as Silver Mountain. Both of these names were given because of the gold and silver mines. Quicksilver Mountain and Cinnebar Mountain were also originally known as War Eagle Mountain.

War Eagle mine was named for an Indian chief.

Warbonnet Peak (Boise/Custer). 10,500'. T9N R12E sec 34,35. On the Boise-Custer county line in the Sawtooth National Recreation Area.

Named for its configuration.

Ward Creek (Shoshone). T46N R7E sec 20. In the E part of the county; a 3-mi tributary of Loop Creek from the W; St. Joe River drainage.

Named for a worker for the Winton brothers who built the Taft RR tunnel. He found a prospect in this vicinity and went back E to get financial support. During the winter of 1911 he was killed by a cook named Forest, because of a grudge. His discovery was known as the Altona mine, for a town in Michigan.

Wardboro (Bear Lake). 5950'. T13S R44E sec 26/35. In the SE part of the county, 2 mi N of Dingle.

Settled by Mormons in 1865 and named Preston for Preston Thomas, a local Mormon leader. When a post office was applied for, the Post Office Department refused that name, and the Edgar, Henry, and Oscar Dalrymple families suggested the name Wardsboro for their home town, Wardsboro, Vermont. Post office, 1894-1910.

Wardner (Shoshone). 2400'. T48N R2/3E sec 12/7. In the W part of the county 2 mi E of Kellogg on Milo Creek. Post office, 1886-.

Founded in 1885 and named first Kentuck, or Kaintuck, both of which were rejected by the Post Office Department; then named Wardner, for James Wardner, a well-known and popular citizen, a promoter of the Bunker Hill and Sullivan mine.

Wardrop Creek (Camas). T1N R14E sec 9. A 2-mi stream flowing SW to Soldier Creek 4 mi N of Soldier, a Camas Creek tributary; Big Wood River drainage.

Jack Wardrop made his home on Soldier Creek in 1883 and raised a family here.

Wards Butte (Lemhi). 8371'. T17N R19E sec 21. On the Lemhi-Custer county border, at the head of Big Hat Creek.

Named for Ward Jones, homesteader in this area.

Wards Gulch (Lemhi). T22N R20E sec 21. Runs S 2 mi to enter Napias Creek drainage; 1/2 mi E of Leesburg; Salmon River drainage.

Named for T. Ward Girton, who along with Elijah Mulkey, Joseph Rapp, William Smith, and F. B. Sharkey sank a shaft near the mouth of the gulch on 16 July 1866 and encountered rich gravel. This started the Leesburg gold rush, which eventually led to the formation of Leesburg, Salmon City, and Lemhi County.

Warm Creek (Teton). T3N R45E sec 25/26. Rises at Sherman Spring and flows NW to empty into Teton River at sec 5; 7 mi long.

Named by Dr. F. V. Hayden, USGS, in 1872, because the water does not freeze.

Warm Lake (Valley). 5300'. T15N R6/7E sec 12 and 13/7 and 18. One mi E of S Fk Salmon River and 1 mi S of Knox Cabin.

Named for the warm springs nearby. The water in the lake is cool.

Warm River (Fremont/Madison). T9N R43E sec 12. Rises in a spring and flows W and SW to N Fk Snake River, 2 mi N of Marysville; fed almost entirely by springs; its flow is quite uniform in view of its drop of 1740' from source to mouth, 200′ in the last 1 1/2 mi. It is 20 mi long; drainage is 145 square miles.

Warm River (Fremont). 5284′. T9N R43E sec 12. Town 4 mi SE of Gerrit Siding. Post office, 1907-1924.

The water temperature of the river is no higher than any of its neighbor streams, but the flow is sufficiently swift to prevent freezing.

Warm Springs Creek (Ada). T4N R3E sec 11. NE tributary of Boise River; rises NW of Lucky Peak and flows SSW to T3N R3E sec 29, at Warm Springs.

A descriptive name.

Warm Springs Creek (Boise). T10 R4E sec 34. Flows 6 mi E into Middle Fk Payette River 2 1/2 mi N of Crouch.

There are hot springs on the creek. Women did their washing there, and people bathed in the natural tubs.

Warren (Idaho). 5908′. T22N R6E sec 12. An early mining town; now a ghost town. In S Idaho County at the head of Slaughter Creek. Post office, 1885-.

James Warren led a prospecting party across the Salmon River Canyon into this area in 1862 and discovered a new gold field.

Warren Creek rises on Warren Summit and flows 18 mi NW then NE to Salmon River, 9 mi N of the town of Warren. Drains Warren Meadow.

Named for James Warren. The name also was transferred to the meadow drained by the creek. Local residents refer to the community as Warrens.

Warren Island (Bonner). T56N R1E sec 3. On Lake Pend Oreille, 1 1/4 mi SW of Hope; 2 1/4 mi ENE of Glengary.

The island is named for General Charles S. Warren, a Civil War veteran, who built a summer home here in 1890. It was once known as Wasunka, "Mother of Twins" with Cottage and Pearl islands being the twins.

Warrens (Canyon). 2390′. T1S R2W sec 23. An agricultural community situated near Melba.

Named for a local resident.

Warrens Meadows (Latah). Early name for Bovill, which see.

Named for Francis Warren, early settler in the Bovill area.

Wasatch Range (Caribou/Utah). T9/10/11S R41E in Idaho. Extends from the bend in Bear River at Soda Springs S to the mouth of San Pete River in San Pete County, Utah, including the Bear River Range.

Wasatch is a Ute word, said to mean "mountain pass."

Wash Creek (Boise). T9N R4E sec 36. Rises on the NW slope of Mineral Mountain and flows 4 mi N into the S Fk Payette River 1 1/2 mi S of Garden Valley.

Wash Kegers homesteaded on this creek.

Washington (Idaho). T22N R6E. Founded shortly after gold was discovered in the Warren Mining District in 1862 and named to honor the capital of the Union; became the county seat in 1868, but lost the seat to Mt. Idaho in 1875. Formerly called Washington in Warren Camp, since it was within that district. Post office, 1868-1881, when it was absorbed by Warren.

Washington County. County seat, Weiser. Established in 1879 and named for the first president of the United States; included the area now in Adams County until 1911.

Bounded on the N by Adams County, on the E by Adams and Gem Counties, on the S by Payette County, and on the W by Oregon.

Washington Creek (Clearwater). T39N R7E sec 22. Rises in the central part of the county 7 mi NE of Jaype and flows erratically 12 mi NE to N Fk Clearwater River.

The name was given by miners when this was still part of Washington Territory.

Washington Creek (Custer). T7N R16E sec 30. Rises in Washington Lake and flows S to Germania Creek; E Fk Salmon River drainage. Washington Basin lies E of Washington Peak. Washington Lake lies about 3 mi NE of Washington Peak; accessible up Fourth of July Creek. Washington Peak (10,527′) is in the White Cloud Peaks.

George Washington Blackman, a black miner, prospected this creek. All these features are probably named for him, as he was an important and popular person in this area. Another feature is named Blackman Peak.

Washington Gulch (Boise). T6N R6E sec 17. Trends 3 1/2 mi SE into Mores Creek 5 mi NE of Idaho City; Boise River drainage.

The name comes from the Washington mine, which was located on the banks of the gulch. The mine was named for George Washington.

Washoe (Payette). 2143′. T8N R5W sec 4. An early ferry, store, and settlement near Welch Island on the Snake River; said to have been owned and operated by Alex Stewart and E. D. Holbrook in the 1880s. Post office, 1873-1898.

Named for the Washoe tribe in northwestern Nevada; Washo, "person."

Watchtower Peak (Idaho). 8780′. T29N R16E sec 20. On the Idaho-Montana boundary, 10 mi SW of Trapper Peak, Montana.

Named because this was a USFS lookout.

Waterdog Lake (Custer). T9N R16E. Lake 400′ long, one of the Boulder Chain Lakes.

Named for the waterdogs (newts) found in the lake.

Waterfall Canyon/Creek (Bonneville). T1N R45E sec 12. Extends 2 mi to N in the NE quadrant, in Targhee National Forest near the Idaho-Wyoming line. The creek flows 1 1/2 mi N into Upper Palisades Lake; Snake River drainage.

Named for the waterfall in the creek.

Waterfall Creek (Lemhi). T20N R14E sec 3. Heads in the vicinity of Puddin Mountain; runs generally W 4 mi to enter Middle Fk Salmon River near Big Creek Bridge.

Named for the large waterfall at its confluence with the Middle Fork of Salmon River.

Waterhole Creek (Latah). T42N R4W sec 21. Rises between Crane and Gold creeks and flows S 2.3 mi to Gold Creek; Palouse River drainage.

Named for Waterhole Spring, a natural hole containing water.

Waterspout Draw (Owyhee). T7S R4E. In the Chalk Hills area.

The excessive flood discharge through a stream drainage following a cloudburst is called a "waterspout" in some regions.

Watson Mountain (Bonner). T61N R4W sec 6. Located 5 1/2 mi E of Idaho-Washington border; 2 mi WSW of Distillery Bay.

Named for a local resident, 1926 or 1927.

Watson Peak (Custer). 10,453′. T9N R15E sec 1/2. Eight mi S of Robinson Bar in the Sawtooth NRA.

Named for a miner who prospected in the area in the late 1890s.

Waugh Gulch (Lemhi). T16N R27E sec 5. Heads E of Grizzly Mountain; flows 2 mi E to enter Canyon Creek drainage 6 mi NE of Leadore; Lemhi

River drainage. Waugh Mountain (8882'), T25N R14E sec 19, is situated on the border between Idaho and Lemhi county about 1 1/2 mi due N of Lost Packer Peak.

Named for Alec Waugh, an early-day stage driver and employee of the Gilmore and Pittsburgh RR.

Wayan (Caribou). 6438'. T5S R43E sec 23/24. In the NE part of the county, 3 mi SE of Grays Lake and 9 mi NE of Blackfoot Reservoir. Post office, 1894-.

Named for Wayne and Ann Nevils, who housed the first post office.

Weaver Creek (Clearwater). T35N R5E sec 11. In the SW extremity of the county, 7 mi E of Weippe. Flows 4 mi SW into Jim Brown Creek; Clearwater River drainage.

Named for a homesteader, Joe Weaver.

Webb (Nez Perce). 1336'. T35N R4W sec 28/27. Town in the center of the county, SW of Lewiston Orchards. Post office, 1901-1921.

Webb Creek. T35N R4W. Flows 15 mi NW to Sweetwater Creek. Formerly Soldiers Meadow Creek. Webb Hill (2323'), the highest promontory in Webb Ridge, is 3 mi SW of Webb.

Named for a Nez Perce Indian, Wapp (sic).

Webster Range (Caribou). T6/7/8S R44/45E. Part of the Peale Mountains; extends in a curving course from the upper waters of Lanes Creek, a distance of about 25 mi between Lanes and Diamond creeks on the W, and Crow, Tygee, and Stump creeks on the E. Its highest summit is Draney Peak (8151').

Named for Webster Canyon, where a man named Webster settled.

Weippe (Clearwater). 3000'. T35N R4E sec 15. Town. Pronounced WEE-ipe.

A site where Indians assembled for councils and camas digging, and where

they camped on the way to buffalo grounds. In 1805 and 1806 Lewis and Clark came through here and enjoyed the hospitality of the Nez Perce. In 1877 it was the scene of the retreat by the Nez Perce from General Oliver O. Howard. Post office, 1872-.

The name came from an Indian word "o-yi-pe" or "o ippe", which may mean "gathering place," although some say the Indians had no meaning for the term.

Weiser (Washington). 2115'. T11N R5W sec 32. County seat. In the SW part of the county at the confluence of the Weiser and Snake rivers. Post office, 1866-.

In 1864 Reuben Olds established a ferry at Farewell Bend on the Snake River. The same year a settlement was established 10 mi above the ferry by Jacob Weiser, William Logan, Thomas Galloway, and others.

This town was named Weiser, probably from the founder; but some say for the Weiser River.

Weiser River (Washington/Adams). T11N R5W sec 32. E tributary of Snake River at Weiser. Rises at an altitude of 5500' in Payette National Forest, Adams County; flows S, SW, and W 85 mi to Snake River, altitude 2110'. Its Middle Fork, T15N R1W, about 5 mi SW of Council, is 15 mi long and has a drainage of 75 square miles. W Fk Weiser at Fruitvale, T17N R1W, is about 18 mi long. Major tributary: Crane Creek.

The origin of the name is in dispute. Peter Wiser/Weiser of the Lewis and Clark Expedition is probably the source, for Wisers River appears on Arrowsmith's 1818 map. Despite this evidence, there are proponents for others: a trapper named Jacob Wayer/Wager, a member of Donald McKenzie's party, 1818; Jacob Weiser, a prospector in the Florence gold rush, 1861, who is in all likelihood the same

Jacob Weiser who was one of the founders of the town of Weiser.

Weiser Valley lies along Weiser River between Weiser and Starkey; about 40 mi long by 2-5 mi wide, a fertile valley.

Weitas Creek (Clearwater). T38N R8E sec 15. Rises in Idaho County on Indian Grave Butte and flows W, then N about 26 mi into N Fk Clearwater River. A second Weitas Creek empties into N Fk Clearwater River at T39N R4E sec 18.

This name developed as a euphemism from the original name, Wet Ass. The name may have originated with the soldiers in Howard's Nez Perce campaign or with the engineers laying road here. The USFS changed it.

Welcome Lake (Lemhi). T21N R16E sec 21. In Bighorn Crags, about 1 mi NE of Skyhigh Lake and 2 mi SW of Cathedral Rock.

Named ca.1938 by Lester Gutzman and an exhausted USFS trail crew, because they thought the little lake was a welcome sight after clearing trail through The Crags this far.

Wellesley (Latah). T41N R5W sec 7. WIMRR station 4 mi N of Viola.

One of 8 WIM stations bearing the names of colleges.

Wellington Creek (Bonner). T57N R2E sec 15. Heads 4 1/4 mi E of Hope; flows 3 mi NE then 1 1/2 mi SE into Lightning Creek 10 mi N of Clark Fork. Tributary: S Fk Wellington Creek.

Named for Wellington Sharai, a miner in the Hope area.

Welty (Bonner). Early town. See Dover. Post office, 1909-1914.

Wendell (Gooding). 3467'. T7S R15E sec 33. In the SE part of the county, 12 mi S of Gooding, on State Highway 25 and the UPRR. Post office, 1908-.

Established in 1907 and named for Wendell Kuhn, son of W. H. Kuhn,

financier of the Twin Falls North Side Irrigation Project.

Wendover Creek (Idaho). T37N R13E sec 35. W Fk Wendover Creek flows 2.8 mi SE to Wendover Creek, which flows 3.2 mi S to Lochsa River 11 mi S of Rhodes Peak. This stream drains Wendover Ridge, on which there is an old trail that Lewis and Clark followed on their westbound expedition in 1805.

Named for a trapper who worked this stream.

Wepah Creek (Latah). T42N R3W sec 1. Flows 5 mi SW to E Fk Meadow Creek; Palouse River drainage; runs parallel to and about.5 mi S of Piah Creek.

Named by W. H. Daugs, USFS ranger, in 1928 with the Indian word wepah "dry," because, like Piah Creek, the area had been burned over and the stream would dry up every summer.

Wesleyan (Gooding). 3576'. T6S R15E sec 6/8. Formerly a Post office, at Gooding College, a Methodist institution. Post office, 1925-19??.

Named for John Wesley, founder of Methodism.

West Plowboy Mountain (Bonner). 5140'. T63N R5W sec 26. Located 3 3/4 mi E of Idaho-Washington border; 3 mi W of Upper Priest Lake. Also Plowboy Mountain.

Named because the long ravines in its rocky slopes give it the appearance of having been plowed.

Westlake (Idaho). 4080'. T32N R1W sec 18. In the NW part of the county, 9 mi S of Ferdinand on the edge of the Craig Mountain timber belt; 5 mi from Salmon River, which runs through a gorge at this point. Post office, 1893- .

Westlake townsite was located in 1887 by J. B. Rice as a preemption. A store was built in 1889. Formerly Mason, for Mr. and Mrs. Thomas Mason. Rivalry with a newer townsite,

Morrow, resulted in a temporary discontinuance of the name Westlake.

Named for the wife of the founder, Sarah Westlake Rice.

Westmond (Bonner). T55N R2W sec 5. Town 2 mi N of Cocolalla on US 95. Westmond Creek, a tributary of Cocolalla Lake, lies 1/4 mi W of Westmond.

Named for George Westmond, president of the Westmond Lumber Company, which had a sawmill here.

Weston (Franklin). 4605′. T16S R38E sec 14. In the SW part of the county, 5 mi from the Utah line and W of Franklin. Post office, 1873-.

First called West Town because of this location. The second Mormon settlement in Idaho (1865) when 15 families crossed Bear River on ice to make their homes here.

Named by Ezra T. Benson because it was the only settlement W of Franklin at that time.

Wet Meadows (Latah). T41N R2W sec 25/36. Five mi due W of Bovill.

So called because water stands here during the rainy season.

Weyer Gulch (Shoshone). T48N R4E sec 35. A 1.5-mi gulch from the NW to S Fk Coeur d'Alene River 1.5 mi E of Wallace.

A man named Anderson owned a sawmill at the mouth of this gulch and a man named Weyer owned two 40-acre tracts farther up the gulch. Some called the gulch Anderson and others, Weyer. The USGN decided the question in 1955.

Wheat Creek (Lemhi). NW of Corn Creek; heads in vicinity from Corn Lake NW to Skunk Camp, and flows SW 2 1/2 mi to enter Salmon River.

See Corn Creek. The name was given because of the creek's nearness to Corn Creek.

Wheaton Mountain (Bonneville). 7000′. T3N R42/43E sec 7/12. In the NE quadrant.

Named for Charles Wheaton, settler.

Wheetip Creek (Lemhi). T15N R28E sec 3. Originates 1 1/2 mi SE of Mountain Peak; flows N 2 mi to enter Big Bear Creek; Lemhi River drainage. Pronounced WHEET-ip.

Possibly means "to defecate" in Shoshoni. A local story says that an Indian who was dining with a family in this vicinity could eat no more pie until he wheetipped.

Whiskey Bob Creek (Idaho). T24N R6E sec 3. A 3-mi tributary of Salmon River, 26 mi E of Riggins.

Named for Whiskey Bob, an old miner, who was buried at the head of this creek under a pile of rocks and antlers.

Whiskey Creek (Boise). T8N R5E sec 2. Flows 2 mi S into Danskin Creek 11 mi W of Lowman; Payette River drainage.

Whiskey Creek (Boise). T7N R5E sec 15/16. Flows 2 1/2 mi W into Grimes Creek 2 mi N of Centerville; Boise River drainage.

Stills were located on these creeks.

Whiskey Creek (Clearwater). T36N R2E sec 10. Rises on Whiskey Butte (4407′) and flows 13 mi SW into Orofino Creek; Clearwater River drainage. The butte is 9 mi SW of Headquarters.

Some say the name came from the saloon that was located on the creek. It was just outside the Nez Perce Indian Reservation, so much whiskey was sold to the Indians. Others, that it originated from a pack string taking whiskey from Walla Walla to Pierce in 1861 and getting stopped by snow. The party camped on what was called Whiskey Flats with their cargo of 20-gallon kegs; however, when it was possible to continue, they discovered every keg was empty. The packers had to return to Walla Walla for another load.

Whiskey Mountain (Owyhee). 6100'. T3S R4W sec 15. Four mi N of The Democrats.

One local story says that when an army train was going into Camp Lyon, a wagon loaded with barrels of whiskey was lost and the load was broken up. Another version says it was a freighter rather than an army train. Still another: that since the mountain is steep, men would stop and have a swig of whiskey en route. Most often called Whiskey Hill by the local residents.

Whiskey Rock (Bonner). T54N R1W sec 4. Rock formation on W shore of lower Lake Pend Oreille 5 1/2 mi N of Lakeview.

Two folk etymologies for this name: one says that the name was given because of a bet made on a swimming match, the winner to receive a jug of whiskey; the other that the name was given because two men were forced to stay here with only their bedding and a jug of whiskey after being caught in a storm on Lake Pend Oreille.

Whiskey Spring (Lemhi). T24N R20E sec 14. At the head of Buster Gulch about 4 1/2 mi NE of Indianola Ranger Station.

An old whiskey barrel was found at this spring by USFS personnel.

Whiskey Springs Creek (Lemhi). T17N R27E sec 28. Flows along Lemhi County-Beaverhead County (Montana) line 2 mi, SW 2 mi, then SE 1 mi to enter Canyon Creek; Lemhi River drainage.

Freighters hauling whiskey from Red Rock, Montana, to Salmon, Idaho, camped here for a night before continuing the trip. It is reported that the whis-

key flowed rather freely during some of these stop-overs.

White Bird Creek (Idaho). T28N R1E sec 22. A stream about 6 mi long heading at the junction of its N (9 mi long) and S (12 mi long) fks and flowing generally SW to Salmon River about 15 mi SW of Grangeville.

White Bird village lies at the mouth of this stream in W central Idaho County near US 95. In 1874 Samuel Benedict built a store here, which was destroyed by the Indians in 1877 and rebuilt by H. C. Brown on the townsite. Post office, 1866-.

White Bird Hill (4613') lies about 4 mi NE of White Bird and 8 mi SW of Grangeville.

White Bird Ridge, 6 mi long with highest elevation of 5421', trends SSW from the junction of Rapid and Little Salmon rivers, along the E bank of Rapid River, to Rattlesnake Creek; 40 mi SSW of Grangeville.

Named for a chief of a Nez Perce Indian band.

White Cloud Peaks (Custer). A group of serrated peaks with elevations above 11,000' in the Salmon River Mountains, about 18 mi E of the Sawtooth Range and 35 mi SW of Challis; the group of peaks encompasses an area about 13 mi across. Not: Whitecloud Peaks.

Named because at times metamorphic silicates cause them to look white when viewed from a distance.

White Creek (Clearwater). T38N R3E sec 22. In the SW quadrant of the county. A 2-mi stream that flows NW into Dworshak Reservoir.

This may have been named for homesteader Bill White.

White Creek (Lemhi). T19N R25E sec 19. Forms just N of the headwaters of Sharkey Creek; flows NW 2 mi to enter Agency Creek; Lemhi River drainage.

Two suggested derivations: two informants say it was named for Harry White, who had a ranch here about 1908 and also had a transfer business in Salmon. Another informant says it was named for the light-colored soil in the area.

White Goat Creek (Lemhi). T16N R17E sec 5. Heads in the vicinity of White Goat Lake; flows NW 2 1/2 mi to enter Camas Creek; Middle Fk Salmon River drainage.

Numerous Rocky Mountain goats inhabit this area.

White Horse Basin (Lemhi). T21N R19E at the intersection of sec 10/11/14/15. Four mi NE of Cobalt.

Named for a wild white horse that used to live in the area.

White Knob Mountains (Custer). Formerly called Cabin Mountains, these form a rectangle W of Mackay, lying between Lost River on the E, NE, and NW and Antelope Creek on the SE. Their E slopes are mounded hills, like knobs. They are visible on State Highway 27 between Chilly and Darlington.

Named for the rounded limestone peaks, mostly covered with snow, though believed by many to have been named for White Knob mine.

White Knob 7800'. T7N R23E sec 31. Ghost town about 5 mi SW of Mackay; founded in 1885, after the gold rush of 1881-84. Post office, 1916-ca.1936.

Named for the first mine in the area, the White Knob.

White Owl Butte (Madison). 6323'. T5N R41E sec 13. In the E part of the county at the head of Dry Canyon; rises out of the surrounding hills and towers above the land.

Named by early travelers for the owls that roosted and nested here.

White Pine Creek (Clearwater). T40N R6E sec 23. In the N central part of the county between Thompson and Beaver buttes, flows 2 mi E into Beaver Creek at sec 23; Clearwater River drainage.

Named for the white-pine forest here.

White Pine Gulch (Latah). T42N R2W sec 12. Seventh of the 10 named gulches running parallel to each other and emptying into N Fk Palouse River from the N.

Named for the stand of white pine that was located in this area. See Banks Gulch.

White Quartz Ridge (Bonner). T55N R1E sec 20. Heads at Schafer Lookout; extends 1 1/2 mi S to Granite Creek.

Named for the quartz deposits.

White Sand Creek (Idaho). T37N R14E sec 34. See Coltkilled Creek.

White Valley Mountain (Lemhi). 9986'. T15N R17E sec 21. About 1 mi NE of Twin Peaks, and 5 mi NE of Parker Mountain.

Soil composition gives the area a whitish color.

Whitehouse Pond (Idaho). T37N R13E sec 36. A small pond on the N bank of Lochsa River 3 mi W of the confluence of Crooked and Coltkilled creeks.

Named by Ralph Space, USFS, because Joseph Whitehouse, a member of the Lewis and Clark Expedition, mentions passing a small pond on 15 Sept 1805.

Whitley Bottom (Payette). T7N R5W sec 5-7. A low-lying grassland located along the E bank of Snake River in the central part of the county. Big Whitley Gulch lies 1 mi S of Whitley Bottom. Little Whitley Gulch is just E of Whitley Bottom.

Whitley is a pioneer-family name.

Whitney (Franklin). 4595'. T16S R40E sec 6. In the S part of the county, just N of Franklin.

A Mormon settlement of 1869, a farming community. Post office, 1892-1939.

Named for Orson F. Whitney, Mormon bishop.

Whoop-um-up Creek (Boise). T7N R7E sec 10. Flows 2 mi E into Edna Creek; Crooked River, 8 mi S of Lowman.

Named by Moses Kempner, a stage driver who settled near this creek. The stage road went by the creek, and he had to whoop and yell at his horses to get them over the nearby hill.

Wickahoney Crossing (Owyhee). T10S R4E sec 21. Crossing on Wickahoney Creek, a 36-mi tributary of Bruneau River from the SW.

Wickahoney (4786'). T11S R4W sec 22. Nine mi NE of Grasmere; once a stage station on the stage road between Bruneau and Mountain City, Nevada. Post office, 1895-1911.

A Shoshoni Indian name already on the land when the emigrants came. It means "beaver," of which there were many.

Wickiup Creek (Owyhee). T8S R3W sec 14. Flows 6 mi NE into Josephine Creek; Owyhee River drainage. Pronounced wick-ee-UP.

A wickiup is a Shoshoni shelter; apparently there was one or more on the creek.

Widow Mountain (Shoshone). 6781'. T43N R4E sec 22. In the SE part of the county, 17.5 mi SE of Avery.

Two widows held a homestead near this mountain. Reported by forester R.H. Rutledge, 1919.

Wiessner, Mount (Kootenai). 6178'. T48N R1E sec 9. In the SE extremity of Kootenai County.

Named in 1859 by John Mullan for a topographer with the Mullan Expedition. The Mullan Trail passed on the N side of this promontory.

Wigwams Mountain, The (Boundary). T62N R3W sec 15/22. In Kaniksu National Forest.

Local name descriptive of the two small peaks on its top.

Wilburn (Washington). 4067'. T11N R2W sec 31. An early community and post office, 16 mi SE of Midvale on Big Flat Creek, tributary of Crane Creek, and 6 mi W of Wilburn Butte. Post office (under the name Wilburus), 1891-1924.

Named for a Mr. Wilburn, who owned the land on Big Flat Creek. But the Postal Department confused the name on the post office application and wrote it Wilburus, instead of Wilburns.

Wild Goat Creek (Boise). T6N R4E sec 26. Flows 4 mi SE into Grimes Creek 5 mi S of New Centerville; Boise River drainage.

At one time there were many mountain goats in this area.

Wild Horse Butte (Owyhee). 2776'. T3S R1E sec 27/28. One mi S of Thomas Flat, near the Snake River.

Located in the wild horse ranges of the county.

Wild Horse Creek (Elmore). T2S R13E sec 6. Rises in the Mount Bennett Hills, Elmore County, and flows SE to Camas Creek; Big Wood River drainage.

Named for a wild horse that ran here. She was a blue roan named Pigeon, so wild no one could corral her.

Wildcat Creek (Lemhi). T16N R27E sec 3. Forms near the head of Rocky Canyon; flows N 3 mi to enter Cruikshank Creek; Lemhi River drainage.

Many wildcats were found here in the early days.

Wilder (Canyon). 2240′. T4N R5W sec 14/23. Town about 4 mi N of the Homedale-Snake River Bridge, and 12 mi W of Caldwell. Post office, 1916-.

The town was named for Marshall P. Wilder, editor of a women's magazine, *The Delineator*, in return for a favorable article about the place. This more or less thwarted investors, who wanted to name it Golden Gate, and who had great plans for making the spot a second San Francisco.

Known for one month in 1916 as Wilderia.

Wildhorse Creek (Adams). T18N R5W sec 36. Rises SE of the Seven Devils Mountains at the junction of Bear and Lick creeks and Crooked River in the Payette National Forest and flows 14 mi SW to Snake River just N of Heath. The elevation drops from 5000′ at the source to 1790′ at the mouth. Wildhorse Falls about 1/4 mi from the mouth of No Business Creek, a small tributary of Wildhorse Creek.

Wildhorse. 5257′. T18N R4W sec 13. Community located on Wildhorse Creek. Post office, 1907-ca.1965.

In the 1880s John McCullough owned a herd of horses that went wild and ranged throughout the drainage of the creek, until they were killed off by prospectors and other ranchers who feared the wild horses would lead their own astray.

Wilford (Fremont). T7N R40/41E sec 24/19. Town 4 mi S of St. Anthony. Post office, 1889-1904.

Named for Leonard Wilford Hardy, presiding bishop of the LDS Church when the town was established ca.1879.

Wilkeson, Mount (Bonner). Across Lake Pend Oreille from Hope.

Named for an NPRR secretary.

Wilkins Gulch (Owyhee). T6S R6E sec 2/3. Located along the Snake River 3 mi NE of Bruneau. Runs W into C. J. Strike Reservoir. Wilkins Island lies in the Snake River near Bruneau.

Named for the Kitty Wilkins family, who ranched near Bruneau.

Williams Creek (Clearwater). T39N R13E sec 22. In the extreme NE part of the county. Rises on Rhodes Peak and flows NW into S Fk Kelly Creek; Clearwater River drainage. Williams Lake and Williams Peak (7705′) lie at the head of this creek, 3 mi NW of Blacklead Mountain.

Named for Lafayette "Lafe" Williams, who located mines in the Blacklead country.

Williams Creek (Lemhi). T20N R14E sec 15. A short stream, less than 1/2 mi long; flows W to enter Middle Fk Salmon River.

Named for an early-day prospector who was a partner of Joe Porterfield and Jess Woolard.

Williams Creek (Lemhi). T20N R22E sec 7. Heads near Williams Creek Summit; flows E 9 mi to enter Salmon River.

Named for Henry V. Williams.

Williams Peak (Custer). 10,700′. T10N R12E sec 36. In the Sawtooth Range, 5.5 mi SW of Stanley.

Named for David M. Williams, local outfitter and guide who with Mr. and Mrs. Robert Underhill made the first ascent of this peak in 1934.

Williams Peak (Valley). T19N R6E sec 1. In Payette National Forest 3 mi E of the confluence of E Fk of S Fk Salmon River.

Named for Hubert C. Williams, former forest ranger in Idaho, who as a lieutenant in World War I leading his troops of Company D, 20th Engineers, in an attack on a German position was fatally wounded.

Willis Gulch (Boise). T9N R8E sec 24. Rises on the W slope of Jackson Peak

Lookout (8124') and flows 3 mi N into the S Fk Payette River 8 mi E of Lowman.

The Willis family had a ranch near the mouth of this creek.

Willow Creek (Camas). T1S R16E sec 15. Rises in the mountains on the Blaine-Camas county line and flows 20 mi generally SW then SE to Camas Creek, 12 mi E of Fairfield; Malad River drainage.

Willow as a place name occurs where there is or has been a heavy growth of willow along a stream. The name of the stream may transfer to other features, such as promontories and meadows. (There are 75 willow names in 28 counties of Idaho.)

Wilmot Gulch (Lemhi). T12N R29E sec 28. Runs SW 2 1/2 mi to enter Birch Creek Valley 1 mi SE of Nicholia.

Named for Bill Wilmot, an old rancher and miner who patented ground in this vicinity in 1921.

Wilson (Owyhee). 2300'. T1S R3W sec 12. Town on Wilson Creek; SE of Givens Springs and W of Walters Ferry. Post office, 1897-1925.

Wilson Bluff lies 6 1/2 mi W of the townsite and 2 mi NW of Wilson Peak (5400'). Wilson Creek rises on the bluff and flows 15 mi generally E to Snake River.

These locations were named for Marvin R. Wilson, the first settler in the area.

Wilson Bar (Idaho). T27N R1E sec 24. On the Salmon River, 16 mi N of Riggins.

Named for Howard Allen "Haywire" Wilson.

Wilson Butte Cave (Jerome). T7S R19E sec 27. In the N central part of the county, 11 mi N of Eden. Named for Wilson Price Hunt, explorer for the Pacific Fur Company in 1811.

Wilson Creek (Clearwater). T35N R4E sec 34. In the SW part of the county. Flows 4 mi W into Miles Creek 5 mi SE of Weippe; Clearwater River drainage.

Thomas Wilson and his family homesteaded here in the late 1800s.

Wilson Creek (Lemhi). T20N R14E sec 34. Heads in the vicinity of Wilson Lake; runs S 4 mi, SW and finally W for about 7 mi to enter Middle Fk Salmon River. Wilson Lake is in the Bighorn Crags, just S of Fishfin Ridge. Wilson Mountain (9561') lies about halfway between the mouth of the creek and Wilson Lake; about 3 mi NW of Sugarloaf Mountain.

Named for "Puddin River" Wilson, who ran a saloon in Yellowjacket during the early mining days (1870s).

Wimpey Creek (Lemhi). T20N R23E sec 3. Heads on the Idaho-Montana border; flows SW 7 mi to enter Lemhi River 1/2 mi NE of Baker.

Named for Major William Wimpey, who settled on this stream in 1867.

Winchester (Lewis). 3968'. T34N R2W sec 31. Town in the W central part of the county, 35 mi S of Lewiston on US 95. Post office, 1899-. Old Winchester came into existence shortly after the Nez Perce Indian Reservation opened for white settlement. The town was moved to its present site when the Craig Mountain Lumber Company constructed its sawmill in 1909-1910.

The town was named at a meeting in 1908. Since most of the rifles brought to the meeting were Winchesters, the people chose that name.

Windy Point (Bonner). T55N R1E sec 7. On the S side of Lake Pend Oreille, 2 mi W of Green Monarch mine.

Named because there is usually a strong wind here.

Winecup Creek (Cassia). T15S R19E sec 31. Rises in the SW corner of the county, Sawtooth National Forest; flows SE 2 mi to its confluence with Goose Creek.6 mi E of the Twin Falls line and 5.6 mi N of the Nevada line.

Named for the Wine Cup Cattle Company, with headquarters on Goose Creek and on the Nevada side of the mountains, and with a herd of cattle in the area of Tincup Creek.

Winona (Idaho). 3282'. T32N R3E sec 8. A logging community in the NW part of the county, 17 mi NE of Cottonwood; formerly named Lowe, for the first postmaster in 1898. Post office, 1898-1945.

Founded by Daniel M. Day, a Montana freighter, who homesteaded 160 acres in 1896. Soon thereafter, Day laid out a townsite and within 6 months what had been his wheat ranch was a little town, dedicated in 1905 as Lowe. Mail was constantly being missent to Lane; therefore in 1906 Arthur McBoyle's widow, Katherine, decided to change the name. Since they were near an Indian reservation, she wanted an Indian name; but "Nez Perce" having already been chosen, she selected Winona, a word from an Indian tribe in Minnesota.

Winsper (Clark). 4872'. T10N R34E sec 31. A farming and livestock area in the SE part of the county 2.5 mi NE of Lidy Hot Springs. Post office, 1915-1948.

Named for the first and apparently only postmaster.

Winter Camp (Owyhee). 3910'. T10S R8E sec 15. Town 21 mi SE of Bruneau; a stopping place for ranchers coming from Bruneau to Three Creek.

It received its name because ranchers from Bruneau wintered their cattle here. Sometimes called Winter Camp Ranch.

Winter Camp Butte (4301') lies 5 mi NE of Winter Camp.

Winter Camp Butte (Owyhee). 4418'. T9S R8E sec 21/22/27. Located 5.7 mi SSW of Pot Hole Reservoir, 25 mi SW of Glenns Ferry.

Named for an old stage stop.

Winters Blowout (Power). T6S R29E sec 17/18. A depression in the Great Rift .3 mi long; 5 mi SE of Crystal Ice Caves and 14 mi WSW of Aberdeen. Winters Ranch lies 2 mi S of the depression.

Named for Adolph Winter, who homesteaded this area in 1914 and lived here until his death in the 1940s.

Wiseboy Lake (Idaho). T27N R6E sec 34. Located .5 mi N of Buffalo Hump and 20 mi SW of Elk City. The larger lake is.25 mi long.

Named for the Wiseboy mine, located 1 mi N of the lakes.

Withington Creek (Lemhi). T20N R23E sec 3. Originates 1 mi N of Sal Mountain; flows generally NE 7 mi to enter Lemhi River.

Named for Lester Penny Withington, a pioneer settler, who had one of the largest herds of cattle in the valley. He patented his land in 1886.

Wittenburg Draw (Benewah). T46N R1E sec 20. A canyon on the N side of St. Joe River near the town of St. Joe; 4 mi long, trends NE to SW.

Emil Wittenburg homesteaded in this area.

Wolf Canyon/Creek (Bonneville). T2N R43E sec 15. Extends 4 mi NE to SW in the NE quadrant. The creek flows 4 mi SW into Pine Creek; Snake River drainage.

Named for the wolf, once a visitor to the area.

Wolf Creek (Latah). T42N R1E sec 31. Flows 1.8 mi S to Porcupine Creek; Potlatch River drainage.

One of three creeks bearing animal names within an area .5 mi long. An office name.

Wolf Fang Peak (Valley). 9014'. T21N R8E sec 12. Near Elk Summit. It is distinctive in a setting of sharp crags, overlooking a deep canyon.

The name is descriptive of the shape of this peak, long and sharp.

Wolf Mountain (Caribou). 7437'. T9S R43E sec 1. Promontory in the E part of the county on the E side of Webster Range.

From the earliest days of settlement in this area, wolves preyed on herds of sheep; as late as 1922 the Dry Valley Cattlemen's Association paid William Cozzens $180 in bounties on wolves he had killed. Cozzens had brought in wolf pelts from the Johnson Creek and Henry Peak areas in 1922 and the Fall Creek Basin Cattle Association had paid $4400 for wolf-pup scalps in 1921.

The presence of wolves in Caribou County was the source of this name.

Wolffs Point (Bonner). T60N R5W sec 19. Near Luby Bay, Priest Lake.

Named for regional forester Meyer Wolff, who landscaped the area several times until told not to do so.

Wolverine Canyon (Bingham). T1/2S R38/39E sec 31. In the NE part of the county, drained by Wolverine Creek; 15 mi E of Blackfoot. Wolverine Creek rises in Blackfoot Mountains, at the confluence of Sellars and Williams creeks, and flows 17 mi generally W to empty into Blackfoot River; drains a green, willow-lined canyon with rocky cliffs on either side.

Named by Presto Burrell, 1889, because he had killed a wolverine here.

The bench where he settled was called Presto Bench.

Wood (Ada). T3N R1E sec 3. An old BVTRR station in the NW part of the county.

Woods Gulch. T5N R1E sec 9. Flows SW 2 mi to T5N R1E sec 28, N of Eagle Island.

Named for W. E. Woods, who homesteaded on the gulch in 1863, owned a ranch on Eagle Island in 1864, and the same year, with five other settlers, constructed an irrigation ditch on Eagle Island.

Woodfell (Latah). T42N R3W sec 23/24/35/36. A general store and halfway house N of Harvard. Post office, 1903-1916.

Named by a packer, farmer, and manager of several enterprises named Johnson, perhaps for the great amount of timber felled in this area. Formerly Hoodoo.

Woodland (Idaho). 2500'. T34N R3E sec 3/10. In the NW part of the county, 9 mi N of Kamiah, 35 mi N of Grangeville, and 5 1/2 mi E of Pardee; a mining town at the terminus of a branch of the NPRR. Post office, 1898-ca.1935.

Settled in the 1890s mostly by Kansans.

Named for its location in the middle of a flat, wooded country.

Woodland Creek (Adams). T18N R1E sec 6. Rises about 1 1/2 mi SW of Pine Ridge and flows 1 1/2 mi E to Weiser River.

The C. E. Woodland family moved to the Weiser area from Iowa in 1883, perhaps to this creek.

Woodrat Mountain (Idaho). 4983'. T33N R5/6E sec 24/19. In the N central part of the county, 8 1/2 mi NW of Lowell; in the Clearwater Mountains.

Named because an old log cabin located here was full of wood rats.

Woodruff (Oneida). 4400′. T16S R36E sec 15/22. In the SE part of the county, 10 mi S of Malad City, on Malad River. Settled by Mormons in 1891 and named for a former president of the LDS Church, Wilford Woodruff. The name is preserved in Woodruff Road. Post office, 1894-1909.

Woods Canyon/Creek (Bonneville). T3N R42E sec 11. Extends 2 mi N to S in the NE quadrant. The creek flows 2 mi S into Snake River.

Named because of the timbered canyon.

Woodside (Lewis). T34N R2W sec 20. Abandoned town 4 mi N of the present town of Winchester in the W part of the county. Woodside served as a trading point for sheep and lumbermen until the RR took trade to Winchester. Post office, 1903-1913.

Named by Alexander Marr, the town's promoter and first postmaster, for its location on the edge of heavy timber.

Woodtick Creek (Lemhi). T18N R16E sec 17. Originates near Woodtick Summit; flows NW 6 mi to enter Camas Creek; Middle Fk Salmon River drainage.

Named because ticks infest this area.

Woodville (Bingham). 4635′. T1N R37E sec 17/18. An agricultural area 2 mi N of Shelley. In the early days, settlers came to this area to cut and haul wood for both fuel and construction. Those who stayed in the area dug irrigation ditches on the W side. Post office, 1901-1905.

Woof Creek (Boise). T8N R4E sec 23. Rises on Alder Creek Summit and flows 3 1/2 mi S into Granite Creek 2 mi S of Placerville; Boise River drainage.

Originally Wolf Creek. A USFS cartographer, who was making a new map, misunderstood the pronunciation by the residents and placed the new name on the map.

Woolard Creek (Lemhi). T20N R14E sec 23. Heads 1 mi SW to enter Middle Fk Salmon River just S of Williams Creek.

Named for Jess Woolard, an early prospector in this region.

Worley (Kootenai). 2654′. T47N R5W sec 23/24. In the SW part of the county, 29 mi S of Coeur d'Alene; in the N half of the Coeur d'Alene Indian Reservation. Platted in 1909 and named for the superintendent of the reservation. Post office, 1911-.

Worthing Canyon (Lemhi). T11N R30E sec 32. Heads 1 mi W of Lemhi-Clark county line; runs SW 4 mi, near Lemhi-Clark county line on the S.

Two brothers, Frank G. and Chester J. Worthing, mined lead and silver in this area.

Wrencoe (Bonner). 2075′. T56N R3W sec 4. Town 10 mi NE of the town of Priest River. Also Wrenco. Post office, 1901-1916.

Named for a local incident involving the GNRR and a local settler. A train was stopped on a passing track waiting for another train to pass from a different direction. As the other train came, some cows belonging to Constantine Speck were frightened and one cow ran down the track in front of the oncoming train. Speck began shouting "Run cow, run! Run cow." The train crew were so delighted by the incident that they referred to the siding as Run Cow. When the railway later named its sidings, they changed the name to Wrencoe, which was more aesthetic but could still be used for purposes of identification.

Wright Creek (Lemhi). T17N R23E sec 20. Originates near Long Mountain; flows NE 4 1/2 mi to enter Bear Valley Creek; Lemhi River drainage.

Named for Dr. Frank Wright, one of the early physicians at the Lemhi Indian Agency.

Wylies Peak (Idaho). 7799'. T31N R12E sec 33. In the E part of the county, about 25 mi NE of Elk City; in Nezperce National Forest. Wylies Ridge lies NE of the peak.

Named for a prospector who marked the first trails in its vicinity in 1890.

Υ–Z

Yakala Creek (Latah). T41N R2W sec 2. Rises at 4000' and flows 2.1 mi SW to Big Sand Creek at 3200'; Palouse River drainage.

The word is of Chinook Indian origin, perhaps from yakwa "here" and kwa "surprise," as this creek flows in a dense forest and is not easily seen.

Yale (Cassia). 4350'. T10S R27E sec 34. In the NE part of the county, 21 mi E of Burley. A ranching area on US Highway 30 and on Raft River. Post office, 1890-ca.1936.

Named for Yale University by several local graduates, one of whom was George Burroughs.

Yale (Latah). T41N R3W sec 34. WIM railroad station 2 mi E and 5 mi S of Harvard; one of 8 stations bearing names of colleges.

The name was suggested in 1906 by William Deary, General Manager, WIM, in a letter to the WIM president.

During construction, this point was called Big Summit and rail tickets were so printed. The final naming of the siding as Yale followed the pattern set in naming Harvard, with Princeton already established in 1896.

Yankee Fork Creek (Custer). T11N R15E sec 18. NE tributary of Salmon River. Heads S of Challis Lakes and flows 25 mi SW and S to Salmon River.

In 1876 prospectors made a strike that they named for General George Custer, who had just suffered disaster with the Sioux on the Little Big Horn. Most of the prospectors who subsequently flooded this area were Yankees and named this creek "Yankee" as a slap at the Confederate miners of Secesh Creek, Warren Diggings.

Yeaman Creek (Bonneville). T1N R44E sec 35. Rises in the NE quadrant and flows 6 mi SE into Snake River about 1 mi SW of Irvin.

Named for Miles Yeaman, who with his family settled on this creek in 1888.

Yearian Creek (Lemhi). T17N R24E sec 4. Forms on the Idaho-Montana border; flows SW 3 mi, S 3 mi, and then W 2 1/2 mi to enter Lemhi River. Pronounced YEAR-yun.

Named for George Yearian, who had a ranch here that he purchased from Joseph Pattee in 1871. He brought in the first cattle to the upper Lemhi Valley from Corrine, Utah, and also ran a general merchandise store at Junction when it was a thriving town.

Yellow Belly Lake (Custer). T8N R13/14E sec 24/30. Near the center of Sawtooth Valley about 2 1/2 mi off US 93, and 1 1/2 mi from Pettit Lake.

Named for a species of fish found in the lake.

Yellow Cat Creek (Lemhi). T16N R13E sec 12. Heads just S of Panther Creek; flows SW 1 mi to Loon Creek; Salmon River drainage.

Named for a big yellow house cat that lived at the mouth of this creek for several years.

Yellow Dog (Latah). T42N R6W sec 13. An early community with a blacksmith shop and grocery store; in 1905, a stop on the Spokane and Inland Empire RR; located in the NW part of the county. Formerly Almeda, which see.

The name Yellow Dog arose when a resident remarked that he did not like the name Almeda and would rather call the area Yellow Dog.

Yellow Peak (Lemhi). 10,968'. T14N R25E sec 19. Situated in the Lemhi

Range, at the head of Rocky Creek 3 1/2 mi NE of Big Creek Peak.

Named for the predominant color of the rock formation.

Yellow Pine (Valley). 4765'. T19N R8E sec 21. On the E Fk of S Fk Salmon River in the center of the county. Originally this was a mining community that served as a supply and postal center for miners and ranchers along Big Creek. Post office, 1906-.

Named for the ponderosa pine abundant in the area.

Yellowjacket Creek (Lemhi). T18N R16E sec 18. Heads in the vicinity of Yellowjacket Lake and in the area NE; flows about 3 mi SE, 3 mi S, and then 8 mi generally SW, to enter Camas Creek; Middle Fk Salmon River drainage.

Yellowjacket. T19N R16E sec 9. Once a mining community. Post office, 1893-1912.

Yellowjacket Lake. 8000'. T20N R16E sec 14. Near the NE portion of Hoodoo Meadows.

Yellowjacket Mountains. T20N R16E sec 29 NE 7 mi to T21N R16E sec 26. Group of mountains, with elevations above 8000', in the Salmon River Mountains around the head of Yellowjacket Creek.

A local story says that miners coming into this area for the first time had their horses stung by yellowjackets, causing them much grief.

Yip Creek (Boise). T7N R9E sec 4. Flows S into Bear River in the SE part of the county; Boise River drainage.

A coyote heard yipping near the creek suggested the name to the USFS.

Yuba City (Elmore). T5N R11E sec 15. An early mining site located up the Yuba River just below the mouth of Decker Creek, on the old road from Rocky Bar to Atlanta. A rich mining area, of which little remains.

The name was probably brought here from California by miners and transferred to Yuba River, a 15-mi long stream that empties into the Middle Fk Boise River 1 1/2 mi SW of Atlanta.

Zeph Creek (Lemhi). T17N R24E sec 10. Just N of Swartz Creek; flows E 2 mi then N 3 1/2 mi to about 2 1/2 mi SE of Lemhi.

Zephaniah (Zeph) Yearian patented land here in 1888.

Zimmer Creek (Boise). T9N R3E sec 16. Flows 2 1/2 mi SW into the N Fk Payette River 6 mi W of Crouch.

The Zimmer family homesteaded near this creek, ca.1870.

Zumwalt Lake (Boise). T10N R10E sec 12. In the NE corner of the county.

A family by this name came to Boise Basin in 1864.

Bibliography

ADAMS, WILLARD. *100 Years of Jefferson County Progress.* N.p., 1960-.

BAILEY, ROBERT GRESHAM. *River of No Return.* Rev. ed. Lewiston: R.G. Bailey Printing Co., 1947.

American Development, Inc. *Magic Valley Atlas and Rural Directory.* Caldwell: American Development, Inc., 1969.

BANCROFT, HUBERT HOWE. *History of Washington, Idaho and Montana, 1845-1889.* Volume XXXI of *The Works of Hubert Howe Bancroft.* San Francisco: The History Co., 1890.

BANKSON, RUSSEL A. AND HARRISON, LESTER S. *Beneath These Mountains.* New York: Vantage Press, 1966.

BEAL, MERRILL D., AND WELLS, MERLE W. *History of Idaho.* New York: Lewis Historical Publishing Co., 1959.

BEAL, SAMUEL M. *The Snake River Fork Country: A Brief History of Peaceful Conquest in the Upper Snake River Basin.* Rexburg: Rexburg Journal, 1933.

BENSON, SIMON, ED. *History of North Idaho: Latah County.* Reprinted from *Illustrated History of Idaho,* n.p., 1903. Provo, Utah: n.p., 1973.

BIRD, ANNIE LAURIE. *Boise, the Peace Valley.* Caldwell: Caxton Printers, 1934.

BROSNAN, CORNELIUS JAMES. *History of the State of Idaho.* 5th edition, revised. New York: Charles Scribner & Sons, 1948.

_____. *Jason Lee, Prophet of the New Oregon.* New York: Macmillan, 1932.

CARREY, JOHNNY, AND CONLEY, CORT. *A Guide to the Middle Fork of the Salmon River and the Sheepeater War.* Riggins: Backeddy Books, 1977.

_____. *River of No Return.* Riggins: Backeddy Books, 1978.

_____. *Snake River of Hells Canyon.* Riggins: Backeddy Books, 1979.

CLARK, BARZILLA WORTH. *Bonneville County in the Making.* Idaho Falls: Barzilla W. Clark, 1941.

CLEMENTS, LOUIS J., AND FORBUSH, HAROLD S. *Pioneering the Snake River Fork Country.* Foreword Merrill D. Beal. Rexburg: Eastern Idaho Publishing Co., 1972.

CLEMENTS, LOUIS J. *History of the Upper Snake River Area to 1840.* Rexburg: Eastern Idaho Publishing Co., 1974.

CONLEY, CORT. *Idaho for the Curious.* Riggins: Backeddy Books, 1981.

DAHL, JAMES CARL. "Place Names of Bonner County, Idaho." Master's Thesis, University of Idaho, 1969.

DAKE, HENRY C. *Northwest Gem Trails: A Field Guide for the Gem Hunter, Mineral Collector, and Tourist*. Boise: Gem Books, 1962.

Daughters of the Pioneers. *The Trail Blazer: History of the Development of Southeastern Idaho*. Preston: Daughters of the Pioneers, 1930.

DAWSON, ALSON WILLIAM. *Western Saga Guide Book: Cassia Country Crosstrails of the Pioneers*. Burley: Cassia County Historical Society, 1974.

D'EASUM, CEDRIC G. *Sawtooth Tales*. Caldwell: Caxton Printers, 1977.

DEFENBACH, BYRON. *Idaho, The Place and its People: A History of the Gem State from Prehistoric to Present Days*. 3 vols. Chicago: The American Historical Society, Inc., 1933.

_____. *The State We Live In, Idaho*. Caldwell: Caxton Printers, 1933.

DELUCIA, ALAN A., ET AL. *The Compact Atlas of Idaho*. Moscow: Cartographics Laboratory, University of Idaho, 1983.

DERIG, BETTER, AND SHARP, FLO. *Idaho Rambler*. Weiser: Rambler Press, 1982.

LEWIS, MERIWETHER. *Journals of Lewis and Clark*. Ed. Bernard DeVoto. Boston: Houghton Mifflin, 1953.

DRIGGS, BENJAMIN WOODBURG. *History of Teton Valley, Idaho*. Caldwell: Caxton Printers, 1926.

DRISCOLL, ANN NILSSON. *They Came to a Ridge*. Moscow: News Review Publishing Co., 1970.

EHRENBERGER, JAMES L., AND GSCHWIND, FRANCIS G. *Smoke Down the Canyons*. Callaway, Nebraska: E. & G. Publications, 1966.

ELLIS, ERL H. *That Word "Idaho"*. Denver: University of Denver Press, 1951.

Elmore County Historical Foundation, Inc. *A Glimpse at Early Elmore County*. N.p., Elmore County Historical Foundation, Inc., 1963.

ELSENSOHN, SISTER M. ALFREDA. *Pioneer Days in Idaho County*. 2 vols. Caldwell: Caxton Printers, 1947, 1951.

ESTES, JAMES F. *Lost Mine of Priest Lake*. N.p., 1967.

_____. *Tales of Priest Lake*. Spokane: Steptoe Publications, 1964.

Federal Writers' Project, Idaho. *Idaho: A Guide in Word and Picture*. Caldwell: Caxton Printers, 1937.

_____. *Idaho: A Guide in Word and Picture*. 2nd ed. rev. New York: Oxford University Press, 1950.

_____. *The Idaho Encyclopedia*. Caldwell: Caxton Printers, 1932.

GEIDL, MARY JO. "Place Names of Clearwater County, Idaho." Master's Thesis, University of Idaho, 1972.

GIBBS, RAFE. *Beacon for Mountain and Plain: The Story of the University of Idaho*. Moscow: University of Idaho Press, 1962.

GOLDSMITH, CLAIRE. *In the Shadow of the Squaw: The History and Development of the New Plymouth Community in Idaho as Told in Records, Reminiscences, and Pioneer Stories*. New Plymouth: n.p., 1953.

GORDON, ELIZABETH ANN. "Place Names of Boise County, Idaho." Master's Thesis, University of Idaho, 1972.

GRAHAM, MARIE HARGIS. "Place Names of Fremont County, Idaho." Master's Thesis, University of Idaho, 1972.

HAMMES, JOJANE, ED. *Living: 1906-1908*. St. Maries: Western Historical, Inc., 1962.

HULT, RUBY EL. *Lost Mines and Treasures of the Pacific Northwest.* Portland, Oregon: Binfords and Mort, 1968.
————. *Northwest Disaster: Fire and Avalanche.* Portland, Oregon: Binfords and Mort, 1960.
————. *Steamboats in the Timber.* Caldwell: Caxton Printers, 1952. 2nd ed. Portland, Oregon: Binfords and Mort, 1971.
————. *Treasure Hunting Northwest.* Portland, Oregon: Binfords and Mort, 1971.
Idaho Department of Commerce and Development. *Idaho Almanac: 1963.* Boise: Syms-York Co., 1963.
————. *Idaho Almanac: 1967.* Boise: Syms-York Co., 1967.
Idaho Poets and Writers Guild. *The Idaho Story.* 2 vols. Iona: Ipas Publishing Co., 1967-68.
Idaho Yesterday and Today. *Souvenir Handbook: Fort Hall Centennial, 1834-1934.* Pocatello: Graves and Potter, ca. 1934.
Illustrated History of North Idaho. N.p., Western Historical Publishing Co., 1903.
JORDAN, GRACE. *Home Below Hell's Canyon.* New York: Crowell, 1954.
————. *The King's Pines of Idaho: A Story of the Browns of McCall.* Portland, Oregon: Binfords and Mort, 1961.
KRAMER, FRITZ. *Idaho Town Names: Twenty-Third Biennial Report of the Idaho State Historical Department, 1951-1952.* Boise: Idaho State Historical Department, 1952.
McLEOD, GEORGE A. *History of Alturas and Blaine Counties, Idaho.* Hailey: The Hailey Times, 1930.
MAGNUSON, RICHARD G. *Coeur d'Alene Diary: The First Ten Years of Hardrock Mining in North Idaho.* Portland, Oregon: Metropolitan Press, 1968.
MILLER, DON C. *Ghost Towns of Idaho: Early to Present.* Boulder, Colorado: Pruett Publishing Co., 1976.
MILLER, JOHN B. *The Trees Grew Tall.* Moscow: Review News Publishing Co., 1972.
MULKEY, SELWAY LYSLE. "Place Names of Lemhi County, Idaho." Master's Thesis, University of Idaho, 1970.
MULLAN, CAPTAIN JOHN. *Miners' and Travelers' Guide.* New York: W.M. Franklin, 1865.
National Archives. Records of the United States Post Office Department. Idaho, microfilm. Record Group 28, 1860-1929.
OGLE. *Standard Atlas of Latah County.* Chicago: n.p., 1914.
OBERG, PEARL M. *Between These Mountains.* New York: Exposition Press, 1970.
100 Years of Progress, 1870-1970: The Story of a Full Century of Progress. Burley: South Idaho Press, ca. 1970.
OTNESS, LILLIAN WOODWORTH. *A Great Good Country: A Guide to Historic Moscow and Latah County, Idaho.* Moscow: Latah County Historical Society, 1983.
PARKE, ADELIA. *Memoirs of an Old Timer.* Weiser: Signal American Printers, 1955.
PARKER, AARON F., AND CARREY, JOHN. *Forgotten Tragedies of an Indian War: The Sheepeater Indian Campaign.* Grangeville: Idaho Free Press, 1968.
PLATT, JOHN A. *Whispers from "Old Genesee" and Echoes of the Salmon River.* Fairfield, Washington: Ye Galleon Press, 1975.

411

Potlatch Lumber Company, Potlatch, Idaho. *Potlatch Lumber Company, Manufacturers of Fine Lumber: Idaho White Pine, Western Pine and Larch*. Spokane, Washington: F.D. Straffin, 1907.

RANNEY, AGNES JOHNSON. *The Valley I Remember: Meadows Valley, Idaho*. Portland, Oregon: n.p., 1973.

REES, JOHN. *Idaho: Chronology, Nomenclature, Bibliography*. Chicago: W.B. Conkey Company, 1918.

RIEDESEL, GERHARD A., ED. *Arid Acres: A History of the Kimama-Minidoka Homesteaders, 1912-1932*. Pullman, Washington: G.A. Riedesel, 1969.

RHODENBAUGH, EDWARD F. *Sketches of Idaho Geology*. 2nd ed. Boise: Rhodenbaugh, 1961.

RUSSELL, BERT. *Caulked Boots and Other Northwest Writings*. Harrison: Lacon Publishers, 1968.

SAUNDERS, ARTHUR C. *History of Bannock County, Idaho*. Pocatello: The Tribune Co., 1915.

SCOTT, GAIL EILEEN KELLER. "Place Names of Lewis County, Idaho." Master's Thesis, University of Idaho, 1972.

SCOTT, ORLAND A. *Pioneer Days in the Shadowy St. Joe*. Coeur d'Alene: n.p., 1967.

SELBY, HAZEL BARRINGTON. *Home to My Mountains*. Princeton, New Jersey: Van Nostrand Company, 1962.

SHUPE, VERNA IRENE. *Caribou County Chronology*. Colorado Springs: Print Craft Press, 1930.

SPACE, RALPH. *The Clearwater Story: A History of Clearwater National Forest*. Orofino: Tribune Printers, 1909.

————. *Lewis and Clark through Idaho, 1805-1806*. Lewiston: Tribune Publishing Co., ca. 1964.

————. *The Lolo Trail: A History of Events Connected with the Lolo Trail since Lewis and Clark*. Lewiston: Printcraft Printing, 1970.

STRINGHAM, MIRANDO. *Bassalt-Firth Since 1900: A Locality History of the Two Communities and of the People*. Idaho Falls: Hansen Printing, 1972.

TAYLOR, MARGARET WATSON. *Memories of a Wagon Trip*. Weiser: Signal-American Printers, 1954.

TAYLOR, MARY WALSH. "Owyhee and Nez Perce County Place Names." Master's Thesis, University of Idaho, 1968.

THURSTON, MARION JILL MOONEY. "Place Names of Bonneville County, Idaho." Master's Thesis, University of Idaho, 1971.

TULLIDGE, EDWARD WHEELOCK. *Tullidge's Histories, I*. Salt Lake City, Utah: Press of the Juvenile Instructor, 1889.

Twin Falls County Idaho, Idaho Territorial Centennial Committee. *A Folk History of Twin Falls County*. Twin Falls: Standard Printing Company, 1962.

United States Department of the Interior. *Decisions on Geographic Names in the United States*. Washington, D.C., 1906-1983.

United States Department of the Interior. United States Board on Geographical Names. Idaho section, archives. Washington, D.C.

WALGAMOTT, CHARLES SHIRLEY. *Six Decades Back*. Caldwell: Caxton Printers, 1936.

WOODS, JEWELL M. *Lives to Live By*. Council: Woods, 1968.

Maps used for the research in this book include all of the county maps produced by the Idaho Department of Highways, Metsker, and Big Sky; maps of the 16 national forests by the United States Department of Agriculture; and Geological Quadrangle Maps for Idaho County and North Idaho, United States Department of the Interior.